THE IRWIN SERIES IN ECONOMICS

CONSULTING EDITOR

LLOYD G. REYNOLDS

YALE UNIVERSITY

BOOKS IN THE IRWIN SERIES IN ECONOMICS

ANDERSON, GITLOW, & DIAMOND (Editors) *General Economics: A Book of Readings*

BEAL & WICKERSHAM *The Practice of Collective Bargaining*

BRANDIS *Economics: Principles and Policy*

BUCHANAN *The Public Finances*

BUSHAW & CLOWER *Introduction to Mathematical Economics*

CARTTER *Theory of Wages and Employment*

DAVIDSON, SMITH, & WILEY *Economics: An Analytical Approach*

DUE *Government Finance: An Economic Analysis* Revised Edition

DUE *Intermediate Economic Analysis* Third Edition

DUNLOP & HEALY *Collective Bargaining: Principles and Cases* Revised Edition

GAMBS & WERTIMER *Economics and Man*

GRAMPP & WEILER (Editors) *Economic Policy: Readings in Political Economy* Revised Edition

GROSSMAN, HANSEN, HENDRIKSEN, MCALLISTER, OKUDA, & WOLMAN (Editors) *Readings in Current Economics*

GUTHRIE *Economics* Revised Edition

HALM *Economics of Money and Banking* Revised Edition

HARRISS *The American Economy: Principles, Practices, and Policies* Third Edition

JOME *Principles of Money and Banking*

KINDLEBERGER *International Economics* Revised Edition

KUHLMAN & SKINNER *The Economic System*

LEE *Economic Fluctuations: Growth and Stability* Revised Edition

LOCKLIN *Economics of Transportation* Fifth Edition

MEYERS *Economics of Labor Relations*

PEGRUM *Public Regulation of Business*

SCITOVSKY *Welfare and Competition: The Economics of a Fully Employed Economy*

SHAW *Money, Income, and Monetary Policy*

SIEGEL *Aggregate Economics and Public Policy*

SIRKIN *Introduction to Macroeconomic Theory*

SNIDER *Introduction to International Economics* Revised Edition

SPENCER & SIEGELMAN *Managerial Economics: Decision Making and Forward Planning*

WILCOX *Public Policies Toward Business* Revised Edition

ECONOMICS OF MONEY AND BANKING

ECONOMICS OF MONEY AND BANKING

BY GEORGE N. HALM

PROFESSOR OF INTERNATIONAL ECONOMIC RELATIONS

THE FLETCHER SCHOOL OF LAW AND DIPLOMACY

TUFTS UNIVERSITY

REVISED EDITION

1961

RICHARD D. IRWIN, INC.

HOMEWOOD, ILLINOIS

REVISED EDITION

First Printing, May, 1961

PRINTED IN THE UNITED STATES OF AMERICA

Library of Congress Catalogue Card No. 61-11420

TO

LORE

PREFACE

This book has been designed as a text for an introductory course in money and banking. It is not a guide for the vocational training of future bank employees but is intended for a liberal arts course which continues the training in economics with the aim of helping the student to understand the monetary problems of today. Therefore the title "*Economics* of Money and Banking."

In the selection of the material I followed Professor Machlup's rule "to give a minimum of explicit information and a maximum of mental exercise with a maximum of social significance."[1] Nevertheless, questions of money and banking cannot be discussed in an institutional vacuum. Wherever necessary, institutions, facts, and historical data have been introduced as working material and for illustrative purposes. Mere description, however, was not my purpose and I left out what could not be formulated as an interesting problem; but I realize, of course, that what is not controversial can still be important.

Throughout I have emphasized theory. Only theoretical analysis leads to an understanding of our problems. Nevertheless, the theoretical discussions have been interspersed with historical and institutional chapters, partly to prevent the student from getting tired of abstract analysis and partly because it is unavoidable to absorb facts into the theoretical treatment and desirable to apply theoretical conclusions to the problems of the present and the past. Rather than describe monetary and banking institutions in minute detail I try to show why they evolved, what they aimed to do and why they may have fallen short of achieving their objectives. My opinions on policy aims need, of course, not be accepted; I am satisfied if they provoke controversy.

---

1 *Journal of Finance,* September, 1949, p. 228.

I hope to have done justice to both the older and the newer (Keynesian) theory since I believe that both have contributed to our fuller understanding of monetary problems.

A modern course in money and banking must not only deal with the domestic supply of money and credit but also with the monetary implications of fiscal policy and with the international payments problem. This accounts for the fact that the second half of the book deals with the problems of capital, interest, aggregate expenditure, and foreign exchange. In many schools some of these problems are the subject matter of special courses. The use of the book will thus depend to some extent on the whole economics curriculum at a given institution.

The book as a whole is designed for the basic one-year course in money and banking. If only a half-year course is offered, Books I and II supply enough coverage in the narrower field. Another possibility for the half-course would be to omit the historical chapters of Book II and to spend the time thus gained on selected chapters of Books III and IV. On the graduate level it should be possible to cover the whole volume or at least the first three books in one term.

The present volume is not a third edition of my earlier book, *Monetary Theory*. Only about 20 per cent of the older formulations have been used. In arrangement, objective and treatment *Economics of Money and Banking* differs decisively from *Monetary Theory*. The earlier book was not intended as a text. Owing to its strictly theoretical character it reduced institutional facts to generalizations applicable to all financially developed countries. Book II of *Economics of Money and Banking* deals with the monetary and banking problems of the United States. Books I, III, and IV are of a more general nature and, with minor exceptions, apply to all developed, non-totalitarian countries. I hope that those who know my older book will find many improvements in the theoretical chapters, both as to content and presentation.

This revised edition of *Economics of Money and Banking* emphasizes even more than the first the general economic aspects of money and banking. By rearranging various chapters and reducing their number I have tried to simplify the structure and improve the teachability of the book. All statistical data, charts, and figures have been brought up to date. Innumerable changes in content and style aim at greater clarity. New materials covered concern Federal Reserve policies since 1951, the problem of creeping inflation, and the foreign deficit of the United States. This foreign deficit at a time of domestic recession supports the belief expressed earlier in the Preface that domestic monetary and fiscal policies and international monetary policies must be studied together.

I am deeply grateful to Professor Edward S. Shaw for his penetrating criticism. Though he is in no way responsible for anything I said, the book owes much to his untiring help. I am grateful, also, to Professor William P. Snavely of the University of Connecticut for reviewing the manuscript. In the earlier stages of the writing of this book I had the great advantage of Professor Fritz Machlup's advice; thus I owe him still another debt of gratitude. Finally, it is pleasant to acknowledge the valuable assistance of Professor Ralph E. Fretty and Mr. Raymond C. Malley in the preparation of this revised edition.

GEORGE N. HALM

WINCHESTER, MASS.
March 18, 1961

TABLE OF CONTENTS

BOOK THREE: MONEY, INTEREST, AND EMPLOYMENT

PART VI. THE CREDIT MARKET

PART VII. MONEY AND ECONOMIC STABILITY

INDEX

BOOK ONE
Monetary Theory

PART I

Money and Money Economy

Chapter 1 THE FUNCTIONS AND SERVICES OF MONEY

The Unit of Account

Let us imagine that we live in a modern economy—but one in which money does not exist. The inadequacy of barter would soon become apparent, for our activities are too specialized; we are mutually dependent and our economic process rests on innumerable exchange transactions. Without the help of money these indispensable exchanges could not take place.

Without a monetary unit we would have to express the value of a commodity in units of whatever other commodities for which the first commodity is to be exchanged. If we want to barter a hundred different kinds of commodities, their mutual exchange ratios already become quite unmanageable. A hundred different products would give rise to 4,950 exchange ratios.[1] Every intelligent person faced with this difficulty would instantly invent money as a unit of account or measure of value. By expressing the values of 99 commodities in units of one standard good, the 4,950 exchange ratios can be reduced to 99

[1] According to the formula $\frac{n^2 - n}{2}$, where n is the number of commodities.

prices. The unit of the standard good itself, being the unit of account, has a price of one.

The Means of Exchange

While a unit of account greatly facilitates exchange transactions, exchanges would still remain awkward and rare were it not for the use of a means of exchange which everybody agrees to accept because everybody else is equally willing to take it in exchange for commodities. On the basis of barter it would be next to impossible to find the persons who are in need of our products and services and are, at the same time, able to offer in exchange exactly those goods and services which we happen to need. Suppose that we select one article as means of exchange and that the article gains the quality of general acceptability. We are now quite willing to take the article in exchange even though we do not want to use it as a commodity. We take it because we can exchange it for other commodities.

The use of a means of exchange allows independent sales and purchases. Barter is now divided into two separate transactions which need no longer be simultaneous. This independence of our sales from our purchases is of supreme importance because it eliminates the need for people's wishes to coincide not only with regard to the time and place of the exchange but also with regard to the kind, quantity, and quality of the mutually desired goods.

Because we are thus concerned with independent sales and purchases, we can hereafter call the means of exchange a means of payment.

Money

Once we have introduced a unit of account and a means of payment, our economy has become a monetary economy. We may hesitate to refer to money both as a unit of account and as a means of payment, but if a little care is taken no confusion need result from this somewhat ambiguous terminology.

It is easy to keep the two functions of money conceptually apart. As a means of payment, money is something concrete (a coin, a dollar bill, a credit entry in a bank account). As a measure of value, money is an abstract unit (the United States dollar, the pound sterling, the cruzeiro, the drachma), even though it may have originated as the weight unit of a precious metal and even though most countries still define their monetary unit in terms of gold.

The unit of account and the means of payment are not identical, as the abstract character of the first and the concrete character of the second sufficiently indicate. But the price of the means of payment must be expressed in units of account. This is not always easy. Where real commodities are used as means of payment, individual units may differ in quality; one head of cattle, for instance, may be younger, heavier, or healthier than another. Not even among mere tokens is uniformity easily accomplished, as will be shown in Chapter 15. Once units of the means of payment are perfectly identical, however, the means of payment and the unit of account form a kind of symbiosis: the abstract unit of account is the price of the unit of the means of payment, that is, we reckon in terms of the dollars which we actually use in making payments.

Price of Money and Value of Money

Money, as the unit of account, is distinguished from commodities by the fact that its price cannot change; its price is always one.[2] Prices of commodities, on the other hand, as a rule are free to fluctuate. Price rigidity, therefore, is a characteristic quality of money.

Money, as a means of payment, is distinguished from commodities by its general acceptability. Commodities are bought when they are needed for consumption or production. Money, by contrast, is always taken in exchange. Once general acceptability becomes the outstanding feature of the means of payment, the means of payment can become a mere token which has no use value as a commodity. We attach value to money because we can exchange it at any time for commodities which have use value. Our valuation of money, therefore, is merely a reflected valuation of the goods which money is able to buy.

This leads to a distinction between the price and the value of money. We saw that the price of the unit of money is always one because the unit of money is the unit of account: "a dollar is always a dollar." Inflation experiences, however, tell us that the value of money may fall while its price stays the same. This is because in a so-called price inflation the prices of almost all commodities tend to rise, so that the dollar exchanges for fewer commodities than before. During price deflation the opposite happens. The dollar exchanges for more commodities and services because commodity prices fall on the average; and since the value of money is the reflected valuation of the commodities which money can buy, we say that the value of money rises.

[2] We shall see that the term "price of money" is often used in a different meaning, namely, as the price for the borrowing of money, the rate of interest.

That money maintains a fixed price may create the illusion that its value stays the same, and since money is the measure of value, this illusion may be dangerous. It can, for instance, lead to unjust shifts in income distribution, as when long-term contracts, based on money, favor debtors during a price inflation because these debtors can repay their debts in money of lower value. The same illusion may lead to mistakes in business calculations, just as a carpenter's job would suffer if the carpenter used an expanding or contracting yardstick for his measurements.

Here it may also be mentioned that money is important not only because it permits an easy comparison of the values of goods and services but also because the expression of the value of commodities in monetary units (prices) enables us to add up values and to express the total value of such aggregates as the national income. In saying that the national income is $400 billion, we make use of the only available means for expressing as a sum total the infinite variety of things which constitute the real income of the nation. However inadequate such an aggregate expression for dissimilar things may often be, money is the only common denominator which we can use.

Again, however, we must beware of the monetary illusion. Increasing national income figures do not necessarily mean that our wealth in terms of commodities and services has grown. Only if the value or purchasing power of the monetary unit has remained stable during the period of comparison is such a conclusion valid.

Money and Liquidity

Price stability and general acceptability combined make money the most liquid asset a person can hold. Other assets, commodities as well as securities, can be "liquidated," that is, sold for money. If they could always be sold immediately and at a fixed price, they could claim to be almost as liquid as money. Most assets, however, can be sold instantly only at greatly reduced prices. Therefore we say that assets are the more liquid the more readily they can be exchanged for money without loss.

Every person or firm must hold a reserve of money to be sufficiently liquid. Since money splits exchanges into sales and purchases, some time, however short, will elapse before money earned through a sale is spent in making a purchase. Money will rest for a while in the pockets, drawers, tills, or bank accounts of those who received it. But only the miser keeps money for its own sake; a sane person earns money to spend it, sooner or later, on commodities or securities.

There are several reasons why we try to hold a sufficiently large reserve of money. We do not receive our income as a continuous stream but rather in the form of payments at regular or irregular intervals. Thus, if we should spend an approximately equal amount each day, we should hold, on the average, a liquid reserve equal to about half of our weekly or monthly pay. In addition we may desire to have a money reserve in case of emergencies, or we may postpone the purchase of commodities or securities when we expect prices to fall.

Money reserves are sometimes referred to as a "store of value," that is, a means by which to shift purchasing power from the present into the future. But we should not overstate this "store-of-value" quality of money since we have seen that price rigidity of money does not guarantee a stable value of money. In times of a roaring price inflation money may become the worst asset by which to store value. Such times are characterized by people's desire to get rid of money as fast as possible. Any commodity, particularly any physically durable commodity, is then rightly considered preferable to money as a store of value. In such times the illusion of money is finally destroyed.

Money and Credit

Money, credit, and debt are closely connected in a number of ways. In a modern society many payments are accomplished by a transfer of claims. A man who pays his rent by check orders his bank, which owes him money, to pay the landlord, that is, he transfers his claim on the bank to the landlord. Indeed, we can envisage a society in which all sales are made on credit and in which all the resulting claims are canceled every day or week in one comprehensive clearing process.

In discussing the need for money reserves we assumed that sales always precede purchases. By introducing credit transactions into our discussion, we can assume that purchases precede sales. The debt which the buyer owes the seller can immediately be wiped out through a payment in money. Often, however, the payment will follow only later, say, after three months. In this case a sales transaction and credit transaction are combined and a promise of a future settlement takes the place of an immediate transfer of money from purchaser to seller. This promise of a future payment can take many forms. In certain cases, when the promise is generally acceptable, the promise to pay money can become money (as, for instance, in the case of the bank note). Most acknowledgments of debt, however, do not possess the quality of general acceptability so that, in the end, a payment in money will have to take place. Some authors have emphasized the role which money plays in connection with debts so much that they have defined money as a means by which we can rid ourselves of debts.

Let us consider still another connection between money and credit (or debt). Suppose that we desire to save part of our earned income and that we use these savings to buy securities (that is, acknowledgments of debt) by which the debtor promises to make specified payments in the future. Such credit transactions are eminently important for our economy. Without them a temporary transfer of purchasing power from the creditor to the debtor would be impossible and much entrepreneurial initiative would run to waste. Also, those who save could not make use of their savings unless they want to go into business. Credit instruments (securities), as a rule, are transferable. They can be sold and thus enable the creditor to terminate his connection with the debtor, provided that somebody can be found to take the creditor's place by purchasing the credit instrument. Without these debt contracts in terms of money it would be next to impossible to collect the enormous amounts of loanable funds which modern corporations must invest in the construction and operation of their gigantic plants. Without these credit instruments the creditor would not enjoy the advantage of diversifying his risk through the purchase of different types of securities and of securing, when needed, increased liquidity through their sale.

Of course, it is possible to borrow goods in a barter economy against the promise to hand these or other goods back after a certain period. In this case we should have as many credit markets as we have different kinds of goods which may be subject to borrowing. It would be impossible to have a uniform market for the special economic service involved, namely the exchange of present for future goods. This service is quite independent of the kinds of goods involved and can adequately be expressed only by the borrowing and lending of money. The development of a money market, furthermore, is the precondition for the formation of a uniform price for the uniform service which is the object of credit transactions. This price is the rate of interest.[3] What people demand and supply on this market is not the disposal of special goods and services but the disposal of money for a certain period of time: the disposal of money through which any other good may be procured.

All these connections between money and credit (or debt) have

[3] The rate of interest is often called the price of money, for example, when we speak of a "cheap-money policy" by which we mean a policy of low interest rates. See footnote 2 of this chapter.

in common that money payments are deferred, are shifted from the present into the future. Money, therefore, is often called a "standard of deferred payments."

Summary

First we studied the two basic functions of money as a unit of account and as a means of payment. By contrasting the use of money with the clumsiness of barter we were able to convince ourselves that money is absolutely indispensable in a modern economy. From the two basic functions of money we then derived several important services which money performs. We saw that as a unit of account, money enjoys price rigidity, while as a means of payment, it is generally acceptable. From these two qualities money derives a degree of liquidity unmatched by other assets. We saw, however, that in spite of its liquidity money may not be a very reliable store of wealth. Price rigidity does not guarantee a stable value of money in terms of the commodities which money can buy. The purchasing power of money changes with the price level of the goods. Money's price rigidity, therefore, can create an illusion of stability which may dangerously interfere with orderly and just economic relationships between persons or firms. A changing value of money may also impair the use of money as a common denominator. Finally, we studied money as a standard of deferred payments. We became acquainted with money as a means for ridding ourselves of debts, with certificates of indebtedness, and with the important part which money plays in the exchange of present for future goods, that is, in credit transactions.

SUGGESTIONS FOR FURTHER READING

For practical reasons frequent reference will be made to two readings volumes which offer a wide coverage in an inexpensive and handy manner. They are:

Ritter, Lawrence S. *Money and Economic Activity.* Boston: Houghton Mifflin Co., 1952.

Whittlesey, Charles R. *Readings in Money and Banking.* New York: W. W. Norton & Co., Inc., 1952.

For further reading on the functions of money:

Robertson, Dennis H. *Money,* chap. 1. New York: Pitman Publishing Corp., 1948.

Coulborn, W. A. L. *A Discussion of Money,* chaps. 1–3. London: Longmans, Green and Co., 1950.

Lerner, Abba P. "Money," *Encyclopaedia Britannica,* Vol. 15. Chicago: Encyclopaedia Britannica, Inc., 1956. Reprinted in Ritter, *Money and Economic Activity,* pp. 11–16.

The close connection between money and debt is very well stated in:

Hart, Albert G. *Money, Debt and Economic Activity,* chap. 1. New York: Prentice-Hall, Inc., 1948.

Hawtrey, R. G. *Currency and Credit,* chap. 1. London: Longmans, Green and Co., 1928. Reprinted in Whittlesey, *Readings in Money and Banking,* pp. 3–10.

Excellent on liquidity:

Simmons, Edward C. "The Relative Liquidity of Money and Other Things," *American Economic Review,* Vol. XXXVII Supplement (March, 1947), pp. 308–11. Reprinted in *Readings in Monetary Theory,* chap. 3 (Homewood, Ill.: Richard D. Irwin, Inc., 1951).

QUESTIONS AND PROBLEMS

1. Why is money indispensable in a modern market economy?
2. Explain the chief difficulties involved in bartering.
3. "Every prudent man in every period of society, after the first establishment of the division of labor, must naturally have endeavored to manage his affairs in such a manner, as to have at all times by him, besides the peculiar produce of his own industry, a certain quantity of some one commodity or other, such as he imagined few people would be likely to refuse in exchange for the produce of their industry" (Adam Smith). Discuss.
4. "If cattle are the medium of exchange, each unit has to be estimated separately in units of a standard good which may be only the 'idea' of a real good, e.g., 'normal' cattle." Discuss.
5. Explain the need for a means of exchange and a unit of account. Logically, which comes first?
6. Our valuation of money is but a reflected valuation of the goods money is able to buy. Correct? Explain.
7. Distinguish between the price of money and the value of money.
8. Under certain conditions the use of money can create dangerous illusions. Explain.
9. Why can it be said that money is the most liquid asset? Which qualities make an asset liquid?
10. How do you determine how much money you want to hold?
11. Is money a good store of value?
12. Discuss the importance of money for credit transactions.

Chapter 2 MONEY, INCOME, AND EXPENDITURE

The Circular Flow of Money

We turn now to a brief introductory study of the circular flow of money through the economy. Money has often been referred to as the blood circulating in the economic body or as the oil which lubricates the economic machine. Our discussion of the flow of money will show that these metaphores are not badly chosen, that money is indeed of basic importance for a healthy economy, and that a disease which affects the bloodstream of the economy may become very dangerous.

The object of this chapter is a limited one. As yet we cannot aim at a full understanding of the forces which determine economic activity, employment, and national income. An analysis of these forces will be attempted in Part VIII. Nevertheless, it seems desirable at this early stage of our discussion to emphasize the vital part which money plays in the determination of income and employment, of prosperity and depression.

Looking at our economy as a whole, we see the breadwinners of family households earn their personal income by contributing, in one way or another, to the productive activities which go on in business firms, that is, in the farms, factories, offices, and stores of the nation. Personal income may be earned as wages, salaries, rents, interest, or dividends.

We can watch a flow of personal income, consisting of repeated payments of money by business firms to family households. Where does the money come from which firms pay, at weekly or other intervals, to family households? The answer is obvious: firms sell their products (which we assume at first to consist exclusively of consumers' goods) to family households which purchase them by spending their income on consumption. Thus consumption expenditure by families leads to a return flow of money to business firms.

Figure 2–1 shows in a very simplified way how personal income, earned by family households through the sale of productive services to business firms, is spent on the purchase of consumers' goods which are the products of these business firms. The money paid out by the firms

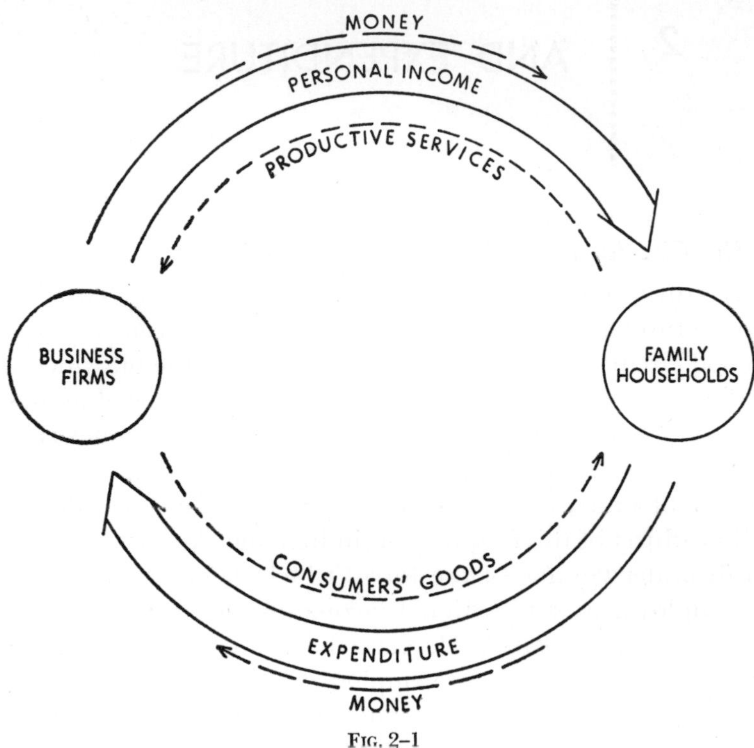

FIG. 2–1

flows back to the firms, so that the firms again can make these payments upon which the steady flow of personal income depends. In this way money circulates through the economy.

Income and money are not identical, of course, but income is received in the form of money, is used up by spending money, and is expressed as a total amount for some period, say a year, in terms of money.

It is perfectly proper to speak, as we have done, of a circular flow of money. Yet, as we watch carefully, we see this difference between the income flow and expenditure flow, on the one hand, and the flow of money, on the other. A picture of the income flow and expenditure flow can be taken, as it were, only with a movie camera. Money, on the other hand, can be the object of both a snapshot and a moving picture.

The snapshot shows most of the money resting in the money reserves of families and firms; only a relatively insignificant part is caught in the act of transfer from one reserve to another. Thus we can visualize a given total supply or stock of money as the sum of all money reserves. A moving picture, however, would reveal movements of the individual units of money from hand to hand and from account to account, and this movement is essentially circular in the sense described above.

Here we can add one more distinction between money and commodities to those enumerated in Chapter 1: commodities pass through the market; they are produced, sold, consumed, and replaced through continuous production. By contrast money stays in the market and is used over and over again.

Since the total amount of money (revealed by our snapshot) is limited and smaller than annual personal income, we see that total expenditure per year depends not only on the supply of money but also on the speed with which money circulates. This velocity of circulation of money is measured by the number of times money is transferred from one owner to another during a period such as a year or a month.

A Decrease in the Flow of Money

Our discussion according to Figure 2–1 revealed a flow of income and expenditure which could maintain itself indefinitely. At the end of each week workers and others are paid and they buy, during the following week, what they produced the week before, and the firms accumulate during the week the money needed for the next payday. Since our example was full of identities (income equals expenditure, which equals the value of production, which equals the cost of production, which equals income), we did not meet with any difficulties. Difficulties, however, may easily occur.

Suppose, for instance, that many people decide to hold larger money reserves than before. If the total supply of money is not increased, they will, as a group, not be able to achieve their aim. We saw that the total supply of money is equal to the sum of all money reserves. Thus if A wants to hold a larger reserve of money, somebody else must necessarily get along with a smaller one. If there is a general tendency to hold more money, the consequences may be serious because those who want to increase their money reserves can do so only by spending less than before.

Figure 2–2, which illustrates this process, is divided into two pictures referring to two consecutive rounds of the money flow. Assume

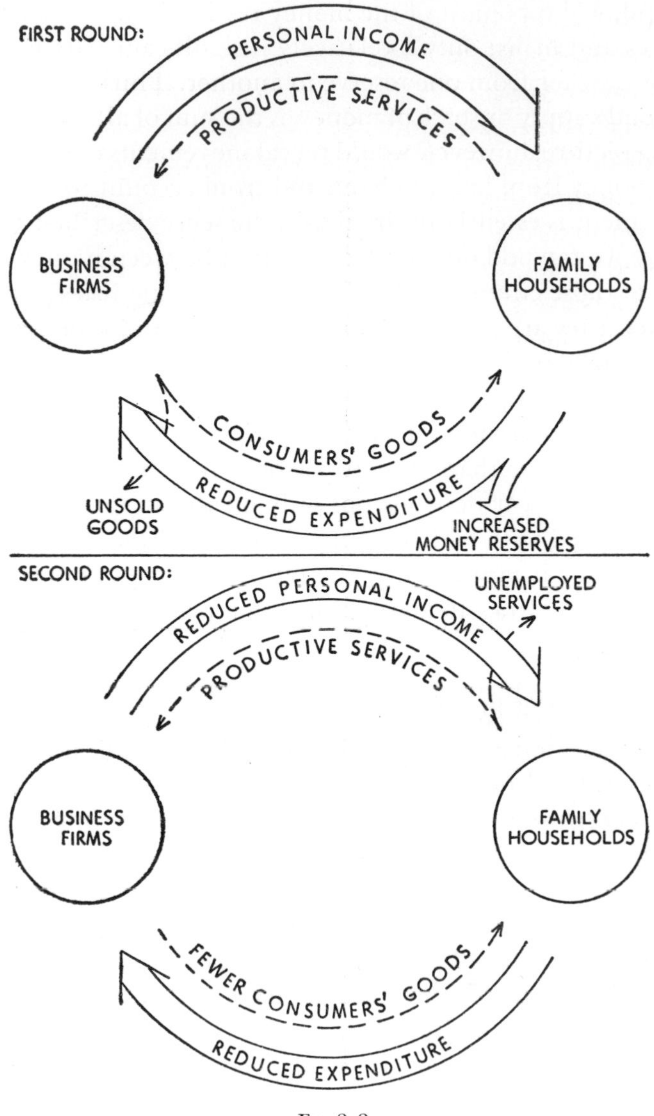

FIG. 2–2

that the first round starts at the firms. The firms pay out the same amount of personal income as in Figure 2–1 and employ all persons previously employed, for they sold all the consumers' goods produced in the preceding period at prices which covered the cost of production. As in Figure 2–1 the flow of money from firms to families is marked by an arrow *Personal Income,* whose width indicates the size of this income flow. Some families now decide to keep part of the income formerly spent on consumption. Their money reserve increases but their expenditure decreases. This is indicated by a split in the *Expenditure* arrow of Figure 2–2. The part of the arrow reaching the firms is narrower than it used to be and is also narrower than the arrow which left the firms. The firms' receipts are smaller than anticipated. As far as consumers' goods are concerned, two assumptions are possible: (*a*) consumers' goods remain unsold and/or (*b*) consumers' goods will be sold at lower prices than anticipated. Disappointed, the managers of the firms decide to produce less during the next round and to employ fewer men. Having received less money, the firms have less money to spend on productive services.

In the second round the firms' income payments are reduced, a fact that is illustrated by the narrower *Personal Income* arrow leading from firms to families. Families, earning less income than before, spend less than before and the *Expenditure* remains as narrow as in the first round. This is so not because of a desire to increase money reserves still further but simply because the personal income of families is decreased.

Families which find their income decreased and firms which have reduced their production will hold less money than before. We had to expect this result since we knew already that, with a fixed supply of money, the higher money reserves of A had somehow to lead to lower reserves of B.

An Increase in the Flow of Money

The opposite case of that shown in Figure 2–2 would be an increase in the flow of money. Such an increase could be caused either by a release of money reserves (Figure 2–3, Part 1) or by the borrowing of additional money by firms (Figure 2–3, Part 2). Either case might result in expanded production and an increase in the personal income flow.

Let us follow the second suggestion. The producer of a new product, which is sure to sell, borrows from the bank. The loan consists of additional money. If unused resources and unemployed labor are available, our manufacturer will meet no difficulties in expanding production. He will pay out additional income to family households and will produce additional products which can be sold because personal income and expenditure will have increased. If, on the other hand, the economy was fully employed before our new production process started, the effects of a creation of additional money will be different. Then personal income will have increased not because of the hiring

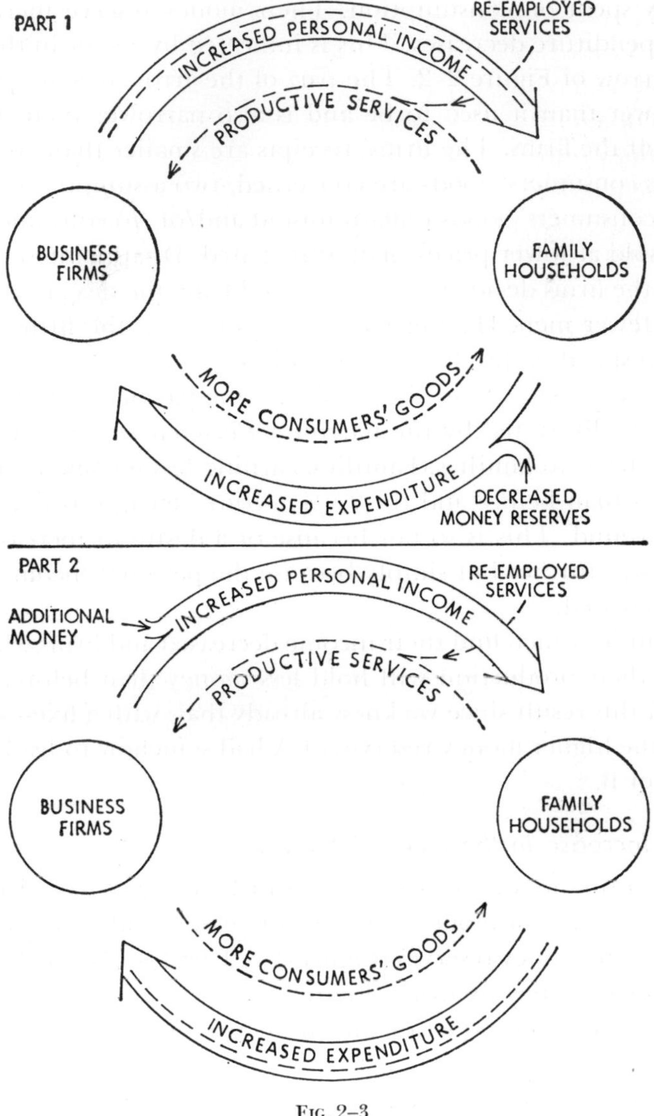

FIG. 2–3

of unemployed workers but because of the hiring away of employed workers from other occupations. Wage rates and wage payments will increase, but since there will not be more goods for sale, the prices of consumers' goods will rise so that the total value of goods sold will correspond to the increased flow of expenditure and also to the increased cost of production.

When this process takes place on a large scale, we have before us the well-known picture of price inflation. Incidentally, with higher personal income and with increased cost of production, families and firms will tend to hold larger reserves of money. Since we assumed the creation of additional money, and since the supply of money is equal to all money reserves, we see how this demand for larger reserves will be satisfied and where the additional money goes.

Saving, Investment, and the Flow of Money

Our discussion of the circular flow of money was oversimplified. Investment goods production was left out of consideration because our firms were assumed to produce only consumers' goods. Furthermore, we left out of account the process called "saving," or we considered it only in connection with increased money reserves. How do investment goods production and saving change our picture of the circular flow of money?

We define investment as the purchase or production of new capital goods by business firms. Capital or investment goods are goods which serve production purposes. They are bought with the intention of making a profit and not for the direct satisfaction of human wants. Capital goods (such as machines, tools, materials, factory buildings) are bought by firms from other firms which specialize in their production.[1]

Where do the funds come from which business firms spend on these capital goods? This question leads us to the problem of saving. A man is said to save when he does not spend all his income on consumers' goods. Suppose that a worker receives $100 on payday. Instead of spending the whole $100 the following week on consumption he spends only $90. He has saved $10. For the economy as a whole we can say that total saving per period amounts to the total income earned in one period (Y) minus the money spent on consumption (C) in the succeeding period. S equals Y minus C.

If we stopped here we could be tempted to assume that the act of saving interrupts the flow of money because income received by the families does not return to the firms. However, this is by no means necessary. If we assume that savings are eagerly borrowed by business firms for investment purposes, if we assume that what is not spent by families on consumers' goods is spent by firms on capital goods, no interruption of our money flow need occur.

[1] This treatment of investment is an oversimplification. It does not allow for inventory accumulation, for government investment, for investment in residential housing by the owner, etc. Investment problems will be taken up in Part VI.

In Figure 2–4 we see how the saved portion of personal income is used to purchase credit instruments.[2] This act of purchasing securities, incidentally, is also often referred to as "investment." In order to distinguish this concept of investment from the one used above (the purchase or production of new capital goods), we can speak of financial investment if we want to indicate the purchase of credit instruments.

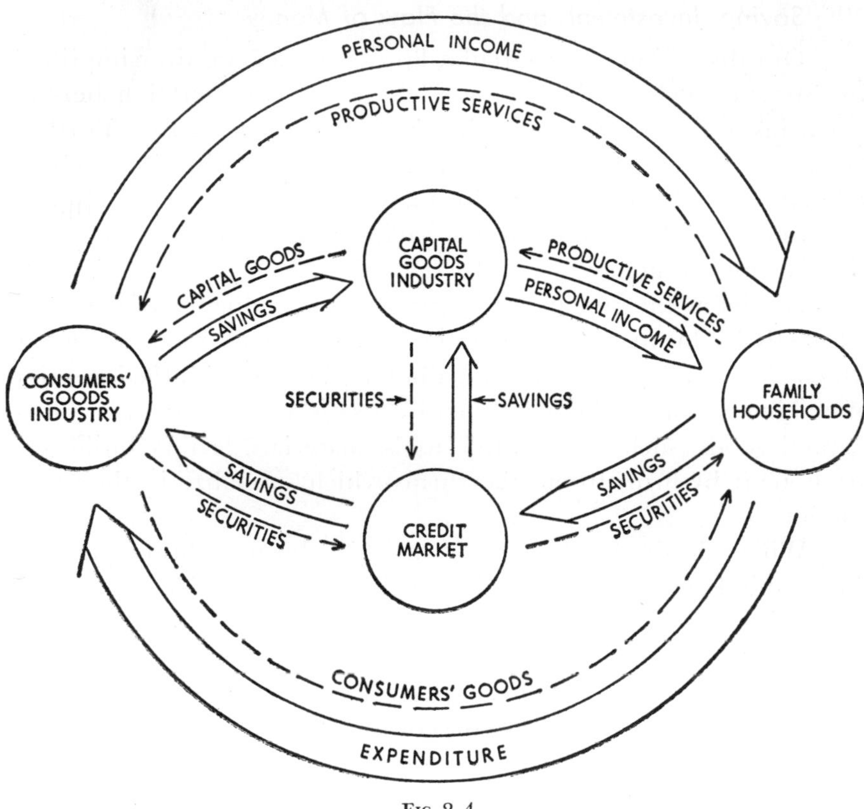

FIG. 2–4

We have seen in Chapter 1 that these securities permit the temporary transfer of money from the creditor to the debtor, from the man who saves (consumes less than he is entitled to) to the manager of the firm who has entrepreneurial initiative.

The firms spend the money which they receive through the sale of securities on capital goods of all kinds. Capital goods are produced by firms in the capital goods industry. These firms employ workers

[2] We assume that these securities are newly issued. The purchase of existing securities which constitutes merely a transfer for one owner to another is not matched by physical investment. See Chapter 21.

and make income payments to family households just like firms in the consumers' goods industry. The only difference is that their products are bought by other firms rather than by consumers.[3]

Following Figure 2–4 we can see how the circular flow of money has been changed, but not interrupted, by the inclusion of saving and investment in our model. Starting at the family households we notice how part of the personal income earned is spent, as before, on consumers' goods. But the saved portion of personal income is used to purchase securities sold by business firms. The saving public and the business firms are brought together by a variety of credit institutions (commercial banks, savings banks, and investment banks) which operate on the credit market. Through this credit market the saved portion of personal income flows to firms and is used to purchase capital goods or productive services for the production of capital goods. It is important to notice that through these investment expenditures the circular flow of money is maintained in spite of the reduction of consumption which is implied in the very concept of saving. The saved portion of the personal income finds its way back to family households as income payments to those who work in the capital goods industry.

Were it not for the fact that families save part of their income, the total expenditure on consumers' goods would tend to be greater than the supply of consumers' goods at stable prices. This is because the families' income is now earned in producing both consumers' and capital goods and therefore larger than the value of the consumers' goods. We see that, far from being necessarily harmful, the process of saving has made it possible to increase the productivity of the economy through the creation of more and better productive equipment. Productive resources which would have been devoted to consumers' goods production had the families insisted on spending their whole income on consumption are freed through the process of saving, thus permitting the production of additional capital goods, which will turn out more and better consumers' goods in the future. This also explains why in debt contracts the borrower is able to promise more future money for a given amount of present money.

These beneficial effects of saving depend on investment. If we should not be able to find investment outlets for additional savings, the consequences would be those shown in Figure 2–2. Income which is saved would fail to be spent on capital goods, total expenditure

[3] Again it must be kept in mind that we are here working with a simplified model which does not do justice to such cases as the purchase of a newly built home by the owner.

would decrease, and total income would fall. This contractionist spiral would continue until, at lower income levels, saving would decrease far enough to match investment or until, for one reason or another, investment would sufficiently increase to match saving.

As saving can exceed investment, so can investment exceed saving.[4] We have already discussed the case of a creation of additional money which causes a broadening of the income-expenditure flow. New investment can be financed by the creation of additional money. In this case additional saving is not a precondition of an increased production of capital goods. The economic consequences will depend, in part, on the existence or nonexistence of unemployed productive resources and unemployed men (as already discussed in connection with Figure 2–3, Part 2).

SUGGESTIONS FOR FURTHER READING

The relationship between money and national income will be discussed in Chapters 23 to 28 of this volume. If a fuller discussion is desired at this time, consult:

RITTER, LAWRENCE S. *Money and Economic Activity,* chap. 1. Boston: Houghton Mifflin Co., 1952. The great similarity of Ritter's and the author's exposition justifies the remark that Chapter 2 of this volume was written before the publication of Ritter's book.

CHANDLER, LESTER V. *An Introduction to Monetary Theory,* chap. 6. New York: Harper & Brothers, 1940.

For an example of the interruption of the money flow see:

KEYNES, J. M. *A Treatise on Money,* Vol. 1, pp. 176–78. New York: Harcourt, Brace & Co., 1930. Reprinted in Charles S. Whittlesey's *Readings in Money and Banking,* pp. 200–201 (New York: W. W. Norton & Co., Inc., 1952). Also reprinted in Whittlesey's *Readings,* pp. 196–99, is a brief passage of the report *National and International Measures for Full Employment.* Lake Success: United Nations, 1949. This passage contains a clear account of the circular flow of money and its interruptions. It points to many issues which had to be excluded from our simplified model.

QUESTIONS AND PROBLEMS

1. Why has money so often been referred to as the oil which lubricates the economic machine?
2. "Money and income are not identical but important relationships exist between the two." Explain.

[4] The reader will see later that modern theory often assumes an accounting identity of saving and investment according to which any increase in investment will be matched automatically by an increase in saving. See Chapter 23, pp. 322–23.

3. If the total amount of money is much smaller than the gross national product and much, much smaller than the volume of all transactions during a year, how can all the goods and services be sold?
4. Is it possible to add newly created money to the income stream of the economy without inflationary consequences? Explain and illustrate.
5. Suppose that suddenly everybody wants to spend his money faster. How would this sudden decrease in money reserves affect the circular flow of money? Where would the money go?
6. Draw a diagram which shows that saving does not interrupt the flow of money if we assume that the savings are spent on capital goods. This diagram should also show how savings flow through the credit market.
7. Show the effects of a situation in which (*a*) saving exceeds investment; (*b*) investment exceeds saving at full employment.
8. "The long-run growth of an economy depends on saving." Discuss.
9. Workers in both consumers' goods industries and capital goods industries spend their wages on consumers' goods. How can price inflation be avoided when both groups tend to buy what only one group produces?

Chapter 3 MONEY, PRICES, AND PRODUCTION

Money and Economic Freedom

In Chapter 2 we were concerned with the circular flow of money and its changes. We saw that expenditure and income may expand and contract and that these fluctuations are connected with changes in the supply and the use of money. However, our picture of the money flow distinguished only consumers' goods and capital goods; it was concerned only with aggregate expenditure and the general level of economic activity. It did not show that many thousands of firms are engaged in the production of a bewildering variety of commodities and services nor how each firm decides on the kind and quantity of its prospective output.

Production in a modern economy is an intricate process whose ramifications and interrelations elude detailed description. Millions of persons contribute daily to the production of our consumers' goods; a fantastic variety of materials and machines is needed, and the materials and machines, in turn, are the result of other lengthy and complicated production processes. We have to find out how this "collective" effort, whose branches and stages are interdependent to a bewildering degree, results in the output of just the right commodities, namely, the commodities which we decide to consume.

At first it may be natural to assume that this whole process of co-operation should be predetermined in detail by one comprehensive central plan, so that each stage and branch of production would fit the requirements of the other stages and branches and so that the aims of production would be known in advance. Yet our economy is not regulated by a central planning board. The factors of production are privately owned and are used according to the decisions of their owners;

private firms are free to plan their own production programs, and the consumer is permitted to spend his income on any selection of goods which he cares to choose. Production, far from being centrally planned, has to adjust itself to the changing wishes of consumers.

Free choice of consumption implies the use of money. An economy without money would have to use rations of consumers' goods in the distribution of the social product and would leave but little leeway for the expression of individual preferences. The right to unrestricted spending of a given sum of money, on the other hand, enables the consumer to choose that combination of commodities which will give him the greatest satisfaction.

It should clearly be understood that free choice of consumption means more than a choice among articles already produced. Even in a centrally planned economy citizens may receive a money income and may be permitted to buy, without rationing cards, whatever they may be able to purchase at prevailing prices in government stores. This freedom, however, does not constitute free choice of consumption in its full meaning as consumers' sovereignty unless the effects of these choices upon prices are used as a guide for future production. Being so used, free choice of consumption will lead to that composition of the social product which corresponds to consumers' wishes.

To underline this important point, namely, the guidance of production according to consumers' preferences, we can speak of dollar ballots which consumers cast when they determine how much to buy at given prices. We must remember, however, that the market counts the dollar of the poor and the rich alike and that free choice of consumption must not be taken to mean a uniform restriction or maximization of the satisfaction of wants. In other words, the willingness to spend a dollar cannot be used as a common denominator for subjective valuations in an economy with unequal income distribution.

The freedom which the consumer enjoys in our economic system is only one of several basic economic freedoms. Within the limits of our training we are free to choose our occupation, we are free to save part of our income, that is, to choose future rather than present consumption, and we are free to borrow and invest whenever we feel induced to do so. If these freedoms are not logically dependent on the use of money, they are at least practically inseparable from it. A moneyless economy would greatly reduce the exercise of personal choice.

For our economic freedoms we must, however, pay a price. They create economic problems since individuals' ever-changing decisions require that production be constantly adjusted. It is characteristic, therefore, that the centrally planned economy abolishes these freedoms whenever and wherever they interfere with the plan.

In the centrally planned economy of Russia the producing units are owned or controlled by the government. The managers of these units have to fulfill production quotas expressed in physical units, and they have at their disposal means of production which are allocated in kind: so much steel, coal, labor, etc. There are prices set on these items, but these prices do not have a guiding function. As a rule, a Russian manager does not produce because receipts are high and costs relatively low, that is, because he wants to make a profit; he produces his quota because the government tells him to. He pays the industries which supply him and, in turn, is paid by other producing units upon delivery of his product. These payments between producing units are, in the main, accounting devices. Monetary transfers from one account to another in the state bank are used to check up on plan fulfillment.

We shall see that the part played by money is more important in the free than in the planned economy. But it is interesting, too, that the centrally planned economy cannot abolish money altogether. Wages are still paid in money, consumers' goods are still purchased with money, and productive agencies pay one another by check. The Russian planners, furthermore, use so-called financial balances (for example, total wages paid during a period versus total value of consumers' goods during the same period) because only in monetary units is it possible to express aggregate quantities of dissimilar things (for example, to compare the total output of an industry with its input).

Money and the Price Mechanism

Where there is no central plan, the direction of production has to rest with the many private economic units, the families and firms. Consuming units, enjoying free choice of consumption, decide what they want to buy at prevailing prices, and producing units translate consumers' demand into a demand for factors of production (labor, natural resources, capital goods). These factors can be used in an immense variety of combinations, and it has to be decided in which fields of industry they shall be employed. The decision depends on what was called the "consumers' ballot." As the demand for a commodity increases its price will rise, other things remaining equal. The producer of the commodity will now expand production because he anticipates higher profits owing to increased prices and is, therefore, also willing to offer higher prices for the services of the factors of production. For example, as consumers shift from coal to oil, the producers of oil and oil burners will hire the men who used to produce coal and coal furnaces. Of course, we cannot be sure that the factors needed for the expansion of one industry are the same as those which are set free by the contraction of another. In the long run, however, the necessary adjustments will take place in spite of temporary frictions.

Each firm must at least earn enough through the sale of its products to be induced and enabled to embark on a new round of production. In other words, the firms' decisions rest on business calculations, that is, on comparisons between costs and the anticipated prices of products. These business calculations could not be carried out in terms of tons, liquid ounces, passenger miles, or bushels. A common denominator, a monetary unit, is indispensable.

Since those who are offering the services of the factors of production (the family units) are eager to obtain the highest prices possible, the pricing process in factor markets will tend to bring about the employment of factors in those industries and firms where they command the highest prices. But only those firms which can obtain sufficiently high prices for their products can successfully compete for the services of factors. Thus, in trying to maximize profits, business firms employ factors where they should be employed according to consumers' ballots.

The pricing process of our economy presents itself as a series of reciprocal price relationships which tend to bring the economy to a state of equilibrium. This state will have been reached when every factor is employed where it is paid the highest price equating demand and supply; that is, where it satisfies the most powerful demand in terms of dollars. Such an ideal state of equilibrium will never exist. There will always be outside disturbances, like weather or war, to which the economy has to adjust; there will be a constant recurrence of technological change; and changing consumers' tastes and fashions will continuously lead to relative price movements. Thus even a perfectly working economy would have to reconcile itself forever to changing conditions.

From the monetary standpoint we must distinguish between two reasons why the demand for a commodity may increase:

1. An increase in the demand for commodity A may be accompanied by a decreased demand for commodity B because total expenditure did not increase. In this case the price of commodity A will tend to rise and that of commodity B, to fall. Given enough time, the final result will depend on adjustments of production and supply to these changed demand conditions. It may be said that price adjustments up

and down will *tend* to cancel one another in their effects on the value of money.

2. An increased demand for commodity A may have been caused by an increase in total expenditure as a result of a larger supply or a faster turnover of money. Now the increased demand for commodity A need not be accompanied by a decreased demand for commodity B. This time there will be a tendency for the price of commodity A to rise without a corresponding fall in the price of commodity B, and the average price level will rise, depending on the reactions of the supply of commodity A to the increase in demand.

The first case is concerned with relative price adjustments, while the second case is most likely to involve both general and relative price movements. It may seem as if, from the monetary standpoint, we were interested only in general price movements which change the value of money. However, we must not lose sight of those relative price movements which accompany general price movements. The two cannot be disentangled. If, owing to increased aggregate spending, the price of commodity A rises without a corresponding rise in the price of B, then price relationships have been changed. If all prices would rise in exactly the same ratio, a change in the value of money would lose much of its importance. But such a lifting of prices of commodities and of factors of production in exactly the same proportion is extremely unlikely to happen. Increasing expenditure hits selected goods and services harder and earlier than others, and the whole relative price structure will change with economic effects which are perhaps more important than the concurrent change in the general price level. We are justified in saying that changes in the value of money are important mainly because they go hand in hand with changes in the relative price pattern and influence the economy through these changes.

Reactions of Supply to Increased Expenditure

The effects of changes in aggregate expenditure on the general level and on the structure of prices will depend on reactions of the supply side of all markets. As we shift demand curves to the right they will intersect supply curves (which are less than perfectly elastic) at higher points. Prices will increase and the amount of commodities supplied will increase, too. Here we move along given supply curves. In the long run, however, increased profits may lead to increased supply. Now we shift the whole supply curves to the right, and there should be a tendency for prices to fall again.

What will be the final effect of changes in total expenditure on the prices of different commodities and productive services? The answer to this question depends on our assumptions regarding the possibility of supplying more of the commodities and services which are in greater demand. We can distinguish three sources of an increased supply:

1. When unused factors of production are available in the technically needed proportions, we can expand production without having to cut production in other places.

2. Even at "full" employment of the factors of production we may produce more of one commodity and still maintain the previous supply of other commodities if improved techniques of production permit an increased output without an increased input of factors.

3. At "full" employment of the factors of production and with unchanged technical conditions of production, we can increase the production of one group of commodities only if we simultaneously decrease the production of others.

Increased total expenditures need not cause price inflation in cases 1 and 2, but in case 3 inflationary effects on prices will be felt as the producers of some commodities begin bidding away factors of production from other producers. We see that price inflation and changes in the purchasing power of money are as much dependent on the conditions of production and supply as they are on the monetary determinants of effective demand.

Real life will present a mixture of the assumptions made above. For purposes of theoretical clarification Keynes made the extreme statement that

> an increase in the quantity of money will have no effect whatever on prices, so long as there is any unemployment, and that employment will increase in exact proportion to any increase in effective demand brought about by the increase in the quantity of money; whilst as soon as full employment is reached, it will thenceforward be the wage-unit and prices which will increase in exact proportion to the increase in effective demand. Thus if there is perfectly elastic supply so long as there is unemployment, and perfectly inelastic supply so soon as full employment is reached, and if effective demand changes in the same proportion as the quantity of money, the Quantity Theory of Money can be enunciated as follows: "So long as there is unemployment, *employment* will change in the same proportion as the quantity of money; and when there is full employment, *prices* will change in the same proportion as the quantity of money."[1]

[1] J. M. Keynes, *The General Theory of Employment, Interest and Money* (London: Macmillan & Co., Ltd., 1936), pp. 295–96.

Keynes then hastens to remove his simplifying assumptions which amounted to the omission of the following complications:

1. Effective demand will not change in exact proportion to the quantity of money.
2. Since resources are not homogeneous, there will be diminishing, and not constant, returns as employment gradually increases.
3. Since resources are not interchangeable, some commodities will reach a condition of inelastic supply whilst there are still unemployed resources available for the production of other commodities.
4. The wage-unit will tend to rise before full employment has been reached.
5. The remunerations of the factors entering into marginal cost will not all change in the same proportion.[2]

Keynes' qualifying statements show that price stability will, as a rule, not change suddenly to pronounced price inflation. Rather, the appearance of bottlenecks of production will cause a more gradual transition. We can also draw the important conclusion that it would be wrong to deal with partial unemployment (that is, unemployment caused by *shifts* in demand) by stimulating aggregate demand through an increased supply of money. Increased total expenditure might only accentuate the inflationary tendencies in the fully employed industries without necessarily creating jobs in the distressed areas.

The Neutrality of Money

Changes in the pattern of prices can take place as a reaction to monetary influences even though the general level of prices remains stable. If total production increases in proportion to an increase in effective demand, we may avoid price inflation. Nevertheless, the increase in effective demand will affect some fields of industry more than others with concomitant adjustments in production. Are these adjustments dangerous in spite of the fact that price inflation was absent?

Suppose, first, that total production grows owing to increased efficiency in many fields of industry or agriculture. If total expenditure does not increase simultaneously, prices, on the average, are going to fall. This price deflation does not originate with monetary changes but with changes in production techniques. A price deflation, due to increased efficiency, rests on reduced unit costs of production. The social product increases in quantity and improves in quality though

[2] *Ibid.*, p. 296.

the total input of factors of production remains the same. Economic development of this kind is, at least theoretically, not incompatible with a stable supply of money; price deflation is not necessarily dangerous. If unit costs of production decline in many firms, *and if competition forces prices to correspondingly lower levels,* there is no reason why production should react adversely. As the Gold Delegation of the League of Nations suggested:

> When the decline of prices is due to improvements in industry and agriculture which have lowered production cost, the decline of prices is, on the whole, beneficial, for it is in this way that the fruits of industrial and agricultural progress are made available to society as a whole. . . . It is only when the attempt is made to sustain prices in the face of decreasing production costs that disequilibria occur, for this encourages overproduction and causes an accumulation of goods which results ultimately in a breakdown.[3]

This quotation is a typical expression of the theory of neutral money which advocates a monetary policy designed to protect the economy against the disturbing effects of money. According to this theory creation as well as destruction of money may easily spoil the healthy equivalence of total demand and total supply. Any creation of additional money (unless counteracted by an increased demand for money to hold) creates an increase in effective demand which is not immediately and exactly counterbalanced by an increase in the supply of goods and services. On the other hand, if money is destroyed, the existing supply of goods does not find its demand counterpart on the markets without painful price adjustments downward. Creation as well as destruction of money thus injects a disturbing monetary germ into the economic body.

Suppose, secondly, that the techniques of production remain unchanged but that the economy expands owing to geographical or population growth. More people produce, but unit costs in, say, terms of labor hours remain the same. If the supply of money is not increased the economy will suffer from a painful deflationary process. Commodity prices will be forced down and since unit costs are not lowered production, employment, and national income will decrease until the prices of the factors of production are also brought to a lower level. Only on very artificial assumptions concerning the smoothness

[3] Gold Delegation of the League of Nations, *Final Report* (Geneva: League of Nations, 1932).

of downward price adjustments and wage adjustments could it be argued that this type of price deflation would not harm the economy.[4]

Thus even neutral-money theory is driven to the conclusion that in the case of geographical or population growth, without technological improvements, enough additional money has to be supplied to maintain existing prices and to provide the new territories or the new members of the economy with adequate money reserves.

The most important criticism of the neutral-money theory has to do with the state of employment. If we assume "full" employment, it does make sense to watch the money supply carefully and to permit even deflationary adjustments if they are justified by improved efficiency under competitive conditions. But for an underemployed economy the theory of neutral money loses much of its otherwise impressive logical cogency.

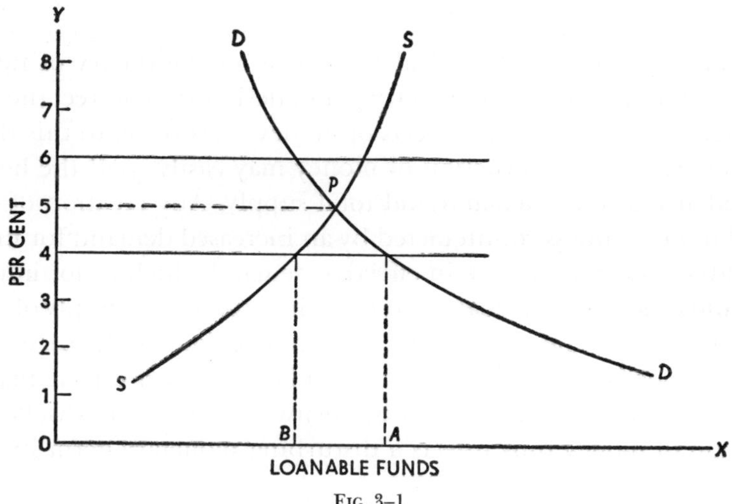

FIG. 3–1

The neutral-money theory holds that, with minor exceptions, any creation or destruction of money will disturb the relative price pattern because it artificially changes a group of prices which have a strategic position in the whole pricing process: the rates of interest. On

[4] It ought to be pointed out that this case, which may seem to be artificially chosen, portrays in reality a situation in which some countries found themselves at the time when modern states began to develop and when the supply of money depended chiefly on the supply of the precious metals. Those countries which did not produce these metals tried to increase the supply of money by a "favorable" balance of trade. Heckscher and Keynes have shown that mercantilist writings, so often branded as entirely nonsensical, permit of a much kinder interpretation when we remember that the mercantilists faced the problem of an insufficient money supply in a quickly growing economy, which severely hampered economic development. See Keynes, *op. cit.*, chap. xxiii.

these rates of interest, when compared with anticipated rates of profit, rest the investment decisions of business firms. Whether or not we share this critical attitude of the neutral-money theory, it is indeed true that changes in the supply of, or the demand for, money will affect the economy directly through changes in interest rates.

Suppose that the rate of interest *P* in Figure 3–1 equates the demand for loans and the supply of savings. If we lower the rate artificially from 5 per cent to 4 per cent while demand and supply remain unchanged, the amount demanded (*OA*) will be larger than the amount supplied (*OB*). On a commodity market, say the market for gasoline, such an artificially low price could be maintained only through rationing. Equilibrium between gasoline demand and supply, which the "ceiling" price cannot establish, must be obtained by measures of government control. On the credit market, too, we could use rationing in the form of lending or investment controls. The market for loanable funds, however, has the peculiar feature that the artificially lowered price can be maintained without rationing provided we fill the gap *BA* with additional money. Since one money unit is identical with another, it makes no difference to the borrower whether the loan consists of savings or of additional money.

We see how the supply of money can be changed by a manipulation of interest rates. As these rates are set below the point at which the supply of savings and the demand for loans are equal, the amount demanded will exceed the amount supplied and additional money can be brought into circulation. Similarly a raising of the level of interest rates above the equilibrium point will make persons and firms borrow less than the saved portion of the national income, and the money flow will be reduced. Changes of interest rates are an instrument by which changes in the supply of money are accomplished. But interest rates together with anticipated rates of profit determine investment, national income, and the level of employment. These connections explain why the most important book in economics which the Twentieth Century has as yet produced has the title *General Theory of Employment, Interest and Money*.[5]

Inflation and Deflation

If we follow the neutral-money theory, we come to the conclusion that even a stable level of consumers' goods prices does not guar-

[5] These very incomplete and sketchy remarks on the relationship between money and interest rates must suffice for the time being. Chapters 19–21 will be devoted to a more thorough study of interest rates.

antee a perfectly neutral behavior of money and that it would be better if we stabilized money income per capita and permitted prices to fall as technical progress reduces production costs. We know from practical experience, however, that we are quite often not even able to keep the level of consumers' goods prices stable. Therefore we have to find out how price inflation and price deflation will influence the economy.

That the value of money should be kept reasonably stable follows logically from money's function as a measure of value. As a measure of value money may succeed or fail depending upon whether its value in terms of goods or services is comparatively stable or subject to uncertain and violent fluctuations. As Barbara Wootton has so convincingly argued:

> One has only to imagine what would happen to business calculations and plans if the number of ounces in a pound, or of inches in a foot, were . . . variable, and then to remember that, whereas these measures enter only into contracts concerning goods sold by weight or length, the monetary unit enters into every single economic contract of any kind whatever, to get an idea of the extent of the damage to economic efficiency for which a monetary system that is unreliable, or imperfectly understood, may be responsible.[6]

It is evident that considerable variations in the value of money—which we refer to when speaking of price inflation and price deflation—would seriously impair the usefulness of money as a unit of account. If a movement of all prices, up or down, would leave the relative price structure undisturbed, price inflation and price deflation would perhaps be a nuisance, but they would not be dangerous. General movements of prices, however, are bound to lead to distortions in the relative pattern of prices. When additional money causes a price inflation, the distribution of the national income is affected. Privileged groups get hold of the additional money, and their power to purchase rises to the disadvantage of persons with fixed or comparatively slowly rising incomes who are compelled to reduce their purchases to the benefit of the *nouveaux riches.*

Much of this injustice is caused, as shown in Chapter 1, by a monetary illusion, the pretense that the price rigidity of money signifies a stable value of money. This pretense underlies all contracts which are based on the unit of money. The terms of contracts, as a rule, do not vary with changes in the purchasing power of money. Thus in times of price deflation, the position of debtors is made harder because

[6] Barbara Wootton, *Plan or No Plan* (London: Victor Gollancz, 1934), p. 142.

their obligations grow in terms of real goods. They must produce and sell more to reach the amounts stipulated in their debt contracts, and their very effort to sell more drives prices further down. It is easy to see that creditors, in turn, suffer during periods of price inflation.

Variations in the real value of debt change the cost of borrowing. A 5 per cent rate of interest per annum is practically a zero rate if all prices rise during the year by about 5 per cent. We shall see later how important for the investment decisions of businessmen is the comparison of rates of interest with anticipated rates of profit. Price inflation may lead to both abnormally high profits and abnormally low *real* rates of interest, to excessive investment and to grave maladjustments in the process of production. Profits appear large when current high prices of finished goods are compared with the costs of production which were incurred at an earlier time. Once price inflation has reached major proportions many businessmen and others will try to avoid losses by buying and producing "real" values such as jewelry or real estate regardless of their usefulness under normal economic conditions.

Price deflation—unless accompanied by a corresponding reduction of production costs through technical improvements—can be even worse than inflation. Price inflation, at least, is accompanied by hectic economic activity, however misled this feverish bustle may be. Deflation may lead directly into depression and mass unemployment. When prices decline generally, and when the decline is expected to continue, buyers will be inclined to purchase less and less in expectation of further price falls while growing unemployment, the result of declining economic activity, will reduce expenditure even further.

Since both price inflation and price deflation may dangerously influence production, distribution, and the level of employment, it must be clear from the outset that the injustices and damages produced by price inflation cannot be removed by a succeeding price deflation or that a new inflation cannot always deal successfully with the destruction brought about by deflation. A man dangerously injured by an automobile is not brought back to health if the car is driven over him once more in the opposite direction.

While it is always essential to avoid excessive fluctuations of the general price level, absolute price stability is not necessarily the most important aim of monetary policy. The creation of additional money may prove beneficial even though it may cause an upward trend in prices. Just as a drug, deadly when taken in large doses, may have a reviving effect on the body to which it is administered with caution, so may the creation of additional money, when carefully handled, be a means of lifting the economy out of a state of depression and unemployment. Experience has shown us, however, that a state of "full" employment is also a state of serious inflationary pressures, and we know that a conflict between a full-employment policy and an anti-inflationary policy may easily arise. Only in the abstract world of theoretical assumptions can the ideal of a fully employed economy with stable or even falling prices—and yet free from price controls—be achieved. In the real world our goal must be the best possible compromise between conflicting aims and the best possible integration of monetary and general economic policies.

Until recently it was generally believed that price inflation could result only from an increase in monetary expenditures which is not met by an increased supply of goods. This assumption is correct as long as the pricing process is sufficiently competitive. It need not be correct, however, if wages and prices are "administered" by monopolistic agencies. It is possible that wages and prices rise even when aggregate expenditure decreases. This was the case in the United States during the recession of 1957–58 (see Chapter 28).

SUGGESTIONS FOR FURTHER READING

A fuller discussion of the pricing process can be found in:

HALM, GEORGE N. *Economic Systems, A Comparative Analysis,* chaps. 3 and 4. Rev. ed. New York: Holt, Rinehart and Winston, 1960.

The advantages of money for consumer and producer as well as the dangers of monetary instability are discussed in:

ROBERTSON, DENNIS H. *Money,* chap. 1 New York: Pitman Publishing Corp., 1948.

The problem of inflation will be discussed in Chapter 28. For an introduction see:

FISHER, IRVING. *Stabilizing the Dollar,* chap. 3. New York: Macmillan Co., 1920.

HABERLER, GOTTFRIED. *Inflation, Its Causes and Cures.* Washington, D.C.: American Enterprise Association, 1960.

KEYNES, J. M. *Monetary Reform,* chap. 1. New York: Harcourt, Brace & Co., 1924.

On the integration of monetary and general price theory:

HAYEK, FRIEDRICH A. *Prices and Production,* Lecture 1. London: George Routledge & Sons, Ltd., 1931.

Keynes, J. M. *The General Theory of Employment, Interest and Money,* chap. 21. London: Macmillan & Co., Ltd., 1936.

Machlup, Fritz. *The Stock Market Credit and Capital Formation,* chap. 12. London: William Hodge & Co., Inc., Ltd., 1940.

Robertson, Dennis H. *Essays in Monetary Theory,* chap. 11. London: Staples Press, Ltd., 1940.

QUESTIONS AND PROBLEMS

1. "Man values highly this privilege of spending his money income, that is of taking his real income as he pleases" (D. H. Robertson). Comment.
2. Distinguish between free choice of consumption and consumers' sovereignty.
3. Compare the role of money in a market economy with the role money plays in a centrally planned economy.
4. "An increase in total expenditure is likely to involve both general and relative price movements and we are justified in saying that changes in the value of money are important mainly because they go hand in hand with changes in the relative price pattern and influence the economy through these changes." Discuss.
5. Under certain qualifying assumptions, J. M. Keynes assumed "that an increase in the quantity of money will have no effect whatever on prices, so long as there is any unemployment, and that employment will increase in exact proportion to any increase in effective demand brought about by the increase in the quantity of money; whilst as soon as full employment is reached, it will thenceforward be the wage-unit and prices which will increase in exact proportion to the increase in effective demand." Discuss Keynes' qualifying assumptions.
6. "Any violent and prolonged exhibition of instability in the value of money affects not only the distribution but also the creation of wealth: for it threatens to undermine the basis of contract and business expectation on which our economic order is built up" (D. H. Robertson). Comment.
7. "Not a money which is *stable* in value but a *neutral* money must . . . form the starting point for the theoretical analysis of monetary influences on production . . ." (F. A. Hayek). Comment.
8. If we accept Hayek's statement in question No. 7, when should the supply of money be increased?
9. Show how changes in the supply of money may be brought about by changes in interest rates. Use diagram.
10. Does social justice require that a period of inflation be followed by a period of deflation?

PART II
Evolution and Kinds of Money

Chapter 4 COMMODITY MONEY, FULL-BODIED MONEY, AND TOKEN MONEY

Commodity Money

Numerous commodities could be mentioned which served, in one society or another, as the unit of account and/or as the means of payment. The article serving as the means of payment may originally have been a good which was readily taken in exchange because of its obvious use value. It depended on the pattern of the society in question which goods possessed general desirability. Oxen and sheep served among nomads, fishhooks among Eskimos, and tobacco among Virginian planters. In addition to general acceptability, commodity money had to have the following qualities: relatively high exchange value which assured easy transportability; reasonable durability which permitted some storage; relatively steady value in relation to other commodities; and availability in reasonably uniform and convenient units.

It was easier for an article to serve as the unit of account than as the means of payment since as the measure of value it soon became an abstract ideal anyhow, a value concept, with which its real embodiments rarely corresponded exactly. The ox as unit of account was an ox of average size, weight, and age. Real specimens of the standard good had to be expressed in this abstract unit of account, the difference between the abstract and the real commodity being, to paraphrase J. M. Keynes, that between the President of the United States and Mr. Kennedy.

For obvious reasons real commodities such as knives, skins, or tea were never quite satisfactory as money. Real commodities differ in quality, they may deteriorate or even perish with age, and they may be rather awkward to transport or to store. In some cases their supply may be subject to sudden changes thus affecting their value in relation to other commodities. Only by the use of precious metals was it possible to create a reasonably close union of commodity and money.

Before we leave commodity money in its original form it may be interesting to turn to a recent case in which a commodity emerged spontaneously as the unit of account and as the means of payment. The cigarette served as money both in POW camps and in the black markets of postwar Europe. The precondition of this recent case of real commodity money was, of course, the deterioration of regular currency through price controls, rationing, price inflation, and general chaos. That cigarettes were taken by nonsmokers as well as by smokers underlines the fact that once general acceptability is established, the use value of the commodity is temporarily of no consequence. During the time it is used as money, a good ceases to be a commodity. Nevertheless, its general acceptability will still depend on its latent use value.

The cigarette possesses some of the characteristics which money must have. It is reasonably uniform in quality so that individual units may be substituted for one another; it can be used in different "denominations" (single cigarettes, packs, cartons); it can be easily transported and stored; and finally, it is scarce in supply and maintains a reasonably steady value of exchange vis-à-vis other commodities.

Thus we could see what had taken place in bygone times: the spontaneous creation of commodity money, the emergence of cigarettes as unit of account and means of payment because under the circumstances they best answered the quest for an article possessing to some degree the qualities of modern money. It is needless to add, that cigarettes were not an ideal money substitute because the identity of the individual units was not perfect, the durability was not sufficient, and the exchange value fluctuated with an uncertain and accidental supply. Certainly, we should not dream of using cigarettes as money when healthy money in its modern form as coins, bank notes, and demand deposits is at our disposal.

Full-Bodied Money

Let us now turn to the next important step in the development of money, the creation of full-bodied coins.

The following qualities made gold and silver especially suitable as a means of payment:

1. The early evolution of the precious metals as a means of payment was probably due to general acceptability based upon their ornamental usefulness. Gold and silver are symbols of wealth, satisfying deeply rooted human desires to accumulate and exhibit wealth in an indestructible form.

2. Precious metals are relatively scarce and, therefore, so valuable that small weight units command large quantities of other goods in exchange.

3. Precious metals can easily be transported and stored.

4. Metal is divisible into small units without any loss in use value. Most other commodities cannot be cut to pieces without being destroyed. Conveniently divided into small units, gold and silver can be adjusted to the value of the commodities which have to be exchanged. Thus they satisfy the desire for monetary units of different denominations.

5. Precious metals are completely homogeneous. Different pieces of the same weight and fineness are identical in value, a fact of great importance for the practical identification of the means of payment and the unit of account.

6. Precious metals, at least in the form of modern alloys, are indestructible in use.

7. Precious metals are relatively independent of cultural differences among communities and societies; this makes them internationally acceptable.

8. Precious metals maintain a comparatively stable value, at least over shorter periods. This stability in value emerges from the fact that very little of the amount produced is destroyed by wear and tear or industrial use. Thus a year's new production is relatively small in comparison with the existing amount, a situation which promotes relative stability in value. We shall see, however, that this point must not be overstressed.

Precious metals could be used as means of payment even before the development of the coin. All that was needed were small pieces, preferably of equal weight. And since these weight units of metal could be chosen at will, it was only natural that they should be so picked as to conform to the previously established unit of account. The use of weight units of metals can still be recognized in such designations as pound, mark, ruble, or lira.

Uncoined pieces of precious metals were, however, not very satisfactory as the means of payment since doubts could arise as to their weight and fineness. This difficulty, which involved frequent weighing and testing, was overcome by covering the whole surface of carefully weighed pieces of metal with a stamp which indicated weight or value and, perhaps, the issuing authority ("crown").

An additional difficulty was that before the use of modern alloys coins of precious metal were not very durable and deteriorated from wear and tear. To overcome these difficulties required considerable time, and before complete uniformity of coins of the same metal and denomination was achieved, the heavier coins often disappeared from circulation and were melted down. This fact led Sir Thomas Gresham (1519–79), financial adviser to Queen Elizabeth, to formulate the famous law which bears his name, that "bad" money drives out "good" money.

The full-bodied coin is still commodity money. It has the same value whether it is used as money or as metal. Identity of the coin as money and as metal is guaranteed when two conditions are fulfilled: when we have the right to melt the coin and use the metal for industrial and barter purposes, and when we have the unrestricted right to have the metal coined into money. Under these conditions the value of the coin cannot be higher or lower than the market value of a piece of the metal of the same weight and fineness. If the value of the coin as money should be higher than the market value of the metal of which it is made (if, in other words, the coin could buy more metal than its own body contains), it would be profitable to buy metal with the coin and have the metal coined until the increased supply of coins and the increased demand for metal would lead to the desired identity of value and thus stop the process. If the value of the coin should ever fall below the value of the metal contained in its body, we could profit from melting the coins and exchanging the metal for more coins until increased demand for, and decreased supply of, coins would arrest this practice.

The full-bodied coin is the ultimate development of commodity money, for it has intrinsic value. It carries its value with it and is, therefore, of value not only in the country of origin but anywhere in the world where the metal has a market value. These statements must not create the impression, however, that the value of the full-bodied coin is entirely and solely derived from its quality as a commodity. Value depends on demand and supply, and in the case of gold and silver it soon became obvious that the demand was largely determined by their monetary rather than their industrial use. If gold were ever demonetized, that is, not used any longer for monetary purposes of any kind, it would, without doubt, suffer a great fall in value resulting from this fall in monetary demand.

Taking the identity of the value of money and metal as given, under conditions of free coinage, we must avoid the mistake of assuming that the value of the metal always stays the same because its price is fixed in terms of money and is, therefore, always unity; in other words, we must not be deceived by the monetary illusion which we discussed in Chapter 1. We must admit, however, that the monetary metal, say gold, finds itself in a special position. Its costs of production are determined by the prices of the productive resources which are needed in gold mining, while its own price is fixed. During a price inflation these cost prices will rise, and since the price of the gold remains the same, production will fall and marginal mines will be closed. Thus the supply of full-bodied money rises less rapidly, and the inflationary development is arrested. Vice versa, when insufficient gold supply or any other reason leads to falling prices, gold production costs decline while the price of the product, being identical with the monetary unit, stays the same. Thereupon gold production will expand and the deflationary trend will be reversed through an increased supply of money.

We must not exaggerate this self-regulating tendency of gold production and money supply, however, for at best it would be a very slow process. Changes in production techniques and discoveries of natural gold deposits would still remain independent data in the process. We can imagine what would happen to the value of gold, and to any monetary system based on gold, if future developments would enable us to produce gold at a fraction of the present cost of gold mining.

Bimetallism

A monetary system which used only one metal and only full-bodied coin would not be practical. We could hardly use golden ten-cent or silver ten-dollar pieces. Early in the history of coinage, therefore, the problem arose as to how several metals could be used simultaneously for monetary purposes.

The solution seems to be simple enough. Let us have, we might be tempted to argue, full-bodied silver and gold coins, silver for coins of smaller and gold for coins of larger denominations. But what if the market value of silver should change in relation to the market value of gold owing, say, to a sudden increase in silver production at greatly lowered cost?

Obviously, the use of two metals under such conditions would imply two units of account and two price systems. The silver prices of commodities would, in our example, rise in comparison with the gold prices of the same commodities. Since it is inconvenient to have two independent price systems in a country, one system with a fixed ratio between the two precious metals was established. This system is known as "bimetallism." Within a nation the government was powerful enough to establish such a fixed ratio through its standing offer to mint both gold and silver in predetermined weights per unit of money. But internationally there was no such power or agreement, and the ratio between gold and silver was liable to differ among various countries. We have already seen that a situation cannot persist in which the value of full-bodied money differs from its metal value within any one country, and also that bad money will drive out good money. In case of two countries with differing gold and silver price ratios, these rules lead to interesting results.

Let us assume that in country A both gold and silver can be freely coined and melted and that the legal or mint ratio between silver and gold is 15 to 1, that is, that the country's monetary unit consists either of 15 weight units of silver or of 1 weight unit of gold. In country B the same situation exists, except that the legal or mint ratio is set at 16 to 1. Within each country the market ratio cannot differ from the legal ratio. In country A, for instance, nobody would be willing to pay more than 15 units of silver for 1 unit of gold, since one could get gold officially at that price. But gold is more valuable in country B because it exchanges in B for 16 units of silver, compared with 15 units in A. Gold, therefore, will flow from A to B. For the same reason silver will flow from B to A. It pays to exchange silver for gold in A, send the gold to B, exchange it for more silver in B, send the silver to A, exchange it again for gold, and so forth, until all gold has left A and all silver has left B.

This process by which one country loses its silver and the other country its gold is another application of Gresham's law that "bad" money drives out "good" money. We see that a bimetallic system cannot keep both metals in circulation as long as different countries maintain diverging ratios between the two metals. Historical experience amply substantiates the working of Gresham's law. Instead of having two monetary metals and two types of full-bodied coin, bimetallic systems kept losing one metal and had to get along either without silver or without gold.

Even regionally limited international agreements, such as the Latin Union of 1865, did not succeed in maintaining a bimetallic system. When silver was demonetized in other countries, the countries of the Latin Union had to abolish the free coinage of silver.

The solution of the problem of maintaining coins of different denominations in circulation was simple. But it involved one of the most decisive steps in the evolution of money: the creation of token money.

From Full-Bodied Money to Token Money

In leaving commodity money we may at first find it rather hard to give up the idea of an "intrinsic" value of money. Practically everyone who begins to study money tends to cling to the idea that money must be made of valuable material or that there must be a full backing somewhere, so that it could be exchanged in its total amount for gold or silver even though it is only paper. The great philosopher Immanuel Kant considered it an indispensable quality of "good" money that the article which is to serve as money should have the same cost of production as the commodities which it can buy. This difficulty which misled Kant is not to be belittled.

We can easily understand why some people like full-bodied money so much. They do not fully trust the ability of money to command other things in exchange, and they are, therefore, comforted by the possibility of using the coin as a commodity. It is as if they insisted that theater tickets be made of chocolate, so that they could be eaten in case the management should have issued too many tickets for the capacity of the theater. What those who want full-bodied money are really afraid of is a future decline in the purchasing power of mere tokens. They put their trust rather in the permanent value of gold or silver. Historical experience suggests that, in this respect, they are not entirely foolish after all.

Money which is not full-bodied is token money, that is, money whose monetary or face value is greater than the value of the material of which it is made.

A simple example will show that token money can be as good as or even better than full-bodied money. Suppose that a country uses full-bodied silver coin but that in all other countries silver is being "demonetized" in favor of gold. The price of silver falls everywhere except in our first country which maintains free coinage of silver at the official price. The result is that great quantities of silver will be exported to this country, the circulation of silver coin in the country will greatly increase, and, accordingly, commodity prices will rise. We see that full-bodied money is no insurance against price inflation.

Now, in order to avoid price inflation this country, too, suspends the free coinage of silver, thus limiting artificially the supply of silver coin. The inflow of silver can no longer exert its inflationary pressure since silver can no longer be exchanged for silver coin at the fixed price and in unlimited amounts. The interesting result is that in this particular case greater monetary stability is achieved by giving up full-bodied money in favor of token money. The value of the silver coin is permitted to rise above the metal value of its body, the silver coin has become token money. The artificial scarcity of silver coins, accomplished through the abolition of free coinage, makes the monetary system immune against the falling price of silver. The more the price of silver falls, the more does the value of the silver coin exceed the value of its metal content.

These considerations show that money does not have to be full-bodied to be good money. And once we realize that money can be worth more than its content, the bodily manifestation of money becomes a matter of secondary importance. As a matter of fact, the means of payment may be reduced to a mere piece of paper with a special imprint (paper money). It makes no difference whatsoever how far the value of money surpasses the commodity value of its body. To paraphrase Irving Fisher: if a pillar is not high enough to support the ceiling, it is a matter of indifference just how tall it is. If money need not be full-bodied, it need not have any value as a commodity.

Token or Subsidiary Coin

We can now solve the problem which a system using only full-bodied money could not solve. We saw that to get coins of convenient denominations we have to use different metals. We also saw that in actual practice it has been impossible to keep even two metals in circulation together under conditions of free coinage for both metals. This difficulty can be overcome by the use of token coins which are characterized by the following principles and regulations:

1. Token coins are not full-bodied. Their metallic value is so low as to eliminate the danger that they are melted down whenever the market value of the metal increases.

2. The legal limitation of the supply of token coins prevents them from causing undesirable fluctuations of the value of money. This limitation of the supply of token coins can be secured only when their free coinage is forbidden. There is danger, however, of an over-expansion of token money since the very fact that the monetary value of token money exceeds its bodily value can lead to a substantial gain for those who have the power to create it. We keep in mind that token money is managed money.

3. Although token coins are as a rule not definitive or standard money they are convertible into definitive money. Definitive or standard money is money in which even the monetary authority can discharge its obligations. Suppose that full-bodied gold coins are the standard money and that token silver coins can be converted into gold coins. Under these conditions nobody will take less than their face value for the token silver coins, which cannot depreciate.

It need hardly be added that token coins can be made of any suitable material and do not have to be limited to silver.

Evolution of the Bank Note

We shall now leave the coins and concentrate on a quantitatively much more important type of token money, the bank note, which is paper money. How did the bank note come into being? How could it maintain its monetary value? And why were people willing to accept a flimsy piece of paper as money?

A brief reference to historical facts may prove helpful.

Before the development of modern coinage much of the metallic circulation in Europe's financial centers was of a dubious character. And since there were in addition so many regional authorities issuing coins, it became difficult to ascertain the real or specie value of money. Businessmen, therefore, developed the habit of employing specialists (goldsmiths) who ascertained the weight and fineness of the various coins in circulation and offered storage facilities to increase the safety of money holdings. Upon the deposit of coins the goldsmith would issue to the depositor a certificate of deposit stating in the monetary unit of the country the specie value of the deposited coins and promising payment in specie on demand. These certificates of deposit were backed to 100 per cent by actual specie and were, therefore, representative full-bodied money.

It soon became the habit to use these convenient certificates as a means of payment instead of the dubious coins. Several technical improvements of the certificates supported this development. The goldsmiths promised payment to the "bearer" rather than to the depositor personally, and they issued these certificates of deposit in round sums of money rather than in those accidental amounts which a depositor happened to deposit. These improvements greatly increased the general acceptability and usefulness of these new means of payment.

Thus far this new money was still representative full-bodied money which merely took the place of an equal amount of full-bodied coin. The monetary circulation had not been increased; the monetary system had been improved in convenience but was not essentially changed.

Our goldsmiths soon noticed that the depositors preferred the use of certificates to the use of coins and that they rarely claimed the deposited metal. In addition occasional withdrawals were usually matched by new deposits. The result was that most of the full-bodied coin remained in the goldsmiths' shops. It seemed quite a waste to have all this money lying idly around, and our goldsmiths began to lend it out. At this critical point in the development of money they changed, thereby, from mere bullion dealers into real bankers.

Since the business community preferred by then a mere promise to pay to the dubious full-bodied coin, our goldsmith-bankers were willing to lend, not the idle coins themselves, but rather claims on these coins which we shall call bank notes. In other words, the borrower was getting claims on coins as if he had deposited coins himself.

This was a most basic change in the evolution of money. Before this all money had consisted of full-bodied coin (since the development of the token coin, discussed above, came long after the development of the bank note) and the supply of money was, therefore, determined by the production of silver and gold. Now, for the first time, money was being created out of nothing. A debt was being monetized. The borrowing customer owed the banker money, that is, he promised to pay in the future. The banker, on the other hand, in giving bank notes to the customer actually promised to pay out full-bodied coin on demand. Customer and banker were thus mutually indebted. The result of this mutual indebtedness was the bank note, whose quality as money could not be doubted since it performed the function of a means of payment as long as it was generally accepted.

When the banker issued bank notes to those who did not first deposit full-bodied money, he added to the amount of money in circulation. He increased the purchasing power of those who received these bank notes on the basis of a loan, while the real depositors went on using their deposit certificates as money. Thus the total supply of money was increased and the total amount of bank notes or certificates was greater than their backing in terms of full-bodied coin.

Note that we gradually changed from the word "certificate" to the words "bank note." This is not inconsistent terminology but rather illustrates what actually took place. The original deposit of full-bodied coin led to the issue of certificates of deposit which were representative full-bodied money. The issue of additional claims to the same amount of specie deprived all the certificates in circulation of the character of representative full-bodied money and changed them into token paper money whose backing in gold and silver was less than 100 per cent. We must hasten to add that an amount of full-bodied coin far below 100 per cent sufficed as a rule to redeem those bank notes which were actually presented for conversion into full-bodied money.

Economic Effects of the Creation of Money

We could be tempted to assume that the consequences of this policy of credit expansion were decidedly inflationary, that more money was available to buy the same amount of goods, that commodity prices rose with this increased demand, and that the purchasing power of the previous owners of full-bodied coin or deposit certificates was sufficiently decreased to make room for those who got the additional money without having first deposited coin.

What actually happened in such a case depended on the development of production in consequence of the creation of additional money through credit expansion. If the factors of production were rather fully employed at the time the additional money was created, inflationary pressures had to develop. If, on the other hand, the additional money was injected into the economy at a time of substantial underemployment or if the economy expanded rapidly owing to a technological or similar advance, a rise in production counterbalanced the increase in expenditure. Prices then either did not increase or increased less than in the case of full employment or in the case of a stationary economy.

At the moment we shall not discuss the important problems of whether and when an artificial creation of money is beneficial or harmful. Here we are only concerned with the fact that such an artificial creation of money out of nothing is possible, and that its first appearance was indeed the most revolutionary step in the evolution of money.

It may seem strange that private persons (goldsmiths and bankers) could usurp the right to create money when we severely punish counterfeiters. But it was not so strange after all. The bankers did not break any existing law since the government had not monopolized the extension of credit. Furthermore, the development of the bank note was probably not understood as a creation of money. The bankers felt perfectly justified in making use of already existing idle money for the benefit of the business community as long as they maintained convertibility. Quickly expanding economies eagerly absorbed the money created in excess of the gold or silver supply, and the newly created money, therefore, became extremely useful.

Unregulated credit expansion by private institutions did cause much trouble. The history of banking is a story of overexpansion, illiquidity (inability to redeem convertible money), bank failures, and inflation. Very gradually the considerable drawbacks connected with this new type of money led to remedial action, the upshot of which was government control or government monopoly of bank-note issue. That the necessary controls came late and were often inefficient shows that governmental control of money often follows economic developments with a time lag of many years.

The Limitation of the Supply of Token Money

The basic problem connected with the control of token money was that of keeping the amount of token money sufficiently limited, as has already been shown in the case of token coin.

There are essentially two different ways by which this limitation can be accomplished:

1. The total supply of money can be so managed that the value of a unit of money will coincide with the value of a weight unit of the metal in terms of which the monetary unit is defined. The bank notes in this system are convertible in unlimited amounts into full-bodied coin (or at least into bullion) and cannot differ in value from the full-bodied coin as long as convertibility can be maintained. If I can always get a gold coin worth ten dollars for a ten-dollar bank note, the value of the bank note cannot fall below the value of the coin. To maintain this convertibility it is not necessary to have available a 100 per cent backing in the form of full-bodied coins or bullion. It is obvious that a system with convertible bank notes is still tied to the monetary metal, say gold, and that the total amount of money in circulation is still to some extent, but by no means exclusively, dependent on the metal supply.

2. Having understood that money can be token money and still maintain its value, we may well draw the logical conclusion that limitation of the quantity of token money can be achieved merely by the decision of an issuing authority to keep it limited. In this case we speak of inconvertible managed money or fiat money. Fiat money is no longer convertible into full-bodied coin or bullion. Monetary management ought to rest with an authority which can be trusted not to misuse its power, but this authority need not be a department of the government.

SUGGESTIONS FOR FURTHER READING

CASSEL, GUSTAV. *The Theory of Social Economy*, chaps. 9–10. New York: Harcourt, Brace & Co., 1932.

COULBORN, W. A. L. *A Discussion of Money*, chap. 5. London: Longmans, Green and Co., 1950.

ROBERTSON, D. H. *Money*, chap. 3. New York: Pitman Publishing Corporation, 1948.

WICKSELL, KNUT. *Lectures on Political Economy*. Vol. 2, *Money*, chap. 2. New York: Macmillan Co., 1935.

About cigarette money see:

RADFORD, R. A. "The Economic Organization of a P.O.W. Camp," *Economica*, New Series, Vol. XII (November, 1945).

On the role of gold as the basis of the monetary system:

CHANDLER, LESTER V. *An Introduction to Monetary Theory*, pp. 86–102. New York: Harper & Brothers, 1940.

For a modern account of bimetallism see:

FROMAN, LEWIS A. "Bimetallism—Reconsidered in the Light of Recent Developments," *American Economic Review*. Vol. XXVI (March, 1936).

QUESTIONS AND PROBLEMS

1. Name several commodities which have been used as money and explain how the economic environment determined their choice. Why were commodities never quite satisfactory as money?
2. Discuss the use of such commodities as cigarettes or coffee as money substitutes in some European countries after World War II.
3. Explain the special qualities of the precious metals which led to their monetary use. Is it true that full-bodied money, such as a coin, has always the same value?
4. The full-bodied coin is supposed to have the same value whether it is used as money or as metal. How is this identity of values maintained?

5. Explain Gresham's law according to which "bad money drives out good money."
6. Assume that in country A both silver and gold can be freely coined and melted, and that the legal mint ratio between silver and gold is 16 to 1; and that in country B the same situation exists, except that the legal mint ratio is set at 15 to 1. Which country would lose gold and why? What would happen to silver? Incidentally, can mint and market ratios differ within one and the same country?
7. The German philosopher Immanuel Kant considered it an indispensable quality of good money that it should have the same cost of production as the commodities which it can buy. Was he right?
8. "Sweden by the passing on the 8th February, 1916, of a special law . . . had freed her economy from its connection with gold, and the value of the Swedish krona was thus enabled to rise above the gold parity" (Gustav Cassel). Explain and discuss.
9. Irving Fisher suggested that if a pillar is not high enough to support the ceiling it is a matter of indifference how tall it is at all. Is it then true to say that if money need not be full bodied, it need not have any value at all as a commodity for use (other than exchange)?
10. Explain the principles governing the issue of token coins.
11. Explain the creation of the bank note and comment on the economic importance of the fact that money is being "created." Why is the public willing to accept mere tokens? Because of their backing?
12. Why can convertibility of bank notes into gold be assured even if the backing amounts to only 25 per cent?

Chapter 5 DEPOSIT MONEY

Currency and Deposit Money

When speaking of currency we may be referring to any one of the kinds of money mentioned so far (full-bodied coin, token coin, bank notes). Currency is recognized by everybody as money and is sometimes referred to as "common money" or "money proper."[1]

Currency, as a rule, is generally accepted without hesitation because its monetary value is independent of the personal circumstances of its owner. A bank note changes hands without difficulty where a check cannot be used. We may accept a check readily enough if we know the person tendering it, but we should hesitate to accept a check from a stranger. We cannot, for example, pay by check at the railroad station, for the ticket agent has no way of ascertaining quickly whether or not we have a deposit with the bank on which the check is drawn.

Only currency conforms fully with our definition of the means of payment as something which is generally accepted. Should we, therefore, limit the term "money" to currency and expressly exclude demand deposits in commercial banks against which checks are drawn?

If checks were always cashed, that is, converted into currency, there would be no point in considering demand deposits as money. In the end payments would always be accomplished by a transfer of currency. It would make little difference whether the buyer of merchandise first withdraws currency from the bank to make the purchase or whether he pays by check and the seller cashes the check. Often, however, the receiver of a check deposits it with his bank. If A makes a payment to B, if both have their accounts with the same bank, and if B deposits the check, the bank transfers the amount in question from

[1] Currency is sometimes identified with cash, but cash is also frequently used in a much broader sense and is then supposed to include demand deposits.

A's to B's account. Payment has been accomplished just as if currency had changed hands, yet currency was not used at all.

If A and B have their demand deposits in different banks, we could be tempted to argue that currency would still have to be moved from A's bank to B's bank. As a rule this is not necessary. We can assume that both banks have accounts in a central bank. Now B's bank sends the deposited check to the central bank. The central bank credits B's bank and charges the amount to the account of A's bank. Again, a transfer of currency has been avoided.

Since millions of check payments are made every day the chances are that a bank's customers will make approximately as many payments to customers of other banks as they will receive. Many check payments, therefore, simply cancel each other as to the total amounts involved, and only relatively small residual amounts must be transferred between the accounts which the commercial banks hold with the central bank. In other words, the central bank is able to clear most check payments.

Advantages of Check Payments

This modern way of making payments without the use of currency has its great advantages and has become predominant in advanced economies.

Many transactions are continually carried on among persons and firms who exhibit enough trust in each other to make check payments possible. We are well-enough known in our home community so that our check payments—to the grocer, the electric company, etc.—are accepted without hesitation. Between business firms also checks are almost exclusively used.

Thus a broad area exists where the necessary conditions for a system of check payments are established. In this area check payments offer considerable advantages, for they are often more convenient and safer than payments in currency. The very fact that currency is generally accepted means that a thief can use stolen currency with impunity. Check payments are safer because a check is an order to a bank to pay a specified amount to a specified person or firm and because the check must be endorsed before it can be cashed.

In studying the development of currency we saw that it was important that the individual pieces of money should represent round sums, that is, simple multiples or fractions of the unit of account. In case of check payments, where the check is only a transitory manifestation of a transfer from one demand deposit to another, it is a convenience that the check can be made out for any exact amount. Check payments, furthermore, help us to keep track of our monetary transactions. The stubs in our checkbooks record our outpayments, and since the canceled checks are returned to us, we have proof in hand that we made the payments.[2]

Even aside from the consideration of check payments, bank accounts are often superior to currency, for where money is to serve as a reserve of highest liquidity it can be held with greater safety and convenience in deposit.

The Creation of Demand Deposits

From the fact that we can accomplish payments without the use of currency we must draw the conclusion that demand deposits, subject to transfer by check, are part of the supply of money. We are justified, therefore, in calling demand deposits "deposit money" in contradistinction to currency or common money.[3]

If demand deposits are money, we must be able to answer the question how this most substantial part of the supply of money is regulated, particularly in view of the fact that deposit money is created by commercial banks and not by the monetary authority.

Demand deposits are credit entries in the check accounts of the customers of commercial banks; they are bank liabilities, acknowledgments of debt, which can serve as substitutes for currency when transferred from one account to another. Demand deposits are not stores of currency. If they were, if demand deposits were backed to 100 per cent by currency, the volume of demand deposits would be controlled by the authority which regulated the supply of currency. As a rule, however, they are not backed by currency but by reserve deposits in the central bank.

Demand deposits originate in two ways: (1) A commercial bank credits the check account of a customer upon the deposit by the latter of currency or checks; or (2) a commercial bank credits the check account of a customer as the result of a loan extended to the customer or a purchase of securities from him.

[2] The usefulness of checks as an accounting and auditing device is emphasized in the Russian payments system. In Russia payments between industrial units are made upon delivery through transfer from one account to the other in the state bank. Since payments may only be made for goods whose delivery was authorized by the plan, the check payments can be used to verify plan fulfillment. Debits and credits in the state bank mirror the movements of goods according to plan.

[3] Irving Fisher used to distinguish between checkbook money and pocketbook money. J. M. Keynes' term "bank money" has the disadvantage that it may be interpreted to include bank notes which belong to currency.

The owner of a demand deposit (check account) has the right to withdraw currency on demand and also to transfer on demand his claim against the bank to others. A commercial bank thus constantly receives currency and pays out currency; similarly, it is constantly credited or debited by the central bank in the clearing process whenever its customers receive check payments from, or make check payments to, customers of other banks.

It may seem as if a commercial bank would have to limit its lending and investment activities to the funds deposited by its customers, for the extension of credit leads to an outflow of currency and to negative clearing balances which must be matched by the deposit of currency and checks. Actually it is more correct to say that the deposits (of currency and checks) by bank customers are the result of the lending and investment activities of the banking system and that these activities are not limited to the funds deposited by the banks' customers.

Suppose that commercial bank A has extended a loan to a customer by crediting his check account with the amount of the loan. As the customer spends the borrowed funds to purchase commodities, his check is received by the seller and is then deposited in the seller's bank, say B. Now picture this example occurring in all commercial banks, assuming that they all extend credit in a similar fashion. If all the banks move in step, that is, if all extend credit simultaneously and to a proportionate degree, debit and credit entries in their accounts in the central bank will tend to offset each other. When a bank extends credit, its central bank reserve account decreases as the borrowing customer makes payments; when other banks extend credit, the first bank's reserve account with the central bank tends to increase as its customers deposit checks which they received from the borrowing customers of other banks. We see that credit creation is not limited by the previous deposit of checks or currency in a bank but rather that the deposit of checks is the result of a process of simultaneous credit expansion by all commercial banks.

The Importance of Reserves

The individual bank manager may not see the situation in this light. He is, indeed, only lending out funds which he, according to his experience, or according to legal reserve requirements, does not need for reserve purposes. On these reserve accounts, which the commercial banks hold in the central bank, hinges the problem of the limitation of deposit money.

Reserves of commercial banks consist to a small extent of currency. Since the daily deposits of currency tend to match the daily withdrawals, and since a bank can replenish its currency supply from the central bank, a special problem does not arise. There have been times in the past when it was difficult for commercial banks to secure more currency in an emergency, but where a central bank keeps the reserves of the commercial banks and where the central bank creates and supplies most of the currency (bank notes), difficulties need no longer arise.

The public's demand for currency, though subject to seasonal variations, is on the whole a rather stable proportion of the total demand for money.[4] And it is this total demand for, and supply of, money that counts. A modern monetary system should be so designed that, within a given total, it can furnish the people with exactly the kind of money they want. Thus if the people desire to use less currency they will deposit currency in the commercial banks and the commercial banks, in turn, will deposit any excessive amount with the central bank. The reverse process takes place when the commercial banks are called upon to pay out more currency; the central bank supplies more currency to the commercial banks and debits their reserve accounts.

Much more important than the small amount of currency which the banks keep on hand are the banks' reserve deposits with the central bank. While these deposits may be drawn upon to replenish a bank's currency supply, their main function is to serve as a buffer in case of unfavorable clearing balances. The ratio of these reserves to the commercial banks' demand deposits will depend on swings in the banks' clearing balances, which, in turn, will be determined by the payment habits and general economic circumstances of the banks' customers.

Once we assume that each bank has decided on a reserve ratio which it considers safe and that, accordingly, an average reserve ratio for all banks has been established, the total amount of deposit money that the banks can create has been determined. If the reserve ratio should be one tenth, the supply of deposit money could reach an amount ten times larger than the reserves of the commercial banks in the central bank.

Suppose that each bank will strive to maintain a chosen reserve ratio. If its reserves fall below this ratio it will consider the situation not entirely safe and reduce its loans or investments until an improvement in its clearing balance has brought the ratio back to normal. On the other hand, if our bank has been overly careful in its lending

[4] Nevertheless, fluctuations may be caused by such factors as lack of confidence, war dislocations of industries, or tax evasions of black-market dealers.

policy, credits will exceed debits in its reserve account, the reserve ratio will rise above normal, and the bank will be induced to expand credit. We must remember that whenever a bank expands its credit further and faster than other banks it must face an unfavorable clearing balance. Concern about their reserves, therefore, forces all banks to follow a roughly similar policy of expansion or contraction, the total supply of deposit money being limited by the amount of reserves and the average reserve ratio.

These considerations show that the reserve deposits which the commercial banks hold in the central bank are of strategic importance. If the central bank can manage the size of these reserves, it can, indirectly, influence the supply of deposit money in spite of the fact that deposit money originates with commercial banks.

The central bank can make it more or less attractive for the banks to hold reserves. A solvent commercial bank has earning assets (for example, government securities) with which it can replenish its reserves. It can sell these assets to the central bank or use them as collateral when borrowing from the central bank (or from other commercial banks). Here the central bank has an opportunity to influence the decisions of bank managers through its own loan and investment policies.

In addition the central bank may determine the reserve ratio to which the commercial banks have to adhere. Legal reserve requirements may supplant customary reserve ratios, and changes in legal reserve requirements may become a rather drastic weapon with which to influence the supply of deposit money.

Legal reserve requirements may seem to be a rather contradictory proposition. A reserve is something one can fall back on in times of need, yet a minimum reserve requirement actually says that the reserve may not be used. If, nevertheless, a central bank introduces such a system of minimum reserves, it is a clear sign (1) that these reserves are now considered a means of monetary control, and (2) that the central bank may be willing to make more reserves available when needed.

Thus we see that deposit money, though created by the commercial banks, is in its supply regulated to some extent by the central bank, which influences the size of the commercial banks' reserves and may even determine the legal reserve ratios. This regulation, however, is rather indirect and leaves, as we shall see, substantial leeway to the commercial banks. Furthermore, while the central bank may be successful in setting an upper limit to the supply of money, it may be much less successful in an attempt to bring about an expansion to this upper limit. The commercial banks may not be able to induce prospective customers to borrow.

The central bank may not be entirely free in its policy of influencing the reserves of the commercial banks and, thereby, the supply of deposit money. In some modern central banks the reserve deposits of the commercial banks are still subject to gold reserve requirements just as are the bank notes in circulation. These backing requirements were originally designed for the purpose of tying the total supply of money to the supply of the monetary metal but are an anachronism in times when the domestic supply of money rarely follows the international movements of gold.

SUGGESTIONS FOR FURTHER READING

For a fuller discussion of the creation of deposit money see Chapters 13 and 14 and:

BOARD OF GOVERNORS OF THE FEDERAL RESERVE SYSTEM. *The Federal Reserve System. Purposes and Functions,* chap. 2, 3d ed. Washington, D.C., 1954. Copies of this excellent book can be obtained free of charge by writing to the Board of Governors of the Federal Reserve System, Division of Administrative Services, Washington 25, D.C.

KEYNES, J. M. *A Treatise on Money,* Vol. 1, chap. 2. New York: Harcourt, Brace & Co., 1930.

PHILLIPS, CHESTER A. *Bank Credit,* chap. 3. New York: Macmillan Co., 1931.

On the nature of bank reserves:

BURGESS, W. RANDOLPH. *The Reserve Banks and the Money Market,* chap. 3. New York: Harper & Brothers, 1946.

QUESTIONS AND PROBLEMS

1. Explain why demand deposits in commercial banks are money. Would your argument also apply to savings deposits?
2. Would it be possible to conceive of a highly developed monetary system in which all payments are made by check so that, theoretically, no currency were needed?
3. Discuss the relative merits of payments by check and by currency.
4. Explain the nature of demand deposits. Are they stores of currency deposited in and held by banks? Do demand deposits derive their value from currency and is their volume determined by currency reserves?
5. "The aggregate deposits in the banking system as a whole represent mainly funds lent by banks or paid by banks for securities, mortgages and other forms of investment obligations. It may seem that it should

be the other way round—that bank loans and investments would be derived from bank deposits instead of bank deposits being derived from loans and investments . . ." (*The Federal Reserve System. Its Purposes and Functions,* Washington, D.C., 1939). Discuss.

6. If demand deposits are mainly derived from loans and investments of private banks, how is it possible to limit the supply of deposit money?
7. Discuss the crucial importance of the commercial banks' reserve deposits with the central bank.
8. "Legal reserve requirements may seem to be a rather contradictory proposition. A reserve is something one can fall back on in times of need, yet a minimum reserve requirement actually says that the reserve may not be used." Explain.
9. Many bankers have persistently denied that they have the power to create money, arguing that they only lend out money which was deposited with them and would otherwise remain idle.
10. "The strange impression that all creation of money by private institutions is a kind of legalized counterfeiting, of orderly theft and robbery, may be mitigated by the knowledge that the increase in the supply of money can be highly beneficial to the economy as a whole." Discuss.

Chapter 6 STATE CONTROL AND THE SUPPLY OF MONEY

Monetary Functions of the State

In our survey of the evolution of money references to monetary activities of the government or the central bank became increasingly frequent. While money certainly is not a mere "creature of law,"[1] it cannot be denied that the government performs important monetary functions.

The state, first of all, names the unit of account, for example, by calling it a dollar. Then a monetary standard can be defined by fixing the price of something, for example, gold, in terms of the unit of account.[2]

Secondly, the state declares that certain kinds of money are legal tender. Legal-tender money must be accepted by the creditor when used in the discharge of monetary obligations. When money is not certified as legal tender, we can call it "optional money." Optional money may enjoy general acceptability if it is full-bodied or convertible into legal-tender money. The legal-tender quality of some kinds of money is limited. The subsidiary coin, for example, may enjoy legal-tender quality only up to a specified amount to protect the public against the use of an inconvenient means of payment (like the discharge of a $1,000 debt in one-cent pieces).[3]

The state's willingness to accept money of its choice or even to force it upon others at face value assures a perfectly elastic demand for money. The price of the monetary unit is thus fixed in terms of

[1] This the state theory of money taught. See G. F. Knapp, *The State Theory of Money* (London: Macmillan & Co., Ltd., 1924).

[2] Art. IV–1 of the Bretton Woods Agreement (International Monetary Fund) of 1944 states that "the par value of the currency of each member shall be expressed in gold as a common denominator. . . ."

[3] Since 1933 all token coins in the United States enjoy unlimited legal-tender power.

itself. We saw, however, that we must distinguish between the price of the monetary unit (which is always one) and its value or purchasing power. The state as the regulator of the supply of money is supposed to follow a monetary policy which avoids extreme fluctuations in the value of money. Different monetary standards are fundamentally nothing but different methods of regulating the supply of money, and it is this regulation of the money supply which constitutes the third and most important function of the state.

Monetary Standards

A standard is a basis of comparison. Standard money is money whose unit serves as unit of account. It is the basis of the monetary system of the country, and all other kinds of money in the system must bear a certain relationship to standard money through convertibility and reserve requirements. Standard money is definitive money, that is, money in which even the monetary authority can discharge its obligations.

The choice of the standard money and of the methods by which other kinds of money are related to standard money establishes what is broadly and vaguely referred to when we speak of a monetary standard, such as the gold standard, silver standard, bimetallic standard, or inconvertible paper standard. Suppose that a country chooses the gold standard. The government declares that the monetary unit of the country is equal to a piece of gold of a given weight and fineness. The monetary unit is given a name (dollar, franc, krona, lira) and serves as the unit of account in all transactions. There may be gold coins in circulation whose denominations are multiples of the monetary unit (for example, ten- and twenty-dollar pieces) and everybody will be free to have gold coined in unlimited amounts and to melt coins. This arrangement guarantees the identity of the value of the coin as money and as metal. We call such a standard a "gold-coin standard." It would, however, be just as satisfactory to achieve this firm relationship between gold and money through the government's offer to buy and to sell gold in the form of bullion at a fixed price in unlimited amounts. Even though there would be no monetary circulation other than of token and deposit money, the standard unit would still be the gold dollar.

It is a mere terminological question whether gold bullion ought to be called standard money, considering that it would not circulate as means of payment. The fact that all kinds of money (demand deposits and currency) are convertible into bullion would still be important. This convertibility implies arrangements which permit the commercial banks and the government to keep their promises. The reserves must at least be large enough to permit the exchange of currency for deposit money and of gold for currency on demand. In detail these arrangements may be of an infinite variety.

All metallic standards want to make the regulation of the supply of money the object of forces beyond the control of the government (such as gold production or the balance of international payments). The friends of metallic standards do not trust governments; they renounce such new-fangled ideas as government deficit spending. To be consistent they must construct a system in which the money supply follows changes in the supply of the metallic base of the system quite automatically. Conscious management of the monetary superstructure is to be avoided.

If the government prevents purely automatic and passive responses of the supply of money to changes in the quantity of the standard metal to any extent, it is already leaning toward a managed standard. Since no system has as yet been found which could be fully automatic in its operation, the difference between metallic standards and inconvertible paper standards is not quite so important as it may seem. Even a gold-standard system today would be a highly managed affair. The growing tendency to manage the money supply independently of the supply of gold violates the original philosophy of the gold standard and explains why the relics of the gold standard which are still found in modern monetary systems are so incongruous. We will hear more of this later.

When the government decides to abolish convertibility of money into gold, it decides openly on some kind of management which frees monetary policy from limitations imposed by the gold supply. Even the monetary authority will now pay only token money in exchange for other kinds of money, that is, paper money becomes definitive or standard money. Inconvertible token money, however, may be so managed that its unit still coincides with the value of a given weight unit of gold.

Apart from this somewhat distant connection of the monetary unit with gold (which may periodically be revised through appreciation or depreciation) there are many possible criteria for monetary management. For instance the government may try to keep the purchasing power of money stable ("market-basket" standard), to raise the purchasing power (that is, to lower the price level) in order to export more, or to gradually lower the purchasing power of money in order to stimulate production or to lower the burden of debtors.

We see that the problem of monetary standards includes the aims and objectives of monetary policy as well as the instruments and institutional arrangements at the disposal of the monetary authority. Mere reference to a monetary standard, such as the gold standard or the inconvertible paper standard, answers none of the more interesting questions concerning monetary policy.

A Model of the Potential Volume of Money[4]

We can construct a simple model of the potential volume of money on the basis of the following assumptions:

1. The supply of the monetary metal, gold, is the result of gold production, gold consumption, gold imports, and gold exports. This supply is not arbitrarily managed and is thus to be taken as a given quantity by the monetary authority. Suppose that this gold supply equals $400 of which $200 circulate as full-bodied coin while $200 are kept as monetary reserves. We will disregard in our model small quantities of token coins.

2. The monetary authority, the central bank, issues bank notes. These bank notes are convertible into full-bodied coin. In order to ensure convertibility, the central bank has to hold a gold reserve of 25 per cent against bank notes in circulation. Suppose that $100 in gold are set aside for this purpose. The central bank can now issue up to $400 in bank notes.

3. In addition, the central bank has to hold a 25 per cent reserve in gold against the reserve deposits of the commercial banks in the central bank. If we set aside our remaining $100 of gold for this purpose, the central bank is authorized to hold up to $400 in reserve deposits of the commercial banks. We should note, however, that these $400 are not money in active circulation because they must be kept as a reserve against the demand deposits of the customers of the commercial banks.

4. Commercial bank reserves, whether they are legally required or merely customarily considered as adequate, we assume to be 20 per cent. On the basis of reserve deposits of $400 then the total amount of demand deposits in the commercial banks (deposit money) could be

[4] I am indebted to Professor Fritz Machlup for his suggestions in connection with this model.

as much as $2,000, that is, five times the sum of the commercial banks' reserve deposits in the central bank. See Figure 6–1.

The total amount of money that could be supplied according to our model is $2,600, namely, $200 in full-bodied coin, plus $400 in bank notes, plus $2,000 in deposit money.

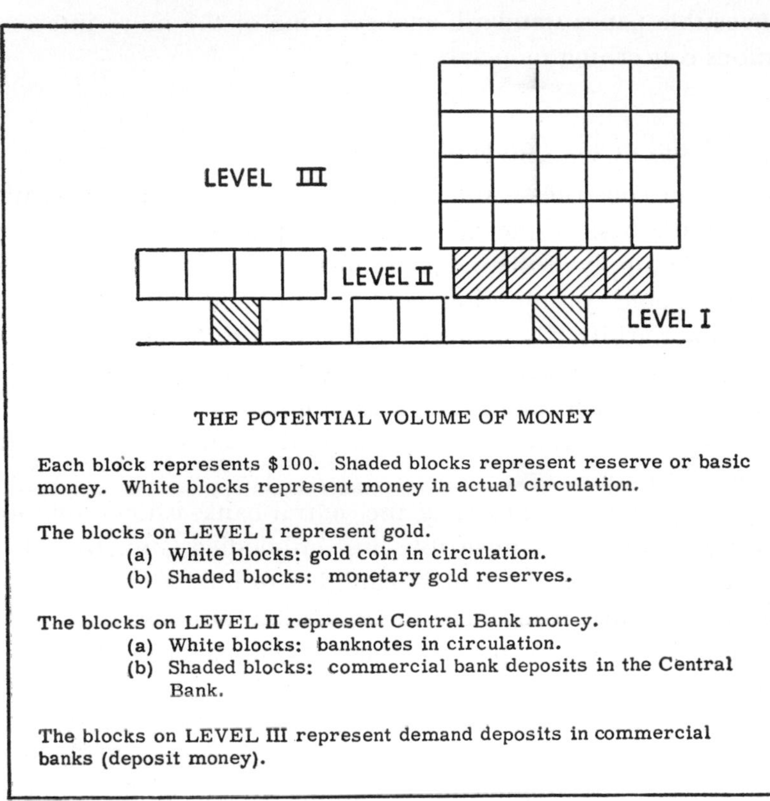

THE POTENTIAL VOLUME OF MONEY

Each block represents $100. Shaded blocks represent reserve or basic money. White blocks represent money in actual circulation.

The blocks on LEVEL I represent gold.
- (a) White blocks: gold coin in circulation.
- (b) Shaded blocks: monetary gold reserves.

The blocks on LEVEL II represent Central Bank money.
- (a) White blocks: banknotes in circulation.
- (b) Shaded blocks: commercial bank deposits in the Central Bank.

The blocks on LEVEL III represent demand deposits in commercial banks (deposit money).

Fig. 6–1

It must be understood, however, that the assumed reserves and reserve ratios do not determine this total volume in any causative sense. Much will depend on the demand for money, and this demand in turn depends on several factors which are not under the control of the monetary authority. The central bank can limit the total volume of money to $2,600, more or less, depending on the use of gold for reserve purposes, but it cannot guarantee that this amount will be reached.

The distribution of the gold for reserve purposes was quite arbitrary. Which part of the gold will be used as reserve against bank notes in circulation and which part as a reserve against central bank deposits will have to depend on the public's choice. We note that one dollar of gold reserve is the base of either $4 in bank notes or $20 in deposit money.

Active Money and Reserve Money

We have to distinguish between active money and reserve money. Reserve money can also be called "basic money." Basic money consists of gold held as reserve against bank notes and against deposits in the central bank. But these deposits are themselves basic money for they are the reserves against the demand deposits of the commercial banks' customers. The gold coins in circulation, the bank notes in circulation (plus the token coins), and the demand deposits, which are subject to transfer by check, are all active money. Clearly, we could not count reserve money in the volume of active money.

Money circulates only until it is presented for redemption. As soon as we insist on payment of gold coin for our bank notes, reserve money becomes active money while the bank notes in question cease to circulate. Similarly, as soon as demand deposits are withdrawn in the form of currency, reserve money is changed into active money. The total supply of money, however, is not increased when reserve money becomes active. On the contrary, we see that insistence on the withdrawal of deposits or on conversion of bank notes may lead to a contraction of the money supply because on each unit of reserve money a larger amount of active money was based. Only if we had 100 per cent reserves could reserve money fully replace bank notes redeemed or deposits withdrawn.

A system of fractional reserves may thus seem to be dangerous. If reserves are less than 100 per cent, how can we prevent the conversion of bank notes into gold or of deposit money into currency from leading to perilous contractions in the supply of money with the consequences of deflation and unemployment?

These are indeed crucial questions. For the present it will suffice to enumerate several reasons why a system of only fractional reserves will work when adequately managed.

1. We saw that in normal times the conversion of one kind of money into another is limited to a predictable amount which depends in the main on the payment habits of the community.

2. The reserves of basic money are as a rule large enough to take care of some deviation from the normal behavior. These deviations themselves may be predictable (such as seasonal variations) or they

may be only regional so that they are offset by opposite tendencies in other areas.

3. The reserve system may be elastic so that the volume of reserves can be increased or that the reserve ratios can be reduced.

These matters will be discussed in detail later on.

Our model illustrating the potential volume of money was so chosen as to include gold reserves because these gold reserve requirements indicate a still existing connection with the earliest form of money: commodity money.

A monetary system in which one kind of money serves as the fractional reserve for another kind which, in turn, serves as the fractional reserve for a third kind can be likened to an inverted pyramid. Following Irving Fisher's expressive terminology, we call the basis of this pyramid, the monetary metal (gold), "supercharged money" to indicate that its broadening may lead to a much greater expansion of the total volume of money. For the same reason we can call the reserve deposits of the commercial banks in the central bank "high-powered money." Both "supercharged" and "high-powered" money are, of course, basic or reserve money.

When circulation of full-bodied coin is abolished, the monetary metal can be used in its entirety as reserve money. When we abolish

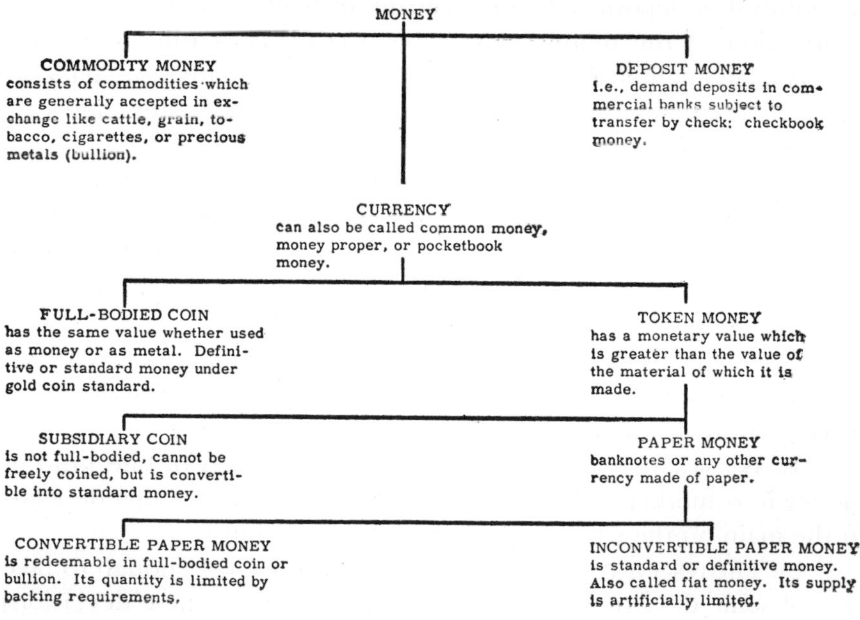

Fig. 6–2

gold reserve requirements altogether, bank notes are no longer convertible into gold and become fiat money whose amount is arbitrarily managed by the monetary authority. In a similar manner the abolition of gold reserve requirements against commercial bank reserve deposits will give the central bank greater freedom in the regulation of the supply of deposit money.

Classification of the Kinds of Money

Figure 6–2 shows the most important categories of money which have been discussed in Part II. The relationships are obvious. No attempt has been made to indicate the distinctions between legal-tender and voluntary money or between active and reserve money. The difference between active money and reserve money is clearly visible in Figure 6–1. The legal-tender power of money is not considered in Figure 6–2 because it rests on more or less arbitrary decisions of the government. It may be interesting, though, to check briefly the possible legal-tender character of the tabulated kinds of money. Commodity money can have legal-tender character when the government declares it to be legal tender, as some colonial governments in America did with regard to wheat, tobacco, rice, and corn. Deposit money, on the other hand, cannot be legal tender. It rests, as we have seen, on personal circumstances of the depositors for which the government cannot assume responsibility. In case of full-bodied coin as standard money the legal-tender character is implicit. But full-bodied coin has been known to circulate on an optional basis as, for example, the Maria Theresa dollar in the Middle East. As far as token coin is concerned, we have already seen that its legal-tender power may be limited to specified amounts. Paper money, finally, may be optional money like the Federal Reserve note before 1933 or legal-tender money like the Federal Reserve note since 1933.

SUGGESTIONS FOR FURTHER READING

For a comprehensive account of the creation of money see:

HANSEN, ALVIN H. *Monetary Theory and Fiscal Policy,* chap. 2. New York: McGraw-Hill Book Co., Inc., 1949.

Concerning the volume of money in the United States:

SHAW, EDWARD S. *Money, Income, and Monetary Policy,* chap. 1, pp. 9–15. Homewood, Ill.: Richard D. Irwin, Inc., 1950. Reprinted in Lawrence S. Ritter's *Money and Economic Activity,* pp. 42–45 (Boston: Houghton Mifflin Co., 1952).

THOMAS, WOODLIEF. "Money System of United States," in *Banking Studies*, pp. 293–319. Washington, D.C.: Board of Governors of the Federal Reserve System, 1941.

Classifications of different kinds of money can be found in:

KEYNES, J. M. *A Treatise on Money*, Vol. 1, chap. 1. New York: Harcourt, Brace & Co., 1930.

ROBERTSON, D. H. *Money*, chap. 3. New York: Pitman Publishing Corp., 1948.

QUESTIONS AND PROBLEMS

1. How should we define "monetary standard"? Distinguish several monetary standards.
2. Discuss the proposition of the so-called "state theory of money" that "money is a creature of law."
3. Is it true to say that the state can determine the value of money by mere fiat.
4. "It is the primary, most indispensable and fundamental doctrine that first and foremost money frees us from debt toward the state" (G. F. Knapp). Do you agree?
5. Assume that the central bank of a given country must hold a gold reserve of 25 per cent against reserve deposits of commercial banks and a reserve of 33⅓ per cent against its bank notes in circulation. The commercial banks, in turn, are required to hold reserve deposits with the central bank equal to 20 per cent of their customers' demand deposits. Assume, further, that the demand for credit is sufficient to cause the fullest monetary expansion which is technically possible. What would the total monetary expansion (currency plus demand deposits) be if $3 million of newly mined or imported gold were available for monetary purposes and if the central bank decided to use $2 million as backing of bank notes in circulation and $1 million as backing for reserve deposits of commercial banks. Use a diagram to illustrate the potential volume of new money.
6. Define the following terms: standard money, legal tender money, active money, basic money, supercharged money, high-powered money.
7. How and under which conditions do the terms used in question 6 apply to Federal Reserve notes in circulation, demand deposits, Treasury currency, member bank reserve accounts, and gold?

PART III

The Value of Money

Chapter 7 MONETARY EQUATIONS

The Quantity Theory

The value of money depends on the amount of different goods and services which can be purchased with a unit of money and, therefore, on the prices of these goods and services.

Among the factors which determine prices, attention was historically first focussed on the quantity of money supplied. This view excluded any other factor which might possibly have some influence on the value of money. Thus it was assumed that if we double the supply of money we automatically double prices; prices, in other words, would vary in direct proportion to the amount of money in existence.

This statement was of course much too one-sided. It is true that the total effective demand on all markets of the economy is one decisive factor in determining the value of the monetary unit. With more money to spend buyers compete with each other and tend to bid up the prices of supplied goods to the point where the total supply can just be disposed of. Collective demand in terms of money (aggregate expenditure over a period of time) acting on a given supply of commodities and services determines prices and, in inverse ratio, the value of money.

But the naïve quantity theory did not consider the important fact that an increased supply of money need not raise commodity prices if simultaneously the velocity of circulation of money decreases. Suppose that the monetary authority increases the supply of money through the purchase of securities with newly created money. The public might not want to hold larger money reserves than before and, accordingly, might spend the additional money on consumers' goods or investment goods. If other things remain equal, prices will tend to rise. However, had the monetary authority increased the supply of money in response to a greater desire of the public to hold money reserves, the additional money would be absorbed by larger money reserves without an increase in expenditure and in prices. When not met by an adequate supply of additional money, the desire to hold larger cash balances leads to decreased expenditures and a lowering of commodity prices.

Another shortcoming of the naïve quantity theory was that it often ignored the supply of goods and services to be exchanged during a given period of time, the so-called trade or transaction volume. Prices, whose aggregate level expresses the purchasing power of money, are the result of the many price-making processes in all markets of the economy. It is by influencing these price-making processes that changes in the supply of, and the demand for, money influence the value of money and, simultaneously, the pattern of relative prices. A direct and immediate relation between the supply of money and the average price level does not exist. Changes in price levels are only statistical abstracts. Decisive are the numerous and interdependent price variations which changes in the supply of, and the demand for, money call forth.

Although there is no other expression for the value of money, we should not overestimate the importance of price averages. General price averages should not be allowed to dominate the analysis of monetary problems so as to give the impression that the price structure responds *as a unit* to monetary changes. It is individual prices and their variations which are the basic data of price analysis, and the consequences of monetary changes must be worked out in terms of these variations.

Monetary Equations: Transaction Type

The effects of money expenditures upon prices have been expressed in a number of equations which, while basically similar, differ in several respects.

The equation best known in the United States is Irving Fisher's transaction equation:

$$PT = MV, \text{ or } P = MV/T.$$

This formula is only a simple way of expressing the truism that the average level of prices (P) depends on the total money supply (M) and its velocity of circulation (V), in relation to the total volume of sales transactions (T). An increase in the supply of money or an increase in its velocity of circulation would work in the same direction, that is, tend to raise prices. An increase in the supply of money could be counteracted in its effect upon prices by a decrease in the velocity of circulation, that is, a desire to hold larger money reserves. An increase in the trade volume (the supply of money and its velocity of circulation remaining unchanged) would lead to decreased prices, and a stabilization of prices under these conditions would, therefore, require an increased supply or an increased velocity of circulation of money.

Two examples may illustrate these abstract statements.

The stabilization of the German mark after the hyperinflation of 1923 shows how an increase in M can be substituted for a decreased V while P remains stable. Although both M and V were increasing during the inflation period, the main cause for the fantastic rise in prices by 1923 (which finally lowered the purchasing power of the mark to one trillionth of its former value) was an enormous increase in the velocity of circulation of money. Everybody was spending the mark as fast as was technically possible, for its purchasing power declined hourly. In order to achieve stabilization the government had to reduce the velocity of circulation of money. For this purpose a new type of money, the so-called "rentenmark," was issued. It was backed by mortgage bonds behind which, so the Germans were told, stood the German soil. Impressed by this backing the people were willing to give the new money a try, that is, to hold it in hopes that prices would remain stable. And P did remain stable because of this reduction of V. Decisive for the success of the measure, however, was that once the velocity had returned to normal it became necessary to create large amounts of additional money in order to accomplish the turnover of commodities at the enormously inflated price level. With this new money private business as well as the government could be tided over until normal sources of revenue reappeared. Thus we see how an increased M took the place of a decreased V in the German stabilization of 1923.

For another illustration of the Fisher equation we can turn to the prosperity of the twenties in the United States. In spite of a rather substantial increase in the supply of money and some increase in the velocity of circulation, commodity prices, on the whole, tended downward. The explanation is to be found in the greatly expanded trade volume. The efficiency of the American economy had grown so much that had it not been for increased expenditure based on monetary expansion, prices would have fallen much more as a result of reduced unit costs of production.

The Trade Volume

The T in the Fisher equation stands for the trade or transaction volume. This includes everything that is being sold, as often as it is sold during the period (consumers' goods, new and secondhand, capital goods of all kinds, labor, securities, government transactions, etc.). Here we must realize that every good which is part of the national product gives rise to numerous monetary transactions between firms in the succeeding stages of its production. The production of bread, for example, requires previous monetary transactions on the part of the flour mill, the grain dealer, the farmer, and the producer of farm implements.

The definition of T encounters considerable difficulties. We could perhaps avoid these difficulties by calling T "goods sold." "Goods sold" indicates ex post what has happened after market forces have done their work, but it says little about what may be expected to happen ex ante to production, supply, and the amounts of "goods to be sold" in the future. "Goods to be sold" may be a larger or a smaller amount than "goods sold," and it is important for monetary policy to estimate the amount of T under the influence of prospective changes of M or V.

It goes without saying that a definition of T as "goods in existence" would be wrong, for an overwhelming part of these goods does not enter into monetary exchanges during the period. And "goods produced" is, as Arthur W. Marget has pointed out, at once too inclusive and not inclusive enough. The term is too inclusive because it counts products which have not been produced for the market, and it is not inclusive enough because the goods sold may consist partly of goods produced in preceding periods.

Our conception of T as seen ex ante and implying, therefore, the possibility of increased or decreased production and supply of goods (T, in other words, not only as the whole of the supply curves in the different markets of the economy but also implying possible shifts of these supply curves) may best be expressed as the physical volume of "goods intended for sale" (Marget) under varying circumstances as compared with T ex post, which stands for the physical volume of goods actually sold.

Monetary Equations: Income Type

Instead of using the transaction volume and of studying the total of all monetary transactions during a period, we can limit ourselves to what may be called the "income circulation of money." We have already used this approach in Chapter 2 where we watched, in simple models, the flow of money from business firms to family households and back to business firms. We saw money continually making a complete circuit, and using a given time period, we could understand that the frequency of this circular flow can be measured by the number of times money passes a given point in the circuit (for instance by finding out how often it is received as income during the period). Providing that we can measure such aggregates as the national income, we can determine the circular velocity of money or income velocity of money by comparing the national income with the supply of money.

We can change Fisher's transaction equation into an income equation which reads:

$$P_y = MV_y/T_y, \quad \text{or} \quad MV_y = T_yP_y, \quad \text{or} \quad MV_y = Y.$$

In this new equation only M remains the same as before, namely, the total supply of currency and deposit money. T_y is the physical national product and stands for all the things which constitute the national income in real terms. P_y is the price average of all these goods and services. T_yP_y, therefore, is identical with Y, the national income. If we define V_y, the circular or income velocity of money, as Y/M, we can see that the circular velocity must be much slower than the transaction velocity (PT/M) since PT is much larger than Y, while M remains the same in both equations.

The National Income

National income figures are products of quantities of real goods and services and their prices. If a comparison of national income figures of different years indicates a substantial change, the result will often be due to price changes, that is, to changes in the value of money. We see, therefore, that it is important to have information about price changes of the goods and services which compose the national income. When we adjust national income figures inversely to these general price changes, we gain a knowledge of quantitative changes in the national income which a direct quantitative approach (in pounds, fluid ounces, miles, etc.) could not supply.

When the statistician tries to measure such aggregates as the national income or the national product, he cannot proceed by adding up locomotives and cosmetics, houses built and concerts performed. He must make use of money as a common denominator. But this does not mean that he will include only items of services and things actually sold for money. He will include, for instance, goods and services produced by the government (highways built, police services rendered), the rental value of homes occupied by their owners, and goods consumed by their producers in spite of the fact that a sale for money has not taken place in these cases. Yet, rather arbitrarily, he will leave out the monetary value of the services performed by housewives. The statistician will not consider certain other items even though they have been objects of monetary transactions. For example, the purchase and sale of goods produced in an earlier period will not be included because in trying to measure the national product we are interested in the productive activities of a given period only.

In measuring the national product we must avoid counting a product at its full value each time it moves through a new stage of production. This procedure was appropriate when we were interested in the trade volume or transaction volume. Now, however, we may only count the value *added* in each stage of production. Since this method would prove rather difficult in practice, one can achieve the same result by counting only *final* purchases of consumption and capital goods (by persons, firms, government agencies, and foreigners) and by not counting anything that was used up in the production process. Here lies the main difference between Fisher's *TP* and the aggregates used in modern income analysis.

So far we have referred only to national income or national product. These terms, however, stood for a whole group of concepts whose distinction will reveal several other interesting statistical problems.

Let us begin with the broadest of these concepts, the *gross national product*. This concept may be defined as the market value of a year's output of the nation's economy before any deduction for depreciation is made. It is larger, therefore, than the amount which normally can be consumed or considered as net addition to the inventories or the capital stock of the nation. The concept gross national product is important for the following reasons: (1) It shows what the nation can produce in the short run. In case of all-out war, for instance, it would show how much armament production could be stepped up while we temporarily ignored depreciation. (2) It is the broadest of all national product concepts and is equal to total expenditure, at market prices, of all spending agencies for currently produced output. In other words, being the most inclusive concept, it has not been adjusted by those deductions which we shall now use to come to less inclusive national income concepts.

When we deduct depreciation from the gross national product, we get the *net national product*. From the net national product we deduct indirect business taxes to get the *national income*. The net national product is now counted at factor prices rather than at market prices because this enables us to look at the national income as indicated in our models in Chapter 2. There we could watch the circular flow of money as a flow of income payments to the owners of productive services (including the owners of firms) and as a flow of expenditure of identical size in payment for goods consumed. This identity requires that we include in cost of production not only wages, salaries, interest payments, and rents but also business profits, whether paid out as dividends, retained as undisturbed corporate earnings, or paid as corporate taxes to the government.

The national income is not identical with *personal income*. From national income we deduct first those parts of business profits which (as undistributed earnings or corporate taxes) did not find their way into personal income. In addition we must deduct social insurance contributions. On the other hand, we must add payments by the government. These are interest payments on debts and so-called transfer payments, such as old age and unemployment insurance benefits.

Finally we come to the last and smallest of the national income concepts: *disposable income*. It is equal to personal income minus personal income taxes and other direct taxes levied on persons. Disposable personal income is either spent on consumption goods or saved.

In Figure 7–1 these national income concepts are arranged as a money-flow diagram.

Monetary Equations: Cash-Balance Type

We can express the transaction velocity of money V as PT/M and the circular velocity or income velocity V_y as P_yT_y/M. This shows that the velocity of circulation of money must depend on the amount of money which persons, firms, and agencies want to hold as money reserves. Since the desire to hold money reserves can be considered a demand for money and since M is the supply of money, it is possible to approach the problem of the value of money as a problem of the supply of, and the demand for, money. The demand for money is the aggregate of cash balances which the community wants to hold. This amount can be expressed as a fraction of the annual monetary transactions (PT) or of the national income (Y). A person, for instance, may desire to hold an average reserve equal to one fourth of his annual income. If everyone should decide to hold about the same proportion, the total amount of money reserves would be one fourth of Y, and M circulating four times a year would be able to buy the goods and services constituting the national income.

Exactly the same idea can be expressed by using k instead of V or k_y instead of V_y. In the example used above, k_y is the proportion of Y which the community desires to hold in the form of money reserves. Since k_y is one fourth, it is an amount equal to 3 months' income. Money must circulate four times annually so that the national income can be received and spent at prevailing prices. This shows that k_y is $1/V_y$ and that V_y is $1/k_y$. We have written the income type of the Fisher equation as $P_y = MV_y/T_y$. Since $V_y = 1/k_y$, this can also be expressed as $P_y = M/T_y k_y$. By transposing we get $P_y T_y k_y = M$, and since $P_y T_y$ is the national income or Y, we can write the income type of the cash-balance equation as $k_y Y = M$. Similarly the transaction equation which we have stated as $P = MV/T$ can be expressed as $P = M/Tk$.

The cash-balance-type equations are often referred to as the Marshallian or Cambridge equations since they have been used by Alfred Marshall and other economists in Cambridge, England.

The Fisher and the Marshall equations are actually identical: k is the reciprocal of V and V is the reciprocal of k. Marshall, however, wanted to emphasize the importance of changes in the community's desire to hold money reserves. These changes are important. Suppose that the desire to hold money reserves increases and that this desire is not instantly satisfied by an increase in the money supply. Expenditures will fall off as people and firms hold larger reserves, and through a lower level of prices and output the desired larger ratio between money reserves and national income will be brought about. A similar process is seen when an increased money supply unaccompanied by an increased desire to hold money leads to a rising price level and thus permits the maintenance of the former ratio of M and Y.

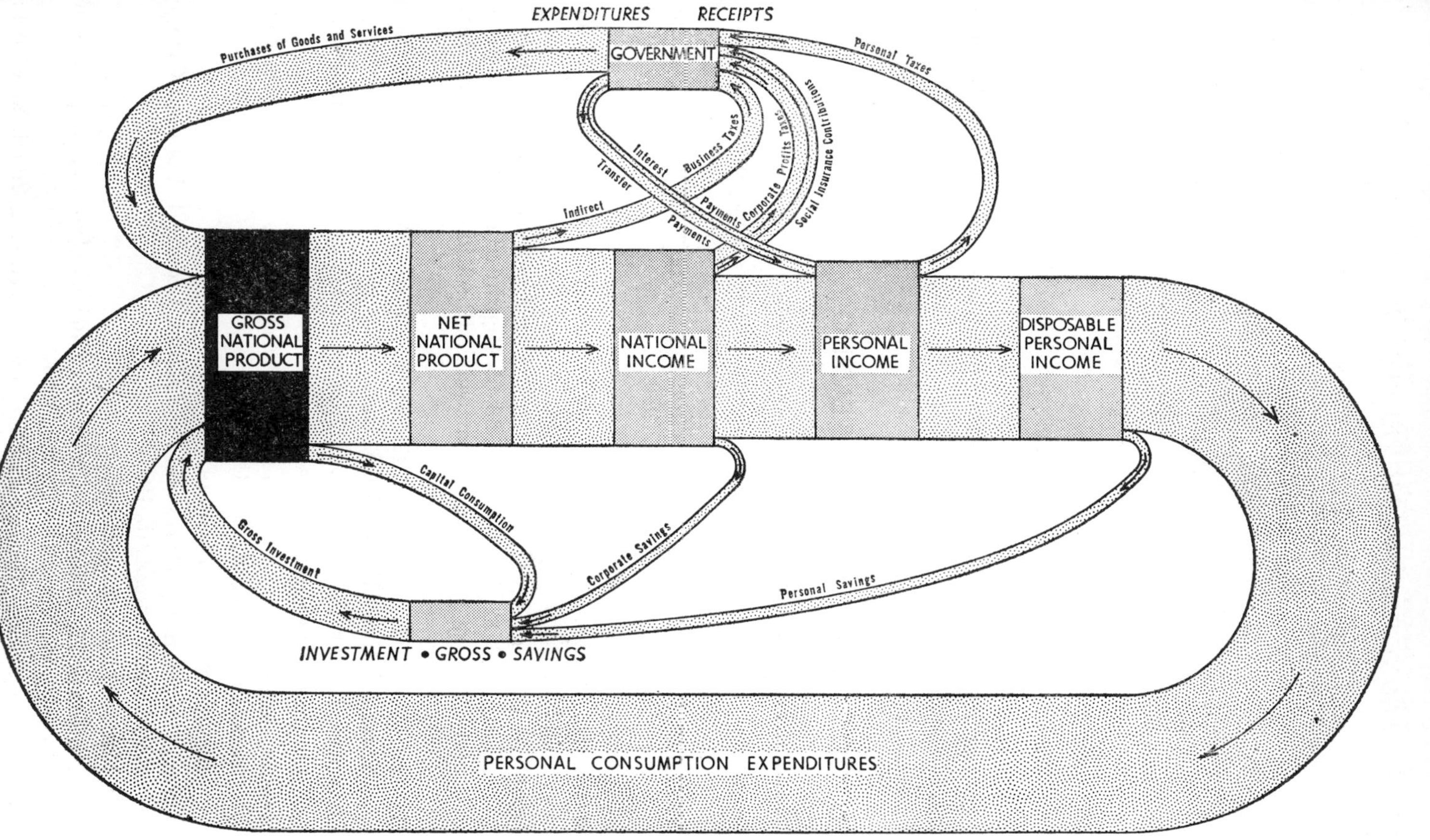

Fig. 7–1

Source: J. Frederic Dewhurst and Associates, *America's Needs and Resources: A New Survey* (New York: The Twentieth Century Fund, 1956).

In conclusion we can arrange the four main equations as follows:

	Transaction Approach	Income Approach	$T_yP_y = Y$
Fisher or V-type approach:	$P = MV/T$	$P_y = MV_y/T_y$	$V_y = Y/M$
Marshall or k-type approach:	$P = M/Tk$	$P_y = M/T_yk_y$	$k_y = M/Y$

We see that the V- and k-type equations can be used for both the transaction and the income approach. The Fisher equation, however, is commonly written in its transaction form, while the Marshall equation is usually seen in its income form.

SUGGESTIONS FOR FURTHER READING

The Fisher equation:

FISHER, IRVING. *The Purchasing Power of Money.* New York: Macmillan Co., 1926.

CHANDLER, LESTER V. *An Introduction to Monetary Theory,* chaps. 2–3. New York: Harper & Brothers, 1940.

The Marshall equation:

MARSHALL, ALFRED. *Money, Credit and Commerce,* Book I, chap. 4. London: Macmillan & Co., Ltd., 1924.

PIGOU, A. C. "The Value of Money," *The Quarterly Journal of Economics,* Vol. 32 (1917–18), pp. 38–65. Reprinted in *Readings in Monetary Theory,* chap. 10 (Homewood, Ill.: Richard D. Irwin, Inc., 1951).

HANSEN, ALVIN H. *Monetary Theory and Fiscal Policy,* chap. 3. New York: McGraw-Hill Book Co., Inc., 1949.

CHANDLER, LESTER V. *An Introduction to Monetary Theory,* chap. 4.

On the trade volume T:

MARGET, ARTHUR W. *The Theory of Prices,* Vol. I, chaps. 17–18. New York: Prentice-Hall, Inc., 1938.

Against overemphasis on price averages:

HAYEK, FRIEDRICH A. *Prices and Production,* Lecture 1. London: George Routledge & Sons, Ltd., 1931.

National income concepts:

HANSEN, ALVIN H. *Business Cycles and National Income,* chap. 6. New York: W. W. Norton & Co., Inc., 1951.

MORGAN, THEODORE. *Income and Employment,* chap. 2, 2d ed. New York: Prentice-Hall, Inc., 1952.

QUESTIONS AND PROBLEMS

1. "It might be supposed, that all goods for sale in a country at any one time, are exchanged for all the money existing and in circulation at that time: or, in other words, that there is always in circulation in a country, a quantity of money equal in value to the whole of the goods then and there on sale. But this would be a complete misapprehension" (John Stuart Mill). Explain.
2. "There is little more resemblance between the modern 'quantity theory' and the 'quantity theory' of the late Middle Ages than there is between the houses of the two periods" (Lester V. Chandler). Explain.
3. Illustrate the so-called "transaction equation" of Irving Fisher by references to the following:
   a) Hyperinflation and stabilization in Germany in 1923.
   b) Prosperity and price stability in the United States 1922 to 1928.
   c) Post–World War II currency stabilization, e.g., in Belgium or West Germany.
   d) Cost-push inflation or administrative price inflation, in which prices rise without increasing expenditure (MV).
4. Should T in the transaction equation be defined as "goods in existence," "goods produced," "goods sold" or "goods to be sold"? Should, for instance, securities, new and old, be included and counted as often as they are sold (or are intended to be sold)?
5. If many complementary means of production have remained unemployed, could this fact influence your estimate of T ex ante and your willingness to have MV increased?
6. Explain the changed meaning of V, T, and P as you use an income-type equation rather than a transaction equation.
7. Why is the income or circular velocity of money much smaller than the transaction velocity?
8. Draw a diagram which pictures the flow of income and expenditure in the United States and explain the terms "gross national product," "net national product," "national income," "personal income," and "disposable income."
9. "The cash-balance equation tries to apply a demand-and-supply analysis to money and starts, accordingly, from the sums of individual demands for money to hold." Discuss.
10. Show that both the Fisher and the Marshall approach can be used for transaction as well as for income equations.

Chapter 8 MONEY AND INDEX NUMBERS

How to Express the Value of Money

Money, as a unit of account, enables us to express the exchange value of commodities and services by their prices. Instead of enumerating the quantities of many other articles for which a pair of shoes can be bartered, we say simply that the pair costs, say, ten dollars. This clear-cut expression serves as an indicator of the exchange value of the commodity.

The system of expressing exchange values in terms of prices, that is, in units of money, puts money itself into a peculiar position. The "price" of the unit of money is always one and is thus nominally constant according to the truism that a dollar is a dollar. How then are we to find the exchange value of money? Obviously, the purchasing power of money does not stay the same during times of price inflation and price deflation. Money will exchange for fewer goods when prices rise in general and for more goods when prices fall. Thus, while the price of the unit of money is fixed, its power to command goods and services in exchange may well fluctuate.

The value of money, therefore, cannot be expressed with the same ease with which we quote commodity prices. In case of money we are driven back to the clumsy method of comparison which we abandoned in the case of commodities when we changed from barter to a monetary system: we have to find out which quantities of various commodities and services the unit of money will buy. For each single commodity this is very easy since commodity prices are already expressed in units of money. The trouble is that there are so many different commodities; there are too many to undertake even a mere listing of all the things which are bought with money.

Thus we see that the value of commodities can be expressed in terms of money, but that the value of money depends upon the prices of a nearly infinite variety of things on which money can be spent.

Nevertheless, it would still be easy to express the value or purchasing power of money if all prices always changed in the same direction and in the same proportion. But this they hardly ever do. As a matter of fact, the whole structure of our unplanned economy rests, as we have seen in Chapter 3, on relative price movements. As the demand for commodity A increases and that for commodity B falls, there will be price and production adjustments up and down. There will be shifts in the demand for the factors of production, and all these changes will be accompanied by further alterations in the pattern of prices.

Clearly, it would not be permissible to take only one commodity, watch its price, and say that the purchasing power of money is doubled when this one price falls to half its former level, for most likely some other prices are increasing at the same time. It is possible that price increases and price decreases may cancel out, but whether or not they do will be known for sure only when we consider all prices or at least a group so large and so well chosen that we can feel reasonably certain that the law of averages had a chance to work.[1]

Price Averages and Monetary Policy

Should we consider as many prices as possible in our attempt to find an expression for the purchasing power of money? Should we try to consider everything that is bought and sold? It seems logical that since money can buy everything that is for sale, the prices of all salable things should be considered and not just the prices of limited categories of commodities such as consumers' goods or internationally traded goods.

Many economists, however, argue that we are mainly interested in consumers' goods prices. J. M. Keynes, for instance, was of the opinion that there need not be any doubt as to what we mean by the purchasing power of money. We mean, he said, "the power of money to buy the goods and services on the purchase of which for purposes of consumption a given community of individuals expend their money income."[2]

[1] Only during extreme price inflation will it become practical to guess at changes in the purchasing power of money by watching the price of only one commodity. In 1923 in Germany, for instance, barbers used to charge for their services in terms of coffee rolls. Rolls were not used as means of payment, but the customer was supposed to know how the bread price had risen since yesterday and to pay a corresponding sum of millions or billions. Relative price changes were drowned in the fantastic increase in all prices.

[2] J. M. Keynes, *A Treatise on Money* (New York: Harcourt, Brace & Co., Inc., 1930), Vol. I, p. 54.

Keynes offered no explanation, but an explanation can perhaps be found in the argument that all our productive efforts aim at the production of consumers' goods, that most of our personal income is spent on consumption, and that we are all consumers although, as receivers of income, we can be divided into such groups as wage earners, farmers, *rentiers,* etc.

It is true that we think first of consumers' goods when the purchasing power of money is mentioned. But it is equally true that consumers' goods prices alone will not even satisfy the layman's need for information when he worries about inflation. What a price inflation or deflation means to us depends as much on the prices of what we have to sell as on the retail prices of the consumers' goods which we buy.

Let us look at our problem from the standpoint of monetary management and the political forces behind monetary management. If we decide to establish a so-called market-basket dollar, we declare our intention to stabilize consumers' goods prices, and a representative assortment of consumers' goods on the retail market will serve our purpose. This declaration of intention, however, may mean little. Consumers do not have much political influence. Monetary policy is more likely to be exposed to pressure from politically more articulate groups which are interested in special prices. Many union members are more interested in wage rates than in retail prices; security holders may, above all, insist on pegged security prices; farmers, on a parity of farm prices with industrial prices—and so with each group, with the exception of those who know that they have little chance to change the distribution of the national income in their favor and for whom the development of consumers' goods prices is of particular concern.

The reason for this interest of members of pressure groups in the prices of the things they sell rather than in consumers' goods prices is easy to understand. Anything they can gain for themselves through skillful bargaining or political pressure seems more important, immediate, and safe than the uncertain result of disciplined co-operation in a common effort to avoid price inflation. The members of privileged groups who are enjoying the advantages of a seller's market hesitate to forego a certain gain for the dubious hope that price inflation can be avoided through sacrifices all around. What if other groups should act selfishly? Here lies the reason for the fact that it is practically impossible to avoid price inflation by exhortation.

These considerations show that it is difficult to say what constitutes a stable value of money and that a stable value of money, say in terms of retail prices, is not necessarily the aim of monetary policy. Actually the value of money differs from person to person because each person is interested in a very special selection of goods.

Nevertheless, we cannot carry this relativism too far. We could not get along without any attempt to ascertain general price movements of broader categories of goods and services such as wholesale prices, retail prices, security prices, or wages. Which averages we are interested in depends on our aims. Our monetary policy may require us to compare the movement of different price groups rather than mix them all together in an attempt to find an expression for *the* purchasing power of money. For instance our policy may be to increase money wages and to stabilize consumers' goods prices, so that an increase in real wages takes the visible and gratifying form of increasing money incomes; we may pursue a parity program where we support farm prices through subsidies as long as they stay below certain industrial prices; we may try to lower export prices to be able to export more and yet maintain a given gold parity; we may try to maintain the prices of government securities so as to peg interest rates and protect security holders against losses; we may try to create a price inflation on purpose so as to lower real wages or to reduce the burden of debtors—and so on ad infinitum. Whether these policies are good or bad is at the moment beside the point. What matters is that there are many possible aims of general economic policy and that different aims imply different price averages as criteria of monetary policy. A search for a price level which is an expression for *the* value of money is a relic from times when monetary theory and policy seemed to be guided exclusively by the desire to keep the price level stable without even bothering to decide which price average was to be kept stable.

Thus we are driven to the conclusion that price averages should be so chosen as to suit particular purposes of monetary or general economic policy and to the admission that there exists no general average of prices which could claim the distinction of being par excellence the expression of the purchasing power of money. However, it can be said that the prices of the items which constitute the national product have gained in importance with the increasing emphasis which modern economic analysis and policy have placed on national income figures.

The Making of Index Numbers

Suppose we have decided on a certain monetary policy which makes it imperative to watch the behavior of prices of a large number of commodities. How can the average behavior of a large number of prices be expressed in simple figures whose movement can easily be followed?

This technical problem can be solved by the construction of so-called index numbers, that is, numbers which show the average rise or fall of prices in percentage terms with reference to a base year. According to our policy aims we assume we have already decided on the commodities whose composite price is to serve as our gauge. This selection of the commodities is a problem which the economist or the politician rather than the statistician has to solve. The statistician's task is then to gather the price data at different points of time and to compute a satisfactory average.

We shall assume that the prices of the selected commodities are given in dollars and cents. To simplify our example we shall now deal with three commodities only: gasoline, milk, and bread. To indicate the hypothetical character of our example we shall compare the prices of the year 1990 with those of the year 2000. Our assumed facts are as follows:

	Year 1990	*Year 2000*
Gasoline (gallon)	$0.30	$0.50
Milk (quart)	0.20	0.25
Bread (pound)	0.10	0.15
Total	$0.60	$0.90

We shall now take 1990 as the base year, that is, we shall assume that the total for this year is 100 rather than $0.60. An equivalent expression for the year 2000 is 150 because $x/90 = 100/60$ or $x = 9{,}000/60$, or 150. Thus we have come to the result that the level of prices has increased by 50 per cent. The reason for this procedure is that comparisons in terms of percentage figures reveal the decisive proportions of a change much better than do comparisons in terms of absolute prices in dollars and cents.

We see that the use of index numbers implies the choice of a base year with whose prices the prices of previous or subsequent years are compared. The choice of the base year is often a matter of convenience. Sometimes it will be a year before the outbreak of a war, or a year which was characterized neither by mass unemployment nor by overfull employment and price inflation.

Would our result have been the same if we had used quarts for gasoline and gallons for milk? Let us try again:

	Year 1900	*Year 2000*
Gasoline (quart)	$0.075	$0.125
Milk (gallon)	0.800	1.000
Bread (pound)	0.100	0.150
Total	$0.975	$1.275

According to the formula $x/1.275 = 100/0.975$, we find that the level of prices has risen by only 30 per cent, from 100 to 130 rather than by 50 per cent as in our first example. Obviously, the units we had chosen as the basis for our absolute price quotations were not irrelevant. In our first example we emphasized gasoline more than milk; in the second example we reversed the procedure, using gallons for milk and quarts for gasoline. Since we did not change our assumption concerning the price changes during the period, inflating gasoline prices in both cases more than milk prices, it is only natural that the first example, which tended to emphasize the relative importance of gasoline, led to a more inflationary picture.

Note that this problem stays with us even after we have solved the question of what commodities are to be included in the index. The two problems shade into each other, however, as is shown by Sauerbeck's index numbers. Sauerbeck took care of the relative importance of certain categories of commodities by including in his index more commodities belonging to one category than another, for instance eight items of vegetable food and seven items of animal food.

The more usual procedure, however, is the use of weights. Each price is multiplied by a figure which corresponds to the relative importance of the commodity in question. The choice of these weights should correspond as nearly as possible to the relative expenditure on the different items (for example, rents will be more important than bread, bread perhaps more important than milk, and milk more important than ink or newspapers). Items which are negligible were probably omitted when the commodities were chosen.

Once we use weights it makes little difference whether we choose gallons or quarts for our original quotations. Suppose we assume that people spend more on gasoline than on bread, and more on bread than on milk. Our first example is now changed as follows:

	Weight	Year 1990		Year 2000	
		Price	Expend.	Price	Expend.
Gasoline (gallon)	4	$0.30	$1.20	$0.50	$2.00
Milk (quart)	1	0.20	0.20	0.25	0.25
Bread (pound)	3	0.10	0.30	1.15	0.45
Total Expenditure			$1.70		$2.70

This time our index changes from 100 to 159: the inflation was worse than even our first example suggested.

Other Difficulties Listed

We are not too concerned here with the technical difficulties which the statistician may encounter in the compilation of index numbers. A few problems, however, may be mentioned.

1. The quality of commodities may change: for example car models in different years, candy bars of changing size, and movie shows in air-conditioned as against hot and stuffy theaters.

2. Many new goods will appear on the list of important goods, while others fade into oblivion. Air transportation and LP records are illustrations of the first category; the horse and buggy and music boxes illustrate the second.

3. Climatic differences between North and South or cultural differences between social classes will have to be considered in the choice of weights or in the choice of commodities.

4. The weights will have to be changed when, over a period of time, expenditures on a given commodity increase substantially, for instance, when the article changes from a luxury to a necessity. Again the automobile may serve as illustration.

5. Often we must beware of double counting. As long as we limit ourselves to consumers' goods the danger is not great, but in the case of investment goods the item may be counted several times as it moves through different stages of production (for example, cattle, hides, and leather are all investment goods on their way to becoming shoes). Again our decision will depend on our aim. If we want to include in our index everything money is being spent on, we should include the purchase of hides by the tannery and the purchase of leather by the shoe manufacturer. If, on the other hand, we are concerned with the national income, we consider mainly shoe prices and include hides and leather only where they are bought to increase inventories.

6. Price level comparisons are often undertaken between different countries, for example, to compare the relative purchasing powers of two currencies. The difficulties which beset these studies of the so-called purchasing power parities will be discussed in Chapter 32. A translation of foreign into domestic prices on the basis of a given rate of exchange must be handled with care and ought not lead to premature conclusions concerning respective living standards. Again it be-

comes evident that factor prices must be considered in addition to consumers' goods prices. In such studies it might be best to find out what an hour of a given kind of work is able to buy in terms of consumers' goods.

7. Where price controls are in force, price averages change their meaning. Price controls lead to rationing, and rationing means that the consumer cannot buy all he wants even though he has the money. Thus, even when price ceilings succeed in maintaining a given price average, the situation is so changed that money can hardly be said to have maintained its purchasing power.

Several Index Numbers Briefly Discussed

Among the numerous possible price indexes some are considered to be expressions of the value of money. We have seen that such claims are exaggerated. All we can say is that some indexes are considered as useful criteria of monetary management.

1. *Indexes of retail prices,* such as the Bureau of Labor Statistics Index of Consumers' Prices (see Chart 8–1). It is a matter of taste whether we consider such index numbers as expressions of *the* value of money. A good index of consumers' prices should include all important commodities and services entering final consumption, weighted in proportion to the money spent on them. It should be noticed that consumers' goods and the goods which constitute the national income are not identical. The national income includes investment goods which have been added to the stock of capital or to inventories during the year.

Against an index of retail prices it can be argued that retail prices react more slowly than wholesale prices to changes in supply and demand and that it is not, therefore, a sensitive index which would promptly indicate when inflationary or deflationary forces are at work.

2. *Indexes of wholesale prices.* It is claimed that such index numbers emphasize commodity prices which are sensitive to monetary influences and that they are a good gauge for the instrument panel of the monetary authority.

Again this all depends on what our monetary policy ought to be. Suppose that an economy is characterized by strong monopolies. Monopolistic prices are not sensitive. Would it be wise to disregard those prices? Should competitive prices be made to bear the whole adjustment burden, for example, be made to fall when monopolistic prices

CHART 8–1

CONSUMER PRICES

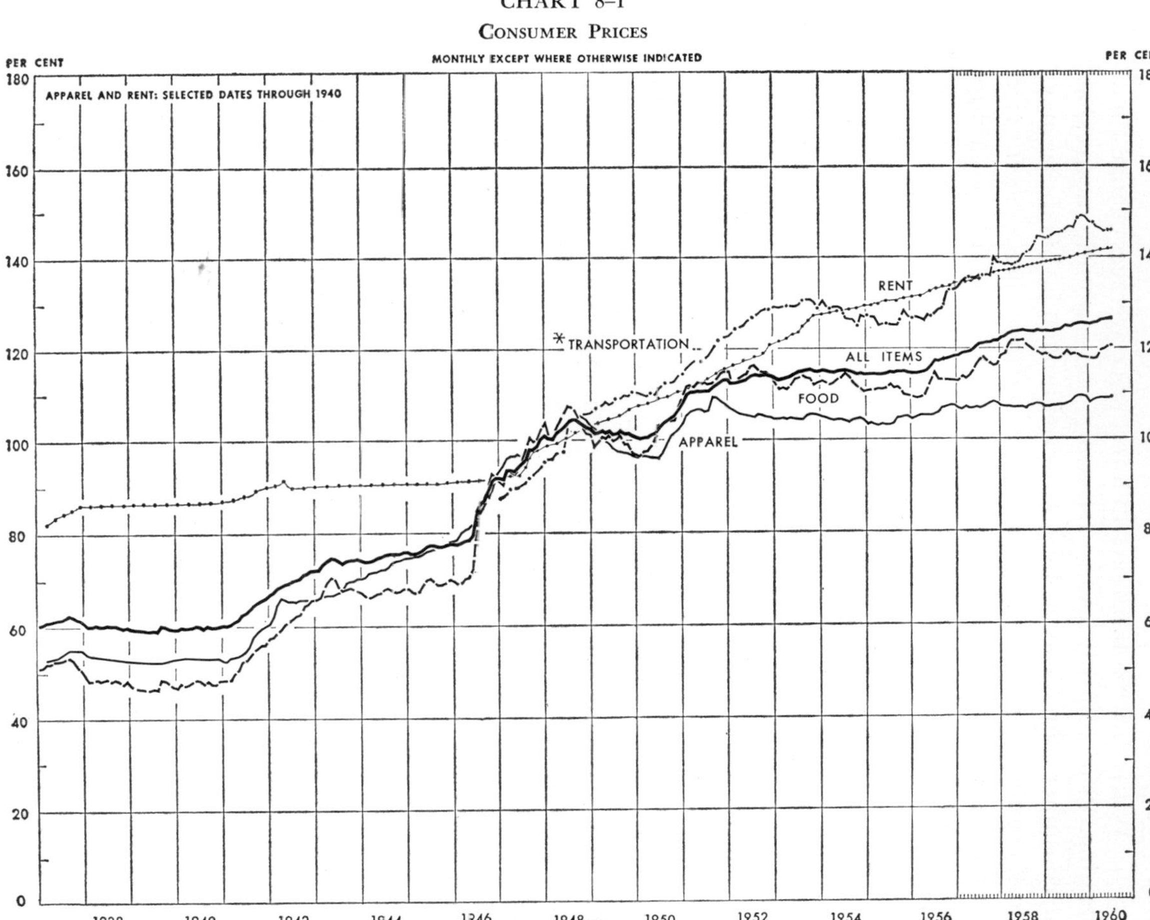

Bureau of Labor Statistics Indexes, 1947–49 = 100

* Transportation not available prior to 1947.

CHART 8–2
Wholesale Prices

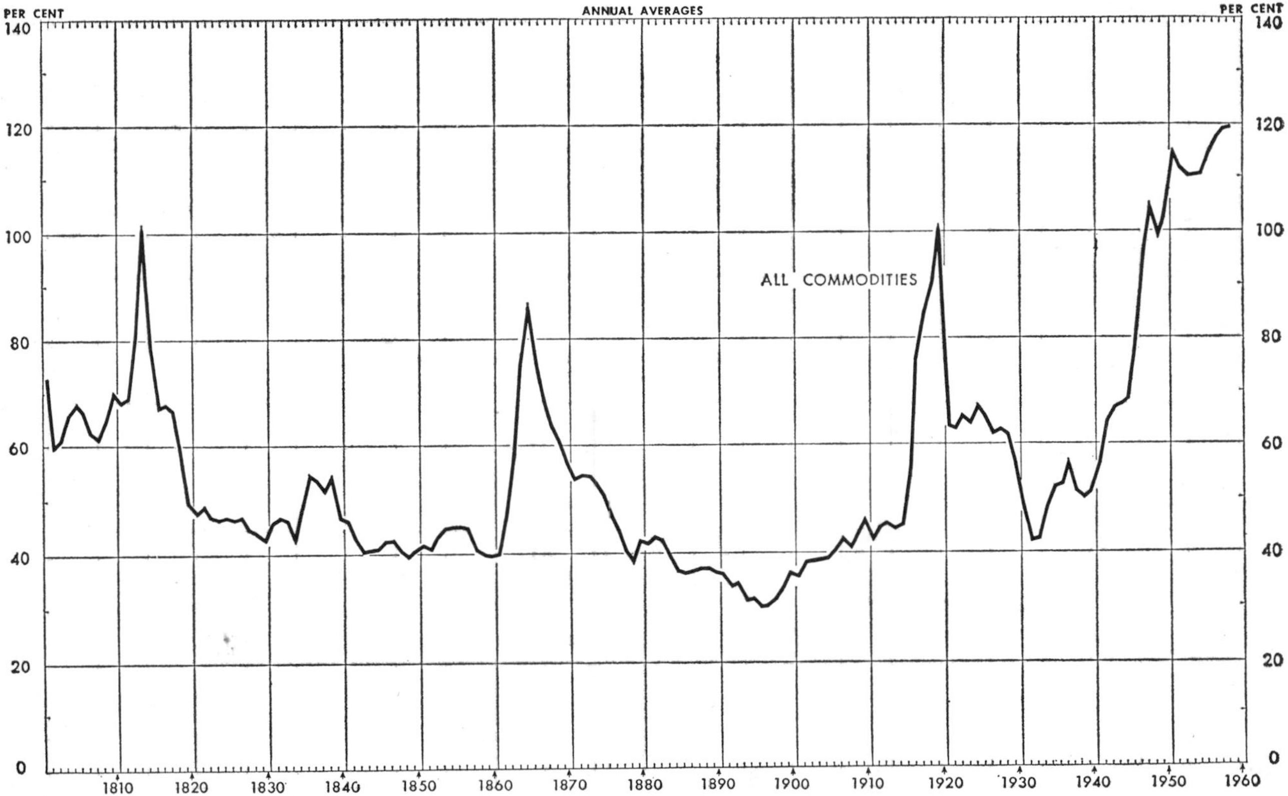

Bureau of Labor Statistics Index, 1947–49 = 100

Source: *Historical Supplement to Federal Reserve Chart Book on Financial and Business Statistics* (Washington, D.C.: Board of Governors of the Federal Reserve System, September, 1960), p. 111.

CHART 8–3

PRICES PAID AND RECEIVED BY FARMERS

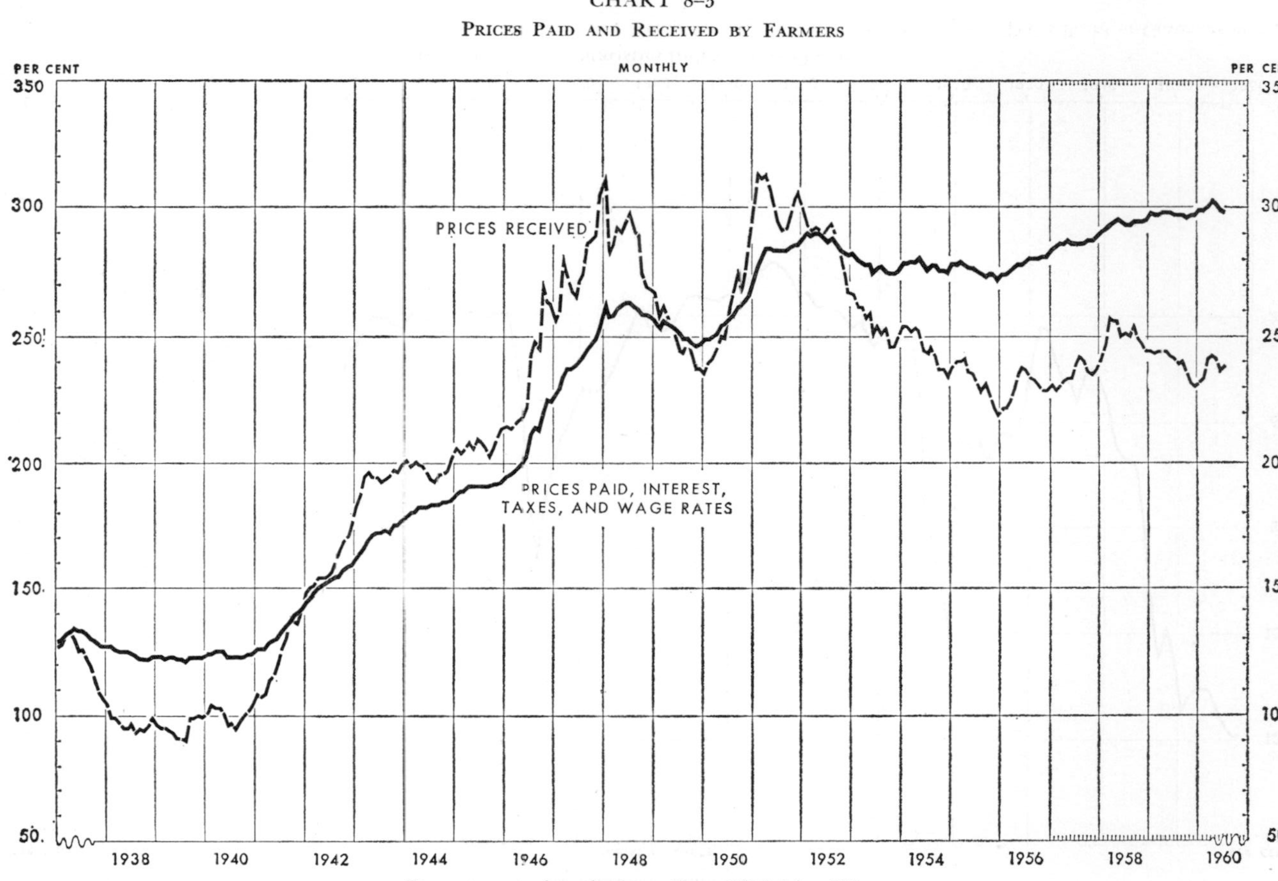

Department of Agriculture Data, 1910–14 = 100

SOURCE: *Historical Supplement to Federal Reserve Chart Book on Financial and Business Statistics* (Washington, D.C.: Board of Governors of the Federal Reserve System, September, 1960), p. 113.

rise so that the average stays the same? Or should sensitive prices be raised to the level of monopoly prices to maintain a reasonable equilibrium between prices?

Chart 8–2 shows the fluctuations of wholesale prices in the United States for the last 160 years. The inflationary influences of wars are clearly visible. Of particular interest is the relative price stability preceding the depression of the early thirties and the absence of a major price deflation after World War II.

3. *A general index.* This index comes nearest to the ideal of those who want to include, as far as possible, all the things that can be bought with money. Against the inclusion of wages Gustav Cassel argued that "wages cannot be included, because, being the share of the worker in the total fruits of economic production, they normally rise in a progressive economy, even if commodity prices remain unchanged."[3] The quotation illustrates how our choice of index numbers is determined by our political aims. Cassel could not include wages because he had already decided on a monetary policy which would keep consumers' goods prices stable and would permit wages to rise.

4. *Special group indexes.* For particular tasks of monetary and general economic policy we may have to compare different series of index numbers. The ratio between indexes of export prices and import prices, for instance, will enable us to measure the so-called terms of trade which are important in connection with balance of payments problems. Another example would be a comparison of prices paid and received by farmers, which will reveal the changing economic position of farmers (see Chart 8–3).

SUGGESTIONS FOR FURTHER READING

FISHER, IRVING. *The Purchasing Power of Money,* chaps. 9–10. New York: Macmillan Co., 1926.

HAWTREY, R. G. "Money and Index Numbers," *Journal of the Royal Statistical Society,* Vol. 93 (1930), pp. 64–85. Reprinted in *Readings in Monetary Theory,* chap. 8 (Homewood, Ill.: Richard D. Irwin, Inc., 1951).

MORGAN, THEODORE. *Income and Employment,* chap. 3, 2 ed. New York: Prentice-Hall, Inc., 1952.

QUESTIONS AND PROBLEMS

1. Why can we not express the value of money in the same way in which we express the value of commodities, viz. by mentioning its price?

[3] Gustav Cassel, *The Theory of Social Economy* (New York: Harcourt, Brace & Co., Inc., 1932), p. 463.

2. "We mean by the Purchasing Power of Money the power of money to buy the goods and services on the purchase of which for purposes of consumption a given community of individuals expend their money income" (J. M. Keynes). Discuss.
3. "But if we have to recognize that, on the one hand, under a stable price level, relative prices may be changed by monetary influences, and, on the other that relative prices may remain undisturbed only when the price level changes, we have to give up the generally received opinion that if the general price level remains the same, the tendencies towards economic equilibrium are not disturbed by monetary influences, and that disturbing influences from the side of money cannot make themselves felt otherwise than by causing a change of the general price level. This doctrine, which has been accepted dogmatically by almost all monetary theorists, seems to me to lie at the root of most of the shortcomings of present-day monetary theory and to be a bar to almost all further progress" (F. A. Hayek). Discuss.
4. List several possible aims of monetary policy and indicate the price averages which would serve as criteria in each case.
5. Assume that between the years 1980 and 1990 the milk price increases from 100 to 200 and that the bread price falls from 100 to 50. Average prices increase from 100 to 125. But suppose that we take the year 1990 as base year. Then the milk price has risen from 50 in 1980 to 100 in 1990 and the bread price has fallen from 200 to 100 in the same period. This time average prices have fallen from 125 to 100. Explain.
6. "An index number may be so dependable that the instrumental error probably seldom reaches one part in 800, or less than three ounces on a man's weight" (W. T. Foster). Do you agree?
7. Enumerate some of the difficulties involved in the computing of index numbers.
8. It is not a precise enough statement if we say that prices should be stabilized. Why not?

Chapter 9 THE VELOCITY OF CIRCULATION OF MONEY

Velocity of Circulation and Money Reserves

On several occasions we had to refer to the fact that the quantity of money supplied is not identical with effective demand. Effective demand depends on the money spent during a period and is the product of the quantity of money and its velocity of circulation.

The velocity of circulation of money can be expressed as the ratio of total transactions or of national income to the quantity of money ($V = PT/M$; $V_y = Y/M$). The first ratio is the so-called transaction velocity and the second is the income or circular velocity. In Chapter 7 we defined k and k_y, respectively, as the reciprocal of V and V_y, or as the portion of the volume of transactions or of the national income which is equal to the money reserves the public wants to hold ($k = M/PT$; $k_y = M/Y$).

In general we may say that the more rapidly receipts and disbursements of money follow each other, the smaller are the money reserves which persons and firms must hold in order to handle a given amount of transactions and the greater, therefore, is the velocity of circulation of money. If money reserves are comparatively small, the velocity of circulation of money has to be comparatively high for a given volume of business or income transactions to be accomplished. Thus when we analyze the motives according to which persons and firms determine the size of their liquid reserves, we analyze the fundamental principles governing the velocity of circulation of money.

Under the impulse of profit maximization there must be a strong tendency toward the reduction of cash balances to a practicable minimum. No one will hold too much cash, which yields no interest if attractive interest-yielding financial investments are available. Cash reserves, therefore, tend to be kept at a minimum in proportion to the anticipated amount of transactions and their fluctuations over a period of time. If no other adjustment is possible, the cash reserve has to be large enough to meet the maximum demands of these fluctuations in receipts and expenditures. The credit system, however, makes it possible to substantially reduce the total amount of reserves through recourse to the money market.

We see that the attitudes of persons and firms toward money reserves are characterized by two opposed tendencies: the desire to hold a part of their resources in a perfectly liquid form and the countervailing propensity to keep this part small because it does not earn an income. To analyze the principles governing the velocity of circulation of money we have to study, first, what J. M. Keynes called the psychological and business incentives for liquidity and, second, the devices used in satisfying this liquidity preference with a minimum of money reserves.

The Liquidity Preference

Keynes pointed out that each individual, after having decided how much to consume and how much to reserve in *some* form for future consumption, will be faced with a further decision, namely, in what form he will hold his command over future consumption. He can hold it in the form of money as immediate, liquid command or he can part with this liquid command, "leaving it to future market conditions to determine on what terms he can, if necessary, convert deferred command . . . into immediate command over goods in general." This second decision depends on a person's liquidity preference.[1]

According to Keynes we have to distinguish three divisions of liquidity preference, which depend, respectively, on the transaction motive, the precautionary motive, and the speculative motive.

The transaction motive Keynes defined as "the need for cash for the current transactions of personal and business exchanges."[2] These needs are determined by such factors as payment habits, the frequency and regularity of payments and receipts, the size of the national income, the degree of business integration, and the ease with which the necessary funds can be borrowed.

A few examples may serve as illustrations.

It is obvious that payment habits will influence the size of money reserves. Services, for example, can be paid for daily, weekly, monthly,

[1] J. M. Keynes, *The General Theory of Employment, Interest and Money* (London: Macmillan & Co., Ltd., 1936), p. 166.

[2] *Ibid.*, p. 170.

or quarterly. A person who receives a yearly income of $9,000 in monthly payments of $750 will hold an average reserve of money of $375, provided that he spend his money in approximately equal daily amounts and does not want to build up an extra reserve for other reasons. The same spending habits would necessitate an average money reserve of $4,500 were he paid in advance for a full year and of about $90 in case of weekly payments. The same thought can be expressed by saying that the average period of rest of his yearly, monthly, or weekly earnings is, respectively, 6 months, 15 days, or 3½ days. Thus, the more frequently income is received, the higher is the velocity of circulation of money.

Our example rested on the assumption of an absolute regularity of inpayments and outpayments. Were our income receiver not sure that his pay checks would arrive at regular intervals, he would tend to hold a larger money reserve even though his income would be the same. A similar influence will be exerted by irregularities in expenditures. We have to set aside money for unforeseen expenses, for doctor's bills, and the proverbial rainy day. Through different kinds of insurance we may change these uncertain anticipations of future needs into regular payments. Insured persons pool their contingency reserves, and the sum total needed by the group is obviously less than the aggregate amount of such reserves for an equal number of uninsured persons.

In connection with the transaction motive for liquidity we must also consider the building up of money balances in anticipation of the purchase of larger items such as automobiles, TV sets, or refrigerators. This tendency, however, may be substantially reduced by the possibility of buying in installments. Installment buying splits lump-sum disbursements into repeated smaller payments and removes the necessity for large reserves on the part of the prospective buyer. This gives money an opportunity to circulate faster.

Business firms, too, will have to arrange for money reserves according to payment habits, regularities of receipts and disbursements, seasonal fluctuations, and the degree of integration of different stages of production. Later we shall discuss how business firms succeed, between them, in reducing the aggregate amounts of liquid reserves which must be held.

If we assume that the amount of money reserves for current transactions is established by rather stable financial habits of persons and firms, we must conclude that changes in economic activity and national income must bring about changes in the demand for money reserves.

We shall see that these changes in demand, unless they are met by equivalent changes in the supply of money, will affect the rates of interest.

Keynes defined the precautionary motive for liquidity as "the desire for security as to the future cash equivalent of a certain proportion of total resources."[3] This is not so much a motive which gives additional reasons why money may be needed at future dates as a reminder that an attempt toward a quick liquidation of earning assets may result in considerable losses. Given the need for money because of current transactions, the demand for money reserves in response to the precautionary motive depends mainly on the organization of the credit market, that is, how fast and at what cost income-yielding assets can be changed into money. The slower the speed or the greater the cost, the greater will be the desire to hold money reserves.

The speculative motive, finally, Keynes defined as "the object of securing profit from knowing better than the market what the future will bring forth."[4] The speculative motive may be understood as the tendency to postpone purchases if one expects prices to fall or to hasten expenditures (and to postpone sales) if one expects prices to rise. These attitudes are particularly important on the security market where they influence security prices and interest rates.

The speculative motive plays an important part in times of severe price inflation or price deflation, when the velocity of circulation of money may become a force which propels the economy further and further away from equilibrium. In severe price inflation people tend to spend money with ever-increasing rapidity, while in price deflation they reduce expenditure and increase their money reserves. In both cases the changing velocity of circulation of money helps to bring about the anticipated price changes.

The Economizing of Money Reserves

While persons and firms desire to hold money reserves for the above-mentioned reasons, money reserves are usually kept as small as possible under given circumstances. Only the speculative motive in times of price deflation would be an exception to this rule. We must now investigate the possibilities of reducing money reserves to a practicable minimum.

If there existed a perfect money market, hardly any money re-

[3] *Ibid.*, p. 170.
[4] *Ibid.*, p. 170.

serves would have to be held. Any surplus cash would be lent out, and any deficiency in money reserves would be made up by borrowing. Nevertheless, recourse to the money market is not always possible or advisable. We have to consider the following two points:

1. We cannot assume that those who desire to borrow additional reserves can always be accommodated by persons or firms whose reserves are temporarily too large. When fluctuations in individual demands for money have been offset, there remain fluctuations in aggregate demand, which are not automatically met by compensating changes in the supply of money.

2. It is quite often more expensive to borrow than to hold money reserves, particularly if a frequent change between borrowing and lending operations should be required to keep reserves at a minimum. The frictions in the form of costs of manipulation become too great.

While the ideal of a perfect money market cannot be attained, every improvement in the organization of the money market will help reduce the aggregate of needed reserves, other circumstances remaining the same. Assuming that the maximum reserves needed do not coincide for different persons or firms, there must exist a possibility of reducing the aggregate amount of reserves by making temporarily excessive cash balances of some persons or firms available to others whose money reserves are temporarily deficient. Whatever methods are used to carry out these credit transactions, they all result in a more frequent use of a given money supply.

Commercial banks can facilitate this mutual accommodation by acting as intermediaries between persons or firms whose financial requirements permit successive use of the same money reserves. Firms in consecutive production processes may also directly support each other by some form of credit operation. If, for instance, a firm has reserves which are large enough to meet its maximum requirements, it may be willing to finance producers in previous stages of production whose demand for credit is at its peak immediately before the output is sold. In this case the credit operation may take the form of a payment in advance of delivery. In other cases credit may be extended to firms in subsequent stages of production in the form of sales on open book account or against promissory notes. In the preharvest period farmers' demand for money tends to be high while corn merchants' demand for money is low, but after the harvest the situation is reversed, and the depleted money reserves of the corn merchants are gradually restored as their inventories are sold. Similar examples may be found wherever technically interdependent but financially separated stages of production succeed one another with each having its peak demand for money reserves at a different time.

That a highly developed credit market also tends to reduce money reserves in other ways is implied in Keynes' precautionary motive. The more easily earning assets can be liquidated, that is, speedily sold for money without loss, the smaller, *ceteris paribus,* may be money reserves. Ease of financial investment, too, will tend to reduce cash balances. Money which is being saved for investment purposes will accumulate until it is worth while to go through the trouble and expense of security purchases. Sometimes it does not pay to invest money for too short a period since the cost of buying and selling securities may well be higher than the profit from investment for the interval. Thus it is obvious that a well-organized credit market will tend to bring about a greater willingness to part with liquidity.

Effects of a Changed Velocity of Circulation of Money

An increased demand for money balances on the part of persons or firms can be satisfied only when either the total supply of money is increased or when other persons or firms reduce their money reserves accordingly. When the supply of money is kept stable, the desire to hold larger money reserves reduces spending. In this case an increased liquidity preference will lower economic activity, income, and prices until the total demand for money reserves can be satisfied with the given supply of money (as shown in Chapter 2, p. 15).

Opposite effects will result when the desire to hold money balances decreases: the desire to economize cash reserves will in the end lead to an increased desire to hold money. If an increased velocity of circulation of money tends to raise production, income, and prices, money reserves will tend to increase owing to the higher money volume of transactions, and the money released through economizing money reserves accommodates this desire for larger reserves. Other things remaining equal, the stimulating effect of an increased velocity of circulation of money will have worked itself out when the money released through economizing reserves is absorbed by the increase in reserves necessitated by the general increase in economic activity. If the increased total demand is matched by increased employment of formerly idle factors of production, prices will not increase, but in this case money reserves are needed for the newly employed persons and the expanded activities of business firms (as shown in Chapter 2, pp. 15–17).

The Velocity of Circulation of Goods

It is sometimes said that the velocity of circulation of money cannot influence the value of money because money and goods are always exchanged against each other, unless money can be made to circulate against nothing. A changed velocity of circulation of money, it is argued, has to be accompanied by an equivalent change in the "velocity of circulation of goods" because money transactions cannot increase if commodities are not offered for sale more often in exactly the same measure.

It is not difficult to explain the fallacy of these arguments.

1. The concept of a velocity of circulation cannot be applied to goods in the same sense as it is applied to money. Money usually remains in circulation; goods are produced, marketed, and consumed. Money stays in the market; goods merely pass through the market.

2. Commodities and services can be paid for in different ways depending on habits of payment and the development of the credit system. The same physical turnover of goods, therefore, can be associated with different velocities of circulation of money.

3. Goods can be produced and traded by many or few independent firms, the number of firms depending on the measure of integration of business organization. The greater the degree of integration, the less numerous will be the monetary transactions connected with the same amount of physical production.

4. Fluctuations of inventories are important, but they are not related to variations in the velocity of circulation of money so as to guarantee parallel changes in the circulation of money and the circulation of goods.

5. In the absence of offsetting changes of other factors an increase in the velocity of circulation of money leads to price inflation, and this rise in prices accounts for the increased values against which additional transfers of money are made.

Methods of Expressing Velocity of Circulation of Money

The transaction velocity of circulation of money refers to the total value of monetary transactions over a period, such as a year or a month, divided by the average quantity of money in circulation during the period (the total of money reserves or M). We include absolutely every monetary transaction, whether in connection with the earning or spending of income, with production and distribution processes, or with purely financial transactions, such as the buying and selling of new and old securities.

How are we to find the figure which, when multiplied by the given quantity of money, will equal the total value of monetary transactions over the period? It is impossible to choose a representative dollar bill and follow it in its course from pocket to till, to bank, to pay envelope, to pocket, etc. to find out how many times it is spent during a year. In the case of demand deposits, moreover, individual dollars lose their identity completely and cannot even theoretically be traced in successive transactions.

Fortunately this tracing of individual units of money is not at all necessary for our purposes. In order to get a rough idea of the average velocity of circulation of deposit money, we compare an average of demand deposits over a period with the value of transactions accomplished by transfers between demand deposits. The value of transactions is expressed in debits to deposit accounts. The sum total of all debits over a period of time, compared with the total of demand deposits, will show how often a dollar on deposit had to be used, on the average, to accomplish the total monetary transfers. Such a calculation may refer to any segment of demand deposits, for example, to demand deposits in major financial centers. See Chart 9–1.

To express the circular or income velocity of money we use another method. We divide the national income or gross national product[5] figures by the average quantity of money for the period. Thus, if the gross national product should be $200 billion and the total amount of money in circulation, that is, demand deposits and currency, $100 billion (roughly the situation in 1945), the income velocity would be two. That is, the total amount of money ($100 billion) would have circulated throughout the economy twice during the year and would, therefore, have been received as income twice during this period.

We have already seen that the gross national product is much smaller than the monetary value of all monetary transactions (*PT*). It is not surprising, then, that the rate of turnover expressed by the ratio of gross national product to the quantity of money seems rather slow. We must remember that for each final purchase of a consumers' or producers' good there have been many transactions in earlier stages

[5] For purposes of comparison over the years it makes little difference whether we use national income or gross national product figures.

CHART 9–1

TURNOVER OF DEMAND DEPOSITS AT BANKS IN SELECTED CITIES

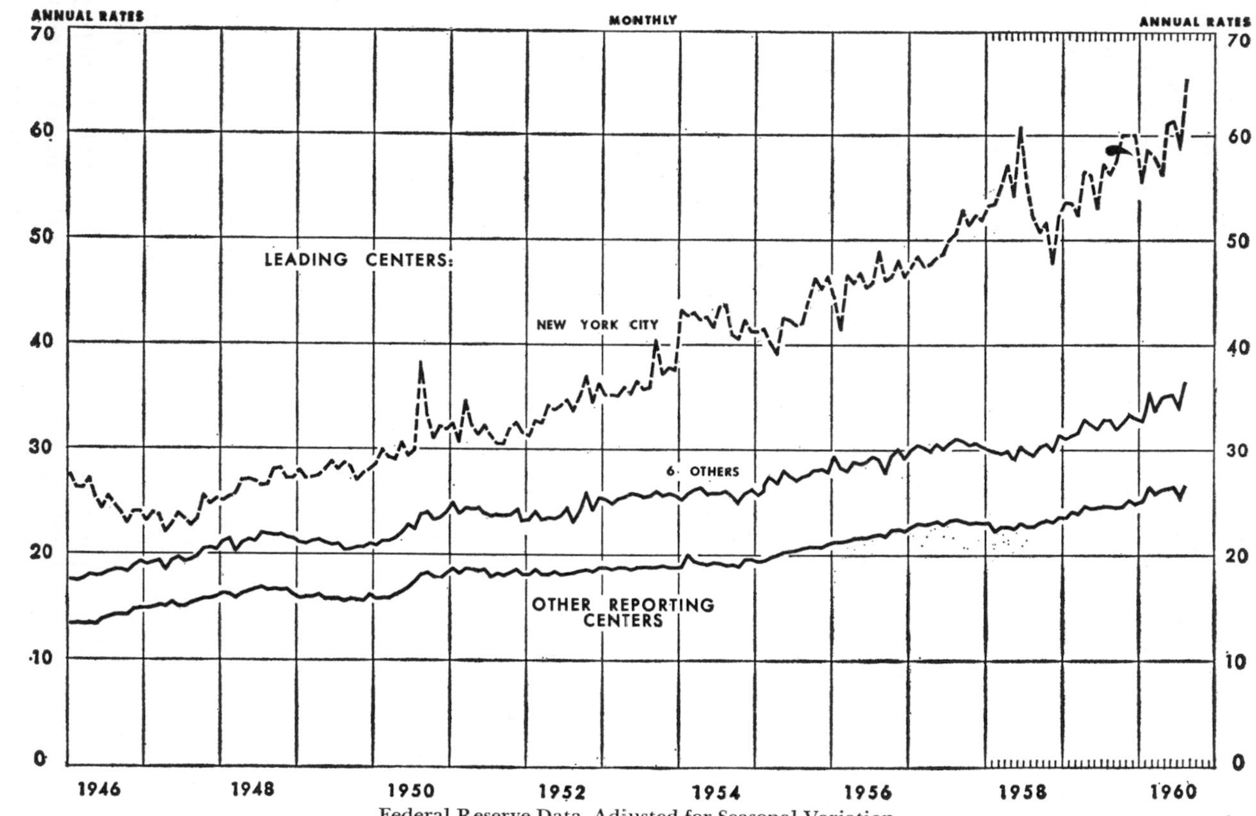

Federal Reserve Data, Adjusted for Seasonal Variation

SOURCE: *Federal Reserve Chart Book on Financial and Business Statistics* (Washington, D.C.: Board of Governors of the Federal Reserve System, September, 1960), p. 8.

of production: purchases of raw materials, of semimanufactured and manufactured goods, payments in connection with transportation and distribution processes, and the like. These many transactions are, as it were, the gear which brings the slow circular velocity to the relatively high transaction velocity.

As circular velocity the ratio of national income or gross national product to M indicates the average time duration of the flow of money from ultimate income recipient to ultimate income recipient. On its way from one income receiver to another money passes through such stages as retailing, wholesaling, and different manufacturing processes. In each of these steps money received is distributed as income among those who contributed to that particular process, while the balance is passed on as the purchasing price of materials and parts to preceding stages, where some of the money is again distributed as income and the rest is passed on. This successive spending approach enables us to distinguish between monetary transactions in general and income transactions, and to understand why it may take months before the last cent of a consumer's dollar becomes the income of, say, a steelworker.

Chart 9–2 shows the ratio of money supply to gross national product.

It is an interesting fact that the income velocity of money (Y/M or GNP/M) has decreased very substantially during the last 150 years. Comparing the ratio of money (demand deposits plus currency) to national income (M/Y or k_y) for different years, Alvin H. Hansen finds that the ratio was 0.05 in 1800, 0.15 in 1850, 0.51 in 1900, and 0.75 in 1945.[6] There were fluctuations around this trend, of course, but it is obvious that "the spectacular rise in income has been accompanied by a far more rapid increase in the money supply" and that "the amount of money which people wished to hold in relation to income, has grown decade by decade."[7]

How can one explain this trend which seems to run counter to the desire to economize money reserves? Two suggestions may provide an explanation: (1) Since the Y/M ratio disregards all monetary transactions which precede the final purchase of the items which constitute the national income, the increased supply of money may be necessitated, in part at least, by the growing intricacy of the modern produc-

[6] Note that the figure of 2 for GNP/M and, therefore, of 0.50 for M/GNP given above for 1945 rests on a comparison of money supply with the gross national product rather than with the national income.

[7] Alvin H. Hansen, *Monetary Theory and Fiscal Policy* (New York: McGraw-Hill Book Co., Inc., 1949), pp. 5–6.

Gross National Product and Demand Deposits Adjusted and Currency

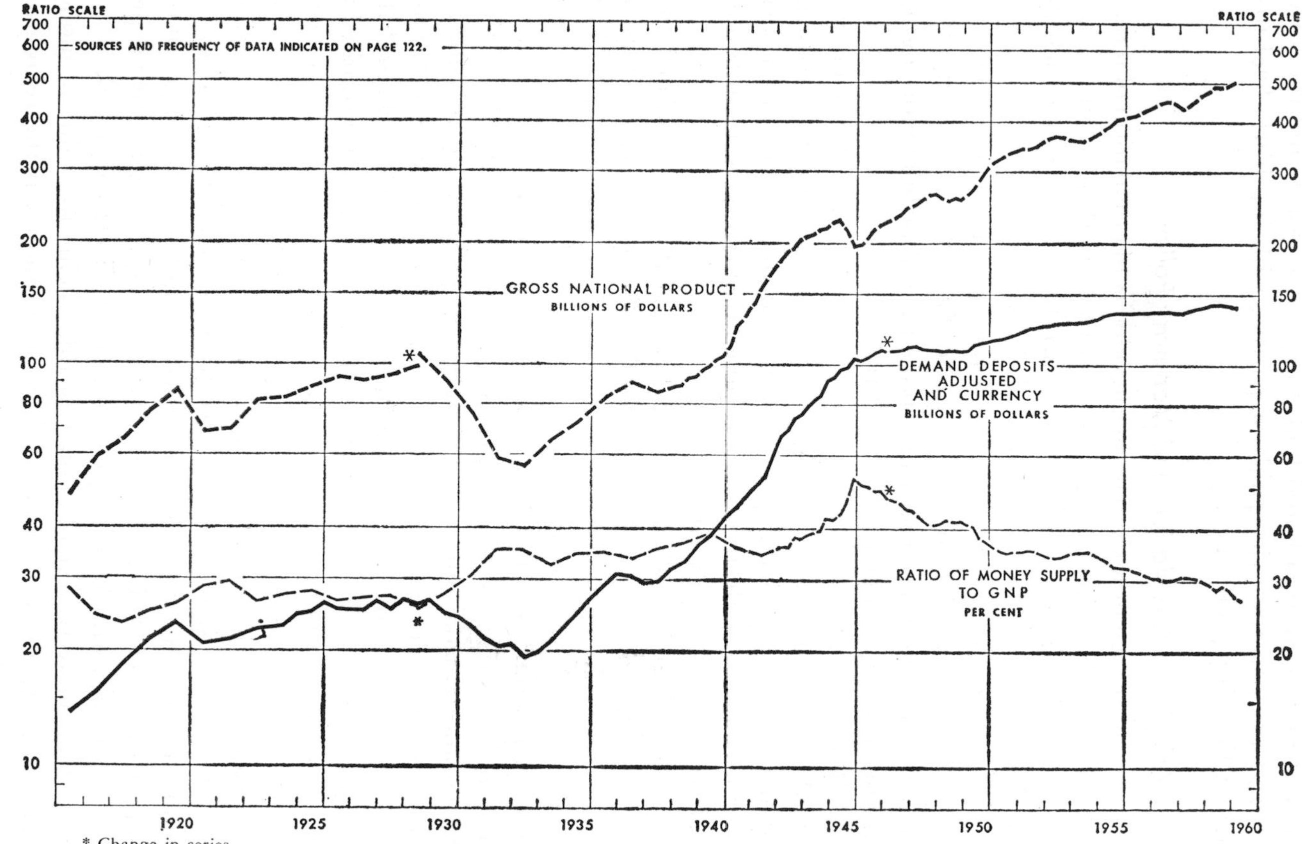

* Change in series.

SOURCE: *Historical Supplement to Federal Reserve Chart Book on Financial and Business Statistics* (Washington, D.C.: Board of Governors of the Federal Reserve System, September, 1960), p. 11.

tive and distributive processes. (2) As the nation's wealth increases, interest rates tend to fall, and both the greater wealth and the lower interest rates (as the price paid for parting with liquidity) lead to a higher liquidity preference.

Velocity of Circulation and Monetary Policy

We have seen how changes in the velocity of circulation of money can influence the value of money. Does this mean that we can manage the purchasing power of money by controlling the factors which determine the demand for money reserves?

Often it is impossible to control both the supply of money and the velocity of circulation. As a matter of fact, an increased supply of money will often succeed only in making the public hold more money without leading to increased expenditure.

Two methods which have been used to influence the velocity of circulation of money will be discussed briefly. One constitutes a strange attempt to increase total expenditure by bringing about a faster turnover of money, while the other is designed mainly as an anti-inflationary instrument in wartime.

Silvio Gesell (1862–1930) suggested that the danger of deflation and depression could be avoided if the public could be made to spend money faster. Gesell proposed the issue of currency notes which would retain their full value only if stamps were affixed each month ("stamp scrip"). The stamps would have to be purchased from the government. The idea was tried in several places in Bavaria, Austria, the United States, and Canada, but each time the attempt failed, mainly for the obvious reason that it was impossible to apply the measure simultaneously to all kinds of money. Gresham's law started to work, and the expensive and bothersome money (which the government promised to accept in payment of taxes) was driven out in no time by the "cheap" regular money. To apply such a measure equally to all kinds of money and money substitutes would be a very difficult task, particularly since the value of the stamps would have to be changed according to our desire to stimulate or to retard the turnover of money. Changes in the supply of money and changes in government spending are by far preferable to such strange attempts to influence effective demand.

A far more reasonable policy of influencing the value of money via changes in the velocity of circulation of money is the regulation of installment buying. We have seen that installment buying increases the velocity of circulation of money. Anything that decreases installment buying, therefore, will tend to be deflationary. To exert this anti-inflationary pressure is the purpose of Regulation W. Under specific and temporary emergency powers the Federal Reserve authorities may at certain times reduce installment buying (1) by limiting the amount of credit that may be granted for the purchase of any article listed in the regulation, and (2) by limiting the time that may be agreed upon for repaying the obligation.

SUGGESTIONS FOR FURTHER READING

In addition to the literature suggested in connection with the Fisher and Marshall equations:

HANSEN, ALVIN H. *Monetary Theory and Fiscal Policy,* chap. 1. New York: McGraw-Hill Book Co., Inc., 1949.

HICKS, J. R. "A Suggestion for Simplifying the Theory of Money," *Economica,* New Series Vol. 2 (1935), pp. 1–19. Reprinted in *Readings in Monetary Theory,* chap. 2 (Homewood, Ill.: Richard D. Irwin, Inc., 1951).

KEYNES, J. M. *The General Theory of Employment, Interest and Money,* chaps. 13 and 15. London: Macmillan & Co., Ltd., 1936.

WHITTLESEY, CHARLES R. *Readings in Money and Banking,* pp. 176–78. New York: W. W. Norton & Co., Inc., 1952.

On Silvio Gesell:

KEYNES, J. M. *The General Theory,* chap. 23, pp. 353–58.

MORGAN, THEODORE. *Income and Employment,* pp. 238–40. New York: Prentice-Hall, Inc., 1952.

On Regulation W:

BOARD OF GOVERNORS OF THE FEDERAL RESERVE SYSTEM. *The Federal Reserve System. Purposes and Functions,* 3 ed., pp. 60–63. Washington, D.C., 1954.

QUESTIONS AND PROBLEMS

1. Explain the equations $V = PT/M$ and $V_y = Y/M$.
2. "It will appear, on consideration, that changes in the rapidity of circulation of money are themselves incidental to changes in the amount of ready purchasing power which the people of a country find it advantageous to keep in their own holding" (Alfred Marshall). Comment.
3. "Every successful attempt to economize cash balances leads to an increase in the demand for goods and services and, other things remaining equal, to an increase in their prices." Explain.
4. Explain the transaction motive, the precautionary motive, and the speculative motive for liquidity.

5. Does a well-organized credit market increase or reduce our willingness to part with liquidity? What effect would rising rates of interest have on our liquidity preference?
6. Suppose that the supply of money remains the same and that many persons and firms decide to reduce their money reserves, where does the money go which these persons and firms no longer desire to hold?
7. "A change in the velocity of circulation of money has to be accompanied by a change in the 'velocity of circulation of goods' because money transactions cannot increase if commodities are not offered for sale more often in exactly the same measure." Correct?
8. Since it is impossible to follow the course of individual dollar bills and since individual dollars lose their identity in the case of demand deposits, how are we to find the transaction velocity of money?
9. How can we express the circular or income velocity of money?
10. The income velocity of circulation of money has by and large greatly decreased during the last century and a half. How can you explain this development?
11. Explain the regulation of consumer credit by the Federal Reserve (Regulation W) as an attempt to influence the velocity of circulation of money.
12. Explain and criticize the proposal by Silvio Gesell according to which currency notes would only retain their value by being stamped each month with stamps purchased at a post office.

Chapter 10 OBJECTIVES OF MONETARY POLICY

Introduction

Monetary institutions and instruments cannot properly be understood before we know the objectives of monetary policy which led to their peculiar design. The objectives of monetary policy have often changed. This can be seen in our present monetary system, which still bears the imprint of theories and policy aims which have by now been discarded. In enumerating several possible objectives of monetary policy we shall proceed from simple to more complex aims, thereby following in the main actual historical development.

First we shall discuss the attitude, found among classical economists, that money is essentially insignificant and that a monetary policy is not needed because the supply of money will adjust itself without any special arrangements to the needs of the economy.

Then we shall turn to those who wanted to limit monetary policy to the designing of simple mechanisms which would keep the supply of money under automatic control. In this category belong the gold-standard mechanism and the commercial-loan theory of money.

A third group of writers does not believe in such automatic solutions. Monetary policy to them is a conscious effort which cannot rely on simple recipes like the gold flow or the discounting of commercial paper. But again, as in the first two cases, money is to be kept passive and neutral, both as a measure of value and as a means of exchange.

The fourth group is both more modest and more ambitious. It is more modest because it does not think that any simple automatic device will work or that we can succeed in maintaining a stable price level with monetary weapons alone. It purports to combine the instruments of monetary policy with other measures to achieve the ambitious aim of a high level of employment at reasonably stable prices. It trusts less than the proponents of the older monetary policies in the automatic forces of the exchange and price mechanism. The problems which are to be solved by conscious effort and by fiscal as well as by monetary policies are seen to be much more complicated than earlier writers believed.

The "Insignificance" of Money

Consciously or unconsciously monetary policy must be based on monetary theory. When it is denied that money influences the economy, monetary theory and monetary policy are equally impossible. Classical economists considered money as a veil behind which the really important exchange transactions are hidden. In their impatience to tear away this veil they did not pay much attention to money. John Stuart Mill (1806–75) believed that "there cannot . . . be intrinsically a more insignificant thing, in the economy of society, than money."[1] He wanted his readers to see that in the last analysis we pay for commodities with commodities.

> Each person's means for paying for the productions of other people consists of those which he himself possesses. All sellers are inevitably, and by the meaning of the word, buyers. Could we suddenly double the productive powers of the country, we should double the supply of commodities in every market; but we should, by the same stroke, double the purchasing power. Everybody would bring a double demand as well as supply: everybody would be able to buy twice as much, because every one would have twice as much to offer in exchange.[2]

Mill conceded that there could be a superfluity of certain things and that this would require adaptations in production, but an insufficiency of money supply, a total overproduction of goods, or an insufficiency of total expenditure did not worry him. He argued that the supply of money would always tend to match an expanded production because

> money is a commodity; and if all commodities are supposed to be doubled in quantity, we must suppose money to be doubled too, and that prices would no more fall than values would.[3]

Even a general fall in prices, owing to an insufficient supply of money, would not have been considered dangerous by Mill, who argued that

[1] J. S. Mill, *Principles of Political Economy* (London: Longmans, Green & Co., 1936), Book III, chap. vii.

[2] *Ibid.*, chap. xiv.

[3] *Ibid.*

the value of things will continue to conform to their cost of production.... If values remain the same, what becomes of prices is immaterial, since the remuneration of producers does not depend on how much money, but on how much of consumable articles, they obtain for their goods.[4]

Mill only repeated what Jean-Baptiste Say (1767–1832) had said before him, namely, "that a product is no sooner created, than it, from that instant, affords a market for other products to the full extent of its own value."[5] Say, too, had been of the opinion that

there is always money enough to conduct the circulation and mutual exchange of other values, when those values really exist. Should the increase of traffic require more money to facilitate it, the want is easily supplied, and is a strong indication of prosperity—a proof that a great abundance of values has been created, which it is wished to exchange for other values. In such cases, merchants well know how to find substitutes for the product serving as a medium of exchange.[6]

Both Say and Mill were sure that the seller of a commodity would be anxious to spend the money which he received because he could not make use of it otherwise. Therefore, they did not anticipate a slowing-down of the velocity of circulation of money and any resultant difficulties.

As a basis of monetary theory and policy, the Say–Mill argument was quite insufficient because it neglected to show how the supply of money would adjust itself automatically to the supply of goods or why a general price deflation would be without danger.

Mill compared money with a machine "for doing quickly and commodiously, what would be done, though less quickly and commodiously, without it" and admitted that, like any other machine, "it exerts a distinct and independent influence of its own when it gets out of order."[7]

This remark can lead us on to those who looked at the monetary system as a mechanism which, when well constructed, will solve all monetary problems automatically as long as the mechanism is kept in good working order.

The Gold-Flow Mechanism

Metallic standards had the attractive feature that they seemed not to require a positive monetary policy. If new gold deposits were discovered or improved mining or metallurgical techniques were de-

[4] *Ibid.*

[5] Jean-Baptiste Say, *A Treatise on Political Economy* (Philadelphia: John Grigg, 1830), p. 78.

[6] *Ibid.*

[7] Mill, *op. cit.*, chap. vii.

veloped, the resulting increase in production would exert an inflationary influence. Then, however, gold production would become less profitable since cost prices would rise while the price of the product would remain fixed.

Even when, with the use of token money and deposit money, a given amount of gold was made to serve as basis of a much larger monetary supply, the belief in this automatic adjustment continued to prevail. Gold was made to serve as an automatic brake in the credit machine. Even more, it was used as a device by which the monetary policies of the different gold-standard countries could be integrated.

Let us assume that all countries are on gold, that is, that their monetary authorities are willing to buy and sell gold in unlimited amounts at a fixed price. Currency and demand deposits are convertible into gold, and the amount of money in circulation is limited by reserve ratios, as discussed in Chapter 6. The price levels in different countries will be established by the forces discussed in Chapter 7. Prices expressed in different currency units, for example, in dollars and in pound sterling, can be compared when we know the rate of exchange which, in the case of two gold-standard countries, is the gold-weight ratio of the two currency units. Decisive for international trade are relative commodity prices. Price differences among countries are caused by the fact that some countries are better endowed with, say, skilled labor while others abound in natural resources.

To simplify our picture let us consider only two countries. In equilibrium country A will pay for its imports from country B by exports to country B. But it may easily happen that A's importers bought more from B than its exporters sold to B. This situation will arise, for example, if A's prices were, on the average, higher than B's prices as a result of a domestic price inflation. We now assume that, in the absence of international borrowing, country A pays for its excess of imports over exports in gold. The gold outflow has the effect of reducing the supply of money in country A. Since the gold supports a superstructure of currency and demand deposits, a multiple contraction of the domestic monetary circulation is brought about. Price deflation results in decreasing imports and expanding exports until equilibrium in international trade is achieved. Opposite effects in the gold-inflow country B help in restoring equilibrium.

Chapter 31 will show how oversimplified this picture of the gold-flow mechanism is. But in this oversimplified form it suited to perfection those who wanted to find a foolproof system of automatic monetary controls.

The Commercial-Loan Theory

Running parallel to the attempt to make the supply of money dependent on the supply of gold is the attempt to connect the supply of money with the supply of commodities which exchange for money. The commercial-loan theory of credit tries to prove that money created through the granting of short-term loans on goods in process would neatly follow the trade volume and thus constitute an ideal supply of money. The commercial-loan theory shares Say's and Mill's optimism about an automatic adjustment of the money flow, provided money is brought into circulation through discounting and rediscounting commercial paper.

The typical commercial loan is based on the promise of the buyer to pay the price of the purchased commodity in, say, three months. The buyer will either sign a promissory note, that is, an unconditional promise to pay at a determined future date, or the seller will draw a draft on the buyer ordering him to pay. If the seller does not wish to wait for his money, he may sell the promissory note or the endorsed acceptance for its nominal value minus interest for three months (or whatever time the note has still to run).

This is the point where, according to the commercial-loan theory, the commercial banks and the monetary authorities have an excellent opportunity to create just the right amount of money by controlling the discount rate and the type of paper eligible for discount or rediscount.

Three interconnected trends of thought can be distinguished in this attitude:

1. The emphasis on short-term commercial credit (rather than on long-term investment credit) rests on the idea that a change in the discount rate is all that is required to bring about a change in the quantity of money in circulation. Since each individual loan will be paid back automatically within a relatively short period, a constant circulation of credit is maintained. When, therefore, the discount rate is lowered and when accordingly more discounting of commercial paper takes place, the outflow of money will exceed the return flow; vice versa, when the discount rate is raised, the return flow will exceed the new outflow and the monetary circulation is reduced.

2. It has been argued that, in this manner, the monetary circulation can be reduced without unnecessary inconvenience to the debtor because his process of production (for the duration of which he needed the credit) is now finished. He has produced the product, has sold it,

and has come into possession of the money out of which he can pay the creditor. Hence it is concluded that the commercial banks, in reducing the quantity of outstanding commercial credit, need not exert a disturbing influence.

This is the theory of the self-liquidation of commercial credits, which has greatly influenced monetary policy in the past. Unfortunately, this theory is wrong. It rests on a very shallow conception of the complexity and the ramifications of modern processes of production. True, merchants may be sensitive to changes in loan rates and, for example, decrease their inventories when anticipated profit margins are wiped out by increasing rates of interest. But decreasing inventories mean decreasing orders for goods already in process. Not being able to sell their products, producers in the earlier stages of production will have to adjust themselves, one after another, to diminishing salability of their products at existing prices. Thus their ability to pay back the loans through which their production processes were financed is reduced. Every step in the process of production depends for its liquidity on the demand of the following step, and the often overrated liquidity of the final stages of production, when really counted upon, may prove to be the cause of an avalanche of illiquidity throughout the whole economic system.

3. The discounting of commercial paper has been considered an ideal way of bringing about an adjustment of the supply of money to the circulation of goods. The real "backing" of money, it has been argued, consists of goods flowing through the production and marketing processes. Thus, whenever money is created on the basis of commercial paper, the goods to be bought with the money are already on their way to the market and no price inflation will arise. Conversely, when goods are sold to final consumers, businessmen will pay back their bank loans out of the proceeds of their sales, and thus the circulation of both money and the goods in trade channels will be reduced in roughly equal amounts.

As D. H. Robertson has pointed out,[8] this argument neglects the velocity of circulation of money. Once issued, the additional money will circulate, that is, be used for purchases again and again before the loan is paid back. Furthermore, the argument ignores the fact that the demand for and the supply of credit are dependent on rates of interest. Rates which are too low can lead to price inflation even though the outstanding credits can still be "secured" by goods passing, at inflated

[8] A. C. Pigou and Dennis H. Robertson, *Economic Essays and Addresses* (London: P. S. King & Son, Ltd., 1931), p. 111.

prices, through the production and marketing processes. Thus, if the rate of discount has the power to influence borrowing, the supply of money is not merely a passive and neutral product of the volume of trade.

The commercial-loan theory obviously assumed the rate of discount to be determined by the gold-flow mechanism. Since both the theory of the gold flow and the commercial-loan theory aimed at the construction of a foolproof system, they joined forces. The gold flow determined the discount rate, and the discount rate determined how much commercial paper would be discounted. While this did not detract from the logic of the gold-flow mechanism, it certainly ruined the notion that credit and the supply of money are following the volume of trade.

This combination of two theories which aimed at an automatic monetary system led to the rule, found in several central banking acts, that currency as well as deposit money should be backed by gold and commercial paper. This view excluded government securities as a backing, for they were titles of credit indicative of long-term investment and did not, therefore, represent "goods in process."

Exclusion of securities points to another major weakness of the commercial-loan theory. The tenets of this doctrine cannot be squared with the fact that commercial bills are only one of many possible methods of financing production processes and that, for this reason alone, they cannot possibly be indicative of the "legitimate" demand for money in its entirety.

The great faith placed in the self-liquidation of commercial loans was bound to be disappointed when, in times of financial crisis, the central bank was not willing to rediscount. If, on the other hand, the central bank was permitted to purchase government securities, security holdings were just as liquid as portfolios of commercial paper.

Hand in hand with this discovery went a change in the instruments of monetary policy. To an ever-increasing extent the discount policy was overshadowed by so-called open-market operations, that is, buying and selling of government securities and other credit instruments by the central bank. But open-market operations were always considered only as tools; they were never believed to be an end of monetary policy like the discount operations under the commercial-loan theory. As mere tools the open-market and discount operations can be used for many purposes, whether for adjustments in accordance with the gold flow or for any kind of independent monetary management.

Price Stabilization

Once we abandon belief in the working of automatic devices, which characterized the gold-flow mechanism and the commercial-loan theory of credit, we are confronted by several conflicting monetary objectives. Among these objectives the seemingly most obvious and most generally accepted is price stabilization: the neutrality of money as a unit of account.

Price stabilization seems to have the great advantage of simplicity. It seems to be a clear-cut aim; we can check whether it has been reached; and it helps us to avoid the admitted evils of price inflation and price deflation.

Unfortunately, these first favorable impressions are deceptive. In Chapter 8 we noticed that no general agreement exists as to what constitutes a price index which could be used as an ideal gauge for changes in the purchasing power of money. Since differently constructed index numbers can show wide discrepancies over the years, the decision to stabilize one index rather than another is tantamount to selecting one monetary policy rather than another. What exactly do we want to stabilize? A general reference to price stabilization is not enough.

Should, for instance, prices of consumers' goods be kept stable and wage rates be permitted to increase in a growing economy? Or should consumers' goods prices be permitted to fall so that fixed income groups can share the fruits of progress? In other words, should wages rather than prices be stabilized? Or should we compromise by stabilizing a price average in which wages are included and given a relatively heavy weight?

More recently the discussion has moved away from these detailed questions of price stabilization. During the great depression the impact of price deflation and economic instability was such that it was generally felt that the foremost monetary aim should be economic stability and a high sustained level of employment, while effects on commodity prices were considered of secondary importance. During and after World War II, on the other hand, full-employment conditions created such inflationary pressures that the refined discussions of different shades of price stabilization lost all practical significance.

A Policy of Neutral Money

Price stabilization and a neutral money policy are alike in that they both seek to relegate money to a wholly *passive* role in economic affairs. The policy of price stabilization wants to stabilize the exchange value of a unit of money by stabilizing the *general* price level; the neutrality policy, in the narrower sense, tries to keep money from having a disruptive effect on the structure of *relative* prices.

Concerning a policy of neutral money we have already seen in Chapter 3 that it is closely connected with a philosophy of *laissez faire*. The supply of money would be so controlled that the effects on production and distribution would be exactly the same as in a magic nonmonetary economy which has overcome the shortcomings of barter. There is some similarity between this attitude and the theories of Say and Mill, but the difference is that the neutrality policy requires a highly complicated administration of the monetary system, whereas Say and Mill thought that money would not have any disequilibrating effects and that monetary policy was unnecessary.

According to the theory of neutral money a stable price level is no proof that all disturbing monetary causes are eliminated. As Friedrich A. Hayek puts it:

> If we have to recognize that, on the one hand, under a stable price level, relative prices may be changed by monetary influences, and on the other that relative prices may remain undisturbed only when the price level changes, we have to give up the generally received opinion that if the general price level remains the same, the tendencies towards economic equilibrium are not disturbed by monetary influences, and that disturbing influences from the side of money cannot make themselves felt otherwise than by causing a change of the general price level.[9]

While one can fully agree with Hayek's statement, it remains extremely difficult to formulate criteria for a neutral money policy. Even if we assume that a state of high employment is reached and maintained, the monetary authority would be expected to accommodate changes in liquidity preference; it would have to distinguish extensive and intensive expansion of production; it would be expected to keep the amount of money stable if prices fell owing to increased efficiency; it would have to provide an increasing population with more money; and since it could not influence individual prices, it would have to keep an eye on monopolistic prices and increase the quantity of money if this were necessary to prevent dangerous changes in the structure of relative prices.

If these requests seem formidable already, then a neutrality policy would even become self-contradictory under conditions of under-

[9] Friedrich A. Hayek, *Prices and Production* (New York: Macmillan Co., 1932), pp. 24 ff.

employment where additional money must be created to bring about an expansion of effective demand.

Limitations of Monetary Policy

Advocates of gold-flow mechanism, commercial-loan theory, neutral money, and price stabilization have in common that they believe their respective monetary policies would simultaneously solve all major problems of a market economy. Nationally, a high employment level would prevail; and internationally, integration of different national economic policies would balance international payments. Only monetary controls would be needed, and only monetary controls would fit the basic character of a market economy.

Today we tend to expect much less of monetary policy. We know that market processes are not always sufficiently competitive and that an unplanned economy does not always maintain a high employment level. We admit that unemployment can be the result of a monetary policy which was not neutral. But we doubt that monetary policy *alone* could lead the economy back to a high level of economic activity. We shall see that monetary policy must be supported by fiscal policy when changes in the supply and cost of money are not strong enough to raise aggregate demand in times of mass unemployment.

Even according to classical theory full employment equilibrium cannot be reached if wages tend to rise faster than productivity per man-hour and if the monetary authority keeps the supply of money limited. When the general price level is not permitted to rise, increasing wage costs cannot be met by increasing product prices and marginal firms must close down. Price stability will then be maintained at the cost of unemployment. If monopolistic organizations raise wages and prices in the face of a given level of demand, the necessary adjustment will be brought about by a fall in economic activity which permits a smaller turnover of goods and services at increased prices. This is the phenomenon called cost-push or administrative price inflation. It will be discussed in Chapter 28.

SUGGESTIONS FOR FURTHER READING

On the insignificance of money:

SAY, JEAN-BAPTISTE. *A Treatise on Political Economy,* Book I, chap. 15. Philadelphia: John Grigg, 1830.

NEISSER, HANS. "General Overproduction: A Study of Say's Law of Markets," *Journal of Political Economy,* Vol. XLII (August, 1934), pp. 433–65.

MILL, JOHN STUART. *Principles of Political Economy,* Book III, chaps. 7 and 14. London: Longmans, Green and Co., 1936.

On the gold-flow mechanism, see literature to Chapter 31. A simple introduction can be found in:

HALM, GEORGE N. *International Monetary Cooperation,* chap. 2. Chapel Hill: The University of North Carolina Press, 1945.

Criticisms of the commercial loan theory:

ROBERTSON, D. H. *Money,* chap. 5, pp. 99–102. New York: Pitman Publishing Corp., 1948.

ROBERTSON, D. H. *Essays in Monetary Theory,* chap. 2. London: Staples Press, 1948.

CURRIE, LAUCHLIN. *The Supply and Control of Money in the United States,* chap. 4. Cambridge, Mass.: Harvard University Press, 1934.

On price stability:

BOARD OF GOVERNORS OF THE FEDERAL RESERVE SYSTEM. "Proposals to Maintain Prices at Fixed Levels Through Monetary Action," *Federal Reserve Bulletin,* Vol. XXV, No. 4 (April, 1939), pp. 255–59. Reprinted in Lawrence S. Ritter's *Money and Economic Activity,* pp. 241–45 (Boston: Houghton Mifflin Co., 1952).

On monetary antirecession policies:

COMMITTEE FOR ECONOMIC DEVELOPMENT. *Monetary and Fiscal Policy for Greater Economic Stability.* New York, 1948.

———. *Defense Against Inflation, Policies for Price Stability in a Growing Economy.* New York: 1958.

FRIEDMAN, MILTON. *A Program for Monetary Stability.* New York: Fordham University Press, 1960.

HELLER, WALTER W. "CED's Stabilizing Budget Policy After Ten Years," *American Economic Review,* Vol. XLVII (September, 1957). See also the literature referring to Chapter 27.

QUESTIONS AND PROBLEMS

1. "There cannot . . . be intrinsically a more insignificant thing, in the economy of society, than money; except in the character of a contrivance for sparing time and labor. It is a machine for doing quickly and commodiously, what would be done, though less quickly and commodiously, without it: and like many other kinds of machinery, it only exerts a distinct and independent influence of its own when it gets out of order" (John Stuart Mill). Discuss.
2. "A product is no sooner created, than it, from that instant, affords a market for other products to the full extent of its own value" (Jean-Baptiste Say). Do you agree?
3. Can it be said that the gold standard does not require a conscious monetary policy because gold serves as an automatic brake in the credit machine?

4. "Nine out of ten advocates of 'elastic' monetary systems neglect that phenomenon called the velocity of circulation of money . . ." (D. H. Robertson). Explain.
5. "If the loan is for a short time and secured by goods passing from the producer to the consumer, there emerges at time of sale of goods the proceeds by which the loan can be paid off; consequently short-time commercial paper is regarded as the safest form of liquid assets a bank can take" (J. Lawrence Laughlin). Comment.
6. "The commercial-loan theory of money disregards the facts that the supply of commercial paper is not independent of the rate of discount and that short-term commercial credit is just one form of financing among many." Explain.
7. Is it correct and sufficient to state that the aim of monetary policy is price stability?
8. "The aims of price stabilization and of neutrality of money are not identical. Taken together they would amount to the stabilization of money in its two functions as a unit of account and as a medium of exchange. But these two aims are often incompatible." Discuss.
9. Discuss the aims and limitations of modern monetary policy.

BOOK TWO

Monetary Policy

PART IV

The Supply of Money

Chapter 11 TREASURY AND MONETARY POLICY

The Monetary Authority

In previous chapters we repeatedly had to refer to the monetary authority which determines the objectives of monetary policy and, through use of its various instruments, influences the supply of money. The term "monetary authority" permitted us to remain in the realm of generalities, to ignore differences between the monetary systems of various countries, and to hide the fact that we must deal with not one but two monetary authorities: central bank and treasury.

For a more detailed study of the monetary system we must operate with more definite assumptions. Because monetary institutions differ from nation to nation, we choose the monetary system of the United States. But much of what we shall learn will be applicable to other countries as well because the basic problems are essentially the same. For instance, in spite of variations in details, all monetary systems suffer from a potential conflict between central bank and treasury.

In the United States the monetary authority rests, in the last analysis, with the Congress. The Congress, however, has delegated the authority over current monetary decisions to several agencies, particularly the Treasury and the Federal Reserve.[1] Unfortunately, it did this without providing clear guiding principles and without distinctly demarcating areas of responsibility. Moreover, little has been done to co-ordinate and integrate the activities of different government agencies in the field of monetary and fiscal policies.

Could we not avoid these difficulties? Could not the power to act in monetary matters be lodged firmly in one agency only? This has been tried in many countries. It was thought best to completely divorce the central bank, the monetary authority, from the executive branch of the government and particularly from the treasury, the government's fiscal agent. Monetary policy, it was argued, has only one aim, that of regulating the supply of money in the best interest of the whole economy, and this policy aim must be protected against any temptation on the part of the government to solve its financial problems by inflationary means.

It was long taken for granted that the central bank, as monetary authority, should enjoy complete independence. This attitude implied belief in an autonomous and automatic monetary policy of the types discussed in Chapter 10. Monetary policy had to be reduced to such simple terms that they could be written into the very charter of the central bank. Simple objectives, such as stable exchange rates or stable prices, were to be reached by automatic mechanisms which left no leeway for conflicting interpretations. If, for instance, the monetary gold reserve declined, rediscount rates had to be raised. The ideal central bank was to be constructed like a foolproof camera where the same motion winds up the shutter and moves the film to make double exposures impossible. Such a system, it was believed, would be the best protection against unbalanced budgets and government deficit spending.

When a central banking system was created for the United States in 1913, the new structure, characteristically, was based both on the gold-flow mechanism and on the commercial-loan theory: a combination of the two automatic devices for regulating the supply of money.

It proved impossible, however, to keep central banks in this independent position, and the Federal Reserve was no exception. We know now that monetary policy cannot be completely divorced from general economic policy. It is still true, of course, that governments

[1] The Federal Reserve System of the United States is distinguished from other central banking systems by the fact that twelve regional central banks (Federal Reserve banks) are co-ordinated by a Board of Governors in Washington. By referring to "the Federal Reserve" we treat the whole system as if it were one central bank.

are often tempted to solve their financial difficulties by resort to deficit financing, and such a policy will normally have undesirable inflationary consequences in times of high employment. On the other hand, both modern economic analysis and practical experience have shown that in times of depression a co-operation of monetary and fiscal policies may become imperative, and government deficit spending, formerly considered a sin, may become a virtue after all.

Thus, whatever the devices for keeping monetary policy independent, the dualism in modern monetary systems will continue until it is resolved by a perfect integration of monetary and fiscal policies.

The Treasury and Gold

The United States Treasury is not an agency which is primarily concerned with monetary policy, but it performs several monetary functions, and its fiscal and debt management policies may powerfully support or obstruct monetary management by the Federal Reserve.

The Treasury buys and sells gold in unlimited amounts at a fixed price of $35.00 an ounce, which means that one dollar is equal in value to 13.714 grains of fine gold. As long as the Treasury is willing and able to buy and sell gold at this fixed price, the value of gold and dollar are firmly connected.

The Treasury does not have the right to change the price at which it buys gold. This is done, if at all, by the ultimate monetary authority of the United States, the Congress. The Congress may lower or raise the price of gold, that is, appreciate or depreciate the dollar. But the United States, as a member of the International Monetary Fund, would have to abide by the Bretton Woods Agreement concerning changes of par values of currencies (see Chapter 35).

Since the Treasury buys most imported or domestically mined gold, how is it to pay for it? The answer to this question is important because the Treasury's financing of its gold purchases determines in part the domestic money supply. Furthermore, these purchases involve rather large amounts. At the end of 1959 the gold holdings of the Treasury were $19.5 billion.

The Treasury pays for gold with checks drawn on its deposit with the Federal Reserve. The purchase will have a potential expansionary effect on the money circulation. It may seem as if purchasing power had only changed hands from the Treasury to the seller of the gold. But in the process the reserve position of the commercial banks has been improved so that they can create more demand deposits. The seller of the gold deposits the Treasury check with his commercial bank, and the bank, in turn, deposits it with its Federal Reserve bank. We assume that the commercial bank, a member of the Federal Reserve System, is required to hold a reserve of, say, 20 per cent against its customers' demand deposits and that this reserve must consist of deposits with its Federal Reserve bank. The commercial bank has increased its reserve deposit and its customers' demand deposits by the same amount and has, therefore, an excess reserve equal to 80 per cent of the amount of the Treasury's gold purchase. No other bank's reserve position has been weakened by the transaction because the check was drawn not on another commercial bank but on the Treasury's account in the Federal Reserve. In Chapter 14 we shall see how on the basis of these excess reserves a multiple creation of demand deposits can take place in the banking system as a whole.

The Treasury, as a rule, will reimburse itself for these gold purchases by issuing gold certificates to the Federal Reserve. The Federal Reserve banks will credit the Treasury's deposits with the amount in question, while the gold certificates will appear as an asset item in the balance sheet of the Federal Reserve banks. But while this policy finances the Treasury's gold purchases, it lays the foundation for an even larger potential expansion of the money circulation. On the basis of the gold certificates the Federal Reserve banks can, for example, through open-market purchases of government securities, increase commercial banks' reserves by a multiple amount, and the commercial banks, in turn, can embark on a creation of credit several times the amount of their newly gained reserves. This process, too, will be discussed in Chapter 14.

The Treasury may want to "sterilize" the purchased gold. By gold sterilization we mean a policy which prevents gold purchases from having an expansionary effect upon the domestic monetary circulation. The Treasury can sterilize gold (1) by abstaining from issuing gold certificates to the Federal Reserve and (2) by selling securities to commercial banks or their customers.

When the Treasury abstains from issuing gold certificates, it sterilizes "supercharged" money (see Chapter 6, p. 64) on which the Federal Reserve could superimpose a multiple amount of commercial bank reserves, that is, "high-powered" money.

When the Treasury sells securities, it not only reimburses itself for the gold purchase (that is, for the reduction of its deposit with the Federal Reserve) but it also reduces commercial banks' reserves (which had been increased through the gold purchase) to their previous level. Thus, when the Treasury refrains from issuing gold certificates, it prevents credit expansion on the central bank level, while the selling of securities compensates for the remaining expansion on the commercial bank level.

The Treasury and Silver

The Treasury also supplies part of the currency in circulation, though in quantity the Federal Reserve notes are far more important (in April, 1960, the circulation of Federal Reserve notes was 5.7 times that of Treasury currency). As a matter of fact, our monetary system could be greatly simplified if Treasury currency were replaced by Federal Reserve notes of smaller denominations. Only subsidiary silver coin and minor coin would then remain as Treasury currency.

Why, then, do we have seven kinds of Treasury currency? In part, the answer is historical. Some kinds of Treasury currency are mere relics, remains of issues which grew out of one emergency or another and are still not fully retired. The amounts involved are negligible.[2]

More serious is the case of silver certificates, which constitute

[2] $149 million silver dollars and $2,251 million silver bullion were held as reserve against silver certificates. The Treasury notes of 1890 are silver certificates. Subsidiary silver- and minor-coin need no explanation beyond that given in Chapter 4. United States notes are the remainder of the so-called greenbacks which were issued during the Civil War. The national bank notes were issued by national banks during the period of the National Banking System which preceded the Federal Reserve System. They were backed by government bonds. To increase the supply of currency during the emergency of 1932, the Home Loan Bank Bill permitted a potential issue of $900 millions in national bank notes for a 3-year period. Since 1935, when the national banks ceased to issue national bank notes, the notes which were still outstanding were classified as Treasury currency since the federal government assumed responsibility for them.

To facilitate the change-over from national bank notes to Federal Reserve notes, the Federal Reserve banks were permitted to issue Federal Reserve *bank* notes which were, like the national bank notes, backed by government bonds. Federal Reserve bank notes were issued in 1918 to replace silver certificates (when part of the silver reserve was sold to England) and in 1933 during the banking crisis. Federal Reserve bank notes, already printed in 1933, were issued in 1942–43, as a Treasury liability, to meet an increased demand for cash. Since June, 1945, Federal Reserve bank notes can no longer be issued.

Treasury Currency in Circulation, April 30, 1960
(In Millions of Dollars)

Standard silver dollars (in circulation)	$ 300
Silver certificates and Treasury notes of 1890	2,094
Subsidiary silver coin	1,467
Minor coin	543
United States notes	312
National bank notes	56
Federal Reserve bank notes	102

Source: Adapted from *Federal Reserve Bulletin*, June, 1960.

the largest item of Treasury currency. Silver certificates are claims on silver on deposit in the Treasury. The Silver Purchase Act of 1934 requires the Treasury to buy, with newly issued silver certificates, newly mined silver at a price well above the market price. These purchases are to continue until the total amount of silver held by the Treasury (and valued at $1.29 per ounce) has reached one fourth of its combined gold and silver stocks.

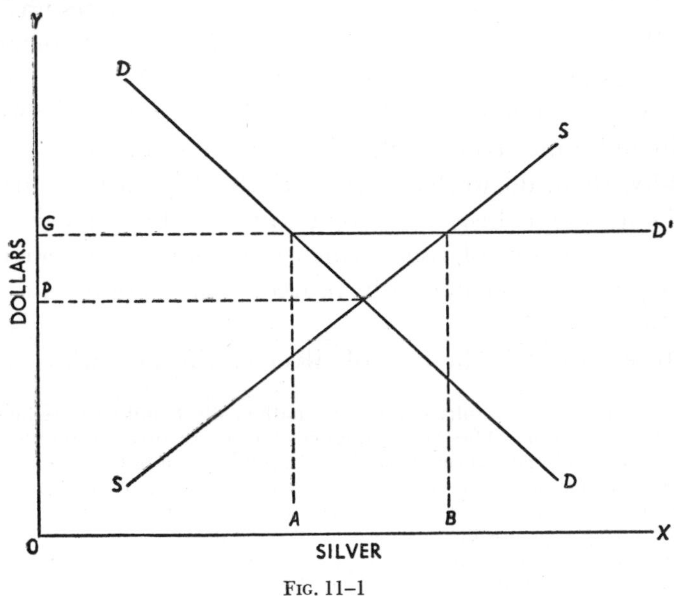

FIG. 11–1

This silver-purchase policy cannot be defended on monetary grounds. If more currency is needed, it can be created with ease through the issue of Federal Reserve notes on the basis of existing gold reserves. If gold reserves should ever become inadequate, gold reserve requirements can be relaxed or abolished. To add silver certificates to the Federal Reserve notes in circulation is costly and an unnecessary complication of our monetary system. The silver-purchase policy can be explained only on political grounds. A small, but politically powerful, industry has succeeded in having the Treasury maintain a perfectly elastic demand for its product at an artificially high price.

Figure 11–1 illustrates what happens when the Treasury buys silver in unlimited amounts at a price above the market price. *SS* represents the supply and *DD* the normal or market demand for silver.

Without interference by the Treasury's silver purchases the market price *P* would equate demand and supply. Now the Treasury is forced to buy all newly mined silver which is not industrially used at price *G*. Since the demand curve *DD'* becomes perfectly elastic at price *G*, the market price is now established at this level and the Treasury has to store away amount *AB*. This amount is not needed as monetary reserve and should have been either used for industrial purposes or not produced at all.

When this nonsensical policy was advocated, it was said that the silver purchases would aid silver standard countries like China or Mexico, whose monetary units would exchange for more dollars than before. Actually, the United States' silver purchases greatly embarrassed these countries because the raised dollar price of silver amounted to an appreciation of their currencies which was not justified by their domestic price levels or their international payments position. Their export goods were made too expensive, and they were forced off the silver standard since, according to Gresham's law, silver flowed to the market where the highest price was paid, that is, to the United States.

The political pressure which silver producers were able to exert seems to indicate the persistence in some quarters of the belief that gold as the single monetary base is not large enough to support a sufficient monetary superstructure and that an adequate supply of money can be assured only when some kind of bimetallism is used. In times when the supply of currency is no longer of any consequence within the total money supply, this is a specious argument.

Consideration of the Silver Purchase Act shows that it would be naïve to assume that our monetary policies are always parts of a consistent effort to supply the economy with the right amount of money in the cheapest possible way.

Monetary Implications of Fiscal Policy

The United States Treasury is the greatest single spender of money in our economy. Its actions, therefore, are of monetary importance whether the Treasury is conscious of this fact or not. When the Treasury collects revenue through taxation or through borrowing from savings, it reduces the purchasing power in the hands of the public; when it spends money, it also increases the public's spending power. When the Treasury spends more than it collects through taxation, a budget deficit is created and must be financed by borrowing: the national debt increases. When tax revenues exceed expenditures, the Treasury accumulates a budget surplus, which can be used to reduce the national debt. The effects of these deficits and surpluses depend on the ownership of the debt and the general state of economic activity.

The Treasury can borrow part of the public's savings and will, in this case, reduce the purchasing power of the public. When the Treasury spends the borrowed money, the result is not inflationary since the total amount of spending tends to remain the same. If, on the other hand, the Treasury borrows formerly hoarded funds from the public,[3] total expenditure increases. When the Treasury borrows from commercial banks or from the Federal Reserve banks, the effect will also tend to be inflationary. Since both categories of banks can create money, assuming that they are still able to fulfill their reserve requirements, the monetary circulation increases, and the government spending out of borrowed funds is added to the previous level of spending.

This second type of deficit spending is extremely important for monetary policy. When the monetary authority has in vain tried to increase aggregate spending by supplying additional money, it is only logical that the money should then be brought into circulation by some form of government deficit spending. Here we see monetary and fiscal policy co-operate in an attempt to increase effective demand.

A budget surplus means that taxpayers had to limit their expenditures but that the Treasury has not spent the money. The money may just remain idle so that the velocity of circulation of money is reduced. It is more likely, however, that the government will use its budget surplus to retire part of the national debt. The economic effects of this operation will depend on the ownership of the retired part of the debt. If the debt was held by the public, the purchasing power of the bondholder is now increased while that of the taxpayer has been decreased. These effects may be of some interest, depending on the consumption and investment habits of the persons involved. No great changes in aggregate expenditure can be expected, however.

If the retired bonds were held by commercial banks, excess reserves may increase since the banks' deposits with the Federal Reserve banks will rise when the Treasury's checks are deposited. It is possible,

[3] "This will occur, for example, if the net effect of . . . refunding operations is to shorten the maturity structure. As the debt shortens, ownership tends to shift from 'savings-type' investors to investors who hold 'Governments' as a 'money substitute.' Thus the Treasury, in effect, borrows funds that would otherwise be idle and releases longer term funds that flow into active use." Federal Reserve Bank of New York, *Monthly Review*, Vol. 41, No. 9 (September, 1959), p. 144.

though, that the Treasury will transfer an equal amount of its deposits from commercial banks to Federal Reserve banks at the same time. In this case the reserve position of the commercial banks remains unchanged.

Deflationary effects would be achieved if the Treasury decided to retire part of the national debt held by the Federal Reserve banks. In this case we should find that in the balance sheets of the Federal Reserve banks both Treasury deposits and securities are decreased by the same amount. The money collected from the taxpayer would not reappear in circulation, and the reserve position of the commercial banks would be weakened.

In Chapter 27 we shall see how this enormous spender, the United States Treasury, can be used to exert an equilibrating effect upon the economy by dampening economic fluctuations: in times of depression smaller tax receipts and increased government spending can help maintain a higher level of expenditure; while in times of prosperity, with higher tax revenues and cautious government spending, a surplus can be employed to exert a retarding effect in an otherwise overexpansive situation.

Treasury and Debt Management

We have already seen that the Treasury's debt retirement policies may be of great importance from a monetary point of view. Actually, everything the Treasury does concerning the public debt is of monetary importance because we find large holdings of government securities among the assets of both the commercial banks and the Federal Reserve banks. Furthermore, since one of the main instruments of the Federal Reserve is its open-market operations, it is obvious that Federal Reserve and Treasury must co-ordinate their activities in the securities market.

To understand the monetary importance of security prices we must become aware of the relationship which exists between security prices and interest rates. Rising rates of interest are connected with falling security prices, and rising security prices, with falling rates of interest. If a government bond pays 4 per cent, or $4 per $100 face value, the yield or actual rate of return will change with the bond's market price. If I have to pay more than $100, my actual yield will be less than 4 per cent; if I pay less than $100, my yield is higher than 4 per cent. Bond prices depend on many factors influencing demand and supply and, in the case of individual issues, on such qualities as maturity and gilt-edgedness. We shall return to these problems in Chapter 21.

The Treasury as the largest borrower is very much interested in the cost of borrowing, that is, in security prices and interest rates. In order to keep the cost of borrowing down it may be eager to keep security prices up. Suppose that in wartime the Treasury has to borrow enormous amounts and that it cannot be sure that these amounts will be forthcoming as a demand for securities by the saving public. Security prices may fall; interest rates may rise. At this point the Treasury requests the help of the Federal Reserve banks and the commercial banks, that is, the institutions which have the power to create money. In the extreme case the Treasury will ask the banks to purchase at a fixed price all the securities which the public is not willing to buy at that price.

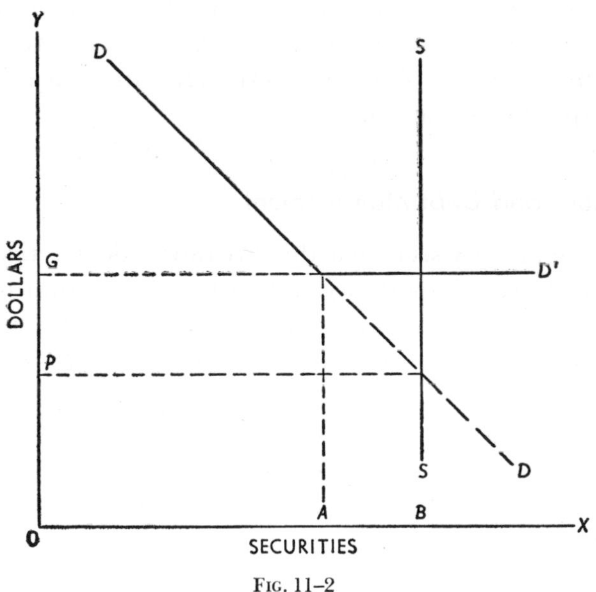

Fig. 11–2

This situation can be illustrated by Figure 11–2. *DD* indicates the normal market demand for securities out of savings, and *SS* the supply of securities. The *SS* curve is assumed to be completely inelastic because the Treasury takes the attitude that financial reasons, such as the cost of borrowing, must not be permitted to limit the war effort. However, the Treasury is not willing to sell its securities at price *P*, which would be the market price under prevailing conditions, but insists that price G be maintained through the readiness of the banks to take the excessive supply at that price. The amount AB is purchased with newly created money. This is the modern way of financing a war through inflation. The Treasury, instead of using the printing press as in former times, simply makes the creators of money buy its securities. This is a "monetization" of the public debt.

Here we see the Treasury and the Federal Reserve co-operating in the creation of inflationary conditions. If, on the other hand, the Treasury wants to maintain a high level of expenditure while the Federal Reserve is mainly concerned with alarming signs of price inflation, a conflict may arise, and there may be room for some honest disagreement as to whether the objectives of fiscal or monetary policy ought to prevail.

SUGGESTIONS FOR FURTHER READING

HARDY, CHARLES O. "Fiscal Operations as Instruments of Economic Stabilization," *The American Economic Review,* Supplement, Vol. XXXVIII (May, 1948), pp. 395–403. Reprinted in *Readings in Monetary Theory,* chap. 16 (Homewood, Ill.: Richard D. Irwin, Inc., 1951).

RITTER, LAWRENCE S. *Money and Economic Activity,* Part III. Boston: Houghton Mifflin Co., 1952.

SHAW, EDWARD S. *Money, Income, and Monetary Power,* chap. 11. Homewood, Ill.: Richard D. Irwin, Inc., 1950.

QUESTIONS AND PROBLEMS

1. "Whoever is to dominate the policy decisions, fiscal policy and monetary (credit and debt) policy obviously must be considered jointly if lack of coordination and direct conflict between the two major monetary-fiscal arms of the government are to be avoided" (G. L. Bach). Comment.
2. What are the immediate and the possible future effects connected with the purchase of gold by the Treasury and the issue of an equivalent amount of gold certificates?
3. How can the Treasury achieve a "sterilization" of the purchased gold?
4. "Debt management policy, which is the responsibility of the Treasury, and credit and monetary policy, which is the responsibility of the Federal Reserve, must constantly be coordinated" (*The Federal Reserve System. Purposes and Functions,* Washington, D.C., 1954). Explain.
5. Illustrate by diagram the effect of silver purchases by the Treasury at a price above the market price.

6. "The silver policy of the United States can be condemned on so many scores that even the most cautious economist may venture upon an *ex cathedra* denunciation" (Kenneth E. Boulding). Discuss.
7. Can it be said that rising rates of interest are always connected with falling security prices? Explain the existing connection.
8. "When the Federal Reserve undertakes to prevent yields on Government securities from rising above a pattern agreed upon with the Treasury, it has to buy all Government securities which others want to sell and loses its control over the supply of money." Correct? Explain.

Chapter 12 THE FEDERAL RESERVE

The Federal Reserve as Monetary Authority

The Treasury shares its monetary powers with the Federal Reserve. By Federal Reserve we mean the twelve Federal Reserve banks and the Board of Governors of the Federal Reserve System, whose function is to give cohesion to the whole central banking system of the country and, in co-operation with the Treasury, to guide the country's monetary policy. In speaking of the Federal Reserve, therefore, we refer to what would be called a central bank in most other countries.

Frequently our interpretation of the term "Federal Reserve" will be even broader and include the so-called member banks, that is, those commercial banks which are members of the Federal Reserve System. Member banks must hold their legally required reserves mainly in the form of deposits with the Federal Reserve banks.[1] For the time being we assume that all commercial banks are member banks.

The strictly monetary tasks of the Federal Reserve are far greater than those of the Treasury. It issues more currency than the Treasury, and through the reserve accounts of those commercial banks which are members of the system, it controls to a large extent the potential volume of deposit money. In addition, the Federal Reserve performs such service functions as the collection and clearing of checks or the distribution of currency. Again, these services outweigh the Treasury's technical activities in the monetary field.

Nevertheless, it would be wrong to jump to the conclusion that the Federal Reserve is the stronger of the two monetary arms of the United States government. The Federal Reserve can see that the commercial banks are put in a position which enables them to expand credit. But neither Federal Reserve banks nor commercial banks can

[1] About membership requirements see Chapter 18.

actually cause increased borrowing and increased expenditure. In this respect the Treasury is in a much stronger position. We have seen, furthermore, that the Federal Reserve operates in an economic climate which to a large extent is conditioned by the Treasury's actions. Thus, even in the monetary field, the Treasury may be stronger than the more specialized Federal Reserve.

The activities of the Federal Reserve banks are mirrored in the so-called "Statement of Condition of the Federal Reserve Banks." The four most important items of this consolidated balance sheet, therefore, can be used as an introduction into Federal Reserve problems. See Table 12–1.

TABLE 12–1

THE FOUR MOST IMPORTANT ITEMS OF THE STATEMENT OF CONDITION OF THE FEDERAL RESERVE BANKS*

(Rounded Off in Billions of Dollars, End of May, 1960)

ASSETS		LIABILITIES	
Gold certificates	19	Federal Reserve notes	27
Total loans and securities	26	Member bank deposits	18
	45		45

*Adapted from the *Federal Reserve Bulletin*, June, 1960. How important the four items are is shown by the fact that total assets were about $51 billion.

Federal Reserve and Gold

In Chapter 11 we followed the Treasury's activities in relation to gold and saw that a gold purchase reduces the Treasury's deposits but increases the reserve deposits of commercial banks, thereby creating the basis for a potential credit expansion. We saw, furthermore, that the Treasury will issue gold certificates to the Federal Reserve banks, which credit the Treasury's account for the amount in question. The Treasury's deposit in the Federal Reserve is now the same as before the gold purchase, because the sale of the gold certificates equals the original gold purchase. In the balance sheet of the Federal Reserve banks we find an increase in the commercial banks' reserve deposits and an increase in gold certificates. The increase in reserve deposits is the result of the Treasury's gold purchase because the sellers of the gold deposited the Treasury checks with their commercial banks, which in turn deposited them with the Federal Reserve banks.

At present the Federal Reserve banks are required to hold a 25 per cent reserve in the form of gold certificates against (1) their deposit liabilities and (2) Federal Reserve notes in circulation. $100 of gold certificates, therefore, may support either $400 of Federal Reserve notes in circulation or $400 of member bank deposits. Suppose that the original gold purchase of the Treasury was $100 and that the Treasury issued $100 of gold certificates to the Federal Reserve. The Treasury's deposit with the Federal Reserve is now unchanged, while gold certificates and member bank deposits are each increased by $100. This means that the Federal Reserve banks have $75 more gold certificates than they need for the backing of $100 of member bank reserve deposits. They can now insure that member bank reserve deposits increase by another $300, for $100 of gold certificates permit the Federal Reserve banks to satisfy the 25 per cent reserve requirement for a total of $400 of reserve deposits. We shall see that they can achieve this increase of reserve deposits by buying $300 of government securities on the open market. The member banks, in turn, can then use their increased reserves as a basis of multiple credit creation through loans and investments, whose limits are determined by the member banks' legal reserve requirements. If, for example, the member banks have $400 of additional reserves and if the legally required reserves are 20 per cent, the total creation of deposit money could reach $2,000.

But while the Federal Reserve's gold reserve sets an upper limit to credit expansion, we cannot be sure that this limit will always be reached (1) because the demand for credit may be lacking and (2) because the Federal Reserve may not want to have credit expanded to such an extent. If the Federal Reserve does not want to increase the money supply, it can follow a gold sterilization policy of its own: the Federal Reserve banks will not use their increased gold certificate holdings as backing for increased member bank reserves and may even sell securities on the open market to reduce the reserves of the commercial banks if these reserves should increase alarmingly in consequence of the Treasury's gold purchases. The Federal Reserve banks may also increase the reserve requirements of the member banks within limits.

We see that the Federal Reserve and the Treasury, between them, have a number of methods by which to undo the real or potential expansionist effects of gold purchases.[2] Such policies of gold sterilization are, of course, a violation of the rules of the gold-flow mechanism. The very structure of the Federal Reserve System with its gold reserve requirements still shows that gold movements were once supposed to

[2] In Chapter 17 we shall learn that these powers may prove insufficient in case of a very large gold inflow.

exert expansionist or contractionist effects on the domestic monetary circulation.

When we now turn to a study of the techniques by which the Federal Reserve banks increase or decrease member banks' reserves, we must remember that these policies are today rather independent of gold reserves. If a lack of gold reserves should really become a roadblock to an otherwise desired monetary expansion, congressional action could lower or even remove gold reserve requirements. If, on the other hand, a very large gold inflow should lead to undesirably large excess reserves of the member banks, the Federal Reserve could be given the right to change the reserve requirements for the member banks beyond the present statutory limits.

Federal Reserve Credit

The item "Total loans and securities" in the balance sheet of the Federal Reserve banks is the result of these banks' lending and investment operations. Federal Reserve banks rediscount commercial paper, make advances to banks, or buy securities from banks or from nonbank investors. Total loans and securities, therefore, marks the amount of Federal Reserve credit outstanding.

Gold purchases are largely independent of Federal Reserve policy. The Federal Reserve takes all gold certificates issued by the Treasury, while the Treasury, in turn, buys at a fixed price all gold offered for sale. Federal Reserve credit, on the other hand, is supposed to be under the conscious control of the Federal Reserve, unless the Federal Reserve is persuaded or compelled to buy at a fixed price or within a given price range all government securities which the Treasury cannot sell to investors at that price.

The Federal Reserve's main instruments, lending and open-market operations, are designed to change the volume of member bank reserves and to indirectly influence the supply of money. The member banks can at any time borrow from their Federal Reserve banks when they find themselves short of reserves. However, the fact that banks do not like to be forced to borrow in order to fulfill their reserve requirements tends to restrain bank credit expansion. This tendency is enhanced when the Federal Reserve increases the discount rate to signify its wish that member banks restrain their borrowing customers.

More important today are the Federal Reserve banks' open-market operations in government securities.[3] If the securities are bought

[3] In May, 1960, the Federal Reserve banks' holdings of U.S. government securities were \$20,035,129,000, while total loans amounted to only \$371,203,000.

from member banks, member bank deposits in the Federal Reserve banks are increased; if the securities are bought from nonbank investors, the result is about the same, inasmuch as the seller deposits the check with his commercial bank. The sale of securities by the Federal Reserve banks diminishes member bank reserves by the same process in reverse. Selling operations, of course, are limited by the amount of "ammunition" previously accumulated in the form of government securities held by the Federal Reserve banks.

The principle of open-market operations is so simple that it is important not to overestimate the powers of this instrument of monetary policy. Existing excess reserves of the member banks, for instance, indicate that open-market purchases would not lead to credit expansion, for the member banks are already technically able to expand credit but have not succeeded in doing so. Furthermore, the expansive effect of open-market purchases will be counterbalanced if banks are the newly gained reserve accounts to reduce their indebtedness with the Federal Reserve banks. However, it must not be concluded that open-market and discount policies always counterbalance one another in their effects on bank reserves and the supply of money. For instance, open-market sales can put the commercial banks in a reserve position where a rising bank rate will be more effective.

Where do the funds come from which the Federal Reserve banks use in their attempts to regulate the supply of money? Certainly we cannot point to the principal asset items (gold certificates, government securities) for we are trying to find out how the Federal Reserve banks can buy these titles. It might seem more reasonable that the funds come from the Federal Reserve banks' capital accounts or from the deposits of the member banks. But the capital accounts amounted in May, 1960 to only $1¼ billion compared with $45 billion of gold certificates and securities; and the reserve deposits of the member banks come into existence in connection with gold and security purchases.

The source of the Federal Reserve funds is indicated by our frequent reference to credit entries in the accounts of the Federal Reserve banks. The funds with which the Federal Reserve banks buy are mainly *created,* for the Federal Reserve, as monetary authority, has the power to create money. Whether this is done by issuing paper money (Federal Reserve notes) or by book entries is of only secondary importance.

It is evident that the Federal Reserve banks can also completely destroy money through open-market sales of securities and the sale of gold certificates. Once more, however, it must be stressed that the Federal Reserve, though potentially able to create and destroy money, is not always in full control of the monetary situation. For instance, it may not be able to absorb (through open-market sales or increased reserve requirements) the excess reserves of the member banks and thus guarantee protection against price inflation. But it may be even more handicapped when credit expansion is desired. The power of the Federal Reserve banks ends when they have made additional reserve money available. In doing so they may have exerted a stimulating effect by lowering rates of interest. If they cannot induce increased private investment, however, they can increase expenditure only by financing some sort of deficit spending by government agencies.

Federal Reserve Notes in Circulation

The Federal Reserve banks issue the principal kind of currency, the Federal Reserve notes. They also receive Treasury currency from the Treasury, for which they credit the Treasury's deposits. Federal Reserve notes, when in circulation, are a liability of the Federal Reserve banks which issued them. Treasury currency in the Federal Reserve banks is an asset item called "Other cash." In May, 1960 it amounted to $340,835,000. Other cash and Federal Reserve notes not yet issued but held in readiness constitute the stock of paper money and coin out of which the Federal Reserve banks can satisfy an increased demand for currency.

Whenever the public wants to draw more currency out of the commercial banks, the commercial banks, in turn, can get more currency from the Federal Reserve banks and have the amount charged to their reserve accounts. Nonmember banks get needed currency through member banks.

The Federal Reserve does not try to limit the use of currency in any way. Rather, it stands ready to supply the public with any amount and kind of currency desired within a given total supply of money. Thus, as the seasonal demand for currency increases, more currency flows into circulation. Currency is automatically retired when the public deposits it with the commercial banks and when these banks, in turn, deposit it with the Federal Reserve banks, deeming it surplus to their need for cash.

This problem of an elastic currency supply can be handled with ease when member banks and Federal Reserve banks command sufficient reserves. It must be remembered that a demand for more currency on the part of the public weakens the reserve position of the commercial banks since it reduces the commercial banks' demand deposits and reserves by the same amount. A greater demand for currency will have a disturbing effect unless the commercial banks possess excess reserves or unless they can borrow from the Federal Reserve banks.

On the Federal Reserve level a similar reserve problem in connection with an increased demand for currency may arise. The same gold reserves of 25 per cent are to be held against both Federal Reserve notes and member bank reserve accounts. Suppose that before the increased demand for currency, credit had been expanded to the utmost, so that no "free" reserves of gold were available. If the public wants to change from deposit money to currency to the extent, say, of $1 million, a credit contraction would have to follow. Assuming a 20 per cent reserve requirement for commercial banks, $1 million deposit money requires a gold reserve of $50,000, while an equal amount of Federal Reserve notes in circulation needs a gold backing of $250,-000. The $50,000 in gold serves as a 25 per cent backing of $200,000 of member bank reserve deposits on the basis of which the member banks can create up to $1 million deposit money. If the public shifts to $1 million Federal Reserve notes, $250,000 of gold will be required as backing, that is, five times as much as in the case of deposit money. The substitution of Federal Reserve notes for deposit money could, therefore, lead to a contraction of deposit money of $5 million.

With large free reserves of gold or with excess reserves on the part of member banks, a problem does not arise. But it is possible to envisage a situation where the asymmetrical construction of the monetary reserves for currency and deposit money could cause trouble.

Member Bank Deposits

The item "Total deposits" in the Statement of Condition of the Federal Reserve Banks includes the reserve deposits of the member banks, the general account of the U.S. Treasurer, the deposits of other government agencies, and the deposits of foreign banks. With $17,849 million out of a total of $18,975 million the member bank reserve deposits were by far the largest in May, 1960. We have already seen that these reserve accounts are of crucial importance for monetary policy since they limit the credit creation by commercial banks and, therefore, the supply of deposit money. This item, as a matter of fact, gives the whole Federal Reserve System its name, and much of Federal Reserve policy consists of actions designed to influence member bank reserves, as the core of the monetary system, through open-market and lending operations.

The Federal Reserve has a more direct means of control, however. It is empowered to change, within limits, the legal reserve requirements, thus changing not the size of the existing reserves but the multiplying factor in the process of multiple credit expansion by commercial banks.[4]

The altering of reserve requirements is not a normal everyday instrument of Federal Reserve policy. It is too powerful and too abrupt. Its main purpose is to do away with excess reserves which hinder the application of discount or open-market policies.

Apart from their function in the process of regulating the total supply of deposit money, reserve accounts of the member banks serve as the basis for the process of check clearing. This process is handled by the Federal Reserve banks and constitutes their most important service function.

An example will explain the technicalities of check clearing. Suppose that a corporation in Boston, Mass., makes a payment by check, drawn on the First National Bank of Boston, to a corporation in Chicago, Ill. The Chicago corporation deposits the endorsed check with the First National Bank of Chicago, which credits the amount to the account of the Chicago corporation, conditionally at first and then unconditionally after collection. The Chicago bank sends the check on to the Federal Reserve Bank of Chicago and is given a deferred cerdit. This credit is changed to an unconditional credit according to a somewhat arbitrary time schedule, which corresponds roughly with the time involved in the collection of the check. The Federal Reserve Bank of Chicago sends the check to the Federal Reserve Bank of Boston and informs the Interdistrict Settlement Fund, which the

[4] Depending on the geographical location of the member banks (that is, their classification as central-reserve-city, reserve-city, or "country" banks) the Federal Reserve can change reserve requirements on net demand deposits for central-reserve-city banks and reserve-city banks between a minimum of 10 and a maximum of 22 per cent, and between 7 and 17 per cent for "country" banks. Reserve requirements for all three categories on time deposits can vary between 3 and 6 per cent. The legal requirements in effect June 1, 1960 were, for example, 18 per cent for central-reserve-city banks, 16¼ per cent for reserve-city banks, and 11 per cent for "country" banks on demand deposits. Reserve requirements on time deposits were uniformly 5 per cent. It may well be argued that the powers of the Federal Reserve be improved and increased to enable it to deal with large excess reserves which may result from gold inflow or monetization of government securities.

twelve Federal Reserve banks maintain in Washington.[5] The Interdistrict Settlement Fund credits the account of the Federal Reserve Bank of Chicago and debits the account of the Federal Reserve Bank of Boston. When the Federal Reserve Bank of Boston receives the check, it charges the account of the First National Bank of Boston and sends the check on to this bank, which, in turn, debits the account of the Boston corporation which made the check payment. Finally, the canceled check is handed over to the Boston corporation, which can use it as proof that its obligation to the Chicago corporation has been paid.

SUGGESTIONS FOR FURTHER READING

BOARD OF GOVERNORS OF THE FEDERAL RESERVE SYSTEM. *The Federal Reserve System. Purposes and Functions,* 3d ed. Washington, D.C., 1954.

BURGESS, W. RANDOLPH. *The Reserve Banks and the Money Market,* rev. ed. New York: Harper & Brothers, 1946.

DAY, A. C. L., and BEZA, STERIE T. *Money and Income,* chap. 13. New York: Oxford University Press, 1960.

GOLDENWEISER, E. A. "Instruments of Federal Reserve Policy," *Banking Studies,* pp. 389–414. Washington, D.C.: Board of Governors of the Federal Reserve System, 1941.

GOLDENWEISER, E. A. *Monetary Management.* New York: McGraw-Hill Book Co., Inc., 1949.

RITTER, LAWRENCE S. *Money and Economic Activity,* Part II, chaps. 6–7. Boston: Houghton Mifflin Co., 1952. Many selections in these two chapters are reprints from the second edition of the above mentioned Federal Reserve publication.

WHITTLESEY, CHARLES R. *Readings in Money and Banking,* Part V. New York: W. W. Norton & Co., Inc., 1952.

See also literature to Chapters 16 to 18.

QUESTIONS AND PROBLEMS

1. Can the Federal Reserve, if it so desires, always increase the amount of money in circulation?
2. Gold certificates, discounts and securities, deposits, and notes in circulation are the principal items in the Federal Reserve banks' statement of condition. From the *Federal Reserve Bulletin* find the most recent figures for these items. Is it true to say that no one of them can change without a corresponding change in one or more of the other three?

[5] The Interdistrict Settlement Fund is a gold certificate fund in Washington through which money "is constantly being transferred by telegraphic order from the account of one Reserve Bank to that of another." See *The Federal Reserve System, Purposes and Functions* (Washington, D.C.: Board of Governors of the Federal Reserve System, 1954), p. 159.

3. Discuss the importance of gold in the Federal Reserve System.
4. Explain the main instruments at the disposal of the Federal Reserve and show how their use influences the reserves of the member banks.
5. Enumerate and discuss the major factors which supply and absorb member bank reserves.
6. Where do the funds come from which the Federal Reserve banks use in their lending operations?
7. Is it correct to say that substitution of currency for demand deposits by the public could possibly lead to a multiple contraction of the total quantity of money? Under what circumstances?
8. What happens when a customer of a bank in San Francisco makes a check payment to a firm in St. Louis?

Chapter 13 THE COMMERCIAL BANKS

The Commercial Banks as Monetary Institutions

Commercial banks are institutions which extend credit out of funds which they own, borrow, or create. The most characteristic feature of commercial banks, one which distinguishes them from other private credit institutions, is their ability to create money. Commercial banks hold the checking accounts of their customers. These accounts are payable on demand and subject to transfer by check. Since demand deposits are money, the commercial banks can create money by creating claims (that is, demand deposits) against themselves in favor of borrowers or of sellers of securities. In Chapter 14 we shall follow this process of credit creation.

Other private credit institutions cannot create money because they do not hold checking accounts. Savings banks in the United States, for instance, depend in their investment operations almost entirely on the savings of their depositors. When they lend or invest they do not add to total purchasing power because the purchasing power of their depositors is temporarily reduced. In other words, savings banks act as intermediaries only, not as suppliers of additional money. We shall see that commercial banks act in both capacities.

Since they create deposit money, the commercial banks play an important part in the monetary system. They are the link between the monetary authorities and the public but are not a part of the monetary authority. They neither determine the aims of monetary policy nor are they mainly motivated by the desire to reach objectives set by the monetary authority. They are in business to earn profit for their stockholders. The Federal Reserve banks, on the other hand, are not prompted by profit considerations. They pursue their policies in the best interest of the economy, as they see it, and are willing to incur losses when necessary.

Another distinction between commercial banks and Federal Reserve banks is that the former are under the control of the latter in spite of the fact that the member banks own the stock of the Federal Reserve banks. However, as we have already seen, the control of the Federal Reserve banks over their member banks is not perfect. The commercial banks may own excess reserves which free them from the limiting influences of the monetary authority; or they may be unable to expand their loans and investments at the urging of the monetary authority because of a lack of demand for credit on the part of the public.

One Hundred Per Cent Reserves

It may seem strange that private credit institutions should have the power to create money. Would it not be better to reserve this right for the monetary authority and to transform commercial banks into mere intermediaries of credit which perform monetary services without being able to influence the supply of money?

Irving Fisher proposed that the commercial banks be legally required to hold a reserve of 100 per cent against their demand deposits in the form of currency, reserve accounts with the Federal Reserve banks, and government bonds. To get this plan started without dangerous deflationary consequences the monetary authority would have to bring the reserves of the commercial banks up to 100 per cent. One method of doing this would be to lend newly printed currency for reserve purposes. From then on the monetary authority alone would create additional money and put it into circulation through purchases of government securities on the open market. The newly created money would either stay in circulation as currency or be deposited, that is, exchanged for deposit money. The selling of government bonds would in a similar but opposite fashion reduce the total amount of money in circulation.

Introduction of a 100 per cent reserve system would have the following effects: (1) it would make a multiple credit creation or contraction on the basis of fractional reserves impossible. This would be a great improvement according to Irving Fisher, who saw in the fractional reserve requirement the "chief loose screw" of our monetary system; (2) it would give the monetary authority the fullest possible control over the supply of money without necessitating anything as drastic as nationalization of the commercial banks; and (3) it would, in the long run, substantially reduce the national debt, for the government would create the money which it now borrows from the commercial banks.

Loss of earning power by the commercial banks could be overcome, for instance, by permitting them to increase their charges for checking services rendered or to hold additional reserves in the form of interest-bearing public debt.

The main weakness of the plan lies in the fact that it tries to control only the quantity of money, ignoring the velocity of circulation of money. If the Federal Reserve creates more money, this additional money supply may be absorbed in the form of increased money reserves. We have seen that not even the monetary authority has the power to make people borrow and spend. The plan, therefore, is not a panacea. As formulated by Fisher, furthermore, it overestimated the importance of a stable price level.

Profitability, Liquidity, and Solvency

Under the present fractional reserve system the commercial banks are hybrid institutions. They are credit institutions whose managers endeavor to earn profit for the stockholders, and they are also institutions which have the power to create money because their deposit liabilities are money (demand deposits) or near-money (time deposits). With such liabilities the commercial banks face a liquidity problem which is more acute than that of other private credit institutions, for the commercial banks must stand ready to pay out currency on demand and, therefore, to transform part of their assets instantly into currency.

The basic problem for commercial bank management is the conflict between profitability, liquidity, and solvency. Perfectly liquid assets, the so-called cash assets, do not earn income; the more profitable assets cannot be turned into money instantly and without loss; and solvency requires that the value of bank assets be sufficient to cover the contractual value of its liabilities. Overemphasis on profitability may lead to a situation in which the sudden liquidation of earning assets impairs a bank's solvency. The management of a commercial bank has to work out a compromise. Assets must be so chosen that a proper balance between profitability, liquidity, and solvency is maintained.

The Liabilities of Commercial Banks

In discussing a consolidated balance sheet for all member banks we shall look first at the liabilities and then at the assets. To be able to evaluate the assets and their composition, we must know how much liquidity the banks need. If commercial banking is characterized by a conflict between profitability and liquidity, the required degree of liquidity must be the limiting factor in a bank's lending and investment policies. See Table 13–1.

TABLE 13–1

ALL MEMBER BANKS
PRINCIPAL ASSETS AND LIABILITIES
(In millions of dollars, December 31, 1959)

Assets		
Cash assets		43,000
Loans	95,000	
U.S. government obligations	47,000	
Other securities	16,000	
Total Loans and Investments		158,000
Total Assets		201,000
Liabilities		
Total Capital Accounts		16,000
Demand deposits	111,000	
Time deposits	53,000	
Interbank deposits	16,000	
U.S. government deposits	5,000	
Total Deposits		185,000
Total Liabilities and Capital Accounts		201,000

Adapted from *Federal Reserve Bulletin*, June, 1960.

We defined the commercial banks as institutions which extend credits out of funds which they own, borrow, or create. The division of the liabilities side of the balance sheet corresponds to our definition. These liabilities are indications of external claims: by the "owners" (capital accounts), by "lenders" (time deposits), and by bank customers who hold their money reserves in the form of perfectly liquid claims (demand deposits). That the demand deposits have resulted from a process of credit creation will be shown below.

The capital accounts of the commercial banks represent the amount by which the total assets exceed the contractual value of the liabilities. These funds are derived from capital subscriptions by stockholders and from net earnings. A glance at the balance sheet will show that the capital accounts are not the main source of the commercial banks' operational funds. Rather, the main function of the capital accounts lies in the protection which, as a buffer, they offer to the banks' creditors.

The ratio between capital and deposits is sometimes treated as decisive for the solvency of a bank, just as the ratio between deposits and reserves is considered as decisive for its liquidity. It has been argued, for instance, that the capital/deposit ratio should be better than 1 to 10, though no satisfactory explanation has ever been offered as to why this ratio ought to be chosen. Without reference to the composition of a bank's assets, a rigid capital/deposit ratio makes little sense. Although the ratio may decrease over a period, the bank may be more sound than before if, simultaneously, the bank's cash assets and security holdings have increased. What really counts, in addition to liquidity, is the ratio of capital to risk assets.

Time Deposits and Demand Deposits

The distinction between time deposits and demand deposits is important, and yet it is less clear-cut than we might wish it to be. Demand deposits are money. Time deposits come near to being money but they just miss making the grade. They are highly liquid since they can be turned into money without risk and, as a rule, without delay. But they are not payable on demand and not subject to transfer by check. Thus they do not fully qualify as money. Another distinction is that commercial banks pay interest on time deposits but, at least since 1933, not on demand deposits. Also, reserve requirements are much lower in the case of time deposits than in the case of demand deposits. Thus a shift from demand deposits to time deposits on the part of bank customers sets free bank reserves and increases the power of banks to create deposit money.

Time deposits essentially are savings deposits. The depositors, as a rule, do not plan to use the deposited funds in the near future. By contrast, demand deposits are money reserves or cash deposits of bank customers. The distinction, however, seems to be more precise than it is, since some holders of time deposits treat them as if they were money reserves while some holders of demand deposits may actually be accumulating savings. The depositor's choice between time deposits and demand deposits will depend on such factors as the rate of interest paid on time deposits, the charges levied on small check accounts, and provisions concerning the withdrawal of time deposits.

The commercial banks do not separate their assets into those held against time deposits and those held against demand deposits. But the composition of the banks' assets will, nevertheless, depend on the character of the deposit liabilities.

We saw that time deposits come near to being money. We can also say that in some respects demand deposits come near to being savings. The depositor may not have decided how he will use these funds, and the bank manager may look at money deposited in checking accounts as if it constituted savings which can be lent out or invested provided reserve requirements are met. The bank managers know that the total amount of demand deposits is not likely to be reduced as a result of withdrawals or transfers by check since individual inpayments and outpayments tend to cancel, not counting minor fluctuations caused by payment habits, tax collections, and other seasonal variations.

But do these considerations not contradict the statement made earlier in this chapter that commercial banks are basically different from other private credit institutions, such as savings banks, because they can create money and because they are, as the holders of the public's check accounts, faced with a more acute liquidity problem? To resolve these doubts we must distinguish two kinds of demand deposits.

Primary and Derivative Deposits[1]

A commercial bank can "create" demand deposits *passively* against the receipt of currency or checks from its depositors. These are the so-called *primary* deposits arising from an actual deposit of money in the bank. These passively created primary deposits may be considered as money reserves of the depositors, entrusted to the banks to be drawn upon and replenished at the will of their owners. For a large number of depositors the inflow and outflow of money will nearly balance, and the sum total of these demand deposits will tend to stay the same with the exception of seasonal fluctuations. While money inflow and outflow will never exactly balance, a commercial bank, as a rule, will be able to take care of occasional inbalances with relatively modest reserves.

A commercial bank can also create deposits *actively* by creating claims against itself in favor of a borrower or a seller of securities. These actively created deposits are *derivative* deposits. In contradistinction to primary deposits, which rest on the actual deposit of money, the derivative deposits arise from lending and investment operations. Primary deposits do not increase the supply of money; derivative deposits do. Primary deposits merely take the place of already existing money. Derivative deposits are the result of an act of credit creation;

1 The following treatment combines terminological suggestions made by C. A. Phillips in *Bank Credit* (New York: Macmillan Co., 1931), chap. iii, and by J. M. Keynes in *A Treatise on Money* (New York: Harcourt, Brace & Co., 1930), Vol. I, chaps. iii and iv.

they add to the money at the disposal of the borrowers and do not reduce the purchasing power at the disposal of others.

While primary deposits may be considered as the money reserves of the depositors, derivative deposits, as a rule, do not have this reserve character. Once people or firms borrow they tend to spend the borrowed money on commodities and services. In this case the bank manager has to take an attitude which is basically different from that taken towards primary deposits. He cannot expect that, on the whole, inpayments and outpayments will cancel in connection with derivative deposits. Rather, he must be ready to face a one-sided outflow of the deposit money which he has actively created. The nature of derivative deposits is such that they tend to be spent promptly by the borrowers, and since we have a banking system which is characterized by a very large number of commercial banks, it is very probable that most of the payments made from derivative deposits will be payments to accounts in other banks. Thus our first bank will be called upon to pay out the entire amount which it created as derivative deposits.[2]

Having now distinguished between primary and derivative deposits, we can understand why the nature of demand deposits is so often misunderstood and why even commercial bankers sometimes deny that they have the power to create money. If derivative deposits come from primary deposits, it seems, indeed, as if the commercial banks were only intermediaries; if, however, primary deposits come from derivative deposits, the commercial banks create money. The important question, then, is which come first, the primary or the derivative deposits?

Suppose we start with the creation of derivative deposits. A bank manager who finds his reserves larger than required decides to extend a loan to a borrowing customer. We assume that the loan equals in amount the bank's excess reserves. This amount is credited to the check account of the customer. As the customer purchases materials and pays for them by check, the checks are deposited in other banks, and our first bank finds its reserve account with the Federal Reserve bank accordingly reduced. Since this reduction merely eliminates excess reserves, the bank's position is safe as far as its liquidity is concerned. Quite possibly the manager looks at such lending operations not as a creation of money or credit but rather as the lending of funds which

[2] If the bank does not lose an amount of its cash assets equal to the newly created derivative deposits, this will be due to one or both of the following two cases: (1) It may be that some derivative deposits are used as money reserves, that is, people or firms may borrow to satisfy their liquidity preference. (2) Some of the derivative deposits may be used in making payments to persons or firms whose accounts are with the same bank.

were previously deposited but not needed for reserve purposes. The manager considers himself in this case as an intermediary rather than as a creator of credit. This is quite natural. But we must notice that derivative deposits become almost instantaneously, that is, as soon as they are spent, primary deposits in other banks. This causes demand deposits and reserves in the other banks to increase by equal amounts and results in the creation of excess reserves. It was from just such an excess reserve that we started. Should we say, therefore, that the process begins with derivative deposits or with primary deposits?

The following considerations will provide an answer.

As long as we deal with a given quantity of demand deposits, as long as no new deposits are created, we cannot study the process of credit creation. Suppose that the banks have no excess reserves, and that demand deposits are as large as reserve requirements permit, that is, five or ten times as large as reserves if the legal reserve ratio should be 20 or 10 per cent, respectively. For each individual bank new deposits tend to be equal to withdrawals; for all banks together an excess of deposits over withdrawals in one bank would be matched by an opposite state of unbalance in other banks. In this situation derivative deposits cannot be created. Whenever a bank overexpands it will fall short of the required reserves and will have to correct its mistake.

Now we assume that the reserves of the commercial banks expand because one bank's reserves increase without a corresponding reduction in another bank's reserves. The increased reserves of bank A are, for instance, the result of a sale by the bank of $100 of securities to its Federal Reserve bank. On the basis of $100 of excess reserves bank A can create $100 of derivative deposits for a borrower. As the borrower makes a check payment the $100 becomes a primary deposit in bank B, whose reserves also increase by $100. Assuming a reserve requirement of 20 per cent, bank B now has $80 of excess reserves and can create $80 of derivative deposits. Continuing with our simplified assumptions, we can have the money flow to bank C which, in turn, creates $64 of derivative deposits. In Chapter 14 we shall see how this process will lead to a total credit creation by all banks together of $500.

We see that the process of credit creation rested on the lending activities of the commercial banks and that the primary deposits played a passive role in the process. It is rather a misnomer, therefore, that the derivative deposits should be called derivative. It is the primary deposits which are the derived ones. But it is dangerous to change an accepted terminology.

Once more we must emphasize that primary deposits are not savings deposits but money reserves of bank customers and that the process of multiple credit creation in superimposing on each primary deposit a new, though somewhat smaller, derivative deposit, adds money to money. When a bank expands credit because a primary deposit has increased its reserves, it gives money to customer B while customer A retains the full present control over his money reserves.

The Assets of Commercial Banks

The balance sheet in Table 13–1 (page 144) shows that the principal assets of the commercial banks are divided into cash assets and loans and investments. Cash assets are assets of perfect liquidity. They include the reserve balances with the Federal Reserve banks, balances with other banks, and cash in vault. The reserves with the Federal Reserve banks are of paramount importance in connection with the legal reserve requirements, the creation of deposit money, the check-clearing process, and the distribution of currency. We have already discussed these reserves in Chapter 12 since it is through these reserves that the Federal Reserve banks try to regulate the supply of deposit money.

The earning assets of the commercial banks must be examined as to profitability and liquidity. Originally commercial loans were supposed to be the basis of a commercial bank's lending activities in contradistinction to investment in securities. This wrong attitude has been abandoned.

The typical commercial loan, extended to customers after a careful investigation of their cerdit-worthiness, is not easily marketable and, therefore, not very liquid. But some categories of commercial paper (for example, promissory notes made out by well-known firms in round sums and payable to the bearer) have the quality of broad marketability. In distributing loanable funds among borrowers who do not have access to the open market, the commercial banks perform an important economic function. It should be emphasized at this point that the allocation of credit is not, as is sometimes naïvely assumed, solely a function of interest rates. Not every borrower who is willing to pay the price can get a loan in the way a consumer can buy all the commodities he wants. In the distribution of credit there is an element which is akin to rationing.

The commercial banks are not limited to short-term commercial loans. They have shown increasing willingness to extend relatively long-term loans which are to be repaid serially over the life of the loan.

Through proper timing and the steady turnover of credits a reasonable degree of liquidity and flexibility can be maintained. The discarding of the commercial-loan theory has also removed objections against consumers' loans, real estate loans, and loans with securities as collateral.

The liquidity of all these loans does not depend so much on inherent qualities of the processes or purchases which they finance as on careful timing, staggering, and diversification. In the last analysis, however, liquidity will always depend on the actions of the Federal Reserve banks. If the latter are willing to buy or lend on the basis of the commercial banks' earning assets, these assets may be considered to be as liquid as the degree implied in the Federal Reserve's attitude. If we accept this fact, the division of earning assets into loans and investments loses much of its former importance.

Short-term government securities (bills and certificates), which have maturities from 3 to 12 months, are issued in anticipation of assured revenue from taxation or long-term borrowing. They yield very little income for the investor, but they are readily changed into money, either through maturity at face value or through sale at a price which can never fall far below the face value since maturity is always close at hand. Treasury notes, which have several years to run, and Treasury bonds, which have much longer maturities, pay higher interest but are subject to more uncertainty in their market prices due to their longer maturities.

Price fluctuations of government securities need not be a deterrent to commercial bank investment. A drop in security prices means a loss only when securities have to be sold. If a commercial bank has staggered the maturity dates of its investment portfolio and has fortified its position wisely with cash assets and earning assets of relatively high liquidity, it should feel justified in taking a long-range view and not be unduly disturbed by a temporary decrease in the value of its long-term investments. Since falling security prices mean higher rates of interest, it is wrong to argue that falling security prices basically endanger the position of institutions whose earnings depend on interest rates.

State and local government securities usually have a somewhat higher yield than the more easily marketable United States government securities. The same is true for the many types of corporate bonds which the commercial banks buy for investment purpose. Commercial banks generally are not permitted to buy corporate stock on the grounds that such investment would be too risky for institutions which depend on a relatively high degree of liquidity of their earning assets.

The main exception from this rule for the member banks is the obligation to buy stocks in the Federal Reserve banks.

The Commercial Banks' Customers

The commercial banks' customers play a decisive part in the creation of money, at least in our economic system. Whether money can be created, whether it will stay in circulation, and under which conditions, depends on the attitude of the public. Without an increased demand for loanable funds the banks are largely powerless: you can lead a horse to water but you cannot make him drink. In buying securities the initiative seems to be with the banks. But, again, the banks have no way of determining the use to which additional money will be put by the seller of securities. He may repay bank loans or he may be induced to hold larger money reserves in expectation of falling security prices. In the latter case the supply of money is increased but the velocity of circulation of money is decreased.

These considerations show that, as far as total expenditure is concerned, the attitude of the public is just as important as the behavior of the commercial banks or the policy of the monetary authority.

Apart from the public's attitude concerning borrowing, spending, and hoarding, the actions of the public are of importance to the commercial banks because the public decides which amounts it wants to hold in the form of currency, checking accounts, and time deposits. Since demand deposits and time deposits require different reserves, the public's choice influences the power of the banks to create credit. Similarly, the public's demand for more currency reduces the banks' reserves.

SUGGESTIONS FOR FURTHER READING

Board of Governors of the Federal Reserve System. *Banking Studies,* pp. 87–109; 169–86. Washington, D.C., 1941.

Ritter, Lawrence S. *Money and Economic Activity,* chap. 4. Boston: Houghton Mifflin Co., 1952.

Whittlesey, Charles R. *Readings in Money and Banking,* Part II. New York: W. W. Norton & Co., Inc., 1952.

On Fisher's 100 per cent proposal:

Fisher, Irving. *100 Per Cent Money.* New York: Adelphi, 1935.

Morgan, Theodore. *Income and Employment,* pp. 242–45. 2d ed. New York: Prentice-Hall, Inc., 1952.

On the distinction between primary and derivative deposits:

KEYNES, J. M. *A Treatise on Money,* Vol. 1, chap. 2. New York: Harcourt, Brace & Co., 1930.

PHILLIPS, CHESTER A. *Bank Credit,* chap. 2. New York: Macmillan Co., 1931.

QUESTIONS AND PROBLEMS

1. What are the distinctive features of commercial banks as compared with central banks and savings banks?
2. "It is because the Federal Reserve can regulate the volume of reserves available to banks that it can influence the availability, cost, and supply of credit" *(The Federal Reserve System. Purposes and Functions.* Washington, D.C., 1954). Explain.
3. Is the contention correct that "the chief loose screw" in modern banking systems "is the requirement of only fractional reserves behind demand deposits" (Irving Fisher)?
4. Discuss the advantages and shortcomings of Irving Fisher's 100 per cent reserve scheme.
5. Explain the difference between liquidity and solvency.
6. "The rate at which a bank can, with safety, *actively* create deposits by lending and investing has to be in proper relation to the rate at which it is *passively* creating them against the receipt of liquid resources from its depositors" (J. M. Keynes). Explain.
7. "A derivate deposit is extremely variable in magnitude. A primary deposit, standing as it does for funds placed in the bank for safekeeping and to be currently checked against as well as currently replenished, is not marked by the extreme ups and downs to which a derivative deposit balance is subject." Explain the importance of this statement by Chester Arthur Phillips for the theory of multiple credit creation.
8. Some commercial bankers deny that they ever create money. They claim that they only lend out already existing money which they do not need for reserve purposes. Do you agree?
9. Can it be said that the distribution of credit by commercial banks is solely a function of interest rates?

Chapter 14 THE PROCESS OF MULTIPLE CREDIT EXPANSION

Introductory Remarks

The purpose of this chapter is to describe the technical process of money creation and its limitations. For the purpose of simplification we shall assume that the expansion of credit by both Federal Reserve banks and commercial banks goes to the maximum amount permitted by reserves and reserve requirements.

We shall make use of simple balance sheet examples. In these balance sheets assets are always equal to liabilities, according to the double-entry bookkeeping practice. Our assumed transactions, therefore, will either change both assets and liabilities by the same amount and in the same direction or they will change two items on the same side, increasing one and decreasing the other. If, for example, a commercial bank sells securities (an asset item) to a Federal Reserve bank, it adds an equal amount to another asset item, its reserves with the Federal Reserve bank. If a loss is incurred in this sale (reserves increase less than securities decrease), an adjustment is made on the liabilities side through a reduction in capital accounts. An extension of loans, to use another example, increases both loans (an asset item) and demand deposits (a liability item).

Changes in these balance sheet items will be shown by plus and minus signs. We shall also assume throughout either that our conclusions are strictly limited to our examples or that there are no excess reserves not shown on the balance sheet.

Our process of credit expansion begins with an addition to the monetary gold reserve on which a superstructure of credit can be built. While this return to gold-standard assumptions may seem to emphasize features in our monetary system which are outmoded, it has the advantage of covering all the possible influences to which the system might be exposed. In the preceding three chapters we have eliminated the danger that our technical model of credit expansion will be taken as a realistic description of the reactions of money supply to a change in gold reserves.

Gold Purchases and Excess Reserves

Suppose that $1,000 worth of gold has been sold to the Treasury, which pays for the gold by a check drawn on its account with the Federal Reserve. The seller of the gold deposits this check with commercial bank A, which credits his checking account with $1,000. Bank A will send the check to its Federal Reserve bank which will credit bank A's reserve deposit with $1,000 while the Treasury's deposit is charged with the same amount.

The changes shown in Tables 14–1 and 14–2 will have taken place in the Balance Sheet of Bank A and in the Statement of Condition of the Federal Reserve Banks.

TABLE 14–1

BALANCE SHEET OF BANK A

ASSETS		LIABILITIES	
Reserve with F.R.	+1,000	Demand deposits	+1,000

Our example shows that the reserve deposits of bank A have grown. Since they have grown by the same amount as demand deposits ($1,000 in each case), bank A now has an excess reserve whose size depends on the legal reserve requirements; these we shall assume to be 20 per cent of demand deposits. Required reserves are, therefore, $200, owing to the increase in demand deposits of $1,000; and excess reserves are $800 (namely, the $1,000 by which the reserves have increased minus the $200 required reserves).

TABLE 14–2

STATEMENT OF CONDITION OF THE FEDERAL RESERVE BANKS

ASSETS	LIABILITIES	
No change	Deposits	
	a) Treasury	−1,000
	b) Commercial banks	+1,000

In the Statement of Condition of the Federal Reserve Banks we find this increase in bank A's reserve as an increase in the deposits of commercial banks. This is counterbalanced by a decrease in Treasury deposits. Obviously, bank A's account with the Federal Reserve was not increased at the expense of other banks' reserves. This is important, for most check payments are transfer payments between customers of commercial banks, and debit and credit entries in commercial banks' accounts in the Federal Reserve banks tend, therefore, to cancel each other. In our present case, however, the addition to the reserves of bank A is, at the same time, an addition to the reserves of all commercial banks. Our transaction has created excess reserves on which a larger amount of deposit money can be based.

How Far One Bank May Extend Credit

Bank A can now lend its customers an additional amount equal to its excess reserves, as the following transactions will show. Loans to the extent of $800 are given to borrowers in the form of credit entries to their demand deposits. The Balance Sheet of Bank A will now read as shown in Table 14–3.

TABLE 14-3

BALANCE SHEET OF BANK A

ASSETS		LIABILITIES	
Reserve............	+1,000	Demand deposits............	+1,000
Loans..............	+800		+800
	1,800		1,800

Table 14–3 seems to indicate that we have been much too careful. Reserves are now more than 55 per cent of demand deposits—much more than the required 20 per cent. How about raising loans to $4,000? The balance sheet would change as shown in Table 14–4.

TABLE 14-4

BALANCE SHEET OF BANK A

ASSETS		LIABILITIES	
Reserve............	+1,000	Demand deposits............	+1,000
Loans..............	+4,000		+4,000
	5,000		5,000

Now the demand deposits are five times larger than reserves, the reserves are 20 per cent of total demand deposits, and it seems that we have created the maximum amount of credit permitted under the legal reserve requirements.

This answer seems plausible—at first. What was correct in the case of our first $1,000 of demand deposits ought to be correct in the case of the newly created $4,000 of deposits. If $200 were sufficient as a reserve for $1,000, why should our excess reserve of $800 not be enough to serve as "backing" for $4,000?

The answer to this question has already been given in Chapter 13 where we distinguished between primary and derivative deposits. The first deposit of $1,000 was a primary deposit, while the $800 or $4,000, respectively, were derivative deposits. Primary deposits, we remember, are money reserves and are normally not expected to be withdrawn on the average. Derivative deposits, however, are almost sure to be withdrawn in full and to be transferred to other banks. Suppose, therefore, that the $4,000 had been borrowed in order to make immediate purchases from other firms. If these other firms had their accounts with bank A, everything would be in order because bank A could clear these payments internally. Its reserves with the Federal Reserve bank would remain $1,000 just as its demand deposits would remain $5,000; one customer's payments would always be another customer's receipts.

Since there are many thousands of banks in the United States, it is more probable that the $4,000 will be used for check payments to firms with accounts in other banks. This means that in the check-clearing process bank A will have the $4,000 charged to its reserve account, while it could afford to "lose" only $800, namely, its excess reserve. Bank A's reserve would then become inadequate. To follow the principle of expanding credit to five times its excess reserves would be ruinous for our bank.

Only in two cases could bank A embark on this otherwise forbidden policy.

1. If bank A were the only commercial bank in the country, it could be sure that all persons and firms would have to hold their checking accounts with it and that check clearing in such a closed system could not reduce its reserves. This case is conceivable in a country which has nationalized all commercial banks so that they are but branches of one bank.

2. If all commercial banks expanded credit simultaneously at an equal pace, such parallel action would tend to leave any individual bank's reserves undiminished, short of those increased payments of currency over the counter which accompany a creation of deposit money because a certain proportion of the payments made by the borrower are likely to be made in currency rather than in deposit money.

Since there are thousands of banks rather than one, and since bankers cannot know in advance what the behavior of other bankers will be, a bank to be on the safe side must follow the basic rule to limit its new loans to an amount equal to its excess reserve. If the borrowers make check payments to customers of other banks, the situation can be handled as is shown on the balance sheet of bank A. Originally, after extending loans equal to the excess reserve, the balance sheet stood as shown in Table 14–3. After the borrowed amounts have been used to make check payments to customers of other banks the balance sheet reads as shown in Table 14–5.

The payments were charged to the check accounts of the borrowing customers (therefore demand deposits were reduced from $1,800 to $1,000), who still continue to owe the bank the $800 which they borrowed. The reserve account of bank A with the Federal Reserve is now only $200 because $800 have been charged to this account in the clearing process. These $800 have at the same time been credited to

TABLE 14–5

BALANCE SHEET OF BANK A

ASSETS		LIABILITIES	
Reserve...........	+200	Demand deposits...........	+1,000
Loans............	+800		
	1,000		1,000

the accounts of other commercial banks. The Statement of Condition of the Federal Reserve Banks is not affected.

Multiple Credit Expansion

To simplify our example let us assume that the $800 which bank A lent and which were spent by the borrower have been deposited in bank B rather than in numerous other banks. This transfer of $800 from the reserve account of bank A to that of bank B creates an excess reserve of $640 in bank B because both its demand deposits and its reserves are increased by $800. If we deduct the 20 per cent legal reserve requirement from the new deposit of $800, we get $640 as an excess reserve of bank B. This handling of our problem implies that we treat the new deposit of $800 in bank B as a primary deposit since it has come into being by the deposit of a check and not by a new process of credit creation.

Since we are satisfied that bank B now has an excess reserve of $640, there is no reason why bank B should not use this sum to make loans (or buy securities) and thereby create derivative deposits of $640.

Since $640 are the bank's excess reserves, bank B can afford to have this amount charged to its reserve account. The balance sheet of bank B will show the following changes: First, when the new loans are extended, it changes from $800 for both reserves and demand deposits to the figures shown in Table 14–6.

TABLE 14–6

BALANCE SHEET OF BANK B

ASSETS		LIABILITIES	
Reserves..........	+800	Demand deposits...........	+800
Loans............	+640		+640
	1,440		1,440

And when the borrowed money is spent, the balance sheet of bank B reads as shown in Table 14–7.

We can see that bank B fulfills its reserve requirement: $160 is 20 per cent of $800.

Now we can ascertain what the total effect of this process of credit expansion by all commercial banks together will be. If we assume that the $640 created by bank B will be deposited as a primary deposit in bank C, then the deposits of bank C will increase by $640 and will require an additional reserve of $128 (20 per cent of $640). The increase in total reserves is $640, and the excess reserve of bank C is accordingly $512. Bank C can then create an amount of derivative deposits equal to its excess reserve, leading to a primary deposit of $512 in bank D. If bank D and other banks follow suit, this is the process of multiple credit expansion illustrated in Table 14–8.

TABLE 14–7

BALANCE SHEET OF BANK B

ASSETS		LIABILITIES	
Reserve...........	+160	Demand deposits...........	+800
Loans............	+640		
	800		800

Only the last line in Table 14–8 requires further explanation. How do we know that the process will end when we have added $4,000, in the form of newly created derivative deposits to the $1,000 of primary deposits which were the result of the Treasury's original gold purchase? The answer is obvious. Since the additional reserve for all banks together was $1,000, the commercial banks must stop this process of multiple credit creation when the whole $1,000 have become legally required reserves. The process ends automatically when in the manner described above, these reserves have been distributed throughout the banking system.

In our example the banks created $4,000 in derivative deposits. One thousand dollars of primary deposits resulted from the gold purchase itself, and since derivative deposits turn into primary deposits,

TABLE 14–8

MULTIPLE CREDIT EXPANSION BY ALL COMMERCIAL BANKS

	Primary Deposits and Additions to Total Reserves	Required Reserves	Excess Reserves and Derivative Deposits
Bank A.........	$1,000.00	$ 200.00	$ 800.00
Bank B.........	800.00	160.00	640.00
Bank C.........	640.00	128.00	512.00
Bank D.........	512.00	102.40	409.60
Bank E.........	409.60	81.92	327.68
Bank F.........	327.68	65.536	262.144
Bank G.........	262.144	52.4288	209.7152
A to G.........	$3,951.424	$ 790.2848	$3,161.1392
All other........	1,048.576	209.6352	838.8608
Total.........	$5,000.00	$1,000.00	$4,000.00

In reality each bank, when creating credit, will lose its excess reserves to "other" banks rather than to one specific bank. The assumption according to which payments go from bank A to bank B, from there to C, etc., is a simplification which may be dropped now that it has helped to explain the process of multiple credit creation.

we end up with $5,000 of primary deposits and see that the gold purchase, so far, has led to a fivefold expansion of the monetary circulation.

Gold Certificates and Federal Reserve Credit Expansion

When the Treasury buys gold it does not, as a rule, buy it with the taxpayers' money. Rather, the Treasury will sell gold certificates to the Federal Reserve banks. When this happens the Statement of Condition of the Federal Reserve Banks, shown in Table 14–2, will be changed as shown in Table 14–9.

With this transaction the Treasury has replenished its account and the Federal Reserve banks have increased their gold reserve.

We shall assume that the Federal Reserve wants to make the utmost use of its increased gold reserves, that the demand for credit in the economy is brisk, and that the Federal Reserve banks are required to hold a reserve of 25 per cent in gold certificates against both Federal Reserve notes in circulation and deposits.

Since the deposits increased by $1,000 and since a reserve of 25 per cent must be held against them, there now remains an excess reserve of $750 in gold certificates which is not yet engaged for backing purposes. How can the Federal Reserve make use of this reserve for purposes of credit expansion?

TABLE 14–9

STATEMENT OF CONDITION OF THE FEDERAL RESERVE BANKS

ASSETS		LIABILITIES	
Gold certificates....	+1,000	Deposits	
		a) Treasury.............	+1,000
			−1,000
		b) Commercial banks.....	+1,000

For one dollar of gold four dollars of Federal Reserve notes in circulation or four dollars of commercial bank reserve deposits may be created because the same 25 per cent reserve rule applies to both of these liability items. Federal Reserve notes in circulation are already currency, but on each dollar of reserve deposits five dollars of deposit money can be created. Since we are interested in the maximum credit expansion practicable on the basis of a given addition to the monetary gold base, we ought to concentrate on deposit money rather than currency. It has to be remembered, however, that with payment habits fixed, an expansion of deposit money will cause an increase in demand for currency. And since we have assumed all along that the Federal Reserve should try to regulate only the total supply of money while leaving the public free to choose what kind of money it desires to hold, we should set aside enough of our gold reserve to enable us to issue more Federal Reserve notes in case of an increased demand for currency. Suppose, therefore, that we leave $500 of gold certificates for this purpose.

There remain $250 of gold certificates, enough to serve as backing for $1,000 in additional reserve deposits. The commercial banks' reserve accounts can be increased by open-market purchases. The Statement of Condition of the Federal Reserve Banks now stands as shown in Table 14–10.

It may seem as if we had violated our rule that a bank should lend out only an amount equal to its excess reserves. Our excess gold reserve, after setting aside $500 for the future issue of Federal Reserve notes, was only $250. Should the Federal Reserve have limited its open-market purchase to $250 rather than to $1,000?

The answer is that our rule of thumb does not apply in this case because we can treat the twelve Federal Reserve banks as one central bank. Check payments from one commercial bank to another stay within the Central Banking System, and there is not much danger that the increased reserve deposits will lead to an equally increased demand for gold. We should note, however, that a greater demand for gold may develop if, as a result of credit expansion, prices rise and imports increase while exports fall.

The expansion of commercial bank reserve deposits by $1,000

TABLE 14–10

STATEMENT OF CONDITION OF THE FEDERAL RESERVE BANKS

ASSETS		LIABILITIES	
Gold certificates....	+1,000	Deposits of com. bank......	+1,000
Securities.........	+1,000		+1,000
	2,000		2,000

has created the basis for a new round of multiple credit creation by the commercial banks.

The Federal Reserve has bought securities from, say, bank M. Bank M's balance sheet will show the changes given in Table 14–11.

Since reserves are increased by $1,000 with no change in demand deposits, the full amount of $1,000 can be counted as an excess reserve. Bank M, therefore, can create $1,000 of derivative deposits, and the money becomes, according to our simplifying assumptions, a primary

TABLE 14–11

BALANCE SHEET OF BANK M

ASSETS		LIABILITIES
Reserves..........	+1,000	No change
Securities.........	−1,000	

deposit of bank N, which can then lend out $800, while banks O, P, and the rest can create $640, $512, and $2,048, respectively. The total creation would be $5,000, an amount five times larger than the excess reserve of $1,000.

Had the Federal Reserve banks bought the securities from the public rather than from bank M, the picture would be very similar. The sellers of the securities would deposit the Federal Reserve check in bank M, and the Balance Sheet of Bank M would be as shown in Table 14–12.

This time the excess reserves would be only $800, because a reserve of $200 must be held against the demand deposits of the sellers of the securities. Excess reserves of $800 would serve as the basis for a credit expansion in the whole commercial banking system of $4,000 which, together with the $1,000 of deposits created through open-market purchases, would put the same total of $5,000 of additional purchasing power into circulation.

TABLE 14–12

BALANCE SHEET OF BANK M

ASSETS		LIABILITIES	
Reserves..........	+1,000	Demand deposits...........	+1,000

Increasing the Supply of Federal Reserve Notes

Demand deposits have now increased by a total of $10,000, namely, $1,000 through the gold purchase itself, $4,000 through the first round of multiple credit expansion, and $5,000 through the second round.

We must assume that the increase in deposit money leads to an increased demand for currency and that more Federal Reserve notes must be issued. For this purpose we have set aside $500 of gold certificates, and we are able, therefore, to fulfill the gold reserve requirement and issue an additional $2,000 of Federal Reserve notes for circulation.

When the commercial banks increase their cash in vault to accommodate their customers' increased demand for currency, they have the Federal Reserve notes charged to their reserve accounts. Since we have carried the commercial banks' credit creation to its very limits, the commercial banks will have to borrow from, or sell securities to, the Federal Reserve banks in order to increase their reserves.

Tables 14–13 and 14–14 indicate the transactions involved in issuing the additional supply of Federal Reserve notes.

The commercial banks increase their reserves by selling $2,000 of securities to the Federal Reserve banks. Then reserves are reduced because $2,000 of Federal Reserve notes, delivered to the commercial banks, are charged to the banks' reserve accounts.

The Statement of Conditions at first shows an increase in securities and in the reserve accounts of the commercial banks with the Federal Reserve. Then, as the commercial banks replenish their cash in vault, a decrease in deposits and an increase in Federal Reserve notes in circulation takes place. Since we have set aside $500 of gold certificates for the purpose of fulfilling the reserve requirement in connection with the issue of additional Federal Reserve notes, we do not meet with any difficulties: first these gold certificates serve as backing for the increased deposits and then for the Federal Reserve notes in circulation.

We see that changes in the public's demand for currency will influence the maximum amount of credit which can be created on the basis of a given amount of monetary gold reserves. When the public changes from deposit money to currency, the change involves a proportional change in the banks' reserves and implies a multiple contraction of credit unless the Federal Reserve is willing to increase member bank reserves. In our example the Federal Reserve was willing to purchase securities from the member banks. Had the Federal Reserve not accommodated the banks, the public's increased demand for currency would have caused the reserves of the commercial banks to fall below the legally required minimum.

TABLE 14–13

ALL COMMERCIAL BANKS

ASSETS		LIABILITIES
Cash in vault......	+2,000	No change
Reserves..........	+2,000	
	−2,000	
Securities.........	−2,000	

TABLE 14–14

STATEMENT OF CONDITION OF THE FEDERAL RESERVE BANKS

ASSETS		LIABILITIES	
Securities.........	+2,000	Deposits..................	+2,000
			−2,000
		F.R. notes.................	+2,000

Whether the Federal Reserve is able to accommodate the commercial banks depends on its gold reserve. In our example the Federal Reserve could issue $2,000 of Federal Reserve notes because we had foreseen the increased demand for currency by the public. If we had used the whole $1,000 of gold certificates to back up $4,000 of member bank reserve deposits, we could have fulfilled the reserve requirement for $20,000 of deposit money but would have been unable to furnish the public with additional currency; and unless reserve requirements would be changed instantly and drastically, the system would be illiquid because the banks would be unable to pay currency on demand.

Since it is almost certain that an increased total supply of money will cause an increased demand for currency, the System's credit expansion must be determined in anticipation of this induced rise in the demand for currency. We assume that this demand equals 20 per cent of the total increase in loans. Thus, if the banks together expand loans by $10,000, demand deposits will increase by $8,000 and currency in circulation by $2,000. This means that the banks together need $1,600 as required reserve against the demand deposits and that, in addition, their reserves are reduced by $2,000 because of the increased demand for currency. A given excess reserve permits in this case a credit expansion by approximately 2.8 and not by 5 times.[1]

The Process of Multiple Credit Contraction

Just as it can be created, so can money be destroyed. It will not be necessary to trace this process of destruction of money in detail since it is simply the opposite of the process of credit creation.

Suppose that gold is bought from the Treasury and paid for by check drawn on bank A. In bank A we find both reserves and demand deposits reduced by $1,000. In the books of the Federal Reserve banks the commercial banks' deposits are reduced by $1,000 and the amount is credited to the Treasury's account.

If bank A's reserve was just adequate before the transaction began, it is now inadequate. With an assumed legal reserve requirement of 20 per cent, bank A will be short of $800 of reserves, and it will have to increase its reserves by selling securities or by calling in loans. Since we are concerned with an analysis of the process of multiple credit contraction, we shall assume that the Federal Reserve banks will not embark on open-market purchases, for these would tend to counteract the contraction; instead, bank A calls in loans. Normally bank A would immediately relend what it receives in payment for loans falling due, and thus the money would be received by customers of other banks

[1] The expansion coefficient x can be found according to the equation $x = \frac{1}{c + r(1 - c)}$, where c is the ratio of currency to total money and r the minimum reserve ratio. In the above example we get an expansion coefficient of 2.77 because

$$x = \frac{1}{0.20 + 0.20(1 - 0.20)} = \frac{1}{0.20 + 0.16} = \frac{1}{0.36} = 2.77.$$

See the excellent article "The Internal Drain and Bank Credit Expansion" by Stephen L. McDonald in *The Journal of Finance*, Vol. VIII, No. 4 (December, 1953), pp. 407–21.

and deposited in turn with other banks. Now that the money is being used to increase bank A's reserve, it is not lent out again, and another bank finds itself short of $800 both in demand deposits and reserves. This bank is, therefore, in a reserve position which is $640 below the minimum. Thus the process of credit expansion is reversed, as is shown in Table 14–15.

The process will come to an end when demand deposits have fallen by a total of $5,000, when required reserves have decreased by $1,000, and when the loans of commercial banks have been reduced by $4,000.

We must assume that the Treasury would not sell gold bullion without repurchasing an equal amount of gold certificates from the Federal Reserve. The Federal Reserve, unless it holds excess gold reserves, has to reduce its combined deposits and Federal Reserve notes

TABLE 14–15

MULTIPLE CREDIT CONTRACTION FOR ALL BANKS

	Reduction of Both Demand Deposits and Reserves	Deficiency in Reserves
Bank A	$1,000	$800
Bank B	800	640
Bank C	640	512
	Etc.	Etc.

in circulation by an amount four times greater than the reduction in its gold-certificate holdings. Suppose that this was accomplished through the sale of $4,000 worth of securities to the public. Now the reserves and the demand deposits of the commercial banks would be reduced by the same amount and, with no excess reserves to fall back on, another process of cumulative credit contraction would follow.

QUESTIONS AND PROBLEMS

1. Suppose that a commercial bank sold $100,000 of securities to a Federal Reserve bank and increased its reserves by the same amount. The legal reserve requirement against demand deposits is 20 per cent. On the basis of this increase in reserves, by how much can this commercial bank increase its loans and investments: $100,000, $80,000, $400,000, or $500,000? Explain your answer.
2. Would your answer to question 1 have been different if our commercial bank were assumed to be the only commercial bank in the country?

3. Would your answer to question 1 be different if the Federal Reserve bank had bought $100,000 of securities not from the commercial bank but rather from a customer of that commercial bank?
4. The Treasury issues $10 million of gold certificates to the Federal Reserve. Assuming that the Federal Reserve banks are required to hold a gold reserve of 25 per cent against the reserve deposits of their member banks, by how much could open market purchases be expanded on the basis of the additional gold reserve of $10 million: 7.5, 10, 30, or 40 million dollars? Explain your answer.
5. Suppose that the Federal Reserve, having gained an additional $3 billion of gold certificates, wants to achieve a maximum expansion of the monetary circulation permitted by the legal reserve requirements (25 per cent in gold against both Federal Reserve notes in circulation and also against member bank reserve deposits). The Federal Reserve decides to use one third of the new gold reserve to back up member bank reserve deposits and two thirds to back up Federal Reserve notes in circulation. The commercial banks in turn expand credit to the maximum permitted by their legal reserve requirements which we assume to be 10 per cent. How much money could be created? Use a diagram like Figure 6–1 on p. 62.
6. The Treasury purchases $1 million of gold from a gold importer who deposits the Treasury's check in a commercial bank in the United States. The Treasury issues $1 million of gold certificates to the Federal Reserve. Using balance sheets, explain step by step how these original transactions can lead to a multiple credit expansion. Further assumptions are: an unlimited demand for credit; only deposit money is to be considered; gold reserve requirement for the Federal Reserve is 25 per cent of member bank reserve deposits; reserve requirement for member banks is 20 per cent.
7. Change question 6 to read: "The Treasury *sells* $1 million to a gold exporter" etc. and show, step by step, the maximum credit contraction which could follow.
8. Assume that the public needs more currency during the holiday season and that the Federal Reserve makes more currency available both in the form of Treasury currency and in the form of its own Federal Reserve notes. Show the changes in the balance sheet of a typical commercial bank which gets more currency from the Federal Reserve and in the latter's statement of condition.
9. If a continued gold outflow would lead to a deficiency in legally required gold reserves, would we have to face a multiple credit contraction? What policy conclusions can you draw from your answer?

PART V

The Federal Reserve System

Chapter 15 U. S. MONEY AND BANKING BEFORE 1914

Introduction

Chapter 15 concerns monetary and banking experiences in the United States prior to the establishment of the Federal Reserve System in 1914. It will furnish illustrations for the theoretical discussions in Parts I to IV. With the advantage of hindsight we shall follow the monetary problems of the past, study the discussions they evoked, and watch the effects of the policies which were adopted. Since the economist cannot use controlled experiments, by which physicists or chemists check their theories, he must use the laboratory of history and learn from past mistakes.

A second reason for our interest in the monetary history of the United States stems from the fact that our present monetary institutions are the outgrowth of past problems, theories, and policies. Much of our present monetary policy represents the struggle to escape from past ideas and from the limitations which they still impose on us through obsolete institutions. At the same time experience with past mistakes can serve as a warning against monetary sins which each new generation seems to feel the urge to repeat, as the history of inflation proves.

The history of money and the history of banking are closely related and must be studied together. However, this does not prevent us from following particular problems through the years, provided these historical strands are properly interwoven.

The Colonial Period

American monetary history during the colonial period is a mixture of deflationary and inflationary troubles.

Deflationary difficulties arose when a region which expanded rapidly in area and population was inadequately supplied with full-bodied coin, the only reasonably trustworthy type of money at the time. Since full-bodied coins were of foreign (Spanish, British, French, Portuguese) origin and came only reluctantly to the new country,[1] their supply could not be easily adjusted to the increasing demand for money. The monetary policies of the colonies consisted in attempts to draw coins away from one another and to substitute other types of money for full-bodied coins.

The unit of account was the British pound sterling, while the Spanish silver dollar was the most frequently used means of exchange. Since the British pound had (from 1600 to 1816) a fixed silver price, it would have been easy to establish a fixed ratio between the pound and the silver dollar. Instead, individual colonies purposely overvalued the silver dollar in terms of shillings to cause an influx of full-bodied coin from the other colonies.

When the scarcity of full-bodied coin became too inconvenient, the colonial authorities tried to alleviate the situation by declaring commodities such as tobacco, wheat, rice, or corn as legal tender. To make the commodity money attractive the official shilling price of the commodity was set above the market price. This overvaluation made it possible to retain the clumsy commodity money in circulation while specie flowed out and the scarcity of full-bodied money was further increased.

The colonial authorities also started to issue paper money of different kinds. Had its quantity been carefully regulated, the value of paper money could have been kept at par with the shilling. Overissue of paper currency and bank notes, however, soon led to yet another application of Gresham's law: paper money drove the full-bodied coin out of circulation and it soon became impossible to re-

1 One of the reasons is given by Daniel Defoe's Moll Flanders. This clever woman decided to take but little of her money from England to Virginia, "for money in that country is of not much use where all things are bought for tobacco." She left most of it behind "to be sent afterwards in such goods as I should want when I came to settle."

deem paper money in anything but paper. The mother country tried to stop these inflationary practices by forbidding (in 1751) any further issue of paper money in the New England colonies and by extending the prohibition (in 1764) to the rest of the colonies.

The Revolution removed this limitation, and the Revolutionary War became the cause of a substantial credit and price inflation. Reluctance to finance the war through sufficient taxation or through borrowing from noninflationary sources led to a budgetary deficit, which the Continental Congress and the colonies filled by credit creation amounting to about $450 million, or $112 per capita. The effect on prices was such that paper money was eventually exchanged against full-bodied money at a rate of 1,000 to 1; this amounted to the practical repudiation of paper money. Thus the monetary history of the United States began with a very substantial price inflation.

Bimetallism in the United States

The colonial monetary confusion and the inflationary experiences of the Revolutionary War explain why the Constitution provides, in Article I, Sec. viii, that "The Congress shall have power . . . to coin money, regulate the value thereof, and of foreign coin" and, in Sec. x, that "No State shall . . . coin money; emit bills of credit; make anything but gold and silver coin a tender in payment of debts." This formulation implied that the powers of the Congress might include the "emission of bills of credit," since it was not expressly stated that such power was excluded. During the War of 1812, Treasury notes were issued.

The refusal to allow the state governments to issue paper money proved to be of small importance in view of the bank notes which could be created by state-chartered commercial banks. But before we turn to a discussion of banks and bank notes, we must first inquire into the new currency regulations of the Coinage Act of 1792.

Following proposals made by Jefferson and Hamilton, the monetary unit of the United States was so chosen that it coincided in name and, as nearly as possible, in value with the Spanish dollar, the most frequently used type of full-bodied money then in existence. The decimal system was adopted in preference to the British system, and both gold and silver coins were issued to supply commerce with convenient coins of different denominations.

So far the Coinage Act of 1792 was excellent. Unfortunately, however, it also provided for the free coinage of both gold and silver at a fixed ratio of 1 to 15 and thereby established a bimetallic standard.

This was deplorable since it was known at the time that bimetallism cannot work unless it is established on a broad international basis. That Hamilton chose bimetallism must probably be explained by his fear of an insufficient supply of money should only one metal be used. But this argument was untenable. It was already quite obvious that a circulation of nothing but full-bodied coin would never suffice. If, then, both full-bodied and paper money were needed anyhow, the total quantity of money could always be adjusted to the needs of the economy. On the other hand, a regulation of full-bodied money alone without consideration of the monetary implications of the creation of bank notes could never be satisfactory.

Even in the narrower field of coinage it was impossible to supply the country with full-bodied money of both high and low denominations since the bimetallic system was bound to lose one of its two metals in any case. Only the issue of token coins could solve this problem. But not until 1853 was the free coinage of fractional silver abolished and subsidiary coin created.

The simultaneous use of full-bodied silver and gold coin would have been possible in the form of the so-called parallel rather than the double or bimetallic standard. A parallel standard provides for the free coinage of both gold and silver but dispenses with a fixed official gold-silver ratio or else adjusts this ratio frequently according to the changing market ratio in the rest of the world. We must remember that it is the discrepancy between official ratio and market ratio that causes the outflow of one metal which is characteristic of the bimetallic standard. In England, for instance, the value of the guinea was permitted to vary in terms of shillings. This elasticity in the gold-silver ratio permitted the system to retain both silver and gold coins. Nevertheless, as early as 1816, England began to issue token silver coins, thus solving once and for all the difficult problem of having both silver and gold circulate in spite of the changing market ratio of the value of the two metals.

Hamilton chose the 15-to-1 ratio between silver and gold because it was the market ratio of the day. Soon after the establishment of that ratio, however, the international value of gold increased. France, for instance, established an official ratio of 15.5 to 1 in 1803. This meant that gold was now more valuable in France than in the United States since one unit of gold would exchange for 15.5 units of silver in France but for only 15 units in the United States. Accordingly, gold was shipped to France.

In 1834 the mint ratio in the United States was fixed at 16 to 1, while the French ratio remained at 15.5 to 1, with the result that, in the United States, gold drove silver out of circulation. Since this result was a foregone conclusion, it must be assumed that the new ratio was set to please gold producers rather than to achieve the impossible, that is, to make the bimetallic standard work. In discussing these gold and silver movements, however, it must be remembered that the divergence between the official and the international market ratios was not very great and that the export and import of individual coins depended to some extent on their actual weight.

With the discovery of gold in California, Australia, and Russia the international market ratio changed, in 1853, to 15.33 to 1. This led to such an outflow of silver from the United States that an embarrassing shortage of silver coin resulted. The difficulty was overcome by the Coinage Act of 1853, which introduced silver coins which were not full-bodied and could not be coined freely. Since the coins were not full-bodied, a changing gold-silver ratio (unless it was substantial) could not lead to an outflow of silver; and since silver could not be coined freely, it was up to the government to regulate the total supply of silver money.

With the Coinage Act of 1853 the country had in fact accepted the gold standard and abolished the free coinage of silver. Only the silver dollar, which could still be freely coined, retained its full legal-tender power and was, therefore, completely equal to the gold dollar at the then existing ratio of 16 to 1. This exception meant little, since nobody wanted to use silver as money at this official ratio when the market ratio was 15.33 to 1. When silver dollars were coined, it was only to have the weight and fineness of the silver certified at a low cost and was not to provide silver dollars for circulation.

The Gold Standard

The outbreak of the Civil War led to monetary problems which, for a time at least, silenced the gold-silver controversy. Redemption of paper money in specie ceased towards the end of 1861, and the road was open for a credit inflation with which the Civil War, as any other major war, was to a large part financed. Commercial banks created bank notes, and the Treasury issued the so-called greenbacks. The total supply of currency increased by about 120 per cent. Chart 8–2 (p. 87) shows the sharp price inflation caused by the increased monetary circulation. Wholesale prices rose by more than 100 per cent, and the price of the gold dollar in terms of the paper dollar was doubled.

At the end of the war it would have been wise to accept the inflated price level as an accomplished fact and to stabilize the paper dollar at its reduced gold value. This decision would have spared the country the cruel and unnecessary hardships of a price deflation, which became unavoidable once it was decided that the prewar gold content of the dollar was to be maintained. Redemption in gold was resumed in 1879 after 14 years of deflation.

The inflation in the United States had not been accompanied by inflations in other countries. If, therefore, the gold content of the dollar remained officially unchanged, the dollar was overvalued and American products were unsalable on the world market. Devaluation of the dollar, on the other hand, that is, a reduction of its gold content by approximately 50 per cent, would have permitted immediate introduction of convertibility and allowed international trade on a competitive basis. Most important, however, it would have made it unnecessary to carry through the price deflation which the country suffered from 1865 to 1879 and which was accentuated by deflationary trends in other countries.

When the United States returned to a metallic standard, it was the gold standard that was chosen. England has been on gold since 1816 and lent the prestige of its economic strength to gold; the new German Empire had embraced the gold standard in 1871; and most other countries were soon forced to follow.[2] The demonetization of silver, together with the great increase in silver production which happened at the same time, threatened all bimetallic systems with the loss of their gold resources and induced finally almost all countries to turn to the gold standard.

In the United States the free coinage of silver dollars was abolished in 1873. This measure, insignificant by itself, caused enormous political repercussions. By way of a political compromise, the Bland-Allison Silver Purchase Act of 1876 introduced government purchases of silver, the coinage of this silver into silver dollars, and the issue of silver certificates which were to take the place of the heavy coin. What could have been done inexpensively with some kind of paper money was done expensively and clumsily to please the silver producers and many others who believed that their economic problems had been caused by the abolition of the free coinage of silver.

We have already seen that the deflationary policy after the Civil

[2] Even the so-called Latin Union, an international agreement between France, Italy, Belgium, and Switzerland, concluded in 1865 could not maintain the bimetallic system and abolished the free coinage of silver in 1874.

War had been a great mistake. The complaints of those who suffered under the deflation (the debtors, the unemployed) were fully justified. Wrong, however, was the argument that the source of the evil was the demonetization of silver. It was not the gold standard as such which was to blame, but the overvaluation of the dollar. History repeated itself in 1925 when Britain's return to the gold standard after World War I was made unnecessarily painful through an overvaluation of the pound.

In Europe the demonetization of silver coincided with a severe agricultural depression which was aggravated by the competition of exports of the bumper grain crops of the Western Hemisphere. The price decline was popularly attributed to the adoption of the gold standard in a number of countries and the consequent shortage of gold.

The basic mistake in this view was the much too narrow interpretation of the causes of deflation and depression. With full-bodied money constituting only a fraction of the monetary circulation, the question of a proper supply of money was quite independent of the single- or double-standard issue. Neither the increased supply of full-bodied coin nor perhaps any other monetary policy alone could have overcome the depression since, as we have seen, an increased supply of money does not necessarily lead to an increased demand for credit if low rates of interest are still higher than anticipated profits. We find the same error repeated later on, particularly in the nineteen thirties, and, characteristically, we also find new legislation which forced the Treasury to buy silver at an artificially high price.

Obviously, the whole debate about silver and gold is hopelessly inadequate unless it considers the whole supply of money, including bank notes and deposit money. But this belongs to the story of commercial banking to which we now must turn.

The First and Second Banks of the United States

The banking system of the United States before 1914 is characterized by the absence of central banking in the modern sense of the word. Commercial banking prior to the Civil War was, in the main, subject only to state legislation and, accordingly, very decentralized and unco-ordinated. The introduction of the National Banking System in 1863 succeeded in creating a uniform circulation of bank notes, issued by the new national banks operating under federal charters, but it was not a central banking system. Even today part of commercial banking in the United States remains outside the Federal Reserve System, and decentralization is still the most characteristic feature distinguishing American from European banking.

The statement that the banking system of the United States before 1914 was a system without a central bank must be qualified, however, for between 1791 and 1811 and between 1816 and 1836 there had been in operation two banks which in some respects can be considered central banks, though they were not central banks in the full modern meaning of the term.

In 1791 the federal government established, by act of Congress, the (First) Bank of the United States. Of its total capital of $10 million, a very large sum at the time, the government subscribed one fifth, while the rest was financed by private individuals. However, the government then borrowed its total contribution from the Bank, and only $2 million of the private subscription was paid in full-bodied money. If this way of financing seems unsound, it must not be forgotten that the Bank of the United States was founded for the purpose of credit creation and that this reserve of full-bodied money was reasonably adequate when compared with the Bank's limited right to incur debts. The Bank's debts "whether by bond, bill, or note" were not to exceed the amount of money deposited in the Bank by more than the Bank's capital. Deposits were then considered as savings; they enhanced the lending power of the Bank rather than being themselves a newly created liability similar to the bank notes issued by the Bank. We must realize that deposit money was not used at the time and that credit creation was limited to the issuing of bank notes.

The Bank, located in Philadelphia, had eight branches in the major cities and did regular banking business, accepting deposits, issuing bank notes, and making loans. Its customers were the government and the general public. Credit was extended to the federal government, and public funds were transferred through the Bank's facilities. Since the Bank's notes were redeemable in full-bodied money at all its branches, they circulated at par throughout the country. The Bank of the United States also forced note-issuing state banks to carefully limit their money-creating activities. The method was simple. The Bank presented notes issued by other banks for redemption in full-bodied money, and if the bank in question was unable to redeem its notes, the Bank of the United States would henceforth refuse to accept these notes.

During the lifetime of the Bank of the United States the number of state banks increased from 3 to 88, but even in 1811 the Bank of the United States accounted for about one fourth of the notes in circulation and was, therefore, dominant by its sheer size.

Nevertheless the Bank of the United States was not a central bank in the modern meaning of the term: it operated for profit, which ought not to be a major aim of a central bank; it dealt with the public, while the modern central bank is mainly a bankers' bank; it was not the only note-issuing bank, while the modern central bank has, as a rule, the monopoly of note issue; and, finally, it had no direct controlling powers over other banks, for it did not control their reserves. Still, the Bank of the United States was a promising beginning, and had it managed to survive the political opposition which brought its operations and those of its successor to an end, American banking would have had a better start and gone through a healthier development. The nation-wide scope of its operations, the uniform acceptance of its notes, its controlling effect upon the circulation of the notes of other banks, and its valuable financial services for the government, made the Bank of the United States a great stabilizing factor in the monetary system of the United States.

That the institution was not permitted to continue its operations was due to political reasons. It was argued that the Bank of the United States was unconstitutional and that it was owned by foreign capitalists. But these were not the decisive complaints. The states and the state banks were rankled by the way in which the Bank of the United States took upon itself to force its conservative policy upon the country. There were those, then as now, who argued for a cheap-money policy and hated the limiting influence of this huge institution which usurped a controlling function mainly because of its size and its nation-wide activities and, accordingly, was blamed for its "monopolistic" policies. These arguments were used against both the First Bank and its successor.

When the charter of the First Bank of the United States was not renewed, there followed, between 1811 and 1816, a period during which state banks expanded rapidly both in number (from 88 to 208) and in the volume of notes issued (from $23 to $110 million). Redemption in full-bodied money ceased, and the bank notes depreciated in varying degrees. The deterioration was so great and so fast that in spite of the opposition against renewal of the charter of the First Bank a Second Bank of the United States was created; this institution was much larger but otherwise resembled its older sister. Though mismanaged in the early years of its operation, the Second Bank soon performed the same useful and constructive functions which its predecessor had performed. Its end came in 1836 for the same reasons which had led to the fall of the First Bank.

The intervals in American banking during which no nationwide regulating influence was felt (the years between 1811 and 1816 and between 1836 and 1863) show by their chaotic monetary conditions that more rather than less central control was needed. This statement can be defended even if we fully understand the arguments behind easy-money policies and admit that it is difficult to determine the line between inflationary expansion and deflationary contraction. The United States was a quickly growing country which needed credit creation if the supply of money was to keep pace with the volume of business activity. Overly conservative credit policies could easily have done as much harm as overexpansion of credit. The trouble was not so much the expansion of credit in itself as it was overexpansion in a completely decentralized banking system which suffered from a lack of leadership and from a lack of the most elementary precautionary measures which could have maintained some degree of liquidity during a major credit crisis. Had there been a central bank to offer leadership and help, it not only might have reduced the mistakes of overexpansion but also would have reduced the severity of the contraction process through the increase in liquidity which the pooling of bank reserves and the creation of additional reserves would have made possible. As it was, there was no limit to expansion, and when illiquidity forced contraction upon the banks and upon the whole economy, contraction was just as excessive as expansion had been. Cheap-money policies make a central reserve system even more indispensable than do conservative policies.

State Banking Prior to the Civil War

With the exception of some unincorporated "private" banks, most banks before the Civil War operated under state charters and enjoyed the advantages of limited liability. During the first third of the nineteenth century the granting of charters to banks required special chartering acts of the state legislature. Existing banks could secure a monopolistic position for themselves by preventing, through political pressure and bribery, the chartering of competitive institutions. According to the new principle of "free" banking (first introduced in Michigan in 1837) any person or group of persons could obtain a charter provided they complied with some general rules concerning such matters as the backing of notes issued, the amounts of notes issued in relation to bank capital, etc. In some states these limitations were inadequate, and in other states, where stricter rules prevailed, the banks often found ways to circumvent the stipulated requirements.

State banks were generally privately managed, but in many the state had a share and was thereby able to influence lending policies.

Because investment opportunities seemed inexhaustible at the time and capital was very scarce, it is no wonder that there was a great demand for loanable funds and a great temptation to create credit when savings were supplied in insufficient quantities.

The principal means of creating credit then was the creation of bank notes and was not, as today, the creation of deposit money. A bank would issue notes and hope that most of these notes would stay in circulation, that is, that they would not be presented for redemption in full-bodied money. If a bank invested its capital in government bonds, and if, for instance, these bonds could be used as backing for an equal amount of notes in circulation, the bank would earn interest not only on the government bonds but also on the loans made with the newly created bank notes.

Whether bank notes stayed in circulation depended on the confidence in the bank's ability to redeem its notes and to some extent on the distance from the place of issue. If the bank was inconveniently located, as were the "wildcat" banks in the backwoods, the notes, once successfully launched, were less likely to find their way back. Because of their dubious redeemability, however, they would not be able to circulate at face value. There were so many kinds of bank notes in circulation, banking laws differed so widely from state to state, and the reserve position of a bank was often so doubtful, that a weekly published *Bank Note Detector*, which gave information concerning the rate of depreciation of the various issues, had to be used. That this was an ideal time for counterfeiting goes without saying.

This system was not only inconvenient and unsafe for the individual holder of bank notes but also dangerous for the economy as a whole. Periods of boom and bust alternated. The financing of long-term investment projects (roads and railroads) with short-term funds and completely inadequate reserve provisions combined to produce avalanches of illiquidity in depression periods. This erratic expansion and contraction behavior is shown by the fact that the circulation of bank notes of the state banks increased from $95 million to $149 million between 1834 and 1837 and fell to $59 million in 1843.

There are, however, a few bright spots in this dark picture:

1. The above-mentioned two Banks of the United States exerted their stabilizing influence during 40 years of this period between 1791 and 1863.

2. Several regional attempts to improve the situation were successful. In 1824 the Suffolk System in Boston established a scheme

which gave New England a bank-note circulation in which bank notes, though issued by many different banks, were redeemable at par throughout the territory. Before 1824 Boston banks had been redeeming their own notes at par, but the notes issued by country banks circulated at a discount, chiefly because of the expense of redemption at a distant place. Thus the public, when in need of full-bodied money, would tend to redeem the notes of Boston banks at par, while the notes of country banks would stay in circulation. This state of affairs was decidedly unprofitable to the Boston banks and constituted another application of Gresham's law. To protect themselves, the Boston banks offered to redeem the notes of the country banks at par in Boston if the country banks would maintain adequate reserves of full-bodied money in Boston. If the country banks refused to co-operate, the Boston banks would collect the notes of the recalcitrant banks and request redemption at the place of issue. As a member of the Suffolk System a country bank found it easier to make loans since its notes would circulate at par. Soon the whole region enjoyed the advantages of a uniform circulation of bank notes.

3. While the Suffolk System represents one of those interesting cases where private initiative accomplished what the government was not willing or able to do, the Louisiana System must be credited to the government of Louisiana. In 1842 this state made it obligatory for all banks to hold a specie reserve of one third and a commercial paper reserve of two thirds against their note and deposit liabilities. Notes of other banks were not to be counted as reserves and were, therefore, promptly presented for redemption. Here we meet for the first time official emphasis on commercial loans as the normal lending activity of commercial banks. Liquidity was to be assured not only by relatively large and effectively enforced reserves of full-bodied money but also by a careful lending policy which made the banks stay away from those long-term investments which proved fatal to so many banks in other states. The record of the Louisiana System up to the Civil War was excellent. We have seen earlier that the commercial-loan theory of credit must be criticized when overstated. But to say that a system built on this theory does not guarantee an ideal supply of money does not deny that such a system can be a good deal better than was the average situation prevailing throughout most of the United States between 1836 and 1863.

4. Among the bright spots in the American banking picture of pre-Civil War times must also be mentioned the Safety Fund System, which was established by the state of New York in 1829. This system

of compulsory mutual bank liability insurance was a forerunner of our present Federal Deposit Insurance. Both the owners of bank notes and deposits were to be protected against losses through a common fund into which each bank had to pay an amount equal to 3 per cent of its capital. The system failed in 1842[3] and was later changed to protect note holders only. It ended when, with the creation of the National Banking System, the charters of the insured banks expired.

Before we turn to the reorganization of commercial banking under the National Banking System, we must inquire into the relationship between the federal government and the state banks. We have already seen that the two Banks of the United States served as bankers of the federal government. Even before the expiration of the charter of the Second Bank, however, Jackson withdrew the deposits of the federal government and placed them with a large number of state banks. Through an Act of Congress in 1836 the federal government tried to influence commercial banking policies in depository banks by limiting deposits, by requesting reports, and by demanding redemption of bank notes in specie. In other words, the Treasury tried to exert central banking functions. Nevertheless, the federal government experiences with the state banks, which it had so uncautiously emancipated from the sobering influence of the Second Bank of the United States, were not encouraging; and in 1846, 10 years after the end of the Second Bank, an Independent Treasury System was created. The funds of the federal government were from then on held in the Treasury in Washington and in subtreasuries in various other cities. This system reduced the contact between the Treasury and the commercial banks to a minimum and prevented losses by the Treasury from bank failures. It also meant, however, that the already precarious reserve position of the commercial banks was made worse by the withdrawal of much of the available full-bodied money.

The National Banking System: A System without Leader

From the preceding section it can be seen that American commercial banking was in a most unsatisfactory state at the outbreak of the Civil War. More than 1,500 banks had issued bank notes, and many of these bank notes did not circulate at par; the reserves of full-bodied money were inadequate, and there was no central monetary authority to which to turn in a liquidity crisis.

[3] The contributions were too small in comparison with the risks involved and were based on the capital of the banks, thus putting a premium on a small capital/liability ratio, that is, on less rather than more conservative policies.

Before the outbreak of the war it had already become quite clear that a thorough reorganization of the whole commercial banking system of the United States could not be postponed much longer. The war hastened reform measures in hopes that a new system would help finance the war effort. Major emphasis was placed on the creation of a uniform circulation of bank notes. The national bank notes were to be backed by government bonds, and in this arrangement we can detect the desire to create a wider market for government securities. The national banks bought only a very small amount of the newly issued bonds, however, and thus the newly created National Banking System had little to do with financing the Civil War.

We must now study this system which served for half a century (between the Civil War and World War I) as a substitute for what it failed to create: a modern central banking system.

It is best to characterize the National Banking System by the negative feature that it did not constitute a central banking system. The newly created national banks were more uniformly and more strictly regulated than the state banks, but they were still commercial banks without a leader—an orchestra without a conductor.

The National Banking Act of (1863 and) 1864 enabled any group of five or more persons to set up a national bank under a federal charter if certain minimum conditions were complied with. These conditions concerned minimum capital requirements based on the size of the city in which the bank was located, the purchase by the national banks of government bonds in certain minimum amounts in relation to the bank's capital, the backing of national bank notes by these bonds, the reserves in lawful money to be held against bank notes and deposits, and other regulations of lesser importance.

The Act's main purpose was to create a uniform bank-note circulation. Through the amendment of 1865 a tax of 10 per cent was imposed on all bank notes issued by state banks. This tax was prohibitive and led to a wholesale change-over by banking institutions from state to federal charters. In 1863 there were only 66 national banks with deposits amounting to $9.4 million, as against 1,466 state banks with $494 million of deposits. But by 1868 the picture had reversed, the national banks numbering 1,640 and the state banks only 247; their deposits were $744 million and $52 million, respectively. As long as credit creation depended on bank-note issue this result was to be expected.

The fact that the state banks soon began to grow again may seem more astonishing. By 1873 there were 1,330 state banks in existence, and when the National Banking System merged with the Federal Reserve System in 1914, there were 7,473 national banks holding $8.1 billion in deposits, while the deposits in 18,520 state banks reached almost $12 billion.

The explanation of this growth of state banking in spite of the 10 per cent tax on note issue by state banks lies in the ascendancy of deposit money over bank notes. Demand deposits of state-chartered banks were not subject to the 10 per cent tax. As soon as check payments developed, and the commercial banks were able to embark on the process of multiple credit expansion (as described in Chapter 14), the right to issue notes became relatively unimportant. Furthermore, reserve requirements, regulating the creation of deposit money were, as a rule, more lenient in the case of state banks than national banks.

The quick development of deposit money was in part a reaction against the insufficient supply of currency caused by the National Banking System. Since deposit money is convertible on demand into currency, we can guess at the main weakness of the National Banking System: it left the *total* supply of money essentially unregulated while limiting too rigidly the supply of bank notes. Such a system was bound to lead to crises of illiquidity.

National Bank Notes and Their Backing

The regulations concerning the issue of bank notes by the national banks were unfortunately designed. The national banks had to deposit United States bonds with the Treasurer of the United States, who would then issue national bank notes to the banks to the amount of 90 per cent of the par value of these bonds.[4]

So far so good, but how was the total supply of bank notes to be adjusted to the demand for currency, particularly in critical periods when the public desired to change deposit money into currency? No consideration was given to the problem of liquidity, that is, to the need for an adequate supply of bank notes in relation to deposit money. As a matter of fact, the system was so designed that it often

[4] According to the Gold Standard Act of 1900, notes in circulation could be equal to 100 per cent of the par value of the bonds. Before 1874 the national banks had to hold a reserve in lawful money against the national bank notes in circulation equal to the reserve requirements applying to the deposits of their customers which we shall discuss below. This reserve against the national bank notes was abolished by the Amendment of 1874 and was replaced by the regulation that an amount of lawful money equal to 5 per cent of the banks' outstanding notes was to be deposited with the Treasurer of the United States. Thereby all notes were made redeemable at the offices of the Treasury throughout the country. The reason for this measure was that at places distant from the offices of the issuing bank the notes had not always been able to circulate at par.

led to a reduced supply of currency when more currency was needed.

We remember that the national bank notes were backed by government bonds. Bank-note circulation depended, therefore, upon (1) the willingness of the banks to invest in government bonds above the minimum required by the National Banking Act and (2) the Treasury's policy with regard to the retirement of its bonds. If, for instance, a prosperous period led to a budget surplus, the Treasury could retire its bonds and thereby force the banks to reduce their bank-note circulation at just the time when there was a greater demand for currency. It must also be assumed that the banks' desire to keep bonds in their portfolios was dictated by profit expectations, based on anticipated bond prices and yields rather than on the desire to supply the amount of currency which the economy needed.

Thus the bank-note circulation was worse than inelastic; it was unpredictable and liable to decrease when an increase was needed. General and rigid regulations cannot guarantee an adequate supply of currency through the actions of thousands of independent commercial banks. Only a central bank which has the power to monopolize the bank-note issue can be relied upon to competently regulate the circulation of bank notes.

Reserve Requirements and Deposit Money

We must now consider this inadequate arrangement concerning bank-note circulation against the equally unsatisfactory regulation of the supply of deposit money.

The National Banking Act of 1864 divided the national banks, according to their location, into central-reserve-city banks (New York, and later Chicago), reserve-city banks, and "country" banks. Banks in central-reserve-cities had to hold a reserve of 25 per cent of their deposit liabilities in the form of lawful money. Banks in reserve-cities had to fulfill the same reserve requirement but were permitted to keep one half of their reserves in central-reserve-city banks; the "country" banks could hold three fifths of their required reserve of 15 per cent in reserve-city banks or central-reserve-city banks.

These reserve requirements were defective for the following reasons:

1. The reserve requirements applied to national banks only and not to all commercial banks. Most state banks operated under more liberal regulations.

2. The reserve requirements of the National Banking Act scattered a large part of the reserves thinly throughout the country. These

reserves should have been pooled. If a bank is to rely on its own liquid funds, these funds have to be very large. By pooling reserves the law of averages is applied in a way which reduces the total amount of reserves needed. Any member of such a reserve system has access to the common pool and unless all members need more currency at the same time the pool can be much smaller than the sum of separate reserves would have to be.

3. Small and scattered reserves are of little use. This is particularly true when these reserves are legally required at all times and must not be touched even in an emergency. This situation has been properly ridiculed by W. Randolph Burgess, who suggested that the difficulties with such a reserve system

> were analogous to an experience a European city is reported to have had at one time with cabs. The city fathers, as the story goes, were greatly troubled because there were frequently not sufficient cabs available at cab stands. They, therefore, passed an ordinance that each cab stand should have at least one cab waiting all the time. The result of the ordinance was, of course to accentuate the scarcity.[5]

4. The pooling of reserves means that one bank or a group of banks can, in an emergency, be supplied with needed currency from a common reservoir. However, if this pooling is done in the commercial banks of the reserve- and central-reserve-cities, the system will not work in a nation-wide emergency, even though it might be sufficient if the demands for increased reserves were localized and synchronized in such a way that interregional shortages and surpluses were nicely balanced. A nation-wide demand for currency cannot be met by shifting reserves to the points where they are most urgently needed, because they are needed everywhere at the same time. Furthermore, the banks in the central-reserve-cities will try to hold on to their reserves because these reserves constitute legally required minima.

5. The deposits which country and reserve-city banks held in commercial banks of central-reserve-cities were, to a large extent, used by the latter as a basis for credit expansion. The depositary banks aimed at maximizing profits. When, therefore, a depositing bank wanted to withdraw its reserve funds, the depositary bank had to liquidate some of its investments or call in some of its loans. This only magnified the credit crisis with which the system tried to cope.

6. The total supply of lawful money was, at the time, strictly limited. It consisted of full-bodied coin, silver certificates, fiduciary

[5] W. Randolph Burgess, *The Reserve Banks and the Money Market* (New York: Harper & Bros., 1946), p. 25.

coin, greenbacks, and national bank notes. The supply of none of these could be increased on short notice. Only a central bank with the power to issue more bank notes, to create larger reserves for the commercial banks, or to reduce reserve requirements could have solved the liquidity problem. We have already seen that the basic weakness of the National Banking System was that it failed to create such a central bank.

A central bank, had it existed and had it been given the power to extend its command to the field of state banking, could have made an attempt to control credit expansion and to prevent an oversupply of deposit money; and in case of a credit crisis it could have tried to stem the tide of illiquidity connected with such a crisis by making larger amounts of currency instantly available. A run on banks can often be stopped if reserves are courageously used and if larger reserve funds can be procured. In part this is a psychological problem. The attitude of the banks' customers is well expressed by the remark the farmer made when he waited for his turn at the counter during a run on his bank: "If they can pay me," he said, "I don't want my money, but if they can't pay, I want it."

The National Banking System has to its credit the creation of a uniform circulation of bank notes and of a check payment system. In other respects it was disappointing. The country lacked monetary leadership, and the system was so constructed that it produced financial crises rather than counteracting them. Since public attention is always attracted to the more glamorous phenomena of a crisis, we can understand why the main weakness of the National Banking System was believed to be the inelasticity of the currency supply. Much less attention was paid to the other side of the picture: the overexpansion of credit in the form of deposit money, without which an increased demand for currency could not have become so dangerous.

We shall see that the Federal Reserve System, which was created to overcome the basic weaknesses of the National Banking System, solved only part of the problem and that it led the country into a credit crisis far worse than any crisis which the National Banking System had to answer for.

SUGGESTIONS FOR FURTHER READING

From bimetallism to the gold standard:

CHANDLER, LESTER V. *The Economics of Money and Banking,* chap. 6., rev. ed. New York: Harper & Brothers, 1953.

DEWEY, D. R. *Financial History of the United States,* 11th ed. New York: Longmans, Green and Co., 1931.

RUFENER, LOUIS A. *Money and Banking in the United States,* chaps. 6–9. Boston: Houghton Mifflin Co., 1936.

American banking before the Civil War:

BOARD OF GOVERNORS OF THE FEDERAL RESERVE SYSTEM. *Banking Studies,* pp. 3–36. Washington, D.C., 1941.

CHANDLER, LESTER V. *The Economics of Money and Banking,* chap. 12. rev. ed. New York: Harper & Brothers, 1953.

JAMES, F. CYRIL. *The Economics of Money, Credit and Banking,* chap. 11. 3d ed. New York: The Ronald Press Co., 1940.

RUFENER, LOUIS A. *Money and Banking in the United States,* chaps. 15–16. Boston: Houghton Mifflin Co., 1936.

On the National Banking System:

DAVIS, A. M. *The Origin of the National Banking System,* Senate Document No. 582. Washington, D.C.: Government Printing Office, 1910.

JAMES, F. CYRIL. *The Economics of Money, Credit and Banking,* chap. 12. 3d ed. New York: The Ronald Press Co., 1940.

SPRAGUE, O. M. W. *History of Crises Under the National Banking System,* Senate Document No. 538. Washington, D.C.: Government Printing Office, 1910.

QUESTIONS AND PROBLEMS

1. "The simultaneous use of full-bodied silver and gold coin would be possible under a parallel but not under a bimetallic standard." Correct? Explain.
2. Discuss the economic and political repercussions of the abolition of the free coinage of silver dollars in 1873.
3. "The First and Second Banks of the United States were not central banks in the modern meaning of the term." Correct? Why?
4. What were the outstanding shortcomings of the American banking system between 1836 and 1863?
5. Did the National Banking System overcome the shortcomings discussed in Question 4?
6. Discuss the reserve requirements of the National Banking System.
7. How do you explain the fact that the state banks grew in number between 1868 and 1914 from 247 to 18,250 in spite of a 10 per cent tax on their note issue?
8. Is it true to say that the National Banking System left the total quantity of money unregulated while it regulated the supply of bank notes so clumsily that this supply was often reduced when more currency was needed? What were the inherent dangers of the system?

9. "A rigid prescription of reserve ratios would be dangerous, unless some central authority had the power to vary the ratios in case of need. In the United States, the danger was increased a thousandfold by the scattering of reserves in many institutions, and the absence of any authority whatsoever" (F. Cyril James). Discuss.
10. "The difficulties with bank reserves were analogous to an experience a European city is reported to have had at one time with cabs. The city fathers, as the story goes, were greatly troubled because there were frequently not sufficient cabs available at cab stands. They, therefore, passed an ordinance that each cab stand should have at least one cab waiting all the time. The result of this ordinance was, of course, to accentuate the scarcity. Laws as to bank reserves had a corresponding result" (W. Randolph Burgess). Comment.

Chapter 16 CREATION OF THE FEDERAL RESERVE SYSTEM

Central Banking Experiences

In Chapter 10 we have seen that the ideal central bank was supposed to operate mechanically. It was to be so constructed that the supply of money would automatically adjust itself to the needs of business. The central bank would not manage the supply of money consciously but would simply follow principles of behavior which were built into the very structure of the system. The managers of the central bank could not make serious mistakes if they followed to the letter the backing or reserve requirements established by the Central Banking Act. Through these requirements changes in economic conditions would exert a correcting influence on the supply of money.

Up to this point nearly everybody agreed. But as to the principles which would guarantee the automatic adjustment of the money supply to the needs of business, there existed an interesting conflict of opinion. Two basically different attitudes, known as the currency and the banking principles, characterized this great debate during the nineteenth century. To understand the philosophy of central banking which prevailed when the Federal Reserve System was created, it is more important to understand the meaning of this controversy than to study various European banking acts which preceded the Federal Reserve Act.

Before we study the difference between the two principles, it is important to stress the fact that both schools were wrong in the naïve expectation that a mere set of rules, faithfully adhered to, would provide the economy with an ideal money supply. Both the currency and the banking schools, furthermore, supported the gold standard. Since the gold standard required that all money must be directly or indirectly redeemable in gold, redemption in gold was not a point of controversy, it was taken for granted. Modern monetary and banking theory, therefore, must criticize both schools for their overemphasis on the advantages of the price-specie-flow mechanism.

The currency school, whose main representatives were Lord Overstone and Robert Torrens, held the following views: First of all, it counted only currency as money. Secondly, it wanted the total supply of money (currency) to change in exact proportion to the changing supply of full-bodied money. It believed, thirdly, that the necessary adjustments of the money supply to economic needs would come about through changes in the balance of trade. Suppose that a given supply of money proved to be inadequate for a growing economy: prices would fall, falling prices would lead to an excess of exports over imports, and the difference would be made up by a corresponding inflow of gold. Now monetary circulation would increase, and prices would be permitted to rise again.

The viewpoints of the currency school found their complete expression in the Peel Act of 1844, which reorganized the Bank of England. It was assumed that a certain minimum amount of bank notes would always stay in circulation because the volume of trade was sure to require it. This so-called "fiduciary" circulation was fixed by law but was capable of revision from time to time. It was entirely independent of the monetary gold supply and was backed by government bonds. The rest of the bank notes in circulation were backed by 100 per cent in gold, so that bank notes over and above the fiduciary issue were actually gold certificates.

The Bank of England was divided into two entirely separate departments, the Issue Department, whose liabilities consisted of notes in circulation and whose assets were government bonds and gold, and the Banking Department, which performed regular banking business and was to remain unaffected by the monetary transactions of the Issue Department. The assets of the Banking Department consisted of discounts and securities, and its liabilities comprised the Bank's capital and the commercial bank and government deposits. Deposits were not considered as money, as the strict separation of monetary and banking activities shows.

The basic idea was that the total amount of money in circulation should vary with the monetary gold supply. About one third of the circulating notes was backed, pound by pound, in gold, while the fiduciary issue, fixed at 14 million pounds, amounted to about two thirds. The Bank of England, at the time, was not the only note-issuing bank, but the maximum issue of the commercial banks was limited to their circulation outstanding in 1844. Gradually these issues lapsed, and the fiduciary issue of the Bank of England was increased. By 1923, when the last commercial bank issue lapsed, the fiduciary issue amounted to nearly 20 million pounds.

The Act of 1844 tried to achieve a monetary circulation which varied exactly in amount with the monetary gold but was, at the same time, a good deal less costly than a circulation of nothing but full-bodied coin. Figure 16–1 illustrates the basic principle of the Peel Act.

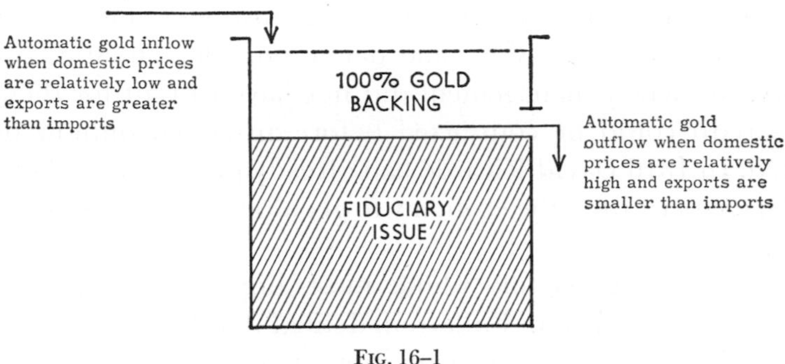

FIG. 16–1

Strict adherence to the principle of the Act of 1844 would have prevented the growth of the British economy. Actually, the necessary adjustment of the supply of money to the demands of a quickly growing economy was accomplished through the following violations of the currency principle:

1. Since the circulation of currency was not elastic enough, the public turned to the use of deposit money whose supply was not limited by the Act of 1844 because demand deposits were not regarded as money.

2. Greater elasticity of note issue was provided by suspensions which permitted the Bank of England to exceed the fiduciary issue. In 1928 a fusion of Treasury and Bank of England notes took place, bringing the fiduciary issue to 260 million pounds. Further adjustments were possible at any time by Treasury directive to the Bank of England. With the end of the gold standard in 1931 the whole system lost its meaning. Neither gold nor the fiduciary issue limited the supply of money. The fiduciary issue is now changed whenever a changing demand for currency requires a changing supply of bank notes.

3. In actual practice the monetary circulation was not expected to change in exact conformity with gold movements. It was pointed

out that gold movements could occur which had nothing to do with changes in price levels. For instance, gold could flow into domestic hoards; it would then be unwise to contract the bank-note circulation.

4. It was seen that the mechanism which the currency school envisaged could do deflationary and inflationary harm: only after insufficient supply of money had resulted in reduced prices, a favorable balance of trade, and an influx of gold would monetary expansion be permissible; and only after an oversupply of money had actually exerted inflationary effects and led to an outflow of gold would the mechanism bring about a contractionist adjustment. This process was much too cumbersome, slow, and dangerous for domestic economic stability. Monetary management did not have to wait for these reactions. Credit could be contracted before an actual outflow of gold occurred. In 1816 David Ricardo had already proposed a policy which would have permitted the economy to get along with a very small gold reserve.

The banking school, whose most important members were Thomas Tooke and John Fullarton, denied that banks had the power to increase the circulation of bank notes over and above the amount that expanding business was willing to absorb. Since, therefore, monetary circulation would grow only in a growing economy, they felt that increased bank-note issues would not lead to rising prices.

When the banking school criticized the shortcomings of the currency school, it showed a greater understanding of the practical financial problems which had to be solved. Its members felt that a strict adherence to the gold-flow mechanism of the Peel Act would lead to serious difficulties. As a "counter theory," as John Stuart Mill called it, the banking principle was not so bad.

The banking school was much less successful when it tried to develop its critical viewpoints into a principle which would provide the central bank with an automatic device for regulating the supply of money. It had been correct in criticizing the Peel Act for its futile attempt to separate monetary and banking policies. But it made the mistake of following the commercial-loan theory of money.

We have seen in Chapter 10 that the commercial-loan theory holds that bank-note issue through the discounting of commercial paper will tie the circulation of money to the circulation of commodities in the most ideal manner possible. Complete liquidity and elasticity would be achieved, and the "legitimate" demands of business would be satisfied by limiting discounting operations to "eligible" commercial paper. Notes of long-term borrowers (securities and, particularly, government bonds) would be excluded as a basis of note issue to ensure the regular backflow of bank notes to the central bank via the repayment of short-term credits. All that was needed was a set of rules which would tie the issue of bank notes to the discounting and rediscounting of commercial paper. In addition, a gold reserve was required, since convertibility of bank notes was to be maintained at all times. The notes not backed by gold were to be backed by eligible commercial paper and not by government bonds.

This view must be criticized on the following grounds:

1. The supply of commercial paper is no indication of the legitimate demand for money. It is certainly no better indication than is the supply of gold, on which the currency school based its principle.

2. Commercial banks do not necessarily consider commercial paper their most liquid asset. It all depends on the willingness of the central bank to buy government bonds. If the central bank is always ready to buy government bonds, these bonds can be a more liquid asset item for the commercial banks than is commercial paper.

3. Regulation of the total supply of money cannot be based on the vague concept of a "legitimate" demand of business. The demand of business depends on rates of interest, profit anticipations, habits of financing, and many other factors. Henry Thornton stated the basic determinants of the demand for loans as early as 1802. He wrote:

> In order to ascertain how far the desire of obtaining loans at the Bank may be expected at any time to be carried, we must enquire into the subject of the quantum of profit likely to be derived from borrowing there under the existing circumstances. This is to be judged of by considering two points: the amount, first, of interest to be paid on the sum borrowed; and, secondly, on the mercantile or other gain to be obtained by the employment of the borrowed capital. . . . We may, therefore, consider this question as turning principally on a comparison of the rate of interest taken at the Bank with the current rate of mercantile profit.[1]

4. The rate of interest was to be determined by the gold-flow mechanism, and the banking school, therefore, acknowledged as "legitimate" only that demand for credit which would arise within the limits of the gold-flow mechanism.

5. The liquidity of short-term commercial paper depends in part on the salability of the goods in process or in inventories and may break down when it is put to a severe test in times of depression.

Thus we see that both the currency and the banking principles

[1] Quoted in F. A. Hayek, *Prices and Production* (London: George Routledge & Sons, Ltd., 1931), p. 13.

were unsatisfactory foundations of central banking. This is not surprising since both principles suffered from the illusion that it is possible to avoid the arduous task of conscious day-to-day monetary management by subscribing to some automatic formula.

European Central Banking before 1914

Since the Federal Reserve Act drew heavily on the experiences of other countries, it seems advisable that some of the principles of European central banking should be enumerated.

1. *The fiduciary issue system.* This system, used by Peel in 1844, has already been discussed. It featured a legally limited circulation of bank notes which were not backed by gold and a 100 per cent backing requirement for the rest. This 100 per cent gold backing, if strictly adhered to, would have meant either that gold reserves could not have been used to achieve a balance of international payments or that their use for this purpose would have led to domestic contraction. Domestic circulation would change in direct proportion to the gold flow.

2. *The percentage method of gold backing* was first applied to bank notes alone. In some countries it was later extended to central bank deposits. It may require more gold than the fiduciary issue system, and it can make gold available for export purposes only through a multiple contraction of the domestic circulation. The system can be combined with a fixed total issue, as in Germany in 1875, where bank notes had to be backed by one third in gold while the total issue was limited, though revised upward from time to time.

3. *Taxing of overissue and discount policy* were connected in the German system by the ambitious attempt to create a foolproof mechanism of bank-note issue. The central bank was permitted to exceed the fixed total, but it had to pay a tax of 5 per cent on the excessive bank-note circulation. This tax, in turn, was supposed to induce the central bank to increase its rate of rediscount, and an increased rediscount rate was to lead to credit contraction and reduced circulation.

4. *A maximum figure of note issue, entirely independent of the gold reserve,* was the basic principle of the system used in France before World War I. The *Macmillan Report* of 1931 called this system "the best form of limitation."[2] It implies frequent adjustments of the maximum figure and to that extent exposes the central bank's activities to constant regulation by government authorities. Connection with the gold standard is maintained through redeemability of the

[2] *Committee on Finance and Industry Report* (London: His Majesty's Stationery Office, Cmd. 3897, 1931).

bank notes, but otherwise gold supply and bank-note issue are entirely independent of each other, so that gold reserves can be used for international payments without directly affecting domestic monetary circulation.

5. *Backing of bank notes by commercial paper rather than by government bonds* was required by some banking acts, for instance, by the German Act of 1875. The backflow of short-term commercial paper was considered essential. Only when bank notes return automatically to the central bank can a rising rate of rediscount be expected to have the result of reducing the outflow of money in comparison with its backflow and, therefore, of reducing the total amount of money in circulation. Where governments bonds were permitted as backing, as under the Peel Act, they were restricted to a fiduciary issue which was considered an irreducible minimum anyhow.

6. *The central bank acquired either immediately or gradually the monopoly of bank-note issue.* Whether or not notes of other banks were still in circulation, the central bank was definitely in control of the bank-note circulation.

7. *No uniform principles concerning deposit money* had been worked out by the banking acts which preceded the Federal Reserve Act. This can easily be explained by the fact that the use of deposit money was as yet relatively unimportant and that the process of multiple credit creation was not understood.

8. *No uniform principles concerning the ownership of central banks existed.* Some central banks were privately owned, some were government owned, and some were jointly owned. The trend, however, was undoubtedly towards management in the public interest. The fact that private ownership was emphasized in some countries in spite of this trend was due to the desire to free monetary policy from interference by a greedy Treasury. Experience, however, has shown that the intricate political problem of a potential conflict between the policies of the Treasury and the central bank cannot be solved by such a relatively superficial feature as the ownership of the shares of stock of the central bank.

9. *The central bank was, as a rule, conceived as a bankers' bank,* but exceptions are known, for instance the Bank of France, which does business with the general public through numerous branches.

10. *The aims of central banking policy were relatively modest.* The central bank was not expected to help achieve "full" employment or maximum utilization of resources. The central bank had only to watch a few gauges: the price level, the exchange rates, the gold move-

ments, the reserves behind notes in circulation. If the supply of money followed the gold movement and the "legitimate" demands of business, as expressed by eligible commercial paper, overexpansion of credit was considered impossible. Insufficiency of money supply during crises caused much concern, but the intricate connection between the creation of deposit money, the supply of currency, and illiquidity was not sufficiently understood.

Novel Features of the American Central Banking System

When the financial crisis of 1907 exposed once again the illiquidity of the National Banking System, a National Monetary Commission was established to make recommendations for changes. The Commission's Report in 1912 proposed the introduction of central banking to overcome the major defects of the old system, particularly the inelasticity of note issue, the inadequacy of reserves, and the absence of a co-ordinated credit policy.[3]

The country, however, had previously been averse to the idea of central banking. Against the establishment of *one* central bank it was argued that the country was too large, that its various regions had to deal with widely diverging economic problems, and, also, that the country's highly decentralized system of commercial banking, characterized by thousands rather than dozens of banks, was quite unlike European banking structures. Behind all these arguments, however, stood the fear of centralization as such, centralization being implied in the concept of a central bank.

By way of a compromise a Central Banking System was created which was quite novel because it consisted of twelve central banks (Federal Reserve banks), whose policies were to be co-ordinated by, as it was then called, a Federal Reserve Board in Washington.

This was a compromise between regionalism and centralization in which the Board was not given much power and the very term "central bank" was avoided. Future developments led, particularly in the Banking Acts of 1933 and 1935, to a strengthening of the Board and a corresponding reduction of the powers of the Federal Reserve banks.

The trend towards centralization was inevitable as soon as central banking outgrew the naïve notion that conscious monetary man-

[3] According to its Preamble the purposes of the Federal Reserve Act were "To provide for the establishment of Federal Reserve banks, to furnish an elastic currency, to afford means for rediscounting commercial paper, to establish a more effective supervision of banking in the United States, and for other purposes."

agement could be avoided simply by adhering to the principles of the gold-flow mechanism and the commercial-loan theory. These two principles were the philosophical basis of the new system. Expansion and contraction of credit were supposed to follow the demands of business and the international flow of gold. The Federal Reserve, therefore, was based on the belief that the supply of money could be adequately regulated by adherence to well-nigh automatic controls. Under these conditions the task of co-ordinating the policies of the twelve Federal Reserve banks was not expected to be difficult or to involve any particular dangers of centralization. "Policy," in the sense of conscious management of the money supply, was to be avoided anyhow.

Another original feature of the new central banking system was the novel idea of letting the Federal Reserve banks be owned by their member banks. All national banks were required, and state banks were permitted, to become member banks by subscribing to the capital stock of the Federal Reserve bank in their district an amount equal, at par value, to 6 per cent of their capital and surplus. In addition, the member banks had to place their reserves in the Federal Reserve banks and became subject to reserve requirements which will be discussed below.

In return, the member banks enjoyed many services which the Federal Reserve banks could render. The member banks could discount commercial paper with their Federal Reserve banks or borrow on their own promissory notes and were thus enabled to increase their reserves more easily than under the National Banking System. The much desired increased elasticity of reserves seemed to be accomplished. In addition, a more satisfactory nation-wide check-clearing system was established. Other important service functions performed by the Federal Reserve banks concerned supplying currency to correspond to the public's demand for pocketbook rather than checkbook money, the handling of foreign exchange transactions, and the performance of important services as fiscal agents of the Treasury. In all these respects the new system was a great improvement over the National Banking System.

To the advantages in the form of direct services must be added the potential benefit of greater financial stability of the whole economy, a supposed result of the new system. After all, the Federal Reserve System had been created to overcome the main shortcoming of the National Banking System—its tendency to lead to credit overexpansion and illiquidity, to boom and bust.

The Resources of the Federal Reserve

At first it was believed that the resources of the Federal Reserve banks were limited to their capital subscriptions and the member banks' reserve deposits which were in gold and lawful money. The member banks subscribed the capital stock of the Federal Reserve banks and transferred their formerly scattered reserves to the common pool, whose administration was supposed to be the main function of the newly created central banks. Soon it became obvious, however, that the Federal Reserve banks had the power to *create* reserves for their member banks. That more reserves could be made available "out of nothing," if only the Federal Reserve banks could fulfill their gold reserve requirements, became the most important feature of the new system.

At first it was not fully understood that the Federal Reserve's control over the reserves of member banks would become the main instrument of monetary policy. At the time of the system's inauguration the main instrument of monetary policy was the rediscounting of commercial paper, and the initiative, therefore, was with the member banks. As a matter of fact, according to the commercial-loan theory, even the member banks were passive; they only accommodated their customers by supplying more money when increased business activity led to a growing demand for cash balances. Monetary policy was limited to changing the rate of interest at which the rediscounting of commercial paper was possible. This rate, in turn, was dictated by the monetary gold supply.

How far the Federal Reserve has moved away from these basic ideas of its conception is shown by the modest part which the rediscounting of commercial paper plays today in comparison with other policies such as open-market operations, the changing of reserve requirements, and qualitative controls. All these policies were then no more than in their infancy. It is also of interest to note that the new instruments became weapons to be used by the Board rather than by the individual Federal Reserve banks.

Reserve Regulations of the New System

The member banks as well as the Federal Reserve banks were subject to reserve requirements which differed substantially from those in force under the National Banking System. These new reserve requirements established the basis for a large potential credit expansion.

The following changes are of importance:

1. The "lawful" reserves which member banks must hold against their deposits have, since the Amendment of the Federal Reserve Act of June 21, 1917, had to consist of deposits with the Federal Reserve banks. The system of scattered reserves was abolished, the principle of "pooling" was consistently applied, and the efficiency of these reserves was greatly increased through their concentration in real central banks.

2. Against these reserve deposits of the member banks the Federal Reserve banks had to maintain "reserves in gold certificates or lawful money of not less than 35 per centum." This was an important change, for gold was promoted from high-powered to supercharged money (see Chapter 6, p. 64). A new multiplying factor could now be applied to the process of credit expansion, and the monetary superstructure, resting on a given amount of gold, could become much larger. Suppose that $100 in gold are transferred from the reserve of a member bank to a Federal Reserve bank. As a deposit with the Federal Reserve bank the gold performs the same reserve function as before, so far as the member bank is concerned. But the Federal Reserve bank is required to hold only $35 (today: $25) against the member bank's reserve deposit; $65 in gold are set free and can, whenever desired, become the legally required reserve for over $185 of additional reserve deposits of member banks.

3. The reserve requirements for member banks were lowered. On the average they had been about 21 per cent under the National Banking Act. Under the original Federal Reserve Act they were about 12 per cent, and after the Amendment of 1917, about 10 per cent. On a given amount of reserves, therefore, the member banks could create more credit.[4]

4. The new system distinguished between reserves against demand deposits and reserves against time deposits, a distinction not made under the National Banking System. Since interest could be earned on time deposits while time deposits could nevertheless satisfy in some measure the liquidity preference of bank customers, it became possible for member banks to induce customers to hold larger parts of their money reserves in the form of time deposits. Against these the member banks had to hold a uniform reserve of only 3 per cent as

[4] We might be tempted to argue that the new reserve requirements permitted about double the former credit superstructure. We have to remember, however, that the reserves in the National Banking System were "telescoped": country and reserve-city banks were permitted to hold part of their reserves with central-reserve-city banks, so that, on the average, the actually required reserves were lower than 21 per cent if we exclude interbank deposits.

compared with 13, 10, and 7 per cent against demand deposits. These variations depended on the character of the member bank (that is, central-reserve-city bank, reserve-city bank, or "country" bank). This distinction was inherited from the National Banking System. Whenever a bank could induce a shift from demand to time deposit, it could set free reserves and create more credit.

5. The circulation of Federal Reserve notes gradually supplanted the circulation of gold certificates, which in 1914 had accounted for about one third of the currency in circulation.[5] For every $100 of the old type of gold certificates replaced by Federal Reserve notes, the Federal Reserve bank gained $60 as an excess gold reserve, for the gold certificates were backed dollar for dollar by gold while the Federal Reserve notes, at the time, required a 40 per cent (today: 25 per cent) backing.

Inconsistency of the New Reserve Regulations

The new reserve regulations show that the Federal Reserve System was based on the gold-flow mechanism and the commercial-loan theory. Closer study of the implications of the new reserve requirements, however, leads to the conclusion that these two time-honored principles of central banking were not consistently applied.

The gold-flow mechanism makes sense only when the credit superstructure closely approaches the maximum figure which the monetary gold reserve is permitted to support. Only then will variations of the reserve, caused by fluctuations in international trade, call forth changes in the domestic money supply. When, therefore, the new Federal Reserve Act lowered the reserve requirements drastically, it exposed the country to a prospective credit and price inflation which would cease only when credit creation and gold outflow had absorbed the "slack" through removal of excess gold reserves and excess reserves of the member banks. Only then could the necessary tightening of the golden brakes of the monetary system be achieved.

The logic of the commercial-loan theory, too, called for the removal of excessive reserves, since only the working of the gold-flow mechanism could provide the system with a quasi-automatic determination of interest rates. Without reference to given interest rates a monetary policy according to the commercial-loan theory becomes indeterminate because at each interest level the "needs of business"

[5] These gold certificates, which were representative full-bodied money, are not to be confused with the gold certificates which the Treasury issues to the Federal Reserve banks.

which are to be accommodated by discounting will differ. The inflationary or deflationary results of the monetary policy will depend on the chosen interest rates rather than on the inherent quality of commercial paper. The commercial-loan theory would be insufficient even if it were possible to distinguish "commercial" from other credits through strict "eligibility" rules.

How inadequate was the Federal Reserve's reasoning behind its monetary policy is shown in the *Annual Report of 1923*. The Board wants to restrict credit "to productive uses" and to "the orderly flow of goods in industry and trade" and to avoid speculative credit which impedes or delays "the forward movement of goods from producer to consumer" and "breeds unwarranted increase in the volume of credit." We note that in these vague generalities speculative credit is blamed both for a shortage and an oversupply of credit.

Member Bank Reserves and Related Items

In discussing the development of the Federal Reserve System we shall make frequent use of Charts 16–1 and 16–2 which reveal, even at a first glance, the tremendous changes which have taken place in the forty-odd years of the System's existence. Since the two charts are not drawn on the same scale, the expansionist story told by Chart 16–2 must be magnified two times to correspond to the dimensions of Chart 16–1.

Let us examine the meaning of the different items whose developments are pictured in our charts.

1. *Gold stock.* Before the Gold Reserve Act of January 30, 1934, the gold stock included gold held by the Federal Reserve banks and the Treasury, and gold coins in circulation. Since then all monetary gold has been transferred to the Treasury. The Federal Reserve banks now hold only gold certificates or gold certificate credits. Gold stock and gold certificates (or gold certificate credits) are not identical in amount. The difference consists of gold held in the so-called general fund of the Treasury.

Changes in the gold stock, as shown in our charts, are, with one exception, not directly caused by monetary policy, since the Treasury's attitude towards gold purchases and sales is passive: it maintains a perfectly elastic demand for and supply of gold at a fixed price. Only indirectly will the gold stock be affected by United States and foreign monetary policies which influence price levels, economic activity, and the balance of payments, thus posing the possibility of gold flows.

A mere glance at the charts will convince us that the gold-flow

CHART 16–1

MEMBER BANK RESERVES AND RELATED ITEMS

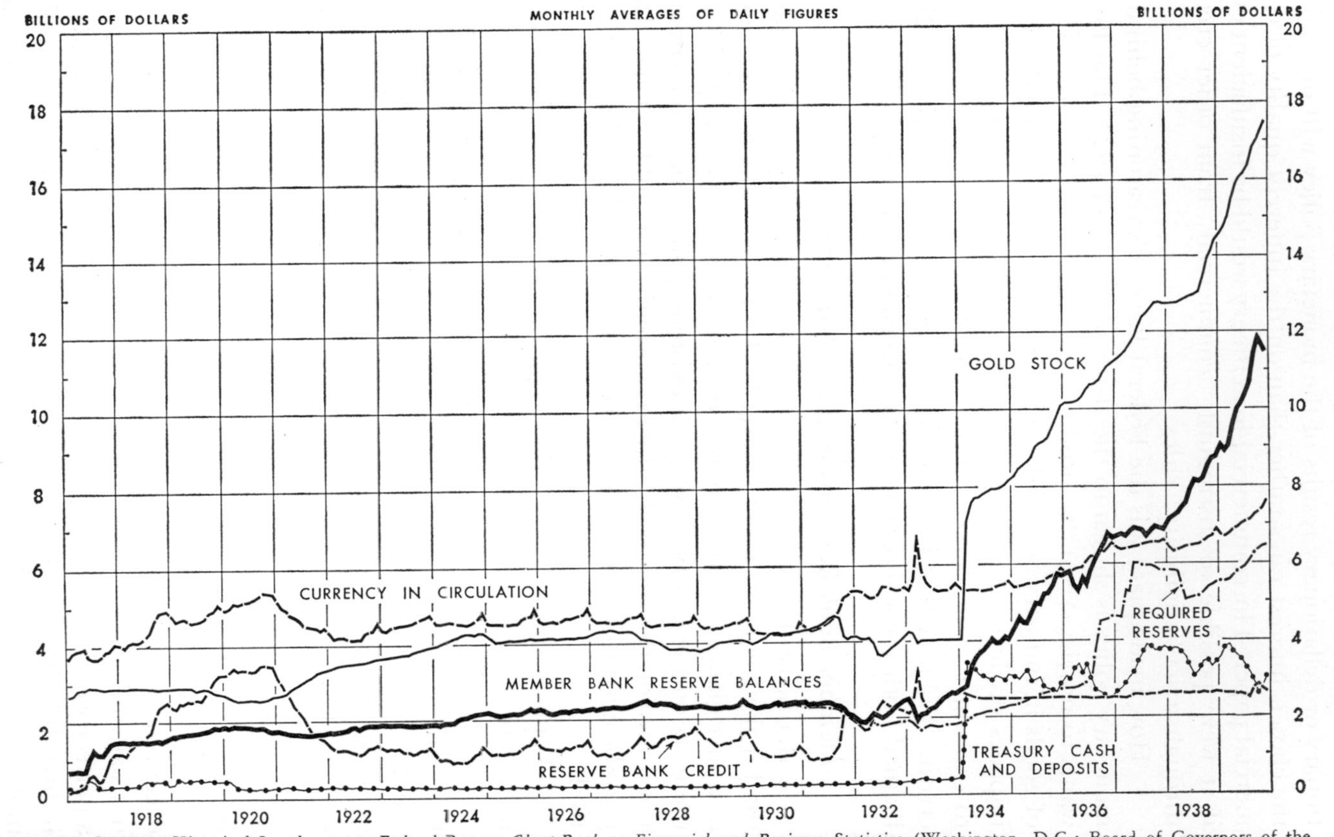

SOURCE: *Historical Supplement to Federal Reserve Chart Book on Financial and Business Statistics* (Washington, D.C.: Board of Governors of the

MEMBER BANK RESERVES AND RELATED ITEMS

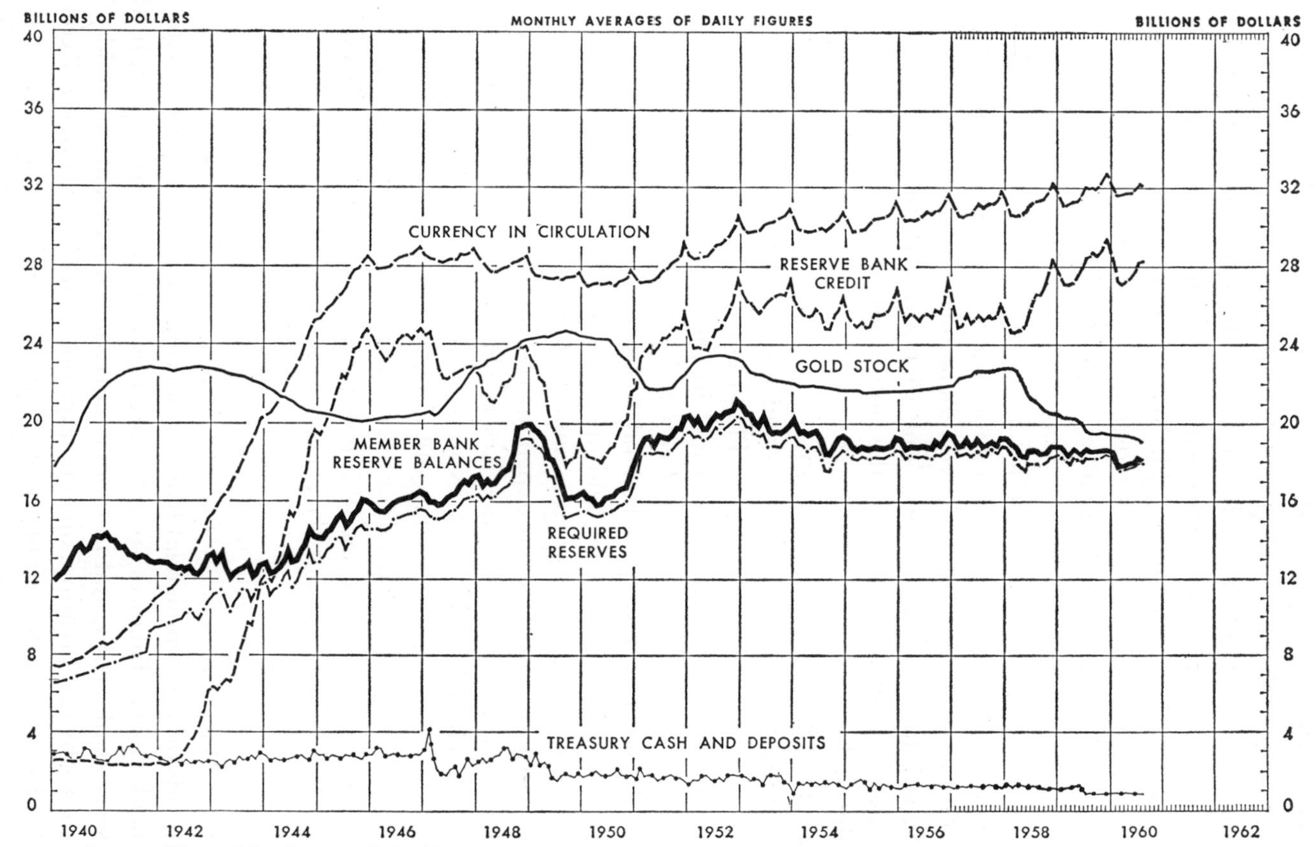

SOURCE: *Historical Supplement to Federal Reserve Chart Book on Financial and Business Statistics* (Washington, D.C.: Board of Governors of the Federal Reserve System, September, 1960), p. 3.

mechanism, as described in Chapter 10, did not dominate monetary events, since it is obvious that the supply of money was not uniquely determined by the gold stock. This does not mean, however, that changes in the gold stock did not affect the other items in our charts. That member bank reserves will increase when the Treasury buys gold was shown in Chapter 14. Nevertheless, member bank reserves do not follow the gold stock closely, since they are also dependent on reserve bank credit and on money in circulation.

The one exception mentioned, where the gold stock changed directly due to monetary policy, is shown in 1934. The tremendous, sudden change of over $3 billion was to a large extent due to the revaluation of gold. The federal government increased the gold price from $20.67 to $35.00 per ounce. The total value of the gold stock was raised by 69 per cent, and the gold content of the dollar was reduced by 59 per cent. The revaluation profit of the Treasury was over $2.8 billion. In Chart 16–1 we see that this amount exceeded member bank reserve balances and reserve bank credit.

2. *Reserve bank credit.* This item it nearly identical with the item "Total loans and securities" in the Statement of Condition of the Federal Reserve Banks (see Chapter 12, p. 132). Reserve bank credit is an expression of Federal Reserve policy since it will change as a result of discounting and open-market operations. As we follow the line in our charts we can immediately see the inflationary credit expansions caused by war expenditures. Interesting, too, is the period between 1934 and 1942 when Reserve bank credit remained at a virtually unchanging low level, expressing the inactivity forced upon the system by the growth of the gold stock and member bank reserve balances. There was no need for open-market purchases, and, as we shall see, open-market sales of all the securities owned by the Federal Reserve banks would not have been enough to absorb member bank excess reserves.

3. *Member bank reserve balances.* This item needs no explanation. We know already that the power to create deposit money depends on the commercial banks' reserves. We also know that member bank reserve balances are influenced by changes in gold stock, in Reserve bank credit, and in money (currency) in circulation. Gold purchases by the Treasury, open-market purchases by the Federal Reserve banks, and the deposit of currency in member banks (and in the Federal Reserve banks) increase member bank reserve balances. A drain of gold out of the country, open-market sales, and a greater public demand for currency have the opposite effect.

4. *Required reserves.* Member bank reserve balances, however, do not indicate proportional changes in the demand deposits of the public because required reserves and member bank reserve balances do not necessarily move together. Required reserves are determined by the demand deposits and time deposits of member banks and the legal reserve requirements. The difference between member bank reserve balances and required reserves constitutes excess reserves. These excess reserves were huge between 1934 and 1942, the period of the enormous increase in gold stock and the unnatural inactivity in Reserve bank credit. These excess reserves show that, technically, the member banks could have expanded credit by many billion dollars, had there been enough demand. It also shows that the description of the process of multiple credit expansion in Chapter 14, which assumed maximum creation of credit, was not realistic. As a matter of fact, if we applied the analysis of Chapter 14 to the situation, say, in 1940, the maximum creation of credit could have reached enormous proportions, as it did a few years later through an expansion of Reserve bank credit on the basis of the increased gold stock.

5. *Currency in circulation.* This item consists of all kinds of currency—Federal Reserve notes as well as Treasury currency—but does not include deposit money. We remember that it is now accepted policy to supply the public with all the currency it cares to use within a given total supply of money. Difficulties could arise only when, with rigid gold reserve requirements and a declining gold stock, the Federal Reserve would be compelled to reduce the total supply of money in consequence of a greatly increased demand for currency rather than deposit money. However, it is hardly conceivable any more that rigid gold reserve requirements would be permitted to stand in the way of an adequate supply of both deposit money and currency.

We remember that an increased demand for currency by the public may cause a dollar-for-dollar reduction in member bank reserve balances. Fluctuations in money in circulation, therefore, influence commercial bank reserve balances and may counteract or accentuate the effects of changes in Reserve bank credit and in gold stock.

6. *Treasury cash and deposits.* This item represents all cash funds of the Treasury other than Treasury deposits with commercial banks. It also includes, in addition to Treasury deposits with Federal Reserve banks, currency held in the Treasury and gold in the stabilization fund and the general fund. If the Treasury wants to sterilize gold by not issuing gold certificates, Treasury cash will grow because

gold in the general fund increases. Since the profit from revaluation went to the Treasury, the increased value of the gold stock was matched by a nearly equal change in Treasury cash in early 1934 (see Chart 16–1).

SUGGESTIONS FOR FURTHER READING

On central banking experiences antedating the Federal Reserve System:

ANGELL, JAMES W. *The Theory of International Prices,* chap. 3. Cambridge, Mass.: Harvard University Press, 1926.

COULBORN, W. A. L. *A Discussion of Money,* chaps. 14–15. New York: Longmans, Green and Co., 1950.

GREGORY, T. E. *British Banking Statutes and Reports 1832–1928,* Vol. I. London: Oxford University Press, 1929.

JAMES, F. CYRIL. *The Economics of Money, Credit and Banking,* chaps. 9–10. 3d ed. New York: The Ronald Press Co., 1940.

KEYNES, J. M. *A Treatise on Money,* Vol. I, chap. 13; Vol. II, chaps. 32–33. New York: Harcourt, Brace & Co., 1930.

MILL, JOHN STUART. *Principles of Political Economy,* Book III, chaps. 23–24. New York: Longmans, Green and Co., 1936.

WITHERS, HARTLEY. *The Meaning of Money,* chaps. 3 and 11. New York: E. P. Dutton & Co., Inc., 1930.

On the original structure of the Federal Reserve System:

CURRIE, LAUCHLIN. *The Supply and Control of Money in the United States,* chaps. 6–13. Cambridge, Mass.: Harvard University Press, 1934.

HARDING, N. P. G. *The Formative Period of the Federal Reserve System.* Boston: Houghton Mifflin Co., 1925.

PHILLIPS, C. A., MACMANUS, T. F., and NELSON, R. W. *Banking and the Business Cycle,* chap. 2. New York: Macmillan Co., 1937.

QUESTIONS AND PROBLEMS

1. Discuss the Peel Act of 1844 as an expression of the ideas of the currency school. Why did the banking school criticize the Act? Which school was right?
2. The commercial-loan theory holds that bank-note issue through the discounting of good commercial paper will tie the circulation of money to the circulation of commodities in the most ideal manner possible. Is this theory correct?
3. Compare the following systems of note issue by central banks: the fiduciary issue system, the percentage method of gold backing, and the system of a maximum issue, independent of any gold reserves.

4. Phillips, McManus, and Nelson remark about the creation of the Federal Reserve System: "The principal and immediate effect of the institution of this new system was to economize reserves—that is, to enable a given foundation of gold to support a much larger superstructure of credit than was previously possible." Comment. Were these increased powers of credit expansion compatible with the gold mechanism and the commercial-loan theory?
5. Can it be said that central banking is inherently inflationary during the period following its introduction?
6. Comparing the reserve requirements of the National Banking System with those of the Federal Reserve System, calculate the maximum monetary circulation which could be supported by a given amount of gold in each system.
7. Discuss the Federal Reserve System as a compromise between regionalism and centralization and indicate how it differed from already established central banking systems.
8. Does the original structure of the Federal Reserve System suggest that the new system was to rest on the twin pillars of the gold-flow mechanism and the commercial-loan theory?
9. "The Federal Reserve promoted gold from high-powered to supercharged money." Explain.
10. Explain the meaning of the following items shown in Charts 16–1 and 16–2: Gold Stock, Reserve Bank Credit, Member Bank Reserve Balances, Required Reserves, Currency in Circulation, Treasury Cash and Deposits.

Chapter 17 HISTORY OF THE FEDERAL RESERVE SYSTEM

World War I and the Postwar Period

The beginning of the operations of the Federal Reserve System coincided with the outbreak of World War I. We saw that the new reserve regulations had created the basis for a huge potential credit expansion. Since the war caused a huge demand for credit, the result was inflationary. Between 1914 and 1920 the deposits of all commercial banks more than doubled, while wholesale prices rose from 100 to 243 (see Chart 8–2, p. 87).

Of course, the war inflation cannot be blamed on the establishment of the Federal Reserve System since conditions favorable to credit expansion would have been created anyhow because of the emergency. It would also be wrong to speak of a Federal Reserve policy for the war period. The system had not had time to get organized when it was already fully dominated by the Treasury. We shall see that 25 years later even the grown-up system could not maintain its independence; how much less can we expect to find a strong Federal Reserve policy in 1917! Furthermore, neither the gold mechanism nor the commercial-loan theory could be used for the formulation of a monetary policy for wartime purposes. The new reserve requirements permitted an enormous credit expansion on the basis of existing gold reserves, and gold was flowing in. The commercial-loan theory could not be adhered to because the Treasury, unable to finance its expenditures wholly through increased taxation or the sale of bonds to the saving public, had to request the banking system to absorb all Liberty Bonds which were left unsold in the closing hours of the Liberty Bond campaigns. When the banks did not buy the bonds themselves they enabled the public to buy them with loans for which the bonds could be used as collateral. In addition the banks increased their loans to industry engaged in war production. The Federal Reserve banks stood ready to lend to the member banks when the original credit expansion possibilities of the new system were used up. Beginning in 1917 we can watch the sharp increase in Reserve bank credit, in member bank reserve balances, and in currency in circulation (see Chart 16–1, p. 200). Gold stopped coming in in 1917 and started to flow out after the lifting of the gold embargo in 1919. To avoid contraction of the monetary circulation in connection with the gold outflow, Federal Reserve credit had to rise even more sharply. Clearly, these reactions of monetary policy had nothing to do with the classical gold-flow mechanism.

The inflation continued after the war. The Treasury's credit demand was high, for the floating debt had to be consolidated, and the Federal Reserve, therefore, was still obliged to keep bond prices stable and interest rates low, notwithstanding a growing uneasiness in Federal Reserve circles about the continuing price inflation. Private investment demand, which had been repressed during the war, was expanding and could not be checked by the mere use of selective credit controls.

Continued increase of Federal Reserve credit and the gold outflow made the gold reserve ratio drop down to very near its legal minimum. This caused some alarm and led to a substantial rise in interest rates by the Federal Reserve, which had by now emancipated itself from domination by the Treasury. Thus the inflationary expansion was brought to an abrupt end, and the economy of the United States was exposed to a brief but very sharp price deflation (see Chart 8–2, p. 87).

That reaching of the minimum gold reserve ratio was an inducement to drastic action seems strange today. The ratio had been artificially chosen; it had not prevented a major price inflation; none of the policies followed had shown any connection with the gold-flow mechanism; and the United States had accumulated one third of the world's gold reserve. Yet so rigid was the thinking at the time that this gold reserve ratio was considered inviolable.

That the monetary deflation of 1921 was harmful goes without saying, but at the time the opinion was widely held that the economic system needed a readjustment of prices and that it was normal and natural that price inflation should be followed by price deflation.

The sharp drop in prices between 1920 and 1921 was accompanied by a fall in gross national product from $86.6 billion to $70.7 billion. Private investment declined from $16.3 to $7.3 billion and investment in inventories from $4.9 to $0.1 billion.

A purely monetary explanation of these business fluctuations without reference to numerous other factors would hardly be fair to the monetary authorities. The Federal Reserve cannot alone be made responsible for expansion and contraction, for prosperity and depression. Only if the business cycle were a purely monetary phenomenon could restraining action by the monetary authority have prevented the collapse of the postwar boom or the great depression of the early thirties. Nevertheless, we shall see that mistakes in the construction of the original Federal Reserve Act contributed greatly to the difficulties of the years between the wars and that substantial improvements in the Federal Reserve structure were made as the weaknesses of the system revealed themselves.

Hidden Inflation and the Great Depression

The period from 1922 to 1929 was characterized by roughly stable prices (see Chart 8–2, p. 87) in spite of a considerable increase in the supply of money. This was the period which called forth the theory of neutral money, which holds that price stability does not guarantee economic stability (see Chapters 3 and 10).

Technological advance led in many fields of industry to falling costs of production. Consequently the increasing social product could be sold at stable prices only if the supply of money either increased or circulated faster. Indeed, both M and V increased, and the rise in T therefore led to only a very modest decline of P. This discrepancy between lowered costs of production owing to technological progress and nearly stable product prices led to high profits which contrasted favorably with low rates of interest. Low interest rates resulted from credit creation. In this difference between low rates of interest and high profits we can also detect a reason for the inflation of security prices in the late twenties. When high profits are capitalized on the basis of low rates of interest, security prices must become very high. An important additional factor was that security speculation was constantly nourished by credit creation: newly created funds found their way into circulation largely through the stock market.

Many nonmonetary factors contributed to the investment boom of the twenties: the technological advance in general, the automobile industry, a housing boom, the development of installment buying, and foreign investment. These investment opportunities created a demand for loanable funds which absorbed not only all available savings but also much newly created credit. It is probably correct to say that without the increased credit supply the investment boom would not have reached equally dangerous proportions. We have already seen that the Federal Reserve did not have an adequate theory to guide its credit policy. Its vague generalizations about the "needs of trade" and its ambiguous reference to the "legitimate" demand for credit on the basis of "eligible" commercial paper did not constitute such a policy. The main danger, however, lay in the inadequate structure of the banking system and its inability to cope with a crisis of illiquidity. The severity of the crisis and the depth of the depression which followed must be ascribed at least in part to misconstructions in the central banking system, and these in turn, were the result of wrong theories.

The crisis and depression were extremely severe and were more disappointing because the preceding period of stable prices had created a false sense of security and even hopes for permanent prosperity. The gross national product, which had nearly touched the $100 billion mark in 1929, fell to $55.4 billion in 1932, and private investment plunged from $17.6 to $1.9 billion. Wholesale prices continued their interrupted decline and reached in 1932 approximately the level at which they had been immediately before the war.

Decreasing economic activity and falling prices are bound to create difficulties for the commercial banking system. Commercial banks' assets drop in value, supposedly self-liquidating credits freeze, and the public may want to change from deposit money to currency and from currency to gold, thereby testing the liquidity of the system at the very time when it is least ready to meet the test.

The extraordinary number of bank failures in the United States, however, calls for additional explanations. More than 5,000 banks, or about one-fifth of all banks, failed from 1930 to 1932. This proved that the banking system of the United States was particularly vulnerable in spite of the fact that the Federal Reserve System had been created for the express purpose of making the system as nearly shockproof as possible. Of the reasons to which the banking crisis can be attributed only the most important will be mentioned.

The Federal Reserve System ought to have been able to extend more help to its member banks by making more reserves available and by furnishing more currency through lending and open-market operations. Unfortunately, the rigid structure of the System prevented such action on the part of the Board and the Reserve banks. Federal Reserve notes could be issued only if more gold or commercial paper were available as backing. There was a decline in the gold stock in

1931, 1932, and 1933, and the attempt to maintain adequate backing in the form of commercial paper limited the Federal Reserve in its vitally important open-market operations. Open-market operations would, through security purchases by the Reserve banks, have increased member bank reserves, and the banks would have been able to reduce their indebtedness with the Reserve banks; this, in turn, however, would have reduced the supply of commercial paper which the Federal Reserve needed for the backing of Federal Reserve notes in circulation!

Needless to say, the banks' supply of eligible commercial paper was very scarce anyhow owing to the deterioration of the whole economic situation. The development was cumulative, for the attempt to liquidate the "self-liquidating" commercial paper was one of the major causes of the decline in commodity and security prices. Many bank loans, of course, had never had the quality of commercial credits, since it was impossible for the Federal Reserve banks to determine the uses to which credits were put.[1]

Bank failures were cumulative because of the interrelationships in banking which make difficulties of one group or region contagious for others. Since the public's nervous demand for cash could not be met promptly because of the limitations under which the Reserve banks had to operate, the commercial banks followed the policy of withdrawing interbank deposits, thus accentuating the stampede.

The credit crisis was international. In 1931 it spread from Austria via Germany to England, where it forced the pound sterling off gold. The British devaluation of 1931 in turn greatly enhanced the difficulties which the banking system in the United States was already experiencing. To the domestic tendency to hoard currency and gold was now added the gold demand of those who expected that the United States would soon raise the dollar price of gold.

That the American banking system was particularly vulnerable was due mainly to its extreme decentralization. There were too many small banks even for normal times, and now when the public tended to transfer its funds to bigger and presumably safer banks, many of the smaller and weaker ones were bound to fail. Bank supervision did not prevent these failures; on the contrary, many banks were declared insolvent by bank examiners when the value of their assets fell below

[1] Already in the *Annual Report 1923* the Federal Reserve Board declared: "There are no automatic devices or detectors for determining, when credit is granted by a Federal Reserve Bank in response to a rediscount demand, whether the occasion for the rediscount was an extension of credit by the member bank for nonproductive use."

the contractual value of their liabilities. Yet some of these banks could have resumed business and regained solvency as soon as the general economic situation had improved.

The banking system of the United States finally came to a complete standstill when all banks remained closed on March 4, 1933, the day of President Roosevelt's inauguration. Having carried our story to a dramatic climax we must now briefly sketch the main trends of the emergency legislation out of which grew some permanent and important improvements in the structure of the Federal Reserve System.

Emergency Legislation and Permanent Improvements

It would be interesting to follow, step by step, the emergency measures which were taken during the credit crisis and to watch the struggle to escape from fixed ideas and regulations which stood in the way of decisive actions. We shall have to limit ourselves, however, to looking at only the final institutional results of these emergency measures. We shall group the policies in question according to the problems which they tried to meet rather than according to the time sequence of the emergency legislation.

1. Thc most basic change which evolved amounted to the discarding of the commercial-loan theory of credit, which had been responsible for the most dangerous structural defects of the Federal Reserve System. The *Glass-Steagall Act of 1932* empowered the Federal Reserve banks temporarily to extend credit to member banks without eligible paper in exceptional circumstances; the *Banking Act of 1935* deleted the temporary emergency character of the regulation by permitting the Federal Reserve banks to make advances to member banks whose notes were secured to the "satisfaction" of the Federal Reserve banks. Government securities could from now on serve as collateral just as well as could commercial paper, and Federal Reserve credit was henceforth freed from the dangerous connection with an untenable theory.

2. Consistency dictated that the reserve requirements for the Federal Reserve banks, too, be divorced from the commercial-loan theory. Consequently the Reserve banks were permitted to use government securities as collateral against their notes and deposits. In addition to the increased flexibility in the supply of Federal Reserve notes which was thus made possible, the *Emergency Banking Act of 1933* permitted the issue of Federal Reserve *bank* notes which could be backed by any sound asset and needed no gold reserve.[2]

[2] See footnote 1 to Chapter 11.

3. The attitude toward gold was not consistently revised. Indeed there were many dramatic changes concerning gold, but after an interval of inconvertibility and after a drastic devaluation the system returned to gold in the *Gold Reserve Act of 1934*. The price of gold was changed from $20.67 to $35.00 an ounce, and a tremendous credit expansion potential was created. An enormous gold inflow further augmented this potential, which we can identify by following gold stock and member bank reserve balances in Charts 16–1 and 16–2 from 1934 to 1940.

4. Excess gold reserves, disequilibrating gold movements, and the discarding of the commercial-loan theory had the consequence that automatic credit controls had to be replaced by a conscious credit policy which presupposed strong credit instruments in the hands of the Federal Reserve. The Board was given new credit instruments in the form of open-market operations, changes in reserve requirements, and the prescription of minimum margin requirements.

5. Open-market operations had evolved as an instrument of monetary policy during the twenties. When, in consequence of the restrictive credit policy of 1920–21, the amount of discounts had fallen, individual Federal Reserve banks began to purchase government securities in an unco-ordinated fashion to increase their earning assets. Very soon it became obvious that these purchases influenced security prices, the reserves of member banks, and the general credit situation. As early as 1922 the Federal Reserve banks appointed a committee to co-ordinate these purchases with regard to their effects on the general credit situation. Though changing in its composition the committee remained active in an advisory capacity until, in the *Banking Act of 1933*, it was built into the System as the Federal Open Market Committee. From now on, individual Reserve banks could no longer engage in open-market operations which did not conform with Committee regulations. The *Banking Act of 1935* established the Committee approximately in its present form and gave it the right to make the Reserve banks engage in certain open-market operations.

The relationship between the new open-market policy and the old discount policy during the twenties and the early thirties is shown in Chart 17–1. The inverse correlation of United States government securities and discounts creates at first the impression that the two policies worked at cross purposes. When the Reserve banks engaged in open-market purchases the rediscounting of commercial paper fell off, and when open-market sales reduced the reserves of member banks the member banks increased their reserves through borrowing from

Chart 17-1

Reserve Bank Credit

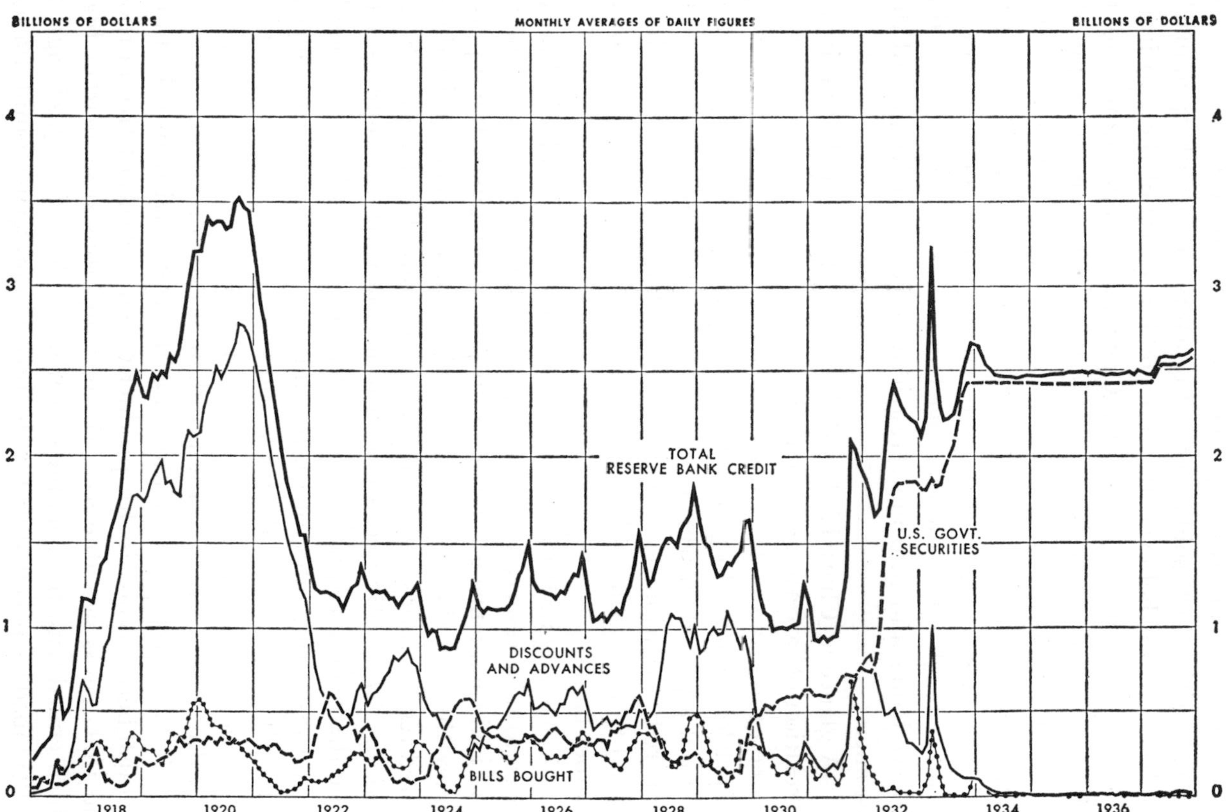

SOURCE: *Historical Supplement to Federal Reserve Chart Book on Financial and Business Statistics* (Washington, D.C.: Board of Governors of the Federal Reserve System, September, 1960), p. 4.

the Reserve banks. This compensatory tendency, however, did not mean that by developing this new instrument the Federal Reserve was destroying its discount policy. As a rule discount rates went up when securities were sold and went down together with open-market purchases. It was believed that the combined use of the two instruments would work more gently. Open-market operations had the purpose of changing member bank indebtedness rather than member bank reserves. Member banks which are out of debt as a result of open-market purchases are supposed to be more willing to expand credit. Reduction of member bank reserves via open-market sales, on the other hand, forces the member banks into borrowing from their Reserve banks and into more restrictive credit policies toward their customers.

A glance at Chart 17–1 will show how this period of an inverse correlation of government securities and discounts was an interlude between the prevalence of discount policy in the early twenties and the predominance of open-market policy in the early thirties. Then followed a period in which neither policy was able to influence the total credit situation very much owing to a large and continued inflow of gold from abroad, which created enormous excess reserves for the member banks.

6. Already in 1916 the Federal Reserve Board had asked for the power to raise reserve requirements. As it became clear that the System's main influence was based on its power to regulate the supply of money through the reserves of member banks, a change in the required reserve ratios suggested itself as the most direct approach. The *Banking Act of 1935* gave the Board of Governors the right to determine the reserve requirements of member banks within a range between the existing rates (of 13, 10, and 7 per cent for demand deposits and 3 per cent for time deposits) and amounts twice as large.[3] Times were soon to come in which even this power proved to be too limited in dealing effectively with the problem of excess reserves.

7. We have seen that the Federal Reserve tried in vain to distinguish between credits for productive and for speculative purposes and that it was not able to curb the dangerous stock-market boom which ended with the collapse of 1929. The *Securities Exchange Act of 1934* made it permissible for the Board to prescribe minimum margin requirements. This Regulation T means that the Federal Reserve

[3] Since July 28, 1959, the minimum and maximum legal reserve requirements against net demand deposits are 10, 10, 7 and 22, 22, 14 per cent respectively.

can limit the amount which security holders can borrow by using the securities as collateral. The margin is the difference between the value of the stock and the value of the loan. A 25 per cent margin, for instance, means that a bank or security broker may make a loan of not more than $750 on stock worth $1,000. A 75 per cent margin limits borrowing in this case to $250, and a 100 per cent margin eliminates altogether borrowing on the basis of securities. The prescription of margin requirements as a qualitative or selective method of credit control enables the Federal Reserve to deal with different fields of the credit market independently.

8. In 1933 a Federal Deposit Insurance Corporation was established. Through it deposits in member banks and voluntarily qualifying nonmember banks were insured up to $5,000 (since 1950: $10,000) for each depositor. This insurance system is financed by compulsory assessments on all participating banks. While not in itself a measure which would guarantee either solvency or liquidity of the insured banks, the FDIC through its very existence will go a long way in preventing those panicky demands for currency which in the early thirties helped to magnify illiquidity and insolvency.

9. The Reconstruction Finance Corporation was created in early 1932. Its capital was subscribed by the Treasury. The RFC had the purpose of giving financial assistance to banks, insurance companies, railroads, and other big corporations. Thus it fulfilled a function which the Federal Reserve was not permitted to perform in view of its specific liquidity problems. The RFC could purchase preferred stock of commercial banks and played a large part in the rescue operations during the credit crisis by lending billions of dollars. Later on the RFC performed various functions, particularly during World War II when it financed war plants and performed other wartime financial services. The *Industrial Advances Act of 1934* empowered the Reserve banks to make medium-term loans to established industrial and commercial enterprises in exceptional circumstances.

10. As important as many of these changes and institutions were, they were not parts of a consistent and comprehensive plan for the reconstruction of the monetary system. Many changes had been introduced belatedly and hesitatingly, while other were boldly experimenting. But it was more an agglomeration of rescue measures than a well-planned reorganization. Particularly inconsistent was the retaining of gold as a factor which was permitted to influence the domestic monetary situation whether this influence was desirable or not. We shall

presently see that the retention of a perfectly elastic demand for gold offset to a large extent the improvements which had been achieved through the forging of stronger monetary weapons.

Gold Inflow and Excess Reserves

A study of Charts 16–1 and 16–2 (pp. 000–00) for the years 1934–41 reveals interesting developments. Throughout this period gold flowed to the United States in huge amounts, the gold flow created enormous member bank reserves, and these reserves condemned the Federal Reserve to relative inactivity as shown by the very minor fluctuations of Reserve bank credit.

Devaluation and gold inflow had raised the gold stock to about $8 billion by the end of 1934; from there it continued to climb until it reached, in 1941, about $23 billion. Member bank reserve balances followed the gold stock, because gold purchases by the Treasury increase the reserves of commercial banks unless these reserves are artificially lowered through a policy of gold sterilization.

Some gold sterilization was attempted. Chart 16–1 shows for 1937 an increase and for 1938 a decrease in Treasury cash, indicating that the Treasury refrained from issuing gold certificates, increased Treasury cash by $750 million, and paid for the gold by selling securities. We can notice the effect of this moderate sterilization policy in the slow growth of member bank reserve balances in 1937.

The Federal Reserve counteracted the gold inflow by using its recently gained power to increase reserve requirements for member banks. Reserve requirements were raised once in 1936 and twice in 1937, and in May, 1937, they reached their legal maxima of 26, 20, 14, and 6 per cent, respectively. The effects are not visible in member bank reserve balances, since the policy changed only the reserve ratio and not the absolute volume of the reserves. Charts 16–1 and 17–2, however, show clearly how a very substantial part of the excess reserves was extinguished during 1936 and 1937. Yet total reserves and excess reserves resumed their rapid increase after the Federal Reserve had exhausted its power to raise legal reserve requirements.

Open-market sales could not have helped materially. In 1940–41 the excess reserves stood at about $7 billion, while Reserve bank credit was still only $2.5 billion. Thus even the selling of all the securities held by the Reserve banks would have left excess reserves of about $4.5 billion! We shall see furthermore that, at the time, the Federal Reserve was inclined to purchase rather than to sell securities.

The enormous and embarrassing gold inflow was caused pri-

CHART 17–2

EXCESS RESERVES AND BORROWING OF MEMBER BANKS
BY CLASS OF BANK

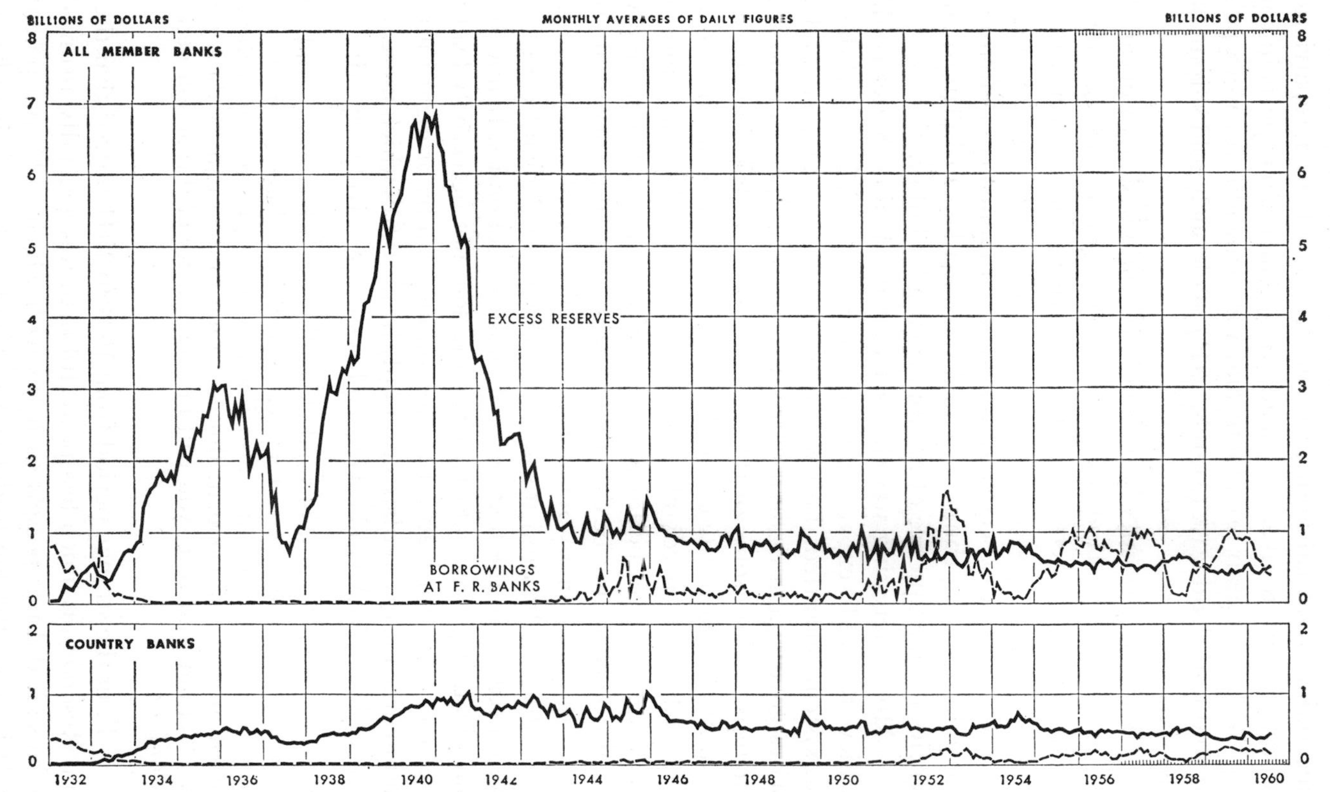

SOURCE: *Historical Supplement to Federal Reserve Chart Book on Fina ncial and Business Statistics* (Washington, D.C.: Board of Governors of the Federal Reserve System, September, 1960), p. 6.

marily by an influx of foreign capital owing to political and economic uncertainties abroad and, to a smaller extent, to a repatriation of American short-term assets. In addition, American exports in connection with European armament and war expenditures were paid for in gold until lend-lease (March, 1941) made such gold shipments unnecessary.

That the Treasury bought gold in unlimited amounts at $35 an ounce was in accordance with the principles of the gold standard. To base a country's system on gold made little sense, however, when capital flight was a major cause of gold movements. The gold-losing countries could not be expected to contract their monetary circulation, and the gold-receiving countries could not be asked to inflate their currencies in consequence of an abnormal gold inflow.

Most interesting was the fact that the United States could not achieve the credit expansion which the excessive liquidity of the banking system permitted. This was the more remarkable since the United States government desired expansion and even price inflation in its attempt to undo some of the worst damages of deflation and depression. According to the classical theory, lower rates of interest should have led to the speedy absorption of all the additional funds which the excess reserves permitted the banks to create. Excess reserves of $7 billion could not be explained by the classical theory of interest or by the quantity theory of money. A combination of excessive liquidity, low interest rates, and insufficient investment demand could not be accounted for in the textbooks of classical economics. It now became obvious that the availability of credit does not necessarily lead to increased expenditure and that more money can be brought into circulation or made to circulate faster only by measures which increase total expenditure. As Alvin H. Hansen has so expressively argued:

> An increase in the flow of total expenditures on final goods and services (which becomes income to the factors) will indeed necessitate an increase either in *M* or *V* or both; so also, if a man grows corpulent he will be compelled to wear a larger belt. But according to the quantity theory, if you first "let out your belt" you will in *consequence* of this action necessarily grow fat![4]

Thus the strange period from 1934 to 1941 proved that the Federal Reserve was much less powerful than was generally assumed: (1) because it did not possess weapons with which to keep a potentially inflationary situation under control; and (2) because it did not have

[4] Alvin H. Hansen, *Monetary Theory and Fiscal Policy* (New York: McGraw-Hill Book Co., Inc., 1949), p. 85.

the power to regulate total expenditure by monetary policy alone.

Of these two shortcomings the second is the more fundamental, for it cannot be cured by structural changes in the banking system but requires the support of monetary by fiscal and general economic policies.

That these two weaknesses became simultaneously obvious was rather strange. Normally the monetary authorities are faced with either an inflationary or a deflationary danger. Here, both problems appeared at the same time, with the advantage that inadequate monetary preparedness did not matter as long as there was an insufficient demand for loanable funds. Nevertheless, the situation was dangerous. On the basis of the $7 billion of excess reserves, a potential credit expansion of some $35 billion of deposit money was possible—even at maximum reserve requirements. With the outbreak of World War II in Europe, the situation became very serious.

Recovery and Recession

Throughout the thirties the economy of the United States was unable to reach a really satisfactory level of economic activity. This does not mean to say that it did not recover. As a matter of fact the recovery was fairly rapid between 1933 and 1937. Then, however, came a short recession, and only under the impact of the war was a high employment level reached. Gross national product, private investment, and public investment developed as follows (in billions of dollars):

	1933	*1937*	*1938*	*1940*	*1941*
Gross national product...	54.8	87.7	80.6	97.1	120.5
Private investment........	2.7	11.1	6.5	13.0	17.7
Public investment.........	9.1	13.6	14.4	16.7	26.5

The Federal Reserve found itself in a difficult position. It wanted to maintain control over the money supply and, accordingly, to absorb those embarrassing excess reserves which were the automatic result of the gold inflow; yet it wanted, too, to stimulate expenditure as far as possible. The latter desire was particularly strong after the somewhat anemic upswing turned into a recession in 1937.

We remember that the Federal Reserve had raised reserve requirements in 1936 and 1937. It is probable that this policy contributed, if perhaps only psychologically, to the forces which halted the upswing. In any case, it became obvious that raising reserve requirements is a rather drastic weapon of monetary control, which must be handled with great care. Already in April 1938 the Federal Reserve reduced reserve requirements again, and the Reserve banks bought moderate amounts of government securities in 1937, 1938, and 1939. These security purchases did not try to influence member bank reserves, as is shown by a comparison of the extremely moderate changes in Reserve bank credit with the development of member bank reserves in Chart 16–1. The reason for these open-market purchases was to attempt to stabilize security prices and to keep interest rates low. The danger at the moment was recession, not inflation. This new monetary policy went under the name "maintaining orderly market conditions." Since it was no longer possible to argue that the supply of money always automatically reaches the maximum permitted by reserves and reserve requirements and since total expenditure rather than money supply was now considered decisive, it is only natural that the Federal Reserve tried to stimulate investment expenditures by keeping interest rates low, that is, by purchasing securities whenever the public desired to sell. We shall see, however, that the same policy was continued when war expenditures created an inexhaustible investment demand.

Federal Reserve policy in 1937 and 1938 was mainly an antidepression policy. When World War II broke out, the Federal Reserve's primary concern became once more the excessive liquidity which was caused by the steep rise of the gold stock. Excess reserves plus war demand created explosive possibilities, while the Federal Reserve lacked the power to control the monetary situation. The situation became so serious that on December 31, 1940, the Federal Reserve sent a special report to the Congress[5] in which it was pointed out that the system's power to cope with the excess reserve problem was inadequate, and that the vast expenditures of the military program made it necessary "to review our existing monetary machinery and to place ourselves into a position to take measures, when necessary, to forestall the development of inflationary tendencies attributable to defects in the machinery of credit control." The report suggested: that the Federal Open Market Committee be empowered to make further increases of reserve requirements sufficient to absorb excess reserves; that "means should be found to prevent further growth in excess reserves and in deposits arising from future gold acquisitions"; that

[5] *Special Report to the Congress* by the Board of Governors of the Federal Reserve System, the Presidents of the Federal Reserve banks, and the Federal Advisory Council, December 31, 1940. *Federal Reserve Bulletin*, January, 1941. It was the first time since the creation of the Federal Reserve System that a joint report was issued.

"such acquisitions should be insulated from the credit system"; that financing of the defense program "should be accomplished by drawing upon the existing large volume of deposits rather than by creating additional deposits through bank purchases of Government securities"; and that "as the national income increases a larger and larger portion of the defense expenses should be met by tax revenues rather than by borrowing."

These suggestions were not acted upon, sharing the fate of so many other New Year's resolutions. The Federal Reserve System remained in a condition which made it impossible to combat the dangers of an overexpansion of credit by monetary means, and worse was still to come.

World War II

The entry of the United States into the war found the banking system in a position similar to that in 1917. Then, the new Federal Reserve System had furnished abundant scope for credit expansion; now, it was the accumulation of enormous excess reserves which performed the same service. Again the country experienced a credit and price inflation, and again the gold standard was suspended only in the sense that international payments were controlled. In 1945, however, the gold reserve requirements of the Reserve banks were reduced from 40 per cent (for Federal Reserve notes in circulation) and 35 per cent (for member bank deposits) to a uniform 25 per cent, indicating that credit expansion and an increased demand for currency had finally succeeded in reducing the gold reserve ratio to more normal proportions.

The phenomenal wartime developments in the monetary field are shown in Chart 16–2, particularly in the steep rise of currency in circulation and in Reserve bank credit. Currency circulation increased from about $12 billion in 1942 to about $29 billion in 1946. This enormous demand for currency by the public would have reduced member bank reserves by an equal amount had it not been for the sharp expansion of Federal Reserve credit, which left the $2.5 billion plateau on which it had stayed from 1934 to 1942 and reached $25 billion by the end of 1944—an increase by ten times!

The over-all financial picture of World War II was approximately as follows: Between July 1, 1941, and June 30, 1946, the federal government raised $383 billion: $169 billion (or 46 per cent) through taxes and $214 billion (or 54 per cent) through borrowing. Of these $214 billion of securities sold, 128 billion was absorbed by nonbank investors, that is, bought with savings. The rest was financed by credit inflation, the commercial banks buying $64 billion and the Reserve banks, $22 billion of securities.

In March, 1942, the Treasury and the Federal Open Market Committee came to the understanding that the existing pattern of prices and yields of government securities should be maintained; in other words, the Federal Reserve should see that all bonds and notes which the Treasury would sell would be bought at fixed prices. This promise implied that whichever amounts the nonbank holders of securities were not willing to absorb would be bought by member banks with newly created money. The Reserve banks, in turn, would purchase securities in the open market (or directly from the Treasury) whenever the reserve position of the member banks made this support necessary. This marked the end of monetary policy as far as the Federal Reserve was concerned. The Federal Reserve promised that the system would supply any amount of additional money which the Treasury's policy of borrowing beyond the supply of savings required; and this policy was continued for 5 years after cessation of hostilities.

To induce the commercial banks to participate wholeheartedly in this inflationary policy, the Federal Reserve Act was amended in April 1942 to exempt the so-called "war loan deposits" of the Treasury from the normal reserve requirements. In addition the Reserve banks stood ready to lend to commercial banks at low rates and to buy all the "Governments" that either the banks or the public wanted to sell. As a matter of fact, the commercial banks could substantially increase their earnings by selling low-interest, short-term securities and by buying, on the basis of increased reserves, a multiple amount of higher-yield, long-term securities. The demand for securities became completely elastic, and the Federal Reserve was willing to monetize the government debt on the initiative of the Treasury, the commercial banks, and the public. The only institution in the country which had no influence whatever over the money supply was the Federal Reserve, the institution which was supposedly responsible for the supply of money.

The supply of money (currency plus demand deposits, but exclusive of interbank and U.S. government deposits) increased from $36.6 billion in 1939 to $103.5 billion in 1945. This expansion was the effect of the banking system's purchases of government securities which increased nongovernment deposits and the circulation of currency whenever the Treasury disbursed the funds which it had raised from inflationary sources.

Had all these facts and figures been foreseen at the beginning of the war, it would have been reasonable to predict that the country was headed for a galloping price inflation. Fortunately, the price inflation was more modest than could have been expected on the basis of monetary policies alone. The reasons for the comparatively mild inflationary effects of war finance in a country which had lost its monetary controls were the following:

1. Repressed inflation was substituted for price inflation. Chart 8–2, p. 87), shows how an initial price inflation from 1941 to 1943 was kept in check during 1944 and 1945 and how repressed inflation erupted as price inflation in the summer of 1946, when price controls were removed.

2. The public was reasonable and did not try to spend money on commodities which were not available. Higher incomes, price controls, and rationing led to a substantial accumulation of unspent purchasing power. The money was either used to buy war bonds or it was left idle. This created the surprising but gratifying phenomenon of a decreasing income velocity of money in times of inflation: the money supply increased faster than the national income.

3. The monetary authorities were able to apply "selective" controls. In 1941 Regulation W authorized the Federal Reserve to limit installment buying (see Chapter 9, pp. 00–00). Margin requirements were raised until they reached 100 per cent. Furthermore, the commercial banks were quite generally requested to limit their loans to strictly productive purposes. It must be remembered that low rates of interest do not imply a practically unlimited supply of credit to anybody willing to pay the going rate of interest. The process of extending credit always involves a more or less conscious distribution of loanable funds, that is, a kind of rationing. Thus it was possible for the Federal Reserve to exert pressure on the commercial banks not to make loans for unproductive purposes.

These brighter spots in the picture, however, cannot hide the fact that because of its policy of maintaining security prices at a fixed level the Federal Reserve had lost effective control over the monetary system.

Postwar Inflation

The situation became even more disquieting after the end of the war when it was obvious that the economy would sooner or later return to a free pricing system. Direct controls which are possible during a war do not always work in peace. The trouble was that wartime financial policies left a legacy of enormous liquidity, which made the commercial banks independent of the Federal Reserve and permitted even nonbank holders of government securities to monetize their assets at a moment's notice.

Why was the policy of pegging security prices and of maintaining a pattern of fixed low rates of interest followed even in the postwar period? A brief examination of the reasons for this policy will lead us to conclude that they were not strong enough to be worth the price. The price was, as we already know, the nearly complete paralysis of monetary control with the result of price inflation.

1. It was said that the cost of government borrowing had to be kept low. This is not a good argument in support of a policy which, through price inflation, cost the government and the people a lot more than it saved in service charges on the debt. It also must be remembered that interest payments on the domestic debt are only transfer payments and not a burden on taxpayers as a whole.

2. It was taken for granted that investors in government securities must be protected against falling security prices. This is hardly a convincing reason even if we believe that public policy should protect special groups against losses and even if we forget that the protected group itself will suffer from inflation. Inflation, as we know, favors the debtor at the expense of the creditor. Increasing rates of interest are not as dangerous to bondholders as often assumed. When we emphasize the fact that security prices fall when interest rates rise, we must not forget that yields are increased when capital values are reduced. The investor cannot lose on both counts. In the long run and after coupon rates are raised, the investor is certain to gain. Capital values, furthermore, will fall only slightly in the case of short-term bonds. The Federal Reserve's great concern about the portfolios of the commercial banks, therefore, was no justification for continuing the policy of "steadying the bond market" in times of price inflation.

3. It was assumed that high rates of interest are always bad for the economy. This is much too broad an argument to be used indiscriminately in war and peace, in depression, and in a period of overfull employment. As far as the war was concerned, it can be argued that even the low rates then in force were too high, since these rates performed no selective function whatsoever. But once it was decided that the economy was not to continue under wartime price controls, it should have been obvious that a period of strong inflationary pressures needed higher rates of interest than those which prevailed under the conditions in the late thirties and which were frozen after the

country went to war. The fear is often expressed that high rates of interest will cause a depression. The question, however, is not one of "high" or "low" rates but of correct rates chosen according to prevailing circumstances. Once we abandon interest rates altogether as regulators of the supply of credit, we abandon monetary policy in favor of a great number of direct price investment, and production controls.

The Treasury–Federal Reserve "Accord" of March, 1951

The inflationary consequences of the paralysis of monetary policy were so obvious and the employment situation was so favorable that a change in the general attitude toward problems of monetary policy came about even before the Korean conflict emphasized the urgency of changes in monetary and debt management policies.

The *Douglas Committee on Monetary, Credit, and Fiscal Policies*[6] recommended in January 1950 that "an appropriate, flexible, and vigorous monetary policy, employed in coordination with fiscal and other policies, should be one of the principal methods used to achieve the purposes of the Employment Act." The Committee stated its belief that "the vigorous use of a restrictive monetary policy as an anti-inflation measure has been inhibited since the war by considerations relating to holding down the yields and supporting the prices of United States Government securities" and came to the following basic conclusion:

> As a long run matter, we favor interest rates as low as they can be without inducing inflation, for low interest rates stimulate capital investment. But we believe that the advantages of avoiding inflation are so great and that a restrictive monetary policy can contribute so much to this end that the freedom of the Federal Reserve to restrict credit and raise interest rates for general stabilization purposes should be restored even if the cost should prove to be a significant increase in service charges on the Federal debt and a greater inconvenience to the Treasury in its sale of securities for new financing and refunding purposes.

The outbreak of the Korean war led to a new inflationary outburst. Wholesale prices in the United States rose about 16 per cent between June 1950 and March 1951. The forces behind this inflation were not exclusively monetary, but it became imperative that a stronger monetary policy be followed to support such direct price and wage freezes as were introduced under the Defense Production Act of 1950.

[6] See *Report of the Subcommittee on Monetary, Credit, and Fiscal Policies* (81st Cong., 2d Sess., Sen. Doc. 129, January 23, 1950).

Chart 16–2, p. 201, shows a steep rise in Reserve bank credit and in member bank reserves. Restraining this expansionist influence were a considerable gold outflow, the raising of reserve requirements (which increased required reserves by about $2 billion), the selective regulation of consumers' and real estate credit, the emphasis on voluntary credit restraint, and the raising of short-term rates of interest in opposition to the Treasury's wishes.

Finally the conflict between the Treasury and the Federal Reserve was officially ended in the joint Treasury–Federal Reserve statement of March 4, 1951, which announced:

> The Treasury and the Federal Reserve System have reached full accord with respect to debt-management and monetary policies to be pursued in furthering their common purpose to assure the successful financing of the Government's requirements and, at the same time, to minimize monetization of the public debt.

After the "Accord"

The "accord" was a victory of the Federal Reserve which had its powers restored. It can even be said that the Federal Reserve had now for the first time in its history the possibility to follow a conscious, flexible monetary policy. It could control the reserve position and lending policy of its member banks.

A sensitive indicator of post-accord policies is given in Chart 17–3 which distinguishes net free reserves from net borrowed reserves. Net free reserves are gained by deducting the borrowings at the Federal Reserve banks by member banks (short of required reserves) from excess reserves of other member banks. Net borrowed reserves remain when excess reserves are deducted from borrowings at the Federal Reserve banks.

Chart 17–3 reveals great flexibility of Federal Reserve policy since 1952. In periods of "active ease" net free reserves are the result of the Federal Reserve's attempt to combat deflationary tendencies. Net borrowed reserves are characteristic for periods of "restraint" during which the Federal Reserve tries to combat inflationary tendencies in favor of slower but more sustained economic growth. We must remember that the ability of member banks to create additional credit depends on the availability of excess reserves and also that continued borrowing by member banks at the Federal Reserve banks is not considered appropriate.

When borrowings exceed excess reserves the expansion of member bank loans must rest on a reduction of member bank security hold-

Excess Reserves and Borrowing of Member Banks

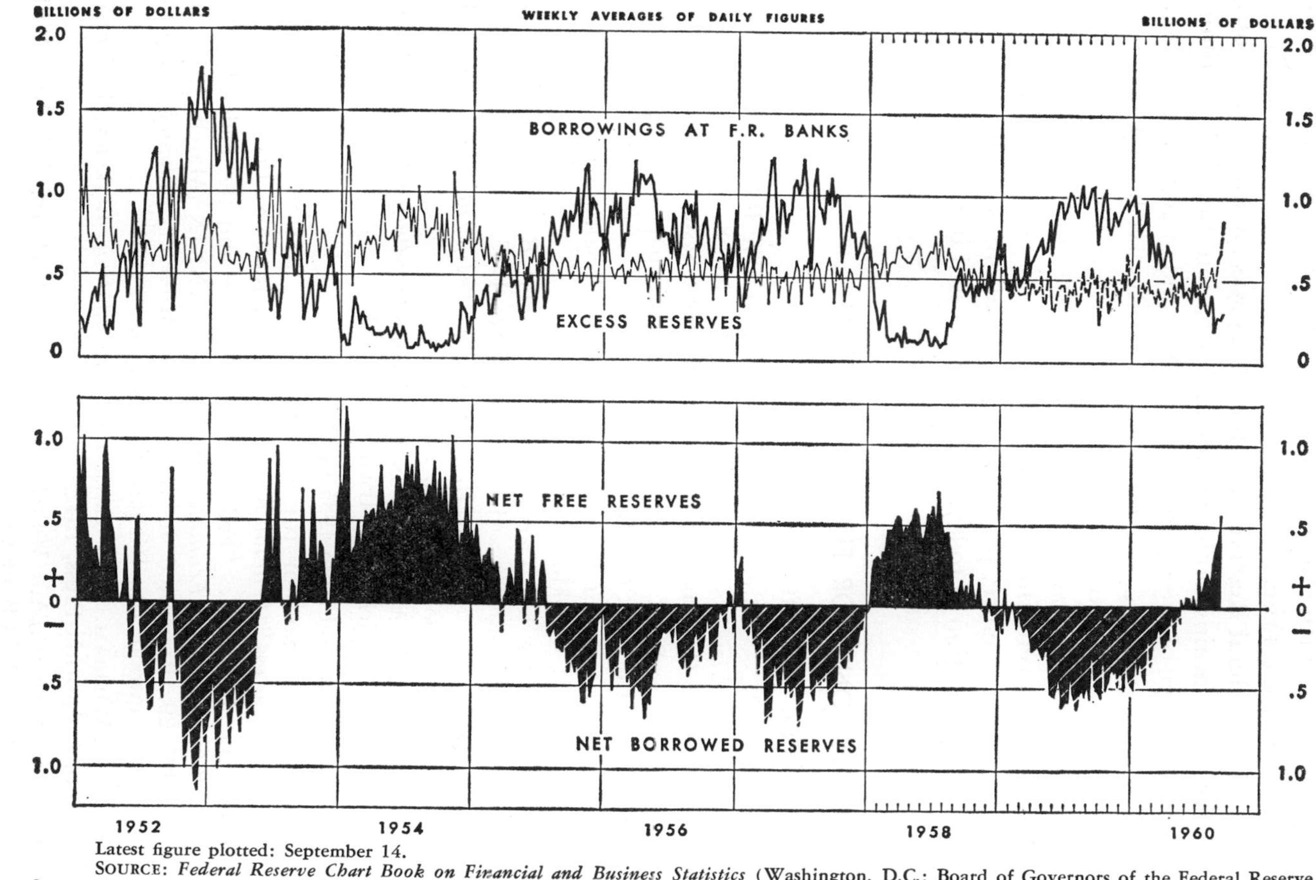

Latest figure plotted: September 14.

SOURCE: *Federal Reserve Chart Book on Financial and Business Statistics* (Washington, D.C.: Board of Governors of the Federal Reserve System, September, 1960), p. 4.

ings. By selling securities to non-bank holders, banks acquire the public's savings and lend them to business. The process is not inflationary and interest rates rise.

The Federal Reserve's flexible policy was an attempt to protect the economy against both inflation and deflation. But both the timing and the dosage of these policies of restraint and of active ease are very difficult to determine. Whether the Federal Reserve leaned too heavily toward restraint or toward ease is hard to judge. We must remember that the Federal Reserve operates in a market economy in which attempts to prevent inflation can easily lead to mass unemployment. Should we, therefore, permit creeping inflation? This is the crucial monetary question of today. It will be discussed in Chapter 28.

SUGGESTIONS FOR FURTHER READING

On the period from 1914 to 1935:

BOPP, KARL R. "Three Decades of Federal Reserve Policy," *Federal Reserve Policy*. Postwar Economic Studies, No. 8. Washington, D.C.: Board of Governors of the Federal Reserve System, 1947.

GOLDENWEISER, E. A. *Monetary Management,* chap. 4. New York: McGraw-Hill Book Co., Inc., 1949.

HARDY, C. O. *Credit Policies of the Federal Reserve System.* Washington, D.C.: Brookings Institution, 1932.

HARRIS, SEYMOUR E. *Twenty Years of Federal Reserve Policies.* Cambridge, Mass.: Harvard University Press, 1933.

REED, HAROLD L. *Federal Reserve Policy 1921–1930.* New York: McGraw-Hill Book Co., Inc., 1930.

SHAW, EDWARD S. *Money, Income, and Monetary Policy,* chap. 18. Homewood, Ill.: Richard D. Irwin, Inc., 1950.

On the period from 1935 to 1960:

BOARD OF GOVERNORS OF THE FEDERAL RESERVE SYSTEM. "Special Report to Congress," *Federal Reserve Bulletin,* January, 1941.

CHANDLER, LESTER V. "Federal Reserve Policy and the Federal Debt," *The American Economic Review,* Vol. XXXIX (March, 1949), pp. 405–29. Reprinted in *Readings in Monetary Theory,* chap. 18 (Homewood, Ill.: Richard D. Irwin, Inc., 1951).

FELLNER, WILLIAM. *A Treatise on War Inflation.* Berkeley: University of California Press, 1942.

GOLDENWEISER, E. A. *Monetary Management,* chaps. 5–6. New York: McGraw-Hill Book Co., Inc., 1949.

GRAHAM, FRANK D. and WHITTLESEY, CHARLES R. *Golden Avalanche.* Princeton: Princeton University Press, 1939.

KEYNES, J. M. *How to Pay for the War.* New York: Harcourt, Brace & Co., 1940.

RITTER, LAWRENCE S. *Money and Economic Activity,* chap. 9. Boston: Houghton Mifflin Co., 1952.

ROBINSON, ROLAND I. "Monetary Aspects of National Debt Policy." *Public Finance and Full Employment.* Postwar Economic Studies, No. 3. Washington, D.C.: Board of Governors of the Federal Reserve System, 1945.

ROOSA, ROBERT V. "Impact of the War on the Member Banks, 1939–1946," *Federal Reserve Policy.* Postwar Economic Studies, No. 8. Washington, D.C.: Board of Governors of the Federal Reserve System, 1947.

SHAW, EDWARD S. *Money, Income, and Monetary Policy,* chap. 19. Homewood, Ill.: Richard D. Irwin, Inc., 1950.

THOMAS, W. and YOUNG, R. A. "Problems of Postwar Monetary Policy," *Federal Reserve Policy.* Postwar Economic Studies, No. 8. Washington, D.C.: Board of Governors of the Federal Reserve System, 1947.

WHITTLESEY, CHARLES R. *Readings in Money and Banking,* Part 10. New York: W. W. Norton & Co., Inc., 1952.

On Federal Reserve policies:

BACH, G. L. *Federal Reserve Policy-Making.* New York: Alfred A. Knopf, 1950.

BOARD OF GOVERNORS OF THE FEDERAL RESERVE SYSTEM. "Objectives of Monetary Policy," *Federal Reserve Bulletin,* September, 1937.

BOARD OF GOVERNORS OF THE FEDERAL RESERVE SYSTEM. "Proposals to Maintain Prices at Fixed Levels Through Monetary Action," *Federal Reserve Bulletin,* April, 1939.

BOARD OF GOVERNORS OF THE FEDERAL RESERVE SYSTEM. "Monetary Measures and Objectives," *Federal Reserve Bulletin,* May, 1939.

"Employment, Growth, and Price Levels," chap. 5, Senate Report No. 1043. Washington, D.C.: 86th Congress, 2nd Session, January 26, 1960.

FELLNER, WILLIAM. *Monetary Policies and Full Employment.* Berkeley: University of California Press, 1946.

GOLDENWEISER, E. A. *American Monetary Policy.* New York: McGraw-Hill Book Co., Inc., 1951.

HANSEN, ALVIN H. *Monetary Theory and Fiscal Policy,* chap. 11. New York: McGraw-Hill Book Co., Inc., 1949.

Monetary Policy and the Management of the Public Debt (Patman Report). Document No. 163. Washington, D.C.: 82nd Congress, 2nd Session, July 3, 1952.

Report of the Subcommittee on Monetary, Credit, and Fiscal Policies (Douglas Report). Document 129. Washington, D.C.: 81st Congress, 2nd Session, January 23, 1950.

RITTER, LAWRENCE S. *Money and Economic Activity,* chap. 10. Boston: Houghton Mifflin Co., 1952.

ROOSA, R. V. *Federal Reserve Operations in the Money and Government Securities Markets,* Federal Reserve Bank of New York, 1956.

SCOTT, I. O., and FAND, D. "The Federal Reserve System's 'Bills Only' Policy," *Journal of Business of the University of Chicago,* 1958.

SHAW, EDWARD S. *Money, Income, and Monetary Policy,* chap. 17. Homewood, Ill.: Richard D. Irwin, Inc., 1950.

WHITTLESEY, CHARLES R. *Readings in Money and Banking,* Part 6. New York: W. W. Norton and Co., Inc., 1952.

QUESTIONS AND PROBLEMS

1. Discuss monetary developments for the periods 1917–22 and 1940–48 and show the similarities and dissimilarities between these two war and postwar periods. Use Charts 16–1, 16–2, and 8–2.
2. The period from 1922 to 1928 is sometimes referred to as a period of "hidden inflation." Explain the term and discuss the period.
3. Can it be said that the gold-flow mechanism and the commercial-loan theory were the basis of Federal Reserve policy during any time between 1917 and 1960. Use Charts 16–1 and 16–2 in your answer.
4. Following "gold stock" in charts 16–1 explain the influence of changes in "gold stock" on "member bank reserve balances." Then discuss the effect of these developments on monetary policy. Can you detect any traces of a gold sterilization policy in Chart 16–1?
5. "Excess reserves of $7 billion could never be explained by the classical theory of interest." Explain.
6. Is it true to say that between 1934 and 1941 the Federal Reserve lacked the power both to prevent a potential inflation and to induce sufficient spending to create a high employment level?
7. How can you explain open market *purchases* in 1937 to 1939 in the face of enormous excess reserves?
8. Discuss the Federal Reserve's *Special Report to Congress* in the light of the monetary developments from 1942 to 1946.
9. Discuss the Treasury–Federal Reserve accord of March 4, 1951.
10. Using Chart 17–3, discuss Federal Reserve policy since the "accord."

Chapter 18 THE STRUCTURE OF THE FEDERAL RESERVE SYSTEM

Introduction

The structure of the Federal Reserve System is intricate because the world's largest and most decentralized commercial banking system was welded into a unit in such a fashion that (1) local characteristics and differences were preserved, (2) a proper balance among a number of agencies was established, and (3) a strong connecting link between the federal government and private enterprise was forged.

We begin our study of the system's structure with a description of the several agencies of the Federal Reserve, moving mainly from top to bottom, from the Board of Governors to the member banks or, more broadly stated, from the federal government down to private enterprise.

The Board of Governors of the Federal Reserve System

The Board of Governors of the Federal Reserve System is an agency of the federal government. The Congress has entrusted to it the main responsibility for forming and carrying out the country's monetary policy. But the Board is not a part of the Executive. The President cannot direct or alter the Board's decisions. The Board is, in this sense, independent from the President, but the seven full-time members of the Board are appointed by the President, subject to confirmation by the Senate.

Since the Board's monetary policy must be co-ordinated with other economic policies of the government, the Board can never be entirely independent from the general economic policy of the Administration. The "independence" of the Federal Reserve, therefore, is a relative concept, "it does not mean independence from Government but independence within the Government."[1]

[1] *Monetary Policy and the Management of the Public Debt,* Report of the Subcommittee on General Credit Control and Debt Management of the Joint Committee on the Economic Report (82d Cong., 2d Sess., Sen. Doc. 163, 1952), p. 51. In the following pages we shall refer to this report as the Patman Report.

The members of the Board are appointed for 14-year terms and are not eligible for reappointment. A new member is appointed every 2 years, and no more than one member may come from the same Federal Reserve district. Behind these regulations we discern the desire to make the Board an impartial body: the long terms of office guarantee continuity of policy; the staggered appointments aim at a gradual adjustment to new ideas; and insistence on representation of different geographical regions tries to guard the system against the dangers of centralization. The Patman Report, however, suggests that a reduction of the number of members, elimination of the geographical restrictions, and perhaps even the possibility of reappointment (connected with shorter terms of office) might help to attract the best possible men.

The Board is not a bank. Its main function is to give cohesion to the whole system and, in co-operation with the Federal Open Market Committee and the twelve Federal Reserve banks, to formulate and carry out the credit policy of the country. Through the Board the system is connected with the executive agencies of the government and with the Congress.

The functions of the Board are the following:

1. Credit policy does not rest exclusively with the Board, but the Board has decisive influence in using two instruments of monetary policy and has sole authority over the other four.

a) Open-market policy is the responsibility of the Federal Open Market Committee, but seven of the twelve members of the committee are the seven members of the Board. The other five members are elected by the Federal Reserve banks.

b) Authority over discount policy is shared with the individual Federal Reserve banks. Although the Reserve banks establish their discount rates, they are also "reviewed and determined" by the Board.

c) The Board has the authority to change the reserve requirements for the member banks. But the range of discretion is narrow, as has already been emphasized.

d) The Board determines the maximum rates of interest which member banks may pay on their time deposits or savings deposits.

e) The Board has sole authority over margin requirements, that is, it determines the amount that holders of securities may borrow on these securities as collateral.

f) Under special emergency powers (as, for example, between 1941–47, 1948–49, 1950–52) the Board may curb installment buying, a measure designed to reduce the supply of credit, the velocity of circulation of money, and the demand for durable consumers' goods.

2. The Board supervises the Federal Reserve System. Only a few of its activities in this respect shall be mentioned. The Board appoints three of the nine directors of each of the twelve Reserve banks, including the Chairman and Deputy Chairman; it examines the twelve Federal Reserve banks and their twenty-four branches; it supervises the Reserve banks' examinations of their member banks; and it supervises international operations of the Reserve banks.

3. Through its excellent Division of Research and Statistics the Board collects and analyzes data which are important for the formulation of its policies.

4. Though not a bank the Board carries on a number of service functions, the most important of which is the operation of the Interdistrict Settlement Fund. This Fund is the capstone of the Federal Reserve System's nation-wide check-clearing system and handles transfers of funds from one Federal Reserve district to another and also transactions between the Treasury and the Reserve banks. The Board also co-operates in other service functions performed by the Reserve banks, such as the distribution of Treasury currency or the preparation of the issue of Federal Reserve notes.

The Federal Open Market Committee

In the Federal Open Market Committee, which determines the use of the system's most powerful monetary instrument, the seven members of the Board of Governors co-operate with five elected representatives of the Federal Reserve banks. The election of these five members (who must be presidents or vice-presidents of Federal Reserve banks) takes place annually on a regional basis. One representative is chosen by the Federal Reserve Bank of New York (district 2) and one each by the following groups of districts: 1, 3, and 5; 4 and 7; 6, 8, and 11; 9, 10, and 12. See Figure 18–1.

The "democratic" character of the system is emphasized by the fact that the member banks elect six of the nine directors of each Reserve bank, while the directors, in turn, choose the president and vice-president of each Reserve bank. It is from these chief officers of the Reserve banks that the banks' five representatives on the Federal Open Market Committee are chosen. But the necessity of integrating Federal Reserve policies with other economic policies of the government made it necessary to emphasize the Board's viewpoint by providing for a larger number of Board members on the Federal Open Market Committee.

BOUNDARIES OF FEDERAL RESERVE DISTRICTS AND THEIR BRANCH TERRITORIES

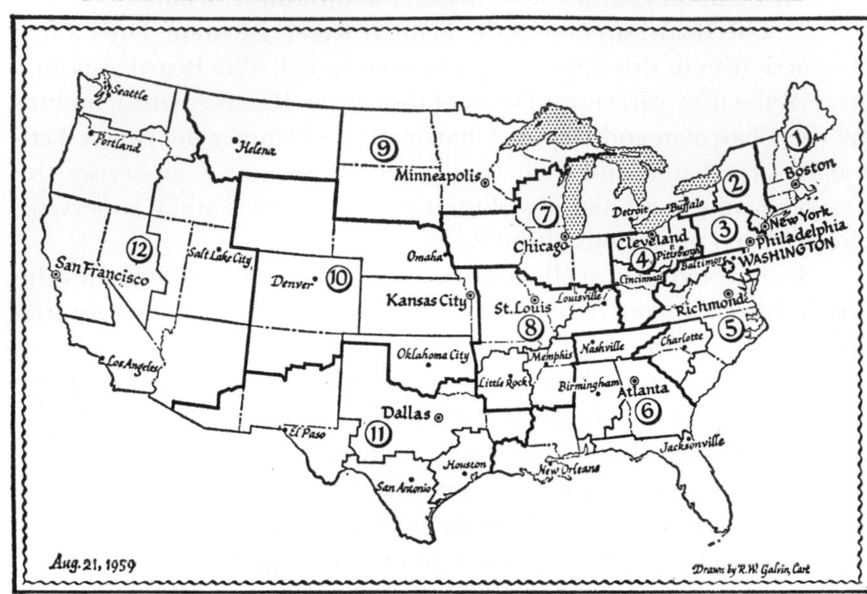

THE FEDERAL RESERVE SYSTEM

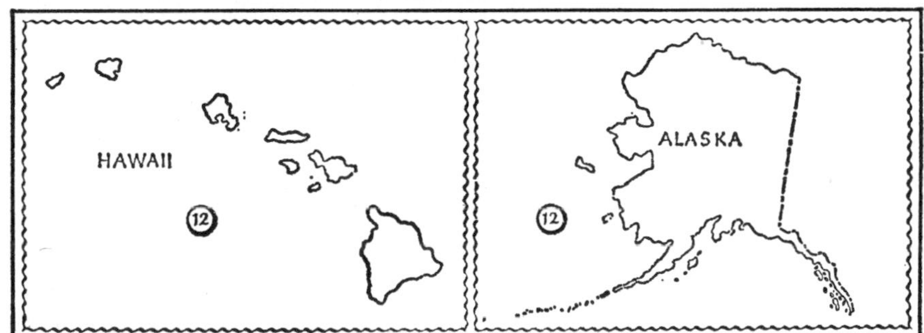

Legend

Boundaries of Federal Reserve Districts —Boundaries of Federal Reserve Branch Territories

Board of Governors of the Federal Reserve System

Federal Reserve Bank Cities • Federal Reserve Branch Cities

FIG. 18–1

SOURCE: *Federal Reserve Bulletin*, September, 1960.

The Patman Report criticizes the present regulations concerning the Federal Open Market Committee as illogical for the following reason:

The three principal instruments of Federal Reserve policy are the determination of rediscount rates, the variation of reserve requirements, and open-market operations. These three instruments must be used in conjunction to serve a common end, and there is no rational basis for the assignment of the most important of them, open-market operations, to a body different from that controlling the other two.[2]

Obviously, the Committee must consult with the Treasury on its policies since these policies influence the prices and yields of government securities.

The Federal Reserve Banks

The boundaries of the Federal Reserve districts, as well as their subdivisions and the location of the Federal Reserve banks are shown in Figure 18–1. Branches of the Reserve banks were established to provide a closer connection between member banks and their Federal Reserve banks in districts with large areas.

A system which combined the preservation of regional characteristics with strong central leadership required a careful balance between centrifugal and centripedal forces. While regional forces had the upper hand in the early years of the system, the system gained in cohesion during the middle thirties.

The Reserve banks' capital stock is owned by the member banks of their respective districts, but they are, nevertheless, institutions which are operated in the public interest. The ownership aspect of this regulation is a very minor matter, since the capital supplies only about ½ of 1 per cent of the system's resources. But private ownership of the Reserve banks' stock emphasizes the stake which private enterprise has in the system, and it also "serves as a memo from Congress to itself that it has chosen to leave to the system as a great deal of autonomy in its day-to-day and year-by-year operations."[3]

The earnings of the Federal Reserve banks are very substantial, as can be expected of institutions which create most of the country's currency and reserve money. But the Reserve banks are not in business to make profit. Profits are indeed incidental to most of their operations in an expanding economy. However, the Federal Reserve banks would carry out policy decisions even though they would involve losses. Out of their earnings the Reserve banks pay for their own and the Board's operating expenses and a dividend of 6 per cent on the capital stock held by member banks. Ninety per cent of the remaining profit is now paid into the federal Treasury.

Each Reserve bank has nine directors, who are divided into three groups. The three class A directors and the three class B directors are

[2] *Ibid.*, p. 54.
[3] *Ibid.*, p. 60.

elected by the member banks, which are, for this purpose, divided into large, medium, and small banks. Each category elects one group A and one group B director. The three class A directors are bankers; the three class B directors are representatives of commerce, agriculture, and industry. Three class C directors are appointed by the Board of Governors, one of them being the Chairman of the Board of Directors and another, the Deputy Chairman. None of the class B and C directors may be officers, directors, or employees of a bank. The Board of Directors elects the President of the Reserve Bank and one or more Vice-Presidents, subject to approval by the Board of Governors.

The Patman Report recommended that the Board of Governors give consideration to including representatives of labor among those whom it considers eligible for appointment as class C directors.[4] This suggestion is important, since the success of anti-inflationist policies will depend to a large extent on the co-operation of organized labor, particularly in times of high employment when labor enjoys a sellers' market.

We have already seen that the Federal Reserve banks share to some extent in the Board's credit policy, mainly through their representatives on the Federal Open Market Committee.

The service functions of the Reserve banks consist of the collection and clearing of checks, the furnishing and retiring of coin and paper money, and the performance of many financial services for the Treasury, particularly those connected with issuing, servicing, and redeeming government securities.

The Federal Reserve Bank of New York serves as agent in gold exchange and foreign exchange transactions and holds the dollar deposits of the International Monetary Fund and the International Bank for Reconstruction and Development (see Chapters 35 and 36).

The Reserve banks hold the reserves of their member banks. This is the core activity from which the system derives its name. There are practically no transactions by the Reserve banks which do not directly or indirectly change the reserves of the member banks, and on these reserves depends the power of the member banks to create deposit money.

The Reserve banks have important supervisory powers over their member banks. They can remove bank officers who violate banking laws; they can exclude banks from recourse to the credit facilities of the system; they can permit the establishment of branches in foreign countries, etc.

[4] *Ibid.*, p. 4.

The Member Banks

Not all the country's commercial banks are members of the Federal Reserve System. Of the 13,477 commercial banks in December 1959 only 6,233 were member banks. Looking at the deposit figures we find, however, that total deposits of member banks were $185 billion while the total deposits of nonmember banks were only $35 billion.

Membership in the Federal Reserve System implies certain duties. Member banks have to buy stock in the Federal Reserve banks; they are subject to reserve requirements which, as a rule, are more strict than those under state law; they must hold their reserves as deposits in the Federal Reserve banks and receive no interest on these deposits; they cannot collect exchange charges on checks; they have to comply with minimum capital requirements which are often higher than those under state law; they are, in the case of state banks, subject to general supervision and examination by Federal Reserve banks; and they must comply with various other requirements concerning investment in securities, restrictions on loans to executive officers, interlocking directorates, etc.

The privileges of member banks consist of (1) their right to borrow from the Reserve banks; (2) enjoyment of services rendered by the Reserve banks (check-clearing, distribution and retirement of currency, etc.); and (3) the participation in the system's democratic processes of policy formulation.

Nonmember banks can indirectly participate in privileges (1) and (2) through correspondent relationships, that is, through the services rendered to them by member banks. One may therefore ask whether member banks are bearing an unfair share of the cost of the monetary system. For this reason and in order to increase the effectiveness of Federal Reserve policy, the Douglas and Patman Reports proposed that all banks which accept demand deposits, including both member and nonmember banks, be made subject to the same set of reserve requirements and that all such banks be given access to loans at the Federal Reserve banks.[5]

The Douglas Report also suggested that the present system of making required reserves dependent on the size of the city in which the bank is located be replaced by a new system which would be geographically uniform but which might require different percentages of reserves against different types of deposits. The Report pointed out that

[5] *Report of the Subcommittee on Monetary, Credit, and Fiscal Policies,* Douglas Report (Washington, D.C., 1950), pp. 3, 32–37; Patman Report, *op. cit.,* pp. 3, 44–48.

for example, a small bank located in New York or Chicago and holding no deposits of other banks must hold reserves almost twice as large, percentagewise, as a similar bank located in a city that has not been designated as a central-reserve or reserve-city bank. And a "country" bank which does hold deposits of other banks is required to hold only about half as large reserves as are required of a similar bank located in a central-reserve-city.[6]

The Federal Advisory Council

The Federal Advisory Council has twelve members who are member bankers (one from each Federal Reserve district) and who are selected by the Directorates of the twelve Federal Reserve banks. The Council advises the Board of Governors and, through the Board, the Federal Open Market Committee, but it cannot require that its recommendations be adopted. The Federal Advisory Council establishes a direct connection between member banks and the highest authority of the system, thus adding another link to the carefully balanced structure of the system and emphasizing its democratic character.

Interrelation of Federal Reserve Agencies

Figure 18–2 tries to illustrate the relationships which exist between the various agencies of the Federal Reserve System.

The solid arrows indicate policy matters. Since the policy of the system originates with the Board and with the Federal Open Market Committee, the solid arrows all point downward.

Arrow (1) concerns the open-market policy of the system and leads from the Federal Open Market Committee through the Federal Reserve banks to the member banks, whose reserves with the Federal Reserve banks and credit policies are influenced by open-market sales and purchases.

Arrow (2) relates to discount policy. It starts at the Board of Governors (which "reviews and determines" discount rates) and leads, via the Reserve banks (which "establish" the discount rates), to the member banks to whose initiative actual rediscounting is left. Policy decisions in this field, however, are not limited exclusively to the determination of interest rates. Considerations of "eligibility" and "acceptablity" introduce a strong element of selectivity.

Arrow (3) refers to reserve requirements. It leads from the Board of Governors directly to the member banks. Changes in reserve re-

[6] Douglas Report, *op. cit.*, p. 37. See also "Proposed Revision of Reserve Requirements," *Federal Reserve Bulletin*, April, 1959.

quirements affect member banks without any further activity on the part of the Reserve banks.

Arrow (4), representing "selective" controls, refers to the regulation of margin requirements by the Board or to such emergency powers of the Board as the regulation of installment buying. Again the member banks and their customers are directly affected. The selective control powers of the Board actually transcend the limits of the Federal Reserve System. Arrow (4), therefore, points also to nonmember banks.

The two-pointed arrows (5) connect the two main policy-making agencies of the Federal Reserve with the Treasury, thus indicating that the policies of the Treasury and the Federal Reserve must be co-ordinated. Similar arrows could be drawn to connect the Federal Reserve with a number of federal or international agencies, such as

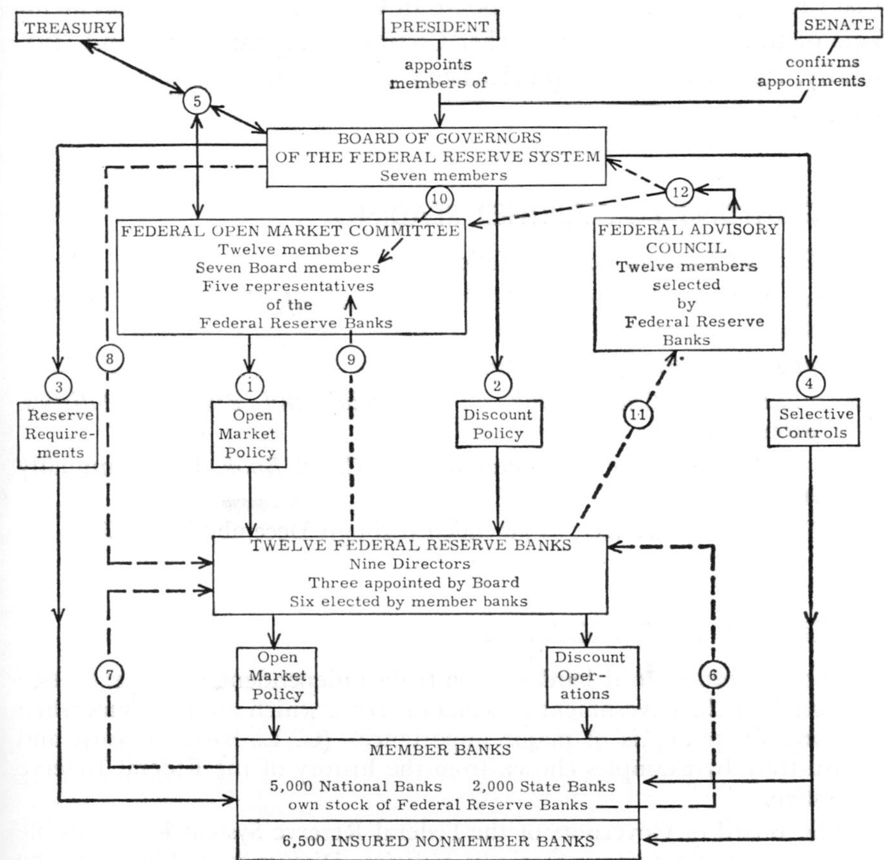

FIG. 18–2

the Federal Deposit Insurance Company, the Farm Credit Administration, the Export-Import Bank, the International Monetary Fund, and the International Bank for Reconstruction and Development.

The broken arrows of Figure 18–2 try to illustrate the administrative relationships among the system's agencies. Some of these arrows point upward, thus characterizing the "democratic" features of the system.

Arrow (6) shows that the member banks own the capital stock of the Reserve banks. Arrow (7) reflects that six of the nine directors of each Reserve bank are elected by member banks; while arrow (8), pointing in the opposite direction, reminds us that the other three directors are appointed by the Board of Governors. Arrow (9) relates to the membership of five representatives of the Reserve banks on the powerful Federal Open Market Committee, while arrow (10) shows that the seven members of the Board of Governors are ex officio members of the Federal Open Market Committee. Arrows (11) and (12), finally, concern the Federal Advisory Council and its consulting activities.

SUGGESTIONS FOR FURTHER READING

Federal Reserve Board Publications:

Annual Report of the Board of Governors of the Federal Reserve System.

Federal Reserve Bulletin. Monthly.

Federal Reserve Chart Book on Financial and Business Statistics. Monthly.

Historical Supplement to Federal Reserve Chart Book. Issued annually in September.

The Federal Reserve Act, as amended through December 31, 1956.

QUESTIONS AND PROBLEMS

1. "No modern central bank can be truly independent of the executive branch of the government in times of stress, which are the times when monetary policy is of major importance" (G. L. Bach). Discuss and illustrate by examples chosen from the history of the Federal Reserve System.
2. The Board of Governors of the Federal Reserve System is responsible for formulating national credit policies. Discuss and show how the Board can carry out its policy decisions via Federal Reserve and member banks.

3. Discuss the "democratic" features of the Federal Reserve System. Can a member bank influence policy formation in the Federal Reserve System?
4. What are the obligations and privileges of membership in the Federal Reserve System?
5. Compare the original with the present structure of the Federal Reserve System.
6. Can you think of minor or major structural changes which would improve the effectiveness of the Federal Reserve System?

BOOK THREE

Money, Interest, and Employment

PART VI
The Credit Market

Chapter 19 — CAPITAL GOODS, LOANABLE FUNDS, AND INTEREST

Introduction

The problems of money, credit, and capital are closely interrelated. In regulating the supply of *money* the monetary authority manages the terms of *credit,* mainly by influencing short- and long-term rates of interest; and interest rates, in turn, together with anticipated rates of profit, determine the volume of investment, that is, the volume of *capital goods* production. Money and capital are not identical, however. Money as a medium of exchange is no more capital than the wire is electric current.

The intimate connection between money and capital has not always received the attention it deserves. The theory of capital used to be treated mainly as part of the general theory of prices, centering on the relative scarcity of capital as a factor of production. Interest was discussed as the income of owners of capital. The theory of capital was part of the theory of distribution, and there existed little if any connection between interest as the price of capital (and the income of owners of capital) and interest as an instrument of monetary policy.

Around the turn of the century Knut Wicksell showed in his *Geldzins und Güterpreise*[1] how the gap between monetary and gen-

[1] Knut Wicksell, *Geldzins und Güterpreise* (Jena: Gustav Fischer, 1898); *Interest and Prices* (London: Macmillan & Co., Ltd., 1936). The English translation is not very faithful as already the title indicates.

eral economic theory might be bridged. He distinguished the "normal" supply of credit through saving from credit creation; and he tried to show that any deviation of the market rate of interest from the normal rate (which equates the demand for credit with the supply of savings) would cause a cumulative process of price inflation or price deflation. This cumulative process arises from changes in the quantity and velocity of circulation of money. The market rate of interest can be kept below the normal rate only when the supply of loanable funds is constantly supplemented by credit creation or dishoarding.[2]

Members of the Austrian—as well as the Swedish—school have further developed and clarified the Wicksellian thesis, and D. H. Robertson followed similar lines of thought independently in England.[3] Another approach by J. M. Keynes and his followers arrives at results partly similar to those of the aforementioned economists.[4] When writing his *Treatise on Money,* Keynes was, as he later pointed out, "still moving along the traditional lines of regarding the influence of money as something, so to speak, separate from the general theory of supply and demand."[5] Subsequently he developed his *General Theory,* in which the supply of and the demand for money are held to play a decisive part in the determination of the rate of interest. The rate of interest and the anticipated rate of profit, in turn, are two determinants of the volume of employment and the national income. Changes in the supply of and the demand for money are thus factors determining not only the general level of prices but—together with other factors—the total volume of output.

Formerly a neglected problem, the interrelation of money, credit, and capital has become a major subject of modern economic discussion.

In what follows emphasis will be placed on what appears to be common ground among participants in the controversy. Having already discussed at some length the present status of modern monetary theory, it seems advisable first to restate some fundamental aspects of

[2] For a fuller discussion of Wicksell's theory see Chapter 20.

[3] See, for example, Friedrich A. Hayek, *Prices and Production* (London: George Routledge & Sons, 1931); Bertil Ohlin, "Some Notes on the Stockholm Theory of Saving and Investment," *The Economic Journal,* Vol. XLVII (1937), reprinted in *Readings in Business Cycle Theory* (Homewood, Ill.: Richard D. Irwin, Inc., 1944); D. H. Robertson, *Essays in Monetary Theory* (London: Staples Press, 1948).

[4] See J. M. Keynes, *The General Theory of Employment, Interest and Money* (London: Macmillan & Co., Ltd., 1936) and the discussion between Ohlin, Robertson, Hawtrey, and Keynes in *The Economic Journal,* Vol. XLVII (1937).

[5] Keynes, *op. cit.,* p. vi.

the theories of capital, interest, and credit as they appear when approached from the capital side of the problem.

Capital Goods

The use of many different capital concepts has been a source of great confusion, "a second Babel," as Eugen von Böhm-Bawerk remarked.[6] This confusion can be reduced, however, once we notice that conflicting uses of the term "capital" often refer to different phenomena and once we assign special names to the various manifestations of the elusive entity called "capital." Most important is the distinction between capital or investment goods and the funds which are available for production of these goods, the so-called "loanable funds."

By capital or investment goods we mean the "produced means of production."[7] Capital goods are the product of labor, natural resources, and already existing capital goods. That they are "produced" distinguishes them from labor and land; that they are means of production differentiates them from consumers' goods, that is, from goods bought and used by final consumers.

Capital goods are usually divided into two categories: fixed capital and working capital.

Fixed capital is mainly represented by the durable means of production, such as factory buildings, machines, and tools. These instruments may have a lifetime of several years and are used during many successive production processes; their services are given up gradually; thus their loss in value is gradual, taking the form of depreciation or obsolescence.

Working capital (or circulating capital) consists of materials, fuels, and semifinished and finished goods used in the successive stages of production (extraction, fabrication, transportation, and marketing). Since each separate stage of production sells its product to the next stage or to the consumer, the working capital of the individual firm is liquidated at the end of each production process.

We can illustrate our two categories of capital goods by using the cigarette machine as an example. The cigarette machine is a fixed capital good whose services can be used for many years. The tobacco and the paper which pass through the machine and the power which drives the machine are working or circulating capital. The cigarettes,

6 Eugen von Böhm-Bawerk, *The Positive Theory of Capital* (New York: G. E. Stechert & Co., 1930), p. 23.

7 Eugen von Böhm-Bawerk, "Kapital," *Handwörterbuch der Staatswissenschaften* (Jena: Gustav Fischer, 1923), Vol. V, p. 578.

when they leave the machine, are physically already a consumption good, but they retain their character as working capital while they pass through the stages of packing, transporting, and distributing. Finally, and still as working capital, they become part of the inventory of a drugstore. Not before they are sold and find themselves in the pocket of a consumer do they cease to be working capital.

This example shows that we deal with rather elusive distinctions. Obviously it depends on the intentions of the owner whether a particular commodity is a capital good or a consumers' good. The cigarettes were bought by the drugstore owner with the intention of making a profit in selling them. For him they are a capital good. For the consumer they are a consumption good, though they remain physically unchanged while they move from one category to the other. Or suppose that a medical doctor uses his automobile both for visiting his patients and for pleasure rides or that a residential building is in one case owned and in another case only rented by the occupant. Is the automobile, or is the house, a capital good or a consumers' good? We see, furthermore, that consumers' goods, too, can be durable goods, goods which render their services only gradually. These durable consumers' goods, like refrigerators, TV-sets, washing machines, and furniture, can give rise to financial transactions quite similar to those connected with fixed capital goods: they are bought on credit and they depreciate.

The most important difference between fixed capital and working capital concerns the length of the period during which the capital good remains in the productive process. Working capital has a relatively short life. Fuel is burnt; nylon thread is woven into stockings; timber is cut and built into frame houses. The house, on the other hand, is a durable good which may last for many years. The process of building the house may take only a few months during which all the building materials are working capital. Once the house is built, or once the cigarette machine is produced, the materials are imprisoned in the fixed capital good, which will render services over a long time, will deteriorate, will need repairs, and will, finally, have to be replaced.

Periods of Production

We see that production processes are time consuming and that the services of durable goods have to be waited for.

We must distinguish different periods:

1. To indicate the average production period in one particular plant or firm, we will assume that the input of labor and materials is

the same every day and that at the end of, say, one week the output (cigarettes, shirts, or sausages) begins to come forth in a continuous flow. If it took one week to transform the first input into the first output, material equal to one week's input will stay continuously in the plant, the annual turnover of working capital will be fifty-two times, and the period of production, in this sense, will be one week.

2. The process of production in one plant or firm, however, is only one stage in a much longer and much more complicated process. Our plant has used a great variety of materials or parts produced by other firms, just as its own products may not be bought by consumers but rather, as intermediate goods, by other firms for use in succeeding stages of production. Thus, in looking at the economy as a whole, we see that many stages of production are both preceded and succeeded by others: preceding others, they distribute their products among various users; succeeding others, they collect necessary materials and parts from a great number of other factories. Seen in this way our whole economy appears as an intricate interdependence of production processes. The *total* length of the production process of a single commodity may reach surprisingly far into the past.

3. The factories whose turnover of working capital and whose technical interdependence have just been described use more or less elaborate machinery. These fixed capital goods had to be produced, and their manufacture, too, was a time-consuming process in which the products of many other plants were used as materials or parts.

4. The life span of a fixed capital good indicates still another period. It may take a long time before a fixed capital good has rendered all the services which it is capable of rendering. Yet, to enjoy even its first service the whole capital good had to be produced. This production may imply a substantial outlay in the present, while the fruits of this productive effort may be enjoyed only over a long period.

Several conclusions may be drawn from these statements about the various periods of production. We see, first of all, that there are definite technical reasons why some production processes need to be financed only for a short interval while in others funds are invested for much longer periods. A builder can build a house and finance the building process through his bank for the necessary 4 or 6 months. After he has sold the house he can pay off his loan or he can repeat the process and build another house. The character of these funds as working or circulating capital is mirrored in the fact that the bank loan retains a certain liquidity provided the builder is able to sell the house.

This salability, however, is the crux of the matter. We learn, therefore, secondly, that the liquidity of working capital depends on the ability of the producer to sell his product. The sale of the product depends on the demand situation. Should the product prove to be unsalable or should it have to be sold below cost, a part of the invested funds cannot be recovered, there will be no new orders, production will be discontinued, and unemployment may be created. The interdependence of production processes means that inability to sell at the end of the line of interconnected stages of production may cause an avalanche of illiquidity.

Still another conclusion can be drawn from our brief analysis of production periods. Fixed capital goods which imply a long period of waiting for all their services must be financed for the whole time necessary for their complete amortization. The sale of a newly produced fixed capital good depends, therefore, on the ability of the purchaser to make satisfactory financial arrangements for this long-term investment. If these financial arrangements cannot be made and the fixed capital good consequently cannot be sold, the funds invested during its production cannot be paid back and become "frozen." The consequences in form of reduced orders, interrupted production processes, and unemployment may be serious.

Loanable Funds

In the preceding section the discussion was largely restricted to technological matters, though it was already possible to see that technology might explain interesting financial phenomena, such as the creation and spread of illiquidity in a system of financially separate but technologically interdependent production processes.

The funds needed by those who produce or purchase capital goods are called "loanable" or "investment" funds. Loanable funds and capital goods are not identical, and confusion will arise if both are indiscriminately referred to as "capital." It is true that we need loanable or investment funds to be able to produce capital goods. But once capital goods are produced, they no longer constitute loanable funds, that is, funds with which anything the producer needs can be purchased.

From the monetary viewpoint we distinguish two main sources of loanable funds: noninflationary and inflationary.

Saving has already been defined as "not-consuming." Income earned and not spent on consumption is income saved. It can be held as a liquid reserve or it can be spent on the purchase or production of capital goods. The purchase of securities which represent these capital goods will be discussed later.

Income is earned in the production of both consumers' and capital goods. If all income earned were spent on consumers' goods, the amount of money spent on consumption would tend to be greater than the value of the consumers' goods at cost prices, and the result would be inflationary. Saving performs the important function of reducing the demand for consumers' goods so that factors of production are set free for the production of capital goods. When savings are spent on capital goods, the result is not inflationary.

While capital goods are, as a rule, produced to increase the future supply of consumers' goods, their production may, for the time being, reduce the supply of consumers' goods. This is due to the time-consuming character of capital goods production, which has already been discussed.

Investment as the production of capital goods means that we embark on "indirect" or roundabout processes of production because we know that in this manner we get in the end a larger supply, a greater variety, and an improved quality of consumers' goods. We shall see how this connection between (1) saving as the willingness to wait for consumption and (2) investment as a time-consuming process which increases efficiency can be used to explain why a given amount of present money is worth more future money. One of the explanations of this phenomenon, called "interest," is found in the increased and improved output of consumers' goods which results from the time-consuming or roundabout processes of production in which we create first capital goods and then, with the help of these capital goods, consumers' goods.

To the savings of individuals we have to add the "corporate" savings of business firms. These firms, instead of paying out all their profits to their owners, retain part of the profits for investment purposes. Since the investment may take place within the firms, the savings may not appear on the credit market. But since the process of building up these business savings tends to be continuous while the process of investment may be discontinuous, these funds may at least temporarily be offered on the credit market.

Government savings may be the result of tax policies or the building up of social security reserves. These savings may raise the saved portion of the national income beyond the amount which voluntary private savings would supply. In a centrally planned economy government savings are the most important source of loanable funds.

When we distinguished net from gross national product (in Chapter 7) we saw that the difference consisted of depreciation. To compensate for depreciation and obsolescence, replacement funds are set aside by business firms. It is obvious that these funds do not represent an increase in the capital resources of the nation. They may, therefore, be included only in gross savings but not in net savings.

But in spite of the fact that replacement funds do not increase the total supply of real capital, they are in many ways of the same significance as investment funds derived from other sources. They may be used for the production of capital goods which are entirely different from those being replaced. The opportunity thus afforded to change to higher quality capital goods or to adjust to changes in demand or techniques is reason for considering replacement funds as part of the supply of investment funds. Occasional terminological inconsistencies can be avoided by distinguishing gross investment from net investment, the latter being gross investment minus the maintenance of capital.

Depreciation allowances represent the "liquidity" of fixed capi tal. Working capital as a revolving fund has a much higher liquidity than fixed capital and can be considered part of the supply of loanable or investment funds whenever the sale of the product whose production it has financed releases it for investment elsewhere. But, as in the case of depreciation allowances, the repeated supply of circulating capital does not mean an increased total supply of loanable funds.

In the case of both replacement funds and liquidated working capital we can speak of funds "disentangled from the embodiment in capital goods."[8] When these funds are re-invested they do not increase our capital resources, but their temporary "disentanglement" permits very important adjustments to changing conditions.

Loanable funds derived from the sources so far mentioned have in common that they do not increase the supply of money, because they merely change the way in which money is spent. Changes in the supply of loanable funds which do not simultaneously alter the supply or active circulation of money imply a corresponding inverse change of consumption. If these funds are invested, total expenditure in monetary terms, total income, and total employment will not be altered except as a result of frictions in the transfer of resources from consumers' goods to investment goods industries.

The inflationary sources of the supply of loanable funds are

[8] D. H. Robertson, *Utility and All That* (New York: Macmillan Co., 1952), p. 84.

credit creation and dishoarding. Commercial banks can create loanable funds when their reserve position and the demand for credit permit the expansion of loans and investments. This creation of additional purchasing power constitutes so-called credit inflation. Whether the credit inflation is accompanied by price inflation depends on the simultaneous development of the volume of production.

Dishoarding is the release of previously held money reserves owing to a reduction in liquidity preference. An increased eagerness to buy securities rather than to hold money makes loanable funds available by withdrawing them from money stocks. As in the case of credit creation the result may be price inflation unless the increased purchasing power is balanced by an increase of production or unless the monetary authority can counteract dishoarding by contracting the money supply.

Invested Funds

All capital goods (and natural resources) belong either to persons or to corporations, which are, in turn, "owned" by their stockholders. To the physical world of plants and factories corresponds, therefore, a financial world in which a great variety of titles of ownership and credit represent the underlying mass of capital goods which produce returns for their owners, or their owners' creditors. The monetary value of securities is determined by market forces and is essentially the capitalized value of income derived from these titles.

Thus we can distinguish (aside from capital goods and loanable funds) still other capital concepts which concern the value of securities, that is, the value of funds which have already been invested.

The Usefulness and Scarcity of Loanable Funds

Interest is the price paid for the use of loanable or investment funds. Anything that has a price must possess utility and scarcity. Our first task in studying interest rates, therefore, is to explain these qualities of utility and scarcity in connection with loanable funds.

Why should loanable funds be considered useful? We saw that loanable funds are used for the purchase or production of capital goods and that the use of capital goods permits greatly increased and improved production of consumers' goods in the future. The reason for this increased productivity is to be found in technical rather than economical facts. As Eugen von Böhm-Bawerk stated:

> That roundabout methods lead to greater results than direct methods is one of the most important and fundamental propositions in the whole the-

ory of production. It must be emphatically stated that the only basis for this proposition is the experience of practical life. Economic theory does not and cannot show *a priori* that it must be so; but the unanimous experience of all the technique of production says that it is so.[9]

The increase in productivity resulting from the use of capital goods is, in percentage terms, most impressive where relatively little capital is available. The ax which permits us to cut wood instead of having to break branches with our bare hands may serve as an example. If Robinson Crusoe had required Friday to give him half of Friday's gathered wood as payment for the loan of Robinson's ax, Friday would be well advised to borrow the ax even at such an enormously high rate of interest, provided this simple tool increases his efficiency by much more than 100 per cent. Later we shall inquire into the marginal efficiency which can be attributed to an additional dollar's worth of capital goods, because on this marginal efficiency will depend the borrower's willingness to borrow at given rates of interest. First, however, we have to find out why loanable funds should be considered relatively scarce.

Capital goods can be produced in larger quantities at any time if we are willing and able to invest a larger portion of our available productive resources in their production. It may seem, therefore, as if the scarcity of capital goods had to be traced back to the scarcity of labor and natural resources; and since natural resources are extracted by the use of labor, we may seem thrown back to the Marxian labor theory of value, which attributes interest and all other kinds of unearned income to the exploitation of labor.

There is, however, a flaw in this argument. It is impossible to requisition just any desired amount of labor and natural resources for the manufacture of capital goods. Assuming full employment of the factors of production, the output of consumers' goods has to be restricted if we want to increase the production of producers' goods. Since we cannot live without a certain minimum supply of consumers' goods, we cannot produce capital goods ad libitum.

With this argument we return once more to the time-consuming character of the process of production. Insofar as labor and materials are first devoted to the manufacture of machines, tools, and factory buildings, a period of time must elapse before such production can result in increased consumption. The satisfaction of wants must be waited for, and the supply of "waiting" is limited, because we must

[9] Eugen von Böhm-Bawerk, *The Positive Theory of Capital* (New York: G. E. Stechert & Co., 1930), p. 20.

have a certain amount of present consumers' goods before we will spare productive resources for the manufacture of additional capital goods.

In an authoritarian economy the production of capital goods is determined by the rulers, who arbitrarily divide the available means of production between consumers' and producers' goods industries. They may enforce a starvation level of consumption, but even they cannot ignore consumers' goods production altogether.

In an unplanned, capitalist economy consumption is normally voluntarily reduced by the desire to save. The decision to save rests on many factors. The most important among these factors are income level and distribution. As the national income increases a greater part of it is saved, because a higher level of consumption carries with it a growing willingness to forego some consumption in the present in hope of bettering the opportunities for consumption in the future. Furthermore, at any given national income level the more unequally income is distributed the more will be saved. The income of many people is so low that they tend to spend all or most of it on consumption.

The so-called waiting theory as stated above can hardly be subject to controversy. As Joan Robinson says:

> When the rate of investment is pressing against the limit set by available resources and all workers are fully employed, then no further increase in the rate of investment can take place unless consumption declines.[10]

When the waiting theory has been criticized, it has been because of a mistaken notion that the theory implies that interest is a price paid for "waiting," while waiting is interpreted as a personal sacrifice. Of course, interest is not a price paid for waiting. "Waiting" means nothing but an explanation of the impossibility of investing more than a part of the available factors of production in the production of capital goods.

Schumpeter[11] denied that we have to wait for the regular fruits of production "because the circular flow (of economic life), once established, leaves no gap between outlay or production effort and the

[10] Joan Robinson, *Introduction to the Theory of Employment* (London: Macmillan & Co., Ltd., 1938), pp. 47–48. Joan Robinson was quoted just because she is opposed to the waiting theory. The main objection to the waiting theory is that it has to presuppose the full use of the productive resources. Provided the productive resources are not fully employed, it is possible to increase the production of capital goods without decreasing the production of consumers' goods.

[11] J. A. Schumpeter, *The Theory of Economic Development* (Cambridge, Mass.: Harvard University Press, 1934), p. 38.

satisfaction of wants." Input and output are, following J. B. Clark's expression, automatically synchronized. The waiting theory, however, does not assume a shortage of consumers' goods in any absolute sense. Clark exemplified the process of synchronization by a forest with 50 rows of trees from 1 to 50 years old, of which the oldest row will be cut every year while a new row is planted.[12] It certainly cannot be denied that first, creation of the forest involved a waiting process; second, in order to ensure a continuous supply of lumber we have to "abstain" from cutting any row less than 50 years of age; and, third, any regular and permanent increase in the supply of lumber necessitates a new process of waiting. A present reduction in the cutting of trees, say half a row, would allow the trees to grow older and bigger, so that more waiting leads to increased future output. Schumpeter's argument thus boils down to the assertion that we enjoy more consumers' goods to the extent that more waiting was done during an earlier period and that we can more easily wait for future consumption to the extent we already enjoy a high level of consumption.

The main objection to the waiting theory is that unemployed natural resources, capital goods, and labor may exist. As long as we have not reached a state of full employment, we can increase the production of capital goods without having to decrease consumption. It is, therefore, quite obvious that the waiting theory does not offer a complete explanation of the rates of interest, since it does not take this case into account. We find rates of interest in periods of unemployment, a phenomenon not accounted for in the waiting theory. In times of underemployment waiting is no longer a precondition of the production of additional capital goods at stable commodity prices, because more loanable funds can be supplied through credit creation without price inflation.

The waiting theory is incomplete, but it is not incorrect as far as it goes. It explains one of the factors which determine the amount of saving, which is, in turn, only one of the factors which determine the supply of loanable funds. Even in times of underemployment it is important to consider that the amount of saving forthcoming at a relatively low income level is dependent on the amount of indispensable consumption. With lower incomes people will save less than before. But this does not mean that the investment possibilities of the economy are now limited by these savings. When the national income decreases as unemployment increases, the potential supply of loanable

[12] J. B. Clark, *The Distribution of Wealth* (New York: Macmillan Co., 1924), pp. 131 ff.

funds for investment purposes becomes increasingly independent of the supply of savings and increasingly dependent on the creation of credit.

The Investment Potential

We can call unemployed factors of production which are available for increased production of capital goods the investment potential of the economy. This investment potential is never large enough to permit unlimited capital goods production. But it explains why investment may be financed by credit creation without price inflation and why, therefore, investment is not always limited to intended savings.

As to the amount and quality of this investment potential, we must consider two points.

1. In times of widespread unemployment of the means of production there is usually available a supply of many kinds of unused resources, capital goods, and labor, and there is, therefore, a correspondingly large choice as to their utilization. As employment increases it becomes more difficult to find all needed means of production in the right proportions. This is the gradual process which is often referred to as reaching bottlenecks of production.

2. With increasing employment both income and consumption will increase. This means that the still available investment potential tends to be simultaneously reduced from two sides: through use of resources for investment purposes and through increased demand for, and production of, consumers' goods.

These considerations show that it is not necessarily safe for credit creation to continue as long as some unused resources remain available. Neither is it certain that unemployment in one field of production can be safely cured by increasing total money supply and total expenditure.

If creation of credit without price inflation is limited by the investment potential of the economy and if the supply of savings is limited by consumption expenditures, loanable funds are scarce. This scarcity, together with the great usefulness of capital goods, provides us with a basic explanation of the price which is paid for the use of loanable funds—the rate of interest.

The Functions of Interest

In a market economy rates of interest perform several important functions:

1. Rates of interest equilibrate the demand for loanable funds with the supply of loanable funds on the various credit markets of the economy. This function can be dispensed with only if we are willing to adjust demand to supply by some other means, for instance, by granting investment licenses.

2. Since the supply of loanable funds comes from inflationary as well as noninflationary sources, the choice of those rates which equate the demand for loanable funds with their supply becomes ultimately the most important instrument of monetary policy. If interest rates are kept below those which bring the supply of savings and the demand for credit into balance, the supply of money will have to be increased. On the other hand, artificially high rates of interest will lead to a level of investment which does not absorb all forthcoming savings, thus causing credit contraction and a fall in total expenditure. Monetary policy, therefore, uses changes in interest rates as a means of influencing the demand for, and the supply of, loanable funds.

3. Interest rates may influence to some degree the supply of savings. Higher rates of interest are supposed to call forth larger amounts of savings. It will be shown, however, that no definite predictions concerning this relation between interest rates and saving can be made and also that the level of income is a far more important determinant of the supply of savings. Apart from their influence on the willingness to save, higher rates of interest may induce the holders of money reserves to part with liquidity. How far a person or firm is willing to go to satisfy liquidity preference depends on the price of liquidity, namely, the income from financial investment which must be foregone if money is to be kept idle.

4. Interest rates serve to distribute loanable funds among different users. The demand for loanable funds comes from those who want to invest (that is, produce or purchase capital goods), from those who want to expand consumption beyond the limits set by their disposable income, and from those who want to satisfy their demand for liquidity (money reserves) through borrowing. Interest rates will influence the allocation of loanable funds among these different uses.

In the field of capital goods production the loanable funds will go to different firms and industries according to their ability to pay going rates. Producers will be able to pay these rates of interest if the consumers of their products, in turn, stand ready to cover the expense by paying sufficiently high commodity prices. However, we must not assume that the willingness to pay the market price for loanable funds is all which is required of the borrower. A bank will not lend money to just anybody promising to pay interest. But while not the only factor influencing the allocation of loanable funds, rates of interest are nevertheless a very important element in the process.

Suppose that an expanding economy wants more steel, more houses, more airplanes, and an infinite variety of goods whose production requires the investment of loanable funds. Which productive facilities should be increased and how far should the expansion go in each case? A consistent answer to this question is possible only if we make the use of loanable funds dependent on the payment of going rates of interest. These rates must be high enough to equate the demand for and the supply of loanable funds in the credit market. Each producer will have to compare the required rate of interest with his anticipated profit. Such comparisons will tend to result in an "ideal" distribution of loanable funds—one wherein the marginal return on each invested dollar will be everywhere the same and production will follow the wishes of consumers as expressed by their willingness to pay commodity prices which cover costs of production, including interest.

Interest Rates, Direct Controls, and Inflation

We must realize that without allocation through uniform rates of interest, loanable funds would have to be distributed in some arbitrary manner, that is, according to the decisions of an authority rather than in response to the wishes of consumers. The government would have to use investment licenses. But how is the government to know which field of industry should be expanded and how far? In a centrally planned authoritarian economy planning agencies will solve the allocation problem by mere command, perhaps without much consideration of the wishes of the people. In the private sector of a market economy, however, the allocation of loanable funds through licensing becomes a dubious instrument of economic policy. As one critic of the investment policy of the British labor government put it:

> Who is to decide between the relative urgencies of a new bridge in Basutoland, a new hospital in Aberystwyth, a new mousetrap factory in Glasgow, or a new cinema in Oxford? The answer is that nobody can decide, and that therefore conscientious officials, fully knowing that they have not the facts on which to base a judgement, will pass everything that seems on the face of it to be reasonable. The result is always that more licenses are granted than the available resources can fulfill, and that there is an unholy

scramble in the course of which many of the most urgent projects are held up because the promoters of the less urgent projects have been more skilled in the arts of acquiring scarce materials.[13]

Even in the public sphere it will become impossible to allocate investment funds economically if the government does not want to be guided by sufficiently high rates of interest.

The Government . . . by holding the rate of interest below the level to which it might rise but for the Government operations specifically designed to keep it down . . . makes itself responsible for substituting some control in place of the brake that high rates of interest might otherwise impose upon capital projects.[14]

Such policies are dangerous because, first, they fail to consistently allocate investment funds and, second, because they are liable to lead to excessive credit creation in an effort to accommodate all who want to borrow.

Cheap money policies are often followed to stimulate private investment. In times of depression such policies may be justified. But if the rate of interest is no longer under the control of the monetary authority (as in the United States before the "accord" of 1951) the result may be price inflation. This is particularly likely if wages are permitted to increase beyond the increase in labor efficiency. D. H. Robertson has pointed out that:

Against this kind of inflation too, monetary management, with its instrument the rate of interest, was, in the bad old days of the gold standard, the ultimate safeguard. Wage negotiations were conducted, as it were, within a steel framework not absolutely rigid indeed, but known not to be indefinitely extensible. . . . If the framework is scrapped, if monetary authorities are always prepared to create without question whatever *flow of money* is needed to discharge whatever *wage-bill* is needed to reconcile full employment with whatever *wage-rate* is demanded by the Trade Unions, they

[13] W. Arthur Lewis, *The Principles of Economic Planning* (Washington, D.C.: Public Affairs Press, 1949), pp. 56–57. It is of interest to note that this book was written for the Fabian Society, a group for the gradual spreading of socialism, founded in England in 1884.

[14] Roy Harrod, *Are These Hardships Necessary?* (London: Rupert Hart-Davis, 1947), p. 33. Harrod illustrates his point by the following example: "On the very day that sterling was declared inconvertible, an extensive scheme for electrifying the Manchester-Sheffield mainline . . . was announced. . . . It is to cost 6 million. No doubt the feelings of the reader were assuaged when he learned that this scheme is calculated to save about 100,000 tons of coal a year. Anything that saves coal must be good! A paradoxical situation for Britain! But it is necessary to be more precise. Even at the present reduced level of output from the mines it only takes 382 men to produce 100,000 tons of coal a year. Meanwhile the scheme will employ at the very least 12,000 man years of labor spread over four years. So we are to expend 12,000 man years now in order, after four years, to save the labor of 382 men in the coal mines . . ." (*Ibid.*, p. 78).

have in effect abdicated from exercising that sovereignty over the standard of value which we thought we had committed to their charge.[15]

Cheap money may lead to a state of affairs wherein we try to accomplish with numerous and often clumsy controls what a correctly chosen rate of interest could have accomplished much better. The difference is that between direct and indirect economic controls. Monetary policy in the form of interest rate changes is one of the most important instruments of indirect economic control. The monetary authority regulates the total supply of loanable funds but leaves its allocation to the general pricing process. Interest rates are chosen so as to create just the amount of additional money needed to fill the gap between the demand for loanable funds and the supply of savings at these rates. If the monetary authority is no longer able to regulate the supply of money in this way, we must use numerous direct controls both to allocate loanable funds and to substitute repressed inflation for price inflation if the latter is to be avoided.

SUGGESTIONS FOR FURTHER READING

Böhm-Bawerk, Eugen. *The Positive Theory of Capital,* Books I and II. New York: G. E. Stechert & Co., 1930.

Cassel, Gustav. *The Theory of Social Economy,* chap. 6. Rev. ed. New York: Harcourt, Brace & Co., 1932.

Clark, John Bates. *The Distribution of Wealth,* chap. 9. New York: Macmillan Co., 1924.

Halm, George N. *Economic Systems,* chap. 21. Rev. ed. New York: Holt, Rinehart, and Winston, 1960.

Hansen, Alvin H. *Business Cycles and National Income,* chap. 16. New York: W. W. Norton & Co., 1951.

Harrod, Roy F. *Are These Hardships Necessary?,* chap. 2. London: Rupert Hart-Davis, 1947.

Hayek, Friedrich A. "The Mythology of Capital," *Quarterly Journal of Economics,* Vol. L (February, 1936). Reprinted in *Readings in the Theory of Income Distribution,* chap. 20 (Homewood, Ill.: Richard D. Irwin, Inc., 1946).

Lewis, Arthur L. *The Principles of Economic Planning,* chap. 4. Washington, D.C.: Public Affairs Press, 1951.

Machlup, Fritz. *The Stock Exchange Market Credit and Capital Formation,* chap. 2. London: William Hodge & Co., Ltd., 1940.

Meade, James Edward. *Planning and the Price Mechanism,* chaps. 2 and 5. London: George Allen & Unwin, Ltd., 1948.

15 D. H. Robertson, *Utility and All That* (New York: Macmillan Co., 1952), p. 91.

ROBERTSON, D. H. *Utility and All That,* chap. 1. New York: Macmillan Co., 1952.

SCHUMPETER, J. A. *The Theory of Economic Development,* chap. 1. Cambridge, Mass.: Harvard University Press, 1934.

QUESTIONS AND PROBLEMS

1. "The problem of credit necessitates a monetary theory which, differently from the quantity theory, is really integrated with the central economic theory" (G. Myrdal). Discuss.
2. Define the terms capital goods, fixed capital, working capital, and loanable funds.
3. Why is it important to distinguish between different periods of production?
4. What did Eugen von Böhm-Bawerk mean when he spoke of roundabout processes of production?
5. Discuss different sources of the supply of loanable funds.
6. Is it correct to call the rate of interest a price for waiting?
7. "A consistent allocation of loanable funds in a market economy is only possible on the basis of interest rates." Do you agree? Would your answer be different for a centrally planned economy?
8. "Interest rates which are kept artificially low lead to misallocations of loanable funds and to inflationary pressures." Correct?
9. "If monetary authorities are always prepared to create without question whatever *flow of money* is needed to discharge whatever *wage-rate* is demanded by the Trade Unions, they have in effect abdicated from exercising that sovereignty over the standard of value which we thought we had committed to their charge" (D. H. Robertson). Discuss.

Chapter 20 THE DEMAND FOR AND THE SUPPLY OF LOANABLE FUNDS

The Decision to Invest

A simple example will illustrate the factors which determine the investment demand for loanable funds. Suppose we have to decide whether it is profitable to build an apartment house. The relevant data are as follows:

1. The yearly net rent, that is, the rent after deductions for such expenses as upkeep and real estate taxes, is expected to be $50,000 throughout the foreseeable future, that is, the house is considered to be a "perpetuity."

2. The construction cost of the house is estimated to be $1 million.

3. The rate of interest, the variable in our example, is assumed to be 5, 6, and 4 per cent, respectively. This is the rate which must be paid both for the short-term loan needed for construction purposes and for the long-term mortgage credit. It is also the rate which we could earn if we possessed our own funds and were to lend them on the credit market; in other words, it is the prevailing rate of interest. The fact that rates of interest are not uniform will be discussed later. To simplify our example we assume the existence of only one rate of interest at any given time.

If under these assumptions the rate of interest is 5 per cent, we might not come to a decision. The net rent of $50,000 would be exactly 5 per cent of the construction cost of $1 million, and the rate of return expected to be obtained in constructing the new capital good would, therefore, exactly equal the prevailing rate of interest. A slight change in the rate of interest, however, will remove our indecision. If the rate of interest were 6 per cent, we should definitely decide against building. The prospective yield of our investment, $50,000, is 6 per cent of $833,333, while the construction cost is still assumed to be $1 million. To induce building under these conditions the prospective yield would have to be at least $60,000, an assumption which we have expressly excluded. On the other hand, if the prevailing rate of interest were as low as 4 per cent, $50,000 would be considered a normal return on $1,250,000, and we would decide to build because we would have to invest only $1 million in order to enjoy the prospective yield of $50,000.

The Marginal Efficiency of Investment

We see that the investment demand for loanable funds depends primarily on a comparison of anticipated yields with the prevailing rate of interest or, in scientific language, on a comparison of the marginal efficiency of investment (or capital) with the rate of interest. The marginal efficiency of investment is the rate of return which we expect to earn in the future when we purchase or produce new capital goods; in our example it was $50,000/$1 million. Since we deal with decisions concerning new investments, which can have only a future return, it is obvious that the marginal efficiency of investment is based on anticipations rather than on known facts.

Other things remaining equal, the marginal efficiency of investment (or capital) will tend to decrease for two reasons as investment increases.

1. The yield will fall as the supply of a given type of capital goods increases: as more apartment houses are ready for occupancy, rents will tend to decline.

2. The costs of production will rise because of an increasing demand for the needed factors of production: as a building boom develops, building materials from bricks to doorknobs will rise in price.

Since the marginal efficiency of investment tends to fall with an increase in investment, it is important to remember that the prospective yields of additional capital goods are not "perpetuities": they are not definitely known in advance and they are not necessarily identical with yields to be expected in the near future. Furthermore, our assumption of "other things remaining equal" suggests that for many reasons unrelated to the additional investment itself, there may occur changes in the marginal efficiency of capital: costs of production may change owing to a change in factor supply; technological improvements may make even newly constructed capital goods obsolete; new taxes may reduce the yield; and the demand for the services of the capital good may change (as when, for example, the population moves away from the city in which the new apartment house is located).

We see that there are many factors which influence our expectations as to the future yields of new capital goods. Since all these influences are more or less uncertain, even the general state of mind which we refer to as optimism or pessimism will have its bearing on investment decisions.

The Investment Demand Schedule

At any moment of time, and assuming given expectations concerning the future value of yields to be derived from new investments, there exists what we can call an investment demand schedule which shows the amounts which people desire to spend on investments at different interest rates. In this functional relation between investment demand and interest we consider the rate of interest as the independent variable and the investment demand for loanable funds as the dependent variable. Since the marginal efficiency of capital falls as more capital goods are produced, we can assume that the amount of loanable funds borrowed for investment purposes increases with a fall in the rate of interest.

It is often said that changes in rates of interest will not influence investment decisions very much because changing rates of interest influence the cost of production only to a moderate degree. Suppose the sum of $1 million has been borrowed for the construction of the apartment house, that the construction period lasts 6 months, and that the house is sold after its completion. If the short-term rate of interest is 4 per cent per annum, the cost of financing the construction process is only $20,000 (namely, ½ of 4 per cent for $1 million). Even a substantial change of the rate of interest, say from 4 to 6 per cent, will increase the construction cost by only $10,000, or by 1 per cent of the total cost. Nevertheless, it would be premature if we concluded that the influence of a changing rate of interest on investment decisions is negligible.

We saw already that a change of the prevailing rate of interest from 4 to 6 per cent would cause the capital value of the apartment house to drop from about $1,250,000 to about $833,333. In this case we have used the rate of interest to capitalize the prospective yield. Thus, while the short-term rate of interest may be an unimportant factor in determining construction costs, the long-term rate as a capitalization factor of a series of prospective yields may become decisive when we compare actual production costs with the prospective market value of the capital good.[1]

[1] See Fritz Machlup, "The Rate of Interest as Cost and as Capitalization Factor," *American Economic Review*, Vol. XXV (1935), pp. 459 ff.

If we change our assumptions concerning the marginal efficiency of capital, for example, if we assume that technological development or increase in income and consumption have led to an optimistic revision of our expectations, the whole investment demand schedule will move to the right of its previous position, that is, at all possible rates of interest will there be a tendency to borrow more funds than before for investment purposes. But the new schedule, too, will slope from the upper left to the lower right, indicating that under the new set of assumptions there will exist the same tendency as before to borrow larger amounts at lower rates.

Investment goods are produced to help produce consumers' goods or, as in the case of the apartment house, to render services to consumers. Changes in consumption, therefore, must affect the investment demand for loanable funds. As the disposable income of consumers increases there will be a greater "derived" demand for the services of capital goods or durable consumers' goods. As a matter of fact, it may easily be that the increased demand for consumers' goods will lead to a "magnified" or "accelerated" demand for investment goods. Suppose consumers' disposable incomes have increased and consumers feel they can now afford increased rents for more modern apartments. The increase in consumers' spending during a month or a year may be modest but it will lead to the construction of an apartment house whose cost of production may easily be twenty times that of the yearly net rent. Thus a relatively small increase in yearly consumption expenditure may give rise to a magnified and accelerated investment demand for loanable funds. Some important implications of this principle of acceleration of derived demand will be discussed in Chapter 24.

Considering the many factors which influence the marginal efficiency of capital, the uncertainty of these influences, the strong reaction of capital values to changes in interest rates, and the acceleration of derived demand, we must conclude that the investment demand schedule for loanable funds can be subject to strong fluctuations and to serious errors of optimism and pessimism.

When discussing the investment demand schedule for loanable funds, we must also consider government investment, that is, purchases of goods and services by government agencies. This investment demand by government units is quantitatively very important. We shall see furthermore that government expenditures may become an important instrument of fiscal policy. When private spending is insufficient and cannot be made sufficient by monetary policy alone, it may become necessary to inject money into the economy via public investment. In terms of an investment demand schedule, however, not much can be said about government investment. Government agencies do not invest because investment is profitable. It is, therefore, as a rule, not possible to speak of a marginal efficiency of capital in connection with government expenditures and to compare marginal returns with interest rates.

Consumers' Demand for Loanable Funds

To the investment demand for loanable funds we have to add the demand for credit by consumers who want to increase their consumption beyond the limits set by their disposable income. The durable character of many expensive consumers' goods such as refrigerators, cars, or houses makes these commodities in some respects very similar to capital goods. The apartment house example can easily be changed so as to cover the case of a consumer credit. A mortgage loan may enable the consumer-owner to purchase a home if his monthly income permits him to pay the monthly interest, amortization, and tax charges, just as purchase on the installment plan permits a purchase many times larger than the amount of the monthly installment.

Consumer credits may be expected to react to changes in interest rates in approximately the same manner as investment demand, even though we cannot here use a marginal efficiency schedule. But much more important than changes in rates of interest will be changes in income. As a person's income increases the availability of credit enables him to borrow funds to purchase a durable consumption good which will render its services over a period of time. Consumer credit, therefore, often finances the "acceleration of derived demand" which was mentioned above.

If we are mainly interested in the investment demand for loanable funds and if we interpret saving as the voluntary reduction in consumption which enables us to produce capital goods, we can treat consumer credit as a reduction of saving or as a kind of dissaving. Consumer credits raise the level of the borrowers' consumption above the amount permitted by their disposable income and can, therefore, be considered as a corresponding reduction of the supply of investible funds.

The Demand for Liquid Balances

In Chapter 9 we discussed a number of reasons which induce individuals and business firms to hold money reserves. Income earned is either spent on consumption or it is saved; the saved amount is either used to purchase interest-bearing securities or held in the form of money. If we decide to hold money, we forego a return in order to enjoy the advantage of that perfect liquidity which only money can secure. It is, therefore, correct to call the rate of interest a price for parting with liquidity or to call the interest which has not been earned the opportunity cost of liquid balances. If the interest rate is low people will be less interested in minimizing their cash balances, whereas a high interest rate may induce them to economize their cash balances to the utmost in order to be able to supply more funds to the credit market.

The decision to hold larger or smaller money reserves influences the supply of and demand for loanable funds. For the theoretical discussion of these influences it makes little difference whether we assume that the tendency to hold liquid balances reduces the supply of loanable funds by those who want to retain a part of their resources in this form or whether it leads to borrowing by others who want to increase their liquidity. A lower rate of interest will either increase the amount which will be borrowed for liquidity purposes or increase the amount which, for the same reason, is withheld from the credit market. These reactions of demand and supply are very important.

The demand for money balances which arises from the transaction motive for liquidity can be assumed to be rather "interest-inelastic" because a certain minimum reserve of money is needed under given conditions, while larger balances would be of little advantage. In case of increasing transactions the demand curve would shift to the right without becoming more elastic.

The influence of the precautionary motive will depend on the prevailing degree of optimism or pessimism concerning not only the future need for money reserves but also the ability to liquidate assets on short notice and without substantial loss. The greater the pessimism and uncertainty in both respects, the greater the demand for cash balances at all rates of interest. Since very low rates of interest make a fall in security prices probable, they will presumably be accompanied by a tendency to hold such precautionary balances. Since the precautionary motive rests in part on our uncertainty concerning the future cash equivalent of assets which may have to be liquidated (for example, to secure otherwise unavailable working capital), it shades into the speculative motive which concerns itself exclusively with the development of security prices.

The holders of speculative balances forego current income from interest in order to wait for a fall of security prices. The gain from a subsequent purchase at lower prices will exceed the temporary sacrifice of earnings. When security prices are not expected to rise any further and when, therefore, the rate of interest is believed to have reached its lowest level, the public will want to hold cash balances and will refuse to bid up security prices still further. That is, at very low rates of interest the demand for money balances becomes highly elastic. On the other hand, when security prices are low and yields are high, the return from investment will tend to compensate the owner for a fall in security prices.

Combining demand attitudes as they are conditioned by the different motives for liquidity, we arrive at a demand schedule for money reserves which indicates that the demand for cash balances is relatively "interest-inelastic" at high rates of interest but tends to become nearly perfectly elastic at very low rates, such as 2 per cent.

The high interest elasticity of the demand for money at low rates of interest is very important from the standpoint of monetary policy. When the monetary authority increases the money supply, the effect will depend to a large extent on the interest elasticity of the demand for money:

1. If the demand for money balances is nearly perfectly elastic at low interest rates, the newly created money will be absorbed without being able to lower interest rates still further and without increasing expenditures.

2. If the demand for money balances is relatively inelastic, the additional money will be spent on the purchase of securities and consumers' goods. Increased security purchases will raise security prices, lower interest rates, and lead to larger investment expenditures. Increased economic activity, in turn, will lead to increased transactions, and the demand for transactions balances will shift to the right. The desire to hold larger transaction balances will finally absorb part of the additional balances, while the rest will go into speculative balances as increased speculative holdings result from rising security prices (lower interest rates).

The desire to hold money balances reduces the supply of loanable funds. Increased willingness on the part of the public to release money with every increase in interest rates increases the supply of loanable funds through dishoarding. It can also be interpreted as an increased velocity of circulation of money.

In this connection it is advisable to distinguish between active and inactive money balances. Balances held to satisfy the transaction motive for liquidity are active balances, while precautionary and speculative balances are inactive. We saw that the first are probably interest inelastic, while the latter are highly interest elastic at low rates. An increase in interest rates will cause a transfer of money from inactive to active balances. As national income and transactions grow the demand for money will rise and, unless satisfied by the creation of additional money, will raise the rate of interest and tend to release inactive balances, thus increasing the velocity of circulation of money. At high rates even money used for transaction purposes may circulate faster, since there is now a high premium on economy in money reserves.

If these arguments are correct, it is possible that total expenditure, income, and employment may increase even if the supply of money does not change.

Interest Rates and the Supply of Money

If we include the demand for money reserves in the demand for loanable funds, we must also include the supply of money in the supply of loanable funds. However, the special position of the monetary authority as regulator of the supply of money makes it impossible to draw a supply schedule of money in which the supply of money is the dependent variable, as in the case of the investment demand and liquidity schedules. The monetary authority cannot be assumed to react to changes in interest rates since it is supposed to influence or even determine these rates. It can try to do this by regulating the reserves of the commercial banks; and the commercial banks, in turn, are supposed to react by expanding credit on the basis of larger reserves or by contracting credit as their reserve position is made less favorable and their indebtedness to the Federal Reserve banks increases.

Our survey of the history of the Federal Reserve System has shown that the monetary authority is not always able to control the supply of money. This may be because its hands are tied, as in the case where it is forced, against its better judgment, to monetize gold or government securities, or where member bank reserves are excessively large. These technical difficulties could be removed by appropriate statutory changes. A more basic weakness of the system is the uncertainty of the responses to measures adopted by the monetary authority. The monetary authority can change the price of government securities and can lower interest rates to some extent, but it cannot make private firms borrow, cannot force the banks to expand credit, and cannot prevent the absorption of additional money by inactive balances. It may be able to control the total supply of money, but it cannot be certain that it will be able to control the supply of money in active circulation.

These statements are not meant to belittle the importance of monetary policy. They merely serve as a reminder that total expenditure cannot always be increased by monetary measures alone, even if we should succeed in perfecting our monetary instruments.

The Supply Schedule of Savings

Last but not least we must now consider the noninflationary source of loanable funds in its relation to changes in rates of interest. The relationship of saving to interest rates is uncertain. Lowering interest rates may either decrease or increase the amount of savings forthcoming. Gustav Cassel[2] observes that

> the ordinary person who saves, with a moderate income, and who tries to accumulate sufficient capital in order to live on the income from it, must, if there is a lower rate of interest, save a larger amount in order to be sure of a certain annual return. So a fall in the rate of interest may stimulate him to greater efforts, and cause him to accumulate more capital.

A second possibility would be that our "ordinary person," instead of deciding to live on his income from capital, may resolve instead to live on his capital through the purchase of an annuity. In this case lowering the rate of interest may lead to a rapid decline of the total supply of savings. Cassel has pointed out that the relative increase in income to be obtained by living on one's capital varies with the rate of interest as well as with the length of the period for which the capital must last. He illustrates this point by a simple example. A person possesses $100,000 and receives, at 4 per cent, $4,000 per annum. If the rate drops to 3½ or 3 per cent, he may be willing to reduce his expenditure and live on $3,500 or $3,000. A rate of ½ of 1 per cent, however, would make it impossible for him to live on his income from capital, which is now only $500. Expecting to live another 25 years, he can still maintain his former standard of $4,000 per year through gradual consumption of his capital. We see that his life expectancy plays an important part in his calculations. As the expected life span increases the purchased annuity will become smaller. The lower the rate of interest and the shorter life expectancy the more attractive it becomes to consume one's savings. Thus it is likely, according to

[2] Gustav Cassel, *The Theory of Social Economy* (New York: Harcourt, Brace & Co., Inc., 1932), p. 239.

Cassel, that if the rate of interest falls much below 3 per cent persons will decide to consume their savings. It is also probable, however, that an increasing average life span will permit the rate of interest to fall to somewhat lower levels before such a decision is made.

In connection with these considerations it must be emphasized that in the long run only the real rate of interest counts. A given market rate means a lower real rate if the price level rises. If prices rise 5 per cent per annum, a market rate of less than 5 per cent becomes in effect a negative rate, and a market rate of 7 per cent becomes a 2 per cent rate. While the public might not immediately react to these subversive changes, price inflation will in the long run have its effect on saving, and this effect will be similar to that which Cassel suggested: a slight rise in prices may induce the public to save more, while a major price inflation will have disastrous effects on saving.

Later we shall see that a far more potent influence on saving is exerted by the size of the national income. While the interest elasticity of saving is probably small owing to the above-mentioned factors, it must be assumed that the income elasticity of saving is generally greater than one because "men are disposed as a rule and on the average, to increase their consumption as their income increases, but not by as much as their income increases."[3] However, we cannot predict what an income receiver will do with an increment of his income and we do not know in advance the marginal propensity to save for all income receivers together. Changes of security prices and security yields, age structure of the population, income distribution, inflationary and deflationary price movements, time-lags in the reaction of spending habits to changes in income—all these factors will influence the propensity to save.

We see that at any given moment of time the rate of interest is only one of several factors which determine saving, and what the response to interest changes will be is impossible to predict. However, since it is indispensable for our purposes that a supply schedule of savings be added to the schedules which were already discussed, we shall assume that the schedule of savings is relatively inelastic at higher rates but relatively elastic at low rates.

The Loanable-Funds Theory of Interest

Figure 20–1 pictures the forces which determine the rate of interest according to the so-called loanable-funds theory. On the vertical

[3] J. M. Keynes, *The General Theory of Employment, Interest and Money* (London: Macmillan & Co., Ltd., 1936), p. 96.

axis *OY* we measure interest rates, and on the horizontal axis *OX*, loanable funds in dollars. The curves show the amounts of loanable funds which would be supplied and demanded at various rates of interest. This picture is abstract and does not pretend to illustrate statistically known quantities. We cannot predict with certainty what would happen at different levels of interest. Historical data would not help very much in drawing our curves, because the situation represented in Figure 20–1 applies only to very short periods and is strictly based on the *ceteris paribus* clause, though in the long run other things

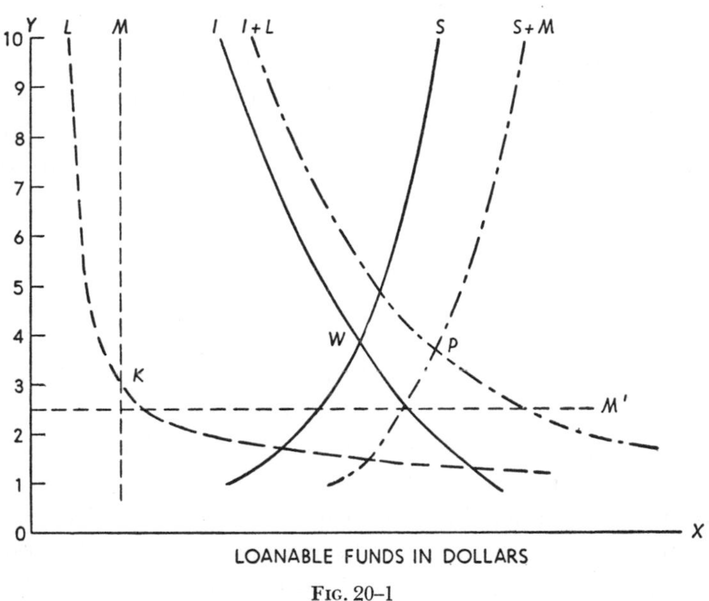

FIG. 20–1

would certainly not remain equal. All our curves would be affected by influences which do not depend at all or do not depend exclusively on interest rates. This is particularly true of changes in the national income, which may prove to be more important in determining saving, money supply, liquidity preference and investment than will changing interest rates.

If we wanted to show the effects of changes in national income on our graph, we should have to use three-dimensional demand and supply curves. The third axis would show different levels of national income. Limiting ourselves in Figure 20–1 to a two-dimensional picture, we must remain conscious of the fact that our curves apply only to very short periods and, therefore, to a given income level. In the longer run they will shift to the right or left, an increase in national income tending to push them to the right. This means that at all rates of interest more savings are supplied and more loanable funds are demanded for investment and transaction purposes. These changes may cancel out in their effects on the rate of interest, though this is by no means certain, because demand and supply curves may move disproportionately and the shapes and slopes of the curves are likely to change in the process.

S in Figure 20–1 represents the supply of loanable funds out of "planned" or "intended" savings. Opposite each rate of interest we mark the point which indicates the amount of savings forthcoming at this level. The *S* curve connects these points. From what we have learned about possible reactions of personal savings to changes in interest rates, we know that we cannot be certain about the shape of this curve. We draw the *S* curve as relatively inelastic at high rates; but below, say, 3 per cent we assume that the supply of loanable funds from savings tends to become relatively elastic owing to a strong tendency to dissave at very low rates.

Figure 20–1 makes no explicit provision for the demand for consumer credit or for dissaving. We must therefore assume either that *S* stands for net savings, that is, savings minus dissavings and minus consumer credits, or that the demand for consumer credit is included in the investment demand for loanable funds, that is, the *I* curve. *S* includes private as well as corporate savings. If current additions to depreciation reserves (replacement funds or amortization quotas) are assumed to be included in *S*, the replacement demand for loanable funds will have to be included in the investment demand *I*. The same holds for the temporary supply of liquidated working capital and the demand for working capital.

M is the supply of loanable funds through money creation. If we assume that the monetary authority is in full control of the supply of money, we can draw the *M* curve as a straight vertical line, signifying that the actions of the monetary authority are not a dependent variable which responds to interest rate changes; on the contrary, the actions of the monetary authority are designed to change the rate of interest. Should the monetary authority be forced to maintain a given rate of interest through a perfectly elastic supply of money at this rate, the supply curve of loanable funds would become perfectly elastic and the rate of interest could not rise above the level indicated by a line parallel to the *OX* axis at the pegged rate (the *M′* line in Figure 20–1).

When the commercial banks possess excess reserves which the monetary authority cannot control, the supply of loanable funds from credit creation may become very elastic though an increase in interest rates may be necessary to overcome the liquidity preference of the commercial banks. In Figure 20–1 we assume that the Federal Reserve is in complete control of the money supply and influences the rate of interest through changes in the money supply. The *M* curve, there fore, is assumed to be perfectly inelastic and to shift to the right or left with every change in money supply.

We included dishoarding in the inflationary supply of loanable funds. This supply could be added to (or in the case of hoarding, subtracted from) the *M* curve. However, it is preferable to indicate the influence of a decreasing or increasing liquidity preference by the shape of the *L* curve, which represents the demand for money balances (liquidity). The *L* curve refers to changes in money reserves which are induced by changes in interest rates. It would not be advisable to measure on the *OX* axis the total of all money balances, for not all money balances are available as loanable funds. It is only *changes* in the demand for and supply of money which are decisive for the determination of the rate of interest.

The *L* curve is not drawn as a straight line for reasons given earlier. While in its upper parts the curve is relatively inelastic, it becomes very elastic at low rates of interest, owing to the combined influence of the speculative and precautionary motives. With a change in the liquidity preference of the population, the whole curve will shift. When under otherwise unchanged conditions the *L* curve moves to the right the rate of interest will rise and inactive precautionary and speculative balances will be released to serve as active transaction balances.

The *I* curve is based on the marginal efficiency of private investment and relates the rate of interest to the amount of loanable funds borrowed for private investment purposes. Whether or not the *I* curve includes the replacement demand or the demand for revolving working capital depends on our interpretation of the *S* curve. Public investment is not considered. It can perhaps be assumed that in normal times public investment demand will react approximately like private investment demand and that interest rates would be watched as a cost item. But it must be remembered that it is impossible in cases of public investment to compare rates of return with interest rates. In emergency periods the government may either neglect the cost of borrowing or, unwilling to permit its continued borrowing to raise interest rates, order the monetary authority to maintain the perfectly elastic supply of *M′*.

Now we can get the total supply of loanable funds, $S + M$, by adding the S and M curves together; and, the total demand for loanable funds, $I + L$, in the same manner. $S + M$ and $I + L$ intersect at point P, which indicates the market rate of interest and marks an equilibrium position until we shift the curves. At low rates the great elasticity of the L and $I + L$ curves will prevent the rate of interest from falling much further even if the M and $S + M$ curves should shift far to the right. Similarly, the perfectly elastic M' curve will prevent a rise in interest rates in spite of a shift to the right of the $I + L$ curve.

The loanable-funds theory of interest assumes that the market rate of interest is determined by the combined effects of all the decisions which are influenced by, and in turn react upon, the rate of interest. It combines suggestions made by less inclusive theories which, accordingly, it criticizes as incomplete rather than wrong. We can use Figure 20–1 for a discussion of these alternative theories. The Wicksell point W at the intersection of the S and I curves marks the rate of interest which Wicksell considered as the natural rate; and the Keynes point K at the intersection of the M and L curves corresponds to the rate of interest according to Keynes' liquidity-preference theory. In calling K the Keynes point we must admit, however, that according to Keynes the rate of interest is determined by the demand for money to hold and the supply of money. The L and M curves depicting Keynes' theory, therefore, should include the total demand for money to hold (not only changes in this demand) and the total supply of money (not only money creation or contraction).

We shall now discuss the theories of Wicksell and Keynes because both are of special interest from the monetary point of view.

Wicksell and the Natural Rate of Interest

Knut Wicksell distinguishes a loan or market rate of interest (P in Figure 20–1) and a real or natural rate (W in Figure 20–1). The loan or market rate is the average of rates actually paid on the credit market. The real or natural rate he defines alternatively as the rate:

> (1) at which the demand for loan capital and the supply of savings exactly agree; (2) which more or less corresponds to the expected yield of the newly created capital; (3) at which the general level of commodity prices has no tendency to move upward or downward; (4) which would be established if one would not make use of monetary transactions but real capital would be loaned *in natura*.[4]

[4] See Knut Wicksell, *Interest and Prices* (London: Macmillan & Co., Ltd., 1936); and *Lectures on Political Economy*, Vol. II, *Money* (New York: Macmillan Co., 1935).

The fourth definition is not very useful, because it is impossible to conceive of a uniform rate of interest in a barter economy. Nevertheless, we shall here use Wicksell's term "natural rate" rather than the term "real rate," because the latter term has been widely accepted to designate the market rate plus or minus changes in the general price level.

It is Wicksell's main contention that any deviation of the market rate from the natural rate causes a cumulative process of expansion or contraction. As long as the market rate is lower than the natural rate, prices must rise for a number of reasons. First of all, saving is discouraged and consumption tends to increase, while businessmen anticipate higher profit opportunities in investment. The producers' increased demand for the factors of production, financed with newly created credit, raises the income of wage earners and others. This in turn leads to a further increase in the demand for consumers' goods at a time when consumers' goods production decreases because of the competitive demand for the factors of production for investment purposes. All these tendencies have the effect of increasing prices, and this process will continue as long as the market rate of interest is kept below the natural rate, which would equate the demand for loanable funds and the supply of savings. At the lowered rate the supply of savings has to be supplemented by a supply of loanable funds out of inflationary sources. The general level of commodity prices will therefore continue to rise. A similar cumulative process of contraction, with price deflation, will result from a market rate which is artificially kept above the natural rate. If the market rate is normal, that is, if it is equal to the natural rate, the ecnonmy will be in equilibrium, loanable funds will be supplied out of savings only, and the rate of interest will be exactly equal to the marginal yield of capital, while the price level will remain stable.

Obviously, Wicksell bases his argument on the assumption of full employment.[5] If, instead, we assume that unused labor and unused resources are available in great variety and in large amounts, consumers' goods production does not have to be contracted and may even expand while investment increases. Under these conditions it is quite possible that a tendency towards increasing prices can be checked, for some time at least, by a corresponding increase in the volume of trade. This means, however, that there would be two dif-

[5] He admits, however, that "if previously there had been unemployment it is, of course, not impossible for the rise in prices to be counteracted to a certain extent by an increase in production." Knut Wicksell, *Lectures on Political Economy*, Vol. II, *Money* (New York: Macmillan Co., 1935), p. 195.

ferent rates of interest which might be called normal, namely, one which keeps the average price level stable and another which equalizes the supply of and the demand for savings. This divergence can be attributed to the fact that the volume of goods offered for sale increases sufficiently to compensate for the artificial increase in the supply of loanable funds out of inflationary sources; or it can be considered as a situation in which the supply of savings falls short of the available investment potential (the supply of savings being abnormally low because the national income is low).

This terminological impasse points to a very real problem: which of the two "normal" rates should guide monetary policy, the one which keeps prices stable or the one which equalizes the demand for and supply of savings? This problem has already been dealt with in the discussion of neutral money in Chapters 3 and 10.

It has been argued that an artificially lowered market rate can become the natural rate and thus establish a new equilibrium once the marginal efficiency of capital, moving along the *I* curve, comes down to the market rate. This argument seems to be implied in Wicksell's second definition, according to which the natural rate is "the rate which more or less corresponds to the expected yield of newly created capital." It is true that at this point no further expansion of investment will take place, but we cannot conclude that the cumulative process of inflation would stop. This would be the case only if at the artificially lowered rate the conditions of Wicksell's first definition were fulfilled, that is, if "the demand for loans and the supply of savings exactly agree." However, it is very unlikely that savings would have increased sufficiently to satisfy the total demand for loanable funds which would prevail at the lowered market rate. As Keynes has pointed out "there is, indeed, a general presumption that the effect on saving, if any, will be opposite in direction to the effect on investment, the easier terms to borrowers meaning less satisfactory terms to lenders, so that what stimulates the one retards the other."[6] The natural rate of interest which is equal to the yield of newly produced capital goods, therefore, cannot be expected to be identical with the natural rate which equilibrates the supply of savings and the demand for loanable funds; and if the two natural rates are different, we have to conclude that the cumulative process of expansion will continue. The demand for loanable funds will be greater than the supply of savings, and the supply of loanable funds will have to be supplemented by credit crea-

[6] J. M. Keynes, *A Treatise on Money* (New York: Harcourt, Brace & Co., Inc., 1930), Vol. I, p. 264.

tion. Thus, once full employment is approached, prices will rise. It has to be remembered, furthermore, that the increase of the general price level continuously lowers the real rate of interest, since credits are paid back in money of decreasing purchasing power. This makes it even less likely that the decreasing yield from investment will arrest the demand for loanable funds in time to stop the cumulative process.

Pre-Wicksellian writers used to limit the theory of interest to nonmonetary factors. Wicksell's great accomplishment at the turn of the century was that he tried to integrate the theories of money and capital, though he was wrong when he diagnosed as pathological all situations in which the market rate differed from the natural rate. By contrast Lord Keynes and his followers took the position that interest rates are determined predominantly by monetary factors.

Keynes' Liquidity-Preference Theory of Interest

Keynes criticized the loanable-funds theory on the ground that it was circular reasoning to argue that the national income is influenced by investment, investment by the rate of interest, the rate of interest by the supply of loanable funds, the supply of loanable funds by saving, and saving, in turn, by the national income. If this is circular reasoning almost all statements concerning demand, supply, and price are circular since in our price system everything does depend on everything else. In Keynes' own theory the rate of interest depends on liquidity preference, that is, on the level of income, which determines the amount of money reserves needed to satisfy the transaction demand for money. "Thus, if the supply curve of saving is on the wobble when the demand curve shifts, so is the 'liquidity preference' curve."[7]

Keynes' critical attitude towards the loanable-funds theory needs a more convincing explanation. Perhaps this explanation can be found in Keynes' rejection of a conclusion which was often drawn from the loanable-funds theory, namely, that downward adjustments of the rate of interest could be trusted to equate investment and savings. It was a characteristic assumption of classical economics that since lower rates call forth enough additional investment when savings increase, a full-employment income level tends to sustain itself. Keynes wanted to explain fluctuations in income and employment. It is possible, therefore, that he was at first under the impression that nothing less than the scrapping of the loanable-funds theory would suffice to make room for

[7] D. H. Robertson, "Some Notes on Mr. Keynes' General Theory of Employment," *Quarterly Journal of Economics*, Vol. LI (1937), p. 186.

a more realistic theory of employment. The loanable-funds theory had, in this case, to be replaced by his liquidity-preference theory according to which

> the rate of interest is not the 'price' which brings into equilibrium the demand for resources to invest with the readiness to abstain from present consumption. It is the 'price' which equilibrates the desire to hold wealth in the form of cash with the available quantity of cash. . . . The rate of interest is the reward for parting with liquidity.[8]

Keynes' liquidity-preference theory can be illustrated by the *L* and *M* curves of Figure 20–1. The Keynesian rate of interest would be *K*, the point where the two curves intersect. This theory is wrong when it claims to be a full discussion of all the forces which determine rates of interest. As a more thorough analysis of the *L* curve, however, it contributes to a more realistic description of these forces, provided we do not banish the factors which were the core of the older theory: the demand for investment credit and the supply of savings. Keynes did not have to discard the loanable-funds theory, he only needed to show that the rate of interest cannot always be counted upon to fall far enough to call forth a sufficient amount of investment. Keynes' analysis of the speculative motive for holding money permitted him to show that there exists, at very low rates, a "liquidity trap," which prevents rates from falling further. This analysis is entirely compatible with the loanable-funds theory, though not with some conclusions which were previously drawn from that theory. Keynes could, therefore, have accepted the loanable-funds theory and avoided many inconsistencies into which he was forced by the one-sidedness of his approach. Only a few of the awkward consequences of Keynes' liquidity-preference theory will be mentioned.

If interest is really the price paid for parting with liquidity, we cannot include anything but cash balances (money) in the supply that satisfies the desire for liquidity. Keynes, however, permits us to draw the line between "money" and "debts" at whichever point is most convenient. We are allowed to include any command over general purchasing power which the owner has not parted with for a period in excess of 3 months.[9] Thus we are permitted to count a substantial part

[8] J. M. Keynes, *The General Theory of Employment, Interest and Money* (London: Macmillan & Co., Ltd., 1936), p. 167. See also J. M. Keynes, "Alternative Theories of the Rate of Interest," *Economic Journal*, Vol. XLVII (1937), p. 250: "The theory of interest might be expressed by saying that the rate of interest serves to equate the demand and supply of hoards—that is, it must be sufficiently high to *offset* an increased propensity to hoard relatively to the supply of idle balances."

[9] J. M. Keynes, *The General Theory of Employment, Interest and Money* (London: Macmillan & Co., Ltd., 1936), p. 195.

of all short-term credits as liquid, and since the rates of interest paid for such credits often exceed the long-term rates (see Chart 21–1, p. 288), we are forced to conclude that those who do *not* part with liquidity are often highly rewarded for their liquidity preference![10] Now it is perfectly true that short-term investments may be preferred to long-term investments for reasons of liquidity. But since in this case liquidity preference becomes a choice between many types of assets, it is obvious "that the demand and supply of every type of asset has just as much right to be considered as the demand and supply of money."[11]

The perfect interchangeability of all units of money makes it impossible for the liquidity-preference theory to account for the phenomenon of diverse rates on various parts of the credit market. Assuming a willingness on the part of the monetary authority to always accommodate an increased desire for liquidity, we could not explain even the existence of a rate of interest. It is true that Keynes did show that the shape of the liquidity demand curve at low rates prevents further lowering of interest rates even if the monetary authority should be willing to create large amounts of additional money. But this liquidity trap depends on the choice between holding money *and other assets.*

Here, as in so many other Keynesian arguments, it becomes clear that the forces which determine interest rates are working *outside* the area of perfect liquidity, a fact already suggested by Keynes' own phrase that interest is the price for *parting* with liquidity. True, the supply of and demand for money do influence interest rates, and the demand for money balances may be a more powerful factor than pre-Keynesian theory assumed. But, as D. H. Robertson has pointed out, "the fact that the rate of interest measures the marginal convenience of holding idle balances need not prevent it from measuring *also* the marginal inconvenience of abstaining from consumption."[12]

Once Keynes noticed that the liquidity trap of the very elastic *L* curve sufficed to explain why rates of interest could not always be expected to call forth sufficient investment and why the monetary au-

10 That Keynes did not clearly distinguish between liquid reserves and working capital is shown when he discusses the "business motive for liquidity" which is defined as the holding of cash "to bridge the interval between the time of incurring business costs and that of the receipt of the sale proceeds." (*Ibid.*, p. 195). How can this be interpreted in terms of the liquidity-preference theory? The funds have been spent and are not held. Did Keynes want to say that *additional* funds would have to be kept liquid? If so he did not explain the reasons and the whole passage remains incongruous.

11 Joan Robinson, *The Rate of Interest and Other Essays* (London: Macmillan & Co., Ltd., 1952), p. 5.

12 D. H. Robertson, "Alternative Theories of the Rate of Interest," *Economic Journal*, Vol. XLVII (1937), p. 431.

thority could not remedy the situation, his attitude towards the loanable-funds theory became more tolerant.

SUGGESTIONS FOR FURTHER READING

CASSEL, GUSTAV. *The Theory of Social Economy,* chap. 6, par. 24. New York: Harcourt, Brace & Co., 1952.

DILLARD, DUDLEY. *The Economics of John Maynard Keynes,* chaps. 7–8. New York: Prentice-Hall, Inc., 1948.

HABERLER, GOTTFRIED. *Prosperity and Depression,* chap. 8. 3d ed. New York: United Nations, 1952.

HAWTREY, R. G. *A Century of Bank Rate,* pp. 189–95, 240–42, 249–50, 277–79. London: Longmans, Green & Co., 1938. Reprinted in Lawrence S. Ritter's *Money and Economic Activity* (Boston: Houghton Mifflin Co., 1952), pp. 166–70.

HAYEK, FRIEDRICH A. *Prices and Production,* Lecture I. London: George Routledge & Sons, Ltd., 1931.

KEYNES, J. M. *The General Theory of Employment, Interest and Money,* chaps. 11–14. London: Macmillan & Co., Ltd., 1936.

KEYNES, J. M. "Alternative Theories of the Rate of Interest," *Economic Journal,* Vol. 47, 1937.

LERNER, ABBA P. "Alternative Formulations of the Theory of Interest," *The New Economics,* Seymour E. Harris (ed.), chap. 45. New York: Alfred A. Knopf, 1948.

LINDAHL, ERIK. *Studies in the Theory of Money and Capital,* part ii. New York: Rinehart & Co., Inc., 1939.

LUTZ, FRIEDRICH. "The Interest Rate and Investment in a Dynamic Economy," *American Economic Review,* Vol. XXXV (December, 1945). Reprinted in Lawrence S. Ritter's *Money and Economic Activity* (Boston: Houghton Mifflin Co., 1952), pp. 171–82.

MACHLUP, FRITZ. "The Rate of Interest as Cost Factor and as Capitalization Factor," *American Economic Review,* Vol. XXV (September, 1935).

OHLIN, BERTIL. "Some Notes on the Stockholm Theory of Saving and Investment," *Economic Journal,* Vol. 47, 1937. Reprinted in *Readings in Business Cycle Theory* (Homewood, Ill.: Richard D. Irwin, Inc., 1944), chap. 5.

ROBINSON, JOAN. *Introduction to the Theory of Employment,* chap. 4. London: Macmillan & Co., Ltd., 1938.

WICKSELL, KNUT. *Lectures on Political Economy,* Vol. 2: *Money,* part iv, chap. 9. New York: Macmillan Co., 1935.

WICKSELL, KNUT. *Interest and Prices,* chaps. 7–8. London: Macmillan & Co., 1936.

QUESTIONS AND PROBLEMS

1. How are private investment decisions made?
2. Discuss the rate of interest as both a cost and a capitalization factor.
3. Is it true to say that the demand for money reserves is relatively interest-inelastic at high rates of interest but tends to become nearly perfectly elastic at very low rates?
4. Explain the concept "liquidity trap."
5. "Lowering interest rates may either decrease or increase the amount of savings forthcoming." Discuss.
6. Draw a diagram illustrating the loanable funds theory of interest.
7. Knut Wisksell's theory has been criticized on the grounds that the rate of interest which keeps the average price level stable is not necessarily also the rate which equalizes the supply of savings and the demand for loans. Begin your discussion of this criticism with a definition of Wicksell's "real" or "natural" rate of interest.
8. Why was J. M. Keynes unwilling to accept the loanable funds theory of interest?
9. What was Keynes' contribution to the theory of interest? Do you find yourself in full agreement with Keynes' attitude?

Chapter 21 CREDIT INSTRUMENTS AND CREDIT MARKET

The Importance of Credit

John Stuart Mill explained the importance of credit as follows:

> . . . though credit is but a transfer of capital from hand to hand, it is generally, and naturally, a transfer to hands more competent to employ the capital more efficiently in production. If there were no such thing as credit, or if, from general insecurity or want of confidence, it were scantily practised, many persons who possess more or less capital, but who from their occupations, or for want of the necessary skill and knowledge, cannot personally superintend its employment, would derive no benefit from it: their funds would either be idle, or would be, perhaps, wasted and annihilated in unskillful attempts to make them yield a profit. All this capital is now lent at interest, and made available for production. Capital thus circumstanced forms a large portion of the productive resources of any commercial country; and is naturally attracted to those producers or traders who, being in the greatest business, have the means of employing it to most advantage; because such are both the most desirous to obtain it, and able to give the best security. Although, therefore, the productive funds of the country are not increased by credit, they are called into a more complete state of productive activity. As the confidence on which credit is grounded extends itself, means are developed by which even the smallest portions of capital, the sums which each person keeps by him to meet contingencies, are made available for productive uses.[1]

J. S. Mill draws our attention to the essential facts that saving and investment are done by different groups of people, that purchasing power must be transferred from the first group to the second, that credit induces people to make funds available which otherwise would run to waste, that even smallest particles of savings can thus be put to use, and that credit allocates the available funds to those able to use them most productively.

[1] J. S. Mill, *Principles of Political Economy* (London: Longmans, Green & Co., 1936), Book III, chap. xi.

Credit is the temporary transfer of purchasing power against a promise of repayment plus interest. Credit could be a barter exchange of present against future goods, but in the overwhelming number of cases it takes place in monetary form. Credit contracts need not be documented by credit instruments, though in most credit transactions we use instruments such as promissory notes or bonds. This representation of credit contracts by transferable credit instruments is of great importance for the following reasons.

Modern production processes use capital equipment of great durability, and this makes it necessary that credit be extended to business firms either without limit of time or for long periods, since repayments have to be geared to the gradual amortization of fixed capital. If creditors should have to wait for repayment until durable capital goods could be written off, many would be deterred from lending, since they cannot afford to part with their funds for long periods. We must have credit instruments which permit lenders to retain some measure of individual liquidity. The sale of a transferable credit certificate permits the individual creditor to disengage himself, for the buyer of the certificate takes his place and the debtor is not inconvenienced by this substitution of one creditor for another. Credit instruments, furthermore, permit reduction of a lender's risk because the creditor can diversify his financial investments by buying claims on a variety of debtors. The borrower, on the other hand, can sell his IOU's to thousands of potential creditors and thus collect the often enormous sums needed for the purchase of modern mass-production equipment.

The principal advantages of the use of transferable credit certificates, therefore, can be listed as follows:

1. Borrowers can obtain the long-term credits necessitated by the durable character of the capital goods needed in modern production.

2. Nevertheless, the individual creditor is under no obligation to continue his connection with any given debtor for any definite period. He can sell the credit instrument and regain his liquidity.

3. The marketability of credit instruments permits, in addition to potential liquidity, a diversification of risk. Individual creditors may hold an infinite variety of combinations of credit instruments.

4. Potential liquidity and diversification of risk induce many persons to supply loanable funds for long-term purposes when liquidity preference, insecurity, or lack of financial investment opportunities would otherwise restrict the supply of loanable funds or limit it to the short-term market.

5. Since the borrower contacts, either directly or indirectly, a very large number of would-be creditors, he can aggregate the enormous amounts needed in modern mass production.

6. The system of using transferable claims is also useful in the case of short-term credit because it allows for a widening of the market, reduction of risk, and increased liquidity for the individual creditor.

7. The usefulness of credit instruments is enhanced by highly organized markets which increase the transferability of these instruments and also by many types of credit institutions which, as intermediaries, permit a further diversification of risk and a further mobilization of even the smallest particles of savings.

Money Market and Capital Market

In order to establish the greatest possible number of debtor-creditor relationships and to thus use to the fullest extent the productive possibilities of the economy, a great variety of credit instruments have been created. They all have in common, however, that they are expressed in monetary units. The essence of credit, the exchange of present for future goods, is made independent of particular commodities. What we demand and supply on the credit market is not commodities but money for a period of time. With the money, in turn, any desired goods or services may be obtained. In the case of commodity credits we would have as many credits and as many commodity rates of interest as we have different commodities which are bartered over time. The lending and borrowing of money, therefore, is the precondition for formation of a uniform price for a uniform service. The interest rate is fixed as a percentage of a sum of money over a period of time, independent of accidental sums and periods.

In spite of the great variety of credit instruments it may seem at first as if there should exist a uniform rate of interest throughout the credit market, owing to the monetary character of all or almost all credit transactions. Loanable funds are sums of money, and units of money are substitutable. If, therefore, the market object is homogeneous, should not price differences in the credit market be only temporary and unimportant? Indeed, we find that many authors assume the existence of a uniform rate of interest throughout the credit market. However, a more careful study should be able to explain the simultaneous existence of a whole pattern of interest rates. The co-existence of different rates must be explained by the fact that loanable funds do not move with perfect freedom among different parts of the credit market.

A glance at Chart 21–1 will reveal that long-term and short-term rates of interest have consistently differed over the years, indicating the existence of separate long-term and short-term credit markets. The basic difference between these two major sections of the credit market, the *long-term* (or *capital*) *market* and the *short-term* (or *money*) *market,* is that short-term funds are usually needed for working capital purposes, while long-term credits are normally used for the purchase of fixed capital goods. Short-term credits are supposed to be liquidated with the sale of the product; long-term funds are needed for the average lifetime of the capital good, for the invested funds can be disentangled only through the slow process of amortization.[2] It is natural to assume that the demand for credit on the part of producers will reflect this basic dichotomy in the time structure of the underlying production periods; and since many suppliers of loanable funds part with their money only for relatively short periods, it seems obvious that demand and supply conditions should differ sufficiently between the main parts of the credit market to account for differences in interest rates.

This plausible explanation, however, is endangered by the following consideration. The marketability of credit instruments permits substitution of the "shiftability" of long-term credit instruments, through sale, for the liquidity of short-term claims, through sale of the products. It seems, therefore, as if lenders could be indifferent as far as the duration of the production processes and the time periods of the credits are concerned. The debtors, on the other hand, are free either to borrow long-term for both long-term and short-term purposes (lending out again such funds as are temporarily not needed) or to borrow short-term and to renew these short-term credits as often as needed for long-term purposes. No doubt, these possibilities exist; and if both borrowers and lenders were indifferent to the long- or short-term character of the credit instruments which they sell and buy, the whole credit market would become a perfectly competitive market with a uniform rate of interest. A brief study of short-term and long-term credit instruments, however, will show why such complete uniformity cannot exist.

[2] Borrowing a term from radio chemistry we could say that in the case of even wear and tear the *total* of the funds is needed for the "half-life" of the capital good.

CHART 21–1

LONG- AND SHORT-TERM INTEREST RATES

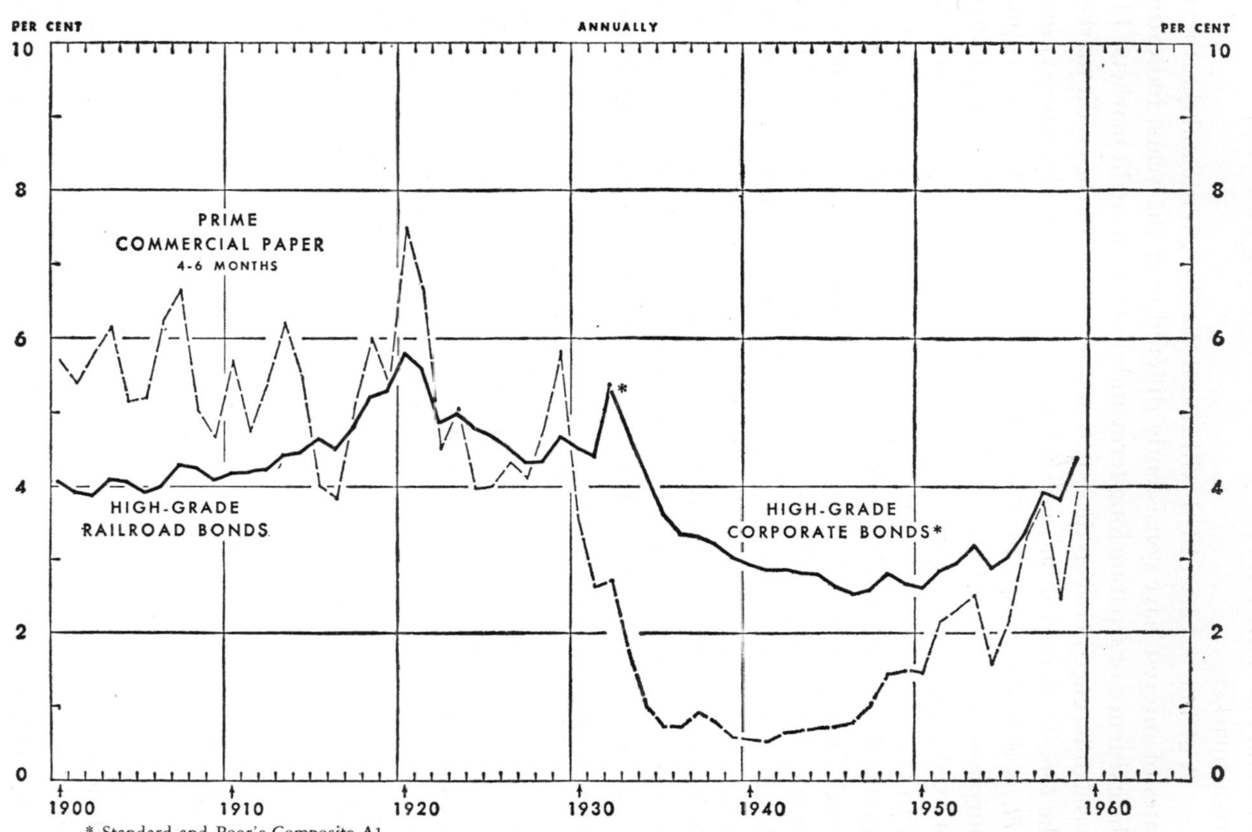

* Standard and Poor's Composite A1.

SOURCE: *Historical Supplement to Federal Reserve Chart Book on Financial and Business Statistics* (Washington, D.C.: Board of Governors of the Federal Reserve System, September, 1960), p. 37.

Credit Instruments

The most important technical distinction between short- and long-term credit instruments concerns the date of maturity at which the creditor will receive the face value stated in the credit instrument. Assuming, for the time being, that the debtor will be able to meet his obligation, the market value of the credit instrument cannot differ much from its face value if the date of maturity is relatively near at hand, as is always the case with short-term claims. All short-term credit instruments, therefore, have the advantage of a high degree of certainty as to their capital value. That the owners of such claims will receive a definite sum of money in the near future establishes the highly liquid character of short-term paper. An asset is more liquid the more easily it can be sold *without loss.*

The disadvantage of short-term paper for the creditor is not necessarily a low interest rate, as might be concluded from Keynes' liquidity-preference theory.[3] Short-term rates can be higher than long-term rates, as a glance at Chart 21–1 will show. The basic disadvantage of a short-term financial investment is that the creditor does not know what his income from capital will be after the present credit contract has expired. The certainty which he enjoys as to the capital value of the credit instrument is thus counterbalanced by a corresponding uncertainty as to future income from his capital. In addition, the substitution of repeated short-term credit transactions for the purchase of a long-term credit instrument means an extra amount of inconvenience and cost.

Long-term credit instruments, that is, bonds, offer the advantage of a certainty of yield for the remaining life span of the credit contract. The yield is not the coupon rate. The coupon rate indicates the fixed amount in dollars to be paid per year, expressed as a percentage of the face value or nominal value of the bond. Since maturity dates may be far removed (or nonexistent in the case of perpetuities), it is likely that a given bond will be bought at a higher or lower market value, depending on demand and supply conditions. If the prevailing long-term rate of interest (that is, the yield that can be expected from similar financial investments) is higher than the coupon rate, the market value of the bond will be below the face value; vice versa, if the coupon rate exceeds the prevailing rate, the market value of the bond will exceed

[3] If interest is the price for parting with liquidity, we should expect the rate to be lower the less we have parted with liquidity.

its face value. Assume, for instance, that we are able to buy a $100 bond for $80. A coupon rate of 4 per cent in this case means a yield of approximately 5 per cent. Yield, therefore, is not the coupon rate but the actual return figured as a percentage of the present market value of the bond.

Since the coupon rate remains fixed, changes in yield will be determined by fluctuations of the market value of the bond. These fluctuations, in turn, will be caused by such factors as changes in the prevailing rate of interest, the relative nearness or remoteness of the date of maturity, and the credit standing of the debtor. While the yield will fluctuate with any change in the market value, it will no longer fluctuate for the person who has made the purchase. As long as he keeps the bond the yield is determined for him by the coupon rate and the purchase price. He also can be certain as to the value of the bond at the time of maturity. However, he cannot be sure of the market value of the bond should he be forced to sell before maturity. Thus, in contrast to commercial paper or Treasury bills, the bond offers the advantage of certain income against the risk of uncertain capital value.

Certificates of Ownership

Should stock certificates be interpreted as credit instruments? Our first reaction is that, as certificates of ownership, shares of stock are decidedly different from credit instruments. We could even be tempted to include stock certificates in the real investment side of our total picture and to contrast them with credit instruments as the financial side. Stockholders, then, would be investors who make investment decisions, who compare the marginal efficiency of capital with the rate of interest, that is, the cost of borrowing. The yield of stock, according to this interpretation, seems nearly identical with the marginal efficiency of capital and clearly distinct from rates of interest. The purchase of stock certificates would be real investment, very much like the purchase or production of capital goods.

This division, however, would be far from realistic. The purchase of stock certificates, like the purchase of bonds, is an event strictly within the financial sphere. Certainly the overwhelming majority of financial investors look at the purchase of stock certificates simply as an alternative to the extension of long-term credit. Similarly, the managers of large corporations, who make investment decisions, consider stockholders as creditors. In most cases the "owners" have practically surrendered control and are, therefore, creditors rather than investors in the real meaning of the term.[4]

Stock certificates are of course different from bonds, since they represent an equity in the corporation and not a creditor's claim on fixed interest. A corporation's assets are balanced not only by what it owes to outsiders, that is, creditors in the narrower meaning of the term, but also by what it "owes" to its owners. What is called owner's equity is equal to the net worth of the corporation, namely, the amount by which the value of the corporation's assets exceeds its contractual liabilities.

Stock certificates differ from bonds in that they do not offer the same certainty of income from capital. Both the earnings of the corporation and the dividends which are voted by the board of directors are liable to fluctuate, whereas the coupon rates of bonds are fixed. Stock certificates "are therefore subject to a double dose of capital uncertainty, for their prices vary both with changes in profit expectations and with changes in the rate of interest."[5]

As shown in Chart 21–2, yields of industrial stock can be expressed either as earnings/price or as dividend/price ratios.

That we are justified in interpreting certificates of stock as credit instruments is shown by the fact that the basic distinction between bond and stock, namely, a fixed coupon rate as compared with the fluctuating dividends, is blurred by such hybrid creations as preferred stock. Preferred stockholders have a first claim on earnings and, in the event of liquidation, on assets; but their rate of return is limited, and they cannot vote. Thus they clearly form a link between bondholders and common stockholders, a link whose mere existence suggests that it would be wrong to overemphasize from the economic standpoint the difference between credit instruments and certificates of ownership.

But how about the rate of interest? Are yields of corporate stock interest or profit? We saw that the decision to invest, that is, to purchase or produce real capital goods, rests upon a comparison between the rate of interest and the marginal efficiency of capital. It is important, therefore, to clearly distinguish interest and profit. Certainly the yield of stock is not identical with the marginal efficiency of capital, since the former does not relate the yield of a physical capital asset to

[4] See Adolph A. Berle and Gardiner C. Means, *The Modern Corporation and Private Property* (New York: Macmillan Co., 1933), pp. 341, 343.

[5] Joan Robinson, *The Rate of Interest and Other Essays* (London: Macmillan & Co., Ltd., 1952), p. 7.

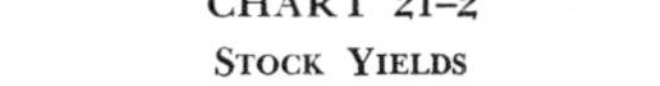

CHART 21–2

STOCK YIELDS

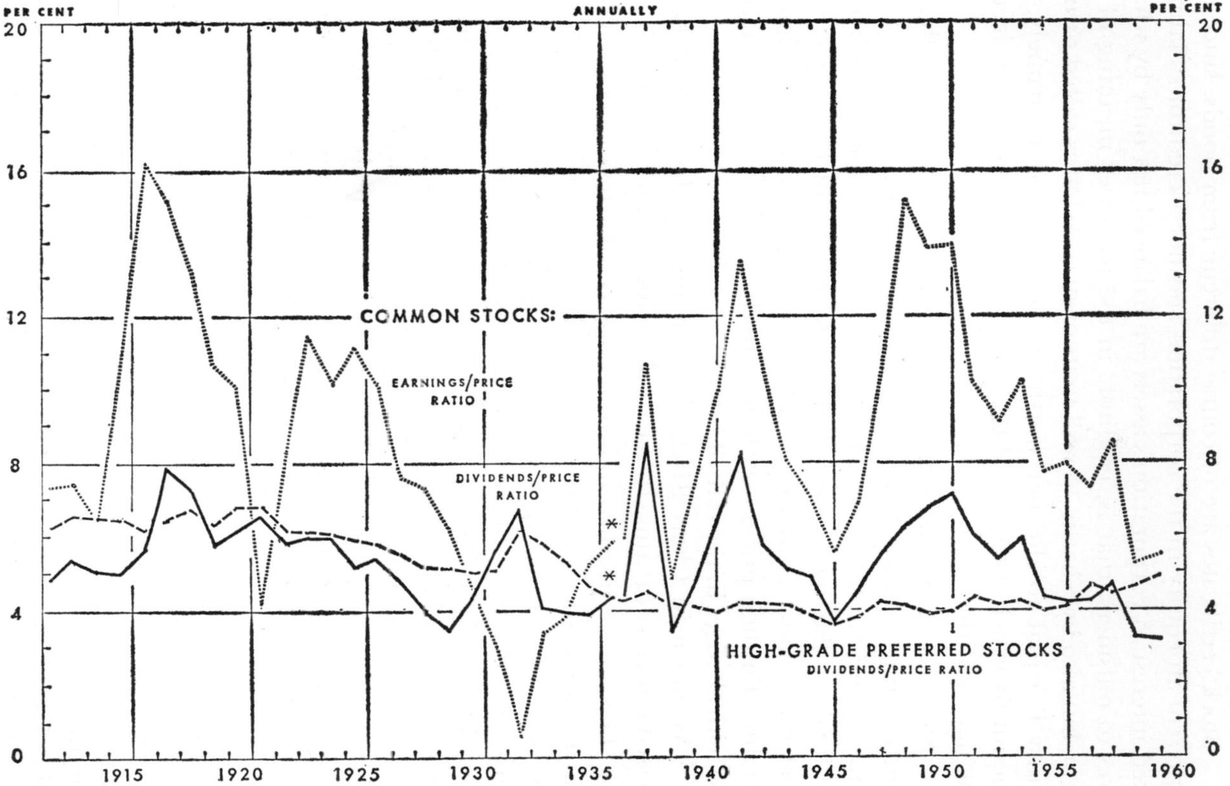

* Change in series.

SOURCE: *Historical Supplement to Federal Reserve Chart Book on Financial and Business Statistics* (Washington, D.C.: Board of Governors of the Federal Reserve System, September, 1960), p. 51.

its supply price or replacement cost. The yield of stock relates either earnings or dividends to the market price of the stock certificate, which, in turn, is determined by a comparison of earnings (or dividends) with the prevailing long-term rate of interest and by other considerations and expectations. But it is also doubtful whether the yield of stock can be considered one of the long-term rates of interest. Against this interpretation it can be said that the corporation is under no obligation to declare dividends and that earnings have the character of profits rather than interest rates. On the other hand, it cannot be denied that corporate managers often consider stockholders a special type of creditor and also that high stock prices permit corporations to raise funds under very favorable conditions, that is, at very low cost. Yields on stock, therefore, indicate the cost of corporate financing very much like interest rates do.

We see that the classification of stock certificates as titles of ownership or as credit instruments is largely a matter of convenience. What would be an impossible construction from the legal point of view may make sense from an economic point of view. This is particularly true when we think of the modern giant corporation, whose development has resulted in "the dissolution of the old atom of ownership into its component parts, control and beneficial ownership."[6] For our purposes the beneficial owner can be regarded as a special type of creditor who is willing to accept uncertainty both as to his income from capital and as to the value of his asset. He is, therefore, a shade more of an entrepreneur than the mere bondholder.

Subdivisions of the Credit Market

We have distinguished short- and long-term credit certificates and certificates of ownership. Most financial assets can be placed in one of these three categories; only a few fall between them, for example, preferred stocks and long-term notes which are the connecting link between short-term credit instruments and bonds.

For our study of the economics of money and banking it is not necessary to describe in detail the bewildering variety of credit instruments. It may be desirable, however, to list some of the qualities whose various combinations lead to many types of credit instruments and to many subdivisions of the major sectors of the credit market.

1. The credit standing of the borrower is important. In reasonably normal times the government, thanks to its power of taxation, is probably the safest borrower from the lender's standpoint. Private bor-

[6] Berle and Means, *op. cit.*, p. 8.

rowers will be considered risky to the same extent that lenders fear the possible partial or total failure of the borrower's enterprise. The monetary character of the credit instrument cannot hide the fact that loanable funds lose their monetary quality as soon as they are used for the purchase of capital goods, such as materials or machines. The lender's risk will depend to some extent on whether the borrower's anticipations will prove correct.

2. Much can be done, however, to protect the lender. Legal stipulations, for instance, can provide for the rapid exaction of claims. Or financial institutions may put their high credit standing at the disposal of their customers by accepting the latters' drafts (bank acceptances).

3. Credit instruments can be made more attractive and the lender's risk can be reduced when real property or financial claims are pledged as security. Typical cases of such secured credit instruments are trade drafts "backed" by the commodities whose purchase they finance or credits for purchasing or carrying securities, when the securities serve as collateral.

4. Because of the lender's desire for liquidity the degree of marketability of the credit instrument will be of great importance. Many lenders will prefer to buy claims which can be easily sold on the open market, where a continuously active demand maintains a relatively high degree of price stability. Borrowers whose notes or bonds are broadly marketable enjoy a position in which the competition of lenders keeps rates of interest at a relatively low level. Again, the federal government finds itself in the most favorable position in this respect. The less marketable credit instruments are, on the other hand, the more expensive will it be for the borrower to acquire necessary funds. If his demand is relatively small and his name is not widely known, it will be difficult for him to attract prospective creditors. Here the lender is in the stronger position. A local banker, for instance, may enjoy a relatively sheltered market where his special knowledge of the borrower's business enables him to combine profitability with a high degree of security.

5. The length of the credit period is so important that it was used to distinguish the long-term capital market from the short-term money market. The same criterion may serve also *within* the main sections of the credit market to account for subdivisions according to maturities. Within the field of short-term credit the time-periods may range from a day or two (with automatic renewal) in the case of call loans to 30- or 90-day maturities in the case of time loans. The different degrees of liquidity expressed in these maturities can account for

differences in interest rates. The time element is even more important in the case of long-term credits, where the distance or nearness of maturity dates encourages or limits fluctuation of bond prices. Maturity dates, however, are not always known in advance and may introduce a considerable element of uncertainty. Term bonds are due on a certain day, other bonds may be callable after a period of time, while others, again, may be so-called perpetuities, which have no set maturity dates.

6. Other things remaining equal, the yields of bonds with different coupon rates must differ. The yields of common stocks will depend on the earning power and financial structure of the corporations. We must remember that bondholders and preferred stockholders have a prior and fixed claim on the earnings of the corporation and that fluctuations in earning power, therefore, will be magnified in the dividends and yields on common stock.

7. Lenders and borrowers have to consider the handling costs of credit transactions in the narrower meaning of commissions paid to middlemen or taxes. These costs will discourage too frequent transfers of funds from one section of the credit market to another. On the whole such costs will weigh more heavily on short-term credits and on credits in small amounts. The amount of work entailed in pre-investment credit analysis is often equally great for short- or longer-term loans; similarly smaller borrowers will have to pay relatively higher charges than large borrowers.

This list of factors, whose various combinations account for the different subdivisions of the credit market and the characteristics of their peculiar credit instruments, is not complete, but it is sufficient to explain why we find even within the major sections of the credit market a variety of different rates and yields. Each combination of characteristics appeals to special groups of lenders and borrowers. We can understand, furthermore, that communication among the various parts of the credit market is less than perfect and that there must exist a whole pattern of interest rates rather than one rate for the whole market.

Short-Term and Long-Term Rates of Interest

The possible substitution for one another of credits of different maturity indicates a tendency toward elimination of differences between short- and long-term rates of interest. If in spite of this equalizing tendency the differences are as pronounced as shown in Chart 21–1, we have to find out why the process of substitution stops long before full equalization is reached. We must also explain why the short-term rates fluctuate in much wider swings. Bond yields, for instance, varied during the last 75 years within a range of only 3 per cent, and their fluctuations over shorter periods kept within a range of 1 per cent. Short-term interest rates, by contrast, showed changes of 3 and even 5 per cent within a few years.

Both short- and long-term rates moved, as a rule, in the same direction during the business cycle. These changes we shall study in connection with our discussion of economic fluctuations. Here we are interested only in accounting for the different degree of oscillation experienced by rates on the money market and capital market respectively.

In Chapter 20 we have seen that investment decisions are much more affected by changes in the prices of capital goods than by changes in short-term rates of interest; in other words, the long-term rate as a capitalization factor is much more potent than the short-term rate as cost factor. It stands to reason that under these conditions we should find more substantial fluctuations in the short-term than in the long-term rate. A change of a fraction of 1 per cent in the long-term rate may be more important for investment decisions than a change of several per cent in the short-term rate. If under these conditions the monetary authority decides to lower the discount rate in order to call forth credit demand, it may be successful only if it resorts to comparatively drastic changes. Open-market operations on the capital market, on the other hand, will have effects even though yields change by only a fraction of 1 per cent.

When we consider changes in demand and supply on the credit market, like those caused by monetary policy, for instance, we must remember that the total dollar volume of credit instruments in the short-term market is incomparably smaller than the volume of certificates of long-term credit or ownership. It is understandable, therefore, that a given increase or decrease in the total supply of credit will affect interest rates on the short-term market more than those on the long-term market.

When lenders or borrowers choose between the money market and the capital market as the place of their operations, they are less interested in the present pattern of interest rates than in the anticipated future development of interest rates. In discussing the influence of interest changes on the value of capital goods, we saw that changes in the prevailing rate of interest by as little as 1 per cent may cause the value of capital goods to fluctuate by as much as 20 per cent. The same relationship holds for interest rates and security prices. Assume the borrower believes security prices will rise and yields will fall. If he waits to sell his newly issued bonds or stocks he may obtain a price so much higher that it will pay him to borrow the needed funds in the meantime on the short-term market, paying for these funds a rate much in excess of the prevalent long-term rate. Under the same conditions lenders, eager to profit from the expected rise in security prices, will buy securities now, thus reducing the supply of funds on the short-term market at the very time when borrowers are eager to borrow short-term in spite of high short-term rates.

Still another explanation for the much more pronounced fluctuation of short-term rates as compared with long-term yields may be suggested. When discussing the periods of production in Chapter 18 we saw that the sale of newly produced durable goods depends on the prospective purchaser being able to secure satisfactory financial arrangements for this long-term investment in fixed capital. Let us assume that the production of fixed capital goods is financed predominantly by short-term credit for the production period, while long-term credit finances their purchase. Continuous turnover of working capital on the money market will depend, under these conditions, on the successful sale of the produced durable capital goods, and their salability, in turn, will be partly determined by conditions on the capital market. If long-term finance is difficult or impossible to arrange, if funding operations are not successful, or if expected sales do not materialize, the short-term funds invested during the production of capital goods will "freeze." In this process short-term credits become long-term credits, contrary to the original intentions of both lenders and borrowers, thus reducing the supply of short-term funds which is dependent on the regular disentanglement and return flow of short-term credits.[7] In the opposite case of an insufficient demand for long-term funds owing to a declining demand for durable capital goods, loanable funds will flow to the short-term market or will be hoarded.

It might be asked what corresponds in terms of real goods or productive services to these funds which flow into the money market because they cannot be absorbed by the capital market. Spiethoff suggests that it is unemployment, unused plant capacity, and stock of

[7] "Those commodities which depend on purchase through capital remain unsold because capital is lacking. The most urgent demands of the capital market stream to the money market and make the situation there even more serious." Arthur Spiethoff, "Krisen," *Handwörterbuch der Staatswissenschaften*, Vol. VI (1925), p. 25.

goods in different stages of completion which constitute the physical counterpart of these funds.[8]

SUGGESTIONS FOR FURTHER READING

BERLE, A. A. and MEANS, G. C. *The Modern Corporation and Private Property,* books i and iv. New York: Macmillan Co., 1933.

EDWARDS, G. W. *The Evolution of Finance Capitalism.* New York: Longmans, Green, & Co., 1938.

HAWTREY, R. G. *A Century of Bank Rate.* London: Longmans, Green & Co., 1938.

KOCK, KARIN. *A Study of Interest Rates.* London: P. S. King & Son, Ltd., 1929.

LUTZ, FRIEDRICH A. "The Structure of Interest Rates," *Quarterly Journal of Economics,* Vol. LV, 1940–41. Reprinted in *Readings in the Theory of Income Distribution* (Homewood, Ill.: Richard D. Irwin, Inc., 1946), chap. 26.

MACHLUP, FRITZ. *The Stock Market Credit and Capital Formation,* chap. 14. London: William Hodge & Co., Ltd., 1940.

MADDEN, CARL H. *The Money Side of "The Street,"* Federal Reserve Bank of New York, September, 1959.

MILL, JOHN STUART. *Principles of Political Economy,* Book III, chap. 11. London: Longmans, Green & Co., 1936.

MOULTON, HAROLD G. *Financial Organization and the Economic System,* chaps. 8–9. New York: McGraw-Hill Book Co., 1938.

RIEFLER, W. W. *Money Rates and Money Markets in the United States.* New York: Harper & Brothers, Publishers, 1930.

RITTER, LAWRENCE S. *Money and Economic Activity,* chap. 8. Boston: Houghton Mifflin Co., 1952.

ROBINSON, JOAN. *The Rate of Interest and Other Essays,* chap. 1. London: Macmillan & Co., Ltd., 1952.

SHAW, EDWARD S. *Money, Income, and Monetary Policy,* chaps. 12–14. Homewood, Ill.: Richard D. Irwin, Inc., 1950.

QUESTIONS AND PROBLEMS

1. "Both entrepreneurial initiative and savings would be wasted without the development of a great variety of transferable credit instruments." Explain.
2. Owing to the monetary character of almost all credit transactions and considering that units of money are substitutible, should we not expect the credit market to be completely uniform and perfectly competitive? How then can we explain the simultaneous existence of different rates of interest?

[8] *Ibid.*, p. 72.

3. "Long-term credit instruments, such as bonds, offer the advantage of certain income against the risk of uncertain capital value." Discuss.
4. Why does Joan Robinson say that stock certificates are "subject to a double dose of capital uncertainty"?
5. Discuss several criteria for distinguishing different classes of credit instruments and for subdividing the credit market.
6. How do you explain the division of the credit market into a so-called short-term money market and a long-term capital market. Which basic economic facts lie behind this division?
7. Looking at Chart 21–1 we must come to the conclusion that short-term rates of interest are more sensitive than long-term rates. How can we explain the fact that short-term rates fluctuate much more than long-term rates?

Chapter 22 CREDIT INSTITUTIONS

Introduction

In the preceding chapter we assumed that lenders and borrowers are brought together through credit instruments and credit markets, but we left out of account the many credit institutions which serve as intermediaries between lenders and borrowers in these markets. Such institutions either bring about a direct connection between debtor and creditor or they remain a permanent link between lenders and borrowers.

Investment banks and security dealers buy newly issued securities from corporations and sell these securities to institutions and persons desiring to purchase them. Thus they are wholesalers and retailers of securities. Obviously there is much room here for the activities of specialists who, on the basis of expert credit investigation and analysis, study the prospects of the issuing corporations, furnish these corporations with definitive sums of money by a given date and recover these funds through the distribution of the newly issued securities among permanent or quasi-permanent holders.

Purchase and sale of these newly issued securities constitute a "primary" securities market. There is also a "secondary" market for old securities. In Chapter 21 we saw that it is very important for credit instruments to be easily salable. Security holders must have the opportunity to regain individual liquidity through shiftability, that is, through sale of their securities. This sale does not create an additional creditor-debtor relationship like the sale of newly issued securities. Nevertheless, the secondary market is just as important as the primary market, since without its existence it would be next to impossible to sell securities on the primary market. The secondary market, too, offers wide scope for the activities of specialists who greatly increase its efficiency and perform important functions. Brokers stand ready to execute their customers' orders, while dealers buy and sell on their own account. Both in the so-called "over-the-counter" market for securities and in the more highly organized stock exchanges we find that dealers stand ready at all times to buy and sell if they expect to profit from such transactions. We shall discuss below both the positive and negative aspects of stock speculation.

A very great variety of credit institutions serve as a permanent connecting link between lenders and borrowers. In this category belong commercial banks in their role as credit intermediaries, mutual savings banks, savings-and-loan associations, life insurance companies, investment trusts, and some others. While differing widely in many respects, these institutions have in common that they pool smaller funds in order to invest them on the basis of expert knowledge. They are able to achieve a combination of profitability, liquidity, diversification of risk, and security which would be unattainable by the individual financial investor.

The financial superstructure of our economy has become so intricate that it is impossible here to enter upon a detailed discussion of all financial institutions. We shall try, however, to examine some features of our financial system which are of general theoretical interest.

The Economic Functions and Dangers of Stock Speculation

The turnover of securities is artificially increased by stock and bond speculation and this makes credit instruments always salable. As Fritz Machlup points out:

> Professional security speculation creates what may be called a reservoir for the easy equalization of supply and demand at any moment of time, so as to prevent wide fluctuations in security prices due to fortuitous circumstances. Without this "reservoir for stray securities" it is unlikely that all shareholders who wanted to realize their securities would be able to find investors who were willing to buy them just at the right moment.[1]

Stock speculation establishes risk bearing as a special economic function. It can be argued that because of its equalizing effect on prices, stock speculation takes on its shoulders part of the uncertainty and risk which the public would otherwise have to bear. Since the speculator wants to profit from his guessing earlier and better than the public, he will buy in order to be able to sell when the public develops a buying mood, and vice versa. He tries to consider in ad-

[1] Fritz Machlup, *The Stock Market Credit and Capital Formation* (London and New York: William Hodge & Co., Inc., 1940), p. 23.

vance everything that may influence the decisions of prospective buyers and sellers, such as future earnings, interest rates, general business outlook, war scares, etc. In acting earlier than the market the speculator may exert an equalizing effect on security prices by spreading price changes over a longer period and by counterbalancing to some degree the impromptu actions of the public. This does not mean that he has the gift of divination; but the speculator probably knows what the "normal" market values are considered to be at the time, and he will, through his sales and purchases, prevent extreme deviations from this norm.

We see that the stock market, and in particular the stock exchange, is a peculiar type of market. Not only does it bring buyers and sellers together through the medium of brokers but it actually can cushion the effect of sudden changes in either demand or supply by inducing, through moderate price fluctuations, instant opposite changes in supply and demand. If we add the stock exchanges' high degree of organization, their communication facilities, the strict rules governing the behavior of their members, and the standards set for the admission of securities, we get the impression that stock exchanges are perfect markets which establish the true value of traded securities. But is it not also possible that stock speculation may cause artificial price fluctuations, that it may induce the public to gamble—in other words, that it may become a disequilibrating rather than an equilibrating force in the economy?

The statement that the stock market will prevent abnormal price fluctuations is true in the sense that speculators will always be ready to buy at a price only slightly below what at the moment is considered normal. But the stock market does not necessarily establish correct prices, that is, prices which correspond to the best possible estimate of long-term developments. In this connection John Maynard Keynes has made some interesting suggestions.[2]

Keynes argues that estimates of prospective yields 10 or even 5 years hence are extremely difficult and that those who attempt to make them are so few that their behavior does not determine market values. If no stock exchange existed, businessmen would not waste time constantly attempting to establish the monetary values of their real investments, to which they are already irrevocably committed. The development of the organized credit market, however, made a constant revaluation of securities imperative because stockholders and bond-

[2] J. M. Keynes, *The General Theory of Employment, Interest and Money* (London: Macmillan & Co., Ltd., 1936), chap. xii.

holders had to be given the possibility to procure for themselves individual liquidity through sale of their securities. These daily revaluations

> inevitably exert a decisive influence on the rate of current investment. For there is no sense in building up a new enterprise at a cost greater than that at which a similar existing enterprise can be purchased; while there is an inducement to spend on a new project what may seem an extravagant sum, if it can be floated off on the Stock Exchange at an immediate profit.[3]

In order to show that the influence of the stock market and stock-market speculation may be dangerous, that price quotations may be wrong, and that investment may be misled, Keynes uses the following arguments. Stock-market prices will not reveal the genuine expectations of professional entrepreneurs, since those who buy and sell on the stock market are not interested in long-run production trends. Either they are devoid of any knowledge concerning corporations in whose shares they deal—the natural result of the already mentioned separation of ownership and management—or they are professional speculators whose knowledge is greater but who do not care to use their knowledge in the interest of correct price determination. Ignorant investors are liable to react violently on sudden changes of opinion which have little to do with changes in prospective yields or interest rates; and professionals use their energies and skills not in correcting the mistakes of the ignorant but in "foreseeing changes in the conventional basis of valuation a short time ahead of the general public."[4] Thus the professional speculator is occupied with his desire "to beat the gun" or "to outwit the crowd"; he has to use his intelligence "to anticipate what average opinion expects average opinion to be."[5] And since average opinion is uninformed and excitable, it may easily be that stock-market quotations are not a true mirror of the best possible appraisal of long-run developments.

Keynes traced these difficulties back to the fact that security markets are organized with a view to so-called liquidity and admitted that this individual liquidity through shiftability is essential if the alternative to financial investment, namely, hoarding, is to be avoided. He suggested that "the introduction of a substantial Government transfer

[3] *Ibid.*, p. 151. In a footnote to this passage Keynes explains "that when a company's shares are quoted very high so that it can raise more capital by issuing more shares on favorable terms, this has the same effect as if it could borrow at a low rate of interest." Less clear is the remark "that a high quotation for existing equities involves an increase in the marginal efficiency of the corresponding type of capital. . . ."

[4] *Ibid.*, p. 154.

[5] *Ibid.*, pp. 155–56.

tax on all transactions might prove the most serviceable reform, with a view to mitigating the predominance of speculation over enterprise in the United States."[6] Keynes did not consider margin requirements, which, by limiting the availability of credit for carrying of securities, are a powerful instrument for correcting dangerous developments in security prices. When security prices increase rapidly we have reason to believe that it is an excess not only of speculation but also of loanable funds from inflationary sources which is responsible for this dangerous development which is bound to reverse itself as soon as the artificial supply of loanable funds is reduced or stopped.

Does the Stock Exchange Absorb Capital?

Security speculation has been attacked on the ground that it diverts capital from potentially productive employment. We are told that loanable funds are absorbed by security trading and do not reach, or reach too late, the businessman who wants to invest them in productive processes.

Some versions of this argument arise from the misconception that the funds which are used by speculators to purchase securities are tied up for the period during which the securities are held by these speculators. But the loanable funds have not disappeared. The economic effect depends on what the sellers of the securities do with the funds they have received from the speculators who purchased the securities. Using Fritz Machlup's penetrating analysis[7] we can distinguish the following cases:

If the speculator has bought newly issued securities, the issuing corporation will receive the sales proceeds and will use them in one of the following ways.

1. To repay bank loans. The supply of loanable funds is not reduced by this action.

2. To buy already produced means of production (capital goods). The loanable funds are now in the hands of the producer of these capital goods, that is, working capital has been liquidated through the sale of his output.

3. To produce capital goods. The loanable funds serve to liquidate the working capital of producers who supplied raw materials and intermediate goods.

[6] *Ibid.*, p. 160.
[7] Machlup, *op. cit.*, chap. iii, sec. 22.

4. To carry through plans 2 and 3 later, supplying the loanable funds in the meantime as short-term credit. The total supply of loanable funds is not reduced.

5. To buy other securities, as in the case of an investment trust. If these securities are newly issued, cases 1 to 4 become relevant again.

If the speculator bought old securities the seller uses the proceeds also in one of the five ways indicated above. The seller of the old securities may dissave, however, by using the sales proceeds for consumption purposes. Dissaving reduces the supply of loanable funds, but it is then dissaving and not security speculation which is to be blamed.

Assuming for the moment that the stock exchange can really absorb loanable funds, we have to ask in which form the capital is absorbed, whither it goes, and where it hides itself until it eventually finds its way back into productive uses. To this question the answer is sometimes given that capital is absorbed by an increase in security prices. If security prices rise by 100 per cent this increase in value, according to these views, has to be financed by loans. Loanable funds have been absorbed; they are no longer available for productive purposes.

The fallacy of this argument lies in the fact that, whatever security prices may be, the purchasing power of the buyer is not lost but is immediately put at the disposal of the seller. The purchase of securities—old or new, at high prices or low prices—never takes from the buyer more purchasing power than is placed in the hands of the seller. The increase of security prices, therefore, does not and cannot absorb the tiniest amount of loanable funds.

The proposition that security speculation does not absorb capital does not necessarily imply that it can never tie up any part of the *money* supply. Increased stock exchange turnover increases the trade volume, and if all other things (especially the transaction velocity of circulation of money) remained unchanged, it could lead to a fall in the price level.[8] Still more important is that the speculative motive for liquidity may lead to an increased demand for money balances, lower the supply of loanable funds, and raise interest rates.

[8] As far as the "inside business" of the stock exchange is concerned, that is, the transactions within the closed circle of members of the stock exchange, the turnover of securities is most frequently carried through without the use of money by a clearing or cancellation process, particularly when the business of several days is brought together in one settlement period; but in any case it is not the gross value of securities traded which is to be paid but just the differences. Compare Machlup, *op. cit.*, chap. vi, secs. 38 and 39.

Credit Intermediaries

There exists no generally accepted definition of the term "bank." This is not astonishing in view of the many different functions performed by banking institutions and considering also their different sources of loanable funds. Somary, for instance, says that banks are institutions whose function is to borrow.[9] According to him it is only on the liabilities side that we find what all banking institutions have in common, for they differ widely as to organization and national tradition as far as their assets are concerned. Macleod, on the other hand, said that a bank is not an institution which borrows money but an institution for the creation of credit.[10] Neither definition is satisfactory. It is not the ultimate function of banks either to borrow or to create money, and the power to create money is limited anyhow to central banks and to those private credit institutions which accept demand deposits. Banks borrow and, in some cases, create money in order to make loanable funds available to those who want to borrow. It would not be advisable to stress exclusively the function of banks as intermediaries, however, for where credit can be created, the banks are not only intermediaries but also original creditors.

Even if we limit ourselves to private credit institutions which are permanent intermediaries between those who want to lend and those who want to borrow—in other words, if we exclude central banks and investment banks—we are faced with a great variety of credit institutions, whose detailed description would interrupt our theoretical argument without aiding it. These intermediaries perform the following economic functions: they pool the savings of their lending customers; they invest these funds (financially) on the basis of careful credit analysis; they diversify risk to a degree unattainable for individual investors; they transform short-term funds into long-term funds through a careful staggering of maturity dates; and they perform insurance and trust functions which also rest on the law of averages.

Not all credit intermediaries perform all these functions. In banking, as elsewhere, specialization has its advantages, and sometimes specialization is enforced by legal restrictions, as when savings banks and commercial banks do not buy industrial stock or when commercial banks are forced to divorce themselves from investment banking affiliates (as in the United States by the Banking Act of 1933). Where no legal bar exists, however, we find also much overlapping of activities:

9 Felix Somary, *Bankpolitik* (Tübingen: Paul Siebeck, 1930).
10 Henry Dunning Macleod, *The Theory of Credit* (London, 1898), p. 594.

both commercial and savings banks, for instance, are interested in mortgage credit; savings banks as well as life insurance companies sell life insurance; and commercial banks as well as sales finance companies finance consumer installment credit—to mention only a few activities which are carried on competitively by a variety of credit institutions.

It is easy to understand why governments have found it necessary to restrict the activities of credit institutions even outside the strictly monetary field. Monetary considerations were of course predominant in regulations applying to commercial banks. Because of the special attention which had to be given to the interrelated problems of liquidity and solvency, it was considered undesirable for commercial banks to purchase industrial stock, even though part of the commercial banks' deposits were not payable on demand. Similar regulations in the case of savings banks are explained by the fact that savings banks receive small deposits of people of modest means and must, accordingly, invest these savings with emphasis on safety rather than profitability.

The division of functions between the banking institutions of a country is to a large extent the result of historical development. Take, for instance, the above-mentioned relationship between commercial and investment banks. Laws which preclude investment banking activities by commercial banks may help to prevent unsound practices, but they should not be considered as a simple solution for an intricate problem. Nor can one and the same rule be applied with equal advantage to different national credit systems. Where industry is largely built on a family basis, the capital being privately provided and expanded out of profits, or where a strong capital market takes care of the long-term financing of industry, it may be possible and advisable to limit the activities of commercial banks to short-term financing of trade and commerce, as was largely true in England. Rapid development of industrial production, on the other hand, may make industry dependent on the financial support of the commercial banks for long-term as well as for short-term financing. In this case (and where a high level of economic activity limits the amount of credit creation) it becomes the function of the commercial banks to rake together even the smallest savings in order to build up the huge sums needed for the equipment of modern industrial plants. And once the commercial banks finance the demand for fixed as well as for working capital, their liquidity depends on how successfully they perform the function of investment banks. They must buy the securities of their borrowing customers and then sell them to their lending customers in order to re-establish the banks' liquidity. This method of combining the activities of commercial and investment banks has certain advantages for the banks as well as for their lending and borrowing customers, advantages which should not be forgotten by advocates of a complete separation of commercial and investment banking.[11]

Federal Credit Agencies

We might be tempted to argue that the government should control the total supply of credit but that it should abstain from any attempt to direct the distribution of credit, since we have already seen that a good case can be made for allocating loanable funds to those able to pay the prevailing rate of interest. Private credit institutions cannot undertake a consistent distribution in any other way, since they are not planning agencies. Are we then correct in assuming that the allocation of loanable funds through private banking institutions fits the logic of our private enterprise system? Are credits to be extended according to the payment of equilibrium rates of interest, the marginal productivity of capital, and consumers' preferences? On the whole the answer to this question must be "yes." As a matter of fact, an unplanned economy has no other way to achieve a consistent allocation of loanable funds among the millions of consumers and the hundreds of thousands of producers who want to borrow.

Yet we find outside the monetary field (in which government control is obvious) a very great number and variety of federal credit agencies, whose very existence indicates that, in practice, we do not rely for the distribution of credit exclusively on our private credit system.

Federal credit agencies outside the monetary field are not part of a coherent system like the Federal Reserve. Instead they are an agglomeration of unco-ordinated offices whose guarantees or direct extension of credit facilitate finance for sectors of the economy which, without such federal aid, would receive a smaller share of the total supply of loanable funds. All these agencies and their policies have in common, therefore, that they change the pattern of credit distribution. Most of them, however, are not interested in credit policy as such. Taken individually they have to be judged, for example, as part of our agricultural policy or as part of our effort to aid other countries.

11 Compare *Committee on Finance and Industry Report* (*Macmillan Report*), Cmd. 3897 (London: His Majesty's Stationery Office, 1931), chap. iv; Adolf Weber, *Depositenbanken und Spekulationsbanken* (Munich and Leipzig: Duncker und Humblot, 1938).

Taken together, under the heading "credit policy," they cannot be discussed as a logical whole, since they were never meant to add up to a consistent credit policy. Indeed, these policies are often contradictory as well as at variance with our monetary policy—for instance, when the monetary authority tries to combat inflationary pressures by mopping up excessive liquidity at the same time that other federal agencies reduce the cost of housing finance.

It has been proposed, of course, that the credit policies of various federal agencies be co-ordinated; but since most of these policies are integral parts of sectional policies, such co-ordination could be successful only as part of a much more ambitious undertaking to integrate all *economic* policies of the federal government.

The various nonmonetary agencies of the federal government in the field of credit are either the result of emergency measures or they are intended to make credit available where private credit cannot be obtained on "reasonable" terms.

The most important example of a federal credit agency which was created during and for an emergency was the Reconstruction Finance Corporation (1932–53). In Chapter 17 we have seen that the RFC extended financial aid to a variety of institutions because the hands of the Federal Reserve were tied by its rigid reserve requirements. Later the RFC was used for a number of purposes, particularly in connection with government deficit spending and war finance. Among the criticisms which led to the abolition of the RFC in 1953 were claims that it helped the Executive to avoid normal appropriation procedures, that its operations exhibited favoritism, and that its really essential functions could be performed by other agencies.

Federal credit agencies can perform important permanent services where for special reasons private banking institutions are not able or willing to make credit available in sufficient amounts, for instance, to agriculture, small business, urban housing, and firms engaged in foreign trade. Accordingly, there were created the Farm Credit Administration (with its many subdivisions), the Small Business Administration (successor to the RFC), the several housing credit agencies, the Export-Import Bank, and others. These agencies either guarantee private credit or extend public credit. A general appraisal of their policies is not possible since they must be studied individually in connection with whatever special economic aim they help to accomplish. Much will depend, furthermore, on the techniques employed. Where private lending is encouraged through public guarantees, where the development of co-operatives is stimulated and unfair public competition with private credit agencies scrupulously avoided, the federal credit agencies cannot be seriously criticized. Where, on the other hand, public credit is extended at low rates, it is not always easy to determine the legitimate scope of public lending. Crucial is the interpretation of what "reasonable" terms of credit are. Federal agencies may be instructed to leave the field to private institutions, provided the banks charge "reasonable" rates of interest. But "reasonable" is a vague concept. Interest rates charged on the credit markets always contain a risk premium, which explains the fact that a well-known corporation may be able to borrow at 3 per cent while the consumer may pay 12 per cent on installment credit. How legitimate is this risk factor in connection with price formation on the credit markets? When and where should the government eliminate risk through its guarantees, and which rate is to be considered "reasonable" after the risk premium has been eliminated?

Since answers to these questions cannot be precise, there exists a broad area in which the activities of private and public credit agencies tend to overlap. Government guarantees may, and public credits at artificially low rates certainly do, constitute a case of subsidization. Rates lower than prevailing market rates guide the flow of loanable funds according to public policy decisions. We may consider it desirable, for instance, to aid low-income groups through cheap housing or underdeveloped countries through low-cost loans and grants. Whether our policy is desirable or not, it is obvious that we are fundamentally altering the principles of credit allocation characteristic of the market economy.

Saint-Simon (1760–1825) and his followers envisaged a centralized banking system through which the government would direct production via credit allocation. More recently it has been argued[12] that after nationalization of the credit system the competitive allocation of funds would cease and that claims for credit would be satisfied according to the urgency, necessity, and usefulness of the production in question. It would then be unnecessary to nationalize industry since the advantages of a centrally planned economy could be achieved through central credit distribution alone.

It need not be pointed out that this naïve scheme underestimates the formidable difficulties of central planning. It has been mentioned only because it illustrates the situation which would be created if we extended subsidization through low interest rates to larger and larger

[12] See, for instance, Robert Deumer, *Die Verstaatlichung des Kredits* (Munich and Leipzig: Duncker & Humblot, 1926).

sectors of the economy. We would allocate the available funds to industries which we somehow consider urgent, necessary, or valuable, and we would try to withhold funds from industries willing to pay higher rates. In a system supposedly based on consumers' preferences, this would lead to contrary results. Fortunately, it would also be impractical as long as private industry could resort to self-financing.

Our criticism is not directed against central planning as such. Central planning may be consistent on its own terms. But for a private enterprise economy with free choice of consumption, arbitrary credit allocation must remain the exception to the rule; it does not fit the logic of our price and credit systems.

SUGGESTIONS FOR FURTHER READING

CHANDLER, LESTER V. *The Economics of Money and Banking,* chaps. 19–20. rev. ed. New York: Harper & Brothers Publishers, 1953.

Committee on Finance and Industry Report (Macmillan Report), chap. 4. London: His Majesty's Stationery Office, Cmd. 3897, 1931.

KEYNES, J. M. *The General Theory of Employment, Interest and Money,* chap. 12. London: Macmillan & Co., Ltd., 1936.

MACHLUP, FRITZ. *The Stock Market Credit and Capital Formation,* chaps. 3–6. London: William Hodge & Co., Ltd., 1940.

MOULTON, HAROLD G. *Financial Organization and the Economic System,* chaps. 9, 12–16, 26–28. New York: McGraw-Hill Book Co., Inc., 1938.

STEINER, W. H.; SHAPIRO, ELI, and SOLOMON, EZRA. *Money and Banking,* chap. 20. 4th ed. New York: Henry Holt & Co., 1958.

QUESTIONS AND PROBLEMS

1. "It is only the existence of professional security speculation that can prevent price fluctuations which are unrelated to judgements as to the yield and safety of the security" (F. Machlup). Discuss.
2. Will the stock market always establish correct prices, that is, prices which rest on the best estimate of long-run economic developments?
3. J. M. Keynes suggested that the professional speculator is not occupied with the correction of the mistakes of the ignorant but rather with the desire "to outwit the crowd" and "to beat the gun." Discuss.
4. Discuss the regulation of stock market credit through margin requirements.
5. "Security speculation diverts capital from potentially productive employment because it becomes absorbed in increased security prices." Discuss.

6. F. Somary said that banks are institutions whose purpose is to borrow while H. D. Macleod insisted that a bank is an institution for the creation of credit. Who was right?
7. "The division of the functions of commercial and investment banks is largely the result of economic development." Discuss.
8. Could nationalization of the credit system short-cut socialism? Would central credit allocation obviate the need for the nationalization of industries?

PART VII

Money and Economic Stability

Chapter 23 INCOME LEVELS

Introduction

The chapters of Part VII have in common that, with particular emphasis on the part played by money, they discuss the forces which cause economic instability and unemployment. This discussion, in turn, will serve as a basis for formulation of appropriate policies for economic stability. If we succeed in diagnosing the causes of unemployment we may be able to cure the disease. Our special emphasis on monetary causes and cures of economic instability does not mean to suggest that prosperity and depression are exclusively or even predominantly monetary phenomena of inflation and deflation and that stability at full employment could be achieved if only the supply of money were properly managed. We have already seen that monetary policy *alone* cannot maintain even stable prices, let alone a high level of employment. The basic weakness of our monetary system is that the Federal Reserve "cannot make the people borrow, and it cannot make the people spend the deposits that result when the banks do make loans and investments."[1]

[1] "Proposals to Maintain Prices at Fixed Levels through Monetary Action," Statement by the Board of Governors of the Federal Reserve System, *Federal Reserve Bulletin*, April, 1939.

But monetary actions may aggravate economic instability, and correctly chosen monetary policies are an indispensable component of government policies aimed at full employment and economic growth. Monetary phenomena such as dishoarding (hoarding) and credit creation (contraction) are indispensable in bringing about economic expansion (contraction), and this implies that adequate monetary management must be *one* of the instruments by which we try to manipulate aggregate expenditure.

"Classical" Equilibrium

Classical theory assumed a permanent tendency towards equilibrium at full employment. The economy would have to adjust itself to disturbances from the outside (such as technological changes), but a sensitive pricing process would lead to the necessary regrouping of the factors of production. Increased savings would press the rates of interest down and thus bring about an increase in investment to offset a decline in consumption; aggregate expenditure would not fall. Improved technical know-how could not cause difficulties, since competitive pressure would translate falling unit costs into falling commodity prices at which more goods could be sold even with an unchanged supply of money. Frictional unemployment would easily be absorbed because at lower prices many more goods could be sold and produced, resulting in a long-run increased demand for labor. Unemployment other than frictional would be voluntary, that is, it would be the result of refusal to work at competitive wages, owing to monopolistic union policies. A growing population would be supplied with just enough additional money to avoid dangerous deflationary tendencies—if deflation could be dangerous in a system which assumes sensitive price reactions and nearly perfect mobility of the factors of production.

Economists, as a rule, did not pretend that the real economy conformed to this ideal model. Disturbances from the outside were frequent: prices, less than perfectly sensitive; and factors, less than perfectly mobile. Frictional problems could be serious and monopolies powerful. Furthermore, the very structure of our economy seemed to transform irregular impulses from the outside into more or less regular fluctuations, the so-called business cycle. Price reactions, instead of leading the economy back to equilibrium, sometimes turned out to be disequilibrating, thus necessitating a more drastic adjustment later on.

Among the possible causes of economic fluctuations, monetary phenomena were often considered prominent. Business cycles were explained as a succession of inflationary and deflationary processes. We shall discuss the monetary characteristics of business cycles in Chapters 25 and 26. Again, however, it must be stated at the outset that while money plays an important part in prosperity and depression, it is not possible to limit the discussion of the business cycle to the field of money.

Before we embark on a survey of those problems of economic instability which are particularly interesting from the standpoint of monetary theory and policy, we must discuss some basic principles of Keynes' *General Theory*. According to Keynes the economy does not necessarily tend towards equilibrium at full employment; it can come to rest at income and employment levels far below the desirable full use of our human and material resources. Though Keynes' theory is a theory of equilibrium rather than of economic fluctuations, we shall be able to use much of his analysis for a better understanding of the inherent instability of our economy.

We have seen that the demand for and the supply of money play a decisive part in Keynes' liquidity-preference theory of interest and that interest rates and the marginal efficiency of capital determine the level of investment expenditures. Now we shall see how consumption expenditures and investment expenditures determine the level of income and employment.

The Consumption Function

When discussing the circular flow of money in Chapter 2, we saw how a given level of income maintains itself indefinitely as long as all income earned in the production processes of the economy is spent either on consumers' goods or, via savings, on investment goods. We also saw that the money flow may be decreased and that income and employment may fall off if the public decides to hold a greater quantity of money idle or if the desire to save by one group is not matched by investment activities of another group. Since we know that hoarding will decrease spending and that credit creation or dishoarding may lift spending above its previous level, we must remain aware of the very close connection between the behavior of money and fluctuations in aggregate expenditure.

Of the two components of aggregate spending, consumption spending is relatively stable and investment spending is highly volatile. Economic fluctuations, therefore, are predominantly caused by changes in investment expenditures—a fact acknowledged by all theorists in face of undeniable statistical evidence.

Figure 23–1 shows the consumption function, that is, the relation between consumption as the dependent and national income as the independent variable. The income = consumption line crosses the figure at an angle of 45 degrees. If all income earned were always fully spent on consumption, the consumption function would be illustrated by this straight line. Actually, however, the consumption function corresponds to curve *C* which illustrates the basic fact that at very low national income levels consumption exceeds income, that at one point (*A*) consumption and income are equal, and that from there on, as

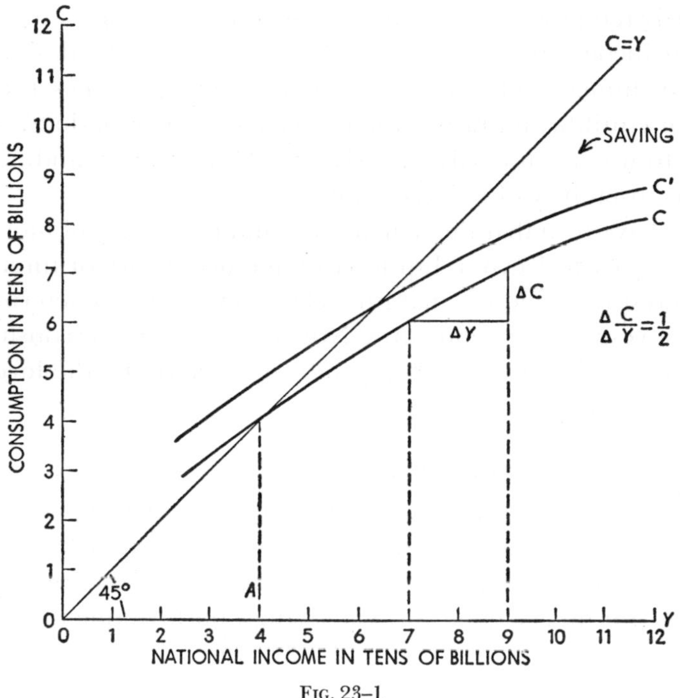

FIG. 23–1

national income grows, consumption grows absolutely but falls relative to income.[2] Since we defined saving as not-consuming, we can also say that the area between curve *C* and the 45 degree line left of point *A* indicates dissaving, while the ever-broadening area to the right of *A* illustrates that with growing income an increasing amount, both in absolute dollar figures and percentagewise, will be saved.

Aggregate consumers' behavior depends on many factors, such as income distribution, tax policies, stocks of goods on hand, expected

[2] See J. M. Keynes, *The General Theory of Employment, Interest and Money* (London: Macmillan & Co., Ltd., 1936), p. 96.

price changes, etc. At any moment of time we can assume the "propensity to consume" to be given and to be related to different national income levels in the manner indicated by curve *C*. This curve, therefore, shows what, under given conditions, consumers will spend at different national income levels. When these conditions change, for instance, when a new tax structure leads to greater equality of individual incomes after taxes, the whole *C* curve will move. In the assumed case of a more equal distribution the curve will be pushed upward to *C′*. This is because people with lower incomes have a higher propensity to consume. *C′*, as compared with *C*, indicates that at the same national income levels consumption expenditures will now be larger than before.[3]

While statistical data suggest that the consumption function follows roughly the pattern indicated in Figure 23–1, we do not know precisely what consumption expenditures would be at different national income levels, other things remaining unchanged. We do have data, however, regarding the consumption habits of different income groups and the changes in their consumption expenditures over the years. Statistics on family incomes and income disposal can be used to plot a curve similar to our *C* curve, with the difference, however, that consumption and income figures would then refer to thousands rather than to billions of dollars.[4]

Time series have to be handled with care since we have to expect that over a period of years the whole *C* curve will be shifted up or down. We cannot assume, for instance, that the saved portion of the national income will substantially increase in percentage terms with an absolute increase in income over the years (see Chart 23–1). Experience has shown that the consumption curve tends to be pushed upward with the passing of time. This may be because the increase in income is inflationary rather than real, because income distribution is altered in favor of the lower-income brackets, or because new consumers' goods and the tendency to "keep up with the Joneses" reduce thrift in favor of consumption.[5] An observed absolute increase in consumption, therefore, can be the combined effect of the slope and of an upward shift of the *C* curve.

[3] The analogy between a shift of the *C* curve and a shifting demand curve is obvious. A demand curve indicates the varying amounts of a commodity people are ready to buy at different prices; a shift of the demand curve to the right shows that people are now willing to buy more than before even at unchanged prices.

[4] See: *Family Spending and Saving in Wartime*, Bulletin No. 822 (Washington, D.C.: U.S. Department of Labor, Bureau of Labor Statistics, April, 1945).

[5] James S. Duesenberry speaks of a "demonstration effect." See *Income, Saving, and the Theory of Consumer Behavior* (Cambridge, Mass.: Harvard University Press, 1949).

CHART 23–1

PERSONAL INCOME, CONSUMPTION, AND SAVING

Department of Commerce Estimates, Quarterly Figures Adjusted for Seasonal Variation

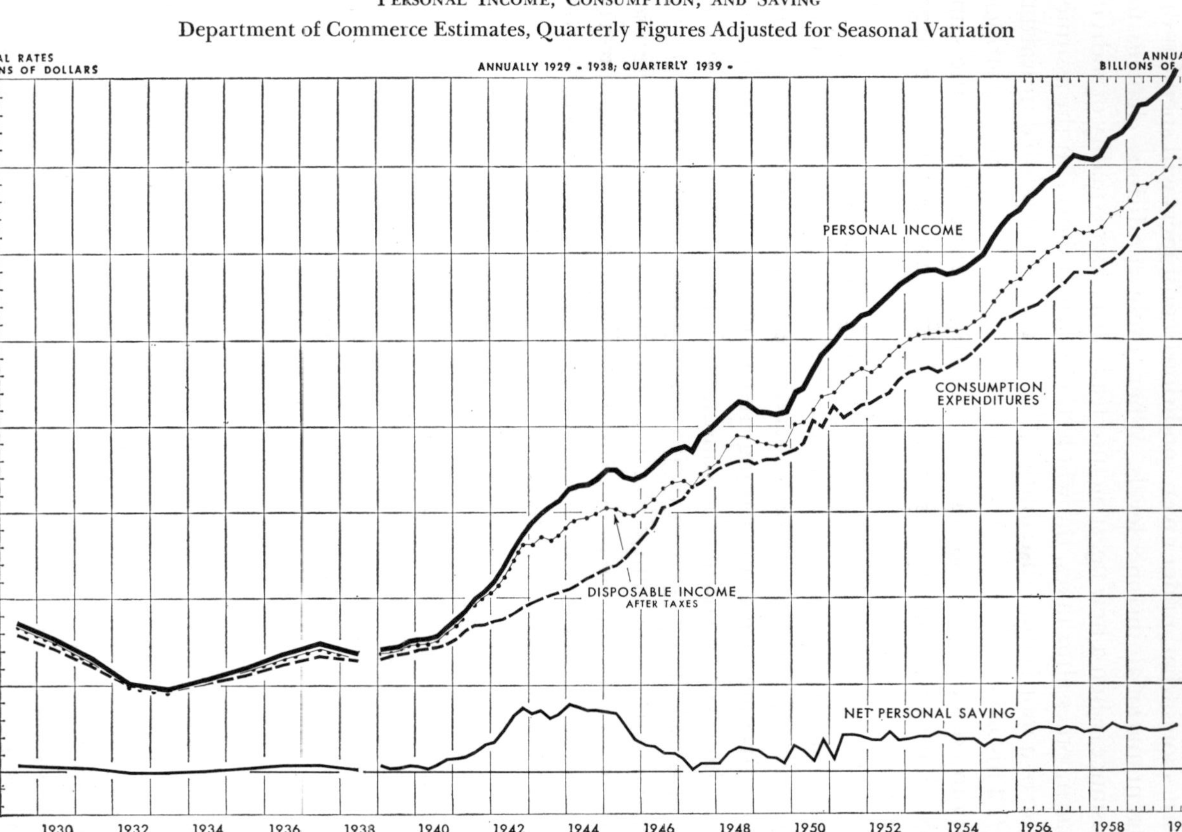

SOURCE: *Historical Supplement to Federal Reserve Chart Book on Financial and Business Statistics* (Washington, D.C.: Board of Governors of the Federal Reserve System, September, 1960), p. 84.

The *C* curve is an expression of the *average* propensity to consume, that is, the ratio of total consumption to total income, or C/Y. Thus at an income level of $90 billion the average propensity to consume would be 70/90. From the average propensity to consume we distinguish the *marginal* propensity to consume which is the ratio of a change in consumption to a change in income, or $\Delta C/\Delta Y$. Thus if income increases from $70 to 90 and consumption from $60 to 70 billion, the propensity to consume is at this margin 10/20, or 1/2. The marginal propensity to consume depends on the slope of the *C* curve as indicated in Figure 32–1. We shall see that the marginal propensity to consume plays an important part in the reaction of the national income to changes in investment.

Saving and Investment

In the discussion which follows we assume that the consumption function is relatively stable while private investment is subject to considerable change. We saw in Chapter 20 how many factors influence the investment demand schedule of loanable funds and how private investment depends on a comparison of rates of interest and the marginal efficiency of capital. We shall return to the determinants of investment when we discuss business cycles. Here we merely assume that the level of investment fluctuates and, most importantly that fluctuations of interest rates do *not* automatically call forth sufficient investment activity to instantly absorb the whole unconsumed part of the national income. This assumption is important because it marks the main point of departure of Keynesian from classical theory. The classical viewpoint was that saving would always call forth an equal amount of investment expenditure via changes of interest rates. The investment demand schedule was assumed to be always very interest elastic at low rates; in other words, it was taken for granted that an inexhaustible number and variety of investment opportunities are always eagerly waiting in a well-ordered line of decreasing marginal efficiency.

Modern economics has discarded this assumption. Some of the arguments used against the classical position are not very convincing, however. For instance, the assumption that we have reached a state of maturity in which lucrative investment outlets are very difficult to find. More satisfactory is the argument that the marginal efficiency of investment may be influenced by such factors as a temporary saturation of markets, a slowed rate of increase in consumers' spending, an increase in production costs, and, quite generally, a pessimistic business outlook. This broad interpretation of the marginal efficiency of investment made it possible to assume temporarily very low or even negative expected rates of return.

Correspondingly, in the theory of interest it was shown that rates of interest are not likely to fall far below such levels as, say, 3 or 2 per cent, owing to the very great elasticity of demand for cash balances at low rates. Thus it could be explained why the investment demand for loanable funds could temporarily fall below the level of intended savings.

For the classical theory it was difficult to admit this discrepancy between saving and investment, for it seemed as if an accumulation of uninvested savings would have to lead to such heavy pressure on interest rates that equality of savings and investments could not be delayed for long. The new theory shows, however, that the national income will shrink when investments fall short of intended savings because money which is spent on neither consumption nor investment cannot be received as income. And when national income falls, saving will decrease, as shown in Figure 23–1. This means that the savings which were supposed to exert the aforementioned pressure actually do not materialize.

Most important is the contention of the new theory that the equality of saving and investment is brought about not by an adjustment of interest rates but by changes in the national income and that, accordingly, the equilibrium position will only rarely be found at the full-employment income level.

Suppose that at full employment 20 per cent of the national income is saved but only 10 per cent is invested. The national income must now decrease by 10 per cent—and probably more, as we shall presently see—because money which has not been spent cannot be received as income. Whether the national income will be maintained at its new level depends again on the relation between investment and saving. Only if savings are far enough reduced or investments sufficiently increased to lead to equality between investment and saving will a new equilibrium be established.

Saving, Investment, and the Level of Income

Figure 23–2 may serve as a very simplified scheme by which we can determine the exact points of equilibrium under varying assumptions. To the consumption curve C we add the I function to get the $C + I$ curve, which indicates in a drastically simplified form what consumption plus investment expenditures would be at various income levels. Of course, in reality the I function is not constant over a wide range of income levels. But given the consumption function C and the investment function I, the corresponding level of national income will be found where $C + I$ intersects the 45° line. In Figure 23–2 the $C + I$ curve intersects the 45° line at point B, that is, at the income level of $80 billion, and we can see that only at this level will equilibrium exist,

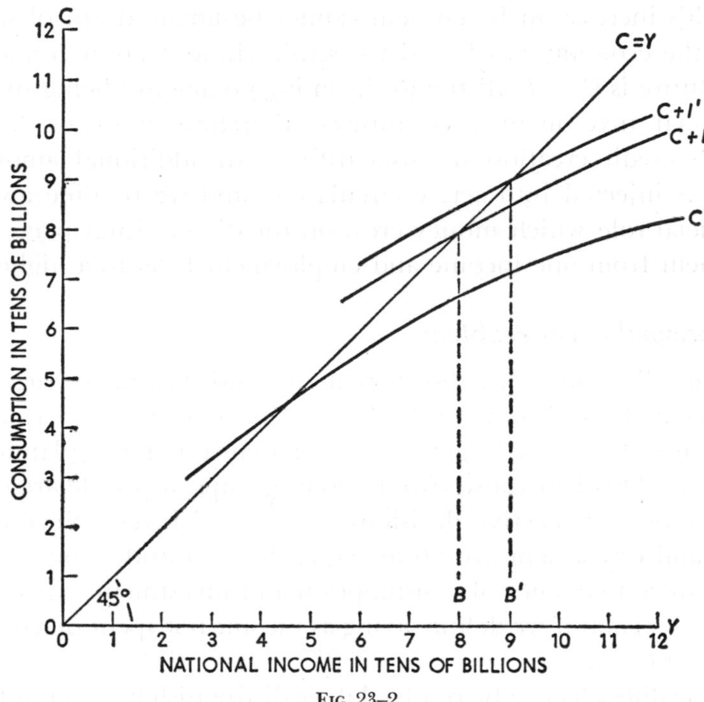

FIG. 23–2

because only here are savings and investments the same. If the national income is to be maintained, the sum of consumption and investment expenditures must be equal to the national income earned in consumption and investment goods production: $Y = C + I$. If we define saving as income not spent on consumption $S = Y - C$ and $Y = C + S$. It follows that in conditions of equilibrium $S = I$. We shall presently return to the terminological problems created by the fact that we are faced with situations in which intended savings are larger or smaller than investments and with equilibrium positions in which $S = I$ by definition.

Suppose now that the C curve remains the same as before but that the $C + I$ curve is pushed up to the position $C + I'$, that is, that investment increases by $5 billion. According to our previous analysis, equilibrium will now be established at point B' or at an income level of $90 billion, because only at this income level will savings and investments be equal. This result is interesting because it shows that a given increase in investment (the distance between the $C + I$ and the $C + I'$ curve) will give rise to a larger increase in income (the distance between B and B'). This is the so-called multiplier effect, which will be discussed in Chapter 24.

This increase in investment cannot be financed out of savings. When the economy has found its equilibrium at point B and total expenditure is $C + I$, all the forthcoming savings are being invested. Additional investment expenditures, therefore, must be financed through credit creation or dishoarding. An additional amount of money is injected into active circulation, and we become aware of the crucial role which money creation (or dishoarding) plays in the movement from one income and employment level to a higher one.

Terminological Problems

Our discussion has shown that, in equilibrium, saving equals investment. It is also probable that at any time intended (planned) savings may be either larger or smaller than intended (planned) investments. This is because two different groups of people are responsible for these respective decisions to save and invest. Nevertheless, saving and investment are always equal if we consider income to be earned in consequence of consumption and investment expenditures ($Y = C + I$) and if we define saving as income not spent on consumption ($Y = C + S$).

The difficulty can be resolved if we distinguish between intended and realized savings or between savings ex ante and ex post.[6] Ex ante, looking into the future, savings and investments may differ. Intended savings, for example, may fall short of planned investments. Investments can exceed savings because they can be financed by credit creation or dishoarding. An increased monetary circulation raises the national income. Ex post, looking backward, we find that the increased I has been matched by an equally increased S, since S is the nonconsumed (that is, invested) portion of the increased national income.

If we follow D. H. Robertson's period analysis,[7] we assume that money received as income in period 1 becomes available for spending

[6] This is the approach of the so-called Stockholm theory. See Bertil Ohlin, "Some Notes on the Stockholm Theory of Saving and Investment," *Economic Journal,* Vol. XLVII (March and June, 1937), reprinted in *Readings in Business Cycle Theory* (Homewood, Ill.: Richard D. Irwin, Inc., 1944).

[7] D. H. Robertson, "Saving and Hoarding," *Economic Journal,* Vol. XLII (September, 1933), p. 399.

in period 2, that is, "earned income" of period 1 becomes "disposable income" in period 2. Saving, according to this approach, is equal to the earned income of period 1 minus the consumption expenditure of period 2. Investment can be greater than saving because it can be financed out of sources other than saving (money creation, dishoarding). If investment is greater than saving, the earned income of period 2 and the disposable income of period 3 increase. Thus the discrepancy between *I* and *S* leads in this case to a rising income.

Keynesian analysis has stressed the *S*-equals-*I* terminology, sometimes to the point of awkwardness. For Keynes and his disciples it was often difficult to show how quantities which were said to be always identical by definition actually had to be made equal by a process of expansion or contraction. The Keynesian method of "implicit theorizing"[8] may sometimes have contributed to a certain disregard for the monetary factors of expansion and contraction.

Fortunately, it is not only easy but also very useful to combine the ex post or accounting identity of *S* and *I* (which has become indispensable for national income statistics) with the ex ante approach. The discrepancies between the ex ante and ex post quantities can serve as a convenient measure of the disequilibrating monetary forces with which our study is concerned.[9]

Income Levels and Interest Rates

How do the statements of this chapter tie in with the results of the loanable-funds theory discussed in Chapter 20? There we saw that the rate of interest is determined by the combined forces of supply of savings and credit creation on the one side and investment demand plus liquidity preference on the other. Since we limited ourselves to a two-dimensional picture we had to draw Figure 20–1, p. 273 without reference to changes in the national income, merely suggesting that such changes would have to be taken care of by shifts of our curves to the right or left. Nevertheless, it was obvious that the supply of savings is much more importantly influenced by changes in national income than by variations of interest rates. And in the present chapter we have seen that the four factors considered by the loanable-funds theory of interest are also factors which influence the level of income and employment and are, in turn, influenced by income changes. How can the two separate analyses be brought together?

[8] See W. Leontief, "Implicit Theorizing: a Methodological Criticism of the Neo-Cambridge School," *Quarterly Journal of Economics*, Vol. LI (1937), pp. 337 ff.

[9] See Edward S. Shaw, *Money, Income, and Monetary Policy* (Homewood, Ill.: Richard D. Irwin, Inc., 1950), pp. 352–53.

Alvin H. Hansen suggests the solution illustrated in Figure 23–3.[10] Equilibrium exists when $L = M$ (that is, when the volume of desired cash balances is equal to the quantity of money) and when $S = I$. Hansen uses an *LM* schedule which shows the relation between income and interest rates when $L = M$. The shape of the curve is based on the assumption that the desire to hold money depends on the size of the national income, so that with a *fixed* amount of money rates of interest will be high at high-income and low at low-income levels. We know already that even a relatively large supply of money cannot push

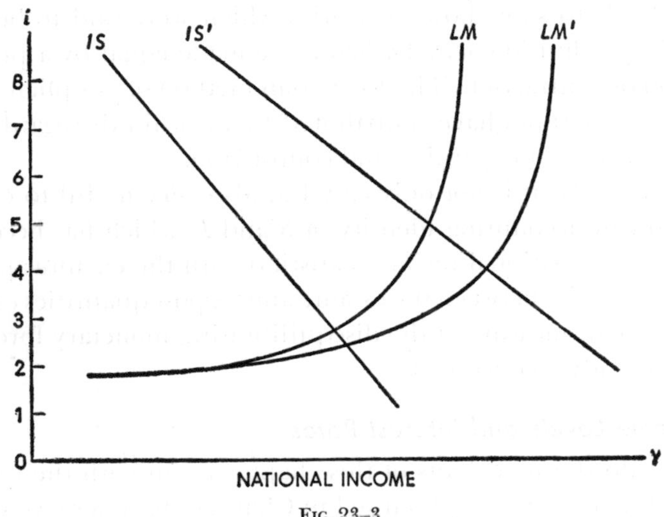

Fig. 23–3

rates of interest down very far at low-income levels, because the demand for liquid balances becomes very elastic at low rates. With high economic activity, on the other hand, the transaction demand for money is very brisk and will drive the rate of interest up unless the supply of money is sufficiently increased.

The shape of the *IS* curve is explained by the following considerations: with a given marginal efficiency of capital a high rate of interest permits only little investment; and since we have seen that the size of the national income is dependent on investment expenditures, high rates of interest lead, other things being equal, to low-income levels. Vice versa, with low rates of interest investment expenditures will increase so that the national income will be higher.

Hansen shifts the *IS* curve to the right when the marginal effi-

[10] Alvin H. Hansen, *Monetary Theory and Fiscal Policy* (New York: McGraw-Hill Book Co., Inc., 1949), chap. v.

ciency of investment increases, since this will lead to an increased investment demand for loanable funds at all interest levels and, therefore, also to an increase in national income. Similarly, an increased money supply will shift the *LM* curve to the right, since the larger transaction demand for money associated with an increase in income can now be accommodated at given levels of interest.

Hansen's picture enables us to indicate the effects of changes in money supply, liquidity preference, saving, and investment both on rates of interest and on income levels. We see that these factors determine simultaneously the interest rate and the income level at which $L = M$ and $I = S$.

SUGGESTIONS FOR FURTHER READING

DAY, A. C. L., and BEZA, STERIE T. *Money and Income,* chaps. 5–7. New York: Oxford University Press, 1960.

DUESENBERRY, JAMES S. *Income, Saving, and the Theory of Consumer Behavior.* Cambridge, Mass.: Harvard University Press, 1949.

HANSEN, ALVIN H. *Monetary Theory and Fiscal Policy,* chaps. 5 and 14. New York: McGraw-Hill Book Co., Inc., 1949.

HANSEN, ALVIN H. *Business Cycles and National Income,* chap. 12. New York: W. W. Norton & Co., Inc., 1951.

HICKS, J. R. "Mr. Keynes and the Classics, A Suggested Interpretation," *Econometrica,* April, 1937.

MORGAN, THEODORE. *Income and Employment,* chap. 12. 2d ed. New York: Prentice-Hall, Inc., 1952.

OHLIN, BERTIL. "Some Notes on the Stockholm Theory of Saving and Investment," *Economic Journal,* Vol. 47, 1937. Reprinted in *Readings in Business Cycle Theory* (Homewood, Ill.: Richard D. Irwin, Inc., 1944), chap. 5.

ROBERTSON, D. H. *Essays in Monetary Theory,* chap. 4. London: Staples Press, Ltd., 1940.

SHAW, EDWARD S. *Money, Income, and Monetary Policy,* chap. 15. Homewood, Ill.: Richard D. Irwin, Inc., 1950.

QUESTIONS AND PROBLEMS

1. "Monetary policy *alone* cannot even maintain stable prices, let alone a high level of employment; but adequate monetary management must be *one* of the instruments by which we try to manipulate aggregate expenditure." Explain.

2. "Classical theory assumed a permanent tendency toward equilibrium at full employment. Unemployment was assumed to be only frictional or voluntary." Discuss.
3. "The fundamental psychological law, upon which we are entitled to depend with great confidence . . . , is that men are disposed, as a rule and on the average, to increase their consumption as their incomes increase, but not by as much as the increase in their income" (J. M. Keynes). Discuss and illustrate with a diagram.
4. Explain the difference between average propensity to consume and marginal propensity to consume.
5. The classical viewpoint was that saving would always call forth an equal amount of investment expenditure via changes in the rate of interest. Modern theory, on the other hand, tries to show that the national income will shrink when investments fall short of intended savings. Illustrate both attitudes with diagrams.
6. Show graphically how an increase in investment changes the level of national income. Why is the marginal propensity to consume important in this process?
7. "At any given income level saving equals investment. Additional investment expenditures, therefore, must be financed through credit creation or dishoarding." Explain. What happens when investment falls?
8. "The difficulty with Keynesian terminology is that it tries to show how quantities which are identical by definition are *made* equal." Do you agree?
9. Discuss B. Ohlin's *ex ante* and *ex post* analysis of saving and investment.
10. Draw a graph which indicates the effects of changes in money supply, liquidity preference, saving, and investment both on rates of interest and income levels.

Chapter 24 MULTIPLIER AND ACCELERATION PRINCIPLE

Multiplier and Income Velocity of Circulation of Money

When newly created or dishoarded money has been spent for investment purposes, it has not yet exhausted its stimulating effect. We have to assume that a substantial part of the newly created money is spent on consumer's goods by those who earned it. The effect of this consumption spending in consequence of additional investment spending is referred to in modern literature as the multiplier.

To explain the meaning of the multiplier we assume that newly created money has been spent for wages of men newly employed in public or private investments. These wages are now spent on food, clothing, cigarettes, etc., that is, on consumers' goods. The money is received by retailers who place new orders with wholesalers, who in turn order new consumers' goods from the various producers. The money spent on wages is thus passed on to retailers, to wholesalers, and to those producers who participate, directly or indirectly, in the production of consumers' goods. In each of these different steps of trade or production, part of the money received is distributed as income among those who contribute to this particular stage, while the balance is passed on, as the purchase price of their product, to preceding stages, where again part of the money is distributed as income while the rest is passed on, and so on and so forth.

The process of distributing the dollars spent on shoes among retailers, wholesalers, shoe manufacturers, tanners, cattle raisers, etc., takes time. Some of the money spent on shoes becomes income of the retailer and his employees comparatively soon, but it may take a long time until all of it is distributed backwards among the ever-increasing number of people who are somehow contributing to the production of shoes. While the last cent of the original amount of money spent on consumers goods becomes "secondary" income in a remote stage of production, and with a considerable time lag, the secondary income of the retailer and his employees has already been spent once again on consumers' goods and has become "tertiary" income in other people's hands. As these people in turn use the money for the purchase of consumers' goods, the money seeps down again through many productive processes and contributes to the income of an ever widening circle of people working in stores, offices, and factories.[1]

These considerations are not new for us. We have already used the successive spending approach to explain the income velocity of circulation of money, which we expressed as either Y/M or M/Y. Suppose that the national income Y equals 100 and the total money supply M equals $50 billion. Y/M or 2/1 indicates the average number of times a unit of money enters the money reserves of ultimate income recipients during a year. This expression corresponds to V_y. M/Y, or 1/2, on the other hand, corresponds to k_y and indicates that the total of all money reserves is equal to half the national income.

If we say that the multiplier is 2, we do not refer to the fact that money completes its circular flow twice during one year. A multiplier of 2 means that an initial investment expenditure of newly created or dishoarded money will tend to raise the national income by twice the amount of the original expenditure. But a connection between a multiplier of 2 and an income velocity of 2 is suggested by the fact that if the relation of Y to M is 2 to 1, an increase in M should lead, via a multiplication of M by a velocity of 2, to an increase of the national income equal to twice the increase in M, so that the 2-to-1 ratio of Y and M is maintained.

Nevertheless, we must clearly distinguish between multiplier and income velocity for the following reasons:

1. The income velocity of money refers to the average income velocity of all money in circulation, while the multiplier analysis is concerned with the effect of newly created or dishoarded money and should, therefore, be compared only with the marginal income velocity of circulation of money.

2. The velocity of circulation of money refers to a definitive time period. If we say that the income velocity is 2, we refer to two completed circuits per year. To say that the multiplier is 2 means that an initial investment expenditure will eventually, but not necessarily within a year, tend to increase the national income by twice the amount of investment expenditure.

[1] See Fritz Machlup, "Period Analysis and Multiplier Theory," *Quarterly Journal of Economics,* Vol. LIV (November, 1939). Reprinted in *Readings in Business Cycle Theory* (Homewood, Ill.: Richard D. Irwin, Inc., 1944).

3. The multiplier analysis treats savings as leakages, while the income-velocity analysis interprets hoarded savings as a reduction of the income velocity, that is, as a lengthening of the income-turnover period.

Schematic Illustration of the Working of the Multiplier

To illustrate the working of the multiplier we make the following simplifying assumptions. To a given level of investment we add new investment expenditures of $100 at the beginning of each of a series of "multiplier periods." We call these expenditures "intial investment expenditures." They are the multiplicand of our multiplier. In each period, furthermore, only one half of the amount of newly earned income is spent on consumption. This means that the marginal propensity to consume is one half and remains one half throughout our analysis.

TABLE 24–1

Multiplier Period	Initial Investment Expenditures	Successive Re-spending (Unit: One Dollar)				
1...........	100					
2...........	100	50				
3...........	100	50	25			
4...........	100	50	25	12.50		
5...........	100	50	25	12.50	6.25	
6...........	100	50	25	12.50	6.25	3.125

The multiplier period is the average period of time which it takes before money received as income and spent on consumption becomes income again. Thus the "secondary" income earned in the second period becomes "tertiary" income in the third multiplier period. Of course, some of the secondary income is earned so fast and spent so soon that some tertiary income is certain to be received and even spent before all of the secondary income has been earned. The process is therefore much less orderly than it appears in Table 24–1.

It is obvious that we arrive at the same sum total whether we follow the effects of an initial investment diagonally through successive periods or whether we add, horizontally, the initial investment of one multiplier period plus the effects in this same period of previous investment expenditures. When carried to completion, both series will show an increase in income of $200. Since the initial investment expenditure was $100, the income multiplier (which relates the initial investment expenditure and the final increase in money income) is said to be two.

If the initial investment expenditures are continued, the national income approaches its new level rather quickly. In the six periods considered in our table, the national income is already increased by $196.875. It will eventually be increased by $200 and remain at this new level as long as the initial investment expenditures are continued at the rate of $100 per multiplier period. When the initial investment expenditures are discontinued, the national income will rather quickly fall back to its original level. The time needed to create this positive or negative effect depends on the length of the multiplier period.

Being by definition the result of consumption expenditures alone, the size of the multiplier is determined by the marginal propensity to consume. A marginal propensity to consume of *one* leads to a multiplier of *infinity*, a marginal propensity to consume of *zero* to a multiplier of *one*, and a marginal propensity to consume of *one half* to a multiplier of *two*.

If the marginal propensity to consume is a, the multiplier is found by the formula $\frac{1}{1-a}$. Thus a marginal propensity to consume of 2/3 leads to a multiplier of $\frac{1}{1-2/3}$, or 3, and a marginal propensity to consume of 3/4 leads to a multiplier of 4. Figures 23–1 and 23–2 (pp. 316 and 321) illustrated the case of a marginal propensity to consume of one half. As we increased investment by $5 billion, the national income found its new equilibrium at a level $10 billion higher than before. Suppose that the marginal propensity to consume is 2/3. A $5 billion increase in investment will now lead to a rise in income by $15 billion, as shown in Figure 24–1. If we make the *C* curve even steeper and assume a marginal propensity to consume of 3/4 and a multiplier of 4, the equilibrium level of the national income will be raised by $20 billion if investment increases by $5 billion. A marginal propensity to consume of one would mean that the *C* curve runs, for a stretch, parallel to the 45° line; a marginal propensity to consume of zero would means a *C* curve running parallel to the income axis.

Savings and Leakages

We have seen that the size of the multiplier depends on the marginal propensity to consume a, and since $1 - a$ is the marginal propensity to save, we can say that the multiplier is the reciprocal of the marginal propensity to save. If, for example, the marginal propensity to consume is 2/3, the marginal propensity to save is 1/3 and the multiplier is 3. To put it differently: if we assume a continued initial investment expenditure of $100, a multiplier of 3 will raise the national income by $300 and, since the marginal propensity to save is 1/3, the amount saved equals exactly the sum needed to finance a continued investment of $100, thus eliminating the need for a further creation of additional money. This result remains the same whichever our assumptions concerning the marginal propensities to consume and to save. Suppose that the marginal propensity to consume is 8/9, the marginal propensity to save 1/9, and the multiplier 9. Again the ninth part of the additional income is saved—enough to permit the permanent noninflationary financing of the continued investment expenditures needed to sustain the new income level.

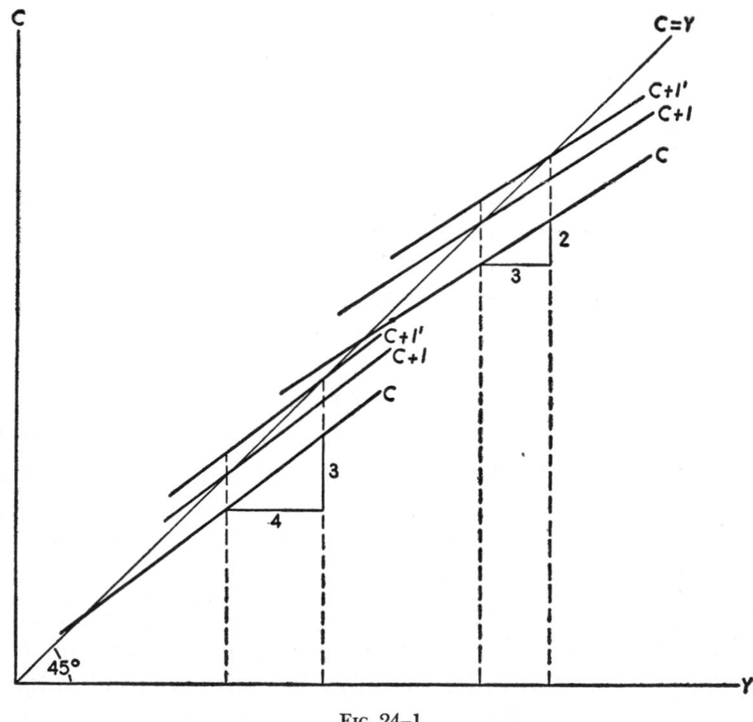

FIG. 24–1

The identity of the increments of saving and investment presupposes that a new equilibrium level has been reached, because only in equilibrium are saving and investment equal. It is obvious, therefore, that an *increase* in investment must at first be based on credit creation or dishoarding. In Figure 23–2 the equilibrium at point B rests on the assumption of $S = I$. If I is increased to I', for example, by $5 billion, these $5 billion must come from credit creation (or dishoarding). At point B', on the other hand, where the national income reaches its new equilibrium level, savings have grown by the exact amount needed to support the new investment and income level without recourse to further credit creation. The importance of this fact was already emphasized by R. F. Kahn in 1931 when he pointed out "that, *pari passu* with the building of roads, funds are released from various sources at precisely the rate that is required to pay the cost of the roads."[2]

So far we have assumed a "closed" system in which all expenditures are expenditures on home-produced goods. If our economy participates in international trade the newly earned income may be spent in part on foreign goods. In this case the multiplier effect will be felt in other countries, too, so that, at least for a time, the domestic multiplier effect is reduced. This "leakage," however, is a short-run effect only since increased imports will most likely lead to increased exports. We have to remember, furthermore, that the temporary leakage may well be compensated for by increasing exports resulting from increasing investment expenditures in other countries.

This positive effect which amounts to a transmission of prosperity from one country to another has its less pleasant counterpart in the case of a fall in investment, namely, a negative multiplier effect, felt both at home and abroad, and a contraction of international trade. We shall discuss the importance of this propagation of economic fluctuations from country to country in Chapter 30.

J. M. Clark treats as another leakage "the amount of the added purchasing power which is absorbed in increasing prices rather than increasing the volume of production and real incomes."[3] Whether we follow Clark's terminology is a question of taste; but his point can be used as a timely reminder that when arguing in terms of the income multiplier we are not allowed to infer that what increases money incomes necessarily increases employment. In translating the income multiplier into physical units, therefore, we must try to eliminate inflationary price rises, which are bound to occur when we reach bottle-

[2] Richard Ferdinand Kahn, "The Relation of Home Investment to Unemployment," *Economic Journal*, June, 1931, p. 189. Reprinted in Alvin H. Hansen and Richard V. Clemence, *Readings in Business Cycles and National Income* (New York: W. W. Norton & Co., Inc., 1953).

[3] J. M. Clark, *Economics of Planning Public Works* (Washington, D.C.: U.S. Government Printing Office, 1935), p. 89.

necks of production. The employment multiplier (which relates the men initially put to work to the ultimate total increase in employment) obviously stops working when "full" employment is reached, while the money-income multiplier can continue to operate indefinitely, though in a purely inflationary way of course.

The Principle of Acceleration of Derived Demand

The multiplier, as explained above, shows the effect upon income of an initial investment expenditure provided we consider only consumption expenditures. To be able to estimate the total effect of initial investment expenditures on income, we have to allow for the fact that a net increase in consumption will, in turn, induce further private investment.

First, retailers and wholesalers will increase their inventories if a net increase in consumption occurs and if it is their custom to keep their inventories in a fixed proportion to the rate of sales. A similar but often much stronger effect is to be expected when the increased demand is for the services of durable consumers' goods (such as houses, automobiles, refrigerators, and washing machines). To enjoy these services it is first of all necessary for the durable good to be produced. Thus the increased demand for services leads to an accelerated demand for goods which render these services. While an increase in income is likely to be only enough to allow regular payments for the services which are rendered—or to make small payments on the installment plan if one seeks to become the eventual owner of such goods—the demand cannot be satisfied unless the durable consumers' goods are first produced. The increased demand for services of durable consumers' goods leads, then, to an accelerated and magnified demand for the durable goods themselves. But the savings resulting from the working of the multiplier cannot cover the cost of this increased production; more loanable funds have to be created. These credits can take the form of loans to either the producers of the durable goods or the consumers who purchase them.

The greater the difference between the sales price of the service (for example, monthly rents or house payments) and the total cost of the durable goods (for example, house) or the greater the number of installments, the greater the magnification of an original increase in demand and the greater the opportunity for new investments, further credit expansion, and the initiation of new multiplier effects.

The principle of acceleration and magnification of derived demand does not work only in the case of durable consumers' goods. It can be stated quite generally that

since the production of any given amount of final output usually requires an amount of capital several times larger than the output produced with it during any short period (say a year) any increase in final demand will give rise to an additional demand for capital goods several times larger than that new final demand.[4]

A simple example will clarify the working of the acceleration principle. We assume that the production of consumers' goods such as shoes, electric fixtures, or cigarettes has been carried on at full capacity when, as a consequence of a general rise in income, the demand for consumers' goods increases by 10 per cent. We assume furthermore that in order to produce any one of these consumers' goods a considerable amount of fixed capital is needed. Let us say that to produce 1,000 units of consumers' goods per year we need 500 units of capital goods. These "units," constituting plant and equipment, have to be replaced at a rate which depends on their average durability. Assuming an average durability of 10 years, we have to replace 50 units each year, and the capital goods industry has to produce these 50 units to maintain the flow of 1,000 units of consumers' goods. Since we assumed that plant capacity was fully used, a 10 per cent increase in the demand for consumers' goods (from 1,000 to 1,100 units) will require 550 units of capital equipment instead of only 500. This new demand for investment goods, added to the normal replacement demand of 50 units, makes it necessary to raise the production of capital goods to 100 units, or by 100 per cent, as a reaction to an increase in consumption of only 10 per cent. Demand in the higher stages of production has thus been magnified and accelerated.

Our example raises some interesting points. Should the demand for consumers' goods increase again in the succeeding period, this time to 1,200 units, the net increase in the demand for capital goods would be only 5 units, as compared with a net increase of 50 units when consumers' demand previously increased from 1,000 to 1,100 units. The net increase of 5 results from 55 units total replacement demand plus the demand for 50 units of new investment goods, or a total of 105 units, as compared with the previous annual demand for 100 units.[5] Should the demand for consumers' goods remain at 1,200,

[4] F. A. Hayek, *Profits, Interest and Investment* (London: George Routledge & Co., 1939), pp. 18 ff.

[5] Since we can argue that new equipment will not be replaced during the first year of its life, it seems advisable to relate the replacement demand to the total of units of capital goods used in the previous period.

the investment goods industry, far from enjoying stable demand conditions, would experience a sharp decline in demand from 105 to only 60 units (which is the replacement demand of 600 units' capital equipment needed for continued production of 1,200 units of consumers' goods).

We can get even more drastic results if we assume that the demand for consumers' goods falls below the 1,200 level, for instance, back to 1,000 units. This assumption is justified by the logic of our example, which has already shown that a mere leveling out of consumers' demand leads to a drastic reduction of capital goods production. As employment falls in the investment goods industry, we must assume that, together with income, consumption will decrease. Since at a consumption level of 1,000 units the number of needed capital units falls back to 500, we must assume that the producer adjusts himself to this situation by the only means available to him: he will delay

TABLE 24–2

Demand for Consumers' Goods in Units	Units of Capital Goods Required to Satisfy Consumer Demand	Replacement Demand When Average Durability Is Ten Years	Expansion or New Demand for Capital	Total Demand for Capital Goods, i.e., Replacement Plus New Demand
1,000...........	500	50	none	50
1,100...........	550	50	50	100
1,200...........	600	55	50	105
1,200...........	600	60	none	60
1,000...........	500	10	none	10

replacements as long as is technically feasible. Let us assume that absolutely indispensable repairs amount to only 10 units. In this case the capital goods demand is temporarily reduced to this very small figure.

Our examples are summarized in Table 24–2.

These simplified examples show that the interrelation between consumers' demand and the "derived" demand for investment goods is of a highly sensitive nature. While superficial examination of currently favorable production statistics might give an impression of stability and equilibrium, the situation may actually be one of grave instability.

Our examples show that the degree of acceleration depends on the ratio between new demand and replacement demand and, therefore, on the durability of the investment goods. If we assume smaller replacement figures, that is, a greater durability of the capital equipment in question, the fluctuations of capital goods production tend to become more violent.[6] A durability of zero, on the other hand, would eliminate the working of the principle of acceleration.

The principle of acceleration of derived demand is so powerful a tool of analysis that it tends to overexplain the observed facts.[7] We hasten, therefore, to introduce several qualifications. First of all, we have to consider the possible existence of unused plant capacity. Obviously, the principle of acceleration does not apply when we are able to expand consumers' goods production without having to produce more investment goods. Furthermore, in case of a mere shift in demand from commodity A to commodity B the principle of acceleration does not have the same effect as in the case of an increase in the total demand for consumers' goods. It would be an overstatement, however, to say that there could be no acceleration of derived demand in this case. The effect of a mere shift in demand will depend, as Gottfried Haberler has pointed out,[8] on the comparative durability of the capital equipment in industries A and B, on the existence of unused plant capacity in industry B, and on whether the equipment of industry A can be used for the production of commodity B. Still another qualification is to be found in the expected nature of the increased demand for consumers' goods. If producers do not expect this increase to last, they will not increase their demand for capital goods.

Interaction of Multiplier and Acceleration Principle

Assuming continued initial investment expenditures and a given marginal propensity to consume, we can explain a net increase, though at a falling rate, in consumption expenditures. This net increase in consumption, in turn, induces further investment at a ratio which depends on such factors as the existence or nonexistence of unused plant capacity and the direction of the new demand. The ratio between a net increase in consumption and the induced investment is referred to as the "relation."[9] The relation, therefore, is a stenographic expression of the effect of the principle of acceleration.

Induced investments financed by newly created money are, in turn, starting points for new multiplier processes because they lead

6 For instance, if we assume an average durability of 20 years, our replacement figures would be 25, 25, 27.50, and 30, respectively. Since the expansion demand would be the same as in our previous example, total demand for capital goods would be 25, 75, 77.50, and 30.

7 R. F. Harrod, *The Trade Cycle* (Oxford: Clarendon Press, 1936), p. 58.

8 Gottfried Haberler, *Prosperity and Depression* (3d ed.; Lake Success, N.Y.: United Nations, 1946), pp. 96–97.

9 See Harrod, *op. cit.*, pp. 53–65.

to successive consumption expenditures. This further net increase in consumption again induces further investment.

Considering the combined effect of multiplier and acceleration we might be tempted to conclude that it is easy to extricate the economy from a state of depression by a relatively small amount of initial expenditures, which do not even have to be continued for long, provided induced investment expenditures are strong enough to carry on. But there is, as a rule, no such "possibility of raising the income to higher and higher levels by the process of lifting yourself by your bootstraps via the interrelation of increased consumption and increased investment in the familiar expansionist process."[10] We shall see that such a result is possible only if we make rather extreme assumptions concerning the marginal propensity to consume and the relation. We have to remember that the multiplier effect of continued equal amounts of initial spending is a limited one and that the multiplier leads to *rising* consumption expenditures only for a short time, after which consumption expenditures are only *maintained* as long as the initial investment expenditures are maintained.

The multiplier analysis explains how under certain assumptions a new income level will be reached, how soon it will be reached, how high it will be, and how it can be maintained. But it cannot explain fluctuations other than those which are already implied in its assumptions. Only fluctuations in initial expenditures or changes in the marginal propensity to consume will lead to fluctuations in income. If we combine the multiplier with the acceleration principle, we introduce a dynamic element which can explain fluctuations as well as permanent increases in national income, depending on our assumptions concerning the marginal propensity to consume and the relation.

Let us assume, for instance, that a net increase in consumption causes "induced" investment to increase by an equal amount. This assumption of a relation of one, added to our assumed marginal propensity to consume of one half, suffices to create damped fluctuations of income. The net increase in consumption leads, according to a relation of one, to an equal amount of induced investment which, financed by newly created money, is the starting point for a new multiplier effect. And since the increase in consumption due to induced investment induces still further investment, we can expect further dynamic effects. These effects, however, will decrease in their quanti-

[10] Alvin H. Hansen, *Fiscal Policy and Business Cycles* (New York: W. W. Norton & Co., Inc., 1941), pp. 283–84.

tative importance the more remote they are from the original stimulus, when the initial investment led to a substantial net increase in consumption.

Table 24–3 illustrates the combined working of multiplier and acceleration. We add to our schematic picture of the multiplier (see p. 329) the further assumption that each *net increase* in consumption over the preceding period causes *induced investment* of an equal amount and that a net decrease in consumption reduces induced investment by the same figure. In other words, the "relation" is assumed to be one. Together with a marginal propensity to consume of 0.5 and an initial investment expenditure of $100 in each multiplier period, we get the results shown in Table 24–3.

The first initial investment expenditure of $100 marks an increase in national income by the same amount (columns 2 and 8). In the second period $50 is spent on consumers' goods (column 3) according to our assumption of a marginal propensity to consume of 0.5. Since consumption expenditure has increased by $50 (column 7) and since the relation is one, induced investment, too, is $50 (column 4). The total effect on national income is $200, namely, initial investment $100, plus $50 multiplier effect of initial investment in the preceding period, plus $50 induced investment.

In the third period we have to consider the multiplier effect of both the initial investment expenditures and of induced investment (columns 3 and 5). Since the net increase in consumption is again $50, induced investment, too, must be $50. The total income effect for the third period is $250.

Since in the fourth period the net increase in consumption is only $25, induced investment, though still positive, is also only $25, and the total income effect remains the same as before, namely, $250. In the fifth period total consumption expenditures are the same as in the fourth period, there is no net increase in consumption and no induced investment. Now the total income effect shows an absolute decline, which continues in the sixth period. Since the sixth period shows a net decline in consumption expenditure, we must also record a net decline of induced investment because our assumed relation is one.

Now we can see that the combined working of multiplier and acceleration causes the national income to increase more and to rise faster than under the influence of the multiplier alone. But we can also see that the national income does not stay on the higher level. Depending on our assumptions concerning the marginal propensity

TABLE 24–3

1	2	3					4	5				6	7	8
Period	Initial Investment	Successive Re-spending					Induced Investment	Successive Re-spending				Total Consumption Expenditure	Net Increase or Decrease in Consumption	Total Income Effect
1........	100						—					—	—	100
2........	100	50					50					50	50	200
3........	100	50	25				50	25				100	50	250
4........	100	50	25	12.50			25	25	12.50			125	25	250
5........	100	50	25	12.50	6.25		—	12.50	12.50	6.25		125	—	225
6........	100	50	25	12.50	6.25	3.125	−12.50	—	6.25	6.25	3.125	112.50	−12.50	200

TABLE 24–4

1	2	3					4	5				6	7	8
Period	Initial Investment	Successive Re-spending					Induced Investment	Successive Re-spending				Total Consumption Expenditure	Net Increase or Decrease in Consumption	Total Income Effect
1........	100						—							100
2........	100	50					100					50	50	250
3........	100	50	25				150	50				125	75	375
4........	100	50	25	12.50			125	75	25			187.50	62.50	412.50
5........	100	50	25	12.50	6.25		37.50	62.50	37.50	12.50		206.25	18.75	343.75
6........	100	50	25	12.50	6.25	3.125	−68.75	18.75	31.25	18.75	6.25	171.87	−34.375	203.125

to consume and the relation, we can expect damped fluctuations of the national income or even inflationary explosions.[11]

Table 24–4 indicates what our results would be if we assumed a marginal propensity to consume of 0.5 and a relation of two.

Our examples assumed that marginal propensity to consume, relation, and initial spending per multiplier period remain the same throughout the process. In reality, of course, these ratios and quantities are constantly changing, since they are all more or less sensitive to variations in employment and income. The relation, for instance, depends on the existence of unused plant capacity, which dwindles as economic activity increases, and on the rate of interest, which in turn depends on the many factors discussed in Chapter 20. The marginal propensity to consume is influenced by the distribution of investment expenditures between wages and profits, by changes in income distribution, by the state of individual indebtedness (for example, debt repayments versus consumption expenditures), and by inflation and deflation and their influence on consumer spending. Multiplier and acceleration, while they supply us with interesting models of economic fluctuations, do not permit us, therefore, to dispense with a far more painstaking analysis of the phenomena of the business cycle.

Our discussion has limited itself to the positive case of an increase in initial investment expenditure and has considered decreasing investment expenditures only in connection with induced investment. It should be obvious that our arguments apply also in reverse, that is, that a decrease in investment spending leads to a multiple contraction

[11] See Paul A. Samuelson, "Interaction between the Multiplier Analysis and the Principle of Acceleration," *Review of Economic Statistics*, May, 1939, pp. 75–78, reprinted in *Readings in Business Cycle Theory* (Homewood, Ill.: Richard D. Irwin, Inc., 1944). If α is the marginal propensity to consume and β the "relation," the model sequences of national income for selected values of α and β are shown by Professor Samuelson in the following table:

Period	$\alpha = .5$ $\beta = 0$	$\alpha = .5$ $\beta = 2$	$\alpha = .6$ $\beta = 2$	$\alpha = .8$ $\beta = 4$
		(Unit: one dollar)		
1.	1.00	1.00	1.00	1.00
2.	1.50	2.50	2.80	5.00
3.	1.75	3.75	4.84	17.80
4.	1.875	4.125	6.352	56.20
5.	1.9375	3.4375	6.6256	169.84
6.	1.9688	2.0313	5.3037	500.52
7.	1.9844	0.9141	2.5959	1,459.592
8.	1.9922	−0.1172	−0.6918	4,227.704
9.	1.9961	0.2148	−3.3603	12,241.1216
. .	. . . . .	. . . .	. . . .	. . . .

of the national income according to the assumed value of the multiplier. This can easily be demonstrated if, in Figures 23–2 and 24–1, we assume a decrease in investment and watch how the national income finds its new equilibrium at an income level perhaps several times lower than the fall in investment expenditure.

SUGGESTIONS FOR FURTHER READING

DUESENBERRY, JAMES S. *Business Cycles and Economic Growth.* New York: McGraw-Hill Book Co., Inc., 1958.

HABERLER, GOTTFRIED. *Propensity and Depression,* chaps. 8, 10 and 13. 3d ed. New York: United Nations, 1952.

HANSEN, ALVIN H. *Fiscal Policy and Business Cycles,* chap. 12. New York: W. W. Norton & Co., Inc., 1941.

HANSEN, ALVIN H. *Business Cycles and National Income,* chaps. 10–11. New York: W. W. Norton & Co., Inc., 1951.

HARROD, ROY F. *The Trade Cycle.* Oxford: Clarendon Press, 1936.

KAHN, RICHARD F. "The Relation of Home Investment to Unemployment," *Economic Journal,* Vol. 41, 1931. Reprinted in Hansen, Alvin H., and Clemence, Richard V., *Readings in Business Cycles and National Income,* chap. 15. New York: W. W. Norton & Co., Inc., 1953.

Readings in Business Cycle Theory, part iii. Homewood, Ill.: Richard D. Irwin, Inc., 1944.

SHAW, EDWARD S. *Money, Income, and Monetary Policy,* chap. 16. Homewood, Ill.: Richard D. Irwin, Inc., 1950.

TSIANG, S. C. "Liquidity Preference and Loanable Funds Theories, Multiplier and Velocity Analyses," *American Economic Review,* Vol. XLVI (September, 1956).

QUESTIONS AND PROBLEMS

1. "To say that the multiplier is two and to say that the income velocity of circulation of money is two means to make entirely different statements." Explain.
2. Illustrate the working of the multiplier under the following assumptions: initial expenditure in each multiplier period is 200; the marginal propensity to consume is three fourths. What would your results be if the marginal propensity to consume were two thirds, one half, one, and zero, respectively?
3. Show graphically how an increase in investment raises the national income by an amount equal to the increase in investment times the multiplier. Identify the marginal propensity to consume in your diagram.

4. Discussing the case for public works, R. F. Kahn points out that "it is always within the power of the banking system to advance to the Government the cost of the roads without in any way affecting the flow of investment along the normal channels. For . . . *pari passu* with the building of roads, funds are released from various sources at precisely the rate that is required to pay the cost of the roads." Interpret.
5. Why did the theorists who developed the multiplier analysis consider only consumption expenditures? Was it justifiable to treat savings as leakage?
6. Explain the principle of acceleration of derived demand under the following assumptions: the demand for a consumers' good increases in the first year from 10,000 units to 11,000 units, in the second year to 12,000 units, in the third to 13,000, stays at 13,000 in the fourth year, and falls to 12,000 units in the fifth. The average durability of capital goods is assumed to be 20 years; 300 units of capital goods are required to produce 10,000 units of the consumer good, 330 to produce 11,000 units, etc. Would your results be different if you assumed the average durability to be 10 years?
7. Assuming the marginal propensity to consume to be one half and the "relation" to be three, show the total income effect of an initial investment of $100 in each period through five periods.

Chapter 25 ECONOMIC FLUCTUATIONS

Business Cycles

Business cycles are successions of periods of prosperity and depression sufficiently uniform to suggest a typical pattern. Special historical circumstances explain why no two cycles are completely alike; and while business fluctuations have recurred with a certain regularity, they were never rigidly periodic. Business cycles, furthermore, are only one ingredient in that mixture of varying business conditions which is so characteristic of the history of capitalism. They are, as it were, statistically distilled from data which are also influenced by seasonal variations, "minor" cycles (which concern inventory changes), general development trends, and, possibly, sudden structural changes. Even the most skillful statistical manipulation cannot cleanly separate these closely interwoven strands. In particular, economic theory does not provide us with a "norm" around which the business cycle fluctuates. Is this norm supposed to be economic activity at "full" employment? In that case the peaks of the cycle would be inflationary excursions into the area of overfull employment. But we know of cycles which turned down before full employment was reached. The equilibrium theory of Keynes, on the other hand, while more realistic than its classical counterpart, offers no definite income or employment level which could be regarded as normal.

Historically speaking, the length of the business cycle has varied between 7 and 10 years for reasons which will be indicated below. We cannot tell whether we shall find the same pattern in the future, since it is our hope to dampen these cyclical fluctuations. The policies used to this end may, if successful, change both the amplitude of the swings and their duration.

A typical cyclical movement of the economy conforms to the pattern of Figure 25–1. This Figure also indicates the terms commonly used in discussions concerning business cycles. In our picture the cycle fluctuates around an upward trend line, indicating an expanding economy. This assumption makes the upswing more pronounced and mitigates the downswing. We note that the upper turning point does not have to be marked by a crisis and that the lower turning point may be a stretch rather than a point, in which case we speak of a stagnation.

The major characteristics of the business cycle are fluctuations in employment, output, and money income, and the most drastic changes occur in the investment goods industries—as our discussion of the acceleration principle suggested. Durable consumers' goods like residential buildings and automobiles will have to be considered similar in many respects to capital goods. The rest of the economy

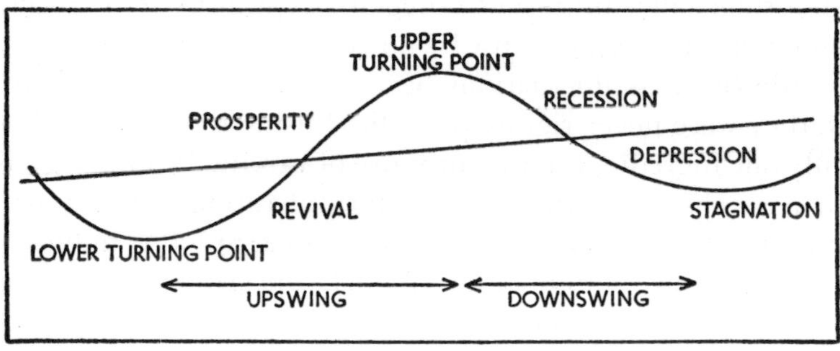

Fig. 25–1

will also be exposed to ups and downs but will fluctuate to a lesser degree; as a matter of fact, many data of a not strictly economic nature will be affected by the state of business, such as political movements, marriages, and births.

Economic depressions have created untold hardships, particularly for those who were willing and able to work but who could not find employment. This personal tragedy must not again be allowed to strike millions of people. The recurrence of mass unemployment would endanger our democratic way of life. The elimination of depression and stagnation must be the first aim of economic policy. But before such a policy can be successfully undertaken, we must understand the causes of economic instability.

Neither the classical nor the Keynesian equilibrium theory explains why the capitalist economy is subject to changes which lead away from rather than towards equilibrium. Exogenous factors like weather, war, or inventions are not sufficient explanations, since they would account for only disturbances and adjustments but not wave-like, self-aggravating movements—movements which temporarily lead away from equilibrium but which are somehow finally forced to reverse themselves. It has been suggested, therefore, that it is not so much these outside impulses but the very nature of the economic system, reacting to these impulses, that constitutes our chief problem. The analogies of the rocking chair and the pendulum have been used to describe the tendency of the capitalist economy to transform irregular pushes into more or less regular swings. Our model of the combined working of the multiplier and acceleration principles suggests the type of quality which makes our market economy subject to cyclical fluctuations.

The "outside" shocks, however, are also of great importance for understanding the ups and downs in economic activity. Knut Wicksell, for instance, believed that the principal and sufficient cause of cyclical fluctuations should

> be sought in the fact that in its very nature technical and commercial advance cannot maintain the same even progress as does the increase in needs . . . but is sometimes precipitate, sometimes delayed. . . . Since new discoveries, inventions, and other improvements nearly always require various kinds of preparatory work for their realization, there occurs the conversion of large masses of liquid into fixed capital which is an inevitable preliminary to every boom and indeed is probably the only fully characteristic sign, or at any rate one which cannot conceivably be absent. If, again, these technical improvements are already in operation and no others are available . . . there will come a period of depression; people will . . . retain the capital as far as possible in a liquid, available form.[1]

From our discussion of Wicksell's theory of interest we know that Wicksell was fully aware of the monetary implications of the problem. But he thought that they were of only secondary importance "although in real life they nevertheless play an important and even a dominating part in the development of crises."[2]

In what follows we consider the theory of the business cycle only to the extent required for a fuller understanding of the aims of modern monetary policy. Since the most ambitious monetary aim is a high sustained level of employment, monetary policy cannot help being business-cycle policy, and it is imperative for us to study the role that money plays—*or may be made to play*—during the different

[1] Knut Wicksell, *Lectures on Political Economy*, Vol. II, *Money* (New York: Macmillan Co., 1935), pp. 211–12.

[2] *Ibid.*, p. 209.

phases of the cycle. Only then shall we be able to see how monetary and fiscal policies should be combined to achieve the desired results.

Deficiencies in Demand

Perhaps the oldest attempted explanation of crisis and depression is the so-called underconsumption theory with its counterpart, the theory of general overproduction. In Chapter 10 we have seen how Say and Mill tried to refute this theory by the assertion that should we double supply we should also double demand since commodities are exchanged for commodities. We noticed, however, that Say and Mill made some monetary assumptions which were not justifiable. Prices and costs do not fall simultaneously and proportionately in the case of a stable money supply and growing production, nor can we be sure that an additional money supply will be automatically forthcoming when a larger volume of exchanges has to be transacted. Furthermore, both Say and Mill admitted the possibility of partial overproduction and, therefore, the development of disproportionality in the structure of the economy.

Our study of monetary policy and practice has shown that money can become a disturbing element in the following two cases:

1. Part of the purchasing power received through sales may be hoarded and fail to reappear as demand. Money earned has then been spent on neither consumption nor investment goods, as shown in the circular-flow diagrams of Chapter 2.

2. The money supply may not expand sufficiently to prevent a fall in prices, and the fall in prices may not be a simultaneous and proportionate decline of all prices, thus disturbing the price and cost structure. This can be caused, for instance, by the prevalence of monopoly conditions in some industries or by an organized labor force which opposes a downward adjustment of money wage rates.

We see, therefore, that deficiencies in demand may be caused by a monetary policy which overestimates either the ease of securing general adjustments in price levels or the ability of the monetary authority to increase total expenditure.

It is clear that an increase in liquidity preference or a deficiency in investment expenditures can be the main cause of inadequate aggregate demand. As long as savings are invested, however, there is no truth to the theory that increased saving results in underconsumption, that is, deficient aggregate demand. It is of course true that saving decreases the demand for consumers' goods, and it is also true that investment in capital goods serves to increase the supply of consumers' goods. But it is wrong to combine these last two statements for the purpose of showing that an increased supply of consumers' goods is faced by decreased aggregate demand.[3] Invested savings do not result in a deficiency of aggregate expenditure. We have seen how saving performs the function of reducing consumption in favor of investment. In a state of full employment saving is an indispensable precondition of investment if price inflation is to be avoided. When, in the future, the newly produced capital goods help to lower the unit cost of production of consumers' goods and when commodity prices are forced down by competition, then it is not at all necessary that consumer demand should be deficient. Those who contrast a decrease in consumption (saving) with an increased output of consumers' goods via investment forget that the two events are not simultaneous owing to the time-consuming character of capital goods production. Thus the decreased demand for consumers' goods will first be compensated for by an increased demand for producers' goods; and when, later on, the producers' goods help to decrease unit costs, they lead to the aforementioned decrease in prices. As the price of consumers' goods falls, purchasing power is set free to absorb the additional output.

Keynesian analysis, however, suggests one basic difficulty: as national income increases, saving increases proportionately more than consumption; and consumption may not be sufficient, after a while, to induce enough investment to absorb all intended savings. This corresponds to the assumptions on which the principle of acceleration rests and explains why an expansion process may have to reverse itself.

Monetary Theories of Economic Fluctuations

The proposition that an ideal money economy does not experience cyclical fluctuations rests on the assumption of a perfectly "neutral" behavior of money. And since, as shown in Chapters 3 and 10,

[3] The best example of this type of argument is found in W. T. Foster and W. Catchings, *Profits* (Boston: Houghton Mifflin Co., 1925); also characteristic is the following passage in Joan Robinson, *Introduction to the Theory of Employment* (London: Macmillan & Co., Ltd., 1938), pp. 4–5: "The mere fact that individuals want to save part of their incomes to add to their private wealth does nothing to encourage entrepreneurs to expect a greater profit from capital. The profitability of capital goods depends upon the demand for the consumption goods which they produce. Thus if individuals decide to save, that is, not to spend on immediate consumption, they reduce rather than increase the motive of the entrepreneurs for acquiring new capital goods, and the decision to save reduces the demand for consumption goods without increasing the demand for capital goods." The difference between Joan Robinson and Foster and Catchings is that Mrs. Robinson assumes that the entrepreneurs are so convinced that they will not be able to sell consumers' goods when people save that they do not even begin to invest.

the conditions of perfect neutrality are extremely difficult to fulfill, it is easy to arrive at an apparent monetary explanation of fluctuations in economic activity. Indeed, some writers tend to blame business cycles entirely on the modern central banking system which alternately expands and contracts credit.

The basic idea of the monetary cycle theory can best be grasped when the cycle is understood as a succession of inflationary and deflationary processes. To be sure, these processes need be neither explosive nor implosive; they stop, as a rule, before hyperinflation has been reached and, certainly, before everybody has become unemployed. But the upswing is a cumulative inflationary process which, if not primarily caused by credit expansion is at least supported by it. We have seen this process result from a discrepancy between the natural and market rates of interest.[4] The process comes to an end when the central bank forces the commercial banks to discontinue further credit creation. Increased demand for currency as a result of increased economic activity and higher wage income will reduce the commercial banks' reserves, and the central bank may not be able or willing to supply additional reserves. Interest rates will rise, and this will disappoint those who based their investment decisions on the artificially low rates which prevailed earlier during the upswing.

With the sudden falling off of investment a cumulative deflationary process is started. Unemployment in the capital goods industries leads to a decrease in consumers' demand, to accumulation of unsold stocks of goods, to cancellation of orders, and to a further fall in investment. Finally the process comes to a halt. With reduced economic activity, currency flows back to the banks, the banks' liquidity increases, and interest rates gradually fall to very low levels in the absence of a desire to borrow for investment purposes. Eventually, when the downward trend of commodity prices has stopped, very low rates of interest may induce new borrowing, the banks will be able to expand credit, and the cycle can begin once more.

A discrepancy of market and natural rates of interest can be explained in several ways. According to Ludwig von Mises[5] it is due simply to a prevailing inflationist ideology which forces the central banks into expansionist policies; R. G. Hawtrey[6] suggests that it may

[4] See Chapter 3, pp. 30–31 and Chapter 20, pp. 276–279.

[5] L. von Mises, *Geldwertstabilisierung und Konjunkturpolitik* (Jena: Gustav Fischer, 1928), p. 58.

[6] R. G. Hawtrey, *Currency and Credit* (London: Longmans, Green & Co., 1928), p. 155.

be caused by the influence of a gold inflow upon the discount rate; and F. A. Hayek[7] assumes that the artificial lowering of the rate of interest is the result of the inherent elasticity of the modern money and credit system.

When the market rate of interest is kept below the natural rate, the demand for loanable funds is larger than the supply of voluntary savings, and the difference is made up by creation of money. Whether prices will increase as a result of this credit inflation depends on the development of the trade volume,[8] but prices will eventually rise as full utilization of resources is approached and as bottlenecks of production begin to appear. It is important to note that rising prices do not help to check this process of expansion but, on the contrary, stimulate the cumulative development. A given market rate of interest means a decreasing "real" or "commodity" rate if it is corrected for upward changes in the general price level. If prices rise by 3 per cent per annum, a market rate of less than 3 per cent becomes, in effect, a minus rate of interest, and a market rate of 7 per cent becomes a 4 per cent rate. In other words, what the creditor earns in the form of interest he may lose in the form of decreased purchasing power at the time the loan is paid back—and the debtor gains accordingly. Thus we see that price inflation will lead to an increased demand for credit and to pressure for further credit creation.[9] The anticipation of rising prices, furthermore, will lower the inducement to save and increase the velocity of circulation of money.

The counterpart of this stimulation via price inflation is the deflationary burden which deepens depressions. Deflation hurts the debtor. As Irving Fisher put it:

> Each dollar debt, still unpaid, becomes a bigger dollar. . . . The liquidation cannot keep up with the fall of prices which it causes. In that case the liquidation defeats itself. While it diminishes the number of dollars owed, it may not do so as fast as it increases the value of each dollar owed. . . . Then we have the great paradox which is the chief secret of most, if not all great depressions: the more the debtors pay the more they owe.[10]

It can easily be seen that under these conditions the real rate of

[7] F. A. Hayek, *Monetary Theory and the Trade Cycle* (London: Harcourt, Brace & Co., Inc., 1932), chap. iv.

[8] See Chapter 3.

[9] See Irving Fisher, *The Theory of Interest* (New York: Macmillan Co., 1930); Mises, *op. cit.*, pp. 51 ff., speaks of a positive and negative price premium.

[10] Irving Fisher, "The Debt-Deflation Theory of Great Depressions," *Econometrica*, Vol. I (1933), pp. 344 ff.

interest is far higher for the borrower than the market rate indicates.

That the inflationary process may be explosive and that prices may rise to astronomical dimensions has been shown by inflationary developments after both World War I and World War II. As a rule, however, a prosperity phase ends without having produced such sensational results. As long as the countries of the world adhered to the rules of the gold-standard mechanism, it was easy to see that if credit expansion in any one country exceeded that in other countries, the first country would experience a gold outflow and credit restriction. But after World War I no such simple explanation was possible. Nevertheless, it can be argued that central banks must sooner or later apply the brakes to credit expansion.

F. A. Hayek suggests that an expansion of investment permitted by voluntary saving is not dangerous, while investment financed by inflationary credit expansion must eventually lead to a process of contraction, deflation, and depression. Suppose that the commercial banks have ample reserves, that they expand credit, and that interest rates do not rise in response to an increased desire to borrow. Investment, therefore, rises beyond the limits set by voluntary saving. The cumulative process begins: wages, money incomes, and the demand for consumers' goods increase. This raises the demand for currency relatively more than the demand for deposit money, reduces the liquidity of the commercial banks, drives up the market rate of interest, and renders unprofitable those investments which were calculated on the basis of abnormally low market rates.[11]

A second reason which Hayek gives for the discontinuation of the expansion process in the capital goods industry is an application of the so-called Ricardo effect. Ricardo's proposition was that a rise in wages will encourage capitalists to substitute machinery for labor, while a fall in wages leads to substitution of labor for capital. Hayek argues that the cumulative process of expansion leads to an increased demand for consumers' goods and, since investment goods production rather than consumers' goods production has been expanded, to a rise in consumers' goods prices, that is, to a fall in real wages. Thus, as real wages decrease, entrepreneurs tend to substitute labor for capital,

[11] Hayek, *op. cit.* It is interesting to note that Hayek and Keynes, though in most other respects miles apart, come here, for once, close together: in Keynes' *General Theory* the rate of interest rises owing to an increased demand for money for transaction purposes, and this rise together with a sudden collapse in the marginal efficiency of capital brings about the crisis. Compare *The General Theory of Employment, Interest and Money* (London: Macmillan & Co., Ltd., 1936), p. 315.

that is, to invest less than before. The fall in investment initiates the depression.[12]

Several things can be said against this theory: (1) Entrepreneurs do not calculate in terms of real wages. (2) Factors of production cannot be shifted with ease from longer to shorter processes. (3) Investment processes, once begun, must be brought to a technical conclusion to avoid complete loss of already expended funds. (4) A rise in money wages may well outweigh the rise in consumers' goods prices.

Overinvestment Theories

Monetary theories which emphasize the artificial lowering of interest rates through credit creation plausibly account for the major characteristics of the business cycle: the fluctuations in employment, output, and money income. They can also explain why investment goods production should show the widest swings. Investment depends on a comparison of anticipated profits with prevailing interest rates, and cheap money is likely, therefore, to stimulate investment goods production. However, the importance of the marginal efficiency of investment in this connection shows why a purely monetary explanation could not be complete.

Many writers have tried to explain why investment goods production proceeds by leaps and bounds rather than evenly. Wicksell reminds us, as we have seen, that "in its very nature technical and commercial advance is sometimes precipitate, sometimes delayed." M. Tugan-Baranowsky suggests that only when the accumulation of savings has pressed down the rate of interest far enough will loanable funds be turned into capital.[13] Schumpeter points out that while inventions may be continuous, innovations (that is, the introduction of new techniques, new organizational methods, etc.) are discontinuous since they depend on the initiative of the "entrepreneur"; and that it is easy for the herd to follow the leader once the first step has been taken.[14]

Particularly interesting is the overinvestment theory of Arthur

[12] F. A. Hayek, *Prices and Production* (New York: Macmillan Co., 1932); F. A. Hayek, *Profits, Interest and Investment* (London: George Routledge & Co., 1939). See also G. Haberler's criticism in *Prosperity and Depression* (3d ed.; Lake Success, N.Y.: United Nations, 1946), pp. 481–91.

[13] M. Tugan-Baranowsky, *Studien zur Theorie und Geschichte der Handelskrisen in England* (Jena: Gustav Fischer, 1901).

[14] Joseph A. Schumpeter, *The Theory of Economic Development* (Cambridge, Mass.: Harvard University Press, 1934).

Spiethoff,[15] for it attempts to explain the nature of the disproportionality in the structure of production caused by overinvestment. Spiethoff assumes that at the end of a period of depression the banking system is liquid, that interest rates are low, and that unused plant capacity, high inventories, and unemployed labor account for low prices and wages. Nevertheless, new investment will not start without new investment opportunities. If businessmen anticipate profits, however, a process of reactivating unemployed productive resources will be made possible through an expansion of credit. Once started the upswing develops as a cumulative process. Investment expenditures increase the demand for productive resources together with their prices, so that profits are now generally high. The end result of this process, however, will not be a state of equilibrium since grave disproportionalities will have developed in the structure of the economy. The capital goods industry will have been overdeveloped.

Spiethoff distinguishes three economic activities: the production of investment goods, saving, and the purchase of investment goods with savings. Since those who save and those who produce investment goods are different people who do not know of each other's actions, a disproportionality between savings and investments will develop.

In the earlier part of the upswing savings tend to outrun the production of investment goods, and since investment goods are bought with savings, their prices tend to increase and profits are high; and out of high profits come more savings, which propel the expansion process still further. During the later stages of the upswing, however, the position is reversed. While, with completion of the technical investment processes, more and more capital goods (and services rendered by capital goods) come to the market, the demand for these goods, which depends on savings, falls off, and prices decline. This situation constitutes a case of general overinvestment.

As wages increase, profits, the main source of savings, decrease. And since Spiethoff does not distinguish carefully between saving and credit creation, we may speculate that credit creation will be stopped to avoid dangerous price inflation once "full" employment is reached. The reduction of savings and the stoppage of credit creation lead to higher rates of interest.

15 Arthur Spiethoff, "Krisen," *Handwörterbuch der Staatswissenschaften* (4th ed.; Jena: Gustav Fischer, 1925), Vol. VI. Very similar to Spiethoff's explanation of the business cycle is Gustav Cassel's in his *Theory of Social Economy* (New York: Harcourt, Brace & Co., Inc., 1932).

Businessmen did not anticipate this dangerous development because of the time-consuming character of investment goods production. Throughout their production, the price of investment goods (and of their services) tended to remain high. But as their production is completed, there develops a situation of increased supply and of a greatly decreased demand.

Spiethoff compares this situation with a pair of gloves, one of which has been lost. The overproduced capital goods (the remaining glove) cannot be used because of the lack of complementary goods (the lost glove). The lack of sufficient savings indicates a desire for consumers' goods rather than investment goods. But the production of consumers' goods has not been expanded in proportion to the production of investment goods. Thus the deficiency in the supply of savings is basically a scarcity of the means of subsistence for labor, that is, consumers' goods. Had investment goods production been carried to the point where these goods would have helped turn out more consumers' goods, difficulty would not have arisen. Unfortunately, lack of sufficient savings led to a discontinuation of investment processes before this strategic point was reached. In other words, in our unplanned economy businessmen have embarked on bigger and longer production processes than could be financed through savings or noninflationary credit creation.

In a barter economy or in a centrally planned economy nothing worse than this would happen. Factors of production would be shifted, and the overproduced investment goods would lie idle until the whole economy had grown sufficiently to fit its prematurely enlarged suit of capital goods. The capitalist economy, however, is unlikely to make a similarly satisfactory adjustment. The drastic cutback in capital goods production creates unemployment, reduces consumption expenditures, and degenerates into a downward spiral of destruction which serves no purpose.

The relatively few remarks which Keynes makes about the business cycle can be included among the theories which emphasize excessive fluctuations in investment. After having pointed out that the interest rate will rise during a period of increasing economic activity (owing to the transaction motive for liquidity), he continues: "But I suggest that a more typical, and often the predominant, explanation of the crisis is, not primarily a rise in the rate of interest, but a sudden collapse in the marginal efficiency of capital."[16] This collapse, in

[16] J. M. Keynes, *The General Theory of Employment, Interest and Money* (London: Macmillan & Co., Inc., 1936), p. 315.

turn, causes a sharp increase in liquidity preference and, consequently, the interest rate, thus aggravating the decline in investment. Conditions will not improve before the marginal efficiency of capital has recovered, not even if the rate of interest is drastically lowered. Keynes uses the time period needed for this recovery to account for the length of the business cycle which depends on "the length of life of durable assets in relation to the normal rate of growth in a given epoch."[17]

Underinvestment Theories

The overinvestment theory emphasizes the prosperity phase of the cycle, while the underinvestment theory is mainly a theory of depression and stagnation. The theoretical framework for a theory of stagnation is given in Keynes' equilibrium theory. Once we have explained that investment will fall below its previous level, the Keynesian analysis shows how the national income will have to fall enough to reduce saving to the size of investment. This is the negative application of the analysis behind Figure 23–2 (p. 321). Where this new low point of equilibrium will be found will depend on the consumption function and on the degree of collapse of the marginal efficiency of investment. Temporarily this point may even be below the intersection of the *C* curve and the 45° line, indicating that consumption is higher than the national income. But since some capital goods must be continually replaced in order to maintain even this low level of consumption, we assume that gross investment will rise again. Whether and when net investment will recover depends either on the emergence of investment outlets which are considered sufficiently profitable by private business or on government spending. This increase in investment will have to be financed by credit creation.

That investment opportunities may be lacking was already suggested more than a hundred years ago by J. S. Mill. In a remarkable passage in his *Principles of Political Economy* he discusses taxes which are taken from capital. In a poor country, he argues, it is impossible to impose any tax which will not impede the growth of national wealth since all taxes are, in some sense, paid out of capital. But he adds that the case is different in a country where capital abounds and where the spirit of accumulation is strong.

Capital having reached the stage in which, were it not for a perpetual succession of improvements in production, any further increase would

[17] *Ibid.*, p. 317.

soon be stopped—and having so strong a tendency even to outrun those improvements, that profits are only kept above the minimum by emigration of capital, or by a periodical sweep called a commercial crisis; to take from capital by taxation what emigration would remove, or a commercial crisis destroy, is only to do what either of those causes would have done, namely to make a clear space for further saving.[18]

Mill's remarks and their political implications anticipated a trend in business-cycle theory which grew out of the stagnation of the thirties. During these difficult years in which full-employment conditions seemed permanently out of reach for the unregulated private enterprise economy, it was argued by Alvin H. Hansen and others that the western world of our generation was undergoing a structural change not less basic or profound than the industrial revolution, that we were passing over a divide which separated the era of growth and expansion of the nineteenth century from an era in which "the combined effect of the decline in population growth, together with the failure of any really important innovations of a magnitude sufficient to absorb large capital outlays" have prevented us from reaching full employment. This situation, it was suggested, accounted for "sick recoveries which die in their infancy and depressions which feed on themselves and leave a hard and seemingly immovable core of unemployment."[19]

These remarks now seem pessimistic and premature. At the time, they were considered as closely related to Keynes' general equilibrium theory. Actually, they are Keynesian only in the sense that the new equilibrium theory could accommodate even such pessimistic assumptions, while the classical theory was not able to plausibly account for the stagnation of the thirties.

Keynes' theory seems to emphasize depression and stagnation by its mere denial that a full-employment equilibrium is the normal state of affairs to which we tend or around which the economy fluctuates. Chapter 22 of the *General Theory* ("Notes on the Trade Cycle") implies that Keynes did not consider stagnation any more normal than a state of high employment. The Keynesian equilibria at different employment levels last as long as the existing level of saving and investment lasts; and since investment, according to Keynes' own analysis, is subject to great fluctuations we must expect fluctuations

[18] J. S. Mill, *Principles of Political Economy* (London: Longmans, Green & Co., 1936), Book V, chap. ii, paragraph 7.

[19] Alvin H. Hansen, *Fiscal Policy and Business Cycles* (New York: W. W. Norton & Co., Inc., 1941), pp. 349, 353.

rather than static conditions. Such fluctuations do not necessarily gravitate towards full employment.

The above-mentioned pessimistic view of the future of "mature" economies rests on a wrong interpretation of the Keynesian consumption function. If this function were to apply historically in the sense that over the years a growing national income would cause savings to grow to unmanageable proportions—unmanageable at least for private investment—then we could indeed begin worrying lest the investment outlets in our economy prove permanently deficient. We have seen, however, that the consumption curve tends to be pushed upwards with the passing of time. This considerably reduces the danger that the investment opportunities of our economy will fall short of the amount needed to absorb all savings.[20] But that the stagnation thesis lacks credibility does not diminish the need for a governmental policy aimed at an amount of aggregate spending which prevents excesses in the directions of both dangerous inflation and mass unemployment.

SUGGESTIONS FOR FURTHER READING

ELLIS, HOWARD S. *German Monetary Theory* 1905–1933, part iv. Cambridge, Mass.: Harvard University Press, 1934.

FELLNER, WILLIAM. "Employment Theory and Business Cycles," *A Survey of Contemporary Economics,* Ellis, Howard S. (ed.), Vol. I, chap. 2. Homewood, Ill.: Richard D. Irwin, Inc., 1954.

FISHER, IRVING. "The Debt-Deflation Theory of Great Depressions," *Econometrica,* Vol. I, 1933.

HABERLER, GOTTFRIED. *Propensity and Depression,* chaps. 2–3. 3d ed. New York: United Nations, 1952.

HANSEN, ALVIN H. *Business Cycles and National Income,* part iii. New York: W. W. Norton & Co., Inc., 1951.

HANSEN, ALVIN H., and CLEMENCE, RICHARD V. *Readings in Business Cycles and National Income,* chaps. 9–12. New York: W. W. Norton & Co., Inc., 1953.

HAYEK, FRIEDRICH A. *Monetary Theory and the Trade Cycle.* London: Harcourt, Brace & Co., 1932.

KEYNES, J. M. *The General Theory of Employment, Interest and Money,* chap. 22. London: Macmillan & Co., Ltd., 1936.

PHILLIPS, C. A.; MCMANUS, T. F., and NELSON, R. W. *Banking and the Business Cycle,* chaps. 6–7. New York: Macmillan Co., 1937.

[20] See William Fellner, "Employment and Business Cycles," in *A Survey of Contemporary Economics,* H. S. Ellis (ed.) (Homewood, Ill.: Richard D. Irwin, Inc., 1954), Vol. I, p. 61.

Readings in Business Cycle Theory, parts iv–v. Homewood, Ill.: Richard D. Irwin, Inc., 1944.

WICKSELL, KNUT. *Lectures on Political Economy,* Vol. 2, *Money,* chap. 4, par. 9. New York: Macmillan Co., 1955.

QUESTIONS AND PROBLEMS

1. "If individuals decide to save, that is, not to spend on immediate consumption, they reduce rather than increase the motive of the entrepreneurs for acquiring capital goods" (Joan Robinson). Do you agree?
2. Discuss Knut Wicksell's cumulative process.
3. Why does Irving Fisher call it the chief secret of most if not all great depressions that "the more the debtors pay the more they owe"?
4. Why does Friedrich A. Hayek believe that an expansion of investment which is financed by voluntary saving is not dangerous, whereas investment financed by credit expansion must eventually lead to depression?
5. Explain the so-called "Ricardo effect."
6. Discuss Arthur Spiethoff's overinvestment theory.
7. J. M. Keynes explains a crisis not primarily by a rise in interest rates but by "a sudden collapse in the marginal efficiency of capital." Discuss.
8. Pessimistic views concerning lacking investment opportunities in mature economics rest sometimes on a wrong interpretation of the consumption function. Explain.

Chapter 26 A MODEL CYCLE

The Upswing

The process of economic revival and expansion must, at least in part, be understood as the result of the economic situation prevailing at the end of the downswing. If we started from a full-employment plateau, expansionist forces would not have much leeway: rising prices and frictions in the transfer of the factors of production from one industry to another would soon check further growth. Only where sufficient unused resources and unemployed labor are available can an expansionist process continue long enough to gather momentum; and only then is it likely that dangerous disproportions will develop in the structure of production.

Let us break into the cycle at the time when a depression (or stagnation) changes into a revival. In other words, our model begins at the lower turning point. This change is due to a combination of conditions and factors. First we must observe that the economy is ready for a revival both in a material and in a monetary sense. Unused plant capacity (the aftermath of a previous period of overinvestment) together with unemployed labor constitute a high-investment potential. And the liquidity of the banking system, characterized by ample reserves, permits a very elastic supply of credit.

Next we have to assume a revival of investment demand. An inducement to increase gross investment may come from the need for replacements. Replacements cannot be postponed forever, capital goods cannot be permitted to deteriorate, nor can one go on indefinitely depleting inventories. The demand for investment goods, therefore, will rise again, and the same will be true for consumers' durables like automobiles. There also may have occurred an accumulation of potential innovations which present increasingly tempting investment propositions under improving price and cost conditions. Historically, most major cycles have been marked by big new investment opportunities associated with the creation of important new industries.

Whether and when such a combination of conditions and factors will be strong enough to overcompensate the forces of depression and stagnation cannot be known in advance. It is likely that the expansionist forces will eventually become strong enough and that in the long run an upturn will come. Fortunately, it is not necessary for us to wait for an automatic, self-generating, or "natural" revival, since an expansion process can be started artificially through a government spending program.

A revival will always be connected with credit expansion. Loanable funds are supplied out of current savings, out of hoards, and through the creation of money. Savings are, as yet, not an important source, since at the prevailing low level of income the propensity to save is small. It is not correct to assume that during the depression savings are accumulated and stored up somewhere to be held ready for future use. Savings simply decline as the national income falls. Dishoarding, on the other hand, is characteristic of the period of revival. Securities and commodities are now preferred to money. Security prices will rise, and rising security prices mean, as we know, falling rates of interest. The main source of loanable funds, in this phase of the cycle, however, is credit creation. The depression is a process of deflation during which money is not only hoarded but actually destroyed through debt cancellation. Bank loans are paid back, and the funds are not lent out again. This destruction of money leaves both the commercial banks and the central bank with excess reserves, with increased liquidity and the possibility of creating credit whenever the demand for loanable funds increases. The supply of loanable funds is thus very elastic at low rates of interest.

The physical counterpart of this very elastic supply of credit is to be found in the idle means of production which constitute the investment potential of the economy. Unemployed labor is available at the lower turning point in a wide variety, and the supply of labor is, therefore, elastic. Employment can simultaneously increase in many industries without causing an immediate rise in wage rates. In addition there is unused plant capacity available, since many firms have been working at less than optimum output. As production expands, overhead costs can be spread over a larger number of units so that unit costs are reduced and profits increased.

Low interest rates, low wage rates, and low unit costs of production will induce investment provided that interest rates are lower than anticipated rates of profit. The lower turning point is marked by this ascendency of rates of profit over rates of interest and marks the beginning of a period during which the climate for investment decisions continues to improve.

As investment increases and as it is financed out of dishoarded and newly created funds, the national income rises. Workers newly employed in the investment goods industries will spend part of their newly earned income on consumers' goods. New consumers' goods will be ordered, and the money spent on consumption will become income of an ever-widening circle of those who participate, directly or indirectly, in the production and marketing of consumers' goods. This is the multiplier effect which has been discussed in Chapter 24.

Part or all of the newly earned income which is being saved may be used to finance further investment, which is either autonomous or induced by the increase in consumption. In addition, however, loanable funds are also continuously supplied through further credit expansion.

Credit expansion tends to keep rates of interest below the level which would be required to equate the investment demand for loanable funds with the supply of current savings. Nevertheless, rates of interest will now tend to rise together with commodity prices while bond prices will begin to fall. The monetary demand begins to outrun the increasing supply of goods. Credit inflation gradually develops into price inflation. However, this price inflation does not halt further expansion, for rising commodity prices put a premium on borrowing: the real rate of interest is lower than the market rate.

Overinvestment

We must be able to explain why cyclical fluctuations are more marked in the investment goods (and durable consumers' goods) industries than in the production of nondurables. Three reasons are prominent:

1. Investment goods production depends on a comparison of prospective rates of profit with rates of interest. Low interest rates increase the capital value of durable goods because the value of durable goods yielding a given amount of revenue varies inversely with interest rates. Assuming that profit expectations improve but that interest rates remain relatively low (owing to credit creation), the production of investment goods will be stimulated. In other words, the

influence of the rate of interest upon the production of durable goods is greater than upon the production of nondurables: the interest rate is more important as a capitalization factor than as a cost factor.

2. The principle of acceleration of derived demand shows that fluctuations in consumers' demand are transmitted to "higher" stages of production with increasing violence. Thus, if an increase in investment leads to an increase in consumption, induced investment will rise and total investment will grow percentagewise much more than consumption. But we know already how temporary this reaction is.

3. The time-consuming character of investment goods production explains the latter's wide swings during the business cycle. If it takes a considerable time until the products or services of capital goods begin to emerge, it also takes time until increased production has its effect on prices. Profits of capital goods producers thus remain high long enough to encourage too many time-consuming processes to be embarked upon.

An increase in investment expenditure will, of course, tend to stimulate consumption, and an increase in consumption will induce further investment. The business cycle, while more pronounced in the capital goods industries than in the consumers' goods industries, is not limited to the former. For some time capital goods industries and consumers' goods industries stimulate one another in a mutually induced process of growth. It is this interrelation which explains the self-propelling character of the expansion process, as long as unused productive resources are available and as long as the expansion can be financed by an elastic supply of loanable funds. Even inflationary developments do not automatically stop this process. Eventually, however, it must come to a halt and it is most unlikely that the structure of production will then be so balanced that it permits the economy to remain in equilibrium at full employment.

The reasons which explained the disproportionate expansion of the investment goods industries can now be used to show that full-employment equilibrium cannot be sustained in an unregulated market economy.

To explain the forces which bring about the downturn we assume that the monetary authority will reduce or discontinue further credit expansion once credit inflation leads to generally rising prices. Once the inflationary supply of loanable funds is reduced, a given investment level can be maintained only if the noninflationary supply of investment funds out of savings increases accordingly. But it is not at all likely that an increased supply of savings can be counted on.

Savings come partly out of profits and profits fall when cost prices rise due to increased competition for the factors of production and when investment goods prices fall as more and more time-consuming processes of production are brought to conclusion.

If we should assume that the supply of savings is increased at the expense of consumption expenditures, we should also have to assume that decreasing consumption would reduce induced investment.

With a reduction of the supply of investment funds out of inflationary sources rates of interest will rise and rising rates of interest, together with falling rates of profit, will lead to rapidly declining investment expenditures. Falling investment expenditures, in turn, lead to falling income and consumption. Both autonomous and induced investment are declining.

Recession and Depression

In an unregulated market economy it is impossible to maintain consumers' demand (let alone a given rate of increase in consumption) when investment goods production falls to the level of mere replacement demand or to an even lower level. As soon as investment declines the driving forces of the upswing, multiplier and acceleration, begin to work in reverse.

The fall of the national income is accompanied by a process of hoarding and credit contraction. Loanable funds, rather than being invested and paid out as income, are used for debt cancellation. With the general falling off of demand the liquidity of short-term commercial credit is impaired. The tendency to turn from holding commodities to holding money (that is, an increased liquidity preference) leads to a general fall in commodity prices, and the anticipation of a further fall reinforces the trend towards liquidity; in other words, the velocity of circulation of money is reduced. The general scramble for liquidity leads momentarily to sharply rising interest rates and falling security prices. Normally commodity prices and interest rates move in the same direction, but temporarily we see now rising rates of interest accompanied by falling commodity prices. Rising rates of interest make further investments even less attractive.

As the downswing continues and investment demand for loanable funds is very weak, interest rates begin to fall. The demand for liquidity is satisfied, and securities are being preferred to the holding of idle money. Once more both commodity prices and interest rates fall simultaneously. Some of these downward price adjustments are quite natural in an economic system whose allocation of productive resources depends on relative price movements. Unfortunately, these healthy price changes can be drowned in a general price deflation which defeats its own purpose by raising the real rate of interest and by lowering total wage income rather than by adjusting selected wage rates.

Multiplier and acceleration principle, working in reverse, plus the destructive influence of a monetary contraction, lead away from equilibrium rather than towards it, and the depression feeds on itself just as previously the prosperity had done; and pessimism makes conditions look even worse than they really are.

Fortunately, the contraction process cannot go on forever. It will stop long before everybody has ceased to be employed. When and where the lowest point will be reached depends on the shape of the consumption function and on the minimum investment demand that can be maintained. If no net investment takes place, the national income must fall to a level at which, on the average, no net savings are forthcoming. Temporarily the national income can fall even farther if even the regular replacement demand for investment goods is reduced.

The lowest point reached, however, is not necessarily a turning point. Stagnation rather than revival may follow the downturn. To understand this situation, we must recall the following facts:

1. It takes time for the marginal efficiency of capital to recover. The time involved depends on the longevity of investment goods and on the extent of previous overinvestment in relation to the normal growth of the economy.

2. We have already seen that it is theoretically always possible for the monetary authority to stop a credit expansion and to bring about a contraction of economic activity but that it is not certain that the monetary authority will be able to lift the economy out of a state of depression. Monetary policies are not equally strong in prosperity and in depression.

3. Classical theory had relied on accumulation of savings to put pressure upon interest rates. Such pressure will not develop, however, because savings do not accumulate during depression. Savings decrease together with a fall of the national income. We saw, furthermore, that at relatively low rates of interest the demand for money becomes nearly perfectly elastic, thus preventing interest rates from falling farther. The marginal efficiency of capital, on the other hand, may well be a negative quantity.

These considerations show that we cannot be sure that the conditions which prevail at the end of a depression will automatically produce an upturn in the same manner prosperity causes a downturn. But this is only to say that the upturn may be long delayed and not that the economy will have to remain forever at a stagnation level.

Conclusion

From our discussion of economic fluctuations we can conclude that business cycles are a necessary feature of an unregulated market economy. We might, therefore, at first be tempted to propose the abolition of our market system in favor of a centrally planned economy.

The argument for central planning need not pretend that the planning procedure will be free of mistakes; rather, it need only try to show that a centrally planned economy could avoid the "secondary" effects of overinvestment, that it would not be exposed to the destructive effects of a cumulative downward spiral.

Let us assume, for example, that the authorities of a planned economy have decided upon a tremendous investment program which necessitates the reduction of consumption to a low level. The authorities promise that after five years the population will enjoy the fruits of the present capital construction in the form of a higher standard of living. Suppose, however, that the planning board underestimates the magnitude of the capital goods construction which has to be carried out before the prospective gains in final consumption can materialize. Such underestimation is easily possible considering that it is a task of overwhelming difficulty to draw up a central plan for a nation's total production.

If the investment program was too ambitious and if at full employment, production of investment goods can be increased only at the expense of reducing consumption still further, the planning board has a choice between two policies. It can admit its mistake and leave part of the investment projects unfinished, probably causing some temporary unemployment; or it can further cut down consumption in order to free productive resources and labor for the continuation of the yet unfinished investment program. But these frictions and sacrifices exhaust the difficulties which a smoothly working planned economy would have to face. The planned economy would be able, theoretically, to avoid the process of deflationary contraction which is characteristic of a depression in the unplanned market economy. "Concretely: a crisis centering in the cotton industry may in the capitalist order put a stop to residential construction; in the socialist order it may of course also happen that the production of cotton goods has to be drastically curtailed at short notice; but this would be a reason to speed up residential construction instead of stopping it."[1]

But if a centrally planned economy can avoid the cumulative downward process it can do so only at a price, in terms of individual freedom (and perhaps also in terms of productivity), which the citizens of democracies are not willing to pay. Therefore, we must try to find policies which permit us to avoid deflationary contraction and are yet fully compatible with our market economy. These policies cannot be purely monetary, since the monetary authority lacks the power to halt the downward spiral or to induce expansion once the destructive cumulative process has spent its force. To monetary policies we must add policies which involve spending funds which the monetary authority permits the commercial banks to create. These policies are mainly of a fiscal nature. The following chapter tries to outline the combination of monetary and fiscal measures by which the unplanned economy can achieve a measure of stability at a high level of economic activity.

QUESTIONS AND PROBLEMS

1. When do we speak of a revival of economic activity? Which conditions must be given if a revival is to take place? Why may investment increase even in the absence of a deficit spending program?
2. Is it correct to say that savings accumulate during a depression and finally exert such pressure on the rates of interest that private investment increases again?
3. Would it be possible to construct a model of economic fluctuations by choosing appropriate figures for the marginal propensity to consume and the relation?
4. "Cyclical fluctuations are more pronounced in the investment goods (and durable consumers' goods) industries than in the production of nondurables." Why?
5. Can your answer to question 4 also explain why it is difficult to maintain full-employment equilibrium in a market economy?
6. "Once the inflationary supply of loanable funds decreases, a given investment level can be maintained only if the noninflationary supply of loanable funds increases. But then we should have to assume that decreasing consumption reduces induced investment." Discuss.
7. Keynes' *General Theory* supplies us with the theoretical framework for a theory of stagnation. Explain.
8. Could a planned economy avoid the "secondary" effects of overinvestment?

[1] Joseph A. Schumpeter, *Capitalism, Socialism, and Democracy* (New York: Harper & Bros., 1942), p. 195.

Chapter 27 FISCAL POLICY

The Concept of Full Employment

Frequent use of the term "full" employment must not lead us to expect that our economic policy aims at nothing less than full employment. Indeed, it would be difficult to define full employment with sufficient precision, let alone to reach and maintain it.

Some clever definitions have been suggested, but they are too vague to serve as useful guides for economic policy. When it is said that we have reached full employment once price inflation begins, we tend to simplify matters as John Maynard Keynes did when he restated the quantity theory of money.[1] Keynes suggested that the creation of additional money raises employment at stable prices as long as unemployed factors are available, but that after the absorption of these factors prices will rise. Yet Keynes proceeded to show that in reality the transition from increased employment to increased prices will be gradual and that price inflation must be expected long before all the unemployed have been absorbed.

William H. Beveridge's famous definition that full employment means "having always more vacant jobs than unemployed men"[2] may instead describe a situation of overfull employment. Bertil Ohlin has pointed out[3] that a state of affairs in which labor enjoys the advantages of a sellers' market may not be a pure blessing. Such a situation, it is true, has the advantage of guaranteeing a relatively large social product, stimulating rationalization of production, and making labor willing to accept laborsaving devices; also, selling costs will be very low at a time of high economic activity. But Ohlin holds against these

[1] See Chapter 3, p. 27.

[2] William H. Beveridge, *Full Employment in a Free Society* (New York: W. W. Norton & Co., Inc., 1945), p. 18.

[3] Bertil Ohlin, *The Problem of Employment Stabilization* (New York: Columbia University Press, 1949), chap. i.

beneficial effects the disadvantages of bottlenecks, an excessive labor turnover, inflationary pressures, and, if price inflation is repressed by price controls, the administrative cost of rationing. Also, overfull employment can easily lead to an adverse balance of international payments since the tendency to import will be high while inflation militates against exports. In the field of international trade and payments, therefore, it may be necessary to introduce controls which reduce the international division of labor.

Quite possibly these disadvantages of overfull employment may outweigh its advantages. It is possible, for example, that an employment level which is less than "full" may actually be accompanied by a greater production volume. And even if the full-employment output is greater, it may be an output of commodities less suited to satisfy the wants of the consumers. Means of production may have become unemployed because of changes in consumer demand. If we ignore these changes in consumers' preferences, as a totalitarian regime might do, we can maintain full employment by adjusting demand to supply; but this would violate one of the basic individual freedoms which characterize our economic system.

These considerations concerning the frictions, inflationary pressures, and control measures connected with a state of overfull employment suggest that employment policies should seek a compromise between stability and inflation, between freedom and control. The more we insist that direct controls be avoided, the less ambitious we must be in defining the "fullness" of the employment level we desire. Certainly we must avoid the mistake of considering unemployment as always a justification of further credit expansion. Disproportions in our economy cannot always be ironed out by raising aggregate expenditures. The "optimum" utilization of our resources often will leave some factors of production temporarily unemployed.

The Full-Employment Budget

We have seen that monetary policy alone cannot be made responsible for the maintenance of a volume of expenditure sufficient to guarantee a high level of employment. It must be the task of the government, as fiscal agent, to see that aggregate spending is neither too large nor too small. The main instrument of a policy which tries equally hard to avoid the disadvantages of unemployment and deflation, on the one hand and overfull employment and inflation on the other hand is a new type of government budget, which "will be concerned with income and expenditure of the community as a whole, not only with public finance, . . . will take the manpower of the country as a datum and plan outlay to that datum rather than by consideration of financial resources."[4]

The government, first of all, will have to analyze the different sources of expenditure. If aggregate expenditure from these sources is not large enough to employ all who want to be employed at prevailing wage rates, the government must take steps to increase outlays in order to avoid deflation and depression. The nature of the policies used will depend partly on how high we set our sights, that is, whether we consider, say, 5 or 3 or only 1 per cent of unemployment bearable. Furthermore, the full-employment budget does not imply that the government will maintain the desired level of economic activity by simply adding to private expenditure enough government spending to reach the desired total. The government, instead, may try to influence private expenditure.

The elements which make up the aggregate total flow of expenditure are the following:

1. Private consumption expenditures (C).
2. Private investment expenditures (I).
3. Public expenditures out of tax revenues (R).
4. Public expenditures out of borrowed funds (L).
5. The balance of trade (B), which may be either positive (excess of exports over imports) or negative (excess of imports over exports).[5]

Aggregate expenditure E, namely, $C + I + R + L \pm B$, should be equal to F, the national output at full employment. If E is larger than F, the result will be price inflation. If F is larger than E, the difference is unemployment. In both cases the government must propose ways and means by which undesirable developments can be stopped and reversed. The task is not to achieve complete stability at full employment and without inflation. We cannot set our sights that high in a free economy. Rather, we should try to avoid the spiral effects of inflation and deflation, which only lead farther away from equilibrium.

The government can try to influence one or more of the components of aggregate spending. As a matter of fact, these components are so closely interrelated that policies which influence one will also affect one or more of the others. For example, if the government tries to

[4] Beveridge, *op. cit.*, p. 30.

[5] For the present we shall ignore the influence of foreign trade and limit our discussion to a "closed" economy. The connection between international trade, international payments, and domestic employment will be discussed in Chapter 30.

finance increased expenditures through raising the tax rates, it must be assumed that we pay for an increase in *R* by a decrease in *C* or *I* or both. Increased government expenditures out of loans *L*, on the other hand, will increase *C* and *I* if the money which the government borrowed from the banks was newly created money. This money, when successfully injected into the income stream, leads to higher consumption and, via higher consumption, to increased investment. As *C* and *I* increase, *R* will automatically increase, and the government will be able to spend more unless it decides to use the increased revenue to reduce its debt. The effect, in turn, of such an "overbalancing" of the budget will depend on how the former holders of the debt use the money. If the retired debt was held by the central bank or the commercial banks, the effect may be deflationary, since the total amount of money in circulation will be decreased; if the debt was held outside of banks, *C* and *I* may increase.

It would be easy to find numerous other examples of the interdependence of *C*, *I*, *R*, and *L* and to think of many more repercussions in connection with each example.

The Roads to High Employment

We assume that government analysts find that during the next year aggregate expenditure will fall short of the amount needed to maintain a high level of economic activity. The government is charged with the responsibility of proposing ways and means by which total outlay can be sufficiently increased. Which roads are open?

A very conservative administration may decide to balance its budget over the year, that is, to avoid any further increase in the public debt. In this case it will be very difficult to increase total outlay. Nevertheless the government may try, through monetary and tax policies,[6] to influence *C*, *I*, and *R*. *L* is not to be changed according to our basic assumption.

[6] Other government policies which can influence the state of employment are commercial, agricultural, and labor policies. Commercial policies will be considered in connection with international payments. Agricultural policies will enter our discussion only insofar as a farm income support program may constitute one of the major government outlays during the downswing. As to wage policies, it is sometimes suggested that any deficiency in aggregate demand could easily, speedily and pleasantly be remedied by a general increase in wages. Unfortunately, this medicine will not work. If businessmen have to pay higher wages under otherwise unchanged conditions, and when product prices cannot rise, the result is increased unemployment. Equally wrong is the opposite argument that wages should be generally reduced to make producers hire more men. A general wage reduction lowers the purchasing power of consumers. Rejection of these contradictory proposals does not mean to say, however, that wage policies are unimportant in connection with our problem. On the contrary, the inflationary pressures of

Monetary policy can do relatively little to stem a downswing or to pull the economy out of a stagnation. However, we must recall that we can at least avoid monetary policies which aggravate the contraction. If we cannot rely on monetary policy, what can a conservative administration which insists on balancing the budget do to increase total expenditure?

Since, according to our basic assumption, no deficit is permitted to arise, an increase of public expenditure will have to be brought about by changes in *R*, that is, by changes in tax policies. We distinguish three tax policies:

1. Without resulting in a loss of tax revenue, the tax structure may be able to be altered so as to encourage an increase of *C* and *I*, thus increasing total expenditure.

2. If the government combines its refusal to borrow with a policy of stable tax rates during the downswing, the fall of *C* and *I* will reduce *R*, and the government will have to cut its total expenditures at the very time that private spending decreases.

3. If the government tries to maintain or even increase its expenditures during the depression in order to compensate for the fall in private expenditures or because unemployment compensation or farm support programs necessitate increased outlay, tax revenue must be increased in the face of falling private economic activity. The increase in *R* leads to a further fall of *C* and *I*.

Concerning tax policy No. 3, Gottfried Haberler comes to the following conclusion:

> In a serious depression, elimination of the bulk of unemployment by this method would probably require exorbitant increases in expenditures and of tax rates, implying a drastic redistribution of income, and the system would soon become incompatible with a free-enterprise economy. . . . This may sound paradoxical to many, for what most conservatives are afraid of is a deficit and a growing public debt. Their obsession with the public debt may thus lead them into a much more dangerous alley.[7]

We must now drop the assumption that the public debt is not permitted to rise. In the following discussion we permit the government to entail a budget deficit, that is, we free its expenditures from the limiting influence of tax revenues.

---

full and overfull employment are mainly due to the tendency of money rates of wages to rise faster than efficiency in a sellers' market for labor. Furthermore, rejection of a general increase or decrease of wage rates does not argue against the importance of adjustments of wage rates in individual labor markets.

[7] Gottfried Haberler in "Five Views on the Murray Full Employment Bill," *Review of Economic Statistics*, August, 1945, pp. 108–9.

We must distinguish two kinds of government borrowing:

1. If the funds are derived from savings the effect is similar to that of increased taxation, and total expenditure will increase only under special circumstances. The savings, instead of being taxed away, are now borrowed away by the government. Borrowing may be preferable to taxing for psychological reasons unless the increased public debt is considered very dangerous by the business community.

2. The government may borrow from the banks. If newly created money is spent by the government, private expenditure need not decrease and total spending is likely to grow with favorable effects on *C*, *I*, and *R*. Here, then, we find the most powerful instrument at the disposal of the government in its effort to maintain a reasonably high level of economic activity.

Deficit Spending

The government may incur a deficit by reducing taxes while maintaining expenditures, by increasing expenditures without raising taxes, or by combining tax reduction with increased expenditures.

1. By reducing the tax burden the government may stimulate either private consumption or private investment, depending on the nature of the tax reduction. Thus total expenditure would be increased by increasing *C* and *I* while reducing *R* and raising *L*. Such a tax reduction program will be favored by those wanting to keep direct deficit spending by the government as small as possible and endeavoring to achieve the desired effect on total expenditure via the private sector of the economy. The difficulty, however, is that a given amount of deficit produced by tax reduction is much less certain to boost total demand than an equal deficit caused by government spending. Neither *C* nor *I* are likely to increase by the full amount of the respective tax reductions. To achieve the same increase in total expenditure, a larger budget deficit will be needed in case of tax reduction than in the case of increased government spending. Once more, therefore, the seemingly more conservative approach may lead to the bigger deficit.

2. Increased government spending financed by credit creation is the most powerful of the government's means for increasing employment through increasing total outlay. In making sure that newly created money will become active, deficit spending "is the logical sequel to central bank policy."[8] If the monetary authority is willing but unable to maintain enough money in active circulation, deficit spend-

[8] John H. Williams, "Deficit Spending," *American Economic Review*, Vol. XXX (February, 1941), p. 55.

ing can be used as a device to increase expenditure, since fiscal policy is independent of private profit anticipations and private initiative. Government spending of funds which have been newly created or which would otherwise have been hoarded helps to increase or maintain income and employment. Deficit spending, of course, is not independent of monetary policy, but in this relationship between monetary and fiscal policy the monetary authority maintains a passive or a limiting position while deficit spending supplies the driving force.

Priming the Pump

Government deficit spending has often been compared with the priming of a pump. The implication is that government deficit spendis a limited and temporary injection of additional purchasing power and that, once successfully primed, the economy, like a pump, will be able to continue to operate without further outside help. Government spending, therefore, is to taper off as soon as private spending has become strong enough to sustain the upswing. Pump priming rests on the assumption that enough profitable investment opportunities are available; it wants to be only a stimulus, the igniting spark which sets the economic machine in motion.

A policy of pump priming is difficult to administer. Our discussion of the multiplier and the acceleration principle shows that it is not at all easy to taper off primary government investments in such a way that, nevertheless, total investment, employment, and national income continue to increase. In other words, pump priming can succeed only when, with increasing optimism, private investment projects are undertaken which do not depend exclusively on the multiplier and acceleration effect of the government's primary investments. If such autonomous—that is, noninduced—private investment opportunities are not available, government deficit spending cannot decrease without detrimental effects on income and employment.[9]

The chances of successful pump priming are the better, the smaller the primary expenditures needed to stimulate private investment. If deficit spending has to be continued for a long time it may impair private initiative, owing to the widespread belief that continuous increase of the public debt will eventually lead to an unbearable tax burden and to price inflation. Furthermore, should noninduced private investment get under way rather late, when the supply of

[9] See J. M. Clark, "An Appraisal of the Workability of Compensatory Devices," *American Economic Review*, Vol. XXIX (March, 1939), p. 201; A. H. Hansen, *Fiscal Policy and Business Cycles* (New York: W. W. Norton & Co., Inc., 1941), p. 287.

loanable funds is no longer very elastic, then it is hard to see how the expansion process could be sustained by private investment alone, that is, how private investment could outweigh the depressive effect of the tapering off of government deficit spending. On the other hand, we can argue that deficit spending will have the effect of an igniting spark only if it is used courageously in sufficiently large and sustained doses. Thus if primary expenditures are too timid, they will fail to stimulate private investment; and if they are too big, it may be impossible to discontinue the spending program without starting a process of contraction.

But even under the most favorable conditions we cannot expect more of a pump-priming process than the initiation of a period of prosperity. Nothing in the pump-priming idea guarantees well-proportioned economic expansion which will terminate in full-employment equilibrium.

Countercyclical Spending

More ambitious than mere pump priming is a policy of countercyclical or compensatory deficit spending. Its most essential feature is deficit budgeting during recession and depression, and overbalancing of the budget during prosperity. In its milder form this policy proposes stable tax rates which lead to fluctuating tax revenues during the cycle, combined with a shifting of government expenditures, to the extent they can be shifted, into periods of depression. A more extreme application of the same principle would not be content with reduced government revenues at stable tax rates but would lower tax rates during the downswing and raise them during the upswing. In addition to shifting essential government expenditures to periods when private expenditures are falling off, government expenditures would be stepped up, not only in the form of unemployment compensation and farm price supports but also through public works which have been blueprinted in advance and are undertaken for the express purpose of stimulating aggregate demand.

The logic of these proposals is rather obvious. The peaks of the cycle are to be chopped off and the troughs filled in. While economic fluctuations would not disappear, they would be dampened. Theoretically, at least, it would even be possible to carry through this countercyclical taxing and spending policy without a permanent increase in the public debt since the budget could be balanced if we averaged successive deficits and surpluses. It is doubtful, though, that we shall muster the political fortitude to apply the principles of compensatory spending with equal zeal to both depression and prosperity, because during prosperity we should have to raise tax rates, reduce public spending, and pay off the debt which we incurred during the depression.

A countercyclical tax and spending policy requires careful diagnosis of the cyclical position in which we find ourselves at any point of time. To make such a diagnosis presents a problem soluble for the past, with hindsight, but hardly for the present, without the gift of foresight."[10] Obviously, it is very difficult to determine just when the government should stop deficit spending, raise tax rates, and overbalance the budget. The record of economic forecasting is rather poor.[11] We lack simple criteria since it is not possible to measure the seriousness of recession or depression simply by the number of unemployed or by changes in the price level.

To the difficulty or impossibility of exact forecasting we must add the necessary delay before countercyclical measures take effect. For "the appropriateness of the action will depend upon how well it fits the situation when it takes effect, not how well it fits the situation when the decision is made. But when the decision is made no one knows what the situation will be when the action takes effect."[12]

The difficulties of forecasting and timing can be avoided if we are satisfied with so-called built-in stabilizers which function automatically. Government receipts and expenditures play today such an important part that they will influence the economy, for better or worse, in any case. Fortunately, it is relatively easy to use the weight of government taxing and spending so that economic fluctuations are

10 Fritz Machlup in *Financing American Prosperity, A Symposium of Economists* (New York: Twentieth Century Fund, Inc., 1945), p. 455.

11 "The poor record of forecasters in the past warns us to the dangers of this course. Thus in the fall of 1945 virtually all of the economic forecasters predicted that there would be a tremendous postwar slump which would create from 8 to 12 million unemployed by the spring of 1946. This did not occur; and, instead, we had rising production and even more rapidly rising prices with substantially full employment. For us to have embarked on a tremendous program of public works at this time, as the forecasters had urged, would not only have been unnecessary but it would have intensified and heightened the inflation. In fact, the accumulation of a surplus and the retiring of a portion of the public debt beginning in the latter part of 1946 helped to dampen down inflation and prevented matters from becoming still worse. Again in the winter of 1949 the official economic forecasters stated that the real problem was inflation, to prevent which they wanted further restrictive controls. Since it then developed that we were in a recession which continued for some time, the putting into effect of these recommendations could only have deepened the recession." *Monetary, Credit, and Fiscal Policies* (Douglas Committee Report), (81st Cong., 2d Sess., Sen. Doc. 129, 1950), pp. 14–15.

12 Committee for Economic Development, *Defense against Recession: Policy for Greater Economic Stability* (New York: Committee for Economic Development, 1954), pp. 31–32.

automatically lessened. The Committee for Economic Development states the principles of such a policy as follows:

Set tax rates to balance the budget and provide a surplus for debt retirement at an agreed high level of employment and national income. Having set these rates, leave them alone unless there is some major change in national policy or condition of national life.[13]

The advantages of this policy are obvious. When national income falls, government revenues decline in relation to government expenditures, and vice versa. It is important, of course, that we should not arbitrarily destroy this beneficial effect by raising tax rates and cutting expenditures in depression and by cutting tax rates or going on a spending spree during prosperity. The built-in stabilizer rests on the assumption that certain government expenditures will increase automatically as private economic activity declines. Unemployment compensation, farm income supports, and similar relief payments will add to the discrepancy between government receipts and disbursements. Far from being dangerous, this deficit is the crucial feature of the stabilizer. It was a grave mistake of traditional budget policy to avoid or reduce this deficit and to balance the budget annually irrespective of depression or prosperity. Thus the government raised tax rates and cut expenditures during the downswing with the result of accentuating the economic fluctuations which originated in the private sector of the economy. The use of fiscal policy as built-in stabilizer, on the other hand, cushions the effects of declining economic activity when during periods of decline it takes much less purchasing power out of the economy than it puts into it.

Built-in stabilizers offer the great advantage of being automatic in operation and should, therefore, be used to the full. It is doubtful, however, whether their stabilizing effect will be sufficient, whether they will adequately protect the economy against the effects of the self-aggravating downward spiral. We have seen how powerful these destructive forces can be, how the economy does not necessarily fluctuate only moderately around a level of reasonably high activity, and how it may lack recuperative forces once it has fallen to very low levels.

If we cannot rely on the automatic reactions of built-in stabilizers, we can try to strengthen the countercyclical effects of taxing and spending by conscious management. Then, of course, we face the great difficulty of economic forecasting. Instead of leaving tax rates where they are, we can lower tax rates during depressions and raise them during

[13] Committee for Economic Development, *The Stabilizing Budget Policy* (New York: Committee for Economic Development, 1950), p. 8.

prosperity periods; and we can add to the regular and emergency government expenditures under the automatic system expenditures on public works. If these changes could be brought about instantly and could just as speedily be reversed, forecasting would not be much of a problem because our actions could be dictated by the present situation. We still would make mistakes by doing too little too late or too much too soon. But the opportunity to instantly reverse our policies would reduce the danger of wrong decisions. Fiscal policy would then enjoy the great advantage of monetary policy: the advantage of being highly flexible, of being subject to change at a moment's notice. Unfortunately, fiscal measures take time. It may take the Congress months to change a tax law, and it may take much longer to authorize, blueprint, and get under way a work-creation program. Still more time will be required until the effects of these countercyclical measures are felt.[14]

But while these difficulties are great, they are not insuperable. We can increase the flexibility of fiscal policy. As far as tax reduction is concerned "it might be possible to short-cut this process by legislation providing for a tax cut to go into effect automatically under certain conditions, or by giving the President authority to reduce certain taxes under specified conditions."[15] Public works can be authorized and blueprinted in advance so that they can be started with a minimum of delay. This planning is not easy. Apart from political and technical difficulties in the budgeting process, we have to find projects which are useful, noncompetitive with private industry, and of a kind that can be discontinued without loss as soon as general economic conditions demand that government spending be reduced. It should not be impossible to do some long-run planning in the public sector of the economy with a view to doing as much as possible of the necessary or desirable construction work (public building, road construction and maintenance, social housing, flood control, conservation projects) in times of low private investment.

[14] "On the other hand, it is probably true that measures of monetary policy (changes in interest rates and availability of credit brought about by discount and open-market policies) unless applied sharply and abruptly in large doses influence expenditure streams and prices slowly, with a lag, while fiscal policy measures, on the expenditure and revenue side, once they are taken, exert their influence more quickly." Gottfried Haberler, *Inflation, Its Causes and Cures* (Washington, D.C.: American Enterprise Association, June 1960), p. 71.

[15] Committee for Economic Development, *Defense against Recession: Policy for Greater Economic Stability* (New York: Committee for Economic Development, 1954), p. 33. See also "The Problem of Economic Instability," a report prepared under the auspices of the American Economic Association, *American Economic Review*, Vol. XL (September, 1950), p. 524.

The difficulty is, in part, of a psychological nature. Deficit spending is still unpopular. It seems to contradict the "sound" principle that the government should spend in good times when tax revenues are high and when the private sector of the economy, which pays the taxes, can afford the expenditure. An anticyclical fiscal policy requires that we give up these old-fashioned ideas and that we consider deficit budgeting during depressions a virtue rather than a sin.[16] As a matter of fact, even in the private sector of the economy some long-run countercyclical "planning" of expenditures on heavy equipment, inventory accumulation, and financial arrangements (for example, less reliance on short-term borrowing) could exert a desirable stabilizing influence.

Permanent Deficit Spending

The application of a countercyclical policy requires considerable political and moral fortitude. True, we have to rid ourselves of the mistake of conservatively trying to balance the budget yearly. But we must also be careful not to fall into the opposite mistake. The Committee for Economic Development envisages "the really frightening possibility . . . that we shall oscillate between adherence to the annual balance principle in prosperity and belief in compensatory spending in depression."[17] A tendency in this direction certainly exists, since it is the way of least resistance. Deficit spending, in this case, would only be interrupted but never reversed, and the public debt would continue to increase, even in peacetime. Apart from the possible dangers of a growing public debt, such a course could not claim the counterbalancing advantages of compensatory spending, but would instead exaggerate the boom. In addition, the public sector of the economy would be continually enlarged.

Permanent deficit spending would be the necessary outcome of a countercyclical policy if private investment proved too weak to absorb the savings which a high-income level brings forth. Even in this case (which does not seem likely in the foreseeable future) the consequences may not be as extreme as it might seem. First of all, the funds to be spent may come from taxing away the savings which cannot be absorbed otherwise. Secondly, we may be able to change the tax structure so that consumption increases at the expense of saving. If savings can be decreased to the level of private investment, deficit spending will no longer be needed. Thirdly, the government can bor-

16 See Gunnar Myrdal, "Fiscal Policy in the Business Cycle," *American Economic Review*, Vol. XXIX (March, 1939), Supplement, p. 184.

17 Committee for Economic Development, *The Stabilizing Budget Policy* (New York: Committee for Economic Development, 1950), p. 7.

row from the banks without price inflation as long as economic activity can be made to expand fast enough to absorb the newly created funds at stable prices. Fourthly, once full employment is reached in the sense that bottlenecks create price inflation, the government can borrow from the people. In cases 3 and 4 the public debt would grow constantly and this unlimited growth could, psychologically, contribute to the very condition which deficit spending tries to correct—the falling off of private investment.

SUGGESTIONS FOR FURTHER READING

AMERICAN ECONOMIC ASSOCIATION. "The Problem of Economic Stability, A Committee Report," *American Economic Review,* Vol. XL (September, 1950). Reprinted in Lawrence S. Ritter's *Money and Economic Activity,* pp. 372–91. Boston: Houghton Mifflin Co., 1952.

BEVERIDGE, WILLIAM H. *Full Employment in a Free Society,* part iv. New York: W. W. Norton & Co., Inc., 1945.

BOARD OF GOVERNORS OF THE FEDERAL RESERVE SYSTEM. *Public Finance and Full Employment.* Postwar Economic Studies, No. 3. Washington, D.C., 1945.

COLM, GERHARD. "Fiscal Policy," *The New Economics,* Harris, S. E. (ed.), cap. 34. New York: Alfred A. Knopf, 1947.

COMMITTEE FOR ECONOMIC DEVELOPMENT. *Jobs and Markets.* McGraw-Hill Book Co., Inc., 1946.

COMMITTEE FOR ECONOMIC DEVELOPMENT. *Monetary and Fiscal Policy for Greater Economic Stability.* New York, 1948.

COMMITTEE FOR ECONOMIC DEVELOPMENT. *Defense Against Recession.* New York, 1954.

COMMITTEE FOR ECONOMIC DEVELOPMENT. *Anti-Recession Policy for 1958.* New York, 1958.

COMMITTEE FOR ECONOMIC DEVELOPMENT. *Defense Against Inflation. Policies for Price Stability in a Growing Economy.* New York, 1958.

DILLARD, DUDLEY. *The Economics of John Maynard Keynes,* chap. 6. New York: Prentice Hall, Inc., 1948.

Employment, Growth, and Price Levels, chap. 3. Report No. 1043. Washington, D.C.: 86th Congress, 2nd Session, Senate, January 26, 1960.

HANSEN, ALVIN H. *Fiscal Policy and Business Cycles,* parts ii–iii. New York: W. W. Norton & Co., Inc., 1941.

HANSEN, ALVIN H. *Monetary Theory and Fiscal Policy,* chaps. 11–13. New York: McGraw-Hill Book Co., Inc., 1949.

HANSEN, ALVIN H. *Business Cycles and National Income,* part iv. New York: W. W. Norton & Co., Inc., 1951.

HELLER, WALTER W. "CED's Stabilizing Budget Policy After Ten Years," *American Economic Review,* Vol. XLVII (September, 1957).

HOMAN, PAUL T., and MACHLUP, FRITZ (eds.). *Financing American Prosperity.* New York: Twentieth Century Fund, 1945.

MORGAN, THEODORE. *Income and Employment,* chap. 17. 2d ed. New York: Prentice-Hall, Inc., 1952.

OHLIN, BERTIL. *The Problem of Employment Stabilization,* chap. 1. New York: Columbia University Press, 1949.

Report of the Subcommittee on Monetary, Credit, and Fiscal Policies. 81st Congress, 2d Session, Document No. 129, Washington, D.C., January 23, 1950.

WILLIAMS, JOHN H. *Post-War Monetary Plans and Other Essays,* Part V. Oxford: Basil Blackwell, 1949.

QUESTIONS AND PROBLEMS

1. Is it true to say that we have reached full employment when price inflation begins?
2. Discuss the disadvantages of a state of overfull employment.
3. Explain the meaning of a full-employment budget.
4. "The elements of aggregate expenditure are so closely interrelated that policies which influence one cannot help but have some influence on one or more of the others." Explain and illustrate.
5. Would it be wise to try to balance the budget every year?
6. If the government is willing to incur a deficit in pursuit of its full-employment policies, would tax reduction or deficit spending be preferable?
7. Pump-priming can only succeed when private investments are not exclusively induced investments." Discuss.
8. Why are the principles of a countercyclical policy often not appealing to the layman?
9. Discuss the problem of timing in connection with both monetary and fiscal policies.
10. Discuss the so-called "built-in stabilizers."

Chapter 28 INFLATION PROBLEMS

Public Debt and Inflation

Deficit spending in times of widespread unemployment need not lead to price inflation, not even if it is financed by credit expansion. And in times of full employment deficit spending is still compatible with price stability if the deficit is financed in a noninflationary way. In other words, whether or not the public debt leads to price inflation depends on a number of circumstances.

Chapter 27 has shown that government deficit financing may prevent the national income from falling as far and as steeply as it would without fiscal measures or that it may raise an income level which has been permitted to drop. In this case it may be argued that, from a general economic point of view, deficit financing does not "cost" anything. Deficit financing, then, is a net advantage. It does not shift any burden into the future: it is no burden at all.

This argument seems to ignore the fact that the debt must be serviced. Whether we pay interest on the debt or retire it, we have to do this out of increased taxes in future years. Yet if by incurring a deficit of $10 billion we have managed to keep the national income from falling by $20 billion, a net advantage remains, even if the debt service were as great a burden as some people think. From an educational and psychological standpoint it is a pity that we cannot demonstrate by experiment that, in a given case, without deficit finance our position would have deteriorated in terms of national income by much more than the amount of the deficit.

Skepticism concerning the ability of the government to contribute to the size of the real income stems from an attitude which considers all government expenditures as basically parasitic. Whatever the government does, according to this belief, is done at the expense of the private sector of the economy. If, therefore, deficit finance allows the national income to increase by, say, twice the size of the deficit, the enemies of deficit finance would contend that in the absence of these fiscal measures private investment would have used the funds to much greater advantage. Such greater advantage would have resulted because private spending is "profitable" and earns the money which the government only taxes away or creates through price inflation.

Chapter 27 has shown that these and similar arguments are wrong or that they are correct only if, indeed, less is added to total spending on the public side than is destroyed in the private sector as a result of inadequate handling of fiscal policy.

As far as the tax burden in connection with an increasing public debt is concerned, we must not forget that the tax revenue used to service the debt is paid to bondholders who are also usually taxpayers. The national income is not decreased by this transfer from taxpayer to bondholder, although the transfer will influence income distribution, consumption, and private investment. Whether or not this influence is favorable will depend on the general economic situation with regard to private investment opportunities, on the type of taxes used, and on the consumption and saving habits of both taxpayers and bondholders.

A public debt is not inflationary in and by itself. Deficit finance will be inflationary, however, when it leads to total expenditure in excess of the national output at full employment. But if an excess of government disbursements over government revenue injects money into the income stream at a time of substantial and widespread unemployment, little if any price inflation is to be anticipated. In this case the government ought to borrow from the banking system since credit inflation without price inflation is the very purpose of deficit finance.[1]

The inflationary danger of deficit finance lies in the possibility that the program will be continued too long, permitting credit inflation to develop into price inflation. This danger is great in an economy where at near full employment labor's strong bargaining position leads to a tendency for wage rates to rise faster than productivity.

In Chapter 27 we have seen that noninflationary deficit finance is possible at high employment if the government borrows from the public rather than the banks. Since the multiplier is the reciprocal of the marginal propensity to save, there is always available an amount of savings which corresponds to primary investment expenditures.

[1] In this connection it may be useful to remember that the government, instead of borrowing from the banks, could create the money itself. This is part of Irving Fisher's 100 per cent proposal (see Chapter 13, pp. 142–143). The public debt would not increase and, accordingly, there would be no "burden."

Theoretically, therefore, we need no further credit creation in order to continue these primary expenditures and to maintain the level of employment that has been reached.

The really serious danger of a large public debt is caused by wrong policies which are justified with the argument that a large debt makes it imperative to maintain a fixed pattern of security prices and interest rates. In Chapter 17 we have already dealt with this untenable supposition.

Prosperity, Monetary Policy, and Inflation

When recent theoretical advances and practical experiences explained and proved the efficacy of fiscal policy as an instrument of economic stability, monetary theory and policy fell, temporarily, into oblivion. Not only was fiscal policy the sequel of monetary policy during times of depression but it usurped the place of monetary policy altogether. Arguments which were justifiable in times of severe underemployment were applied in times of high employment, and in the United States and many other countries the monetary authority became subservient to the treasury. Since about 1951, however, there has been a resurrection of monetary policy so that since then we have once more been able to integrate monetary and fiscal policies in an attempt to maintain a high level of economic activity without price inflation.

In the co-ordination of monetary and fiscal policy, emphasis will be on fiscal policy during depression and on monetary policy during prosperity. This is explaind by the natural weakness of monetary measures during times of depression and by the restraining influence of monetary policy in prosperity. This restraint implies conscious management. As a matter of fact, it resquires much greater political and psychological fortitude than does deficit spending during the downswing. Monetary policy continues throughout the cycle. Deficit financing implies credit creation and thus the active co-operation of the banking system. And the monetary authority retains—or at least ought to retain—the ultimate power of shutting off the inflationary faucet.

The powers of the monetary authority depend partly on the monetary instruments at its disposal. These instruments may be insufficient. In Chapter 17 we have seen that monetary policy in the United States was paralyzed for nearly 20 years; first because the excess reserves resulting from an enormous gold inflow could not be wiped out by the Federal Reserve, and then because the Federal Reserve was obliged to maintain a perfectly elastic demand for government bonds.

Let us assume, however, that the instruments of the monetary authority have been overhauled and that the central bank can stop an inflationary development. The central bank is not forced to maintain a perfectly elastic demand for securities; it can remove excess reserves through increased reserve requirements; it can raise the discount rate, and through open market operations it can see, via an excess of security sales over purchases, that the commercial banks' reserves are lowered. In addition it can use qualitative controls over margin requirements and installment buying.

Monetary policy has the great advantage that it is more flexible than fiscal policy. Monetary measures can react instantly to changing economic conditions. This high degree of flexibility, however, does not mean that the monetary authority can dispense with economic forecasting. A continuous appraisal of the economic situation is essential for its decisions on credit policy. It has not only to decide whether credit expansion or credit restriction is the right medicine under the circumstances but also what dosage is to be used. Credit policy, of course, is not limited to changes in interest rates. Rather what counts is the general availability of credit, which depends on the reserve position of the commercial banks. We have already seen that credit extension always contains an element of rationing.

Monetary policy which, together with fiscal policy, aims at general economic stability is much more difficult to administer than a policy of stabilizing commodity or security prices. Technically speaking, nothing is easier than the maintenance of a perfectly elastic demand for government securities but this means the end of monetary policy. Stability of commodity prices is more difficult to achieve, but as an *aim* of monetary policy it is relatively simple because it indicates what the monetary authority should try to do. Even a policy of neutrality, though requiring delicate compensations for hoarding or business integration, would not necessitate economic forecasting. But forecasting becomes unavoidable if monetary policy wants to co-operate with fiscal policy in stabilizing the economy.

A policy of neutral money is inapplicable if a state of underemployment necessitates the creation of new purchasing power. Credit creation will then be an essential part of our compensatory efforts. But this does not mean that the monetary authority can limit itself to the task of preventing price inflation when a high level of employment has been reached. Inflation is a gradual process which cannot be stopped abruptly unless we want to upset rather than maintain economic stability. This is the dilemma of monetary policy: only in times of prosperity can it exert a decisive influence, but by that time the expansionist process has already gathered momentum and dangerous disproportions have developed. We have seen that these disproportions between the rate of growth of consumption and investment must finally lead to a downswing. Yet this strain in our economic structure may not be apparent. It will be revealed, however, as soon as the monetary authority slows down the rate of credit expansion. The central bank may thus find itself in the unpleasant position of having to take the blame for either of two evils: if it puts the brakes on early, it will be blamed for spoiling the expansion process at a time when further vigorous credit creation could have sustained the boom; and if it acts too late, it will be blamed for not having checked the inflationary forces, for having let the situation get out of hand, and for having to use, in the end, much more drastic policies than would have been necessary in the case of timely action.

Thus it can easily be seen that actions taken by the monetary authority will frequently be subject to much criticism and that the central bank may be simultaneously blamed for excessive caution and a much too liberal attitude. Not even hindsight will serve as arbiter because we can never be sure what turn economic events would have taken if the monetary authority had acted more conservatively or more liberally during a given previous period.

Once more, as in the case of fiscal policy, some comfort can be found in the knowledge that a very flexible policy can instantly adjust to changes in our economic weather. In the case of fiscal policy we could only stress the importance of making public revenue and expenditure policies as flexible as possible, knowing that by their very nature they are relatively slow in their reactions. Monetary policy, on the other hand, enjoys the advantage of being able to change instantly in both degree and direction as economic facts change.[2]

Creeping Inflation

A glance at Chart 8–2 (p. 87) shows that the development of wholesale prices was in the main inflationary since the outbreak of World War II. Previously, inflation periods had always been followed by deflation periods. Now this fluctuation of prices has been replaced by a one-sidedly inflationary development with occasional brief interruptions. The development of consumer prices (Chart 8–1, p. 86) resembles a stepladder rather than a wave.

This chronic or intermittent inflation is a new phenomenon, indicating a departure from past monetary policy which needs our

[2] See, however, footnote 14 to Chapter 27, p. 376.

special attention. The new inflation is a relatively mild one and has been called *creeping* inflation. Were it not creeping but self-aggravating or accelerating, it could not continue for long. History shows that price inflations which became runaway inflations had to be stopped by drastic means, because no market economy can continue to function without a reasonable degree of price stability. It is not likely that a modern government will let an accelerating inflation develop into hyperinflation. However, a government which delayed remedial monetary action too long may try to cure the symptoms of price inflation by freezing prices, wages, and exchange rates—an attempt which implies production, consumption, and foreign trade controls.

The problems of repressed inflation will be discussed below. For the present we assume that repressed inflation is to be avoided, because price controls contradict the working principles of a market economy. It follows that creeping inflation must not be permitted to become an accelerated or self-aggravating inflation. Neither hyperinflation nor repressed inflation is acceptable, nor must the economy be exposed to the shock of a sudden drastic application of the monetary brakes.

The greatest danger of a creeping inflation, therefore, lies in the fact that it may become self-aggravating and that then no cure could be found which would not seriously hurt a market economy.

Exactly when a creeping inflation develops into accelerated inflation cannot be determined in advance. Reactions of a population to a continuous rise of prices depend to some extent on a country's previous inflation experiences. But in any country inflation can reach a point where the population will find it inadvisable to save money of visibly decreasing purchasing power. With a further rise in prices the population will accelerate the purchase of consumers' goods, that is, the velocity of circulation of money will dangerously increase.

But creeping inflation may be dangerous even if it can be kept creeping. A continuous credit inflation leads to artificially low interest rates and artificially high rates of profit. The result will be overinvestment and recession and the recession must be kept from developing into a depression. But, as Gottfried Haberler has pointed out:

> If an ordinary cyclical depression threatens (not caused by tight money policy) in a period not marked by chronic inflation, the monetary and fiscal authorities have a free hand to counteract the depressive forces with the weapons of monetary and fiscal policy. If such a depression strikes during a period of chronic inflation, the monetary and fiscal authorities lack this freedom to a considerable degree, because of their justifiable pre-

occupation with creeping inflation. Creeping inflation thus carries the double danger that it tends to produce depression and to impede the prompt and effective treatment of depressions that arise independently of the price creep.[3]

But is not recession caused by a falling-off of aggregate demand and, therefore, always accompanied by deflation? In this case we could assume that there would always be room for "reflation," that is, room for expansionist monetary and fiscal policies without price inflation.

Recent experiences have shown that recession and deflation need not be simultaneous and that price inflation can continue even when aggregate demand decreases.

Before we turn to this interesting phenomenon it should be mentioned that creeping inflation may be incompatible with balance of payments equilibrium if it raises costs and prices of a country above those of competing countries. We shall turn to this problem in Chapter 37.

Demand-Pull and Cost-Push Inflation

Substantial price inflations are always demand-induced in the sense that a continuous rise of the general price level would be impossible without continued credit creation and an expansion of aggregate demand which exceeds the growth of production. Nevertheless, a wage push may lead to a supporting credit inflation, that is, a credit inflation which tries to avoid unemployment which may result from a wage push under unyielding demand conditions. While it is often impossible to separate a wage push from other inflationary factors, it becomes clearly visible when aggregate demand falls off but wages and prices rise.

The same holds true for a so-called administrative price inflation which can be the result of monopolistic policies of private firms or of "government operated, sponsored, or induced price maintenance and price support schemes."[4] It is possible, of course, that with unchanging aggregate demand prices of competitively produced commodities will be forced down when administered prices are raised. Then the general price level can remain stable in spite of rising administered prices. However, more likely total output will fall because of frictions which

[3] Gottfried Haberler, "Creeping Inflation," *Ekonomi Politik Samhälle*, published in honor of Professor Bertil Ohlin's sixtieth birthday (Stockholm, 1959), pp. 92–93.

[4] Gottfried Haberler, *Inflation, Its Causes and Cures* (Washington, D.C.: American Enterprise Association, 1960), p. 34.

develop when prices are to be lowered without a fall in costs.[5] If total transactions (T) decrease, monetary demand (MV) purchases fewer goods at higher prices (P). There is nothing new in the assumption that monopolies (private or public) can raise prices at the cost of reduced production and that the pressure exerted on the competitive sector of the economy can cause unemployment. It follows that unless we assume perfect price and wage flexibility in the nonmonopolistic sector, the general price level can rise without demand pull or even without cost push.

Often, however, an administrative price inflation is caused by a wage push. This form of inflation could not occur in an economy with perfectly competitive labor markets, because wages could then rise only as result of a demand pull.

Prices need not rise, however, in consequence of a wage increase, if productivity increases. It is often assumed, therefore, that wage-push inflation presupposes that the average increase in money wages exceeds the average increase in productivity in the economy.

But even in this case of a noninflationary wage push we must consider that organized labor gains its advantage at the expense of unorganized labor and of fixed-income groups. Furthermore, if wage increases absorb the entire increase in output, nothing is left for capital accumulation, the precondition of further economic growth. Under these conditions price stability could become more dangerous than a price inflation which is not too quickly followed by rising wages, because this so-called profit inflation would at least be a means for the accumulation of capital.[6]

The wage push becomes inflationary when wages rise faster than productivity. Prices must then rise to avoid unemployment. This situation puts the monetary authority in an exceedingly difficult position because it must now either support the wage push through credit inflation or it must permit unemployment to rise as result of a conflict

[5] See Alvin H. Hansen, *Full Recovery or Stagnation* (New York: W. W. Norton and Company, 1938), pp. 78–79. F. A. Hayek admits that "if we introduce the further realistic assumption that many long-term contracts have been made in term of this means of exchange in expectation of more or less constant prices and furthermore that all or many of the existing prices show a certain rigidity and are especially difficult to be reduced, very essential frictions turn up against the realization of a 'neutral' money supply which are of the greatest importance for the formulation of a practical criterion for the monetary policy." (F. A. Hayek, "Über 'neutrales Geld,' " *Zeitschrift für Nationalökonomie*, Vol. 4 (1933), p. 660.)

[6] See Gottfried Haberler, *Inflation, Its Causes and Cures* (Washington, D.C.: American Enterprise Association, 1960), pp. 57–58, who reminds us that both Schumpeter and Keynes held this view.

between an unyielding money supply and an increase in money wages which exceeds the increase in productivity.

Wages should not be automatically raised in industries whose productivity has increased. Even if this policy were not inflationary in the long run, the logic of the price mechanism of a market economy would still require that wages should be raised in response to an increased demand for the particular kind of labor involved. For the same kind of labor the same wage rate should prevail—not different wage rates depending on the varying profitability of the firms and industries; or, to be exact, the difference ought to be limited to the amounts needed to bring about the correct allocation of labor in response to changing demand conditions.

If we assume that a union succeeds in raising wages in a given industry in which increased productivity permitted the increase without a price increase, other workers will ask for equalizing wage increases where there has been no increase in productivity.[7] Again, the result will be unemployment unless the monetary authority permits price increases through a supporting credit inflation.

Repressed Inflation

We cannot deny, of course, that the government can try to freeze prices and wages and thus to cure, at least temporarily, the symptoms of price inflation. Such a policy can be defended in special cases. If in time of war it becomes technically impossible to finance government expenditures entirely from noninflationary sources, credit inflation will have to be resorted to and will eventually lead to price inflation. In addition, there might develop such acute scarcities in strategic materials that only extreme price rises could bring about equality between demand and supply. It may be wise to handle such cases through direct allocations and price controls rather than through the competitive process. Furthermore, price controls and rationing will have to be used where we want to enable the members of lower-income groups to buy essential commodities in wartime.

Price fixing, however, implies that the price is kept below that which would be determined by demand and supply in a free market and that, at the artificial price, the demand cannot be satisfied by the forthcoming supply. Price fixing, therefore, must be accompanied by some form of rationing. Rationing of only selected commodities,

[7] See the excellent discussion of the problem by Fritz Machlup, "Another View of Cost-Push and Demand-Pull Inflation," *The Review of Economics and Statistics*, Vol. XLII (May, 1960).

moreover, has the effect of directing excess purchasing power into the markets of commodities which are not yet subject to price controls and rationing, that is, commodities which consumers have considered less important. The production of these less important commodities, whose prices are still free to rise, then becomes more profitable than production of commodities whose prices are frozen. The whole productive process is thus distorted unless all goods are included in the control scheme.

Suppose that all prices are frozen and that the creation of credit continues. Credit inflation cannot find a vent in price inflation, and the pressure mounts. There is a continuous increase in the inflationary gap between the commodities which are for sale at artificially low prices and in restricted quantities and the growing money income which would like to buy more of these commodities. An ever-growing amount of purchasing power remains idle. If this excess can be absorbed by taxation and borrowing, further credit creation may become unnecessary. If the pressure is permitted to increase too much, the government's ability to enforce price controls and rationing may be jeopardized. Repressed inflation will then erupt, sooner or later, into open inflation.

Repressed inflation causes distortions in the production process no less dangerous than those which an open price inflation brings about. When prices are frozen they do not serve as criteria for the guidance of production. We must assume, therefore, that after the unfreezing a totally new pattern of relative prices will emerge, particularly when the period during which the freeze lasted, was one of enormous structural changes in production techniques, world trade, government demand, and the like.

If open general price inflation is to be avoided once price controls are lifted, it will be necessary to successfully carry out either one or both of two policies prior to the lifting of controls. We must greatly increase the output of goods which are for sale and/or must wipe out the excess purchasing power which repressed inflation left idle in the hands of the people.

Consequences of Repressed Inflation

Insistence on full employment was one of the main factors in the inflationary picture of the postwar years. So much had the depression psychology of the prewar years impressed itself on those responsible for economic policy that rising rates of interest and other anti-inflationary policies were ruled out for fear that they might lead to deflation and unemployment. The cheap-money policy, in turn, made it imperative to control investments artificially. This corresponded in many countries with the general aims of socialism. But in economies where by far the largest part of industry is still in private hands and where a central plan of action does not exist, there is no rational means for deciding on the ends of an investment program or for achieving these ends once they are arbitrarily chosen. The normal criterion for allocating investment funds in an unplanned private enterprise economy is a comparison between rates of interest and anticipated rates of profit. The interest rate must be high enough to reduce the total demand for loanable funds to the noninflationary supply of savings, assuming full-employment conditions. Otherwise, resultant credit inflation will deprive the economy of the main criterion for consistent allocation of the factors of production.

Accompanying the arbitrary allocation of investment funds during repressed inflation will be the egalitarian pressures insisting that the socially undesirable effects of open price inflation must be avoided. Subsidies will be used to lower the prices of essential food items, and a broad and expensive program of social services will add to the difficulties which the government faces in balancing its budget. Again, the result will be credit inflation.

Although the existence of widespread controls in a country experiencing repressed inflation may give an impression of "austerity," it should be understood that such controls do not necessarily reflect an abnormal shortage of total resources. They always reflect, however, an allocation of resources other than that which market forces would bring about, and such arbitrary allocation of resources will in many instances aggravate an abnormal shortage of total resources. Furthermore, in an effort to achieve through controls both high investment and high consumption at home, resources may be diverted from the production of goods for export, thus creating a shortage of foreign exchange which leads to foreign exchange controls. Foreign exchange controls must be maintained in any case, since domestic price and production controls are incompatible with a free market for foreign exchange.

Thus a country with repressed inflation offers the not very intriguing picture of a very large number of direct controls clumsily trying to achieve what the pricing process is prevented from doing. It may perhaps be argued that, while repressed inflation necessitates controls, controls do not necessarily imply the existence of repressed inflation. But the overwhelming evidence of postwar experiences seems to be that most peacetime controls are the outgrowth of repressed inflation.

While postwar England under the Labor government provides an example of controls which were able to be enforced with considerable success, many other countries have exemplified a state of repressed inflation in which the government was no longer able to keep the lid on prices and wages. Black markets will then appear, and the economy will be divided into legal and illegal sectors, with the illegal sector rapidly gaining the upper hand. Excess purchasing power then causes a violent price inflation in the black markets, while the legal markets are drained of merchandise. Once the population finds that it cannot buy even its modest rations, black-market operations become the preoccupation of everybody. Where one such black-market transaction earns more money than a week's or a month's hard work, productivity will decline enormously.

This mixture of repressed and open inflation is perhaps the worst type of all inflations.

Stabilization after Repressed Inflation

How can a nation get from repressed inflation to stability without having to pass through a period of price inflation? Obviously, if excess purchasing power is not permitted to burn itself out, it must be removed, that is, the supply of money must be brought into proper proportion to the supply of goods.

Two methods suggest themselves. The whole excess purchasing power could be removed by being changed into public debt through authoritative decree. Future tax revenues would have to service this debt. This method would have the disadvantage of saddling the country with a large public debt and correspondingly difficult budgetary problems at a time when a balanced budget is a precondition of monetary stability. From the standpoint of social justice it can be argued that much of the excess purchasing power is owned by black-market profiteers and that it would be better to deal more drastically with these ill-gotten gains.

The second method of removing excess money consists of temporarily freezing all existing money reserves (currency as well as demand deposits) and then carefully converting this old money into new money at some chosen ratio, such as 10 to 1. The total quantity of new money must be that which meets the needs of the economy at the chosen price level. This more drastic method has the great advantage of avoiding difficult debt and tax problems. Money holdings of profiteers can be detected by comparing present with previous money reserves. That such vigorous and prompt action will be too summary to assure all persons equity and justice cannot be helped. It is above all necessary that the reform create clear price relationships if the economy is to recover. Uncertainty would be an unmitigated evil.

The tasks which remain after the removal of excess purchasing power are difficult: gradual adjustment of the money supply to the supply of goods, that is, regulation of the speed of the unfreezing process; establishment of normal price relationships, somewhere between the previous legal and black-market prices; pursuance of a careful credit policy, which must avoid overinvestment; and, finally, pursuance of a wage policy which rigorously adjusts the standard of living to the productive capacity of the country.

The injustices connected with such incisive action as the removal of excess purchasing power are more acceptable than the tremendous economic loss and chaos which prevail where the controls of repressed inflation cease to work and where black-market operations rather than productive activities absorb the energies of the people.

Several countries have carried through such drastic reforms, for example, Belgium on October 6, 1944, and West Germany on June 20, 1948.[8]

SUGGESTIONS FOR FURTHER READING

Day, A. C. L., and Beza, Sterie T. *Money and Income,* chaps. 19–22. New York: Oxford University Press, 1960.

Bresciani-Turroni, Constantino. *The Economics of Inflation.* London, 1937.

Committee for Economic Development. *Flexible Monetary Policy.* New York, 1953.

Committee for Economic Development. *Defense Against Inflation. Policies for Price Stability in a Growing Economy.* New York: 1958.

Dillard, Dudley. *The Economics of John Maynard Keynes,* chap. 10. New York: Prentice-Hall, Inc., 1948.

Dupriez, Leon H. *Monetary Reconstruction in Belgium.* New York: Carnegie Endowment for Peace, 1947.

Fellner, William. *A Treatise on War Inflation.* Berkeley: University of California Press, 1942.

Graham, F. D. *Exchange, Prices, and Production in Hyper-inflation: Germany, 1920–1923.* Princeton: Princeton University Press, 1930.

[8] See Leon H. Dupriez, *Monetary Reconstruction in Belgium* (New York: King's Crown Press, 1947); Horst Mendershausen, "Prices, Money and the Distribution of Goods in Postwar Germany," *The American Economic Review,* Vol. XXXIX (June, 1949).

HARROD, R. F. *A Policy Against Inflation.* New York: St. Martin's Press, 1958.

KEYNES, J. M. *How to Pay for the War.* New York: Harcourt, Brace & Co., Inc., 1940.

RITTER, LAWRENCE S. *Money and Economic Activity,* chap. 9. Boston: Houghton Mifflin Co., 1952.

WHITTLESEY, CHARLES R. *Readings in Money and Banking,* part xi. New York: W. W. Norton & Co., Inc., 1952.

On demand-pull and cost-push inflation:

BURNS, ARTHUR. *Prosperity Without Inflation.* New York: Fordham University Press, 1958.

CLARK, JOHN M. *The Wage-Price Problem.* The American Bankers Association, 1960.

HABERLER, GOTTFRIED. *Inflation, Its Causes and Cures.* Washington, D.C.: American Enterprise Association, 1960.

MACHLUP, FRITZ. "Another View of Cost-Push and Demand-Pull Inflation," *Review of Economics and Statistics,* Vol. XLII (May, 1960).

MEANS, GARDINER C. *Administrative Inflation and Public Policy.* Washington, D.C.: Anderson Kramer Associates, 1959.

QUESTIONS AND PROBLEMS

1. Discuss the inflationary dangers of a permanently increasing public debt.
2. "Government is not maintained out of surplus of private enterprise. Each segment contributes to the total flow of real income and each takes its share out of the income stream" (Alvin H. Hansen). Discuss.
3. "A policy of neutral money is inapplicable when a state of underemployment necessitates the creation of credit." Correct?
4. Discuss the problems of creeping inflation.
5. Is it possible to have price inflation without demand pull?
6. Explain the possible effects of a so-called "administrative price inflation" in terms of the Fisher equation.
7. Is it safe to say that a wage push is not inflationary when the average increase in money wages does not exceed the average increase in productivity?
8. Should wages be raised automatically in industries whose productivity has increased?
9. How does administrative price or wage-push inflation affect monetary policy?
10. "Repressed inflation will cause distortions in the production process which are not less dangerous than those which an open price inflation brings about." Discuss.

BOOK FOUR

Money and Foreign Exchange

PART VIII

The Theory of International Payments

Chapter 29 INTERNATIONAL PAYMENTS

The Problem of International Payments

Much of the analysis of the preceding chapters has proceeded on the assumption of an isolated country or a uniform monetary system for the whole world. This assumption is now to be removed to make way for a discussion of international exchange, which, no less than trade within countries, requires the use of money to overcome the awkwardness of barter.

The peculiar problem of international payments arises from the fact that there is no unit of account common to all countries, and no means of payment acceptable as legal tender beyond the borders of the issuing country.[1]

Strictly speaking, money can buy only within its own national boundaries—the United States dollar in the United States, the cruzeiro in Brazil, the pound sterling in Great Britain. International money, money which could buy throughout the world, does not exist and will not be created in the foreseeable future. How then, are international payments to be accomplished? English exporters need

[1] Exceptions have been the result of international agreements such as the Latin or Scandinavian Union.

English money to pay English producers, while American importers are paid in American money by their customers. Obviously the American importer will have to acquire pounds sterling for dollars, or the British exporter must accept dollars and sell them for pounds sterling. Payments from one country to another require the exchange of domestic for foreign money. The foreign money, as seen by the domestic buyer or seller, is generally referred to as foreign exchange.

Foreign exchange is bought and sold on the foreign exchange market. On the foreign exchange market of the United States we buy —with dollars, of course—foreign currencies or drafts payable in foreign currencies. The prices paid for the pound sterling, the French franc and the Deutsche mark, expressed in dollars and cents, are foreign exchange rates.[2] The price of the pound sterling on the foreign exchange market of the United States will rise when the demand for pounds sterling increases or when the supply of pounds sterling decreases. We can call this a "rise" in the foreign exchange rate; British money becomes more expensive for American buyers, and American currency becomes cheaper for British buyers.

Assuming sufficient freedom of international payments (that is, excluding foreign exchange control), the dollar price for pounds sterling in New York and the pound sterling price for dollars in London must be closely related. The slightest difference of the two ratios would lead to a process of arbitrage. For example, if less British money were needed to buy a dollar in New York than in London, dollars would be acquired for pounds in New York and sold at a profit for pounds in London until the exchange rates would be consistent for the two markets. The increased supply of pounds in New York and of dollars in London would have this equilibrating effect. The principle of arbitrage (that is, the simultaneous purchase of a currency in one market and its sale in another market) would similarly lead to consistency among the exchange ratios of all currencies, since the dollar-franc rate could not be out of line with the pound-dollar and pound-franc rates, respectively, without setting the arbitrage process in operation.

The Clearing of International Payments

If gold is used as a common denominator for the different national currency units, it facilitates the comparison of relative exchange

[2] Of course, since the "commodity" on the foreign exchange market is foreign money, we have the choice of quoting the price of the pound sterling in dollars and cents or the price of the dollar in shillings and pennies.

values and gives more stability to the pattern of exchange rates. In respect to different currencies gold performs then a function similar to the one that money performs when it enables us to express exchange values of commodities in terms of prices. Gold may also serve as a means of international exchange. Gold is willingly accepted all over the world, and it is therefore possible to make international payments through gold shipments. If the gold parities of the different currency units are fixed and if the residents of the different countries are entirely free to buy and sell gold and to transfer it to other countries, the monetary systems of the world are closely knit together. This is the essential framework of the international gold standard of the old, pre-1914 type, which will be discussed in Chapter 31.

The use of gold as a common anchorage for national currency units does not, however, imply that international payments are generally accomplished through gold shipments. Even when countries are on the gold standard, cumbrous payments in gold are avoided through operation of the foreign exchange market. On the foreign exchange market a country's debits and credits are cleared in the same way that a bank clearinghouse effects the clearance of money claims of different banks on each other.

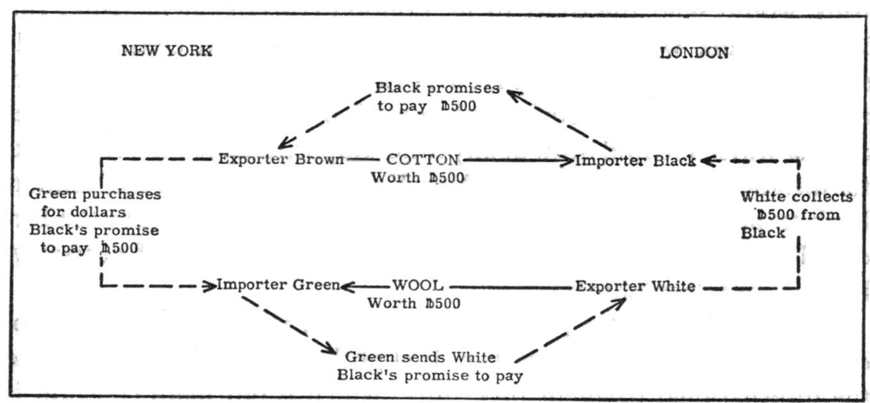

FIG. 29–1

A greatly simplified example (see Figure 29–1) will illustrate the clearing process. Exporter Brown in New York has sold 500 pounds sterling worth of cotton to importer Black in London, and at the same time exporter White in London has sold 500 pounds sterling worth of wool to importer Green in New York. Payments for these purchases can easily be made without inconvenient and expensive shipments of gold. Brown will draw a bill of exchange on Black, ordering him to pay 500 pounds sterling. Brown sells the bill to Green for dollars; Green uses the bill to pay White; and White in turn collects pounds sterling from Black. Two international payments have thus been accomplished with the aid of a commercial paper and one domestic payment in each of the two countries. (This system, incidentally, does not require gold-standard conditions in the trading countries. It would work in essentially the same way between countries on the paper standard.)

This simplified description of the fundamental international payments procedure can be completed with a few additional remarks. The four parties in the above example are, in reality, a multitude of exporters and importers who are brought into convenient financial relationships by bankers and exchange dealers. Brown, for example, would sell his pound sterling draft on Black to a New York bank; the bank would send the draft to its London correspondent bank; the London bank would collect from Black and would credit pounds sterling to the account of the New York bank. Through many similar transactions the New York bank would build up foreign balances against which it could draw at any time. Importer Green in New York, for instance, could buy from the New York bank a draft on the London bank to make payments to exporter White in London. Since the foreign balances are readily available the payments could, if necessary, be made by telegraphic transfer.

If the draft is not payable on sight but, say, in sixty days (a so-called time draft) the transaction is slightly more complicated, since the international payment procedure, which is our main concern, is then connected with a credit operation. The New York bank, when buying a time draft from Brown, will deduct from the purchase price the interest (discount) for the interval between the time of the purchase and the time when the London correspondent bank can collect from Black.

Since foreign exchange transactions are almost always also credit transactions, that is, exchanges of present money of one country against future money of another country, exchange rates for different kinds of international claims will vary according to maturity dates and also according to credit-worthiness (that is, the credit standing of drawee, drawer, and those who have endorsed the credit instrument).

Foreign exchange dealers (usually commercial banks) perform an important function in acting as financial intermediaries between importers who have to buy foreign currency and exporters who have foreign currency to sell. The dealers act as wholesalers and retailers in foreign funds, make their superior credit standing available, act as collectors of claims in foreign countries with the assistance of their correspondents, borrow and lend internationally, and bring about a consistent pattern of exchange rates through arbitrage.

The identical value of the traded goods in the above example is a simplification which will appear less arbitrary if we consider that each country's total receipts and payments must balance and that it is the very function of fluctuations in foreign exchange rates to help bring about this equilibrium. Of course, the payments between any pair of countries will not necessarily balance unless they are artificially equalized through bilateral payment agreements. There is no reason to assume that a country's export markets will coincide with its sources of supply. Country A may have a continuous import surplus with country B and a continuous export surplus with country C.[3] Such a situation is absolutely normal owing to the different economic structures of the countries in question. But it requires that country A must be able to use the proceeds of her exports to country C to pay for her imports from country B. Or stated quite generally, a country must be allowed to spend the proceeds of her exports for purchases from any country. If a country cannot use its export proceeds anywhere for any desired purpose, the consequences are very damaging.

The Balance of Payments

Will commodity exports and imports balance between one country and the rest of the world? Not necessarily, since international payments do not originate only from the purchase and sale of commodities. They may be due to services rendered (shipping, freight, insurance, banking), expenditures of tourists in foreign countries, interest and dividend payments, expenditures by government agencies, capital movements (that is, purchase of foreign securities and sale of domestic securities), unilateral payments (grants or indemnities), and monetary gold movements.

All these and other payments between one country and the rest

[3] "Thus the United States on the average of the three years 1936–8 sold to Britain goods to the value of $499 millions a year and bought from Britain only to the extent of $174 millions a year. On the other hand, in the same three years, the United States bought from British Malaya goods, chiefly rubber and tin, to the value of $174 millions a year and sold to British Malaya less than $8 millions worth a year. . . . British Malaya transferred her surplus dollars, or some of them, to Britain to pay for imports from Britain and by that means Britain was able to pay for some of her imports from the United States." William H. Beveridge, *Full Employment in a Free Society* (New York: W. W. Norton & Co., Inc., 1945), p. 216.

of the world constitute a country's balance of payments. Commodities and securities sold and services rendered to foreigners, as well as interest and amortization payments received from residents of other countries, lead to a supply of foreign exchange on a country's foreign exchange market. Payments in the opposite direction, that is, payments to residents of other countries, similarly lead to a demand for foreign exchange.

To say that the balance of payments always balances is a truism; because records of all international transactions are kept in the form of double-entry bookkeeping, the debit items must equal the credit items. Every transaction leads to a credit and a debit, a receipt and a disbursement, a plus and a minus. An export of merchandise creates a credit entry, but payment for the exported commodity in form, say, of a deposit in a foreign bank leads to a debit entry signifying a capital export. Similarly, if our exporter were paid in gold or by his own government, as in the case of a grant to the importing country, debit entries would result.

Such an accounting balance records, *ex post,* what happened during a past period. But the identity of debits and credits in such an accounting procedure cannot hide interesting surpluses and deficits in the subdivisions of the balance of payments. An excess of imports over exports, for example, may be balanced by a capital inflow or by unilateral transfers (grants, indemnities); a gold inflow may increase the bank deposits of residents of foreign countries in the gold-inflow country; tourists travelling abroad may draw on their balances held in foreign banks. To interpret the meaning of an accounting balance we must watch these changes of selected accounts. Sometimes we notice an enormous imbalance, as when huge export surpluses are financed by government grants of the exporting country.

In a study of the balance of payments we must distinguish the "current account" from the "capital account." The current account can also be called "income account," since it pictures the expenditures of a country for goods and services and its income from sales abroad. Included are not only commodity and service trade but also "payments due as interest on loans and as net income from other investments" and "payments of moderate amount for amortization of loans or for depreciation of direct investments."[4] We can also interpret government grants as belonging to the current account. Our interpretation will depend on the purpose of our analysis. These donations,

[4] See *Articles of Agreement, International Monetary Fund* (Washington, D.C., 1944), Art. XIX, (i).

which are unilateral transfers, perhaps finance a considerable part of the receiving country's imports. Yet for the purpose of showing the basic imbalance of such a situation it may be preferable to set this item aside as compensatory official financing.[5]

The capital account includes all transactions during the period in evidence of debt or ownership. In most cases net lending or borrowing in the international sphere will have as its counterpart an excess of exports or imports of commodities and services—net lending accompanying an export surplus and net borrowing, an import surplus. We can say that the lending country purchases the borrowing country's securities and pays for these securities with commodities. The capital account deals with both short-term and long-term lending. Many of the short-term financial transactions are closely related to payments in connection with commodity trade and often play an equilibrating or compensating role.

The capital account in the balance of payments is not the so-called balance of international indebtedness which lists for a given date (and not for a period) all claims held by the residents of one country against those of other countries, and vice versa. These claims are the result of past capital movements.

That the balance of payments registers monetary gold movements separately is due to the great importance of gold as a balancing item whose movements may have considerable effect on the domestic monetary policies of the countries concerned. It may be clarifying to bracket these gold movements with short-term capital movements and government grants as the equilibrating and compensating items which bear the brunt of the adjustment burden when disequilibria develop in the balance of trade which are not matched by long-term capital movements.

Now that we have acquainted ourselves with the balance of payments, we can see that a so-called favorable balance of trade, that is, an excess of exports over imports, may have a variety of reasons. A country may borrow abroad and may receive, during this period of borrowing, an excess of imports over exports in exchange for an "export" of its securities. When the country's process of economic development, furthered by these loans, has advanced far enough, the country may stop borrowing but will have to pay interest and amortization on the accumulated debt. During this period of repayment the country must develop an excess of exports over imports. This favorable

[5] See International Monetary Fund, *Balance of Payments Yearbook, 1938, 1946, 1947* (Washington, D.C.: International Monetary Fund, 1949), p. 5.

trade balance will continue when our country, now a mature economy, starts to make loans to other countries. As it "imports" the securities of other countries it pays for them by an excess of exports over imports in its commodity and service trade. Should this period come to an end, our creditor country would have to develop an unfavorable balance of trade to enable debtors to pay their debts.[6]

Figure 29–2 may be of some help in studying the balance of payments and its various subdivisions. Charts 29–1 and 29–2 picture the recent historical development of the United States balance of payments.

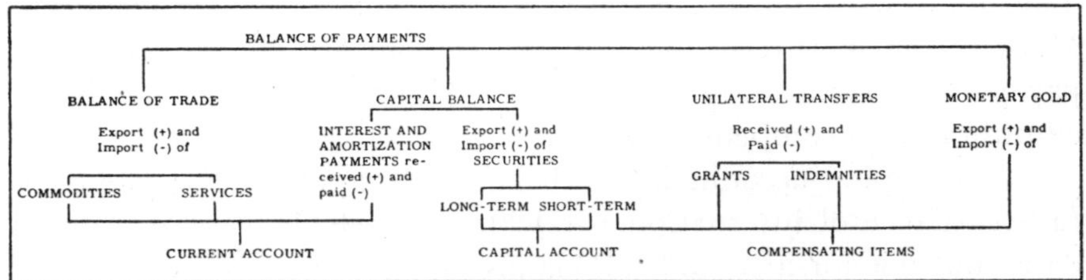

FIG. 29–2

The Market Balance of Payments

Just as the balance of payments always balances ex post in an accounting sense, so it can be said that there must always be some rate of exchange at which demand and supply of foreign exchange will balance if the rate of exchange is permitted to fluctuate freely.[7]

The foreign exchange market, like any other market, is a place of price determination. It has, however, the peculiar feature that the "merchandise" offered for sale is foreign *money* and that we thus find money on both the demand and supply side of the foreign exchange market.

In treating the demand for any good it is generally assumed that as the price goes down the amount bought increases and that with an increase in price the amount bought will decrease. In technical language: the demand curve is assumed to slope from the upper left to

[6] The history of United States trade relations conforms roughly to this development pattern minus the final stage.

[7] See Fritz Machlup, "Three Concepts of the Balance of Payments and the So-called Dollar Shortage," *Economic Journal,* March, 1950. In connection with the following also consult Fritz Machlup, "The Theory of Foreign Exchanges," *Economica,* November, 1939, and February, 1940. Reprinted in *Readings in the Theory of International Trade* (Homewood, Ill.: Richard D. Irwin, Inc., 1949), pp. 104–58.

CHART 29–1

UNITED STATES BALANCE OF PAYMENTS

Based on Department of Commerce Data

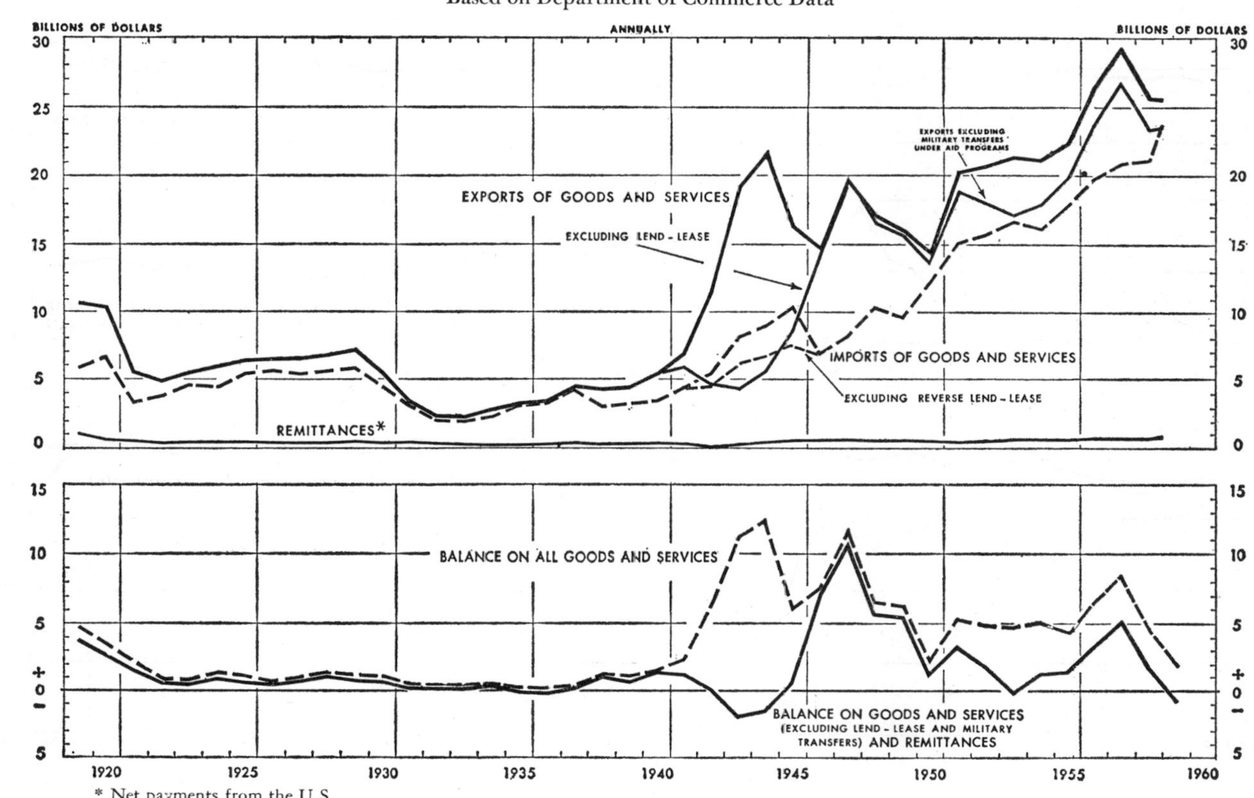

* Net payments from the U.S.

SOURCE: *Historical Supplement to Federal Reserve Chart Book on Financial and Business Statistics* (Washington, D.C.: Board of Governors of the Federal Reserve System, September, 1960), p. 118.

CHART 29–2

UNITED STATES BALANCE OF PAYMENTS

Based on Department of Commerce Data

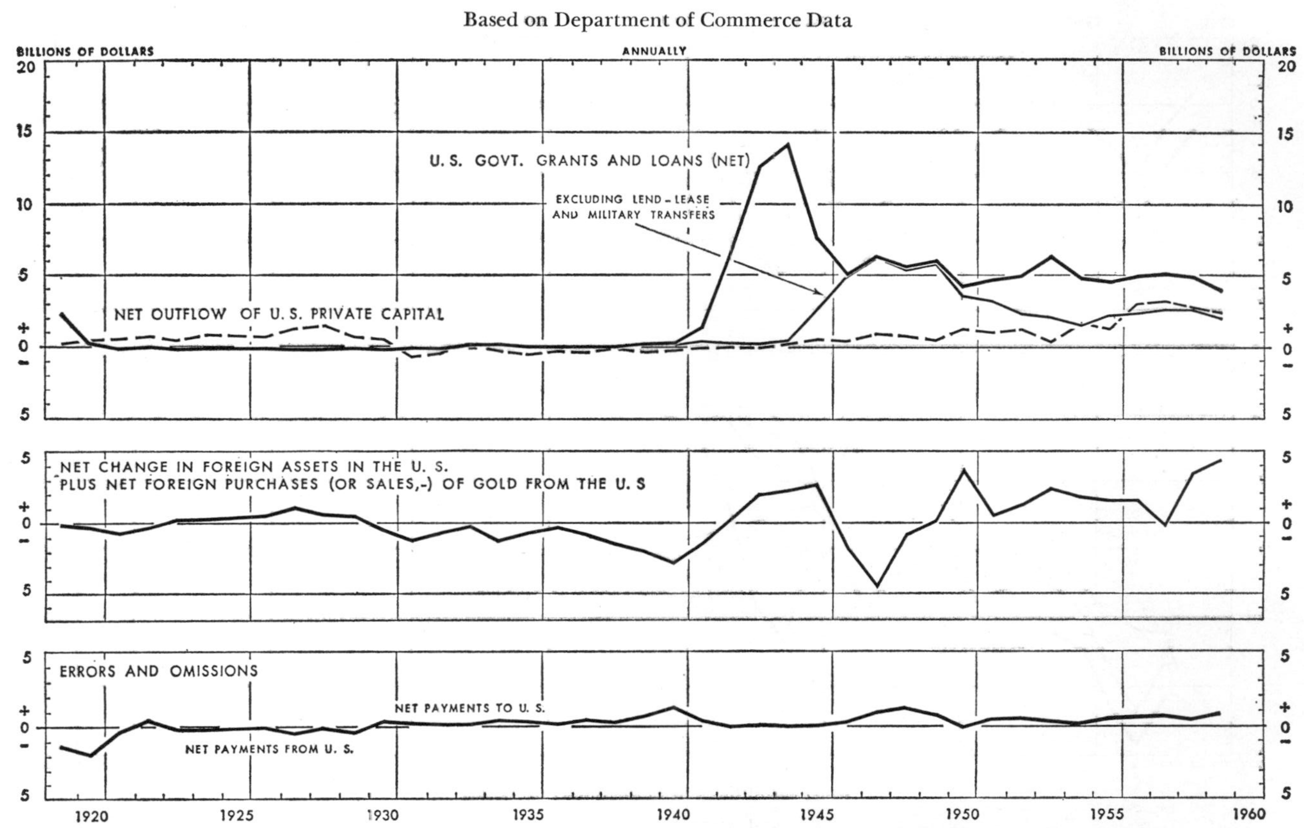

SOURCE: *Historical Supplement to Federal Reserve Chart Book on Financial and Business Statistics* (Washington, D.C.: Board of Governors of the Federal Reserve System, September, 1960), p. 119.

the lower right. The foreign exchange market is no exception to this rule. It is quite natural that, in a normal case, the amount of foreign exchange which buyers stand ready to buy should be the greater the lower the price of foreign exchange in terms of domestic money. Foreign exchange is the entrance ticket to foreign markets. Assuming that the prices of foreign goods in terms of foreign money are stationary, a reduction in the price of foreign money makes all foreign products cheaper and therefore leads to increased imports from abroad. Since these increased imports have to be paid for, importers will desire to buy larger amounts of foreign money. A higher price for foreign money, on the other hand, makes all foreign products more expensive, leads to a falling off of imports and, consequently, of the amount of foreign exchange demanded by importers.

The statement that more is bought at a lower price, while true, is, however, of little significance unless it is qualified by assumptions concerning the elasticity of demand.

We assume with Alfred Marshall[8] that the elasticity of demand for imports and for foreign exchange is, on the average, greater than unity, that is, that a lower price, in domestic money, for the unit of foreign money will result in a larger total amount of domestic money being spent on the foreign exchange market.

It is possible that a section of a country's demand for foreign exchange is perfectly inelastic, that is, that the amount of foreign exchange bought remains the same irrespective of changes in the exchange rate. Consider a country which has to make interest or reparation payments to another country *in the other country's currency* and assume that the amounts in question are fixed. Now the amount of foreign exchange required does not vary with the exchange rate, but the amount of domestic money necessary to buy the foreign exchange increases or decreases in proportion to an increase or decrease in the exchange rate. In technical language this is a *perfectly inelastic* demand for foreign exchange, and the demand curve is a vertical straight line parallel to the *OY* or price axis. Of course, only part of

[8] See Alfred Marshall, *Money, Credit and Commerce* (London: Macmillan & Co., Ltd., 1924), p. 171. It must be admitted, however, that "in the short run the demand for imports is inelastic primarily because both consumers and producers cannot rapidly adapt their purchasing habits or methods of production to a change in relative prices." Lloyd A. Metzler, "The Theory of International Trade," in *A Survey of Contemporary Economics*, ed. by Howard S. Ellis (Homewood, Ill.: Richard D. Irwin, Inc., 1949), p. 228. Later we shall become acquainted with the so-called income elasticity of demand for imports (and foreign exchange). It is often difficult to tell which part of a given rise in imports was due to lower prices in the export country and which part to expanding income in the import country.

a country's demand for foreign exchange will be perfectly inelastic, but this part may be quite important.[9]

The case of a *perfectly elastic* demand for foreign exchange would require that the monetary authority of the country stand ready to buy at a certain price *all* foreign exchange that is offered for sale. The demand curve would be a horizontal straight line parallel to the *OX* or quantity axis. When such a standing offer exists, the price of foreign exchange cannot fall below the official buying rate, since no one would sell for less than the price at which the government buys "any" amount. Of course, only the monetary authority can be expected to undertake to buy unlimited amounts of foreign exchange at a set price, since only the monetary authority can (theoretically) create unlimited amounts of domestic money.

Take, finally, the case where country A has to make yearly payments to country B fixed in country A's own currency—for example, the repayment of a loan contracted in units of A-money. If the price of B-money fluctuates in terms of A-money, that is, if the exchange rate varies, a fixed amount of A-money will buy varying amounts of B-money. A fall in the price of B-money by 50 per cent would, for instance, increase by 100 per cent the amount of B-money which could be bought with the fixed sum of A-money. Conversely, a doubling of the price of B-money would cut in half the amount of B-money obtainable for a fixed sum of A-money. This is the peculiar case of a demand situation in which the amount spent remains the same irrespective of price. In technical language, the demand has an *elasticity of unity* and the demand curve is a rectangular hyperbola.

While at any moment of time the demand curve on the foreign exchange market can be assumed as given, the demand curve may shift over a period of time. Such shifts (an increase or decrease of demand) are due to changes in the demand for foreign commodities, services, and securities. These changes, in turn, are caused by variations in national income, in tastes, in technology, in commercial policies, etc. Also, changes in the price of currency C and D may change country A's demand for currency B.

The supply of foreign exchange on a country's foreign exchange

[9] The period from 1929 to 1932 offers an excellent example. Owing to the decrease in American imports of goods and in long-term investments abroad the dollars supplied by the United States to foreign countries fell from $7.4 billion in 1929 to 2.4 billion in 1932, but in both 1929 and 1932 the dollars required to meet fixed debt-service payments to the United States (assuming no defaults or adjustments) were $900 million. See Hal B. Lary and Associates, *The United States in the World Economy* (Washington, D.C.: United States Government Printing Office, 1943), p. 6.

market depends on that country's exports of goods, services, and securities. These exports are other countries' imports and are, therefore, influenced by numerous factors in both the exporting and importing country. The quantity of foreign exchange supplied will increase with the price paid for foreign exchange (the supply curve of foreign exchange slopes, as a rule, upwards to the right). The exporter sells his receipts of foreign exchange for domestic money, and his profits are increased if he can sell them at a higher price—that is, for more domestic money. Also, as the price for foreign currency rises in country A, A-currency becomes cheaper for foreign buyers. And since A-currency is the entrance ticket to country A's market, all prices in country A become at once more attractive to foreigners.

We assume that the supply of foreign exchange is relatively elastic, that is, that an increase in the price paid for the unit of foreign money will cause a more than proportionate increase in the amount supplied (for example, if the price is doubled, the quantity supplied will more than double) and that a decrease in price will cause a more than proportionate decrease in the quantity supplied.

In the absence of foreign exchange control, the exchange rate is determined by demand and supply, as is any other market price in a perfectly competitive situation. At the rate thus determined international payments equilibrium must exist, that is, the amounts demanded and supplied under free market conditions must be equal. (The rate corresponds, in other words, to the intersection of the demand and supply curves.) When demand for foreign exchange increases (a shift of the demand curve to the right) the price of foreign exchange will increase. Conversely, a decrease in demand (a shift of the demand curve to the left) will lower the price of foreign exchange. Similarly, an increase in supply (a shift of the supply curve to the right) will lower the price of foreign exchange while a decrease in supply (a shift of the supply curve to the left) will increase the price of foreign exchange.

The theory of the foreign exchange market consists mainly in an analysis of the factors which determine demand and supply. Theoretically, these factors can be divided into those which determine the elasticities of existing demand and supply, and those which change the demand and supply situation (that is, shift the positions of the demand and supply curves). The elasticity of demand (supply) will determine whether shifts in the supply (demand) curve will have a greater influence on the amounts bought and sold or on the price at which the sales take place. The greater the elasticity of demand or supply, the more stable the exchange rate will remain and the more will changes in supply or demand manifest themselves in changes of quantities bought and sold. Conversely, the more inelastic the supply and demand, the greater will be the changes in the exchange rate as the result of a shift of the curves and the smaller will be the changes in quantities bought and sold.

The working of the price mechanism on the foreign exchange market with freely fluctuating exchange rates can be illustrated by the following example. Suppose that country A makes a loan to country B, that is, that country A purchases country B's securities. The demand for these securities is added to the demand for foreign exchange arising from current transactions. When the total demand for foreign exchange thus increases, the price of foreign currency will rise. This price rise will decrease the amount of foreign exchange bought for current transactions as well as increase the amount supplied since, as we have already seen, a higher price of foreign exchange will cut down the purchase of foreign goods and services and will step up the sale abroad of domestic goods and services. The difference between the amount of foreign exchange bought for current transactions and supplied by current transactions will equal, at the new exchange rate, the amount desired for purposes of capital transfer.

Fig. 29–3 shows a demand curve *DD* and a supply curve *SS* for foreign exchange, the curves intersecting at point *P*. The demand curve *DD* represents the demand for foreign exchange arising from current transactions. Then the demand curve is shifted to the position *D′D′* owing to the addition to *DD* of a new demand for foreign exchange arising from purchase of foreign securities or from a loan given to another country. The new (total) demand curve *D′D′* intersects the old supply curve *SS* at point *P′*, that is, the price of foreign exchange will rise. At this higher price the amount of foreign exchange bought for current transactions is reduced from *OA* to *OB* while the amount supplied rises from *OA* to *OC*. An amount of foreign exchange equal to the total difference *BC* is now available for the "transfer" of capital.

Classification of International Payments Systems

A real (as distinguished from a mere accounting) balance of international payments can be achieved in several ways. The government can decide to leave all who want to buy or sell foreign exchange entirely free to do so, or it may decide to subject the foreign exchange market to price controls and rationing. This distinction is basic. Exchange control replaces the equilibrating function of the foreign

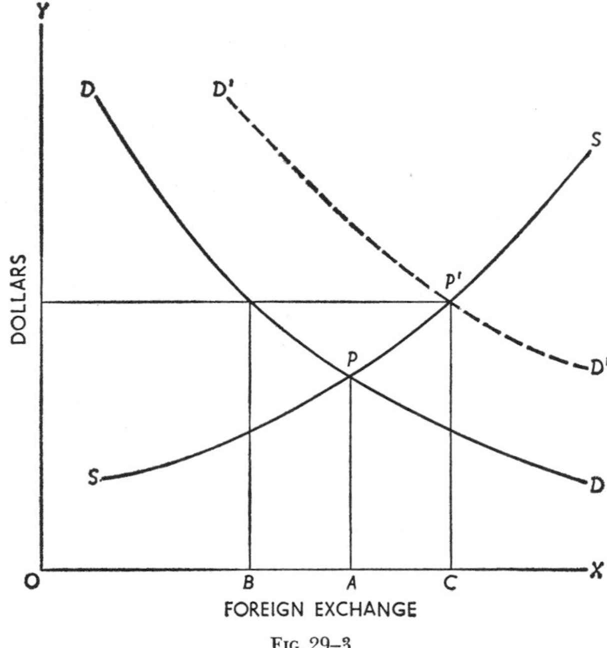

Fig. 29–3

exchange market by regulations which are alien to the pricing process.

Once the market price has been replaced by official quotations, the government can establish several rates. At low rates preferred buyers will be permitted to purchase (though perhaps not freely), others will be charged higher rates for what they will be permitted to buy, while still others are entirely excluded. We see that quantitative controls adjust demand to supply.

Exchange control still implies that foreign trade is carried on by private agents who are free to act within the framework of the control measures. More extreme is the case of a government monopoly in international trade since, by definition, it excludes private traders as agents on the domestic side of international transactions.

Among the free payments systems we can distinguish two major cases:

1. *The system of freely fluctuating exchange rates.* In this system, changes in demand and supply on the foreign exchange market are permitted to change the exchange rate until a new equilibrium position has been found. The adjustment burden rests on the exchange rate, and no attempt is made by the monetary authority of the country to influence demand or supply conditions with the aim of stabilizing the rate of exchange.

2. *A system of relatively stable exchange rates.* In this system everybody is free to buy and to sell foreign exchange, but steps are taken by the monetary authority to guarantee such high elasticities of demand and supply on the foreign exchange markets that the exchange rate can fluctuate only within a narrow margin.

Since exchange control is, by definition, excluded, and since demand and supply on the part of the public are free and unrestricted, the stability of the exchange rate must be achieved by counterbalancing actions on the part of the monetary authority. A free system in which, nevertheless, the exchange rate is to be temporarily or even permanently stabilized must rest on the government maintaining a perfectly elastic supply of both foreign exchange and domestic money. Under these circumstances changes in the demand for domestic money by "exporters" (changes in the supply of foreign exchange) or changes in the demand for foreign exchange by "importers" are automatically neutralized in their effect upon the exchange rate.

Obviously such a counterbalancing policy cannot be continued if the monetary authority should run out of foreign exchange (or gold). In order to keep the supply of foreign exchange perfectly elastic the monetary authority would have to see that its reserves of foreign exchange are filled up again by an increase in the supply of foreign exchange or a decrease in the demand for foreign exchange. This it can do through borrowing from abroad, through a reduction of domestic prices, or through higher tariffs.

Among the free systems with relatively stable exchange rates we can distinguish two cases:

a) *The exchange rate is permanently stabilized through gold parities.* This is the case of the gold mechanism, which rests on the price-specie flow. Adjustments through exchange rate fluctuations are now limited to the very narrow range between the so-called gold points (see Chapter 31). Major equilibrating adjustments are to be brought about by monetary contraction in the gold-outflow country and monetary expansion in the gold-inflow country. Resultant slight deflationary and inflationary price movements are supposed to establish equilibrium. While in the freely fluctuating exchange rate system a changing rate brings about a balance of international payments, the gold-standard system rests on domestic price level adjustments at stable exchange rates, as will be shown in Chapter 31.

Since these price adjustments may not be easy to achieve in case of major disturbances, the system can be made less rigid by replacing the gold parities with flexible exchange rates.

b) *Flexible exchange rates.* These flexible rates do not fluctuate freely. On the contrary, they are always pegged, perhaps to conform to a chosen gold parity. But the rates (and the gold parities) can be changed (adjustable peg: depreciation and appreciation) if it is believed that the change will contribute to international payments equilibrium. Depreciation, for instance, is then being substituted for domestic monetary contraction. This system of flexible rates has been adopted by the International Monetary Fund (see Chapter 35).

Figure 29–4 is a schematic simplification. In reality the systems overlap. Also, we may use other criteria for separating payments sys-

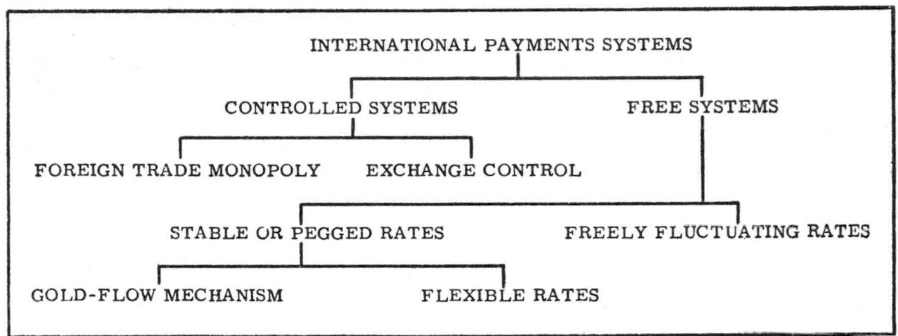

FIG. 29–4

tems or we may disagree on points of emphasis. Bertil Ohlin, for instance, defines exchange control "simply as measures to change directly the demand and supply on the foreign exchange market."[10] If we accept Ohlin's definition, all international payments systems, with the exception of freely fluctuating rates, would be nothing but varying degrees of exchange control.

An overlapping of exchange control and free exchange systems occurs when the freedom to buy and sell foreign exchange is limited to either certain transactions or a certain geographical area. Current transactions, for instance, may be free, while disequilibrating capital movements are subjected to exchange control. We shall see, however, that in practice it is extremely difficult to keep some transactions under control and to grant freedom to others. When exchange transactions are free among the residents of a group of countries but not between the group and the rest of the world, we have another mixture of freedom and control, namely, multilateralism within but not between monetary blocs.

[10] Bertil Ohlin, "Mechanism and Objectives of Exchange Control," *American Economic Review*, Vol. XXVII (1937), Supplement.

Another distinction between international payments systems could be based on the prevalent degree of political agreement and economic integration. As Charles R. Whittlesey puts it: "Stability of exchange rates between any two countries requires approximate reciprocity of conduct. Nothing that any country could do by itself, no matter how orthodox its behavior, would give it stable exchange rates if other countries chose to pursue a contrary policy."[11] Some sort of agreement, whether tacit or formal, must exist to permit that minimum of reciprocity and integration of domestic policies which exchange rate stability or flexibility requires. The gold-flow system rested on tacitly accepted rules of behavior; the International Monetary Fund is based on a formal agreement.

The international monetary policies of modern countries may combine features of the above classifications in great variety, and if technical details were to be included in the classifications, the combinations would indeed be infinite. This does not mean to say that elements of different payments systems can always be combined ad libitum. Some of these elements may be mutually exclusive. For instance, discriminatory exchange control excludes, where it exists, multilateral clearing; exchange depreciation is incompatible with rigidly fixed exchange rates; and monetary nationalism does not permit international co-ordination of monetary policies. Of an infinite number of conceivable international payments systems only a comparatively few are consistent in the sense that the means used to reach the desired ends are adequate or that the ends are not conflicting.

SUGGESTIONS FOR FURTHER READING

MACHLUP, FRITZ. "The Theory of Foreign Exchanges," *Economica,* Vol. VI (November, 1939; February, 1940). Reprinted in *Readings in the Theory of International Trade,* chap. 5 (Homewood, Ill.: Richard D. Irwin, Inc., 1949).

MACHLUP, FRITZ. "Three Concepts of the Balance of Payments and the So-called Dollar Shortage," *Economic Journal,* Vol. LX (March, 1950).

MARSHALL, ALFRED. *Money, Credit and Commerce,* chap. 7. London: Macmillan & Co., Ltd., 1924.

SHAW, EDWARD S. *Money, Income, and Monetary Policy,* chap. 21. Homewood, Ill.: Richard D. Irwin, Inc., 1950.

YOUNG, JOHN PARKE. *The International Economy,* chaps. 4–5. 3d ed. New York: The Ronald Press Co., 1951.

[11] Charles R. Whittlesey, *International Monetary Issues* (New York: McGraw-Hill Book Co., Inc., 1937), p. 11.

QUESTIONS AND PROBLEMS

1. How can international payments be accomplished considering that international money does not exist?
2. Explain the clearing of international payments.
3. "There is no reason to assume that a country's export markets will coincide with its sources of supply." Comment.
4. "To say that the balance of payments always balances is a truism." If this statement is correct, why do countries so often suffer from balance-of-payments difficulties?
5. Draw a systematic picture of the balance of payments. This picture should distinguish current account and capital account and indicate those items which compensate for an otherwise existing disequilibrium.
6. An excess of exports over imports is often referred to as "favorable," an excess of imports over exports as "unfavorable." How did this terminology originate? Is it reasonable? Illustrate your answer with examples.
7. Assume that exchange rates are free to fluctuate on the foreign exchange market and show how different transactions will influence the demand for and the supply of foreign exchange. Give examples for a perfectly elastic and a perfectly inelastic demand for foreign exchange. Which circumstances will lead to a shift of the demand and supply curves? Illustrate graphically.
8. Explain the working of the price mechanism on the foreign exchange market under the assumption that exchange rates are free to fluctuate and that country A buys country B's securities.
9. Is it correct to define exchange control as "measures to change directly the demand and supply on the foreign exchange market" (B. Ohlin)?
10. Arrange the different international payments systems from the completely controlled to the completely free and briefly describe the essential features of each.

Chapter 30 PRICES, NATIONAL INCOME, AND THE BALANCE OF PAYMENTS

International Trade and International Payments

The countries of the world are not equally endowed with productive resources. Some enjoy plentiful skilled labor, capital, and land; others abound in cheap labor but are poor in capital; while still others combine a scarce labor supply with rich natural resources. These various factor combinations in different countries lead to different patterns of factor prices; and since given production techniques often require the use of generally specified proportions of factors, product prices in different countries will differ because factor-price patterns differ. If the structure of commodity prices in country A deviates from the price structure in country B, it must be possible to gain from international trade. Each of the countries will specialize in the production of commodities suggested by its characteristic relative advantage in factor endowment.[1]

The residents of a country will import products which in spite of the cost of transferring them from one country to another are still attractively priced in comparison with domestically produced goods; and they will pay for these imports by exporting commodities whose domestic prices plus transfer cost are competitive on foreign markets. To translate domestic prices into foreign prices we need exchange rates as conversion ratios. Once we know that we can buy or sell a pound sterling for $2.80, we can directly compare British and American prices. When we know, in addition, the cost of transfer (transportation, insurance, tariff duties) we can determine which goods will be imported, which will be exported, and which will not enter international trade. The latter are those whose transfer costs exceed the difference between the domestic and the foreign price.

Every commodity, therefore, has both an export and an import

[1] See Bertil Ohlin, *Interregional and International Trade* (Cambridge, Mass.: Harvard University Press, 1933).

point,[2] the distance between these two commodity points being determined by the cost of transfer. Between the commodity points prices are free to fluctuate without leading to changes in international trade and without affecting exchange rates.

If the price of a commodity should rise beyond the import point, it would automatically attract foreign competition, leading to imports and an increased demand for foreign exchange. A fall below the export point, on the other hand, would lead to exports and an additional supply of foreign exchange.

If transport is impossible or if transport costs are exceedingly high, the good will not be internationally traded. Whether a commodity enters international trade depends, therefore, on the transport (or transfer) cost in comparison with the difference in its marginal cost of production in the respective countries (provided the markets are perfectly competitive in each country). If the transport cost is small enough, it becomes profitable to buy the article in the cheap country and to sell it in the dear country until prices are equalized after allowance has been made for transport (or transfer) costs and after prices have been converted to a common basis by means of the actual exchange rate. Changes in relative prices of individual commodities—even with unchanged general price levels—will bring about changes in exports and imports. Assuming freely fluctuating exchange rates, these changes in trade in turn cause changes in the foreign exchange rate sufficient to equalize exports and imports if there are no other international payments. The effect of changes in relative prices upon international trade and upon the exchange rate depends on the elasticities of demand and supply in the commodity markets of the trading countries. The greater the elasticity of foreign demand for the "domestic" products of country A the more will the amount of foreign money spent increase as the commodity prices in country A decrease, and *ceteris paribus,* the greater will be the elasticity of supply of foreign exchange on the foreign exchange market of country A.

The elasticity of foreign demand depends on factors such as the character of the commodity as a luxury or necessity, the existence of substitutes available in the foreign market, the elasticity of supply of these substitutes, etc. The consumption of raw materials, for instance, which are used for further manufacture, "is not directly responsive to any marked degree to price changes."[3]

[2] See Gottfried Haberler, *The Theory of International Trade* (New York: Macmillan Co., 1937), p. 34.

[3] Hal B. Lary and Associates, *The United States in the World Economy* (Washington: U.S. Government Printing Office, 1943), p. 41.

The elasticity of supply in foreign trade depends on such factors as the competitive or monopolistic character of the industry in question, the ease or reluctance with which domestic demand releases goods for export purposes, and the existence or absence of excess capacity.

The greater the elasticity of foreign demand and the greater the elasticity of domestic supply of export articles, the more elastic will be the supply of foreign exchange in the exporting country and the demand for foreign exchange in the importing country. Conversely, an inelastic demand for imports and an inelastic supply of export products are factors making for an inelastic demand for foreign exchange in the importing country and an inelastic supply of foreign exchange in the exporting country.

The position of countries which produce primary products illustrates the practical importance of the above analysis. Suppose that the production of primary products such as rubber, cotton, wheat, and lead is highly competitive and that it cannot easily be reduced when prices fall. The supply of these products is, consequently, rather inelastic. But the demand, domestic as well as foreign, also tends to be inelastic. The demand for raw materials as well as for foodstuffs is relatively unresponsive to price changes. The combination of inelastic supply and inelastic demand can lead to extremely severe fluctuations in the total amount of domestic and foreign money earned by the sellers of primary products. If the exchange rate is free to fluctuate, a contraction of export values will cause the price of foreign exchange to rise conspicuously.

The smaller one country's share in a product's total export trade, the more elastic is foreign demand for that country's export of the product. If, on the other hand, a country had for its additional exports only a single outlet, that is, if it could sell in the markets of only *one* other country, the foreign demand for its products could prove to be relatively inelastic.

This consideration leads to the important conclusion that, *ceteris paribus,* a system of multilateral trade and payments will experience relatively more stable exchange rates than a system of bilateral arrangements.

Tariffs can be considered a part of transfer costs. They increase the difference between the domestic and foreign price of the protected commodity. When the artificially created price difference outweighs the difference in marginal costs, the tariff becomes prohibitive.

An increase in tariffs is often used as means to achieve balance-of-payments equilibrium by cutting down imports to the "given" size of exports. If stable exchange rates are the aim of such a policy, the result is highly doubtful in the long run. Such tariff increases will seriously reduce the size of the world market and the volume of world trade and will generally lead to an increasing inelasticity in foreign demand. And, as we have seen, the greater the inelasticity of foreign demand, the less stable will be exchange rates and foreign trade equilibrium.

Under a system of import quotas the quantity of imports is rigidly limited if the quotas are small enough to be effective, and the relationship between domestic and foreign prices is disregarded. A quota policy introduces, therefore, "an element of rigidity in the balance of payments."[4] In an extreme case (when all other countries have introduced a comprehensive quota system and when all quotas have been exhausted) the foreign demand for a country's products would become perfectly inelastic, and it would then be impossible to increase the supply of foreign exchange through increasing the physical volume of exports.

Obviously, the elimination of import quotas and the reduction and stabilization of existing tariffs would contribute to a better balanced international payment system and, therefore, to more stable exchange rates.

The foregoing remarks referred to commodity trade. How will the other items in the current account react to price changes? Services will be rendered by the country which enjoys a relative cost advantage in their performance. The demand for and supply of some of these services will closely parallel to fluctuations in merchandise imports and exports and will, therefore, be influenced by the same factors which influence the direction and volume of international commodity trade.

Travel expenditures are interesting as a luxury item among international transactions.[5] They are liable to fluctuate with the national income of the spending ("importing") country rather than with price changes in the "exporting" country.

Personal remittances, depending on such factors as the needs of the recipients, personal relationships, and the financial circumstances of the transmitter, are also rather independent of relative price changes.[6]

[4] League of Nations, *Quantitative Trade Controls* (Geneva: League of Nations, 1943), p. 21.

[5] Lary and Associates, *op. cit.*, pp. 74–77.

[6] *Ibid.*, p. 78.

Interest payments have already been used as an example of perfect price inelasticity of the demand for foreign exchange. Dividend payments, on the other hand, are not predetermined in amount and depend on general business conditions in the paying country—and even on those in the receiving country, if the foreign investment is used to supply raw materials to the investor.

Payments of moderate amounts for amortization of loans will affect the demand for and the supply of foreign exchange very much in the same way as interest payments. But when large settlements of old debts have to be accomplished within a relatively short period of time, the payments can no longer be considered "current transactions" and special problems arise in connection with such debt payments.

Capital Movements and the Balance of Payments

A demand for or a supply of foreign exchange may arise from capital movements, from settlements of old debts, and from such unilateral payments as reparations.

The demand for and the supply of foreign exchange connected with capital transactions cannot be expected to balance. A country will hardly be simultaneously a lender and a borrower of equal amounts or a payer and receiver of reparations. Only if a country should pay reparations out of the proceeds of foreign loans (as was the case with Germany from 1924 to 1929)—thus paying a political debt by transforming it into a commercial debt and shifting the payment problem into the future without solving it—could there be a rough balance on capital account in the period in question.

Payments arising out of capital movements are unilateral in the sense that, for any short period of time, there will be no tendency towards a balancing of the demand for and the supply of foreign exchange connected with them. Payments on current account have the inherent quality that demand for and supply of foreign exchange would tend to be equalized over a relatively short period, say a year, if other transactions were absent. But if unilateral payments are to be made, this self-contained tendency towards equilibrium on current account is deferred or eliminated. The increased demand for foreign exchange, owing, say, to the import of foreign securities, must be satisfied by a supply of foreign exchange which comes from current transactions (export of goods and services). In other words, the transfer of capital from one country to another can be achieved only by an excess of the lending country's exports (including "invisible" items) over its imports, and vice versa for the borrowing country. We have seen how this is accomplished under conditions of freely fluctuating exchange rates (see Chapter 29, pp. 410–11). If foreign lending fluctuates considerably it may be impossible for corresponding changes of imports and exports to materialize with sufficient promptness. Such maladjustments can result from wide variations in long-term leading, and can be even more frequent and violent in connection with certain types of short-term capital movements.

Short-term capital movements may be either equilibrating or disequilibrating. Equilibrating capital movements follow slight declines in the exchange value of the borrower's currency and will help to bring exchange rates back to normal again. Such movements can be expected only when the lender believes that the exchange value of the borrower's currency will fall no further; for they represent movements of capital into a country which suffers from a temporary disequilibrium in its balance of payments. The lender's belief may rest either on an optimistic appraisal of the long-run balance-of-payments situation of the borrowing country or on the certainty that government policies will make it impossible for the exchange value of the borrower's money to deteriorate any further. (For example, the borrowing country's monetary authority may be willing to sell gold or foreign exchange at this price in unlimited amounts.) Since the foreign exchange value of the borrower's money is presumed to have reached the lowest point to which the monetary authority will allow it to fall, it can from now on only rise; and the lender can therefore only gain and not lose through temporary investment of his funds in the currency of the borrowing country. This gain will help to attract short-term capital, and the supply of foreign exchange on the borrowing country's foreign exchange market will increase, thus alleviating a condition of temporary stringency; the foreign exchange rate will tend to return to normal.

Capital movements may, however, be dangerously disequilibrating. When, owing to a disequilibrium in the balance of payments, the price of foreign exchange rises *and is expected to rise still further*, speculators will tend to buy more foreign currency. There are instances of excessively large capital movements when domestic funds, fearing further depreciation, are eager to leave a country (capital flight or hot-money movements) and to move into a country where there already exists a surplus of liquid funds. The effect of such movements is, of course, to raise the price of foreign exchange still further; the anticipation of a price rise is likely to bring about its own realization. Capital movements of this dangerous type may, therefore, easily become cumulative and self-aggravating, especially when domestic credit facilities are not drastically curtailed.

Inflation and the Balance of Payments

In the preceding paragraphs we were mainly concerned with the structure and movements of *relative* prices within each trading country. In reality, of course, relative price movements do not always cancel out. We must assume that general price levels are not always stable.

The countries of the world consider their respective monetary policies as a national prerogative which they are not willing to sign away in favor of international bodies. They may be willing to adjust their domestic monetary policies with a view to better integrating them with those of other nations. But international payments problems which would be ameliorated by such integration cannot monopolize monetary policy. Other aims, such as the maintenance of a high employment level, may be given a prior claim. Accordingly we must consider the case in which the monetary policies of trading countries diverge considerably. Such divergence is important in three respects:

1. As we saw in Chapter 3, general price movements are practically always connected with changes in the relative price structure, whose importance for international payments problems we have already considered.

2. Changes in money supply may accompany changes in national income and employment. These changes are extremely important in connection with the problems of international trade since through international trade such fluctuations in domestic economic activity are transmitted from country to country. We shall deal with this propagation of economic fluctuations later (pp. 424–28).

3. If substantial changes in national price levels are not matched by changes of nearly equal degree and direction in the price levels of other countries, more or less drastic adjustments in the rate of exchange will be unavoidable if freedom of international payments is to be permitted. Even exchange control countries may find it advisable to adjust their official rates (that is, to depreciate) if strong inflationary changes at home have caused the official rate to diverge too far from what the rate would tend to be on a free market.

A system of freely fluctuating exchange rates would adjust the "conversion ratio" to price level disparities. As an inflation in country A (at stable prices in country B) stimulates country A's imports and lowers its exports, the corresponding change in the demand for and supply of foreign exchange will raise the price of foreign exchange in country A. The new equilibrium price should be the old exchange rate multiplied by the ratio of the degree of inflation in the respective countries. If the price level of country A doubled while the price level of country B remained the same, and if 5 units of A-money used to buy 1 unit of B-money, the rate of exchange should now be 10 A-units to 1 B-unit.

Times of violent inflations, however, are hardly times in which we should like to let exchange rates fluctuate freely (see Chapter 32, p. 455). Suppose, therefore, that after years of inflationary changes which had forced countries to seek shelter behind exchange controls, we want to return to a free exchange system and to know the new, correct rates of exchange. Can we follow the so-called purchasing power parity theory, which teaches that, in general, changes in foreign exchange rates are determined by, and are in proportion to, changes in the relative domestic values (purchasing power) of the currencies in question? The answer is no, because there are many other factors which help determine the demand for and supply of foreign exchange, for example, relative price changes, capital movements, unilateral payments, and changes in national income at stable prices (see Chapter 32, p. 456).

The relationship between changes in price levels and changes in the demand for and supply of foreign exchange has been interpreted above as a process leading from changed price levels, via changed demand and supply conditions on the foreign exchange market, to adjustments in the rate of exchange. The so-called balance-of-payments theory, on the other hand, tried to prove during the hyperinflation in Germany in the early twenties that inflation was the result rather than the cause of a balance-of-payments disequilibrium.

Karl Helfferich, for instance, assumed the following chain of cause and effect:[7]

First came the foreign exchange depreciation of the German currency as a result of Germany's overburdening with reparation payments. Then followed a rise in price of all imported commodities. This led to a general rise in prices and wages, which in turn resulted in a greater demand for currency and an increase in the note issue. It was, according to this view, not inflation but exchange depreciation which primarily caused the general rise in prices.

This presentation reverses the actual causal sequence. One of its chief tenets is that a great "need" for imports will result in currency

[7] Karl Helfferich, *Money* (London: E. Benn, 1927), p. 601.

depreciation. It fails to take into account that even the most urgent desire for foreign goods would not lead to imports if they could not be paid for. The "cause" of the upward price movement during those years in Germany was the persistent increase in the quantity of money and its velocity of circulation. Without inflation the German exchange rate could not have fallen indefinitely. If the creation of money had been stopped prices would have ceased rising, and a further fall of the German exchange rate would then have increased exports and decreased imports until a new equilibrium resulted.

There seems to be one point of actually observed fact in favor of this theory: the fall of the German exchange rate often preceded the rise of the domestic price level. This, however, can easily be explained by the purpose for which new money was primarily created. The German governmental budget was heavily unbalanced, partly because of reparation payments, and the deficit was financed by newly created money. To meet reparation payments, and still more to meet payments for imports necessitated by the disruption of the German economy after World War I, a large part of the newly created money was immediately spent in the foreign exchange market. Furthermore, the inflation was generally anticipated to continue and to depress the internal value of the currency. For this reason German currency was "discounted" in the foreign exchange market. A currency which is being rapidly inflated may be quoted in the foreign exchange markets considerably below the purchasing power parity computed from the domestic prices ruling at the moment.[8]

National Income Fluctuations and the Balance of Payments

The classical theory of international trade, as indeed the classical theory in general, proceeded on the assumption of a "full" employment level in the different trading countries. It was admitted, of course, that a disequilibrium in the balance of payments could occur. If, for instance, at stable exchange rates one country's domestic monetary expansion caused prices in that country to rise more than in other countries, that country's imports would increase while its exports would fall off. Gold outflow and domestic monetary contraction were considered the logical and automatic cure for such a temporary state of imbalance. Alternatively, it could be assumed that in the country experiencing inflation the price of foreign exchange would rise and

8 See Gustav Cassel, *Post-War Monetary Stabilization* (New York: Columbia University Press, 1928), pp. 25 ff. See also the excellent critique of the balance-of-payments theory in Walter Eucken, *Kritische Betrachtungen zum deutschen Geldproblem* (Jena: Gustav Fischer, 1923), pp. 5–33.

that this change of the "conversion ratio" would bring about a new balance of international payments. Both adjustment mechanisms were believed to primarily affect prices and costs in the different countries. Changes in output and employment were, as a rule, not sufficiently considered. Economic activity would presumably continue at a high level of employment.

Assumption of a full or high employment level permitted classical writers to show that international trade was favorable for the countries concerned because it made use of the advantages of international specialization. It was the task of the theorist to show which goods would be traded at which terms and how international payments equilibrium could be maintained.

The new economic theory which substituted for the classical assumption of full employment equilibrium a more realistic income-expenditure analysis has had considerable influence on the theory of international trade. Now it could be shown that changes in the national income of one country will affect other countries, that fluctuations in economic activity are transmitted internationally from country to country, and that in the process of transmission the balance of payments will be temporarily disturbed.

For international trade policy some interesting issues arose. If it was possible that a country's employment and income level could be affected by economic fluctuations in other countries—if, indeed, international economic relations could become the cause of unemployment—then a case could be made both for and against international trade. It could now be argued that what we gained through international specialization we could lose through unemployment. This possible conflict can be resolved only if a domestic high employment policy can be made compatible with an international payments equilibrium in which exports pay for imports; and if the advantages of multilateral trade are to be enjoyed, this international payments equilibrium must be possible under a free international payments system.

In Chapter 23 we discussed income levels on the assumption of a "closed" economic system, that is, we excluded economic relations between countries. In Chapter 24, when discussing the multiplier, we found that the domestic multiplier was temporarily reduced by import "leakages." And in Chapter 27 we listed among the elements which make up the aggregate total flow of expenditure an excess of exports over imports (plus) or an excess of imports over exports (minus). The effect of this positive or negative "net international investment" was not pursued. We shall now discuss international monetary relations under the assumption of changing income and employment levels in trading countries.[9]

Assume that in a world-wide depression international payments balance at a low level of international trade. Country A now experiences an increase in net domestic investment. Country A's income and employment expand under the mutually stimulating effects of multiplier and acceleration. The multiplier effect in country A is reduced to the extent that the residents of country A purchase foreign rather than domestic goods. Similarly, we must assume that induced investment expenditures will in part lead to the purchase of capital goods (for example, raw materials) from abroad, that is, from country B (the rest of the world). To refer to the combined imports of consumers' and producers' goods we speak of country A's *marginal propensity to import,* meaning the increment in imports connected with an increment in national income. This marginal propensity must be distinguished from the *average propensity to import,* or the value of imports as a percentage of national income. If we indicate imports by m, the *average* propensity to import is m/Y and the *marginal* propensity to import $\Delta m/\Delta Y$.[10] It may be that the marginal propensity to import is either smaller or larger than the average propensity to import. If the national income of a formerly poor and mostly self-sufficient country rises and if the luxuries which it can now afford to buy are an import article, the marginal propensity to import may well be higher than the average propensity. If, on the other hand, basic necessities had to be imported all along and luxuries, by contrast, are home produced, the marginal propensity to import could be lower than the average propensity.[11]

In connection with our problem of the transmission of economic fluctuations from country A to country B we are interested in the percentage change in imports associated with a percentage change in national income. This relation is known as the *income elasticity of demand for imports.* It can be expressed as $\frac{\Delta m/m}{\Delta Y/Y}$ or $\frac{\Delta m/\Delta Y}{m/Y}$. We see

[9] In connection with the following see: Ragnar Nurkse, "Domestic and International Equilibrium," in *The New Economics,* ed. by Seymour E. Harris (New York: Alfred A. Knopf, Inc., 1948), pp. 264–92; Lloyd A. Metzler, "The Theory of International Trade," in *A Survey of Contemporary Economics,* ed. by Howard S. Ellis (Homewood, Ill.: Richard D. Irwin, Inc., 1949), pp. 210–54; William A. Salant, "Foreign Trade Policy in the Business Cycle," in *Readings in the Theory of International Trade* (Homewood, Ill.: Richard D. Irwin, Inc., 1949), pp. 201–26; Fritz Machlup, *International Trade and the National Income Multiplier* (Philadelphia: Blakiston Co., 1943); Gottfried Haberler, *A Survey of International Trade Theory* (Princeton, N.J.: Princeton University Press, 1955), pp. 31–48.

[10] m/Y must not be confused with M/Y or ky in Chapter 9.

[11] See Charles P. Kindleberger, *International Economics* (Homewood, Ill.: Richard D. Irwin, Inc., 1953), pp. 155–56.

that the income elasticity of import demand is equal to the marginal propensity to import divided by the average propensity to import.[12]

To make our case of a transmission of an economic fluctuation from country A to country B (the rest of the world) a strong case, we assume (1) that country A is a very important country in size and national income; (2) that it is a mature and highly industrialized country with pronounced economic fluctuations; and (3) that its income elasticity of import demand is greater than unity.

With a sharp rise in country A's national income country B should experience a sharp rise in its exports to A. Employment and income in country B's export industries will increase, and its national income will rise even more, owing to the multiplier effect: the receipts of the export industries are to a large part spent on home produced goods. The increment in national income generated by an increment in export is called the *export multiplier.* We see how country A's original expansion has been transmitted to country B. Both country A and country B are now in the process of being lifted to higher income levels. But what has, in the meantime, happened to their balance of payments?

When country A's economy expanded, country A started to import more than before from country B. It is legitimate to assume that these imports are not instantly matched by increased exports since the international propagation of country A's expansion takes time. Country B will in due course increase its imports from country A, but not immediately. Country A, therefore, develops an excess of imports over exports and uses up part of its foreign exchange or gold reserves to pay for this import surplus. Since country A's foreign exchange and gold reserves are limited, it is important that the disequilibrium in international payments be only temporary. Fortunately, it is to be assumed that equilibrium in international payments will tend to be re-established because of country B's economic expansion. This expansion will be accompanied by an increase in country B's imports from country A. These imports will in due time tend to equal country B's increased exports. Thus equilibrium can be established again, without undue difficulties, at a higher level of international trade.

In the re-establishment of international payments equilibrium the payments mechanisms mentioned in Chapter 29 play an important part. We cannot expect exports to equal imports by mere chance. The transmission of economic fluctuations from country to country is not in itself a payments mechanism but implies powerful forces which are

12 *Ibid.*, p. 156.

not one-sidedly and permanently disequilibrating, since country B's imports will tend to catch up with its exports. The more delicate adjustments of imports to exports, however, need the aid of our payments mechanisms, whether they be based on changes in exchange rates or on an integration of domestic monetary policies in country A and country B via the flow of foreign exchange reserves.

For our example of the transmission of economic fluctuations we have chosen the gratifying case of an expansion. Unfortunately, we must also consider the case of a contraction. A falling off of country A's economic activity causes country B's exports to fall, and the negative multiplier effect lowers country B's national income in the wake of country A's depression. This time country B encounters balance-of-payments difficulties, owing to the delayed fall of its imports from country A. If country B tried to boost its exports (and lower its imports) by contractionist monetary policies, it would hasten the downward process of depression and deflation. If country B tried to counteract domestically the contraction which is generated by a decline in its exports, if it embarked on expansionist monetary and fiscal policies, its balance of payments deficit would be magnified. In its dilemma country B may take refuge in exchange controls, tariffs, and import quotas in order to insulate its economy against the contagious depression abroad and in order not to be hampered in its domestic policies by balance-of-payments deficits. Domestic high employment equilibrium may then be achieved at the price of a substantial shrinkage in international trade. If trade is to continue on a multilateral basis, it is essential, therefore, that depressions in the major trading countries be avoided.

These considerations should not leave us with the impression that international payments difficulties for country B are always created by a depression in country A or by a refusal of country A to match expansionist policies in country B. Country B may pursue a policy of credit inflation which, at high employment, leads to a substantial price inflation. If country B refuses to adjust its exchange rate or, after such adjustments, continues to live beyond its means in an inflationary way, it will have to face balance-of-payments difficulties even if country A's employment level and commercial policies are satisfactory.

SUGGESTIONS FOR FURTHER READING

DAY, A. C. L., and BEZA, STERIE T. *Money and Income,* chaps. 30–33. New York: Oxford University Press, 1960.

ELLSWORTH, P. T. *International Economics,* chaps. 3 and 5. New York: Macmillan Co., 1947.

HABERLER, GOTTFRIED. *A Survey of International Trade Theory,* chap. 5. Princeton: Princeton University, International Finance Section, 1955.

LARY, HAL B., and Associates. *The United States in the World Economy.* Washington, D.C.: U.S. Government Printing Office, 1943.

MACHLUP, FRITZ. *International Trade and the National Income Multiplier.* Philadelphia: Blakiston Co., 1943.

METZLER, LLOYD A. "The Theory of International Trade," in *A Survey of Contemporary Economics* (ed., Howard S. Ellis), Vol. I, chap. 6. Homewood, Ill.: Richard D. Irwin, Inc., 1948.

NURKSE, RAGNAR. "Domestic and International Equilibrium," *The New Economics* (ed., Seymour E. Harris), chap. 21. New York: Alfred A. Knopf, Inc., 1948.

OHLIN, BERTIL. *Interregional and International Trade,* chaps. 1–4. Cambridge, Mass.: Harvard University Press, 1933.

QUESTIONS AND PROBLEMS

1. "A country will gain from international trade when its exports cost less to produce than it would have cost to manufacture the imported goods at home." Explain.
2. "One region cannot possibly be superior to others in the production of *all* commodities, in the sense that it produces all of them at lower money cost" (B. Ohlin). Interpret.
3. "*Ceteris paribus,* a system of multilateral trade and payments will experience relatively more stable exchange rates than a system of bilateral arrangements." Why?
4. "Equilibrating short-term capital movements can be expected only when the lender believes that the exchange value of the borrower's currency will not fall further." Explain and contrast with so-called "flight-capital" movements.
5. If inflation in country A has raised the price level by 50 per cent while prices remained stable in country B, and if the exchange rate was 2 units of A-money for 1 unit of B-money, what will the new exchange rate be? Would it be necessary to use the *ceteris paribus* clause?
6. Discuss the so-called "balance-of-payments" theory according to which the German hyperinflation of 1923 was caused by the depreciation of the German currency as a result of Germany's overburdening with reparation payments.
7. "Any expansion or contraction originating in the domestic economy tends to spread abroad through its effect on the demand for imports. A domestic investment boom will 'spill over' to other countries since part of the increased money 'leaks out' for the purchase of additional

imports" (Ragnar Nurkse). Explain. How is the size of the leakage determined? What will be the effect on the balance of payments of the countries involved?

8. Explain the following terms: (*a*) average propensity to import, (*b*) marginal propensity to import, (*c*) income elasticity of demand for imports, and (*d*) export multiplier.
9. What should a country do if its exports suddenly decline owing to a depression abroad? Domestic employment policies call for increased expenditures, but this policy would make the foreign deficit worse.
10. "Domestic monetary and fiscal policies aiming at high employment are quite compatible with multilateral trade." Do you agree?

Chapter 31 THE GOLD-FLOW MECHANISM

Gold Points and Gold Flow

In our discussion of the gold-flow mechanism we assume that all countries are on the gold standard. Their monetary authorities are willing to sell and buy gold at a fixed price in unlimited amounts, and their residents are free to export and import gold. Under these conditions gold can always be used as a means of international payment since nothing but the small cost of transferring gold from one country to another can interfere with an exchange, via gold, of one currency for the other at their respective gold parities.

Where the monetary authority of a country promises to sell gold freely in unlimited amounts at a fixed price, the supply of currencies of other gold-standard countries becomes perfectly elastic, since gold can buy these other currencies in unlimited amounts at a fixed price. Strictly speaking, the supply of foreign exchange becomes perfectly elastic only at the so-called upper gold point or gold export point. The following case will serve as an illustration.

Suppose that one gold sovereign contains 123.274 grains of gold, eleven-twelfths fine, while one dollar contains 25.8 grains of gold, nine-tenths fine. On this basis the pound-dollar rate is established at \$4.866: 1. Assuming further that the cost of sending a pound sterling worth of gold from New York to London is 2.5 cents, an American can always get pounds sterling at a price not higher than \$4.891 (namely, \$4.866 + \$0.025). An American buyer of pounds sterling, therefore, need not pay more for British money, and the price of British money cannot rise above the gold export point. At this level the supply of pounds sterling on the American foreign exchange market becomes perfectly elastic.

Similarly, an American owning claims on English money has, under the same assumptions, the choice of either selling his claims on the American foreign exchange market or collecting in England in pounds sterling, buying gold in England with pounds sterling, shipping the gold to the United States and converting it into dollars. He will, therefore, not sell a pound sterling for less than $4.841 (namely, $4.866 — $0.025) the so-called gold import point or lower gold point. At any lower price it would pay a buyer to purchase foreign exchange in the United States and to use it for gold imports at a profit. The willingness of the United States monetary authority to buy any amount of gold at a predetermined fixed price, therefore, makes the demand for foreign exchange perfectly elastic at the lower gold point.

Since the supply of foreign exchange becomes perfectly elastic at the gold export point and the demand perfectly elastic at the gold import point, the pound-dollar rate in our example cannot fluctuate by more than 5 cents.

The distance between the gold points could be changed artificially. Mutual holdings of "earmarked" gold reserves could reduce the spread to the vanishing point, while the spread could be increased if the monetary authorities establish different buying and selling prices for gold.

Since the gold-standard system rests on a perfectly elastic supply of gold, and since the supply of gold is not inexhaustible, we must explain how international payments equilibrium can be re-established, once it has been disturbed, before the whole of the gold reserve has been drained out of a country. Obviously, when all gold is lost, the basic assumption of the gold standard—free convertibility of money into gold—cannot be maintained and the price of foreign currencies will rise above the upper gold point.

If a country wants to remain on the gold standard in the face of a dangerous decline of its gold reserves, it has to see either that the market demand for foreign exchange decreases or that the market supply of foreign exchange increases—or both. To achieve these results the country has to subordinate its domestic monetary policy to the one objective of equilibrating its foreign payments since a rising price of foreign exchange (above the upper gold point) is ruled out by our assumption that the country remains "on gold."

Suppose that rising prices in country A have led to an international payments disequilibrium since imports now exceed exports. Let country B stand for the rest of the world. On country A's foreign exchange market the demand for B-money is shifted to the right and the price for B-money (which in equilibrium was equal to the gold parities) increases. If the price of B-money were permitted to rise freely, there would be an increase in the amount of foreign exchange supplied by exporters and a decrease in the amount demanded by importers. International payments equilibrium would be achieved at point *P* in Figure 31–1.

But a price of foreign exchange high enough to accomplish this may easily be above the upper gold point and cannot be permitted under gold-standard conditions. Since the supply curve is perfectly elastic at the gold export point, a shift of the demand curve to the right has no further effect upon the price of foreign money (Fig. 31–1).

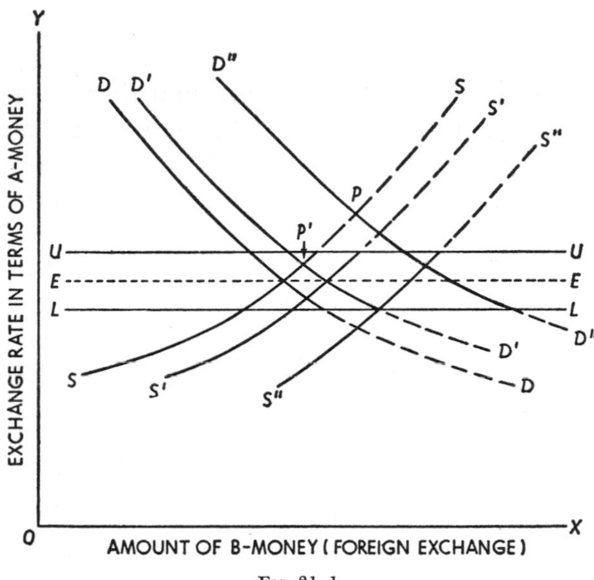

FIG. 31–1

Shifts of the demand curve to the right first raise the exchange rate from its equilibrium position *E*, which is determined by the gold parities of country A and country B currencies, towards the upper gold point. This point is for each demand curve the point at which the demand curve intersects the *U* line. The *U* line lies parallel to the parity line *E*, the distance between them being equal to the cost of transporting gold from country A to country B. Between lines *U* and *L* (the distance being twice the transportation cost) the exchange rate is permitted to fluctuate, and it exerts through its fluctuations an equilibrating influence. For example, equilibrium is achieved at point *P′* in Figure 31–1, well below the upper gold point. But the exchange rate is not permitted to rise above the *U* line or to fall below the *L* line. The equilibrating function of changes in the exchange rate is now taken over by the gold-flow mechanism. The upper gold point establishes, as it were, a ceiling price for country B's currency. Ceiling prices are often lower than market prices would be under the circumstances; in other words, the amounts demanded and supplied are often not equal at the ceiling price. But under gold-standard conditions they are made equal through the provision of additional supply out of gold reserves. The difference between the amounts of foreign exchange supplied and demanded at the upper gold point is made up by gold exports. Gold arbitrageurs send gold to country B, convert gold into B-money and supply B-money in country A's foreign exchange market. Since they buy gold from country A's monetary authorities, the circulation of domestic money in country A will decrease by an amount which is at least equal to, but may be several times larger than, the amount of the gold outflow. In country B, on the other hand, domestic purchasing power is increased by the gold purchases of country B's monetary authorities by an amount at least equal to, but possibly also several times larger than, the amount of the gold inflow.

The restoration of international payments equilibrium is supposed to be the automatic result of the gold flows' effect upon the economies of both the gold-losing and the gold-receiving countries. In the gold-losing country the contraction of monetary circulation will reduce money expenditures and incomes. Prices and costs will tend to fall, attracting foreign purchasers and discouraging domestic importers. But interest rates will rise owing to credit contraction. Increasing rates of interest will attract short-term funds from abroad. This influx of foreign funds will be further encouraged by the fact that A-money is at the moment—while the exchange rate stands at the gold export point—cheap in terms of B-money, so that whoever buys country A's obligations at this price is liable to gain from a future improvement of country A's exchange rate.

All these reactions work in the same direction; they tend to increase the supply of, and to decrease the demand for, foreign exchange in country A's foreign exchange market. As a result of a fall of expenditures, prices, and costs, country A's imports will decline and its exports will rise. The gold outflow has, ultimately, the same effect which a rise in the price of foreign exchange (above the gold export point) would have had immediately; it will re-establish equilibrium between imports and exports. And the possible influx of short-term capital will make for an easier adjustment and may even anticipate and prevent any actual gold movements. The basic features of the gold-standard mechanism are the contraction which it causes in gold-losing countries and the expansion in the gold-receiving countries. These reciprocal contraction and expansion processes constitute an automatic tendency toward integration of the two countries' monetary and credit policies.

How the gold flow is supposed to affect the domestic monetary policies of the gold-standard countries depends on the gold-backing requirements of the central banks and on the reserve requirements of the commercial banks. Chapters 6 and 14 discussed the case under assumptions which correspond to the present reserve requirements in the United States.

Conditions for the Working of the Gold-Flow Mechanism

The logic of the gold-flow mechanism implies a number of conditions which must be fulfilled if it is to work as the classical theory wanted it to work.

1. Obviously, the monetary authorities of the participating countries must be both willing to conform to the rules of the game and able to accomplish what they are supposed to do. The mechanism requires, as Keynes put it, that "the main criterion of the banking policy of each country should be the average behavior of all the other members, its own voluntary and independent contribution being a modest one."[1] In following the rules the monetary authority must abstain from gold sterilization (that is, the accumulation of "buffer" reserves) and must have its "member" banks under control (that is, it must be able to extinguish excess reserves of the commercial banks). We have seen that it is not at all sure that the monetary authority can bring about a desired credit expansion even though it is willing to conform to the rules. Credit contraction is, technically speaking, easier to achieve, but it may be considered politically unwise. Domestic full employment policies may be considered more important than international payments equilibrium.

2. Absence of disturbing capital movements is essential for the working of the gold-flow mechanism. This is true, first of all, for flight capital movements, which lead to gold sterilization in the gold-receiving countries and an uneven distribution of the world's monetary gold. But these flight capital movements are characteristic of abnormal times in which the gold mechanism is not likely to be in operation. Interesting is a second and more normal case. If profits are expected to rise together with prices, capital may be attracted from abroad. Con-

[1] J. M. Keynes, *A Treatise on Money* (New York: Harcourt, Brace & Co., 1930), Vol. II, p. 303.

sequently, a country which is supposed to contract credit in consequence of a gold outflow does not lose gold; instead it sells securities, has its foreign exchange supply increased, and can continue its expansion process.

3. If the mechanism is to rest on the lowering of prices in the gold-losing country and on the raising of prices in the gold-gaining country, two assumptions must be fulfilled:

a) A high degree of price flexibility in the member countries must exist. When the monetary pressures of gold movements are exerted, price levels are supposed to rise or fall like water in a lock, accompanied, of course, by smooth adjustments of costs. In reality, however, these changes are not achieved instantly and without political frictions. Among the many price rigidities which have to be taken into account, one of the most important is the inflexibility of wage rates where strong labor unions firmly resist downward adjustments.

b) The price elasticity of the foreign demand must be relatively high "so that a fall of prices will produce an increase in value of exports relative to imports, and contrariwise."[2]

4. Although free trade is not a necessary condition for successful functioning of the gold-flow mechanism, an increasing amount of control measures and restrictions of international commerce hinder those adjustments which are the very essence of the mechanism. This is particularly true of import quotas which greatly reduce the efficiency and smoothness of any international payments system.

5. For the proper working of the gold-flow mechanism it is essential that it be generally taken for granted that all participating countries maintain their given gold parities. Grave doubts in the ability of a country to maintain a perfectly elastic supply of gold would create the double danger of an internal and external drain of gold; that is, domestically, a run on banks, and internationally a flight of capital (see point 2).

The conditions enumerated above were not always fulfilled and rarely were they fulfilled simultaneously. Yet the gold-flow mechanism worked well before 1914. Indeed it worked so smoothly and promptly that F. W. Taussig remarked: "It must be confessed that here we have phenomena not fully understood. In part our information is insufficient; in part our understanding of other connected topics is inadequate."[3]

[2] John W. Williams, *Post-War Monetary Plans and Other Essays* (Oxford: Basil Blackwell, 1949), p. 272.

[3] F. W. Taussig, *International Trade* (New York: Macmillan Co., 1928), p. 239.

Taussig's bafflement was solved by the new employment and income analysis (see Chapter 23) and its application to the theory of international trade (see Chapter 30). The theory of the gold flow was affected in two ways: it could be shown that the effect of a gold outflow on the domestic economy of the gold-losing country could be more direct and more powerful than the older theory had assumed; and it became clear that the extent of the adjustment to be effected by the gold-flow mechanism as such was smaller than expected, because it was the transmission of economic fluctuations from country to country that actually shouldered the main burden of adjustment.

The new theory, instead of stressing the *price* effect of a gold flow, emphasized the *income* effect. The main influence which credit contraction exerts on the economy of the gold-losing country was now seen to be the decline in investment and consumption expenditures. The negative multiplier effect leads to a fall in the national income and a reduction in imports. This new emphasis showed that the necessary adjustment in the balance of payments could be achieved promptly but only at a considerable sacrifice in terms of domestic employment. Equilibrium in international trade would be achieved by shortening the long leg (fall of imports) rather than by lengthening the short leg (increase of exports).

Fortunately, another conclusion to be drawn from the new analysis of income and employment was less pessimistic in its implications. Assume that country A experiences an increase in domestic economic activity and develops an import surplus which lifts the price of B-money to the gold export point. Assume, moreover, that B-capital is attracted by the prosperity and high profits in country A. Country A's export of securities takes the place of a gold outflow. Our assumptions imply that, in terms of the old gold-flow theory, we are moving further and further away from international payments equilibrium.

Now, however, we must remember that country A's expansionist process is transmitted to country B, that country B's export industries expand, that via multiplier effects country B's national income rises, and that country B's imports will tend to catch up with its growing exports. While these events in country B will not create international payments equilibrium for country A, they will, nevertheless, reduce the imbalance to a manageable size. Furthermore, the adjustment process need not bring about an absolute decline of expenditure, employment, and income in country A. It suffices that the expansion process in country A is slowed down to permit the expansion in country B to catch up. Under favorable world-wide conditions of expansion this can take the sting out of the domestic income effect of a gold outflow. Alvin H. Hansen has drawn our attention to the fact that the successful functioning of the pre-1914 gold-flow system was "greatly facilitated by the circumstance that it operated in a rapidly expanding economy and under the favorable condition of an upward trend in prices."[4]

Of course it is necessary to admit also the possibility of a contracting spiral: a decline in country A's economic activities causes a fall in country B's exports; country B attempts to bring about payments equilibrium through credit contraction; while country A, this time the gold-inflow country, cannot expand its monetary circulation however hard it tries. Under these circumstances the gold-flow mechanism will balance international payments only at the cost of rising unemployment and rapidly shrinking international trade.

Real and Alleged Advantages of the Gold-Flow Mechanism

We are now in a position to evaluate the gold-flow mechanism as a system of international payments. First we shall summarize the real and alleged advantages of the international gold standard; then we shall analyze its major disadvantages.

1. *Stability of exchange rates.* The outstanding advantage of the old (pre-1914) gold mechanism was that it guaranteed stable exchange rates among the countries which decided to become members of the international gold system by adhering strictly to the free purchase and sale of gold at a fixed price. Thus, gold was used as an international unit of account, and exchange rates could fluctuate only within the rather narrow limits of the gold export and import points. Stable exchange rates were a reliable foundation for international trade and for international capital movements. Since the advantages of international division of labor are perfectly obvious from a strictly economic point of view, we can attribute to the gold-standard mechanism at least part of the increased standard of living which was enjoyed by a rapidly increasing world population as the result of international co-operation resting on the secure basis of stable exchanges.

2. *Stability of gold value.* Gold has maintained a reasonable stability of purchasing power over extended periods. Not only have the exchange ratios between different currency units been stabilized by the gold mechanism but the world price level itself has been kept an-

[4] A. H. Hansen, *Full Recovery or Stagnation?* (New York: W. W. Norton & Co., Inc., 1938), pp. 210–12; see also H. D. Henderson in *The Problem of Monetary Stabilization* (Paris: International Chamber of Commerce, June, 1936), pp. 161 ff.

chored to gold. A remarkable stability of the value of gold in several long periods before 1914 cannot be denied; but it must be pointed out that gold contributed to this result only through a quality which it shares with all durable goods—namely that the addition to the total supply in any year is relatively small. As has already been shown on page 40, the value of the standard metal depends at least as much on monetary management as on its own supply. Since the price of gold remains unchanged under gold-standard conditions, the purchasing power of money and gold are identical, and the value of money, in turn, depends on its total quantity—that is, not merely on the supply of the metal but also on the whole superstructure of money which can be based on the gold reserve. Gold determines only the base of the monetary pyramid; the reserve ratios which connect standard money with token and deposit money account for the rest.

3. *Intrinsic value of gold.* By the same reasoning one can easily invalidate the economic significance of the so-called intrinsic value argument, which is so frequently heard in defense of the gold standard. It is absurd to argue that our whole credit structure is sound only when it rests on the intrinsic usefulness and value of the money metal. The intrinsic value argument is correct, however, when it merely refers to the simple fact that gold, when sent from country to country, carries its value with it. It is also true that there exists a tremendous prejudice in favor of gold, and this prejudice may well be used to good advantage when gold is established as the international monetary unit.

4. *The "golden brake" of the credit machine.*[5] The gold-flow mechanism permits small doses of expansion and contraction but rules out deflations and inflations of the more violent and self-generating type. The internal credit policy of any one gold-standard country is kept in line with the average behavior of the participating countries. No single country on the gold standard can embark to any considerable degree or for any considerable length of time upon inflationary or deflationary policies unless such policies are followed by the majority of the members of the international gold-standard system. Any single country or any minority group of countries in which commodity prices are inflated or deflated more than the average are soon forced into line by international gold movements. The gold flow acts as an automatic brake on credit expansion and credit contraction.

5. *Protection against irresponsible governments.* The gold mechanism is thought to be the most reliable protection against irrespon-

[5] See J. A. Schumpeter, "Die goldene Bremse an der Kreditmaschine," *Die Kreditwirtschaft,* Vol. I (1927), pp. 80–106.

sible actions on the part of the monetary authorities at home or abroad and especially against outright inflation. The friends of the gold standard believe that once we have subscribed to the rules of the gold standard we have renounced the dangerous ideas of government deficit spending and pump priming. Of course, if we regard the central bank "as a stupid or weak-kneed creature, which is incapable of taking intelligent charge of events, or which is liable to put its money-creating powers too easily at the disposal of a needy Government, we shall be relieved that its capacity for mischief is kept within bounds by a golden chain."[6] This chain could easily be broken though. "An Act of Parliament is a very ineffective method of curtailing the powers of a government; and in almost every known case of stress and strain, in which the Note Regulations interfere with the wishes of the Government of the day, it is the former which have given way."[7]

6. *Maintenance of sovereignty.* The different countries are kept in line with the average behavior of other gold-standard countries without having to submit to controls by an international authority. This argument that the gold mechanism does not impair national sovereignty is formally and superficially correct; but, as a matter of fact, in playing the gold-standard game the member countries submit to rigid rules and, indeed, sacrifice the sovereign right to carry out whatever fiscal policies their domestic situations may require.

7. *Automatism and simplicity.* The gold mechanism works semiautomatically, is not complicated, and requires few restrictions. Since the rules of the game are known to all players, the actions of the monetary authorities are foreseeable—a fact which introduces a further element of security into international relations. Yet, that the gold standard is simple and easily understood is not quite correct. The fundamental idea is clear. The effects of the gold flow upon the national credit structures of the member countries, however, are complicated and depend on so many factors that conscious management becomes imperative. The main difficulties arise with attempts to adjust prices and costs downwards as well as upwards. These difficulties sometimes prove insurmountable for the monetary authority.

8. *Advantage for gold-producing countries.* Finally, it must not be forgotten that the friends of gold will always find strong political support in countries which gain special advantages through the worldwide use of gold for monetary purposes. A country that produces gold

[6] See D. H. Robertson, "World Finance," in A. C. Pigou and D. H. Robertson, *Economic Essays and Addresses* (London: P. S. King & Son, Ltd., 1931), p. 197.

[7] Keynes, *op. cit.*, p. 264.

at a comparative advantage (or at a comparatively smaller disadvantage) is, of course, from a national point of view, interested in the maintenance of the international gold standard. It produces a product which enjoys the unique advantage (under gold-standard conditions throughout the world) of being salable in unlimited amounts at a fixed price everywhere. Russia's attitude at Bretton Woods in 1944 seems to have been dictated by the advantages it hoped to gain from a reintroduction of the gold standard on a worldwide scale.

Disadvantages of the Gold-Flow Mechanism

In spite of the above-mentioned advantages the gold mechanism has little chance of being reintroduced in its old-fashioned form. This is partly due to the experiences during the interwar period when the gold standard came back to a short and troubled life. The mere mentioning of rampant nationalism, price rigidities, volatile capital movements, and obstacles to international trade (among which foreign exchange control played an increasingly important role) shows that the conditions for successful functioning of the mechanism were then not fulfilled. One could perhaps be tempted to argue that the gold standard was not to blame, because it had been revived at a time when the countries of the world were not willing to play the game according to the rules. Nevertheless, in going back to gold the countries had indicated their willingness to stick to the rules, and that they were unable to do so points to basic difficulties resting in the mechanism itself rather than in a particular historical period.

1. *A fair-weather craft.* Independently of any concrete historical situation, it may be stated as a first objection that perfectly smooth functioning of the gold-flow mechanism requires a degree of flexibility and stability in the economic structure of the world in general which may be obtainable only as the result of a highly fortuitous combination of circumstances. It is a fair-weather craft, of doubtful seaworthiness in stormy waters. When the necessary conditions cannot be fulfilled the gold standard is abandoned, and it becomes the task of "paper" standards to manage the bad situation. This, incidentally, may be an important reason for the rather uncomplimentary esteem in which inconvertible currency systems are held in many circles.

2. *Cause of violent strains.* That the gold standard is abandoned under the adverse conditions of a world-wide depression is, of course, the result of the unwillingness of policy makers to accept the discipline and the sacrifices which it imposes. We have seen that in the face of potent causes of international payments disequilibrium the system

becomes increasingly difficult to handle from the standpoint of domestic economic policy as a whole. This weakens very considerably the argument that the gold standard is superior to other monetary policies because of its automatic character. It has been said that the presumption should be the contrary. "For a nationally managed standard would not subject the country's internal economy to such violent strains as those to which the attempt to continue to conform to an international standard may subject it; so that the inherent difficulty and the necessary sacrifice will be less in the former case than in the latter."[8] As the Macmillan Report has pointed out: "In the modern world, where, on the one hand, inflows of gold are liable to be sterilized and prevented from causing an expansion of credit, whilst on the other hand the deflation of credit set up elsewhere is prevented by social causes from transmitting its full effect to money-wages and other costs, it may be that the whole machine will crack before the reaction back to equilibrium has been brought about."[9]

3. *Anachronism in times of full-employment policies.* The gold-standard mechanism becomes an anachronism when monetary conditions and monetary policy are "recognized as too important and too close to the heart of fiscal sovereignty to be entrusted to any automatic or even semiautomatic system."[10] Since 1914 the governments of most "member" countries have learned to look at their credit and government spending policies as indispensable weapons in their struggle for full employment. It has, therefore, become increasingly impractical for these policies to be subjected to the single aim of keeping exchange rates stable. Following their own often misconceived and shortsighted national credit policies instead of the rules of the gold-standard game, the nations of the world began to pull away from one another and to strain the unifying mechanism to the breaking point.

4. *More contraction than expansion.* The gold-flow mechanism suffers from an "inherent bias towards deflation."[11] The gold-losing country must contract credit in order to maintain its gold reserves. The gold-receiving country, on the other hand, is under no equal compulsion to expand credit to check the gold inflow. In other words, the mechanism lacks sufficient reciprocity. In this connection we should

[8] *Ibid.*, p. 299.

[9] See *Committee on Finance and Industry Report* (London: H. M. Stationery Office, Cmd. 3897, 1931), p. 108.

[10] Robert B. Bryce, "Basic Issues in Postwar International Economic Relations," *American Economic Review*, March, 1942, Supplement, p. 178.

[11] See Joan Robinson, "The International Currency Proposals," *Economic Journal*, June–September, 1943, p. 161; reprinted in Seymour E. Harris (ed.), *The New Economics* (New York: Alfred A. Knopf, Inc., 1948).

also remember that central banks have, as a rule, more power to force their member banks into credit contraction than to force them to expand.

Two more reasons have been mentioned for a lack of reciprocity in the gold-flow mechanism. "One is the unequal importance of the balance of payments as between countries whose foreign trade and other payments are large relative to the home economy and countries for which foreign trade is less important. The other is the unequal size of countries. Gold-standard theory was based on the principle of interaction between homogenous countries of approximately equal size." Referring in particular to the United States it has been pointed out that "a large export surplus, or any other change leading to substantial gold inflow, would be likely to have a far less expansive effect here than contractive effect upon the deficit countries."[12]

5. *Cause of unemployment.* The gold standard and vigorous labor union policies are not compatible with each other. The gold standard confines "the natural tendency of wages to rise beyond the limits set by the volume of money, but can only do so by the weapon of deliberately creating unemployment."[13] If wages rise, prices likewise will have to rise since "each national price-level is primarily determined by the relation of the national wage-level to efficiency; or, more generally, by the relation of money-costs to efficiency in terms of the national unit of currency." If prices are prevented from rising, increasing money costs will squeeze marginal producers out of production. It is suggested, therefore, that the different countries should be allowed "to pursue, if they choose, different wage policies and, therefore, different price policies." To impose a rigid price level upon a country, as the gold standard does, would mean to submit national wage policies to outside dictation. And since it is not feasible to control money wages by monetary measures, the result of the general tendency of money wages to rise against a stable price level would be unemployment. Consequently it is wiser, according to this suggestion, to regard domestic prices as a matter of internal policy and politics, that is, to leave national price levels free to adjust themselves to changing costs of production.

6. *Anarchy in world credit control.* Gold reserves, equally distributed and taken religiously as the institutional basis of the per-

[12] John H. Williams, "The Postwar Monetary Plans," *American Economic Review*, March, 1944, Supplement, pp. 374 ff.; reprinted in *Post-War Monetary Plans and Other Essays, op. cit.*, pp. 170–84.

[13] Lord Keynes, "The Objective of International Price Stability," *Economic Journal*, June–September, 1943, pp. 185–87.

missible credit superstructure, will certainly prevent hyperinflation. They may, however, contribute to considerable inflationary and deflationary tendencies throughout the world, not so much because of changes in the monetary gold supply as because of a tendency for participating countries to expand or contract *simultaneously*. "The value of the yellow metal, originally chosen as money because it tickled the fancy of savages, is clearly a chancy and irrelevant thing on which to base the value of our money and the stability of our industrial system."[14]

The gold standard has been called a state of "anarchy in world credit control."[15] It is not at all certain that the actions taken by the central banks will neutralize each other. They might instead lead to a world-wide contraction or expansion. If contraction prevails in a number of countries while the rest of the world is still free from it, the chances are that the diminishing imports of the depression countries will soon affect the rest.

The often-used analogy comparing the member countries of a gold-standard system to the member banks in a banking system is misleading when driven too far. If the central bank is the conductor of the national banking orchestra, the concert of the members of the gold-flow system can be likened only to an orchestra without a conductor. The gold-flow system lacks a central authority to co-ordinate the national credit policies of the members.

7. *No escape from managed currencies.* "In the modern world of paper currency and bank credit there is no escape from a 'managed' currency, whether we wish it or not;—convertibility into gold will not alter the fact that the value of gold itself depends on the policy of the central banks."[16] We cannot choose between purely automatic and managed standards but only between managed standards of different degrees. A system may be semiautomatic in the sense that international gold movements affect its institutional capacity to grant loans. In smaller countries management of the internal price level is given comparatively narrow scope for independent action. In larger countries, however, the monetary authorities may have considerable freedom of action to manage the credit system for the purpose of securing other objectives (such as domestic economic stability), undisturbed by gold movements.

[14] D. H. Robertson, *Money* (New York: Pitman Publishing Corp., 1948), p. 144.

[15] R. G. Hawtrey, *Trade Depression and the Way Out* (London: Longmans, Green & Co., 1931), pp. 15–18.

[16] J. M. Keynes, *A Tract on Monetary Reform* (New York: Harcourt, Brace & Co., 1924), p. 184.

The distinction between "automatic" and "managed" standards has to give way to the more important distinction between international and domestic stabilization. Here the claim that the *automatic* gold standard combines the advantages of both national and international stabilization has to be rejected. International exchange stability may require some countries to carry out deflationary measures (for example, in cases of unilateral payments) which are incompatible with the chosen objectives of domestic credit policy. It is by no means self-evident that stable exchange rates will be preferred under all circumstances if their maintenance involves deflationary and depressive credit restriction.

A clear-cut decision for either international or domestic stabilization can perhaps be avoided by compromise. Monetary institutions and techniques may be developed to link the different countries together in a manner which guarantees relatively stable exchange rates and gives, nevertheless, time and room for national divergencies ample enough to prevent disturbing repercussions. The International Monetary Fund, discussed in Chapter 35, is designed to be such an institution.

8. *Waste of gold reserves.* Gold as a means of international settlement is wasted needlessly by the gold-standard system in its orthodox form. "Cover reserves" are indispensable only if we want to achieve strictly automatic credit contraction in a country which is losing gold. If monetary and credit policies could be left to the discretion of the monetary authority, we could do without gold-backing requirements whose effect "is merely to lock away a large part, and sometimes the major part, of the gold reserve so that it can *never* be used. . . ."[17] "Unlocked," the cover reserves could serve as a fund of highest international liquidity, help bridge temporary balance-of-payments disequilibria, and afford a reasonable amount of freedom in the pursuance of domestic monetary and general economic policies.

Then, but only then, could it be certain that gold production is less foolish than it must seem to observers from another planet who watch us through huge telescopes and are puzzled as we extract gold laboriously from the bowels of the earth only to bury it in a somewhat more orderly fashion in a different place.

The Future of the Gold-Flow Mechanism

It is safe to predict that the "automatic" gold-flow mechanism will never return. The orthodox gold-flow mechanism stands for rigid

[17] J. M. Keynes, *A Treatise on Money*, Vol. II, p. 265.

exchange rates, rigid gold-backing requirements, reciprocal deflation and inflation according to gold movements, and conservative domestic credit policies with balanced budgets and without deficit spending. All this is unacceptable to those who believe in the government's responsibility for economic stabilization, full employment, and labor union strength. The refusal of many countries to subscribe to the rules of the gold-standard game makes it impossible for the rest of the countries to accept the gold-flow mechanism; for a multilateral payment system depends on the co-operation of all, or almost all, countries. No matter how badly some friends of the gold standard want it reintroduced, they must see that the case for it in its orthodox form is hopeless when some of the major countries refuse to be put into the "strait jacket" of gold.

But to suggest that the gold-flow mechanism will not come back does not mean to say that gold could not perform an eminently useful role in a modern international payments system. The question is partly a terminological one. If we broaden the meaning of the term "gold-flow mechanism" sufficiently, we may even apply it to a payments system in which gold parities are not unalterably fixed and in which the monetary gold serves predominantly or even exclusively as an asset of highest international liquidity (without being locked away by obsolete backing requirements).

In such a system gold would continue to perform several important functions:

1. It would, during the period between alterations of gold parities, help to maintain a perfectly elastic supply of and demand for foreign exchange; that is, it would stabilize exchange rates.

2. It would serve as a stopgap during temporary balance-of-payments disequilibria; that is, it would remain the most liquid international asset.

3. It would serve as a common denominator for the different currencies, the nearest approach to an international unit of account that seems at present possible.

4. It would help to bring those countries which are either large gold holders or large gold producers into the fold of an international payments system. Otherwise, such countries might easily refuse to become members of a system that would dethrone gold entirely.

The issue, therefore, is not whether we shall reintroduce the old-fashioned gold-standard system or discard gold entirely; the issue is rather whether gold can be used to advantage in a more flexible multilateral payments system or whether the world will break apart into separate monetary blocs.

SUGGESTIONS FOR FURTHER READING

BROWN, WILLIAM ADAMS, JR. *The International Gold Standard Reinterpreted.* New York: National Bureau of Economic Research, Inc., 1940.

Committee on Finance and Industry Report (Macmillan Report), chap. 7. London: His Majesty's Stationery Office, Cmd. 3897, 1931.

GREGORY, T. E. *The Gold Standard and Its Future.* 3d ed. New York: E. P. Dutton & Co., Inc., 1935.

HARDY, CHARLES O. *The Postwar Role of Gold.* The Monetary Standards Inquiry, No. 8. New York: The Monetary Standards Inquiry, 1944.

KEYNES, J. M. *A Treatise on Money,* Vol. II, chaps. 35–36. New York: Harcourt, Brace & Co., 1930.

KEYNES, J. M. *Essays in Persuasion,* Part III. New York: Harcourt, Brace & Co., 1932.

RITTER, LAWRENCE S. *Money and Economic Activity,* chap. 11. Boston: Houghton Mifflin Co., 1952.

WHITTLESEY, CHARLES R. *Readings in Money and Banking,* Part XIV. New York: W. W. Norton & Co., Inc., 1952.

WILLIAMS, JOHN H. *Post-War Monetary Plans and Other Essays,* chaps. 16 and 17. Oxford: Basil Blackwell, 1949.

QUESTIONS AND PROBLEMS

1. When can we say that a country is on the gold standard?
2. Explain why the rate of exchange between two gold-standard countries cannot rise above an "upper" and not fall below a "lower" gold point. Use diagram.
3. "The maintenance of international payments equilibrium before 1914 was supposed to be the automatic result of the gold flows' effect upon the economies of both the gold-losing and gold-receiving countries." Explain. Do you agree?
4. The gold-flow mechanism requires that "the main criterion of the banking policy of each country should be the average behavior of all the other members, its own voluntary and independent contribution being a modest one" (J. M. Keynes). Discuss.
5. "The functioning of the gold-flow mechanism presupposes the fulfillment of several conditions." What are these conditions?

6. Discuss the importance of modern income analysis for our better understanding of the relatively smooth working of the gold-flow mechanism before 1914.
7. The gold-flow mechanism suffers from an "inherent bias towards deflation" (Joan Robinson). Do you agree?
8. "In truth, the gold standard is already a barbarous relic" (J. M. Keynes in 1923). Do you agree?
9. The gold standard confines "the natural tendency of wages to rise beyond the limits set by the volume of money, but can only do so by the weapon of deliberately creating unemployment" (Lord Keynes). Discuss.
10. "Monetary stability is a prime condition for economic growth, for the expansion of international trade and investment, as well as for obtaining free convertibility of currencies, and stable exchange rates. It cannot be secured without putting an end to inflation of money and credit, and to inflationary practices by monopolistic labor unions and powerful businesses. In a world divided into so many sovereign and independent countries, monetary stability can be reached and maintained only by the discipline of the international gold standard or by the strict application of the rules of the International Monetary Fund" (Philip Cortney). Discuss.

Chapter 32 THE EQUILIBRIUM RATE OF EXCHANGE

Freely Fluctuating Exchange Rates

Having critically analyzed the effects of the gold-flow mechanism, it seems logical to ask why free fluctuations of exchange rates should not be permitted to exert their equilibrating influence unchecked, that is, beyond gold points or any other kind of upper or lower limits; why domestic economic policies should not be completely liberated from the dictation of outside forces; and why international payments equilibrium should not be achieved through the simple device of changing the one "variable" which connects the price systems of any two countries: the exchange ratio between their currencies.

One critic of the gold standard has stated that "there seems no valid reason to assume, as is commonly done, that, while the principle of supply and demand functions fairly well in goods relationships, it should not be allowed to operate, except within arbitrary restrictions, to determine the price of currencies."[1]

Why, then, the nearly unanimous rejection of the system of freely fluctuating exchange rates? Obviously, the arguments against freely fluctuating exchange rates center around the basic contention "that fluctuating parities, by creating additional hazard and uncertainty, will be prejudicial to international trade."[2] In detail we can distinguish the following criticisms:

1. Freely fluctuating exchange rates seem to be incompatible with domestic stability. As the exchange rate fluctuates the prices of all exported and imported articles are affected. Moreover, articles formerly not internationally traded will enter international trade

[1] Charles R. Whittlesey, *International Monetary Issues* (New York: McGraw-Hill Book Co., Inc., 1937), p. 33.

[2] Hubert Douglas Henderson, "Memorandum on New Technical Arguments for Postponing Stabilization," in *The Problem of Monetary Stabilization* (Paris: International Chamber of Commerce, 1936), p. 160.

while others are excluded, because the commodity points have moved. As Ragnar Nurkse has pointed out, freely fluctuating exchange rates "call for constant shifts of domestic factors of production between export and home-market industries, shifts which may be disturbing and wasteful."[3]

2. It always takes at least two currencies to complete an international trade transaction, and fluctuating exchange rates constitute, therefore, an additional risk for at least one of the parties involved. This argument cannot be brushed aside with the remark that domestic transactions are risky, too, and that we do not make any special efforts "to safeguard the man who deals in particular commodities, the trader in wheat, the manufacturer of tires or the farmer who grows peanuts."[4] First of all, the foreign trader is also a dealer in a particular commodity so that the exchange risk is superimposed upon the regular risk connected with his operation. Secondly, it must not be forgotten that exchange rate fluctuations, like a change in the domestic purchasing power of money, influence the economy much more widely than do changes in any particular commodity price. The change of a rate which instantaneously influences the prices of all internationally traded goods cannot be compared with individual price changes within a country. We must remember that the alternative to variations of exchange rates is a change in price levels. If we are opposed to dangerously deflationary adjustments under the operation of the gold standard, we must be equally willing to acknowledge the widespread repercussions of a change in the exchange rate.

As long as exchange rate variations are kept within reasonably narrow margins, they are relatively harmless because of the fact that the foreign trader can hedge against the risk involved. The exchange risk connected with existing contracts can be adequately covered in the forward exchange market, where future claims on foreign money are exchanged at today's exchange rate (plus a certain premium or minus a certain discount), the risk being transferred to exchange dealers and speculators. But it may be "that the price so paid for this forward covering is so high that the trader can as well run the exchange risk himself."[5] The forward exchange market, furthermore, offers no

[3] Ragnar Nurkse, *Conditions of International Monetary Equilibrium*, Essays in International Finance, No. 4 (Princeton, N.J.: Princeton University Press, Spring, 1945), p. 3. Reprinted in *Readings in the Theory of International Trade* (Homewood, Ill.: Richard D. Irwin, Inc., 1949), pp. 3–34.

[4] Whittlesey, *op. cit.*, p. 77.

[5] A. A. van Sandick, "Memorandum on the Technique of the Forward Exchange Market and the Elimination of Uncertainty," in *The Problem of Monetary Stabilization* (Paris: International Chamber of Commerce, 1936), pp. 303 ff.

protection against losses from anticipated contracts. Possible variations of exchange rates of, say, 10 per cent may, therefore, greatly reduce investments in international trade and in industries producing goods for foreign markets, reducing therewith the international division of labor.

3. In a free payments system capital will tend to flee from a country whose currency is expected to depreciate substantially. The particularly dangerous feature of these capital flight movements is that "such anticipations are apt to bring about their own realization. Anticipatory purchases of foreign exchange tend to produce or at any rate to hasten the anticipated fall in the exchange value of the national currency, and the actual fall will set up or strengthen expectations of a further fall. The dangers of such cumulative and self-aggravating movements under a regime of freely fluctuating exchanges are clearly demonstrated by the French experience of 1922–26. Exchange rates in such circumstances are bound to become highly unstable."[6]

These difficulties are hard to overcome within a system of freely fluctuating exchange rates since the appropriate methods for dealing with such situations constitute, by definition, violations of the freedom for which the system stands. Exchange control abolishes the freedom to buy and sell on the foreign exchange market, and operations of exchange stabilization funds influence exchange rates through buying and selling operations on the part of the government.[7]

4. Connected with these capital flight movements which are likely to prevail with freely fluctuating exchange rates is an abnormally high liquidity preference. "The gains and losses which can be made from the unexpected depreciation of one currency or another have come to be realized more and more widely. People therefore try to invest their money in as liquid a form as possible, in order to be able to convert it at the first sign of danger into some other currency which appears at the moment to offer greater security."[8] This desire for liquidity leads to hoarding and, through the hoarding of gold in

[6] Ragnar Nurkse, *International Currency Experience. Lessons of the Inter-War Period* (Geneva: League of Nations, 1944), p. 118.

[7] Exchange stabilization funds operate in secrecy, and speculators in foreign exchange must always reckon with the possibility that the great resources of these funds may be used against them. The British Exchange Equalization Account was created in 1932 to offset speculative movements in sterling exchanges; the American Stabilization Fund was established in 1934 to promote greater exchange stability. The typical exchange stabilization fund must consist of both domestic and foreign money (or gold) so as to be able to counteract fluctuations in supply as well as in demand on the foreign exchange market.

[8] Gottfried Haberler, *The Theory of International Trade* (New York: Macmillan Co., 1937), p. 45.

particular, to credit contraction, to higher rates of interest, to shrinking investment, and to unemployment—another proof that it is impossible to insulate the domestic economy against the influence of outside forces.

5. It is rather generally believed that exchange rate fluctuations would seriously impede the process of long-term foreign investment.[9] Even though international loans are customarily expressed in the currency of the lending country, stability of the debtor country's currency seems highly desirable: from the creditor's standpoint, because he will consider the investment more secure; from the debtor's standpoint, because a depreciating exchange rate would increase his debt burden in terms of his own currency.

These arguments may be overstated, however. Against them it has been said:[10]

a) Foreign loans are expressed in terms of creditor currencies and a depreciation of the creditor currency does not directly harm the investor in foreign securities since he is not worse off than if he had invested in domestic securities.

b) Depreciation of the debtor country's currency need not be quite as dangerous as it appears. The country may be paying its debts chiefly through export of goods whose prices are predominantly determined in foreign markets and, therefore, are not substantially affected by monetary policies in the country of origin. Although the country's foreign debt is increased in terms of its depreciated currency, the proceeds from exports are similarly increased in terms of its own currency. (This argument, however, fails to distinguish between the individual debtor and the country as a whole. The firm owing the foreign debts may not be an exporter and therefore would not be helped by the higher proceeds from exports.)

c) The danger of severe strain upon the exchange rate and the currency system would be reduced to the extent that equity investments replace bond investments since equity investments constitute a more adjustable item in the balance of payments.

d) Authors who have not denied the detrimental effect of fluctuating exchange rates upon international lending have, nonetheless, pointed out that the damage might be less serious than expected, since it is doubtful whether international capital movements should be en-

[9] See, for example, Arthur D. Gayer, *Monetary Policy and Economic Stabilization* (London: Macmillan & Co., Ltd., 1935), p. 191; E. M. Bernstein, *Money and the Economic System* (Chapel Hill: University of North Carolina Press, 1935), pp. 464 ff.

[10] Whittlesey, *op. cit.*, pp. 154–70.

couraged in times when the international movements of goods, in which capital movements materialize, are seriously obstructed.[11]

Controlled Exchange Rate Fluctuations

In favor of freely fluctuating exchange rates and against pegged exchange rates, it can be argued that freely fluctuating exchange rates are less likely to establish wrong conversion ratios than are pegged exchange rates. Pegged rates are adjustable, but they differ from fluctuating rates in that they are supposed to remain stable until a formal adjustment occurs (depreciation, appreciation). Speculation is more likely to be induced by deviations of the official from the market rate of exchange than by fluctuations of the latter, provided these fluctuations are moderate. Furthermore, as long as these price movements are relatively small, it is possible to maintain orderly conditions in the foreign exchange market through the operations of exchange stabilization funds (see footnote 7 on p. 451). These operations do not necessarily constitute a system of adjustable or pegged exchange rates. The stabilization fund may permit the exchange rate to fluctuate in response to normal changes in supply and demand conditions and limit its activities to the control of excessive speculation. Such a system of controlled fluctuations would be a free payments system. It would combine a reasonable amount of exchange stability with the advantage of prompt price adjustments in the foreign exchange market when such adjustments are equilibrating rather than disequilibrating.

Obviously, such a system can work only under reasonably normal conditions. Where abnormal conditions prevail, as in the case of extreme instability of domestic monetary policies, no free international payments system can be made to work.[12]

The Equilibrium Rate of Exchange

If we want to avoid the rigidities of permanently fixed gold parities and the dangers of violently fluctuating exchange rates, a compromise is indicated. This compromise may take the form of either controlled, moderate fluctuations (as discussed above) or of pegged rates which are held stable for the time being but are promptly adjusted upwards (depreciation) or downwards (appreciation) when a fundamental disequilibrium in the balance of payments develops. We shall

[11] See J. M. Keynes, *A Treatise on Money* (New York: Harcourt, Brace & Co., Inc., 1930), Vol. II, p. 324; J. H. Williams, "The Adequacy of Existing Currency Mechanisms," *American Economic Review*, Vol. XXVI (1937), p. 156.

[12] Gottfried Haberler, *Currency Convertibility*, No. 451 in the Series "National Economic Problems" (New York: American Enterprise Association, Inc., 1954), pp. 1–11.

now discuss this second alternative. The main problem, however, is the same for both cases: we must know approximately what the normal market rate of exchange would be under existing conditions and we must have at our disposal adequate reserves of foreign exchange or gold.

Pegged rates in an otherwise free payments system must be near-equilibrium rates, that is, rates at which balance-of-payments equilibrium can be maintained over longer periods so that what is lost out of reserves in one period can be confidently expected to flow back during the next. The equilibrium rate of exchange has been defined as "the rate which, over a certain period, maintains the balance of payments in equilibrium without any net change in the international currency reserve."[13]

Chapter 31 has shown that rigidly stable exchange rates could always be had at the price of deflation and unemployment in the gold-losing country. In other words, international payments equilibrium would be achieved at the expense of domestic economic prosperity. The equilibrium rate which a country should try to stabilize or establish is, therefore, better characterized "as one that maintains the balance of payments equilibrium without a degree of unemployment greater than in the outside world."[14]

This equilibrium rate could also be specified as the rate which is "neutral" because it would not create artificial export advantages or disadvantages. At the equilibrium rate the currency in question would be neither undervalued nor overvalued.

Thus the equilibrium rate would have to conform to the following criteria:

1. The rate should be compatible with an average degree of domestic stabilization. Unemployment worse than in other countries might indicate a mistaken attempt to stabilize a rate which is not or is no longer the equilibrium rate.

2. To maintain the rate over a sufficient period of time should require neither exhaustion of the country's reserves of foreign balances and gold nor drastic credit contraction which would conflict with criterion No. 1.

3. The rate should not constitute a competitive undervaluation but should conform in a completely neutral manner with the price,

[13] Ragnar Nurkse, *International Currency Experience. Lessons of the Inter-War Period* (Geneva: League of Nations, 1944), p. 124.

[14] *Ibid.*, p. 126; Ragnar Nurkse, *Conditions of International Monetary Equilibrium*, Essays in International Finance, No. 4 (Princeton, N.J.: Princeton University, Spring, 1945), p. 6.

cost, and demand relationships of the countries whose price systems it connects. The rate must not afford artificial advantages or disadvantages in international competition.

Once it could be ascertained that an exchange rate does not, or does no longer, conform to all three criteria, a new rate would have to be chosen. This new rate would then be maintained until it, too, would have to be discarded in accordance with the same criteria.

This compromise between rigid and freely fluctuating exchange rates is often referred to as a system of "flexible" exchange rates. The adjective "flexible" is meant to indicate that the system is manageable, adjustable to changing conditions, and, therefore, less likely than a rigid system to break under strain.

The most important difficulty of such a system consists in the translating into practical guideposts for monetary policy such elusive terms as "equilibrium rate," "fundamental disequilibrium," "overvaluation," "undervaluation," and "competitive exchange depreciation."

How is the equilibrium rate to be found? How is it to be ascertained after long periods of exchange control during which the continuity of the pricing process has been completely interrupted on the foreign exchange market?

At the first glance, the following seems to be an obvious solution: where the exchange rate had been held stable through purchases and sales by the monetary authority in the foreign exchange market, the monetary authority could simply refrain for a time from any interference. Under adverse balance-of-payments conditions the price of foreign exchange expressed in domestic currency would rise (the foreign exchange value of domestic money would fall) and, after some fluctuations, would supposedly find a new level. This technique is not advisable, however. The "transitional" fluctuations may invite capital flight movements, and the speculative forces of the foreign exchange market could easily make true their own pessimistic anticipations. Under these conditions a "self-adjustment" of the exchange rate would not be able to establish a new balance-of-payments equilibrium, and no new equilibrium rate of exchange would emerge.

The trial-and-error technique, the policy of letting market forces decide where the new rate should be established, may be more attractive to a creditor country which finds itself momentarily in grave disequilibrium on current account. The depreciation of the creditor currency would induce debtors to rid themselves of their obligations at the new more favorable rate, assuming the debts are expressed in the creditor's currency. The debtors' increased demand for the depreciated currency would cushion the currency's fall. As a matter of fact, the currency may be pushed temporarily above the long-run equilibrium point.

In general, a temporary return to the system of freely fluctuating exchange rates cannot be regarded as a practicable way of finding the equilibrium rate. Times which call for a search for better adjusted rates, because the old rates are badly out of line, are hardly times in which one can rely on the equilibrating forces of freely fluctuating exchanges.

The Purchasing Power Parity Theory

If it is inadvisable to determine the equilibrium rate of exchange through the free interplay of market forces, can the equilibrium rate be computed on the basis of index numbers? The purchasing power parity theory teaches that exchange rates reflect the ratios of the domestic purchasing powers of different national currencies. It may seem, therefore, that it ought to be possible to compute the correct exchange rates once we have index numbers which express the domestic purchasing powers of the currencies in question.

Unfortunately this is not so. Gustav Cassel, the chief modern proponent of the theory, has pointed out that "it is only when we know the exchange rate which represents a certain equilibrium that we can calculate the rate which represents the same equilibrium at an altered value of the monetary units of the two countries."[15] In other words, the purchasing power parity theory "cannot . . . be applied to absolute levels of prices, but only to changes in the price levels."[16]

In Chapter 30 we could see that changes in general price levels are only one of several factors which determine demand for and supply of foreign exchange. Changes in relative price structures (caused by

[15] Gustav Cassel, *Money and Foreign Exchange after 1914* (New York: Macmillan Co., 1923), p. 142. That the theory is much older than Cassel's restatement is shown in J. W. Angell's *Theory of International Prices* (Cambridge, Mass.: Harvard University Press, 1926). The famous Bullion Report stated in 1810: "In the event of the prices of commodities being raised in one country by an augmentation of its circulating medium, while no similar augmentation in the circulating medium of the neighbouring country has led to a similar rise in prices, the currencies of the two countries will no longer continue to bear the same relative value to each other as before. The exchange will be computed between these two countries to the disadvantage of the former." The purchasing power parity theory as formulated by the late Gustav Cassel was devised primarily to explain the connection between inflationary price changes and the fluctuations of foreign exchange rates during the stormy period 1914–23.

[16] Gottfried Haberler, *The Theory of International Trade* (New York: Macmillan Co., 1937), p. 35.

changes in demand and in technology), in commercial policies, in debtor-creditor relationships, and in the level of economic activity all affect exchange rates quite independently of variations in domestic price levels. If, then, exchange rates are not exclusively determined by the respective price levels in the trading countries, it is impossible to compute equilibrium rates on the basis of absolute prices. Instead, we must start with a base year for which we know ex post that the rate of exchange was an equilibrium rate, that is, a rate which was compatible with international payments equilibrium on a free market. This rate we must then multiply by the ratio of the degree of inflation in the respective countries, as expressed by index numbers.

Such a base year is often hard to find, because not many years are free of disequilibrating influences such as recessions, unemployment, currency depreciations, exchange controls, etc. But suppose even that year *y* can be considered an equilibrium year in international payments. Can we then calculate exchange rates for year *x* on the basis of *y*-rates plus a sufficiently exact knowledge of the changes in the purchasing powers of the respective national currencies since year *y*? We saw that Gustav Cassel assumed that we can calculate the rate for year *x* which represents *the same equilibrium* as prevailed in the base year. This statement meant to imply that the computed rate is correct only *if all other relevant factors affecting the rate of exchange have remained unaltered,* including "that the rise in prices in the countries concerned has affected all commodities in a like degree."[17]

If the period between years *x* and *y* was a period of depression, war, or structural changes in international trade this assumption becomes absurd. Yet it is likely that periods in which countries had to use stringent exchange control measures and were no longer sure about the approximate level of their equilibrium rate of exchange are times of such abnormal events.

Even if we could apply the purchasing power parity theory under favorable conditions, that is, if we could find a satisfactory base year in the recent past and if we could assume that price level changes had been so overwhelming as to drown out the effects of all the other relevant factors, we should still be faced by some baffling problems.

Let us assume that our index numbers include the prices of both commodities which are internationally traded and commodities which are traded exclusively within national boundaries. Only internationally traded goods will influence the demand for and the supply of foreign currency and, consequently, the rate of exchange. Commodi-

[17] Cassel, *op. cit.*, p. 154.

ties which are only domestically traded, on the other hand, have no direct bearing on the exchange of the currency, and their prices may therefore fluctuate without affecting directly and immediately the exchange rate. Which goods *are* internationally traded, furthermore, depends partly on the exchange rate, because a rise in the price of foreign currencies would make a hitherto domestic commodity exportable and would remove hitherto imported articles from the list of internationally traded ones.

Confined to internationally traded commodities the purchasing power parity theory becomes an empty truism because it is obvious that the national prices of internationally traded goods (adjusted to account for transportation costs, tariffs and other delivery expenses) tend to equality as between different markets when translated into each other at the current exchange rates. A process of equalization through arbitrage takes place so automatically that the national prices of these commodies seem to follow rather than to determine the movements of the exchange rates.

To choose the prices of domestically traded goods for purchasing power parity calculations would be even less satisfactory unless we assume that the prices of goods which do and of those which do not enter international trade fluctuate in exactly the same degree. But we cannot expect changes in exchange rates and in internal domestic purchasing power to be exactly or even nearly proportionate. Changes in the relation between exchange rate and internal purchasing power depend in part on the importance of international goods as compared with domestic goods. Where international trade is an important part of the trade of a country, international price changes must strongly influence the internal purchasing power of that country's money. In this case domestic prices and international prices will have a greater tendency to move together than they will have if international trade is a comparatively minor factor in the economic activities of a country. The percentage change in the prices of domestic and international commodities is not likely to be the same, even in the long run.

On the whole we cannot expect much from an application of the purchasing power parity theory and must conclude that purchasing power parities cannot be used to compute equilibrium rates or to gauge with precision deviations from international payments equilibrium. Nevertheless, the purchasing power approach may be used with advantage when we are entirely in the dark, as after long periods of exchange control or after violent inflations. Then it is valuable to use it for finding at least the approximate range within which the equilibrium rate should be located.

Other Criteria Examined

Since the equilibrium rate of exchange is supposed to be neutral in terms of artificial export advantages, the question arises whether a country's export and import position would give a clear indication of divergencies of the exchange rate from its equilibrium position. This method may work ex post facto. Once we know all the data concerned, we may be able to decide that a particularly favorable export position was due to an undervaluation of the country's currency. But exports and imports are subject to so many influences that only historical perspective would enable us, without proof, to attribute a predominant role to one of many possible factors. Deviations from the equilibrium rate which are too small to register when the purchasing power parity test is applied could not be detected either by an analysis of the current export-import situation.

A reduction of the foreign exchange (or gold) reserve of a country is an obvious indication of a balance-of-payments disequilibrium. The loss of foreign balances indicates that the price of foreign money would be higher if the exchange rate were flexible and determined by free market forces; reserves of foreign balances are used up to bridge a discrepancy between the amount demanded and the amount supplied by private sources at the official exchange rate.

Why not take such an outflow (or inflow) of foreign exchange reserves as an indication of the degree of disequilibrium in international payments? The exchange rate would then have to be adjusted whenever the loss or gain in reserves was considered abnormally large.

This suggestion is less satisfactory than it seems, however. The determination of the amount of foreign exchange reserves (a precondition of the determination of a *change* in reserves) is difficult. Reserves often consist not merely of foreign balances or gold but of habitual credit relations or customary borrowing rights.

When discussing the gold-standard mechanism we saw that equilibrating short-term capital movements (capital inflow) may be substituted for an outflow of gold. These loans by foreigners "should be regarded as a draft on the recipient country's stock of international reserves. Whether there is an outflow of gold or an inflow of foreign short-term loans, the country's net international liquidity will be reduced. The foreign short-term funds are a liability, can be withdrawn at any moment, and must be treated as a negative gold reserve."[18]

Supplies of foreign currency resulting from long-term loans obtained from abroad should not be included in a country's normal foreign exchange reserve. An exception would be so-called stabilization loans, since they are especially earmarked to serve as foreign exchange reserve.

Even if it were easier to define foreign exchange reserves and to gauge changes in these reserves than the above discussion suggests, our difficulties in determining the equilibrium rate of exchange by reference to changes in foreign exchange reserves would not be over.

It is the very purpose of reserves that they be used when they are demanded. The lowering of reserves is, therefore, in itself no reason for alarm. The question is that of how long the reserves are supposed to last. The "standard" reserve period clearly must be so chosen that the reserves will not be exhausted before the balance-of-payments situation reverses itself and the reserves of foreign exchange or gold begin to flow back again. If the reserves are in danger of being exhausted without the prospect of a reversal, the exchange rate can no longer be considered as the equilibrium rate.

How long a period should the monetary authority have in mind when it tries to determine the size of international liquidity reserve needed to meet the largest anticipated drain? It would certainly not be sufficient to consider only the drain connected with seasonal fluctuations; it would be more reasonable to prepare for the possible drains connected with cyclical changes.

If the reserve is ample, the country may with equanimity face a temporary deterioration of its international liquidity status. With scanty reserves, on the other hand, the country will try to equilibrate its balance of payments within a short period of time through credit contraction—or perhaps import restrictions—or it will have to depreciate its currency on the grounds that the present rate can no longer be considered the equilibrium rate of exchange. Obviously, the availability of adequate reserves of foreign exchange will prove to be a major factor in a policy which tries to stabilize exchange rates and to prevent all too frequent exchange rate adjustments.

The "adequacy" of foreign liquidity reserves will, of course, depend on the domestic monetary and general economic policies which determine the amplitude of cyclical changes and on corresponding

[18] Ragnar Nurkse, *Conditions of International Monetary Equilibrium*, Essays in International Finance, No. 4 (Princeton, N.J.: Princeton University Press, Spring, 1945), p. 4.

fluctuations in other countries during the same period, that is, on how effectively different national policies are integrated through such international payments systems as the gold-flow mechanism or the International Monetary Fund. Fluctuations in domestic activity will influence foreign exchange reserves only if they are not accompanied by corresponding changes in the other countries. It is not seasonal or cyclical fluctuations as such which are decisive but rather their disproportionate strength and timing in different countries.

Again, the problem of adequate exchange reserves cannot be separated from the question of the country's domestic economic policies. If a country is willing to follow policies conducive to international payments equilibrium at stable exchange rates, irrespective of the consequences of these policies for its domestic economic situation, it can nearly always protect its foreign exchange reserves. If this were not so, the gold-flow mechanism could not have functioned as it did over a long period. But in discussing the gold-flow mechanism we saw that governments are not likely to follow a policy of rigid exchange rate stabilization if this policy means painful income contraction and mass unemployment. Unemployment has become the most important criterion for domestic disequilibrium. Can it also be used to determine the equilibrium rate of exchange?

Suppose that the foreign exchange reserve remains reasonably high, that no excessive amount of short-term borrowing abroad reduces the country's net international liquidity, but that the country suffers severely from mass unemployment. Should the existing exchange rate be considered the equilibrium rate?

If we accept unemployment as a criterion for deviation from the equilibrium rate of exchange, we must immediately qualify our position by emphasizing that it is not the unemployment situation as such that is decisive, but rather the degree of unemployment in relation to conditions in other countries. If mass unemployment per se were taken as the criterion, the conclusion would be absurd because "for periods of world-wide depressions (for example, in 1931) all currencies would have to be considered as overvalued."[19] Only if a country were considerably worse off than other countries could one assume that its currency was overvalued. "But even in that case there are weighty objections against permitting depreciation in the absence of a current balance of payments deficit. The main objection is that depreciation will improve the balance of payments of the depreciating country.

[19] Gottfried Haberler, "Currency Depreciation and the International Monetary Fund," *The Review of Economic Statistics*, Vol. XXVI, No. 4 (November, 1944), p. 180.

Therefore, if the starting point is an even balance, depreciation will lead to a gold [or foreign exchange] outflow from other countries which, under the balance-of-payments criterion, would constitute an overvaluation of other currencies."[20] Domestic full employment policies may bring about a monetary expansion in consequence of which the balance of payments would become unfavorable. Depreciation would then be in order if the loss of reserves rather than unemployment is taken as the criterion of exchange rate policy. Were it not for the danger of competitive exchange depreciation, it would seem to be only a comparatively minor point of timing whether depreciation should precede or follow domestic expansion. Since it is not easy to draw the line correctly, it would be wise to wait until the deficit in the balance of payments resulting from the domestic expansion has actually developed. "As a general rule . . . so long as its liquid international reserves are adequate, a country should be expected to make use of the reserves to meet an actual deficit in its balance of payments before a downward adjustment of its rate can be approved."[21]

Concluding Remarks

It is not at all astonishing that we should have found it difficult to determine the criteria which are to indicate deviations from the equilibrium rate of exchange. An international payments system which wants to avoid both the rigidities of the old-fashioned gold-flow mechanism and the dangers of freely fluctuating exchange rates must have as its very pivot the concept of an equilibrium rate of exchange. Here center all the technical difficulties and political conflicts. Whether, or to what degree, freedom of domestic action is given precedence over exchange stability is expressed in the criteria which are chosen to define the equilibrium rate; the amount of foreign exchange reserves that is to be considered adequate depends on our definition of international payments equilibrium. There is hardly any problem connected with an international payments system of managed flexibility that would not have to be decided according to our basic interpretation of the concept "equilibrium rate."

The lack of unambiguous, objective criteria is obvious; the concept of the equilibrium rate leaves room for many interpretations, from the demand for nearly complete freedom of domestic action to

20 *Ibid.*

21 Ragnar Nurkse, *Conditions of International Monetary Equilibrium*, Essays in International Finance, No. 4 (Princeton, N.J.: Princeton University Press, Spring, 1945), p. 8.

the complete submission to automatic gold-standard rules. Thus, even if certain criteria could be defined more clearly they would still be subject to different interpretations.

In one respect, however, it is actually an advantage that the criteria of international payments equilibrium are not too easily interpreted. "A publicly recognized and recognizable criterion . . . has the disadvantage that it may act as a signal for speculative capital transfers in anticipation of changes in exchange rates."[22] The less easy it is for speculators to determine deviations of the official from the equilibrium rate, the smoother will a system of managed flexibility function.

SUGGESTIONS FOR FURTHER READING

CASSEL, GUSTAV. *Money and Foreign Exchange After 1914,* pp. 137–69. New York: Macmillan Co., 1923.

ELLIS, HOWARD S. "The Equilibrium Rate of Exchange," *Explorations in Economics.* Notes and Essays Contributed in Honor of F. W. Taussig, chap. 3. New York: McGraw-Hill Book Co., Inc., 1936.

HABERLER, GOTTFRIED. "Currency Depreciation and the International Monetary Fund," *The Review of Economic Statistics,* Vol. XXVI, No. 4 (November, 1944), pp. 178–81.

KEYNES, J. M. *A Tract on Monetary Reform,* chap. 3. New York: Harcourt, Brace & Co., 1924.

METZLER, LLOYD A. "Exchange Rates and the International Monetary Fund," *International Monetary Policies.* Postwar Economic Studies, No. 7. Washington, D.C.: Board of Governors of the Federal Reserve System, 1947.

NURKSE, RAGNAR. *Conditions of International Monetary Equilibrium.* Essays in International Finance, No. 4. Princeton: Princeton University Press, International Finance Section, 1945. Reprinted in *Readings in the Theory of International Trade,* chap. 1 (Homewood, Ill.: Richard D. Irwin, Inc., 1949).

WHITTLESEY, CHARLES R. *International Monetary Issues.* New York: McGraw-Hill Book Co., Inc., 1937.

QUESTIONS AND PROBLEMS

1. There seems to be "no valid reason to assume, as is commonly done, that, while the principle of supply and demand functions fairly well in goods relationships, it should not be allowed to operate, except with arbitrary restrictions, to determine the price of currencies" (C. R. Whittlesey). Discuss.

22 *Ibid.*

2. Is it true that exchange rate fluctuations will seriously impede long-term capital movements?
3. Discuss the purposes and functioning of exchange stabilization funds.
4. Compare a system of controlled exchange rate fluctuations with (*a*) a system of pegged rates and (*b*) a system of freely fluctuating rates.
5. Is it correct and sufficient to define the equilibrium rate of exchange as "the rate which, over a certain period, maintains the balance of payments in equilibrium without any net change in international currency reserve" (Ragnar Nurkse)?
6. Explain the purchasing power parity theory. In particular, show why it cannot be applied to absolute price levels but only to changes in price levels on the basis of a known exchange rate which was an equilibrium rate.
7. "It is possible to compute the correct exchange rates once we have index numbers expressing the domestic purchasing power of the currencies in question." True?
8. Can you make a case for purchasing power parity calculations in spite of the obvious shortcomings of the purchasing power parity theory?
9. How long a period should the monetary authority have in mind when it tries to determine the size of the international liquidity reserve according to the definition of the equilibrium rate used in question 5?
10. Should a country which suffers from mass unemployment be permitted to depreciate its currency?

Chapter 33 PATHOLOGY OF INTERNATIONAL PAYMENTS

Exchange Control

When referring to exchange control we mean measures which replace the free foreign exchange market with discriminatory regulations. Buyers and sellers are no longer permitted to purchase and sell foreign exchange in unlimited amounts. Either the quantities purchased or the prices at which they can be purchased or both are now subject to direct regulations. These arbitrary and discriminatory regulations can be of an immense variety in detail.

As a rule, exchange control is used when the price for foreign money is kept below the price to which it would rise on a free market and when it is impossible to maintain this low price through sales out of foreign exchange reserves. Figure 33–1 illustrates this situation.

Suppose that a falling off of the supply of foreign exchange (a shift of the supply curve to the left) or an increase in demand (a shift of the demand curve to the right) or a combination of both would establish a new market price *P′* for foreign exchange. For some reason the monetary authority deems it desirable to maintain the old price *P* and declares it to be the official rate at which all transactions have to be carried through. The line *CC,* therefore, marks the ceiling price above which the exchange rate is not permitted to climb. The *CC* rate constitutes an artificial overvaluation of the domestic currency, because the monetary authority declares that it takes fewer units of domestic money to buy a unit of foreign money than would be needed at the market price *P′*.

At the ceiling price the amount supplied falls so short of the amount demanded (the distance between *A* and *B*) that the foreign exchange reserves of the government would soon be exhausted if it were attempted to bridge the gap through sales of foreign exchange out of reserves. If the government refuses, nevertheless, to let the price rise to or near P', it will have to bring about an artificial "equilibrium" of demand and supply through controls of one kind or another.

First of all, the monetary authority (or foreign exchange control board) must try to get hold of the supply of foreign exchange. All those earning foreign money must be made to sell their earnings to government offices. This is more easily said than done. Foreign traders know full well that the official price is kept artificially low and, accordingly, will try to sell foreign exchange on the black market rather than at the official price. The government, therefore, must know who has earned foreign exchange and how much. Obviously, it will not be easy to subject only certain categories of international

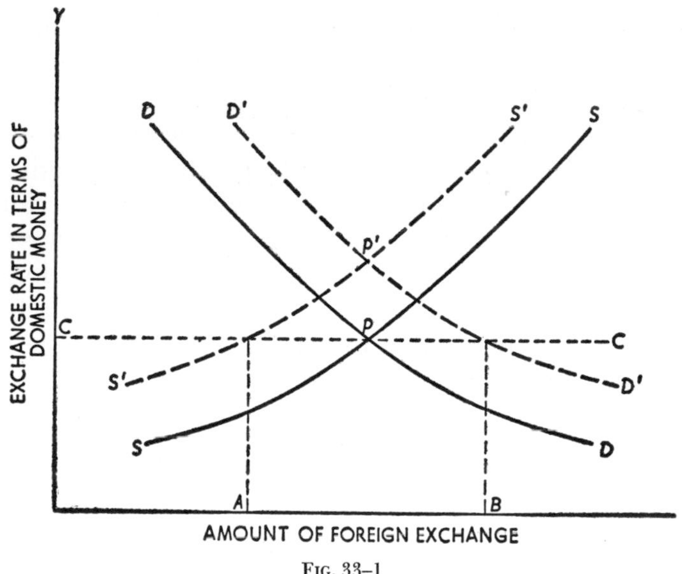

FIG. 33–1

transactions to control (say capital flight movements) and let others remain free (say current account transactions). The opportunities for evasion would be great. In a really tight exchange control system all receivers of foreign exchange are forced to sell their foreign balances to a central office at the official rate. Furthermore, in order to make sure that the proceeds of exports are not left abroad by private traders, exports are closely scrutinized and made subject to export licenses.

This tendency of an exchange control system to eventually embrace all transactions and to control in greatest detail all commodity exports is typical for direct controls in general: they have the tendency to multiply as by chain reaction. We also ought to remember at this point that complete exchange control will require the opening of mail and that, in extreme cases, it may penalize offenders with concentration camp and capital punishment.

Assuming that a central office has succeeded in appropriating all foreign exchange earnings at the official price, it must now allocate this supply through some form of rationing, for the amount demanded far exceeds the amount supplied at the ceiling price. The authority has four decisions to make: "(1) how much to allot for different *purposes* (commodity imports, debt service, tourist traffic, etc.); (2) how to distribute the exchange available for imports among different *commodities;* (3) how to ration exchange among different *firms;* and (4) how to distribute the total among different *countries.*"[1]

The regulations which have been designed to solve these rationing problems are sometimes further complicated by the desire to simultaneously stimulate the supply of foreign exchange. In its attempt to narrow the gap (*AB* in Figure 33–1) the authority will provide exporters with inducements intended to take the place of the lacking stimulation of a higher market price.

Since foreign exchange control measures are infinite in their variety, we can look only at a few typical forms. We assume, however, that changes in the foreign exchange rate are not used as an equilibrating device. Multiple exchange rates as a form of foreign exchange control will be discussed later.

1. The monetary authority may want to confine foreign exchange restrictions to certain kinds of capital transfers. If these controls could be so perfected that they eliminate hot-money movements without interfering with other transactions, they would be a valuable instrument of international monetary policy. But it is next to impossible to sufficiently tighten controls on only one type of transaction. Exporters could leave their earnings abroad and sell claims to foreign currency to those who want to transfer capital.

2. In a case of total exchange control the techniques employed may still aim at the greatest possible neutrality in terms of commercial policy. For example, the supply of foreign exchange may be allocated uniformly on a percentage basis with reference to a base year. This may be done in connection with any or all of the categories mentioned above (purpose, commodities, firms, and countries). The weakness of this system is that it freezes the pattern of international

[1] Ragnar Nurkse, *International Currency Experience* (Geneva: League of Nations, 1944), p. 173.

economic relations which existed in the base year and does not allow for vital adjustments to fundamental changes. When applied to commodity trade the percentage ratio allocation tries to make the rationing of foreign exchange compatible with the most-favored-nation principle,[2] but here, too, it succeeds only in freezing a position which may have been a historical accident and is unjustified under changed conditions.

3. The temptation may be great to use the allocation of foreign exchange as an instrument to circumvent existing trade agreements, for exchange allocation is a weapon admirably suited for discriminatory practices. As such, it becomes the very negation of the most-favored-nation principle.

4. In an attempt to combine the rationing of foreign exchange with an inducement to supply foreign exchange, import licenses may be granted if such imports from country B can be paired with exports to country B in some sort of barter arrangement. The possibilities of matching exports and imports increase if such barter deals are carried through on a national scale via so-called clearing agreements. Clearing accounts are established in the central banks of the trading countries. Importers pay domestic money into this account and exporters receive payment, also in domestic money, out of it. Normally such an agreement must limit the debt which the other country may run up if its imports exceed its exports; and a procedure must be established whereby unpaid claims can be settled. The claims may be carried over to the next period or paid in gold or an acceptable third currency.[3]

5. Payments agreements are similar to clearing agreements, but they use foreign exchange instead of clearing accounts and may be concluded between countries of which only one uses an exchange control system. For example, if exchange control country A, which is a debtor country, has an excess of exports over imports in its relations with creditor country B, country B may insist that at least part of

[2] The principle of unconditional most-favored-nation treatment gives the foreign trader of every country with which a trade agreement has been concluded the right to be treated no worse than the trader of any other country.

[3] A country may find it advantageous to buy more than it can sell under barter arrangements, to accumulate debts, and to use its position as a debtor to exert pressure upon the creditor; if country A buys more from country B than it is able to pay for in kind, it may seem advisable to country B to buy in country A rather than in another country so as to get payment for its previous deliveries. Once a big country has in this fashion crowded out its competitors in the markets of a smaller country, its position as a single buyer and seller may become so strong that it may finally be able to dictate the exchange rate very much in its own favor. This was common practice in the relationships between Nazi Germany and southeastern European countries.

country A's export earnings be used for interest and amortization payments to B. We see, also, that payments agreements are broader in scope than clearing agreements, which are limited to commodity and service transactions.

The Disadvantages of Exchange Control

If multilateral international trade is advantageous, exchange control is bad even though it may sometimes be a necessary evil. Multilateral trade offers us the advantage that we can shop around and purchase where comparative advantages permit a country to quote the most favorable price; while we, in turn, can sell wherever the highest prices are offered for our products. Since we can pay for our purchases in country B with our earnings in C and D, we are not forced to limit our choice of markets by the necessity of pairing exports and imports in barter fashion. Clearing agreements reduce international trade to the level where the trade between any two countries can be equilibrated. Obviously, the volume of international trade must then shrink to a fraction of the trade possible on a multilateral rather than bilateral basis. In addition, the price and quality of bartered goods will be far less favorable.

To these basic disadvantages we must add the danger of discrimination and bureaucratism which bilateral deals imply and the political consequences for smaller countries which deal with larger ones on the basis of clearing agreements. We have seen that exchange control has in extreme cases become an instrument of international blackmail and aggression. Why, then, do monetary authorities often turn towards exchange control in preference to free payments systems?

The Advantages of Exchange Control

1. The monetary authority may be skeptical about the effectiveness of the normal mechanisms under abnormal circumstances. Facing wild speculation and the flight of capital they may, for instance, fear that exchange depreciation might be interpreted as another warning signal and add to the motives of the stampede instead of halting it.

2. The monetary authority, conscious that it has allowed inflationary forces to develop, may wish to conceal the inflation by avoiding official exchange depreciation as well as the drain on its foreign exchange and gold reserves.

3. Government authorities may wish to support and supplement a system of domestic price and production controls. The regulation

of domestic prices would be ineffective without the control of foreign transactions. This illustrates the tendency of direct controls to multiply.

4. Government authorities may anticipate the contagious effect of a depression in foreign countries. They refuse to use domestic monetary contraction as a means to safeguard their foreign exchange reserves, knowing that they would pay with increasing unemployment for a stable balance of international payments. Instead, they use domestic monetary and fiscal policies to compensate for the contraction in their export industries, increasing thereby the balance-of-payments deficit. Exchange control permits the authorities to insulate the economy against the transmission of depression and deflation in other countries, at the price of a reduction in the volume of international trade.

5. The monetary authority may permit itself to be used as an instrument of commercial policy. By allocating foreign exchange for importation of particular commodities, from particular countries, or by particular importers, it may grant protection from foreign (and domestic) competition and exercise wide discriminatory powers in violation of existing agreements.

6. The monetary authority may choose an overvalued exchange rate and the resulting exchange control measures, arguing that the alternative, namely, a higher price of foreign exchange, would constitute a deterioration of the so-called terms of trade, that is, a rise in import prices and a fall in export prices.

Multiple Exchange Rates

Until now we have assumed that the exchange control country introduced exchange control because it refused to let the price mechanism work; accordingly we have taken it for granted that the exchange regulations consisted of direct controls. However, it is possible to have an exchange control system and yet allocate foreign exchange by a system which uses several prices depending on the nature of the demand or the sources of the supply. It is claimed that such a system can avoid the clumsiness of rationing and barter.

Suppose that the monetary authority sells foreign exchange to different groups of buyers at different prices. The rate charged will depend on whether the government considers the imported articles of greater or lesser importance. This system can avoid rationing by setting the price in the different segments of the arbitrarily divided market so that the amount demanded in each segment will closely correspond to the government's wishes. The government can use price differentials also to try to exploit possible monopsonistic positions in foreign markets (through high rates) or to subsidize buying under heavy competitive pressure (through low rates). Similarly, the government can subsidize foreign sales by offering the exporter a high rate for his foreign balances. A low rate will be paid where exports are considered less desirable or where an inelastic foreign demand will permit sales even at high foreign prices.

This system has its advantages when compared with the rationing system, particularly where stimulation of exports is concerned, but it is basically just as discriminatory. We must remember that the list of exports and imports which are to be treated preferentially rests on arbitrary decisions since objective criteria for such a market segregation are not available.

Robert Triffin proposes an exchange control system which he believes avoids the disadvantages of discrimination, incompetence, and favoritism. He wants "exchange restrictions through flexible and impersonal market forces, leaving the importers free to buy whatever they please wherever they please (presumably from the cheapest source of supply), subject only to such automatic restrictions as would normally result from the free interplay of supply and demand."

Triffin's plan is simple:

> (1) The monetary authorities would make exchange freely available, without previous permit or restrictions of any sort, at the normal exchange rates, for payment of all essential and urgent imports or services and of contractual obligations, dividends, or reasonable amortization on approved foreign investments. (2) The remainder of available exchange would be sold by the monetary authorities to provide means of payment for deferrable or nonessential imports, again without quantitative restrictions or import permits, through the functioning of one, or a few, auction markets.[4]

The elegance of Triffin's proposal is deceiving. Imports are still in an artificial and discriminatory way classified as "essential," "urgent," "deferrable," and "nonessential," with plenty of possibilities for pressure groups to exploit the incompetence of a powerful bureaucracy. It also seems that Triffin overestimates the monopolistic and monopsonistic advantages implied in his scheme. He is, for example, mistaken when he assumes that raw material and food-producing countries could avoid making price concessions simply by avoid-

[4] Robert Triffin, "National Central Banking and the International Economy," in *International Monetary Policies. Postwar Economic Studies*, No. 7 (Washington, D.C.: Board of Governors of the Federal Reserve System, 1947), p. 69.

ing depreciation through exchange control. They still would have to consider the danger of competition from third countries.[5]

Competitive Exchange Depreciation

When a country suffers from an overvaluation of its currency and wants neither to use exchange control nor to contract its domestic monetary circulation, it has a choice between three types of exchange depreciation: (1) it can let the exchange rate find its own level; (2) it can choose and try to maintain a new rate as near as possible to the equilibrium rate; (3) it can choose and maintain a rate which constitutes an undervaluation of its currency. Since cases (1) and (2) have already been discussed in Chapter 32, we shall now analyze the consequences of the third case, which is commonly known as competitive exchange depreciation.

Competitive exchange depreciation is, like inflation, particularly dangerous because its consequences are initially favorable. Overvaluation, on the other hand, like deflation, has effects which are disagreeable from the start. Undervaluation can be easily maintained. It implies that the price of foreign exchange is kept *above* the equilibrium point (that is, the point of intersection of the demand and supply curves) on the foreign exchange market. At this artificially high price for foreign currency in terms of domestic currency the amount of foreign exchange supplied exceeds the amount demanded and the gap (between points *A* and *B* in Fig. 33–2) is closed by the monetary authority taking the excess supply off the market, that is, buying it up with domestic currency. This the monetary authority is able to do without limitation, since its resources of domestic currency are, at least theoretically, infinite; it can create, if legally so empowered, any amount of domestic currency. The country proceeding with this policy accumulates foreign balances and gold and causes corresponding depletion of the foreign exchange or gold reserves of other countries. Since a country by undervaluating its currency improves its balance-of-payments position, it can continue to keep its currency undervalued until the disadvantages resulting from international repercussions become too great.

In spite of its monetary advantages, or rather because of them, competitive exchange depreciation must be classified as a most dangerous "beggar-my-neighbor" policy which benefits nobody in the

[5] See Gottfried Haberler, "Comments on 'National Central Banking and the International Economy,'" in *International Monetary Policies. Postwar Economic Studies,* No. 7 (Washington, D.C.: Board of Governors of the Federal Reserve System, 1947), p. 94.

end. Obviously if one country gains an export advantage through artificial reduction of the price of its currency (turning, as it were, its whole market into a big cut-rate store for foreign buyers), it does so at the expense of other countries, whose currencies are now relatively overvalued and whose exports are consequently reduced. The economic consequences in these countries are not difficult to trace. Since they find their foreign exchange reserves depleting at an alarm-

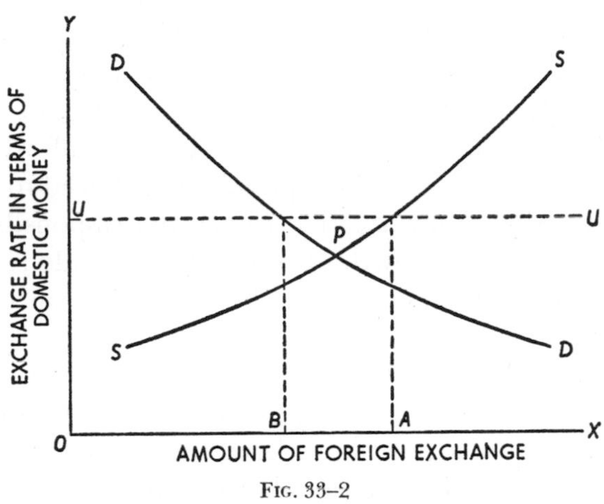

FIG. 33–2

P is the equilibrium rate of exchange.
UU is the official price of foreign exchange constituting an undervaluation.
BA is the excess supply of foreign exchange to be taken off the market by the monetary authority.

ing rate, these countries will try to protect their reserves. They can choose among three possibilities: (1) they can pursue a policy of domestic monetary contraction, with a fair chance that decreasing economic activity at home would prove contagious for the country which started to beggar its neighbors; (2) they, too, can turn to competitive exchange depreciation, thus reducing and finally eliminating the initial advantage of the country which started this depreciation cycle; (3) they can counteract competitive exchange depreciation by protectionism in the form of import quotas or exchange control with the result that excessive competition leads, as so often, to a gradual suppression of competition.

It is easy to see that competitive exchange depreciation does not pay in the long run. Accordingly, it is one of the purposes of the International Monetary Fund "to avoid competitive exchange depreciation" (Art. I [iii]). However, since it is difficult to determine the equilibrium rate of exchange, it will also be difficult to determine whether and to what degree a currency is undervalued.

Inconsistencies

Under the gold standard a country that was losing gold was compelled to contract credit, while, as we have seen before, a gold-receiving country was under no compulsion to expand. Generalizing from this example of a lack of reciprocity of action, we may state that countries whose foreign exchange reserves are endangered ("deficit" countries) are forced into policies designed to equilibrate their balances of payments while countries whose foreign exchange or gold reserves are constantly growing ("surplus" countries) can afford to be indifferent to this situation or to follow policies which lead to even greater disequilibrium. Since they are free to act, the responsibility for the expansion and balanced growth of international trade rests primarily with the surplus countries, though the restrictionism of the deficit countries may be more conspicuous. A surplus country should at least shoulder half the adjustment burden in an unbalanced situation and, from the standpoint of its own long-run advantage, it should not force deficit countries into a position where they will resort to policies which are destructive of international prosperity.

It is easy to perceive the principles of a code of desirable behavior for surplus countries. The ideal surplus country would make more of its own currency available to deficit countries or pursue policies leading to a natural decline of the deficit countries' demand for its currency. These policies should follow the principle that a disequilibrium in the balance of payments be overcome by lengthening the short leg rather than shortening the long leg, that is, emphasis should be on expansionist rather than contractionist measures.

The ideal surplus country would try, first of all, to step up its imports. This can be accomplished in several ways:

1. The surplus country could make every possible effort to achieve and maintain a high level of employment and thus secure a large effective demand for commodities produced at home and abroad. If the surplus country has not yet achieved a high employment level it has the "moral" obligation to lead in an expansionist policy upon which the deficit countries cannot embark alone if foreign trade and payments are to remain multilateral.

2. The surplus country could take the lead in relaxing tariffs and other protectionist policies and thus encourage additional imports.

3. The surplus country could appreciate its currency when a persistent and increasing inflow of gold or foreign exchange indicates an undervaluation of its monetary unit.

4. If these measures are economically or politically impossible, the surplus country must help to bring about a temporary equilibrium situation through purchases of foreign securities, that is, through the extension of credit to deficit countries.

To solve the problem of international payments disequilibrium through international loans means, however, to postpone its real and final solution which, on the part of the surplus country, must be achieved in one or more of the ways enumerated above. Foreign loans should, therefore, be made only if the surplus country is completely conscious of the fact that it will have to receive in the future *even more* foreign payments in the form of an excess of imports over exports of goods and services. Creditor countries are seldom conscious of this necessity when they grant further loans in order to avoid the *immediate* application of policies which would lead to an excess of imports over exports. Nevertheless, as a temporary measure, the extension of loans may be more advisable than the accumulation of gold by the surplus country, since the drain on the deficit countries' reserves could exert dangerous deflationary pressure throughout the world.

During the thirties the United States as a surplus country violated the above code of desirable behavior on all four counts: by not maintaining or successfully restoring a high employment level; by raising tariffs; by depreciating; and by withdrawing short-term loans.

Deficit countries too can be inconsistent. Let us assume that surplus countries follow our code of desirable behavior so that balance-of-payments difficulties do not originate with them. An imbalance may still arise if deficit countries refuse to adjust their domestic policies in such a way that they fit the policies of other countries. A country may, for example, follow a policy of price inflation at full employment. It practices a cheap-money policy and encourages more domestic investment and consumption than sufficient production in its export industries would permit. Its imports will tend to exceed its exports: partially because its resources are drawn into domestic use, leaving insufficient resources for the production of export goods; and partially because its exports cannot be competitive in other markets if the country's inflation is worse than those in other countries. If price inflation is repressed through domestic price controls, the basic difficulties will remain the same. Foreign exchange control then becomes a necessary counterpart of domestic controls, and the allocation of resources will be even more arbitrary than under a price inflation.

The basic difficulty in this situation is easy to diagnose. A deficit country which under world conditions of high employment carries through a more expansionist policy than the other countries tends to live beyond its means: it tries to maintain higher standards of living and of investment than the full use of its resources permits.

The cure for such a situation is not deflation, but discontinuation of inflation plus a correct depreciation of the inflated currency. The cure will not require contraction and unemployment, but reduction of consumption and/or investment to a level which can be sustained under balance-of-payments equilibrium. On the other hand, if depreciation is carried through with the false promise that "the people's wages, salaries and savings will buy just as much as they did before,"[6] the policy is sure to fail.

The Transfer Problem

A particularly interesting case of (potential) international payments disequilibrium is connected with the transfer of unilateral payments of a more or less abnormal character. Such payments may arise from reparations, accumulated war debts, the unfreezing of foreign short-term balances when exchange restrictions are removed, or any other quick withdrawal of substantial amounts of capital.

In Chapters 31 and 32 we have studied the international payments mechanisms. We have now to ask why these mechanisms should not work in the above-mentioned cases. Does a special transfer problem really exist? This question has led to an interesting controversy.[7] One group of writers is inclined to assume that unilateral payments (of the reparation type) do not represent a new problem and that the transfer from one country to the other and from one currency into the other can be accomplished rather easily within the existing international monetary mechanism—provided only that the paying country is able and willing to raise among its nationals the domestic funds for such payments. These writers argue that paying country A

[6] This was promised by Sir Stafford Cripps in his broadcast of September 18, 1949. See *New York Times*, September 19, 1949, p. 6.

[7] See particularly J. M. Keynes, "The German Transfer Problem," and B. Ohlin, "Transfer Difficulties, Real and Imagined," *Economic Journal*, Vol. XXXIX (1929). Both articles are reprinted in *Readings in the Theory of International Trade* (Homewood, Ill.: Richard D. Irwin, Inc., 1949). A very good summary of the Keynes-Ohlin discussion can be found in Gottfried Haberler, *The Theory of International Trade* (New York: Macmillan Co., 1937), pp. 66–76.

would have to decrease its domestic expenditures. The raising of the necessary sums of domestic money would have a deflationary effect in country A and would thus bring about a sufficient increase of country A's exports over its imports. This result would be facilitated if the purchasing power of country B were simultaneously increased, for example, if reparation money were used in B for remission of taxes. Country A's goods and services, furthermore, would not have to be pressed directly into B's markets. In a multilateral payments system country A's goods could be sold anywhere in the world market and the foreign exchange proceeds handed over to country B.

Another group of theorists is less optimistic and considers it very likely that the paying country would have to lower its prices artificially in order to be able to create the necessary export surplus. The flow of gold from country A to country B under the gold standard, with deflationary effects in A and (perhaps) inflationary effects in B, is seen to place an extra burden of debt on the paying country, a burden over and above that of raising the domestic funds for the payment. Lower prices in the paying country mean larger amounts of goods and services in terms of a fixed sum of country A's money even if the exchange rate is kept stable. Generally speaking the barter terms of trade would become less favorable for the paying country and more favorable for the receiving country.

Some writers believe that the receiving country B is not to be envied either, for its industries would have to face increasing competition. While country A's economy suffers from a dangerous deflationary process, B's government may be under pressure to increase its tariffs to offset country A's deflationary efforts. In fact, the inconsistent policy of insisting on unilateral payments which B is loath to receive in terms of imports, and which B actually shuts out by increasing its tariffs, is a source of international difficulties which may have grave consequences.

There is no single, obvious solution for the transfer problem. Whether the optimists or the pessimists are right depends entirely on the prevailing circumstances. If the payments are of moderate size (per period of time and in relation to the economic strength of the paying country) and if the demand for the products of the paying country is rather elastic, it will be comparatively easy to increase exports sufficiently and without much effect upon the barter terms of trade. The employment situation in country A, the paying country, need not suffer at all since the enforced export activity may conceivably create new employment opportunities. If B's businessmen complain about increased competition, they take in effect the strange attitude that country A is to be envied—an attitude from which one could logically deduce the absurd conclusion that the victors had better pay reparations to the vanquished.

If one assumes that the required payments are relatively large and that the demand for country A's products is not elastic the transfer of the payments may cause serious difficulties. If the demand for A's products is of an elasticity of unity or less than unity, efforts to accomplish the transfer may become intolerable, because the attempts to reduce A's prices, even though successful, would not lead to larger exports. Indeed, such reduced prices might even lead to smaller proceeds from exports.

The outcome will depend on the character of the economies of the countries involved, the character of the payments system and the relative size of the payments. A few generalizations, however, are permissible. For it can be shown that under normal multilateral payments conditions the demand for the paying country's products in all probability is quite elastic.

1. It can be assumed that the world market will be large compared with the exports from one single country. In a multilateral payments system the paying country's exports need not be pressed directly into the markets of the receiving country. Any increase in exports from country A to the rest of the world will contribute to unilateral payments from country A to country B.

2. The receiving country's industry does not necessarily have to face increased competition from abroad for domestic consumers' dollars. The purchasing power in country B may have been increased through tax remissions or increased government expenditures. Imports could then be increased without reducing domestic expenditures on home products. A decrease in country A's imports is likely to occur but would have to be borne by all other countries rather than by country B alone.

3. The excess of exports over imports in the paying country need not be accomplished solely by increased sale of those products which have been exported hitherto. New commodities or services may become export articles, while a decrease of imports into country A will also help widen the gap between exports and imports. The broader the variety of articles involved, the smaller will be the necessary price reductions.

4. Since the standard of living in the paying country is falling while that of the receiving country is rising, it may be that the iden-

tical goods whose consumption is reduced in country A will be bought in increasing quantities by country B as a result of the two countries' income changes. This may be true, for example, of coffee imported by the two countries from a third country—a shift with relatively few frictions.

Thus it seems that the transfer of unilateral payments of the reparation type could be accomplished without special obstacles, provided the payments are not excessive and the international payments system is both multilateral and in good working order.

The transfer pessimists are right, however, on the following points:

1. If the respective industries of the paying and receiving countries produce the same commodities and compete with each other in the world market, the transfer of unilateral payments may raise serious complications, economic as well as political. The economic structures of the economies involved are important factors in the solution of the problem.

2. The disturbing effects of the payments are the greater, the more rapidly the export surplus has to be achieved. The rapid enforcement of an export surplus necessitates an artificial deflation process, which may reduce incomes in country A so drastically as to endanger the raising of domestic funds for the payment. Unemployment created by deflation may be disastrous for the paying country, much more so than the worsening of the terms of trade.

3. The problem is made the more difficult, the less country B realizes that it must accept the unilateral payments in the form of an excess of its imports over its exports. Increasing tariffs or introducing import quotas may aggravate country A's difficulties to the breaking point. There is no possible doubt that increasing tariffs in country B or in other countries buying country A's products increases A's burden by forcing A's prices and wages down further.

4. Besides the receiving country the paying country and even third countries may be induced to raise trade barriers, thus further complicating the international payments system. Efforts by country A to reduce its imports through tariffs and other protectionist devices are less inconsistent than they are in B, but the consequences are no less harmful to international trade. When country A uses the proceeds from its exports to country C to pay B, country C in turn, confronted with increased imports from country A and reduced exports to country A, may try to reduce its imports. Of course, we might assume that B will buy from C what country A could no longer afford to buy, but

the commodities demanded by B easily might not be the same as those formerly demanded by A. Shifts in production would become necessary and transition difficulties would be created which might be serious enough to cause a general spread of protectionism.

SUGGESTIONS FOR FURTHER READING

Exchange Controls:

ELLIS, HOWARD S. *Exchange Control in Central Europe.* Cambridge, Mass.: Harvard University Press, 1934.

ELLIS, HOWARD S. "Exchange Control and Discrimination," *American Economic Review,* Vol. XXXVII (December, 1947), pp. 877–88.

HAWKINS, HARRY C. *Commercial Treaties and Agreements,* chap. 16. New York: Rinehart & Co., Inc., 1951.

KINDELBERGER, CHARLES P. *International Economics,* chap. 13. Homewood, Ill.: Richard D. Irwin, Inc., 1953.

LEAGUE OF NATIONS. *International Currency Experience,* chap. 7. Geneva, 1944.

TRIFFIN, ROBERT. "National Central Banking and the International Economy," *International Monetary Policies.* Postwar Economic Studies, No. 7. Washington, D.C.: Board of Governors of the Federal Reserve System, 1947. See also Gottfried Haberler's criticism of Triffin's paper in the same volume.

Transfer Problem:

HABERLER, GOTTFRIED. *The Theory of International Trade,* chap. 7. New York: Macmillan Co., 1937.

KEYNES, J. M. "The German Transfer Problem," *Economic Journal,* Vol. XXXIX (March, 1929), pp. 1–7. Reprinted in *Readings in the Theory of International Trade,* chap. 6 (Homewood, Ill.: Richard D. Irwin, Inc., 1949).

OHLIN, BERTIL. "The Reparation Problem: A Discussion," *Economic Journal,* Vol. XXXIX (June, 1929), pp. 172–73. Reprinted in *Readings in the Theory of International Trade,* chap. 7 (Homewood, Ill.: Richard D. Irwin, Inc., 1949).

ROBERTSON, D. H. *Essays in Monetary Theory,* chap. 14. London: Staples Press, Ltd., 1940.

QUESTIONS AND PROBLEMS

1. "As a rule exchange control is used when the price for foreign money is kept below the price to which it would rise on a free market." Explain and illustrate graphically.

2. Discuss the problems which a central office has to face in the artificial allocation of the supply of foreign exchange under exchange control.
3. "If only a few categories of applicants for foreign exchange are subject to exchange-control restrictions, it proves difficult if not impossible to prevent applicants within this category from disguising their real status . . . and thus evading or avoiding the control" (J. Viner). Give examples.
4. What causes governments to prefer overvaluation and exchange control to a free payments system?
5. Is it possible to insert a most-favored-nation clause in exchange controls?
6. Could the government eliminate discriminatory practices in exchange control through selling foreign exchange on a few auction markets?
7. Why is it one of the purposes of the International Monetary Fund "to avoid competitive exchange depreciation"?
8. "During the thirties the United States behaved as a surplus country should not have behaved." Discuss.
9. "In the case of German Reparations . . . we are trying to fix the volume of foreign remittance and compel the balance of trade to adjust itself thereto. Those who see no difficulty in this . . . are applying the theory of liquids to what is, if not a solid, at least a sticky mess with strong internal resistances" (J. M. Keynes). Do you agree?
10. "Professor Ohlin is undoubtedly correct in maintaining that Mr. Keynes ignores the shifts on the demand side produced by the (reparation) payments themselves" (Gottfried Haberler). Discuss.

PART IX

International Monetary Co-operation

Chapter 34 THE LESSONS OF THE INTERWAR PERIOD

The Return to Gold

The gold-flow mechanism had been working well before World War I. The conditions for its functioning were favorable and its automatic features appealed to the economic philosophy of the period. Exchange rates were stable; exchange markets, free and multilateral; and the monetary authorities, under no obligation to make difficult policy decisions. Since the central banks followed, more or less, the same tacitly accepted rules of behavior, a remarkable co-ordination of the various domestic economic policies was achieved. Full employment policies were not known and could not challenge the primacy of stable exchange rates as the main goal of monetary policy. The gold flow worked with apparent ease since prices and costs were still flexible. The business cycle emphasized expansion more than contraction, and gold outflows could be avoided, as a rule, by short-term borrowing. London took it upon itself to make foreign exchange reserves available to those who were temporarily in need of reserves. Capital movements were equilibrating, and hot-money movements, practically unknown.

To be sure, the gold mechanism, as it operated in reality, was different from the simple textbook model of classical economics. But it worked to the satisfaction of all concerned, and no "member" country showed a desire (or was forced) to go off the gold standard. When the gold standard was abandoned by most countries during World War I, it was done in the firm conviction that after the emergency the world would return to gold and would continue where it had left off in August, 1914.

In Chapter 17 we saw that World War I led to a substantial price inflation in the United States. Other countries, too, experienced inflationary developments, but the degree of inflation differed widely from country to country. Under the circumstances it should have been obvious (1) that nothing could be gained by an attempt to redeem the injustices of inflation through deflationary policies (see Chapter 3, p. 33); and (2) that the old prewar gold parities could no longer be considered as the equilibrium rates of exchange. However, these basic truths were not clearly understood. Even the purchasing power parity theory, oversimplified though it is, was not grasped by the responsible authorities.

The United States returned to gold at the old gold parity of $20.67 for an ounce of gold. This unilateral decision of the United States created problems for the rest of the world. In most countries the inflation had been worse than in the United States, and the dollar shortage was acute. The whole war and postwar period was one of fundamental payments disequilibrium. The United States had a constant export surplus of commodities, and it imported gold and securities to finance this net foreign investment. After the United States returned to gold at the old parity, return to the old gold parity by other countries meant a return to the old dollar parity. It also meant a return to gold under conditions in which the value of gold was determined by the purchasing power of the dollar. Formerly, the gold value was the politically neutral result of the co-ordinated credit policies of the major countries playing the gold-standard game. Now, under conditions of a grave dollar shortage, the value of gold was determined by the credit policy of the Federal Reserve Board in Washington. Thus, to tie a currency to gold meant in effect to tie it to the dollar.

British Overvaluation

Countries whose price levels had risen far beyond the comparative rise in American prices could not possibly contemplate a return to prewar gold and dollar parities by way of domestic price deflation. Thus, their more extreme inflations had at least one favorable effect: to prevent their monetary authorities from following the mistaken example of some of the countries whose inflations had not been hopelessly worse than the American one. For some countries the prewar dollar parity seemed so nearly within reach that it was considered reasonable to attempt to close the gap in purchasing power parities through domestic credit contraction.

This was true of Great Britain, which for so long had been the center of world finance. The attempt to return to the prewar gold and dollar parities in the spring of 1920 meant an appreciation of 44 per cent. The deflation in the United States in 1920–21 made the British task even more formidable.

Today we find it difficult to understand why a country should be willing to undertake a dangerous credit contraction and price deflation in order to return to a prewar parity which had no justification anyhow under completely changed circumstances. Moreover, the United States parity was no longer determined by objective market forces (such as gold production and the world demand for gold).

J. M. Keynes, who argued against a return to gold and even more strongly against overvaluation, has listed the arguments which were made for a return to the old gold parity rates after the first World War:

> 1. To leave the gold value of a country's currency at the low level to which war has driven it is an injustice to the rentier class and to others whose income is fixed in terms of currency, and practically a breach of contract; while to restore its value would meet a debt of honor.
>
> 2. The restoration of a currency to its prewar gold value enhances a country's financial prestige and promotes future confidence.
>
> 3. If the gold value of a country's currency can be increased, labor will profit by a reduced cost of living, foreign goods will be obtainable cheaper, and foreign debts fixed in terms of gold (for example, to the United States) will be discharged with less effort.[1]

Only the second argument has some value, according to Keynes, and then only if the currencies concerned are within 10 to 5 per cent of their former gold value. Arguments (1) and (3), however, are completely mistaken. To undo the damage done to the rentier class one would have to pile the damages of a price deflation upon the wreckage left by price inflation; or in Keynes' words: "in order to do justice to a minority of creditors, a great injustice would be done to a great ma-

[1] J. M. Keynes, *Essays in Persuasion* (New York: Harcourt, Brace & Co., Inc., 1932), pp. 191, 193, 194.

jority of debtors."[2] The third argument is, according to Keynes, "pure delusion." Wage earners lose in a process of deflation. A general process of contraction is successful only if wages can be lowered more than prices; and where wages resist the downward adjustment unemployment will result. As far as the debt burden is concerned it does not make much difference whether exports are stimulated by depreciation or deflation.

Keynes' warnings remained unheeded, and in 1925 Great Britain returned to the prewar gold and dollar parity. The Chancellor of the Exchequer "underrated the technical difficulty of bringing about a general reduction of internal monetary values."[3] Labor strenuously resisted the attempt to reduce wage costs, and England suffered grievously in 1926 under a general strike and a lengthy coal strike. Not until September 1931, when, exhausted from her mistaken overvaluation, England left the gold standard, did the country's economy recover.

The British rate was not the only wrongly chosen rate. The situation was made worse through a substantial undervaluation of the French franc. For a long time France enjoyed the advantages which follow a competitive exchange depreciation. This would have caused disequilibrium in international payments in any case, particularly in conjunction with the overvaluation of the pound sterling. The French policy of insisting on settlement in gold of her enormous surplus, both on current and capital account, made the situation even more critical and contributed to the final breakdown of the system in 1931.

Neither the United States nor France, the two major surplus countries, provided the financial leadership which Great Britain had provided during the prewar years. Yet the postwar gold system was from the beginning more precariously balanced than the prewar system and needed a strong financial center more urgently.

The Gold-Exchange Standard

The Genoa Conference of 1922 recommended adoption of the so-called gold-exchange standard. This proposal was made in order to permit return to a gold system in spite of a menacing gold shortage. Gold production had suffered from the inflationary price developments which raised the cost of gold production but not the price of gold. In addition, the existing gold stock was unevenly distributed. To permit the participation of countries which could not muster sufficient

[2] *Ibid.*, p. 192.
[3] *Ibid.*, p. 250.

gold reserves in a general return to a gold system, it was suggested that these countries link their currencies not directly with gold but rather with gold-standard currencies. The currency of the gold-exchange standard country is then convertible not into gold but rather into a "hard" currency which, in turn, can be converted into gold. The system was widely used after the war and, under the circumstances, was probably the only practicable arrangement of the gold-standard type. Yet the gold-exchange standard had the following drawbacks:

1. The use of a foreign currency rather than gold as "supercharged" money (see Chapter 6, p. 64) impairs the gold-flow mechanism because the currency of country A, the gold-standard country, has a different importance in country A than in country B, the gold-exchange standard country. If A-currency rather than gold flows from country B to country A, the effect will not be very expansionist in A, where A-currency will at best be "high-powered money, but the contractionist effect will be strong in B, where credit will have to contract just as if gold had left the country. The gold-exchange standard tends, therefore, to emphasize the basic weakness of the gold standard, namely, its unsymmetrical character (see Chapter 31, p. 442). It tends to stress contraction more than expansion if we make the legitimate assumption that the gold-exchange standard countries are likely to be deficit countries.

2. The gold-exchange standard system makes it imperative that hard currency countries be fully aware of their responsibilities. They are, as it were, international central bankers for the gold-exchange standard countries and indirectly influence the latter's domestic monetary policies. A policy of loan withdrawals, for instance, can have the effect of a multiple credit contraction in the gold-exchange standard country.

3. The experiences of the interwar period show that the adoption of the gold-exchange standard by many countries was in part instrumental for the formation of monetary blocs. This became obvious when in September 1931 the whole sterling area followed its "key currency" when Great Britain left the gold standard.

The Inconsistent Surplus Country

In spite of the already-mentioned difficulties the return to gold might still have been successful had not the great depression in the United States put the international payments mechanism under an unbearable strain; and even the effects of the depression as such might have been manageable in terms of international payments had the United States not followed policies which in every respect were the opposite of what a surplus country ought to have done under the circumstances.

The falling off of United States imports under the impact of the great depression constituted the classical case of a transmission of economic fluctuations through international trade and payments. It would be wrong to blame the United States government for the depression itself. Nobody knew at the time how to maintain expenditures, and the country did not even have adequate monetary weapons, as was shown in Chapter 17. But criticism concerning the foreign economic policies of the United States during the depression period is fully justified.

When international payments disequilibrium was already excessive, owing to a dramatic fall in imports, foreign lending, instead of being increased was suddenly and drastically curtailed. The supply of dollars to foreigners through purchase of their commodities, services, and securities decreased from $7.4 billion in 1929 to $2.4 billion in 1932, a fall of 68 per cent. Private short-term loans were withdrawn. But the attempt by debtor countries to pay their debts through an excess of exports over imports was answered by raising United States tariffs in 1930 to the highest levels in the history of the country. The restrictionist effect of the tariffs was perhaps not very important when compared with the contractionist effect of the depression itself, but it revealed even more glaringly than the untimely withdrawal of short-term private loans an astonishing inconsistency and irresponsibility in the behavior of a surplus country. The third inconsistency, the devaluation of the dollar, will be discussed below.

British Devaluation and Gold Bloc

Under the impact of these heavy blows the gold-exchange standard system, weak and defective from its beginning, was bound to disintegrate. Yet so strong was the belief in gold parities and in stable exchange rates that a prompt depreciation of the deficit currencies was at first not even considered. The Macmillan Report, for instance, advised against depreciation, saying that "there can be little or no hope for the monetary system of the world as a whole, except as a result of a process of evolution starting from the historic gold standard. If, therefore, this country were to cut adrift from the international system with the object of setting up a local standard with a sole regard to our domestic situation, we should be abandoning the larger problem—the solution of which is certainly necessary to a satisfactory solution of the purely domestic problem. . . ."[4]

Nevertheless, as the pressure mounted, Great Britain followed the course which J. M. Keynes had been advocating for years. The pound sterling was cut loose from gold and permitted to find a new low level. This new level constituted a competitive exchange depreciation which was consciously maintained through sales of sterling by the Exchange Equalization Account when the eagerness of Britain's debtors to rid themselves of debts at the new, unusually favorable rate threatened to push the sterling rate back to the equilibrium level.

Great Britain was followed in its depreciation by a group of countries with which she had close political, commercial, and financial relations. All of these countries exported more to England than they imported from her. Accordingly, it was imperative for them to maintain their competitive position in the British market. A stable sterling rate was more important to them than a stable gold parity. Furthermore, British economic activity was less hard hit by the depression than was production in the United States. The sterling area provided a measure of insulation against the contagious effects of the American depression.

Great Britain now enjoyed the advantages of competitive exchange depreciation, for she was not followed for several years by the most important gold-standard countries. "Thus England achieved the best of two worlds: (1) an export advantage over competitors, and (2) an improvement of trade through exchange stability with countries complementary to her economy."[5] This does not mean to say that Britain's policy was a wise policy in the long run or that years of suffering from overvaluation entitle a country to a competitive depreciation spree. Great Britain was, indeed, "abandoning the larger problem" as the Macmillan Report had warned. The total results were such that only five years later Great Britain joined the United States and France in an attempt to prevent undervaluation through the Tripartite Agreement of 1936.

That France, Belgium, and the other gold-bloc countries refused to depreciate and were instead willing to suffer the hardships of overvaluation (in comparison with the sterling area countries) can be ex-

[4] *Committee on Finance and Industry Report* (London: H. M. Stationery Office, Cmd. 3897, 1931), p. 109.

[5] Alvin H. Hansen, *Fiscal Policy and Business Cycles* (New York: W. W. Norton & Co., Inc., 1941), p. 99.

plained by their fear of domestic inflation and a still persisting belief in the feasibility of domestic deflation. All of them had to learn, however, that attempts towards credit contraction reduce employment rather than wages. As these difficulties became increasingly evident it was easy to predict that the gold-bloc countries would sooner or later have to depreciate their currencies, particularly after the devaluation of the dollar in 1933–34. If depreciation is anticipated, capital flight will cause a constant drain on the reserves of foreign exchange and gold unless drastic exchange controls are used. It is profitable to buy gold or dollars with the overvalued currency and to buy the currency back after its depreciation. These speculative transactions themselves made depreciation finally unavoidable.

The gold-bloc countries, unwilling to depreciate and unable to deflate, could not balance their international accounts. They had to take refuge in direct import controls, and international trade contracted accordingly. It can be argued that the gold-bloc countries ought not to be blamed because the difficulties had not originated with them. But their insistence on overvalued gold parities could be defended only on the assumption that they would be able to successfully bring about deflation. That they were not able to lower the wage level sufficiently must be counted as another of those inconsistencies between domestic and foreign economic policies which plagued the world during the interwar period.

The Devaluation of the Dollar

Outstanding among the inconsistencies of the interwar period is the case of the devaluation of the dollar from $20.67 to $35.00 for an ounce of gold since the United States was at the time (1933–34) a surplus country. It must be assumed that the dollar was already undervalued at the old rate and, therefore, excessively undervalued at the new gold price.

It is difficult to give economically sound reasons for this third inconsistency of United States foreign economic policy (withdrawal of loans and high tariffs being the first two). The main reason may have been a naïve attempt to raise the domestic price level through a depreciation of the currency. The depreciation of the dollar had, indeed, the effect of increasing exports and raising the dollar price of export goods. But the general index of wholesale prices gained only 13.4 per cent in comparison with the rise of the gold price by 69 per cent. Commodity prices rise only in response to an increase in expenditure which cannot instantly be met by a corresponding increase in supply.

As shown in Chapter 17 the enormous liquidity which the devaluation created did not lead to increased expenditures so much as to excessive monetary reserves.

The British devaluation influenced the decision to devalue the dollar but could not justify this exaggerated undervaluation of a surplus currency. The undervaluation of the dollar worsened an already existing fundamental payments disequilibrium and aggravated the enormous gold flow to the United States whose other causes have already been mentioned in Chapter 17.

The German Problem

Our rough sketch of the international payments situation during the interwar period would be incomplete without a glance at the special German problem. Germany suffered from a postwar inflation which annihilated the purchasing power of the mark. German authorities blamed the reparations for this inflation, arguing in terms of the balance-of-payments theory (see Chapter 30, pp. 423–24). How it became possible to stabilize the mark through a reduction of the velocity of circulation of money was shown in Chapter 7. Stabilization had become possible after reparations payments had temporarily broken down and had found a new formula in the Dawes Plan. This formula, however, was not a real answer to the transfer problem, for after the stabilization of the mark, private foreign capital began to flow into Germany. If these foreign funds had been carefully invested, it might have been possible, later, to transfer the interest and amortization payments and, in addition, the reparations. This the Dawes Plan had in mind when it declared that transfer payments could be accomplished only through a German export surplus. Actually, however, only about one half of the approximately 20 billion marks of private foreign loans were invested, the other half being used to convert German marks in the reparations account into foreign exchange. This amounted to transformation of a political into a private debt and explains why Germany could "transfer" reparations while her balance of trade was unfavorable.

This whole development was fraught with danger, particularly since nearly one half of the newly incurred foreign debt was short-term and since the proceeds which were actually left in Germany (that is, not used for transfer purposes) went into investments of dubious productivity. Furthermore, German reparations, Allied war debts to the United States, and United States loans to Germany were linked in a strange circle. As soon as foreign capital stopped flowing into Germany the precarious character of these arrangements became evident. With the success of the National Socialists in the September elections of 1930 and the breakdown of the Austrian Kreditanstalt, confidence in international financial relationships was badly shaken, and the whole international credit fabric started to go to pieces.

Only after the flow of foreign capital to Germany stopped could the transfer possibilities be put to a real test. Germany had to develop an export surplus if she wanted to pay her creditors. Fear of inflation made it seem unwise to the pre-Hitler government to follow the depreciation of the pound sterling, and Germany decided on deflation as an alternative course of action. Since a purely monetary deflation through credit contraction would have been slow and insufficient, prices and wages were lowered directly by emergency decree. This policy caused a rapid increase in unemployment. The student of monetary problems and policies will note that Hitler made his first bid for power on November 9, 1923, at the pinnacle of the German hyperinflation and gained power at the very depth of the German deflation in the spring of 1933. This connection between monetary and political events is too obvious to be missed.

However, the course of events in Germany cannot be taken as proof that the transfer of reparations is impossible. At the time of Germany's belated attempt to pay, the world situation was such that even normal international payments relationships had largely collapsed. Reparations could probably have been transferred under more normal conditions and if all the parties concerned had made a determined and co-ordinated effort. As it was, the reparations issue and the catastrophic consequences of the German deflation helped Hitler to come to power; and once in power the Nazi regime embarked on discriminatory exchange controls which negated the very philosophy of multilateralism.

Conclusion

International payments relationships were so chaotic during the interwar period that it is impossible to describe them in a systematic fashion. The student of the period is left with the impression of a complete lack of co-ordination among the domestic economic policies of the different countries. Only within narrower regional groups or monetary "blocs" can we detect attempts towards integration.

One relatively modest but significant contribution towards improved international payments relationships came in 1936 after the French devaluation: the so-called Tripartite Agreement in which the

United States, Great Britain, and France made arrangements to insure short-run stability of their mutual exchange ratios and took a stand against competitive exchange depreciation, now that the depreciation cycle had run its full course. Unfortunately, the United States recession of 1937–38 and the growing capital flight from Europe made a balance-of-payments equilibrium before the outbreak of World War II impossible.

With the beginning of the war regular international economic relationships soon ceased to exist. Exchange rates were no longer determined by market forces and the domestic economic policies of the countries concerned. But from now on we witness a fundamental change in the attitude of the United States. The ability of the free world to resist aggression became the concern of the United States government, and this implied in the economic field that the dollar shortage, which now reached stupendous proportions, be taken care of by United States government grants. One of the wisest acts of statesmanship was the introduction of Lend-Lease on March 11, 1941, through which the postwar world was freed from a transfer problem of enormous proportions.

SUGGESTIONS FOR FURTHER READING

Beyen, J. W. *Money in a Maelstrom.* New York: Macmillan Co., 1949.

Buchanan, Norman S. and Lutz, Friedrich A. *Rebuilding the World Economy.* New York: Twentieth Century Fund, 1947.

Cassel, Gustav. *Money and Foreign Exchange After 1914.* New York: Macmillan Co., 1923.

Committee on Finance and Industry Report (Macmillan Report). London: His Majesty's Stationery Office, Cmd. 3897, 1931.

Keynes, J. M. *Essays in Persuasion,* chaps. 2–3. New York: Harcourt, Brace & Co., 1932.

Lary, Hal B., and Associates. *The United States in the World Economy.* Washington, D.C.: U.S. Government Printing Office, 1943.

League of Nations. *International Currency Experience.* Geneva, 1944.

Robbins, Lionel. *The Great Depression.* London: Macmillan & Co., Ltd., 1935.

Röpke, Wilhelm. *International Economic Disintegration.* London: William Hodge & Co., Ltd., 1942.

Young, John Parke. *The International Economy,* chaps. 39–40. 3d ed. New York: The Ronald Press Co., 1951.

QUESTIONS AND PROBLEMS

1. Why did the gold-flow mechanism work before but not after World War I?
2. Discuss J. M. Keynes' remark that in returning to gold "Mr. Churchill's experts . . . misunderstood and underrated the technical difficulty of bringing about a general reduction of internal money values."
3. "The gold-exchange standard stresses the assymetrical features of the gold-flow mechanism." Explain.
4. Cordell Hull said in 1940 that the international credit crisis had been caused by "reckless international lending and borrowing." Discuss.
5. Discuss the British depreciation of 1931. Was it a competitive depreciation? Why had the Macmillan Report warned against it? Which alternatives were available?
6. "The operation of an exchange reserve system such as the sterling area involves no doubt certain inconveniences to the reserve centre. It has often been argued that, while the United Kingdom could not 'go off sterling,' the member countries could obtain competitive advantages at the expense of the United Kingdom by pegging their currencies to the pound at an unduly low level" (Ragnar Nurkse). Explain. Does this argument apply to the dollar today?
7. Why were the so-called "gold-bloc countries" unwilling to follow the British depreciation and willing rather to undergo the hardships of overvaluation, quantitative restrictions of imports, and exchange controls?
8. Discuss the economic arguments behind the devaluation of the dollar in 1934.
9. Hitler made his first bid for power at the height of Germany's hyperinflation in November 1923 and actually gained control at the very depth of the German deflation in 1933. Which conclusions for monetary and general economic policy can be drawn from these facts?

Chapter 35 THE INTERNATIONAL MONETARY FUND

Aims of International Monetary Co-operation

The interwar period has taught us how *not* to handle the international payments problem. The difficulties of the period were due to selfish and shortsighted policies, embarked upon unilaterally, without regard for the requirements of other countries. Each nation acted as if exchange depreciation, credit withdrawals, the hoarding of gold, or discriminatory exchange controls were its private affairs. But the results were such that eventually most nations had to see that international monetary problems must be solved by some kind of mutual agreement or some kind of international monetary institution. The need for a compromise between the policies of different nations and, within each country, between its domestic and foreign economic policies was clearly indicated.

The elements of such a needed compromise are the following:

1. All member countries of an international payments system must try to avoid severe fluctuations in employment and national income.

2. Policies aimed at a high and steady level of employment must not lead to permanent inflationary pressures worse than those in other countries, for this is incompatible with balance-of-payments equilibrium.

3. Deflationary pressures, too, must be avoided since they will lead to unemployment. Monetary policy, therefore, must steer a course between inflation and deflation, between balance-of-payments disequilibrium and unemployment.

4. Rejection of deflation as a means for the re-establishment of a balance-of-payments equilibrium implies flexible exchange rates. If

price inflation has led to balance-of-payments trouble, depreciation rather than deflation ought to be the answer; competitive exchange depreciation, however, must be avoided.

5. In case of a balance-of-payments disequilibrium both the deficit and the surplus country should take appropriate measures. A surplus position does not entitle a country to inactivity.

6. In choosing appropriate policies, those measures which tend to "lengthen the short leg" should have precedence over measures designed to "shorten the long leg."

7. Only in extreme cases should discriminatory devices be used, for they violate the basic principle of multilateralism.

8. All members of an international payments system must be supplied with sufficient reserves of foreign exchange; only then will they be able to meet balance-of-payments deficits without having to resort immediately to exchange depreciation or exchange control.

9. The system must be designed to achieve a reasonable amount of integration among the monetary and fiscal policies of the member countries; and disequilibria caused by deviations in these policies must be able to be bridged without the loss of multilateralism.

10. The system must be so designed that an agreement or an international institution will see that member countries follow rules of behavior compatible with the principles enumerated above.

Such an international institution would be the logical conclusion of a development which led to the establishment of central banks within national credit systems. An international bank for central banks can perform functions similar to those which a central bank performs for its member banks (and the member banks, for their customers). It can pool international reserves and make them available where they are most needed; and it can try to harmonize the monetary policies of the central banks of the member countries.

We shall now study the international monetary institution which was created in Bretton Woods, N.H., in July 1944, with the hope to spare the world after World War II the economic ordeals of the interwar period.

Lord Keynes' International Clearing Union

Toward the end of World War II plans were made in both the United States and Great Britain for an international monetary institution which would organize the international payments system on the principles of multilateralism, flexibility, and co-operation. The two plans were known as the *White Plan* and the *Keynes Plan,* after their main authors.[1]

Since the compromise of Bretton Woods, the International Monetary Fund, follows in its main outlines the United States plan, we can limit our discussion of the preliminary proposals to Keynes' Clearing Union. The elegance and simplicity of Lord Keynes' scheme is of more than historical interest.

In the Clearing Union plan the member countries would not have been asked to make contributions to a common reserve pool. Instead, they would have been asked to "agree to accept payment of currency balances, due to them from other members, by transfer of [international bank money called] bancor to their credit in the books of the Clearing Union" (Keynes Plan II–6–6). The foreign exchange reserve gained through membership in the Union would have consisted of the right to accumulate debit balances, up to a "line of credit," equal to the member's quota with the Union. The Keynes Plan was unsymmetrical in its treatment of deficit and surplus countries. Deficit countries could have drawn checks only up to an amount equal to their respective quotas (and counter measures, such as depreciation and exchange control of outward capital transactions, would have been called for long before the quotas were exhausted). Surplus countries, on the other hand, might have had to accept bancor checks far in excess of their quotas, owing to the principle that credit balances must equal debit balances. The Clearing Union did not have to face the problem of "scarce" currencies which, as we shall see, causes complications in the structure of the International Monetary Fund which limits the commitments of members to amounts equal to their quota. Thus the Union would have put a tremendous potential burden on surplus countries. Lord Keynes proposed an aggregate of quotas of about $33 billion, including the United States quota of $3 billion. If we assume a deficit position for the "rest of the world," with only the United States in the surplus category, we see that enormous bancor credits might have piled up in the Union in favor of the United States. Obviously, the American experts at Bretton Woods were unwilling to sign, as it were, a blank check of such potential proportions. But we should remember that our example makes extreme assumptions and, also, that the order of magnitude of Lord Keynes' figures corresponds rather

[1] See *Preliminary Draft Outline of a Proposal for an International Stabilization Fund of the United and Associated Nations* (Washington, D.C.: U.S. Treasury, July 10, 1943); *Proposals for an International Clearing Union* (London: H. M. Stationery Office, Cmd. 6437, April, 1943).

more closely to the actual dollar shortage of the postwar world than the much more conservative figures of the Fund.

Interesting, and to some people shocking, was Lord Keynes' proposal that interest charges be paid on both the debit and credit balances in the Union as "a significant indication that the system looks on excessive credit balances with as critical an eye as on excessive debit balances, each being, indeed, the inevitable concomitant of the other" (Keynes Plan II–6–7).

The Keynes Plan proposed to make frequent and almost automatic use of exchange depreciation by insisting on "a stated reduction in the value of a member's currency" as that member's deficit with the Union mounts. Both this feature and the large size of the quotas indicate that Lord Keynes tried to give substantial leeway to the domestic policies of the members.

The International Monetary Fund

After the American and British experts had already reached a compromise in Washington in April 1944, the Bretton Woods Conference of July 1944 accepted unanimously the Articles of Agreement of the International Monetary Fund.[2] The Fund started operations in Washington on March 1, 1947, and has, as of the fall of 1960, 70 members.

According to Art. I of the Fund Agreement the purposes of the Fund are:

(1) To promote international monetary cooperation through a permanent institution . . .

(2) To facilitate the expansion and balanced growth of international trade, and to contribute thereby to the promotion and maintenance of high levels of employment . . . of all members . . .

(3) To promote exchange stability, to maintain orderly exchange arrangements among members, and to avoid competitive exchange depreciation.

(4) To assist in the establishment of a multilateral system of payments in respect of current transactions between members and in the elimination of foreign exchange restrictions . . .

(5) To give confidence to members by making the Fund's resources available to them under adequate safeguards, thus providing them with opportunity to correct maladjustments in their balance of payments without resorting to measures destructive of national or international prosperity.

[2] *Articles of Agreement. International Monetary Fund and International Bank for Reconstruction and Development.* United Nations Monetary and Financial Conference, Bretton Woods, N.H., July 1 to 22 (Washington, D.C.: United States Treasury, 1944).

(6) In accordance with the above, to shorten the duration and lessen the degree of disequilibrium in the international balances of payments of members.

Purchasing Rights of Members

The resources of the International Monetary Fund consist of member currencies and gold. Each member country subscribes in gold and in its own currency an amount which is called its quota. The obligatory minimum gold contribution is "the smaller of (i) twenty-five per cent of its quota; or (ii) ten per cent of its net official holdings of gold and United States dollars" at the time when the Fund's operations begin (III–3).

Considering that the status of a member as either a deficit or surplus country is not generally predictable, quotas must be so chosen that they satisfactorily determine both the obligations and the purchasing rights of the members. The quota formula used included (aside from political considerations) such factors as "a country's holdings of gold and free foreign exchange, the magnitude and the fluctuations of its balance of international payments, its national income, etc." (White Plan II–4). On April 30, 1960, aggregate quotas amounted to $14,276.55 million.

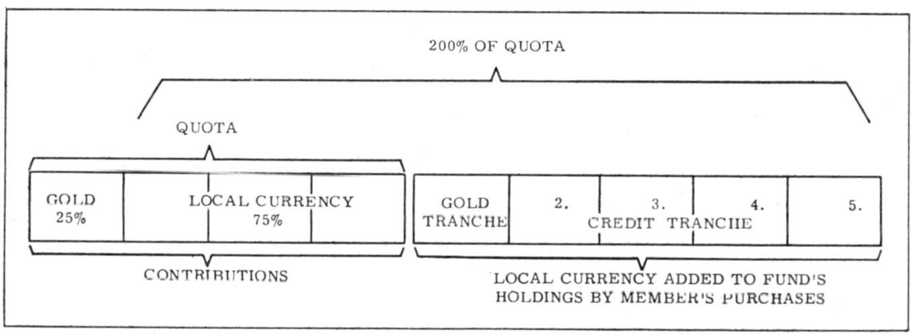

FIG. 35–1

Through the subscriptions of its members the Fund has at its disposal an assortment of member currencies. Gold is the Fund's most liquid asset, since for gold any desired member currency can be bought (VII–2–ii). The members may purchase foreign exchange from the Fund; the Fund is a pool of member currencies from which each member can take the currencies of other members if it adds a corresponding amount of its own currency to the pool.

These purchasing rights are strictly limited (V–3). Let us assume that a member's quota is the equivalent of $100 million, of which it has contributed $25 million in gold and the rest in local currency.

The Fund may sell to the country in each twelve months' period foreign exchange worth 25 per cent of its quota. According to more recent usage we can speak of "credit tranches." As the Fund sells foreign exchange to a member, the Fund accumulates more of the member's currency. The first tranche of 25 per cent brings the Fund's holdings of the member's currency to 100 per cent of the member's quota since we assume that the country contributed originally only 75 per cent of its quota in local currency. Present usage calls this first tranche the gold tranche, since the member receives in foreign exchange an amount equal to its gold contribution. When the Fund's holdings of a member's currency have reached 200 per cent of the member's quota, the member has exhausted its purchasing rights.

Figure 35–1 illustrates these quantitative relationships and shows that it will take *at least* five years to exhaust the purchasing rights of a member.

Since 1953 the Fund has in certain instances concluded so-called stand-by agreements with members, assuring them that they may purchase from the Fund up to a previously agreed limit, on the understanding that they must repurchase their currency from the Fund with foreign exchange within a limited period of time.

The *Annual Report 1959* states the Fund's policy and practice in respect to the use of its resources as follows:

> Members are given the overwhelming benefit of the doubt in relation to requests for transactions within the "gold tranche," that is, the portion of the quota which can be regarded as equivalent to the gold subscription. The Fund's attitude to requests for transactions within the first credit tranche, that is, transactions that bring the Fund's holdings of a member's currency above 100 per cent but not above 125 per cent of quota, is a liberal one, provided that the member itself is also making reasonable efforts to solve its problems. Requests for transactions beyond these limits require substantial justification. They are likely to be favorably received when the drawings or stand-bys are intended to support a sound program aimed at establishing or maintaining the enduring stability of the member's currency at a realistic rate of exchange. In accordance with all the principles outlined above, the Fund has in appropriate cases continued to receive from members seeking to purchase exchange or to enter into stand-by arrangements declarations of intent as to the policies that would be followed.[3]

[3] International Monetary Fund, *Annual Report 1959* (Washington, D.C., 1959), p. 22. The *Annual Report 1960* adds: "A member which finds itself obliged to deviate from the policies specified in its declaration of intent consults with the Fund, in order, where it is appropriate, to reach a new understanding on the basis of which further drawings may be made" (p. 20). The Report for 1960 points out that these policies "have been found to be eminently practicable" (p. 19).

Scarce Currencies

As the Fund accumulates currencies of deficit countries it depletes its holdings of the currencies of surplus countries. When the Fund's supply of a currency becomes low, the Fund may (1) require the member to sell its currency for gold (VII–2–ii); (2) ask the member for a loan ("but no member shall be under any obligation to make such loans to the Fund") (VII–2–i); (3) "formally declare such currency scarce and . . . apportion its existing and accruing supply of the scarce currency with due regard to the relative needs of members . . ." (VII–3–a); (4) authorize "any member, after consultation with the Fund, temporarily to impose limitations on the freedom of exchange operations in the scarce currency" (VII–3–b).

In joining the Fund a potential surplus country faces, therefore, the following obligations: (1) it agrees to accept payments for its goods and services in the local currency which it has contributed to the Fund and which the Fund has sold to other members; (2) it agrees to sell its currency to the Fund for gold in any desired amount; (3) it agrees to accept exchange discrimination through exchange control against itself if its currency is declared scarce and if it refuses to grant loans to the Fund or to other members.

The Repurchase Provisions

We have seen that the Fund may have to introduce exchange control when a member currency becomes scarce. To avoid such a situation, which contradicts the Fund's purpose of eliminating foreign exchange restrictions, the Fund will try to maintain a sufficient supply of demanded currencies in two ways: (1) through the repurchase provisions of Art. V and (2) through special provisions which aim at the maintenance of international payments equilibrium in the long run.

Provided the members are able to maintain long-run equilibrium in international payments, the liquidity of the Fund is assured through the provision that a member must under certain conditions repurchase its own currency from the Fund with gold or convertible currencies. The complicated provisions of Article V–7 can be reduced to the following basic principles:

The members must be prevented from using the Fund one-sidedly. As the Fund helps a member that finds itself in difficulties, so must the Fund participate in an improvement of the member's balance-of-payments position. It is not enough that, according to Article V–3, the member desiring to purchase foreign exchange from the Fund has to prove that the purchase is needed for payments which are consistent with the purposes of the Fund. This provision would only prevent misuse of the Fund by members which are actually not in need of help. In addition, it is necessary that a member which bought foreign currency from the Fund when it needed help should later, as its balance of payments reverses, help restore the Fund's former position by sharing with the Fund its new inflow of foreign currencies.

Each member must at the end of each financial year of the Fund repurchase with gold or convertible currencies one half of any increase that has occurred during the year in the Fund's holdings of its currency, provided that the following special provisions do not apply:

1. Repurchases are not required (*a*) when the country's own monetary reserves outside the Fund are less than the amount of its quota; and (*b*) when the Fund's holdings of the member's currency are below 75 per cent of its quota.

2. The amount required to be repurchased is reduced by one half the amount of a decrease in the member's own monetary reserve during the year. Thus, the repurchase rule does not apply at all "when a member's monetary reserves have decreased during the year by more than the Fund's holdings of its currency have increased" (V–7).

3. The amount to be repurchased is increased by one half the amount of an increase in the member's reserve (unless the country's own monetary reserve is still below the country's quota).

The application of these rules will lead to the following results: (*a*) When a country with reserves above its quota buys, say, $10 million worth of foreign exchange from the Fund during one year but improves its balance-of-payments position by the same amount during the following year, the Fund is not weakened, because the country would have to repurchase $5 million worth of its own currency (with gold or convertible currencies) at the end of the first year and another $5 million worth at the end of the second year. (*b*) When a country is in a weak position, so that its monetary reserves stay below its quota, the Fund loses, for the time being, "surplus" currencies even though the country may balance its international accounts over a period of sufficient length. The loss of surplus currency is occasioned by the fact that even a subsequent increase in the country's foreign exchange reserves does not lead to a repurchase as long as the reserves remain below the country's quota.

Provisions for the Maintenance of Equilibrium

Persistent deviations from international payments equilibrium must be avoided. The repurchase provisions maintain the liquidity of the Fund only if the members manage to balance their international payments when we average one period with another.

As seen by the Fund, a member is in a position of equilibrium when the Fund holds approximately that amount of a country's currency which the country originally contributed. This is the dividing line between surplus and deficit countries. A country becomes a deficit country when the Fund's holdings of its currency grow over and above the Fund's original holdings. That this should happen is quite in order; the Fund is there to be used in the case of normal balance-of-payments fluctuations which tend to cancel out over a period of sufficient length.

When the deficit continues to grow the case becomes more problematic, however. In provision V–8 the Fund has a rather sensitive index for the degree of disequilibrium which has developed in a country's international payments situation. The Fund will levy charges "which shall be payable by any member [in gold] on the average daily balances of its currency held by the Fund in excess of its quota." These charges which have been revised repeatedly increase according to the duration and amount of the excess. The revised schedule of Fund charges of January 1954, which has been repeatedly extended, levies different charges for excesses below 50 per cent, between 50 and 75 per cent, and between 75 and 100 per cent of the quota. The charges begin after three months at 2 per cent and can reach a maximum of 5 per cent.[4]

When the charges have reached 4 per cent, "the Fund and the member shall consider means by which the Fund's holdings of the currency can be reduced."

Since these means depend on the merits of each case, the Fund Agreement does not contain general directives. There are several possibilities. A deficit country will have to either increase its exports or decrease its imports. It can achieve this desired result through (1) deflation, (2) depreciation, (3) protectionist devices plus subsidies, and (4) exchange control.

The Fund, dedicated to the task of facilitating the expansion

[4] Where a stand-by agreement permits a reduction of the Fund's holdings of a member's currency over a period longer than five years, the Fund may apply higher maximum charges.

and balanced growth of international trade (I–ii), will be reluctant to recommend restrictive devices and deflationary credit policy. It may, however, suggest more conservative (that is, anti-inflationary) monetary policies and, in the case of a fundamental disequilibrium, exchange depreciation.

A member is a surplus country (and strictly speaking, also in disequilibrium) if the Fund's holdings of its currency fall below the original contribution in that currency. As seen by the Fund, this "surplus" position becomes critical when "a general scarcity of a particular currency is developing." In this case the Fund "may issue a report setting forth the causes of the scarcity and containing recommendations to bring it to an end" (VII–1). Another report is to be issued when the Fund formally declares a currency as scarce (VII–3).

The Fund Agreement makes no suggestions as to the content of these reports, but the Keynes Plan recommended for a similar situation (*a*) measures for the expansion of domestic credit and domestic demand; (*b*) the appreciation of the country's currency or, alternatively, the encouragement of an increase in money rates of earnings; (*c*) the reduction of tariffs and other discouragements to imports; and (*d*) international development loans. These policies have in common that they would tend to increase the import of commodities and securities. But it would not always be easy to carry them out.

Exchange Rates and Exchange Control

The Agreement, while committed to promotion of exchange stability (I–iii), permits adjustments of exchange rates, particularly when they are necessary to correct fundamental disequilibria (IV–5–a). Exchange depreciation is an extraordinary and rare measure which is either very narrowly limited or dependent on the special permission of the Fund.

The Fund agrees with new member countries on the initial par values of their respective currencies. "Changes in par values may be made only on the initiative of the member and in order to correct a fundamental disequilibrium, and, with minor exceptions, only with the approval of the Fund."[5]

The Fund shall concur in a proposed change "if it is satisfied that the change is necessary to correct a fundamental disequilibrium. In particular, provided it is so satisfied, it shall not object to the proposed

[5] International Monetary Fund, *Annual Report 1956*, p. 82. Compare also Art. IV–5 of the *Fund Agreement* and *Annual Report 1951*, pp. 36–41.

change because of the domestic social and political policies of the member proposing the change" (IV–5–f).

Since the Fund permits unilateral depreciation only within very narrow limits, condemns sharply competitive exchange depreciation, and consequently makes exchange depreciation normally dependent on its permission, we may say that the Fund substitutes for the gold standard's exchange rigidity the principle of managed flexibility in the adjustment of exchange values of the member currencies.

How difficult it will be to determine a state of fundamental disequilibrium or the degree of a given overvaluation was shown in Chapter 32.

It is one of the purposes of the Fund to assist "in the elimination of foreign exchange restrictions" (I–iv). Nevertheless, the Fund uses or permits exchange restrictions in the three cases below:

1. In case of a large or sustained outflow of capital "the Fund may request a member to exercise controls," (VI–1) "but no member may exercise these controls in a manner which will restrict payments for current transactions or which will unduly delay transfers of funds in settlement of commitments" (VI–3).

2. Exchange restrictions may become necessary, as we have already seen, when the Fund formally declares a currency as "scarce."

3. During the transition period "members may . . . maintain and adapt to changing circumstances . . . restrictions on payments and transfers for current international transactions" but "as soon as conditions permit, they shall take all possible measures to develop such commercial and financial arrangements with other members as will facilitate international payments and the maintenance of exchange stability. In particular, members shall withdraw restrictions maintained or imposed under this Section as soon as they are satisfied that they will be able, in the absence of such restrictions, to settle their balance of payments in a manner which will not unduly encumber their access to the resources of the Fund" (XIV–2).

The Fund consults annually with members which have not yet reached a position which permits them to avoid restrictions of current payments and discriminatory currency practices according to Art. VIII. Sometimes these consultations are undertaken in connection with stand-by agreements.

The Fund and Gold

We have seen that the Fund tries to induce both deficit and surplus countries to maintain a reasonable degree of international payments equilibrium or, when this should prove impossible, to adjust their exchange rates in an orderly manner. The gold-standard system did not know these problems. Conscious international monetary management was absent, the pattern of exchange rates rigidly set, and the necessary integration of the economic policies of the gold-standard countries supposed to be accomplished automatically through reciprocal inflation and deflation. It seems, therefore, that Lord Keynes is basically right when he calls the Fund proposal "the exact opposite of the gold standard."[6]

John H. Williams, on the other hand, considered the new currency proposals (White Plan and Keynes Plan) from the very beginning as "essentially gold standard plans."[7] And if we follow the transactions of members with the Fund we can indeed see that, other things remaining equal, a deficit country is in a position similar to that of a gold-losing country, and a surplus country, in a position similar to that of a gold-receiving country. Let us see what happens when a member buys from the Fund.

A member deals with the Fund "only through its Treasury, central bank, stabilization fund or other similar fiscal agency" (V–1). It would be a mistake to picture the Fund as an enormous organization through which all international payments would be cleared. Quite to the contrary, the overwhelming amount of international payments is cleared without the help of the Fund through the foreign exchange market. Transactions with the Fund are of an exceptional nature, very much like gold or short-term capital movements under the gold standard.

Suppose the Banque de France wants to buy dollars from the Fund because of a temporary dollar shortage. The Banque de France will be permitted to draw against the Fund's dollar account with the Federal Reserve Bank of New York. The Fund's dollar account will go down, and the purchase price will be credited to the Fund's account with the Banque de France. The French central bank has acquired the dollars to sell them to commercial banks which, in turn, sell them to their customers. This process will reduce the commercial banks' demand deposits and their reserves with the central bank by an equal amount, and since the commercial banks have to hold only fractional

[6] J. M. Keynes, "The International Monetary Fund," Speech delivered before the House of Lords, May 23, 1944, reprinted in *The New Economics*, ed. by Seymour E. Harris (New York: Alfred A. Knopf, Inc., 1948), pp. 369–79.

[7] John H. Williams, "Currency Stabilization: the Keynes and White Plans," *Foreign Affairs*, July, 1943, pp. 649–50; reprinted in *Post-War Monetary Plans and Other Essays* (Oxford: Basil Blackwell, 1949), pp. 141–54.

reserves, their reserve position is weakened. Unless the commercial banks have excess reserves at their disposal or unless the central bank wants to make additional reserves available, the transaction with the Fund would clearly have a contractionist effect on the French economy.

The opposite would be true for the United States. The dollars bought by France would be received in payment for exports and would increase both the deposits and the reserves of commercial banks in the United States, thus improving the banks' reserve position and enabling them to expand credit.

Transactions with the Fund affect, as we see, "bank reserves in precisely the same way as the movements of gold under the gold standard."[8] But, as in the case of the gold standard, there is, of course, no compelling reason to assume that credit expansion would actually take place. Furthermore, it is now, in contradistinction to the gold standard, quite unlikely that the member countries will accept the deflationary consequences of their transactions with the Fund. None of the provisions of the Fund Agreement suggests deflationary policies on the part of the deficit countries. Rather, it appears almost certain that the Fund was designed to obliterate this part of the gold mechanism or to let it operate only under control.

The members of the Fund do not have to adopt the gold standard but they can adopt it if they desire to do so. A member merely has to express the par value of its currency in terms of gold as a common denominator (IV–1) and to promise not to buy gold at a price above par value plus the prescribed margin or to sell gold at a price below par value minus the prescribed margin (IV–2).

Gold is a more "respectable" *tertium comparationis* than a newly invented unit such as "bancor." That gold has "intrinsic" value may be a rather childish argument. But as long as a strong popular prejudice in favor of gold exists, the Fund is psychologically strengthened through its many connections with gold. Furthermore, the establishment of a permanent market in gold—the Fund's standing offer to buy gold at official parities—was needed to induce gold-producing countries or countries with large gold reserves to join the Fund.

The Fund's gold provisions are not just window-dressing.[9] Gold

[8] *Ibid.*

[9] In the Keynes Plan, gold had no essential function to fulfill. In a letter to the author of June 22, 1945, Lord Keynes admitted: "In discussing the question of why it is advisable to retain a provision for gold, the main point is, of course, that no scheme which did not make such a provision would have the smallest chance of acceptance. . . . In short, there is no option."

plays a really important role as the Fund's most liquid asset and as a common anchorage for member currencies.

Organization and Management

The Fund has a Board of Governors, Executive Directors, a Managing Director, and a staff (XII–1). The Board of Governors, in which all powers are vested, consists of one governor and one alternate oppointed by each member. It has the power to admit new members, to approve a revision of quotas, to approve a uniform change in the par value of the currencies of all members, to require a member to withdraw, and to decide to liquidate the Fund (XII–2).

The Executive Directors are responsible for the conduct of the Fund's operations. They select a Managing Director. He is chief of the operating staff and conducts the ordinary business of the Fund.

The voting rights of the members (exercised by the Governors and by the Executive Directors appointed or elected by the members) depend mainly on the size of the quotas.

Criticism and Performance

That the Fund Agreement is not a perfect document goes without saying. The very nature of a compromise implies that nobody is fully satisfied. Also, where mutual concessions have been made there remain areas of doubt as to the exact terms on which a dispute was settled. However, these minor difficulties can be ironed out.

More fundamental were the criticisms of extremists on the right and left. Conservative opponents believed that, instead of creating an international organization, the different countries should have put their own houses in order, balanced their budgets, and stabilized the internal purchasing power of their currencies. Exchange stability would then have followed automatically without the sacrifice of national sovereignty. These critics, though logically consistent, forgot that we no longer live in an economic climate which permits the gold-flow mechanism to work. Similarly, those critics who considered even the Keynes Plan as much too modest failed to realize that potential surplus countries could not possibly have endorsed plans in which the inflationary policies of deficit countries would have controlled the degree of credit expansion in the surplus countries.

The difficulties of the transition period were much greater than envisaged in 1944 and the Fund made at first only a minor contribution to the solution of the postwar shortage of foreign exchange. With the return of more normal conditions, however, the Fund is now in the position to operate successfully and to make very substantial reserves of foreign exchange available to members.

On April 30, 1960 the Fund's resources amounted to more than $14 billion, of which nearly $3 billion was in gold (including $500 million temporarily invested in U.S. Government obligations) and about $10.6 was in currency. Of the latter sum, more than $7 billion is in the currencies that are most usable in the Fund's operations, viz., U.S. and Canadian dollars and the currencies of the European industrial countries and Japan. The Fund, therefore, has at its disposal effective international assets to the value of at least $10 billion. While the Fund's assets so measured are equal to nearly 20 per cent of the aggregate reserves of all member countries (which were about $53 billion at the end of 1959), their significance is greater than this percentage may suggest. The resources that its members have provided for the Fund are available as a second line of reserves under the policies and practices agreed for their use when members encounter temporary balance-of-payments difficulties. The direction in which they are effectively used can be continuously adapted to the changing conditions of the world economy, the practice of repurchase ensuring that Fund resources which have served their purpose in one country will later be available elsewhere if the need should arise.[10]

The Fund's ability to supply additional foreign exchange is only one of its contributions to the solution of international payments problems. Perhaps even more important is that "the Fund is a forum in which the policies of all members in relation to their foreign exchange arrangements, including changes in their exchange rates, are discussed and examined as a matter of international concern."[11] The more orderly way in which the different countries have tried to solve their balance-of-payments difficulties after World War II can be attributed, to a large extent, to the existence of the Fund and the collaboration in international monetary matters which it managed to achieve. It must be remembered that the transactions of the Fund will be determined by the size of the balance-of-payments disequilibria which it will serve to bridge. These disequilibria depend on the degree of integration of the domestic monetary policies of the members. Successful co-ordination of these policies, therefore, will be more important than repeated upward revisions of the members' quotas.

[10] International Monetary Fund, *Annual Report 1960*, p. 6.

[11] International Monetary Fund, "Fund's Role in World Trade," *International Financial News Survey*, Vol. V, No. 46 (May 29, 1953).

SUGGESTIONS FOR FURTHER READING

Articles of Agreement. International Monetary Fund and International Bank for Reconstruction and Development. United Nations Monetary and Financial Conference, Bretton Woods, N.H., July 1 to 22. Washington, D.C.: United States Treasury, 1944.

HALM, GEORGE N. *International Monetary Cooperation,* chaps. 1, 6–8, 10–11. Chapel Hill: University of North Carolina Press, 1945.

INTERNATIONAL MONETARY FUND. *Reports.* Washington, D.C., Annual.

INTERNATIONAL MONETARY FUND. *Report on Exchange Restrictions.* Washington, D.C., Annual.

INTERNATIONAL MONETARY FUND. *Staff Papers.* Washington, D.C., published at various intervals.

KEYNES, J. M. "The International Clearing Union," *The New Economics* (ed. Seymour E. Harris), chap. 26. New York: Alfred A. Knopf, Inc., 1948.

LOFTUS, MARTIN L. "The International Monetary Fund, 1946–1950. A selected Bibliography," *Staff Papers,* Vol. 3 (1953–1954), International Monetary Fund.

LOFTUS, MARTIN L. "The International Monetary Fund, 1951–1952. A selected Bibliography," *Staff Papers,* Vol. 3 (1953–1954), International Monetary Fund.

Proposals for an International Clearing Union. London: Mis Majesty's Stationery Office, Cmd. 6437, April 1943.

"A Symposium on the International Monetary Fund and the International Bank for Reconstruction and Development," *The Review of Economic Statistics,* Vol. XXVI, No. 4 (November, 1944), pp. 165–93.

TEW, BRIAN. *International Monetary Co-operation 1945–52,* Part II. London: Hutchinson's University Library, 1952.

TRIFFIN, ROBERT. *Gold and the Dollar Crisis,* Part II. New Haven: Yale University Press, 1960.

UNITED NATIONS. *National and International Measures for Full Employment.* Lake Success, N.Y., December, 1949.

WILLIAMS, JOHN H. *Post-War Monetary Plans and Other Essays,* Part IV. Oxford: Basil Blackwell, 1949.

QUESTIONS AND PROBLEMS

1. "The creation of an International Central Bank would be the consistent conclusion of the development which led to the creation of central banks within the national credit systems." Discuss. Is the International Monetary Fund an International Central Bank?

2. The basic idea of the Keynes Plan is "to generalize the essential principle of banking as it is exhibited within any closed system. This principle is the necessary equality of debits and credits." Explain.
3. Article II–6–7 of the Keynes Plan states: "A member shall pay to the Reserve Fund of the Clearing Union a charge of 1 per cent per annum of its average balance in bancor, whether it is a credit or a debit balance in excess of a quarter of its quota; and a further charge of 1 per cent of its average balance, whether credit or debit, in excess of half of its quota." Discuss.
4. Compare the structure of the International Monetary Fund with that of the International Clearing Union.
5. Explain the rights and obligations of the members of the International Monetary Fund.
6. Explain the basic importance of the repurchase provisions in the structure of the International Monetary Fund.
7. Why are repurchases not required (*a*) when the member's own monetary reserves outside the Fund are less than the amount of its quota; and (*b*) when the Fund's holdings of the member's currency are below 75 per cent of its quota? What are the repurchase provisions if these two cases do not apply?
8. What happens when the International Monetary Fund formally declares a currency as scarce. How did the Keynes Plan handle the problem?
9. Explain Article IV–5–f of the Fund Agreement according to which the International Monetary Fund shall concur in the proposed change of a currency "if it is satisfied that the change is necessary to correct a fundamental disequilibrium."
10. Is the International Monetary Fund "the exact opposite of the gold standard" as Lord Keynes believed or a gold-standard plan as John H. Williams suggests?

Chapter 36 THE INTERNATIONAL BANK FOR RECONSTRUCTION AND DEVELOPMENT

Purpose of the Bank

The International Bank for Reconstruction and Development, now often referred to as the World Bank, was created in Bretton Woods as a sister organization of the International Monetary Fund.[1] It has the purpose of promoting long-term foreign investment. The Fund cannot fulfill this task because long-term lending would make it illiquid. Nevertheless, the danger was foreseen that many members of the Fund would need long-term funds so urgently that they might be tempted to use the facilities of the Fund for investment purposes unless long-term loans were made available to them on reasonable terms.

That private capital would begin to flow after the war was not to be expected, nor was a repetition of the type of capital flow which had characterized the interwar period considered desirable. Chapter 34 has shown that principles of sound international private lending were not followed after World War I. Foreign funds were borrowed for purposes of dubious productivity, sometimes at exorbitant rates of interest. Short-term credits were used for long-term investment purposes, and reparations were transferred through the medium of commercial credits, while the basic transfer issues were ignored by both borrowers and lenders. It is no wonder that the whole international credit structure disintegrated.

With these experiences in mind it did not seem likely that private lending would solve the postwar problems of international fi-

1 See *Articles of Agreement, International Monetary Fund and International Bank for Reconstruction and Development*, United Nations Monetary and Financial Conference, Bretton Woods, N.H., July 1 to 22 (Washington, D.C.: United States Treasury, 1944). The articles quoted in this chapter refer to the Bank, not to the Fund. A few passages in this chapter are taken from the author's *International Monetary Cooperation* (Chapel Hill: The University of North Carolina Press, 1945), chap. xiii.

nance. Not even at very high rates (or rather risk premiums) could sufficient private capital be expected to venture abroad and to be allocated according to sound economic principles. Those who are willing to borrow at extremely high rates and other unfavorable or dangerous conditions and those who are willing to lend at usurious rates are not the best judges as to how a limited amount of internationally available funds should best be used.

Nevertheless, the Bank was not created with the intention of replacing the flow of private capital through an international institution. On the contrary, the Bank has the purpose "to promote private foreign investment by means of guarantees or participations in loans and other investments made by private investors; and when private capital is not available on reasonable terms, to supplement private investment by providing, on suitable conditions, finance for productive purposes out of its own capital, funds raised by it and its other resources" (I–ii). The Bank has remained faithful to this basic principle. It believes its role to be a marginal one, marginal with respect to private international investment and to investment in the member countries.

Structure of the Bank

At the end of June 1960 the subscribed capital of the Bank was $19,308 million. Seventy countries were members at that time. In several respects these subscriptions are similar to the quotas in the Fund. They determine the relative share of the members in the management of the Bank (V–3)[2] and they limit the members' obligations (II–6), but they do not, like the Fund quotas, limit the amount of loans or guarantees which the member can arrange with the Bank.

As designed at Bretton Woods, the Bank was expected to act predominantly as a guarantor of private loans placed through normal investment channels. In connection with this function no immediate need of funds would have arisen. Only in case of default would the Bank have had to meet contractual payments of interest and amortization on the guaranteed loans. This explains why 80 per cent of the subscribed capital is not paid in by the members but is only to be made available on call in case of future emergencies.

Of the 20 per cent of the subscribed capital which is to be paid in, 2 per cent must be in gold or gold convertible currencies and the remaining 18 per cent in the currency of the member. However, only

[2] Organization and management of the Bank are so similar to those of the Fund that no special discussion is needed for our purposes. The details can be found in Art. V of the Agreement.

about one sixth of the currencies held by the Bank in June 1960 was "unrestricted." The rest was "restricted," that is, it could be loaned by the Bank "only with the approval in each case of the member whose restricted currency is involved."[3] The still existing restrictions are due to foreign exchange regulations.

The Bank can, with the approval of a member, sell its own securities in the member's market and use the borrowed funds to make loans or participate in loans (IV–1). The Bank has sold its securities in United States dollars and in the currencies of Belgium, Canada, and Netherlands, the United Kingdom, West Germany, and Switzerland. "These bonds and notes are now (1960) held by more than 40 countries, and investors outside the United States hold more than a billion dollars' worth, amounting to more than half of all the Bank's borrowings."[4]

To the extent that the Bank can sell its loans to private investors, it reduces the need to borrow funds in the market. In these selling operations the Bank was particularly successful in 1959–60.

The extent of all the Bank's activities together is strictly limited. "The total amount of outstanding guarantees, participations in loans and direct loans made by the Bank shall not be increased at any time, if by such increase the total would exceed 100 per cent of the unimpaired subscribed capital, reserves and surplus of the Bank" (III–3).

By mid-1960, the gross total of the Bank's loans (including its reconstruction lending) had risen to over $5 billion, consisting of 260 loans for governmental or private projects in 52 countries and territories. Actual disbursements rose accordingly: in the calendar year 1958, they amounted to one tenth of the international flow of capital to the low-income countries from all sources, and accounted for one fourth of the flow from public sources.[5]

Like the Fund, the Bank deals with its members only through their central banks, Treasuries, or other fiscal agencies (III–2). But the Bank can make loans to any business, industrial, and agricultural enterprise in the territories of a member (III–4).

Lending Principles

All guarantees and loans are subject to the following conditions (III–4):

[3] International Bank, *Fifteenth Annual Report, 1959–60* (Washington, D.C., 1960), p. 44.

[4] Eugene R. Black, *The Diplomacy of Economic Development* (Cambridge, Mass.: Harvard University Press, 1960), p. 69.

[5] *Ibid.*, p. 64.

(i) "When the member in whose territories the project is located is not itself the borrower, the member or the central bank or some comparable agency of the member which is acceptable to the Bank, fully guarantees the repayment of the principal and the payment of interest and other charges on the loan."

(ii) "The Bank is satisfied that in the prevailing market conditions the borrower would be unable otherwise to obtain the loan under conditions which in the opinion of the Bank are reasonable for the borrower."

(iii) "A competent committee, as provided for in Article V, Section 7, has submitted a written report recommending the project after a careful study of the merits of the proposal."

(iv) "In the opinion of the Bank the rate of interest and other charges are reasonable and such rate, charges and the schedule for repayment of principal are appropriate to the project."

(v) "In making or guaranteeing a loan, the Bank shall pay due regard to the prospects that the borrower, and, if the borrower is not a member, that the guarantor, will be in position to meet its obligations under the loan; and the Bank shall act prudently in the interests both of the particular member in whose territories the project is located and of the members as a whole."

(vi) "In guaranteeing a loan made by other investors, the Bank receives suitable compensation for its risk."

(vii) "Loans made or guaranteed by the Bank shall, except in special circumstances, be for the purpose of specific projects of reconstruction or development."

As early as 1946–47 the Bank's *Annual Report* showed how the Bank's lending principles gradually evolved as the Bank gained experience and as the problems of the postwar world emerged. This *Report* stressed that the Bank had to accept risks in face of the uncertainties of the international situation; that it had to use its funds so "as to result in the greatest possible increase in productivity in the shortest possible time"; and that "the Bank's resources must not simply be used to relieve the borrowing nation of tasks which that country could justifiably be required to perform itself."

The Bank started its activities in 1947 with reconstruction loans. However, reconstruction proved to be a far bigger task than the Bank could undertake. It was not only a physical job of rebuilding. Needed was a fundamental readjustment in the whole structure of the European economy. When the *European Recovery Program* (ERP) undertook to gradually lower the enormous European balance-of-payments deficit from the 1947 level of nearly $8 billion to more manageable proportions by 1952, the Bank, relieved of a task which it was too small to shoulder, turned to its second and more permanent purpose, namely, that of assisting the economic development of its members. The lending principles which evolved after 1947, therefore, are predominantly concerned with financial and technical assistance to underdeveloped countries.

If, in connection with reconstruction needs, the Bank had soon to find that its resources were far too small, it now made the surprising discovery that, even when measured by its modest means, it was difficult to find in underdeveloped countries enough investment projects which were compatible with its basic lending principles. "Perhaps the most striking single lesson which the Bank has learned in the course of its operations," stated the *Fourth Annual Report* for 1948–49, "is how limited is the capacity of the underdeveloped countries to absorb capital quickly for really productive purposes."

Financing Economic Development

The difficulties which confront investment in underdeveloped countries are formidable. In spite of the fact that underdeveloped countries differ widely as to the nature of their individual problems, a few generalizing statements are permissible.

The basic dilemma of the underdeveloped country is to be found not so much in an insufficiency of its domestic productive resources as in its ability to put these resources to efficient use. The underdeveloped country suffers from inadequate capital formation because it is poor and because its low living standard forbids the use of its productive resources in the investment goods industries (see Chapter 19). But better use can be made of these resources for investment purposes *and without a reduction of consumption* if certain obstacles can be removed. These obstacles can be of a great variety, such as inadequate education, poor health conditions, vested interests opposed to change, inept bureaucracies, insufficient technical and administrative skills, insufficient transportation facilities, inadequate banking institutions, etc. And even if these deficiencies are gradually overcome, conditions conductive to private international and domestic investment will grow only slowly as the domestic markets expand in a process of balanced growth.[6] As the Bank's *Third Annual Report* for

[6] See the excellent discussion of this point in Ragnar Nurkse's *Problems of Capital Formation in Underdeveloped Countries* (Oxford: Basil Blackwell, 1953).

1947–48 points out: until earlier stages of industrialization "have produced sufficiently broad home markets, there will generally be lacking the basis for creation of heavy industries, either to supply domestic needs at economic prices or to compete in world markets."

As we contemplate these obstacles to economic development we can understand why clear-cut specific projects of obvious profitability were not forthcoming and why the Bank had to approach its task in a manner quite different from the one originally envisaged. The specific project provision was in need of reinterpretation. In its *Fifth Annual Report* for 1949–50 the Bank explained that this provision was meant to insure that loans would be used for productive purposes and that "the only requirement which it imposes is that, before a loan is granted, there shall be a clear agreement both as to the types of goods and services for which the proceeds of the loan are to be expended and of the uses to which those goods and services are to be put."

The nature of the investment problem in underdeveloped countries made it imperative that careful consideration be given to appropriate investment priorities, a formidable task which involves nothing less than drawing up a development program for the country as a whole, with special emphasis on proper balance. In the absence of an all-inclusive central plan this is difficult to do since no guidance can be expected through the pricing system. Most of the basic investments which an underdeveloped country needs are to be found in the field of communal demand where the criteria of interest rates and anticipated profits cannot or should not be applied. The Bank has found it necessary to encourage its members to formulate long-term development plans and to extend to them technical assistance in this effort through survey missions.

The Bank's aim has been to strengthen the general economic foundations of the underdeveloped countries and to set free productive resources without having to lower an already low standard of living. The character of the economic fields which the Bank has selected for this purpose is indicated in the following statement:

> The Bank has made more development loans to develop electric power than for any other purpose; but it has lent nearly as much for highways, railways, ports and other means of transportation. Taken together, power and transportation account for two-thirds of the Bank's development lending. Projects in these fields have plainly met the Bank's tests of usefulness and urgency; and in general private capital has not been available for projects of this type, even when they were revenue-producing. For the rest,

the Bank's loans have been made for industry, agriculture, or programs involving several sectors of the economy at the same time.[7]

Local Currency Expenditures and Other Problems

We have seen that the Bank's activities are supposed to be marginal to domestic investment. As a rule, the investment projects selected by the member and the Bank imply not only the importation of capital equipment but also local investment expenditures, as when an imported generator is installed in a powerhouse built by local labor (see *Ninth Annual Report* for 1953–54). The loans of the Bank are meant to finance the foreign exchange expenditures directly connected with the project and not the local currency disbursements which are the responsibility of the member (IV–3–a). However, "the Bank may, in exceptional circumstances when local currency required for the purposes of the loan cannot be raised by the borrower on reasonable terms, provide the borrower as part of the loan with an appropriate amount of that currency" (IV–3–b).

To interpret this passage we have to distinguish between two sources of demand for foreign exchange in connection with an investment project, namely, (1) the demand arising from the importation of investment goods, and (2) the demand arising from the importation of consumers' goods. This second type of demand *for foreign exchange* is what Art. IV refers to when it speaks of local currency expenditures.

The *Fifth Annual Report* for 1949–50 admits that a plausible case can be made for the financing of consumers' goods imports by the Bank. When domestic resources are shifted from consumers' to investment goods production, the consequence may be an increase in the purchase of consumers' goods from abroad. If the Bank hesitates to finance these "local" currency expenditures, the reason is as follows.

Since the Bank wants to be marginal to domestic investment, it wants to encourage the members to do their best in making local resources available for investment purposes. The Bank, therefore, is afraid that a liberal financing of consumers' goods imports will run counter to this policy since it will tend, indirectly, to finance the whole project. If the member is able to increase domestic investment without a reduction of its consumers' goods production, the increased demand for foreign produced consumers' goods should be moderate. In some underdeveloped countries it will be possible to draw labor from agriculture without a reduction of agricultural output. If this

[7] Black, *op. cit.*, p. 64.

can be done "the main problem is to stop the peasant from consuming more of his product when family members living off his output go away to work on capital construction."[8]

As a companion agency to the Fund the Bank is based on the principle of multilateralism. Art. III–5 provides that "the Bank shall impose no conditions that the proceeds of a loan shall be spent in the territories of any particular member or members." However, in a world in which multilateralism is not yet fully re-established, the Bank, too, must make concessions.

The borrowing member must repay its loan to the Bank in the currencies which the Bank has disbursed in connection with the loan. A prudent member, therefore, must seriously consider its future obligations and may hesitate to superimpose yet another hard currency burden on an already existing large hard currency debt. Both the member and the Bank, therefore, may desire to finance a given project with less hard currencies.

In a really multilateral payments system these limitations will disappear. A borrowing member will then be able to shop around for the commodities it wants to import in connection with an investment project, and the Bank, when it borrows, will borrow in the cheapest market. Since currencies will then be fully convertible, no direct connection between lending and commodity exports will exist, that is, loans will no longer be "tied."

In case of an acute exchange stringency a member may be unable to live up to its promises. In this case the member may apply to the Bank for a relaxation of the conditions of repayment (IV–4–c). If the Bank is satisfied that some relaxation is in the interest of the member, the other members, and the Bank, it can do two things: (1) it can accept service payments in the currency of the member and arrange for the repurchase of such currency on appropriate terms; and (2) it can modify the terms of amortization or extend the life of the loan, or both.[9]

Stimulating Private Investment

We have seen that the Bank has not been able as yet to stimulate a direct international flow of capital between private lenders and bor-

[8] Nurkse, *op. cit.*, p. 43.

[9] In case the Bank should only serve as a guarantor these relaxations which concern only direct loans are not applicable. But the Bank has the right to terminate its liability to the creditor of a guaranteed loan by offering to purchase the loan at par value and interest accrued (IV-5-c). After the purchase the above-mentioned relaxations could be arranged.

rowers. Originally this was the aim of the Bank, and the Bank stated again in its *Fourth Annual Report* that "over the long run, it is only the sustained flow of private capital that can provide external financial assistance in amounts sufficient to make a significant inroad on the world's development needs." The Bank pointed out that direct private investment was plainly desirable for two reasons, namely (1) in order to avoid fixed interest charges and (2) "to take advantage of the essential technical and managerial skills which are normally associated with such investments and often are not obtainable in any other way."

That a direct international connection between private lenders and borrowers could be established only to a very modest degree in the postwar period has many reasons. The type of investment which was needed to create the preconditions for the balanced growth of an underdeveloped economy, is not as a rule, profitable, however productive it may be in the long run. But there were other obstacles, too, obstacles which could continue to exist even after a country had reached a state of economic receptiveness for private foreign investment. One barrier has nothing to do with the underdeveloped country itself. It is the state of high employment in the potential creditor countries. Private capital has no desire to take on the added risk and burden of foreign investment when lucrative domestic investment opportunities are plentiful. In going abroad private capital faces the possibility of discrimination, of double taxation, transfer problems, and even nationalization.

The Bank Agreement tried to help pave the road for the flow of private investment by its own guarantees and by the additional requirement that in the case of loans extended to private enterprise the member government in whose territory the project is located "fully guarantees the repayment of the principal and the payment of interest and other charges on the loan" (III–4–i). This well-intended second guarantee seems to have done more harm than good. As the *Seventh Annual Report* for 1951–52 has pointed out, this guarantee has the effect of discouraging private borrowers "who fear that a governmental guarantee might lead to interference by the government in the conduct of their business," while "governments, for their part, hesitate to guarantee loans to private enterprises for fear they might be charged with favoritism."

An additional difficulty from the Bank's point of view was that the Articles of Agreement did not permit the Bank to engage in equity financing.

To overcome some of these obstacles an International Finance Corporation was created in 1956. The IFC is closely affiliated with the Bank to avoid the creation of a large staff, but no financial relationship exists between the two institutions because the IFC is designed to invest *without government guarantees* in productive private enterprises. Although the IFC cannot invest in capital stock, its investments are not conventional fixed-interest loans, for they carry the right to share in the profit and growth of the business. The IFC tries to revolve its modest authorized capital of $100 million by selling its investments at an early opportunity. Private investors can then convert IFC loans into shares of stock.

A second affiliate of the Bank is to be the International Development Association which will provide finance "on terms more flexible and bearing less heavily on the balance of payments of the recipient country than those of conventional loans."[10]

The initial resources of the IDA are to be about $1 billion of which more than three fourths will be available on a fully convertible basis. All member countries will pay 10 per cent of their subscription in gold or freely convertible currencies. Seventeen more developed countries will pay the remaining 90 per cent of their subscriptions in five equal installments in gold or freely convertible currencies. The less developed countries will pay the remaining 90 per cent in their own currencies which the IDA cannot use without the consent of the countries concerned.

SUGGESTIONS FOR FURTHER READING

Articles of Agreement. International Monetary Fund and International Bank for Reconstruction and Development. United Nations Monetary and Financial Conference, Bretton Woods, N.H., July 1 to 22. Washington, D.C.: United States Treasury, 1944.

BLACK, EUGENE R. *The Diplomacy of Economic Development.* Cambridge, Mass.: Harvard University Press, 1960.

HIGGINS, BENJAMIN. *Economic Development: Principles, Problems and Policies.* New York: W. W. Norton & Co., Inc., 1959.

INTERNATIONAL BANK OF RECONSTRUCTION AND DEVELOPMENT. *Reports.* Washington, D.C., Annual.

The International Bank for Reconstruction and Development 1946–53. Published by the Bank. Baltimore: The Johns Hopkins Press, 1954.

KINDLEBERGER, CHARLES P. *Economic Development,* chap. 15. The McGraw-Hill Book Co., Inc., 1958.

[10] International Bank, *Fifteenth Annual Report,* p. 6.

NURKSE, RAGNAR. *Problems of Capital Formation in Underdeveloped Countries.* Oxford: Basil Blackwell, 1953.

QUESTIONS AND PROBLEMS

1. Why was it considered advisable at Bretton Woods to create two international financial institutions rather than only one?
2. Compare the quotas in the International Monetary Fund with the subscriptions to the International Bank.
3. How do you explain the "limited capacity of the underdeveloped countries to absorb capital quickly for really productive purposes" (IBRD, 4th Annual Report)?
4. Discuss the lending principles of the International Bank as stated in the Articles of Agreement. Have these lending principles changed as a result of practical experience?
5. "The nature of the investment problem in underdeveloped countries makes it imperative that careful consideration be given to appropriate investment priorities, a formidable task which involves nothing less than drawing up a development program for the country as a whole." Comment.
6. "Planning is at the same time much more necessary and much more difficult in backward than in advanced countries" (W. Arthur Lewis). Discuss.
7. Is it advisable that the International Bank should finance consumers' goods imports by underdeveloped countries?
8. Why was it considered necessary to create an International Finance Corporation and an International Development Association?

Chapter 37 TOWARD CONVERTIBILITY

Different Meanings of Convertibility

Since the main theme of this chapter is the return to convertibility, we must examine the different meanings of convertibility. Convertibility does not necessarily mean that everybody can exchange any amount of his own local currency for any other currency at fixed rates. Our aim may have to be more modest.

To understand the different types and degrees of convertibility we must distinguish the following cases:

1. Full convertibility into gold is not a prerequisite of multilateralism. It would imply acceptance of the gold standard by all members of a multilateral system. Many countries will not return to gold in the sense that they will promise to sell unlimited amounts of gold at a fixed price for their own currency.

2. Full convertibility, therefore, will be limited to free conversion of one currency into other currencies. Depending on the payments system to be established, this conversion can take place at either a fixed or moderately fluctuating rate of exchange.

3. Full convertibility will not include all countries and currencies in the foreseeable future. Because full convertibility implies the abolition of exchange controls and of state-trading monopolies, it cannot exist between market economies and centrally planned economies.

4. Convertibility may be introduced for all newly earned balances while old balances (such as prewar or war debts) may have to be excluded and dealt with according to special arrangements.

5. Convertibility may be restricted to current transactions while capital transfers remain under control. We have already seen that the International Monetary Fund permits this distinction.

6. Convertibility may apply only within a group of countries

which have formed a monetary bloc. The bloc is fenced in against the outside world by exchange controls. If we call this narrower, regional convertibility multilateralism, then we have to call full convertibility omnilateralism.[1]

7. Even within a regional bloc convertibility may be incomplete, for example, old debts or capital transfers may be excluded. Convertibility may be limited to the central banks of the member countries and not apply directly to residents. The rules applying to residents, furthermore, will differ from the rules applying to nonresident holders of local balances.

8. Whether the still remaining discriminations in a system of only limited convertibility are implemented by exchange controls or other devices is of secondary importance. It is meaningless, therefore, to introduce or broaden "convertibility" through the removal of exchange controls if quantitative restrictions (for example, import quotas) are tightened simultaneously.

As we descend below the level of regional convertibility, we can no longer speak of convertibility. In Chapter 33 we became acquainted with clearing agreements which, in a bilateral way, try to match two countries' trade. Even such barter trade is better than no trade, particularly if the clearing agreement permits some credit swings.

We see that between bilateral trade and fully multilateral trade there exist a great variety of intermediary positions. Whether we accept or even welcome these less-than-fully-multilateral solutions depends on our point of view. Seen against the background of a network of bilateral arrangements any multilateral agreement on a regional basis is an improvement. Yet regionalism will seem inferior when compared with a truly multilateral system of general convertibility (omnilateralism).

During the past decade we could witness an interesting and gratifying transition from bilateralism to regionalism and multilateralism. A report on this encouraging development will conclude our discussion of problems of international monetary co-operation.

The Dollar Shortage

Sir Dennis Robertson described the then existing dollar shortage as "a persistent tendency on the part of the population of the world outside North America to spend more in that region than the sum of what they are earning in that region and what the inhabitants of that

[1] See *The Economist,* London (February 5, 1944), p. 70.

region are disposed to lend to them or invest in their borders under the play of ordinary economic motive."[2]

It was to be expected that after World War II balance-of-payments difficulties would arise between the dollar area and the non-dollar countries. The magnitude of the problem, however, was greatly underestimated, not only at Bretton Woods but also in the *Anglo-American Loan Agreement* of July 15, 1946. This Agreement provided for a loan of $3.75 billion to Great Britain. Great Britain undertook to make sterling convertible on current account within one year. Convertibility became effective on July 15, 1947, but had to be suspended again on August 20, 1947! Insistence on convertibility had been a deplorable mistake. The loan had been much too small in comparison with the dollar deficit; and convertibility was premature considering that the causes of the dollar shortage had not been eliminated. We have to remember that in the summer of 1947 the pound sterling was still overvalued, that inflation was not under control in Great Britain, and that huge sterling balances within the sterling area were insufficiently blocked.

It was unfortunate that this inadequate, premature, and abortive attempt toward convertibility should have been made, because "this expensive miscarriage thoroughly compromised the principle of non-discrimination and made many British statesmen and experts allergic to convertibility and non-discrimination."[3]

The original causes of Britain's and Europe's postwar dollar shortage were fairly obvious: physical destruction and the need for imports from the United States with its undamaged industrial facilities; shipping losses and the liquidation of foreign investments, with the consequent loss of invisible foreign exchange earnings; loss of sources of supply in East Europe and East Asia and the resultant increase of imports from America; loss of export markets during the war; the unfavorable change in Europe's terms of trade; and, finally, the greatly increased military expenditures overseas even after the war. In listing these causes of the acute postwar dollar shortage we must also remember that these difficulties were superimposed on a situation which even before the war had been unsatisfactory.

Europe's balance-of-payments position was made worse in consequence of the particularly hard winter of 1946–47 and the spring drought of 1947. The impossibility of paying for all its needed im-

[2] Sir Dennis H. Robertson, *Britain in the World Economy* (London: George Allen & Unwin, Ltd., 1954), p. 53.

[3] Gottfried Haberler, *Currency Convertibility*, No. 451 in the Series "National Economic Problems" (New York: American Enterprise Association, Inc., 1954), p. 16.

ports of food and raw materials threatened to disrupt Europe's industrial production. Awareness of the magnitude and seriousness of the problem led to the *European Recovery Program*. The program had four goals:[4] (1) Increase of production through modernization of equipment; (2) creation and maintenance of internal financial stability; (3) development of economic co-operation between the participating countries; and (4) increase in exports to gradually remove the dollar deficit. The European Recovery Program was suggested (Marshall Plan) and financed by the United States. The aid extended, on a yearly basis, was actually somewhat lower than that provided during the previous two years. American financial help in the form of net grants and loans from the middle of 1945 to the end of 1952 amounted to nearly $28 billion.

The European Recovery Program was a great success, but it was not expected to lead by 1952 to a situation which would have permitted full convertibility. With the failure of Britain's convertibility attempt fresh in mind, the general attitude towards convertibility had become much more cautious and patient. We shall see, however, how a regional arrangement, the *European Payments Union,* supplanted bilateralism.

We cannot trace in detail the events of the postwar decade. Our main theme, the problem of convertibility makes it necessary, however, to mention at least the devaluation of the pound sterling on September 18, 1949, which was followed within one month by the devaluation of twenty-seven other currencies. All these currencies had been overvalued in relation to the dollar and the question, therefore, is not why these devaluations occurred but rather why they occurred so late.

In Chapter 33 we saw why overvaluation and exchange control may be considered preferable to convertibility. During the immediate postwar period overvaluation was of actual advantage as long as the shortage of supplies was so great that all commodities which could be set aside for export purposes could actually be sold abroad. If exports to the dollar area could not be increased in physical quantity, devaluation could only have reduced the sum total of dollar earnings. But when the sellers' market changed into a buyers' market, exchange rate adjustments could not be postponed for too long.

The devaluation of the pound sterling should probably have come earlier than it did, for exchange controls were not tight enough

[4] *Committee of European Economic Co-operation, General Report* (Washington, D.C.: Department of State, Publication 2930, September 21, 1947), Vol. I, p. 11.

to prevent a severe drain on Britain's foreign exchange reserves. Once the devaluation was anticipated, English exporters were eager to have American importers postpone their payments, and American exporters insisted on prompt payments while sterling still retained its current ratio to the dollar.

The lowering of the dollar price of the pound sterling from $4.03 to $2.80 was a drastic step. A very large physical increase in exports was needed to result in improved dollar earnings. Important for the success of the measure was not only the elasticity of foreign demand but also the ability of the devaluing country to resist domestic price inflation in the face of increasing import prices. To this most essential point, the relation of domestic monetary policy to the dollar shortage, we shall presently return.

Alleged Incurability of the Dollar Shortage

We saw in Chapter 30 how a depression may be internationally propagated through a falling off of the imports of the depression country. If we assume, therefore, that the economy of the United States will continue to be subject to severe economic fluctuations, we might be tempted to argue that a dollar shortage must recur again and again in connection with severe recessions in the United States. This attitude is based not only on experiences of the early thirties (see Chapter 34) but also on the fact that it was the impact of the United States recession of 1948–49 which triggered the devaluations of 1949. In retrospect we can see, however, that the precarious state of health of the European economies was more decisive for the dollar shortage than the recession in the United States. Throughout the fifties the United States had balance-of-payments deficits with the exception of 1957. During 1950–56 the deficits averaged about $1.5 billion while the deficit for 1958 and 1959 amounted to a total of about $7 billion. Certainly, the American recessions of 1953–54 and 1957–58 did not create grave balance-of-payments problems for the rest of the world.

Nevertheless, some economists insisted that the dollar shortage was incurable. They argued that the United States is a huge country with a large domestic market, comparatively self-sufficient, highly industrialized, and much more productive than any other country. Furthermore, the United States is so rich that it can afford to save a large percentage of its national income. Enormous capital formation, in turn, makes possible more rapid technological progress than in other countries. The discrepancy in productivity between the United States and other countries, therefore, is constantly growing with the result that the dollar shortage, too, will become worse rather than better, since there is so much that others want to buy in the United States and so relatively little that the United States will want to purchase from others.[5] Once we take this attitude, a permanently high employment level in the United States seems rather more frightening than reassuring from the standpoint of balance-of-payments equilibrium.

Had this theory been correct the chances for convertibility would have been bad. Fortunately, the theory is in this general form untenable. Over a hundred years ago it was already refuted by David Ricardo and John Stuart Mill. At that time, too, it was customary to assume that one country is more productive than others. Therefore, it was pointed out that it is not absolute but only relative production advantages which count. This was the famous theory of comparative advantage. It was convincingly shown that foreign trade was desirable whenever a country could get products from abroad with less effort than it cost to produce these same products at home. International trade would increase the standard of living of the trading nations independently of the fact that absolute levels of productivity differ widely from country to country. One basic condition, however, had to be fulfilled: wage levels had to be adjusted to levels of productivity.

If, therefore, the United States outproduces all other countries, its wage level must be higher than the wage level of all other countries; and if the discrepancy in productivity increases, the discrepancy in wages, too, must increase. For the less productive countries this means that there are limits, set by their current comparative level of productive efficiency, beyond which their standard of living cannot rise. If money wages are allowed to rise above this level, not only will the attempt soon fail but the country's products will lose their competitive position in world markets.

We see that a country can create a shortage of foreign exchange by seeking for itself a higher level of consumption and investment than the circumstances justify. As Sir Dennis Robertson said: any nation which gives its mind to it can create balance-of-payments difficulties for itself in half an hour with the printing press and a strong trade union movement.[6] If we remember how tempting it has always been to use inflationary policies and if we acknowledge how difficult

[5] Typical of this attitude is Thomas Balogh, *The Dollar Crisis* (Oxford: Basil Blackwell, 1949).

[6] Sir Dennis H. Robertson, *Britain in the World Economy* (London: George Allen & Unwin, Ltd., 1954), p. 56.

to handle the wage problem may become in times of high employment, we must then admit that the main cause of a shortage of foreign exchange lies here rather than in different levels of productivity.

If the pessimists had been right, the dollar shortage could not have been overcome by more conservative monetary policies. Yet this is exactly what has happened. The past decade has in many countries been characterized by the rebirth of monetary policies. Those countries which applied monetary weapons were able to improve their balance-of-payments position surprisingly fast and without having to pay the price of deflation and unemployment.

The European Payments Union

The transition to convertibility in Europe was greatly aided by the European Payments Union. The EPU was an attempt to reconstruct multilateralism within the general framework of the *Organization for European Economic Co-operation* (OEEC). The aims of the EPU were more modest than those of the International Monetary Fund, since the former never wanted to be more than a temporary and regional step on the way to full convertibility.

Before the EPU started its operations in July 1950 (and disregarding earlier attempts in 1948–49), any two European countries had to try to balance their payments bilaterally as best they could. If country A earned B-money it could buy only B-goods with it; it could not spend B-money in third countries. Accordingly, the possibilities of intra-European trade were seriously limited. Compared with this state of affairs, regionalism, as established by the European Payments Union, meant a great improvement. Country A was now permitted to use its earnings from country B to buy from country C or D, that is, it could buy and sell in the most profitable markets of a reasonably large area and was no longer strait-jacketed by bilateralism. This regional payments arrangement, together with gradual and partial dismantling of quantitative trade controls, was the way in which greater European co-operation was achieved, with the result of decreasing dependence on dollar imports and rising productivity through regional division of labor.

The EPU was based on the following principles. At the end of each month the members reported to the *Bank for International Settlements,* as the agent of the Union, their net bilateral balances with each other member. The BIS then cleared these balances, that is, it derived each member's net position with the Union as a whole. Country A did not owe anything to countries B and C, with which it had an import surplus; nor was it owed anything by countries D and E, with which it had an export surplus. Country A either owed the Union or had a claim against the Union, depending on whether it had an unfavorable or favorable trade balance on current account with the rest of the members. The common unit of account was the dollar.

The clearing process described above referred to the transactions of only the previous month. A second operation provided for a clearing over time. Country A's monthly credit balance with the Union, for instance, was added to a previously existing credit balance or used to reduce a previously existing debit balance. Vice versa, a debit balance for the previous month either increased an already existing deficit with the Union or reduced an existing credit balance. The whole arrangement rested on the basic assumption that no member would remain permanently in the surplus or deficit category.

In the short run, of course, balance-of-payments disequilibria would arise so that debtor or creditor relationships between members and the Union developed. A creditor position with the Union meant that a country had sold more to the rest of the region than it had bought and that it had extended credit to the other members. A deficit position meant that a country borrowed through the Union from other members. Obviously, the members could not be permitted to accumulate unlimited debts with the Union.

Concerning the arrangements which limited a potential deficit country's drawing rights as well as a potential surplus country's obligations, the European Payments Union borrowed ideas from the Keynesian Clearing Union and from the International Monetary Fund. The members made no contributions; they simply permitted the accumulation of credit balances with the Union. In contradistinction to the Clearing Union, however, the total amounts of these credit balances were rather narrowly limited. Each country had a quota expressed in accounting units. As in the International Monetary Fund, the quota limited both the obligations and the borrowing rights of the members. The quotas were subdivided into tranches. Originally a creditor country would extend the full amount of the first tranche (that is, 20 per cent of its quota) as credit to the Union. For all following tranches only one half of the net surplus position would be allowed to constitute a credit extension; the other half had to be paid in gold by the Union. The deficit country could originally count on an outright credit of 10 per cent of its quota but had to pay increasing proportions of its deficit in gold to the Union as its deficit with the Union increased over time.

These arrangements were repeatedly changed in connection with the general improvement of the balance-of-payments situation and the desire of OEEC and EPU to bring about a gradual "hardening" through insistence on larger gold payments. In July, 1954, for instance, the system of proportionately increasing gold payments by debtors to the Union was replaced by a straight 50-50 gold and credit arrangement throughout the whole quota; and in July 1955 the ratio was further stiffened to 75 per cent in gold and 25 per cent in credit. However, the quotas had been doubled so that the hardening of the ratio left the credit facilities and credit obligations of the members unchanged.

The EPU was terminated when, in December 1958, EPU members representing more than 50 per cent of EPU quotas decided to make their currencies externally convertible. The EPU was replaced by the European Monetary Agreement which, through a European Fund of $600 million, provides credits to member countries. But these credits, which cannot exceed two years, are not automatic as in the EPU.

The Foreign Deficit of the United States

Since 1958 the United States has incurred a substantial balance-of-payments deficit. To many observers this deficit came as a surprise because it contradicted (a) the opinion that the dollar shortage was incurable, and (b) the belief that a recession in the United States will always cause a deficit in the balance of payments in the rest of the world. However, already the recession of 1953–54 had not had any such detrimental effect; and the recession of 1957–58 was accompanied in 1958 by a gold outflow from the United States of $2.3 billion, the largest such drain ever suffered by a single country in a single year.

The total foreign deficit of $3.4 billion in 1958 contrasted sharply with the unusually favorable payments conditions of 1957 which had been caused by the Suez crisis.

The foreign deficit of the United States was not surprising to those who accept the theory of comparative advantage. Since World War II it had been the policy of the United States Government to help recreate multilateral trade in the free world area and enable the participating countries to regain a competitive position. The very success of this American policy reduced the dependence of other countries on United States exports and increased their ability to sell in the United States. Once reasonably normal conditions were re-established, each country's balance-of-payments position depended on its domestic monetary and fiscal policies and on the prices of its goods in comparison with the prices of its trade partners, assuming given rates of exchange. In this normal situation even the most productive country can incur a balance-of-payments deficit by permitting itself a wage level which exceeds the level dictated by its relative productivity and the general international payments situation.

Chart 29–1 illustrates the deterioration of the United States balance of trade. A continued rise in imports together with a sharp downturn of exports suggest that inflation in the United States was more pronounced than the competitive position of the United States permitted. The deficit in the balance of payments (see Chart 29–2) is explained by the fact that U.S. Government grants and loans and the net outflow of private capital were not balanced by a corresponding excess of exports over imports.

Government grants and loans are motivated by military necessity and foreign policy considerations. They cannot easily be adjusted to reduce the foreign deficit. Private net capital outflow increased. With the return of more normal and stable international financial conditions, American private capital has made use of high profit expectations abroad while foreign borrowers made use of relative low rates of interest in the United States. Once again we see that the present deficit arises to some extent from a transition to more normal conditions.

Even the gold outflow is a return to a more even distribution of gold, a return which was encouraged by the low rates of interest in the United States. These low rates made a transfer of dollars into gold relatively cheap owing to the low cost of liquidity preference.

The free world has shown confidence in the dollar by holding a large portion of its foreign reserves in dollars. This very fact, however, emphasizes the role of the dollar as international key currency and reduces the practicality of a devaluation of the dollar as a means for overcoming the foreign deficit of the United States. A devaluation of the dollar would lead to a dangerous run on the gold reserves of the United States, for then all foreign dollar balances would tend to be converted into gold. At the end of 1959 foreign dollar balances corresponded approximately to those gold reserves which were not needed for backing purposes. We see that we deal here with a problem with explosive and self-aggravating possibilities.

If we want to abstain from protectionist devices, avoid devaluation, maintain or even increase the flow of private capital, and continue foreign aid, we must cure the foreign deficit mainly by keeping domestic inflation under control.

Much can be done, furthermore, by the "surplus" countries which have already started to dismantle those discriminations which are a hangover from the dollar shortage period. The wealthier of these countries must also shoulder a greater share of the burden of defense and development of underdeveloped countries.

Our recent experiences in the international economic field underline some of the conclusions of Chapter 28. Although we may consider a sustained high level of employment more important than stability of the price level, consideration of currency convertibility should strengthen our determination to keep inflation in check.

SUGGESTIONS FOR FURTHER READING

Balogh, Thomas. *The Dollar Crisis.* Oxford: Basil Blackwell, 1949.

Beveridge, William H. *Full Employment in a Free Society,* Part VI. New York: W. W. Norton & Co., Inc., 1945.

Committee for Economic Development. *National Objectives and the Balance of Payments.* New York, 1960.

Dale, William B. *The Foreign Deficit of the United States: Causes and Issues.* Menlo Park, Calif.: International Industrial Development Center, Stanford Research Institute, 1960.

Economic Cooperation Administration. *The Sterling Area. An American Analysis.* Washington, D.C.: U.S. Government Printing Office, 1951.

European Payments Union. *Annual Reports.* Paris: Organisation for European Economic Co-operation. 1951–1958.

Haberler, Gottfried. *Currency Convertibility.* No. 451 in the Series "National Economic Problems." New York: American Enterprise Association, Inc., 1954.

Harris, Seymour E. (ed.) *Foreign Economic Policy for the United States.* Cambridge, Mass.: Harvard University Press, 1948.

Hicks, J. R. *Essays in World Economics,* chap. 4. Oxford: Clarendon Press, 1959.

International Monetary Fund. *The Revival of Monetary Policy.* Washington, D.C., September 11, 1953.

Jacobsen, Per. *Some Monetary Problems—International and National.* New York: Oxford University Press, 1958.

Kindleberger, Charles P. *The Dollar Shortage.* New York: John Wiley & Sons, Inc., 1950.

KINDLEBERGER, CHARLES P. *International Economics,* chap. 25. Homewood, Ill.: Richard D. Irwin, Inc., 1953.

MIKESELL, RAYMOND F. *United States Economic Policy and International Relations.* New York: McGraw-Hill Book Co., Inc., 1952.

ORGANISATION FOR EUROPEAN ECONOMIC CO-OPERATION. *The Internal Financial Situation.* Report by a Group of Independent Experts. Paris, 1952.

ORGANISATION FOR EUROPEAN ECONOMIC CO-OPERATION. *From Recovery to Economic Strength.* Sixth Report of the OEEC. Paris, March, 1955.

RITTER, LAWRENCE S. *Money and Economic Activity,* chap. 68. Boston: Houghton Mifflin Co., 1952.

ROBERTSON, SIR DENNIS H. *Britain in the World Economy.* London: George Allen & Unwin, Ltd., 1954.

QUESTIONS AND PROBLEMS

1. What do we mean when we say that a currency is *fully* convertible?
2. Discuss the advantages of multilateralism. Can you conceive of circumstances under which it would be desirable to work for a less than multilateral solution?
3. Compare the British depreciation of 1931 with the British devaluation of 1949.
4. Discuss Europe's dollar shortage after World War II.
5. "Any nation which sets its mind to it can create balance-of-payments difficulties for itself in half an hour with the printing press and a strong trade union movement" (D. H. Robertson). Do you agree?
6. Discuss the balance of payments of the United States for the period 1951 to 1960.
7. Explain the structure of the European Payments Union. Was it modeled after the International Clearing Union or after the International Monetary Fund?
8. How can you explain the 1958–60 foreign deficit of the United States considering that recessions are supposedly accompanied by an increase in foreign reserves?

INDEX

INDEX

D

G

K

L

M

This book has been set on the Linotype in 11 point Baskerville, leaded 2 points. Chapter numbers and titles are in 18 point Spartan Medium. The size of the type page is 27 by 46½ picas.